LEARNING FROM EXPERIENCE

A RESOURCE BOOK BY AND FOR
CO-OP/INTERNSHIP PROFESSIONALS

by Scott Weighart

Given that this book is clearly the product of the son of a teacher and an engineer, it is dedicated to my mother, Edith Weighart, and to the memory of my father, Fred Weighart.

CONTENTS

Introduction: Becoming Conversational   v

Chapter 1: Assessing Your Program   1

Chapter 2: Developing a Vision   17

Chapter 3: Making Priorities   35

Chapter 4: Striving for Greatness   65

Chapter 5: Making Mistakes   95

Chapter 6: Working with Today's Students   119

Chapter 7: Counseling Students One-on-One   143

Chapter 8: Teaching Students in Groups   187

Chapter 9: Critiquing Resumes and Interviews   215

Chapter 10: Maximizing Student Learning on the Job   253

Chapter 11: Managing Reflection Processes   283

Chapter 12: Handling Moments of Truth   309

Chapter 13: Developing Employer Relationships   333

Chapter 14: Maintaining Employer Relationships   359

Epilogue: Toward Fluency   389

Selected Bibliography   401

Index   403

ACKNOWLEDGEMENTS

This book would not have come to be without the assistance of many people. First, I have to thank the Cooperative Education and Internship Association. Without a CEIA research grant to assist with the cost of producing this book, I would not have attempted to make it happen. Thanks to Ray Easterlin in particular for his assistance, especially given that this is by no means a typical "research project."

My wife, Ellie, played her usual impressive variety of roles, most notably desktop publishing and copyediting the book as well as ensuring are various contributors were on track with all that they needed to do.

Among all the many others, what amazed me most is how many people said yes to help with this project with no hesitation. My Northeastern colleague Linnea Basu surely ended up getting much more than she bargained for when she agreed to be the initial content editor of the book. Regardless, she gave great feedback through all 400+ pages, and this is a much better final product as a result.

I won't attempt to list all of my contributors here, though a complete list is on the back cover. Thanks to all of these great educators for taking the time to be interviewed as well as cleaning up and signing off on the transcripts that appear here. Of that group, I want to single out Nancy Johnston and Anita Todd, who really went above and beyond in many ways. They helped come up with the title of the book and gave feedback when I struggled at times. My material on learning theory is heavily borrowed from Nancy's authoritative thesis on the subject. Thanks to all of this book's contributors of content for an amazing team effort. My only regret is that there are so many other great educators at Northeastern and elsewhere who I could not include, as it would not have made the project's scope impossible to manage.

Many other colleagues played key roles in the book's development. Lynn Hansen from the University of Central Florida was an interviewee for the book. While her busy schedule made it impossible to include her actual words here, her ideas informed the content of many chapters. At Northeastern, our erstwhile curriculum committee of Lorraine Mountain, Kate McLaughlin, Erin Callery, and Theresa Mangan contributed to an early brainstorming meeting. Erin Callery also gave significant feedback on the book's content. Leigh Shea offered edits and suggests on the book in progress and also served as our "juggling" cover model. As we finalized the book, Megan Brodie from the University of Guelph read the whole manuscript and offered many constructive suggestions and caught many subtle errors. I also very much appreciate the great professionals—Michael True, Jean Egan, and Bruce Lumsden—who were willing to write blurbs for the back cover on relatively short notice.

Given the terrific job that she did on the cover of my *Find Your First Professional Job* textbook, I was thrilled that Vicky Arico was able and willing to find the time to design this cover as well. Lastly, I entrusted the final edit of the book to my great friend, Jill Gómez, whose keen eye in the final days before *Exceeding Expectations* went to print resulted in a much better outcome.

Any errors that ended up in this book are no one's fault but my own. To all above, "You, of course, have my most infinite gratitude."

Scott Weighart
March 2009

INTRODUCTION

BECOMING CONVERSATIONAL

*"Whatever your discipline, become a student
of excellence in all things. Take every
opportunity to observe people who manifest
the qualities of mastery."*
—*Tony Buzan*

In my early days on the co-op faculty at Northeastern University, I went to The Gillette Company to visit a first-time co-op student, Renee Middendorf. Like many of our students, Renee had no significant professional experience before landing this first job. However, she was very intelligent and had a high GPA, and she ended up getting an extremely challenging co-op position. She worked in a highly technical field called Electronic Data Interchange, or EDI. EDI enables computer systems to "talk" to each other... eventually. First, though, EDI professionals often had to do several trial runs and fix problems before a major sales order from, say, a nationwide chain of supermarkets could be transmitted automatically to Gillette and processed appropriately.

Renee had only been in the job for about six weeks when I visited her. During our meeting in her cubicle, the phone rang. She picked it up and launched into a conversation that absolutely floored me. I couldn't make heads or tails of 90 percent of it! I can't remember a word of it, but looking at an EDI glossary online I can imagine that she was throwing around some of the following terms: bisync; EFT; flat file; IEA; VANs; transaction sets; and so on.

It blew my mind. Less than two months ago, Renee knew considerably less than I did about technology. Now she had left me in the dust in the matter of a few weeks. It seemed almost magical to me. How could a person immerse themselves in a field so quickly and become competent in a complex area so quickly? It was as if I had plopped her down in Moscow and returned six weeks later to find her conversing effectively in Russian despite no previous exposure to the language.

That's an analogy that I continued to use when explaining that job to students who subsequently applied for it. I told students that this job could make them feel very clueless in the early going but that a day would come when they suddenly would be able to "speak EDI" and surprise themselves by doing so. It might take a month or much longer, but it would happen for them if they kept their ears open, asked questions, hung in there, and focused on learning.

In many ways, I believe that all professionals go through a similar baptism by immersion, if you will. Every intern or co-op student is suddenly thrust into a "community of practice," as learning theorist Etienne Wenger would call it. In his book *Communities of Practice: Learning, Meaning, and Identity*, Wenger talks about a *social* theory of learning. This includes ways in which we talk about the following components:

- Meaning—our dynamic ability to experience life and the world as meaningful

- Practice—the "shared historical and social resources, frameworks, and perspectives" that are mutually engaged in by group members

- Community—the "social configurations in which our enterprises are defined as worth pursuing and our participation is recognizable as competence"

- Identity—the notion that learning changes who we are in a relationship to that community

With this in mind, we can start to appreciate the complexity and richness inherent in the process of starting to become a professional within any field. While Renee's transformation may have seemed magical to me, it is more helpful to think of what I observed as the sum of hundreds of incremental gains in learning over roughly 240 hours of work experience to date. During those six weeks, Renee sat in on meetings in which problems were discussed and resolved. She overheard colleagues on the phone. She was copied on e-mail messages that were initially incomprehensible. Through questioning, conversation, observation, reflection, and practice, she gradually integrated herself into that particular community of practice at Gillette. This inevitably changed her sense of meaning and identity as a professional.

While the realm of cooperative education and internships is certainly a world of its own, it is every bit as much of a community of practice. For those who are outside of our community or new to it, the joys, challenges, tensions, and even the lingo likely will seem to be alien. The first year or two in the job might be a real struggle. As a fledgling educator attempts to become integrated in the community, it will be enough of a challenge just to figure out how to handle the more operational elements of the job. Learning to use technology, getting jobs listed on a system, making sure resumes go to those jobs and that students get hired—that may be enough to keep your hands full for the first referral cycle.

Gradually, though, you will want to immerse yourself much more thoroughly in the field. It really is like learning to speak a foreign language. You begin with learning what is simple, concrete, and unavoidable—how to ask for directions, how to get from point A to B, and how to ensure the most basic needs are met. If you persist, though, you will start to become conversational. You will be able to get beyond the operational in favor of what is abstract, rich, provocative, and profound. How will you get there? There is no magic formula. Some might be able to figure out a new language by reading it and listening to it with little assistance. Others will get it by being immersed in a community in which becoming conversational is the prerequisite for members. Many will benefit with formal instruction and/or informal mentoring. It will take time, but eventually the language learner can grow toward competence and then mastery.

This book is intended to be a resource that will help you increase your fluency as a co-op or internship educator. I was inspired to write this book by making presentations when attending conferences around the U.S. and Canada. Everywhere I go, I see a real thirst for knowledge. Whether people are the sole proprietor of co-op at their schools or the member of one of the larger programs, there is a feeling that we don't always do a great job of sharing best practices across our community. And regardless of whether you are new to the field or if you have been in it for decades, this field is so rich that you will never run out of opportunities to reinvent your approach to running a program, whether working with students or employers.

Given how many amazing professionals there are in our field, I was determined that this book was going to offer much more than my own perspective on all elements of being a great co-op or internship professional. Accordingly, I reached out to many of my colleagues at Northeastern and many other great programs across the U.S. and Canada. I interviewed 17 educators for 45 minutes to one hour each, asking them a variety of questions that were pertinent to the creation of the book. I wish I could have interviewed three times as many, as there are so many terrific professionals and programs that I was unable to include due to concerns about time and space. Ultimately, I compiled a spreadsheet of topics and carefully analyzed the interview transcripts. Each chapter of this book was created by combining the themes that arose in these extended interviews along with my own observations and experiences. The end of each chapter includes many of the actual interview excerpts, so you can hear what these experts had to say in their own words. Bear in mind that these are almost all transcripts of speech: My hope is to capture the feeling of having an expert talk to you directly rather than to have something conveyed in abstract, flowery prose.

The upshot is a book that I hope will be provocative, informative, and entertaining to read. It starts with some big-picture chapters on program management. How do we figure out where we're at so we know where to go? What tools and techniques will help us get to be competent in our roles, and how can we move from competence toward greatness? How do we learn from our mistakes? These are the questions early in the book.

We then proceed to some meaty chapters on students. What do we need to know to understand where today's students are coming from? How can we work with them in large groups, small groups, or one-on-one? What are some tricks of the trade that will help them through the phases of preparation, activity, and reflection in the co-op learning model? It closes with a few chapters on working with employers. How do we build relationships with employers who will be good educational partners? How do we keep those relationships strong, even in the face of inevitable difficulties?

Learning From Experience is not intended to be the last word on how professionals should run their programs, nor is it intended to be a dry manual. Instead, I hope that it will stimulate educators to ask themselves some tough questions about how and why they do what they do. What are you trying to accomplish in your program? When you have students, educators, and administrators pulling you in different directions, where does your loyalty lie? What are you doing to make sure that you are maximizing learning in the face of many pressures to do otherwise? What do you even know about the science behind the learning that happens in co-op jobs and internships? How can you be sure that learning is happening, and to what degree is it possible for an educator to increase it?

These are just a few questions that this book raises. In fact, each chapter ends with a set of reflection questions that are designed to make you think about how you run *your* program and how you might or might not want to rethink elements of doing so.

There definitely were a few surprises for me as I reflected on our field while writing this book. First, it's remarkable how universal many of our struggles turn out to be. Very few educators feel terrific about the reflection element of our students' learning. Many have a sincere interest in real education but get bogged down by workload and pressures to worry more about placement than learning. This book has contradictory opinions on how to handle various "moments of truth," such as the degree to which a coordinator should "play God" when playing a role in determining who works where.

Second, I am amazed to find how much this book has changed *me* as a professional. Although I have been working in cooperative education for 13 ½ years, the 15–20 hours of conversations that led to the creation of this book often made me realize that there is plenty of room for improvement. I already have revamped some of my counseling and reflection tactics in the spirit of helping students learn how to transfer their knowledge from one community of practice to another.

With that in mind, I encourage you to think of this book as an opportunity to become more conversational—or maybe even fluent—as professionals in the realm of cooperative education and internships. Think of the book as a series of conversations: Feel free to eavesdrop, and be prepared to be thrilled or scandalized by some of the opinions that you will overhear... and maybe indifferent to some others. More than anything, I hope that this book will prove to be a resource that will have an impact on your thoughts, actions, and conversations with students, employers, and colleagues.

Scott Weighart
November 2008

CHAPTER 1

ASSESSING YOUR PROGRAM

*"If you don't know where you are going, any
road will get you there."*
— *Lewis Carroll*

As co-op/internship professionals, a major part of our role is ensuring that our students are
prepared for day one in a new role. I often tell my students that they should not underestimate how difficult it is to be a new employee at any organization. At that moment in time,
you are eager to prove to those that hired you that you are worthy of their trust. Yet you
generally know very little about the organization's culture, including its unwritten rules. You
may face Byzantine bureaucracy, mind-addling acronyms, and petty politics.

However, all of the above is just as true for co-op or internship professionals as it is for the
students they counsel. While some new professionals may have a relevant degree or two as
well as experience in higher education or in a directly related profession, it's not unusual for
people to come into our field knowing little or nothing about how it all works.

Many professionals feel that it took several placement cycles before they really knew what
they were doing. So it takes some patience as well as a determination to make things better
each time around. That said, you can ramp up relatively quickly if you can adopt a strategic
mindset to running your program.

One trait that many co-op or internship professionals have in common is a passion for working with college students. As we will see, that is one of the great joys of working in this field
as well as one key to success. But to do the most for those students, you first need to use your
analytical skills and figure out exactly where your program stands. There are many co-op and
internship professionals who are terrific when it comes to working one-on-one with a student
or employer. But it's not as common to see professionals who also are able to step back and
assess where their program is and what it could be after cultivating a vision based on input
from academic counterparts, students, and employers. In this chapter, we will address some
of the first steps you should take when starting a program… or, if you are an experienced

professional, some steps that I recommend that you take periodically to address the changing environment of students, employers, and the economy.

HISTORY

Here are some questions to ask yourself as you assess or reassess your role as an educator: What already has been done at your school? Is there any information from your predecessor, whether on paper or electronically? What is your starting point? What do you have? Who are the driving forces that have tried to make things happen, whether faculty or staff? Who supports the program? What is the curriculum, and how will a co-op or internship program complement that? Are there restraining forces that have stood in the way of the program being all that it can be? Geographical location; interest from students, faculty, and administration; student schedules; job market; economy; and transportation all affect the viability of a program.

Make appointments with academic faculty and administration. Ask them what they know about the program historically, what feelings they have. What impact does the program currently have? What is their vision for what a strong co-op/internship program would be? What do you want your graduates to look like, and how can I help? Make appointments, take notes, and be "damn sure that you follow up with people," as Northeastern co-op coordinator Jacki Diani told me. There will be people who might be frustrated because they expressed interest in the past and attempted to contribute, only to have people drop the ball when it came to following through on good intentions.

In my case, I was hired to be on the co-op faculty for our College of Business Administration students in March 1995. I immediately inherited the Management Information Systems co-op program from two experienced colleagues, Bill Sloane and Charlie Bognanni. MIS is basically what many of you might think of as Information Technology. I would say that my qualifications to run that program were a mixed bag at the beginning. I have an MBA, and I had taken two good courses in MIS as part of that degree. In a previous job, I had managed the development of some computer-based training games, working with some computer science co-ops from Northeastern in the process. However, I lacked any real knowledge of the range of possible co-op jobs for MIS students, and I didn't know anything about career paths. Even worse, I had very limited experience in counseling students. I had been a part-time lecturer in Organizational Behavior years before at Boston University as well as Northeastern, so I had worked in higher education and counseled students through academic challenges. But I had never helped anyone through a job search.

As I gained experience in the field, I learned that some coordinators were like me. They had a relatively strong academic background but needed to ramp up when it came to counseling skills. Others had extensive schooling and experience as counselors but were hired with neither a degree nor experience in the professional field that they were hired to handle. Rarely, there are co-op and internship professionals who walk in the door with substantial backgrounds in both counseling and a directly related functional area—marketing or civil engineering, for example—but that's the exception rather than the rule. There are perennial debates as to whether one is better off to come in with a counseling background or with professional experience, but my sense is that either route can lead to great success. The key is to be aware of what you're lacking and to address your deficiencies aggressively.

I relied on my colleagues to get me up to speed at first. Bill and Charlie told me the short history of the MIS program. It was a relatively young concentration, and they humbly said that they thought I could do much more with it. For them, it was a secondary priority to their primary responsibility, which was placing accounting concentrators.

In short order, I was able to look at placement records and get a feel for how large the concentration was and which employers were hiring the students. I looked over the curriculum and made some inferences about what type of jobs would tie with the coursework. I met with the MIS academic faculty and asked them what jobs they thought students should have, ideally. In the process, I got a good sense of which academic faculty had real interest in the co-op program and could be useful resources for future collaboration as well as those who had less interest.

METRICS

After informally gathering information about your program's history, one critical—but often overlooked—step is to crunch some numbers and put together some metrics about your program. Co-op and internship professionals are not always hired because they are good at analyzing data, so you may need some training to do this effectively. I literally have seen some of my colleagues cringe when I suggested that they need to develop a comfort level with Excel or Access, but it's important to do some data analysis—or find someone who can do it for you—if you really want to understand the big picture of your program.

Frankly, this is a step that you regularly should undergo with your program. Periodically, I put together an Excel document that pulls together all the placement data for my program. For each job that I post for a given work term, I enter the following data:

- Employer name

- Employer location (City, State)

- Employer industry (Financial Services, High Tech, Education, etc.)

- Job Title

- Job Type: For any given field, there is a finite number of types of jobs. For my Management Information Systems students, for example, the types include: PC/LAN Support; Network Administration; Business Analyst; Web Design; Database Manager; Program Manager; Software Tester; and "Hybrid" job (job that strongly combines MIS with another business function, such as Finance or Marketing)

- Accessibility of job: Is the job easily reachable by public transportation? Difficult but possible to reach via public transportation? Reachable only by car?

- Pay rate or range

- Number of positions for each job title

- Number of positions that we were able to fill

- Concentration/major of students who accepted the jobs (e.g., MIS versus Marketing, Computer Science, etc.)

Once I have this data entered into Excel, I start to pull it together to form a picture of the "state of the program." Here are the most intriguing questions for me:

- Given that MIS jobs can be found in virtually any industry, how diversified is my program on that front? Do I have a disproportionate number of jobs in, say, the financial services industry? Do I have less than I should in a field that is large and/or growing in my region?

- How do I feel about my mix of jobs in terms of job type? For example, right now I have been listing over 100 MIS jobs for about 40–50 MIS job seekers each six months. Great, right? Yes, but a ton of those jobs are PC/LAN Support jobs. While there is significant interest in that area, I am weaker on jobs that are more on the analytical, softer side of information technology. So I am putting more energy into developing those jobs and not worrying so much about the roll-up-your-sleeves type of IT positions for now.

- What is the average pay rate for my students? What is the pay range? How is that changing over time? Is it appropriate as a reasonable percentage of what a full-time hire in the field might make? For example, MIS graduates from my program in 2008 often made about $50,000 per year upon graduation if they have two or three six-month co-ops under their belts. $50K is basically equivalent to $25/hour (not counting benefits), so I'd like my co-op pay rates to be progressing toward that figure as they obtain increasingly challenging jobs. One of my colleagues thinks that a third-time co-op should make about 80 percent of their full-time salary in their last co-op. By that standard, my third-time co-ops should make about $19/hour. I want to keep tabs on that data when deciding whether I should be pushing employers for higher pay rates or not.

- What percentage of jobs posted are actually getting filled? More specifically, when employers post but don't hire, what happened? Did we lack the number of students to fill jobs that we should be able to fill? Was the employer not paying enough? Were they only willing to consider a "walk on water" candidate with a ton of experience and an obscenely high GPA? Was the employer so far out in the suburbs that students were unable or unwilling to make the trek? Were there other reasons that made the job less attractive to our students? Or did our students get beaten out by someone from another program? Did the employer pull the job due to budget constraints? Some analysis of these factors definitely will help you catch trends early on.

When you're looking at your data, it's fascinating to notice some facts that eluded you without the analysis. You always think you know what's going on in your program, but inevitably there will be some counterintuitive surprises. For example, our marketing group underwent this exercise several years ago, and we were all surprised to find that there was a much higher percentage of jobs reachable via public transportation than we had assumed. I had been telling students that 70–80 percent of marketing jobs required cars, but the number was much closer to 50 percent. It just seemed significantly higher because we always think of downtown Boston being much better for employers hiring for financial services and accounting. This is true, but the numbers told a more precise story.

When I first did this analysis of my program's metrics back in 1995, the biggest revelation was that I had most of my eggs in not so many baskets. Two employers alone hired about half of my Management Information Systems students. For the moment, that was not a problem in the least. It was great, in fact, as I could visit 10–15 students in a single firm visit. However, I could imagine it being disastrous depending on how the economy affected different industries as well as a specific company experiencing a downturn or an acquisition. That got me thinking about expanding and varying my employer base. What employers were more likely to be recession-proof?

One immediate idea I had was to expand positions at the many branches of Harvard University, as I knew that jobs established there were less likely to disappear due to a blip in the economy. Likewise, it seemed like we had surprisingly few jobs in the technology-rich neighborhood in Cambridge—right on public transportation—so that seemed like a good place to attempt inroads. The biotech industry also seemed ripe for more job development. Within the next few years, I had an opportunity to present the co-op program to about 15 human resources professionals across Harvard and build awareness of our program there significantly. I added a couple of great nearby employers and a key biotech employer.

And wouldn't you know it, a few years later, both of my top two employers were acquired by other corporations! One had been hiring as many as 24 information technology co-ops and quickly went down to hiring three or four, while the other went from about a dozen co-ops to a fraction of that. A more laissez-faire approach to running my program would've really crippled me if I hadn't taken steps to diversify instead of being complacent with most of my eggs in a couple of baskets.

CO-OP AND INTERNSHIP COLLEAGUES

Another important step was getting to know my co-op colleagues. If you are at a smaller program, then this may be an easy step: There may be only one or two other co-op or internship professionals, or maybe you are the program yourself! But if you do have counterparts doing what you do, it's absolutely essential to talk to them—even if they are far-flung around your campus. Why reinvent the wheel by creating program materials, developing a referral process, and figuring out counseling fundamentals on your own if there are individuals who have been doing work that is identical or at least analogous to what you do?

In some ways, this was easy for me. At the time, Northeastern had a centralized co-op program, and there were about ten of us handling business majors right on my floor. Pretty quickly I came up with a useful approach: When I faced a challenging issue, I often ran it by the individual who had the reputation for being the strictest in decision-making… and then I walked down the hall and posed the same question to the colleague who was the most flexible in the face of ambiguity! I also asked each of them their reasons for their decisions. This gave me an excellent sense of the range of possibility for the matter at hand, and I could figure out for myself if I thought a more or less permissive response would work best for me.

I didn't stop with the colleagues who were most readily accessible, though. I talked to several coordinators beyond my immediate area in business. Most (but not all) were extremely willing to share materials that they had developed and to discuss their programs and the philosophy behind it. I could see how some coordinators were especially good at creating programs that fit both their own personality as well as the needs of their students. There were times when I walked away from these meetings realizing that I had heard about some things that I definitely did not want to do in running my own program. To be fair, just about everyone who offered advice was quick to remind me that I needed to figure out that how I chose to run my program was up to me; I had no obligation to heed anyone else's suggestions.

Still, I would say that every single meeting led to at least one element that I incorporated into my ways of working with students and employers. For example, I believe that Mel Simms—a computer science co-op faculty coordinator—was to my knowledge the only one at NU requiring practice interviews at that time, and before long I was the only business co-op coordinator who required them. My colleagues started to see the benefit of having highly prepared students. Now, 13 years later, every business major at Northeastern must complete a practice interview before going on their first official interview. Likewise, my meeting with Mel Simms directly resulted in changing my voice-mail message from a quick and generic one to a more detailed one that probably has saved numerous games of "telephone tag" over the years. I'll describe this in detail in Chapter 3, which discusses maximizing efficiency and effectiveness.

EMPLOYERS

How is the economy doing? How is the job market in those specific fields that you're handling? Are there obvious major or smaller employers in your region? Talk to the Chamber of Commerce, alums, and find out about professional associations in your area. My colleague Bob Tillman can keep tabs on dozens of civil engineering employers by simply going to a few professional association meetings each year.

Don't stop there, though. Go out and visit organizations; get a feel for what their working environments are like. Meet with employers to find out what their needs are and how you can help meet those needs. If they have hired in the past, what feedback do they have, positive or negative, about previous co-ops and interns? "Phone conversations and e-mails are great, but for me personally I'm a big fan of one-on-one conversations and meeting people," Jacki Diani said. "That's not possible all the time between time constraints and location, but if you can set up meetings you can educate yourself better about the employer and their needs and hopefully grow your program. What's worked well in the past? What hasn't worked well? How can we adapt to streamline things for you?"

Perhaps the best advice that Charlie Bognanni and Bill Sloane gave me in my early months was to get out of the office and go visit employers. "You have time to do that now, but it gets harder to make it happen once you've been here for a while," they said. They explained that I would end up working on committees and other on-campus projects that would make it harder to get on the road. So I ended up getting to maybe 15 employers in my first month on the job.

A funny thing happened on that first batch of firm visits. Basically, I learned how dumb I was when it came to understanding my employers. Fortunately, I was smart enough to test out my naïve assumptions by asking questions. Quite simply, I thought I knew what my employers would be seeking when they hired MIS co-op students, and I turned out to be way off the mark. Given that the co-op jobs were computer-related tasks such as PC support, software testing, and developing or maintaining databases, I had figured that most employers would start off by describing the technical skills that candidates needed to possess.

As it turned out, about one-fourth to one-third of my inherited employers did validate my preconceived notion. "At the minimum, the student definitely needs to have some informal experience with troubleshooting or PCs...." some would say. Or "If the student hasn't had a data management course, then he or she would have a tough time in this job." However, I found that at least two-thirds of my employers said something that surprised me at the time. I kept hearing something like this: "Computer skills are useful to have—the more the better," they would say. "But many other qualities are more important: the ability to learn quickly; interpersonal skills; communication skills; the ability to work independently or in a team. We want someone with a positive attitude—someone who doesn't whine or moan when something less enjoyable needs to get done, as that's a part of any job."

I was intrigued and asked several employers why these skills were considered more important than the technical skills—especially as some of these jobs were highly technical. "If you don't know anything about a UNIX operating system, I can teach you that over a six-month co-op—assuming that you're smart and motivated to learn," one employer said. "But if you haven't learned in the first 18 or 19 years of life to have a positive attitude, to be intellectually curious, to get along with people, and so forth, how can I undo 18 years of training in just six months?"

Subsequently, I learned that this is a pretty common view from employers across many majors. My point here, though, is that it's very important to test your assumptions about your program by questioning your key constituencies about their needs. With employers, it's critical to understand what they're seeking and what their motivation is for working with a co-op or internship program. There are many possible motivators for employers when it comes to the rationale for hiring student employees:

- They are seeking cost-effective resources for getting work done.

- They are concerned about the high cost of benefits and like the idea of co-ops or interns as benefit-free labor.

- When the economy is unpredictable, co-ops or interns allow them a way to get work done without making a long-term commitment to a resource that may not be needed in the future. If the economy picks up, the employer could hire a full-time employee or additional co-ops. If business gets worse, they simply can opt against hiring another co-op without having to lay off someone and provide unemployment compensation.

- They have a seasonal or cyclical need or a temporary project.

- A co-op or internship program is a great mutual trial period to help employers and students figure out if they are a good match for each other after graduation. Given how costly it is to hire the wrong individual—as well as the fact that interviewing is not necessarily a highly scientific predictor of job success—this is an important factor in having a co-op program.

Although managers generally enjoy mentoring young professionals, I often tell employers that I would never want to tell them to hire students purely out of the goodness of their hearts. When that happens, it's a sign that it's time for me to seek a new career! Early firm visits are important opportunities to understand why existing employers hire your students and what might lead them to hire more or less of them in the future. With new employers, these visits are an important opportunity to use the aforementioned points to pitch the program. I will revisit employer visits in more detail in Chapter 13.

STUDENTS

What programs are you handling? How marketable are your students in your region or beyond? Who are they competing against—what other options do employers have? What are your students able and willing to do? What are their short and long-term career goals? How realistic are those goals?

Meeting with students is another critical early step in assessing your program. While it's important to meet with students of all academic years, I personally would recommend talking first to those students who are closest to graduation and who took maximum advantage of opportunities to do a co-op or internship. I like the idea of holding roundtable discussions in which small groups of students can respond informally to a variety of questions. You could call these exit interviews. Did they have good work experiences? What made their experiences more or less satisfying? What did they think of the quality and quantity of jobs made available to them through the program? Are there industries, regions, specific employers, or particular types of job that they feel are glaring omissions from the program? How did the co-op preparation process work for them? Did they feel prepared in terms of resume writing and interview skills? Did they have problems arise during any of their jobs, and did they know where to turn if that occurred? What did they think of the reflection process or whatever may have been asked of them upon returning to college?

If you hear critical comments, resist the urge to defend the program or to attempt to convince any students that their views are unfair. That could derail the dialogue in a hurry. Concentrate on asking clarifying questions that help you understand any positive or negative perceptions that exist. If you conduct several roundtable discussions as well as some one-on-one conversations—and surveys are a possibility as well; surveymonkey.com is a good resource that preserves respondents' anonymity—you should start to get a sense of how your program is generally regarded by students. Eventually you can figure out what the existing strengths and weaknesses seem to be and begin to map out some opportunities for improvement.

In my case, conversations with students were generally pretty positive. My predecessors had developed more than enough jobs for the relatively small MIS student population, and that was despite the fact that they admitted that they hadn't put much energy into MIS job development. So I could see that there was a real opportunity to grow the number of jobs along with the number of MIS students.

That said, student conversations also raised some concerns. The less-qualified candidates often ended up doing accounting jobs for their first co-ops. Basically, we didn't have enough good entry-level jobs despite the general surplus of positions. And given that the students were working with coordinators who focused most of their energy on accounting, it was natural enough for them to suggest an accounting position to a student who struggled to find a job in their first choice of an area.

When it came to discussing employers with my students, I found that my conversations also revolved around a small handful of organizations. This corroborated what I had seen when I had analyzed the metrics of my program. It was great to have three or four big employers that each hired many MIS students, but it also made me uneasy and confirmed that my data analysis had yielded correct inferences about the need to diversify my program.

Conversations with first-time co-ops revealed a different set of concerns. In my particular concentration, there was a significant number of international students who were very motivated but who had language skill issues. I also was struck by another dramatic contrast: Although my employer conversations had taught me that a lack of technical skills or professional experience was not going to be a fatal flaw for my first-time job seekers, those inexperienced students indicated to me that they were quite anxious about their job search and often believed that they had nothing to offer a potential employer. Telling them what employers had told me helped to some degree, but I started to think that their confidence needed to be built in a more tangible way. Combined with my conversation with Mel Simms, that led me to experiment with practice interviews as well as to look for workshops and reading materials that might ramp up their technical skills for the IT positions I had available.

At this point, I was still "drinking from a fire hose" as the saying goes at Microsoft, one of my co-op employers. I was taking in a ton of information and processing it, and it gradually came together in a tentative vision for how to approach my program. We'll delve into that in the next chapter.

TOWARD GOALS

As I alluded to in the introduction, I asked numerous professionals a series of questions that were critical to determining the content of each chapter of this book. For this chapter, the question I asked took various forms. In some cases, I asked people to reflect on their early days in the field and to talk about what worked for them. Ultimately, though, the question morphed into the following scenario: "Let's say you suddenly obtained a new position as an educator. Let's assume we've plunked you down at Plankton State University, an institution that you basically know nothing about at all. Walk me through the series of steps you would take to get a co-op or internship program off the ground when you're in unfamiliar territory."

When I mentioned this question in passing to Nancy Johnston of Simon Fraser University—who you will be hearing from quite a bit throughout this book—her immediate reaction was, "Well, I'm curious as to whether anyone who was told that they were plunked down at Plankton State said, 'The first thing I would say is, what am I trying to do here?' Because that really will determine the mechanics piece. I would hope that people would say something about education because it's Plankton State University not Plankton Placement Agency. Why did they hire me? What do they want? If this thing at Plankton State is running tickety-boo in five years, what does it look like?'"

As you'll see with the excerpts that follow, many of my interviewees definitely are on the same page when it comes to remembering that we are developing an educational model as Nancy had hoped. That said, there is less of an emphasis on defining direction initially. I think that this is because there is a bit of a chicken-or-egg first question that comes along when we consider how we can best move toward goals. Do you tackle a new job with an initial philosophy when it comes to goals and vision, or do you really need to gather information and get some sense of the lay of the land before you move toward goals? It's all well and good to say that you are going to create a program revolving around the educational needs of students, but what if those that hired you think that the institution's goals are paramount?

Basically, I think it might be magnanimous to say that a professional could either start off by asking "Why am I here?" or by deferring that question—temporarily—by beginning a relationship-building process with all constituencies (students, employers, academic faculty, the administration of your institution) and then reaching a conclusion of what is both desirable and possible for your program.

With that in mind, let's hear how a handful of professionals describe the process of assessing that Plankton State co-op or internship program in their own words.

IN THEIR OWN WORDS

PROFESSIONAL PERSPECTIVE #1
"MANY HATS"
Ronnie Porter, Northeastern University

My career started a little bit differently than probably a lot of other people's, though here at Northeastern there were other people who started the way I did. I began my career in what was called an assistant to a coordinator position, which was akin to a cooperative education counselor. So it was like having a four-year co-op job of being a coordinator in training, so to speak.

My first assignment in the co-op program was to work with Homer "Doc" Littlefield who, as he put it, was "one of the oldest living co-op coordinators at NU." The first thing he told me was that he was going to describe what he did. He said, "A coordinator wears many hats." And he actually did the motion of taking hats off and putting hats on.

I think that Doc hit the nail on the head as far as describing that co-op coordinators do have several roles. That's really true. He was someone who delegated many responsibilities, and that actually worked to my advantage. I got to try to do a wide range of things during that four-year period that probably a lot of my peers did not get to do. After that I had the basic skills that I needed to become a co-op coordinator and was ready to interview for a position.

Some of the skills that co-op coordinators need are the ability and interest to work with students but also it is necessary to have the ability, the interest, and the skills to work with employers. There are several facets of employer development work. We have to be able to market our programs, so we have to be able to actually sell the program to some extent. We have to do it in a way that brings employers on board as education partners and mentors for our students and not just as employers. I think that that's a big change from when I first started this work until now in terms of the language that we use. We always knew that we had those expectations of employers, but now we really need to be very specific about it—the language that I use with employers about the integrated learning model [consisting of the preparation, activity, and reflection phases], the partnering with NU, and mentoring of students is an integral part of the students' educational process. We need to be able to explain that as educators.

We need to be able to teach the employers about effective mentoring—some of them are very good at it; some of them are not as good at it. We need to work with them on being able to assess student skills and to understand our curriculum, so that the activities that students are doing are supporting the learning process as it relates to the curriculum. So there are a lot of things that we do with employers.

And then the other hat is being strategic about our programs: as co-op faculty we need to be able to effectively plan, and to continually assess the needs of the students, the needs of the employers, and the marketplace. We need an understanding of the labor market in our regions and nationally, what's going on. So we really need to be proficient at understanding the bigger picture.

I do think that we do wear many hats, and that is certainly what has made this work very interesting to me—the opportunity to work with a student here at the university and then see them in action in the field. Helping students integrate their academics and experiential opportunities has been very exciting.

I already had had some background and nuts-and-bolts experience about the workings of the University, which gave me a little bit of an advantage. The first thing I did when I became a faculty coordinator was to find out who my students and employers were. I researched specific information about the curricula for the different programs I coordinated. At the time I was working with four different programs. I actually went to the departments to gain an understanding of the different curricula and got copies of all of the various curricula so that I really understood which courses my students were taking—of course now we can do all of that online. I did some research at that time using the Occupational Outlook Handbook and other career informational materials to try to understand what kinds of occupations that students in these fields of study could go into, what skills were needed for those occupations, what types of industries those occupations existed in, and where those industries were located. I spent a lot of time doing some background exploration and research about the programs and the majors/occupations. I then identified all of the students in the programs that I was assigned to work with. I made sure that I created updated files on the students and established contact with them. I developed a communication process, designed co-op preparation seminars on different topics, as well as collected and compiled information on co-op opportunities. I developed materials on interviewing and resume writing and other career related topics.

At the same time, I identified which employers were already participating in the program. I also did a needs assessment by breaking down the list of employers by occupational areas. In addition, I did some research using a variety of available career and industry information to identify potential job opportunities for students with science academic backgrounds as well as to explore the labor market outlook for potential growth areas. I networked with academic faculty in the programs as well as my co-op colleagues who, although they work with students in other majors, may already work with companies that may have opportunities for science students. A particular marketing coordinator took me under his wing and mentored me. He had marketing students in a number of pharmaceutical companies and was instrumental in helping me make contacts in that industry. After assessing the program, I tried to determine if there were any areas that needed to be developed. At that time, I was working with the allied health fields, and I noticed that there seemed to be an emerging need for science students in industry. I started making connections with biotechnology employers and was able to open up new types of opportunities for students. For example, although Medical Laboratory Science students had primarily worked in hospital settings up to that point, their backgrounds were in demand for positions in industry as well. Though this opened up new types of work experiences for students, initially it didn't fly very well with some of the academic faculty who wanted the students to be working in hospitals; they saw that as a more traditional role. But students were coming to me saying: "You know, I also have this interest in business, and I'd like to do research but not in a hospital." It took some time to expand both the opportunities and the mindset to round out the program to reflect the opportunities that were available in this region.

I don't know what you would call that, but having the ability and interest to do the research and to have the understanding that both the interests of students and the needs of employers are very important is critical. You can have the best counseling skills in the world, but if you don't have good opportunities for students you can't run a good co-op program.

PROFESSIONAL PERSPECTIVE #2
"FOCUS ON STUDENT EDUCATION"
Bernadette Friedrich, Michigan State University

My advice to somebody who's been brought in or is going to be brought into a new program would be to make sure that this is truly administratively backed and to get a feel for the faculty. A program without faculty is not a program; a program without faculty support is not a program. You can do all kinds of programming for students and you can even get money from administration, but if a faculty member says to students "Why would you want to take a semester off?" your program is not going to go anywhere.

Then I would focus on student education and programming. Starting from why this is important and then you need to start pulling employers in even if it's just one or two key employers to spread that message for you. It's great to have a program and say we want 50% of our students to participate in co-op, we're going to bring employers on campus to interview and then have jobs available. But if the students aren't prepared, you've got a problem. They may be academically prepared, but if they're not professionally prepared to create a resume and interview, then you're going to lose your employer buy-in. You need to have an assessment and evaluation process at least in the back of your mind. If you have employers but the students don't get good experiences, it's going to die because students are going to come back and tell their friends. If you have employers and you have students who are ill-prepared, it's going to die because employers can find students who are top-notch at the neighboring college.

PROFESSIONAL PERSPECTIVE #3
"FIRST STEPS"
Kate McLaughlin, Northeastern University

My first advice to you would be to compartmentalize. What particular program are you going to be serving? Which majors? Which portion of the student population? What have they done previously? Is there anything to build off of—any existing internship structure that you can use as a base? Once I had an idea of what I was working with, I would sit down with some of the faculty members of those particular departments and say, "What are the areas of interest for your students? What are the kinds of companies they would benefit from working at?"

As much as you can, I recommend that you look at models at other schools working in the same disciplines. Because the kind of discipline that you're working in will have a significant impact on how you structure the program. If you are working with English majors and math majors and music majors, you're going to have a different program than if you work with accounting majors, and engineering majors, and nursing majors. In some ways, the more professional programs are easier to build a structure around—certainly easier to sell to an employer because it's a much more obvious connection.

Presumably, your school has certain programs that are its strengths. That's probably where you're going to want to start because it's going to be an easier sell to employers. So meet with faculty, but you also might want to meet with development folks or alumni representatives to find out what connections the university has with companies in the area to try to use those as a first entrée into starting this program.

My suspicion, however, is that in this day and age there is really not a university out there that doesn't have some sort of internship program that has done these things in some way, shape, or form. So my first goal would be to talk to whomever has done those programs with students—whether it's overseeing an internship as a directed study, or something that's done not for credit or through Career Services—find out who those players are on campus and pick their brains.

And don't let anybody pressure you to roll out something before it's ready to roll. I might recommend that you start out with a very, very small pool of students to work with because you're going to find a lot of bumps in the road that you didn't know about in the first round of finding employers and helping students find positions. What you want to do is try to build it in a manageable way. So if historically, let's say you're working with five or six disciplines, and each of those disciplines had five or six students go out and do an internship of their own creation during that term. So you take that and you do not advertise this as something new that everybody should be involved in, yet. You kind of take over managing that and work with those students to find out what's worked for them, what hasn't worked for them, what you can help with. Then you start talking to their employers and building the relationship so the next semester, the next summer, you can start building a lot more employers and students into the system. Maybe you go from five or six in the major to ten. One of the things that you definitely want to push back on is to not let them make you go from zero to 60 because if you do that, the students are going to suffer.

PROFESSIONAL PERSPECTIVE #4
"Aligning With Academia and Student Learning"
Tamara Pinkas, Lane Community College

Like any good professional, you go around and you make friends. Our job is so much about communication and to constantly be visible. Part of my job description is to be very active on campus in all kinds of committees. For example, I have been a long-time member of and have chaired the Learning Council—one of the governance councils—because we need to be vigilant about 1) making sure people know what we do and the value that we bring and 2) knowing about and having the ability to influence decisions that come through those organizations. For example, when your institution undergoes a reorganization, you've got all those good relationships and people who are all over the organization who know about how co-op fits in the academic program as well as a role in the decisions related to the reorganization.

I'm not suggesting the results are fast. By participating and being highly visible on campus in ways that are helpful to the whole institution—not just in places that affect your job—you will gain the support you need. Another valuable use of your time is to identify ways in your institution to publicly thank or in some way acknowledge others who help the co-op program. At Lane, we choose a co-op champion every year. We pick a staff person, it can be a faculty member or classified person, who has been particularly wonderful that year and we go out of our way to recognize them. We invite them to a picnic that we have and they get honored, and they get a plaque, and then we also go to their division and we honor them in front of others. It gives us an opportunity to do internal marketing, and that is one of the ways to effect change.

Some institutions are so entrenched that they may never change. I acknowledge that however, the more that you can be a person—a co-op person—who is seen as aligning with academia and student learning and less with job placement the better. Because that's where the value is. One way to ensure co-op is aligned with academics is to have grades associated with the co-op experience. Another way to more effectively align with the academic side of the institution is to require co-op staff to be faculty who have the academic credentials to teach in the areas in which they do co-op as well as choosing co-op faculty who are well regarded within the institution. Also, the more that you can structure it so your co-op program actually brings money to the college through things like tuition and fees—money talks, we know that—the more influence you can have in how co-op is aligned within the institution.

Not every institution can go that way, not everyone will be changed, but I really think that our profession cannot sit on its laurels and think, "Oh, everyone knows how important and valuable we are to student learning." We have to constantly be teaching: meeting new faculty, staff and administrators, making presentations. Every year I help plan and participate in the new faculty orientation. I bring presents; I bring co-op mugs to all the new faculty and I get a chance, because I organize the event, to get up in front of them and say my 30 seconds about who I am and what I do at Lane. I invite them to contact me if they have questions about co-op but more importantly, I want them to know that there is a faculty co-op coordinator in their division who they will want to get to know.

You might wonder what new faculty orientation has to do with students learning at a job? Well, the way I see it, we need faculty support for co-op in every discipline. I want faculty all across campus to know about co-op and recommend it to their students. I see a direct connection between faculty orientation and co-op so that is why I see it as my job to participate. And again that's getting known, getting visible, being useful, and influencing how things go so that we can create the environment that is really supportive for the students, because that's the goal.

PROFESSIONAL PERSPECTIVE #6
"BUILD RELATIONSHIPS"
Tom Akins, Georgia Institute of Technology

That's a great question. As I've matured, you might say, over the years in my career I think what I've begun to realize is how much our business and what we do is based on relationships. Personal relationships that are professional in nature but it's even more like the one-on-one that you have with different individuals. I think that the first thing if you're beginning a program is to realize that they don't know you and you don't really know them, but you need to really build a rapport, build relationships. This needs to happen not only with, say, the upper administration because they have to buy into the idea of having this type of program being offered.

I think that maybe a lot of people don't realize this when they get into cooperative education, but the faculty and academics are the driving force behind the institution, and you have to have the buy-in from the faculty. I believe it's truly a program that's academic in nature, so I think you'd have to build relationships with faculty members so that they don't think that you're trying to do something that's outside the norm. You're going to respect and not interfere with their classroom instruction and what they're trying to teach as far as theory is concerned, but you're there to help facilitate and enhance the method of education. You're there to work with them.

So I think the first key thing that I would do is start to build those relationships not only with the upper administration, because you're working for them, but also with the faculty to let them know that yes, you're working for them as well. You may not work directly for them, and they're not your supervisors, but they need to know you're there to help benefit the students so they have an enhanced form or method of education. So that would be what I would do first, to build that and to realize, look, we're all working together as a team to benefit the students. That's the main thing.

PROFESSIONAL PERSPECTIVE #5
"TAKING STOCK OF YOUR PROGRAM"
Jacki Diani, Northeastern University

I remember it being overwhelming, and I think that's not uncommon when you're a new coordinator. When I started, I didn't have a huge number of majors—three or four within healthcare—but they were all very *different* areas of healthcare. The assessment of the academic and co-op programs can be very overwhelming at first, but I think it's critical for you to be able to grow and develop your program. You don't want to develop positions in the wrong areas because you will disappoint the employers and the students.

In my situation, I inherited a program, so at least I could assess it through files and historical paperwork: what employers had been hiring students and from what majors. I could take some stock of the program from the employer and student side. I also met with academic faculty who gave me feedback and suggestions; it is important to connect with academic faculty. I was also very fortunate to have co-op colleagues to bounce things off of, ask questions and seek advice about problems. These co-op colleagues, even from other majors, were instrumental in my development and success.

Your program starts to pull together when you start talking to people. First you might pull out a drawer and you find folders on employers, and you start reading them, and it's not making a lot of sense. Then you start talking to students and talking to faculty, and then all of a sudden you start to hear recurring themes, and it begins to make sense. By doing this you get a feel for what has generally worked well, and where the challenges lie. For example, the issues for one major might be that the jobs don't pay well, for another that job locations aren't great. With another major, a reoccurring theme might be leveling—that there are plentiful opportunities for a student going out on their first co-op, but not enough for those on their third. By reviewing student and employer files, reviewing curriculums, talking to people, you start to get a grasp on the program and what you need to work on. Much of what we do is cyclical, so in talking to faculty you can try to predict some of what is coming and what you'll need. For example, it may be June and students are placed, but I should be thinking of January—not only focusing on the coming weeks. Can I somewhat predict which students will be going out for January? How many students? What levels? Then you can look at what you have and plan accordingly.

Now that we have covered the various steps in assessing what you've got when you're starting a program, we'll go into more depth on developing a vision that will help you chart your direction for the months and years to come. First, though, you might want to reflect on how you go about assessing your own program by considering and discussing the questions that follow.

REFLECTION QUESTIONS

1. This chapter raises a question as to whether it is best to start off by simply asking yourself "What am I trying to do here?" versus undergoing an information-gathering process before trying to ascertain your program's direction. What do you think? Is it wiser to start off with an educational vision and philosophy that you can bring into your first meetings with students, employers, academic faculty, and administrators, or is it better to use these meetings to develop that vision and philosophy?

2. This chapter talks about metrics as a critical but often overlooked aspect of many co-op and internship programs. What metrics do you track on a regular basis? Are you simply keeping track of placements, or are you doing more to develop a sense of where you are versus where you might aspire to be when it comes to job options for your students? Why or why not?

3. Chapter 1 also discusses the importance of gathering information on an ongoing basis from colleagues, students, employers, academic faculty, and administrators in your institution. You may find that some constituencies have goals that align, while others are incompatible. If you have to choose between doing what's in the best interest of employers, students, and your institution, which is going to be your priority? Why?

4. In her interview transcript, Ronnie Porter talks about how coordinators need to wear many hats. These include marketing your program to employers, counseling students, teaching employers to be become good educational partners, developing some mastery of your students' majors, and creating a big-picture, strategic vision for your program. Which of these areas are natural strengths for you as a professional? Which are your biggest weaknesses? What are you doing or planning to do to become stronger in those areas that are not natural strengths?

CHAPTER 2

DEVELOPING A VISION

"Vision is the art of seeing what is invisible to others."

— *Jonathan Swift*

Once you have done some serious assessment of your program, you can move toward developing a vision for your program. This is critical. I have known several co-op or internship professionals who are perfectly good at dealing with a student who is in their office or who can answer any questions that an employer might ask, and who are really perfectly adequate in their roles. Yet I sometimes get the sense that some professionals never really have stepped back to consider the big picture of what are their guiding principles when it comes to running the best possible program.

There is no one way to run a great co-op or internship program. That said, my conversations with numerous experienced professionals resulted in many recurring themes when it comes to understanding what goes into developing a vision or philosophy for running a program that will have a great impact on your students' educational experience. In this chapter, I'll first discuss where a vision comes from and then what, generally, it looks like.

EDUCATION AND EXPERIENCE

What educational background and prior work experiences do you bring to the table as a professional? Although they can vary dramatically, they often can be useful when it comes to how you look at the world in general and your program in particular. Someone who is trained as an industrial engineer may bring a more analytical and innovative focus to the role, a relentless sense of process improvement and maximization of efficiency. A professional who majored in marketing might use that foundation to inform how he or she sells the program to employers as well as how students can pitch themselves with a resume, cover letter, or interview. An individual trained as a software developer might think of an internship program as analogous to a software development project: Develop a prototypical process, test it with end users, de-bug it repeatedly, and ultimately deliver a final product that is user-friendly, efficient, and great when it comes to usability. With an MBA, you might consider a SWOT analysis, in which you look internally at your strengths and weaknesses and then consider the external opportunities and threats that affect your program.

In addition to your academic background, your previous professional experiences are invaluable. It's not impossible to counsel students effectively if you have never worked outside of academia, but it's undoubtedly more difficult. Being able to tap into your own experiences with a tedious job, a difficult co-worker, or an unreasonable employer give you a better ability to empathize with your students and to model appropriate responses to the challenges they face. We'll discuss how to do this later in the book when we delve deeper into student counseling, but for now just bear in mind that you definitely want to tap into your experiences and be prepared to reflect on them and possibly share them with your students.

In my case, my educational background is in Business Administration with an emphasis on Organizational Behavior. Well before I ever worked in cooperative education, I was a lecturer in Organizational Behavior at Boston University as well as Northeastern University. OB is basically the psychology of business. At BU, I worked with a professor named George Labovitz, a guru in Total Quality Management. In teaching it to students, I internalized the principles and learned to differentiate between how TQM could either be a useless buzzword—after all, who is "against" quality?—or a transformational philosophy in an organization.

Several tenets of TQM are apparent in how I've chosen to run my program:

1. *A dollar invested in preventing a problem from arising ultimately will save anywhere from $10 to $100 in comparison to fixing something after it's broken.* TQM focuses on analyzing processes and doing the "right things the right way the first time." Doing so may take a little more time, energy, or money up front, but ultimately it will save much more time, energy, and money in the long run. This rule is why I began requiring practice interviews when it was unfashionable at Northeastern. "I don't have time to do that," some of my colleagues said. To which I thought, yes, but you apparently do have time to meet with a student again and again over several months because they are interviewing repeatedly without success! Why not increase the student's chance of getting the best job possible with less interviews? Ultimately, an hour spent conducting and critiquing a practice interview may well save at least a couple of hours in counseling time.

2. *Always focus on the never-ending battle of continuous improvement.* Whether you're a factory building bicycles or running an internship program, there is always a way to improve your process to minimize errors and problems. But doing so requires a relentless, honest focus on how things can be better—even when it's not easy to make it happen. You need to talk to everyone your work affects and solicit input on how to make things run better. In co-op, this means reflecting regularly on what's working and what's not, and then making changes. And that never ends.

3. *Satisfy your customers… and everyone is a customer.* In accordance with TQM, I love to think up new ways to satisfy both my internal and external customers—students and employers—in ways that actually buy me quality time to do other activities. For example, I probably get at least two calls per week from prospective employers requesting information about the program. Early on, I would take 20–30 minutes on the phone to try to explain cooperative education. But would I remember all the salient details? And how much information would the employer retain? Eventually, I invested a few hours to develop a co-op

FAQ document. Now when an employer calls, I immediately send the FAQ document, which includes a sample job description that they can use as a template. I can respond very quickly to requests for information, and it only takes a minute or two to e-mail the document. I estimate that this alone probably saves me an hour a week. That's about 50 hours per year freed up to go out and visit organizations or do other "quality time" activities with students!

4. *TQM is a "value-driven" top-down philosophy.* With TQM, the person in charge needs to set the tone. The assumption here is that most people are motivated and want to do a good job, and they will do a better job if their input is valued and utilized. So that had a big impact on my emphasis on being open to criticism from students, employers, and colleagues.

In addition to TQM, I have found that my more general training as an MBA has had an impact in how I manage my program. Remembering my coursework in finance, I often think of how running the employer side of a program is rather like managing a mutual fund. In either case, the goal is to diversify your investments to manage risk. In practical terms, this led me to take steps to ensure that my Management Information Systems program would be more resilient in the face of inevitable fluctuations in the economy.

As mentioned in Chapter 1, my analysis of metrics showed me that I was "invested" heavily in a limited number of companies and industries. As with investments, that can lead to a big payoff or a major loss. I found it useful to think of my program as a somewhat conservative mutual fund—I wanted some stability. I didn't need to double or triple my number of jobs in a hurry; I preferred modest growth with minimal downside when it came to risk. While writing this very chapter, I noticed that the Dow Jones Industrial Average dropped 350 points today. That only reinforced my sense of how important it is to have an array of employers that can withstand the economic roller coaster.

I have seen other coordinators make comparable adjustments after undergoing a similar analysis. Our criminal justice co-op faculty split up career areas among them, and my colleague Steve Williams ended up doing a substantial amount of job development in the areas of adult and juvenile corrections as well as rehabilitation as a result. Even before financial services took a hit, I saw our finance co-op coordinators striving to develop more opportunities in corporate finance. Moves like these are wise, both in terms of offering a healthy variety of educational options for students as well as minimizing the upheaval that can be caused by job market changes.

How you utilize your previous education and training is up to you. Just think about tapping into it to see how it can work best for you.

PERSONALITY AND STYLE

I recall doing an interesting activity as part of diversity training in my early days at Northeastern. A group of a few dozen co-op and career services professionals took a test to determine what our preferred style was at work. The main groups were as follows: people-oriented, process-oriented, and results-oriented.

A handful of my colleagues were in the process-oriented group. I was amused to note that these were the people who tended to drive me nuts at departmental meetings, as they were the folks who just loved to talk about how we should go about making a decision. They loved

Robert's Rules of Order and relished the whole process of making motions, seconding them, and so forth.

By far the largest group in the room was, unsurprisingly, the people-oriented group. Given that our roles all required us to counsel students, it made sense that there would be many people who just loved to work one-on-one with young adults.

Where did I find myself? I was in the results-oriented group—with just one other person out of about 35! That was an illuminating moment for me. Obviously, it's not "better" to have one personality profile rather than another, but there are definite pros and cons to any style. It's important to have self-awareness about your interpersonal style, as this will make you cognizant of what aspects of your role will come naturally to you as well as what your potential blind spots may be.

In my case, a results-oriented style is great when it comes to making a resume look terrific or helping a student strategize for an interview. It drives me when it comes to making my program as good as it can be... or when getting a book written regardless of distractions or interruptions! Yet there are potential problems associated with that style that I've had to address. Taking the Myers-Briggs test underscored these drawbacks. I am an ENTP (Extrovert, Intuiting, Thinking, and Perceiving). In a nutshell, this means that my personality type is strong on big-picture thinking, innovation, and visionary. Yet this style is also characterized by impatience with people and too much emphasis on logic rather than the human element in the equation.

This describes my early years as a professional pretty well. Dealing with a student who was upset about not having a job, I would shrug off their feelings and reel off what he or she needed to do to address the issue as expediently as they could. Working with international students who struggled with English, I got very frustrated with the effect that this had on getting them a good job, and I did a poor job of acknowledging the challenges that they faced every day in our culture.

Some advice that I give to students regarding career choices can also be applied to co-op and internship professionals. When it comes to transferable skills, we all have some strong muscles and weak muscles. We all have a tendency to gravitate toward situations—or even careers—that allow us to flaunt our strong muscles while avoiding our flabby ones. But how wise is this? Yes, you need to capitalize on your strengths and set yourself up with a job or career that makes the most of them, but you also need to think about addressing your weaker areas. As a person and professional, you may not be all that comfortable with technology, confronting bad behavior, discussing strong emotions, or closing your mouth and just listening for an extended period, but these and other skills are all ones that you'll need to master to be the best professional you can be.

The same can be said for any other personality type. My buddies in the process-oriented cluster who I sometimes find annoying probably were better than I was about creating a structured and clear process for working with students and employers, but they also needed to be careful that their love of process didn't come at the expense of valuing people and striving for results with their program. At times, I have seen professionals bog students down with hoops and hurdles that certainly created a sense of order. But did these steps really add value to the student's educational experience, or were they perceived as no more than a pain in the butt? Likewise, I have known people-oriented professionals that loved their students so much that they happily would recite the same information 50 times to 50 students instead of developing a more efficient process that would get results…and, ironically, give them more time to enjoy quality interaction time with those students.

In the terms of Myers-Briggs, someone who is a strong "Feeler" may need to make sure that their preference for harmony doesn't override the need for competence. A feeler still needs to be able to give critical honest feedback to students. Meanwhile a "Thinker" is just the opposite. Thinkers generally aren't shy about nonchalantly criticizing students in the spirit of competence, but their great advice may anger or alienate students if it is perceived as being presented in a cold, uncaring way. In the final analysis, being aware of your own style and that of your colleagues will result in much more understanding and much less irritation in how you set up your program. Now I sometimes work with a strong "J" personality in Myers-Briggs nomenclature, and I'll find myself thinking, "Well, Dan is a strong "J," so I've got to make sure to give him some structure and details when I ask for his assistance…." I have to consciously remind myself to do this, as my "P" personality means that I tend to dislike structure and resent details!

PROGRAM REQUIREMENTS AND WORKLOAD

Workload is probably the most dramatic difference from one professional to the next when it comes to co-ops, internships, career services, and so forth. On one extreme, a good colleague of mine left Northeastern and took a job with an outplacement agency. He did many of the tasks that he once did at NU—career counseling, resume critiques, interview prep, and so forth—but every client had a one-hour appointment, meaning that he saw no more than eight clients per day! On the other end of the spectrum, I have heard of colleagues at other institutions who literally are supposed to assist hundreds of students in their job search efforts simultaneously.

Even within one program, results can vary, as they say. I started off with a very low load of 31 students for my first referral cycle in 1995, and I maxed out at 155 MIS students for one six-month work term back in January through June 2000. At that time, it was the largest load in all of Northeastern, where we tend to think of a load of 60–70 students seeking jobs at one time (with a similar number out working simultaneously) as a fairly reasonable load.

You hate to think of workload as a factor that will influence your vision for your program, but inevitably it plays a significant role. When I had 155 students, I had to cut down significantly on my firm visits, handle more preparation and reflection activities with small or large groups instead of one-on-one, and I just couldn't put in the time really needed to develop and maintain the kinds of relationships that I ideally like to have with students and employers. I had to be pretty ruthless when it came to deciding what companies I really needed to visit and how much energy I could put into the students who were more rough around the edges. I'd like to think that I still lived by my usual vision in many ways, but there is no question that it was somewhat of a pale facsimile of what it ordinarily would be.

So when I proceed to lay out what many professionals have identified as the fundamentals of a solid vision for a program, I know full well that some of you will be thinking "Sounds great, but there is no way that I can do all of that in light of my student and employer load or my wide range of majors." I understand that completely. Still, think about which of the following you can do to make your program as good as it can be. I often like to say that the biggest challenge in this field is not that any element of it is so difficult; it's more the challenge of figuring out how to best use your time. Everyone's time is limited, no matter how big or small their load is. How can you load the deck to maximize the educational value that your students obtain from your program while ensuring that employers are meeting any number of needs that they may have as well?

FUNDAMENTALS OF A STRONG VISION

In my many conversations with experienced professionals about their philosophy or vision, a variety of themes emerged. Some specific, verbatim thoughts on this topic will round out the chapter in a few pages, but first let's look at the concepts that emerged most frequently.

BUILD GOOD RELATIONSHIPS WITH STUDENTS

Almost all educators I spoke to cited the critical importance of building good relationships with students. There are many elements to this.

1. *Managing Expectations*

One key is *managing expectations*. Some students come into their relationships with a co-op or internship coordinator with an incredibly unrealistic notion of what is plausible given their level of experience, schooling, grades, and so forth. Other students are just the opposite: They approach their first job search with great anxiety or even a sense of paralysis; they believe that they are not worthy of any kind of professional job because they may have only worked in retail or in other non-professional environments. Either way, we need to make sure that students understand what is possible. They may have to pay their dues and work their way up the ladder professionally. They might be more qualified right now than they believe. Becoming an expert on the job market in your field and developing a keen sense of how jobs fit into a long-term career path will help you convey to students what they reasonably can expect.

2. *Honesty*

A second key is *honesty*. In the co-op preparation class that I teach, I often make a point of telling the students what is and is not possible given the economy, the job market in their fields, and the effort they put into their job search. I tell them that I will be completely honest with them as to whether I anticipate that they will have a difficult job search, what jobs they can and cannot obtain at this point in their careers, and so forth. It's important that they understand that I'm not going to be a cheerleader and praise them for no reason, but I'm also not going to scare them into thinking things will be really tough in order to make them work harder.

3. *Reality Therapy*

A third key of building strong relationships is what I like to call *reality therapy*. This relates to managing expectations. When students' perceptions or behaviors are inaccurate or inappropriate, you need to point this out to them, right away. As we will see when we take a longer look at the Millennial Generation later in this book, many students today lack self-awareness. They often aren't sure what their strengths really are—let alone their weaknesses—and they may overestimate or underestimate themselves as job candidates. You need to be supportive but honest with students when giving them feedback, as this will build your credibility with them and increase their trust in you as a professional.

A few years ago, a student asked to be on the interview schedule with my best MIS employer. At that time, the employer preferred to have me determine who went on their schedule, given my knowledge of their company and who would fit the jobs. One student was stunned when he asked to be put on the schedule, only to hear me say, "I just can't do it." But I told him exactly why: "There are three reasons: You have a 2.6 GPA, which is borderline at best for this employer. Your last co-op evaluation was okay but not very positive. And this employer always seeks outgoing, energetic, make-it-happen personalities. That's just not how you come across. I can help you find a really good job, but not at that employer."

4. *Use Conflicts and Problems as Learning Opportunities*

A fourth key in building relationships would be to *use conflicts and problems as "teachable moments" or learning opportunities.* There will be many examples of this later in the book, when we consider counseling tactics. In the big picture, though, bear in mind that it's inevitable that some students will make poor choices with bad consequences. Naturally, this will disappoint, frustrate, and maybe even anger you because of the effect it has on your reputation as well as that of the student and your program. Still, most professionals will tell you that you'll have a much greater impact on your students if you can always use the tone of an educator when addressing disappointing behavior. Being solution-oriented and always remembering to talk to the student as if you want them to learn something will teach your students that true professionals take the high road in interpersonal interactions, and it also shows them that addressing problems directly and honestly can strengthen relationships instead of ending them.

When a student is struggling in my co-op preparation class, I tend to make them aware of it in an unemotional, matter-of-fact way. At times, I have told students that they are dead-last in my class in terms of performance. I explain why, and then I probe, unemotionally, to find out what the student can tell me that will shed some light on his or her struggles. Students are often taken aback initially when I give them direct feedback, but soon they can sense that I am using the tone of a teacher. I want to make sure that they are aware of the problem, and then I want to figure out what we're going to do to turn the situation around. I am careful to remind them that I am not branding them as a hopeless case; in fact, I have had such dead-last students evolve into superstars over time. I've had a few students who look back at this fateful meeting with me as the turning point in their co-op career, and it all comes down turning a problem into a learning opportunity instead of an outlet for frustration or a chance to punish.

5. *Model the Right Behavior*

A fifth and final key with students is to *model the right behavior.* Given that some educators may be considerably older than our students, I think that they may have the sense that we can't relate to what they're going through as undergraduates. So it can be helpful to share some of your experiences as a way to show empathy as well as giving them a specific model to follow when facing a predicament. Even for younger professionals—who students may relate to more naturally as near peers but who also need to prove that they are credible mentors despite their relative youth—modeling can be a great way to show that they have had some legitimate experiences to share.

As I get further into my career, I find that I am more willing to share my personal stories of challenge and difficulty. With students who are in real psychological crisis, I will share the story of the second semester of my junior year, which probably was one of the toughest times of my life. If students have an unfair boss, I'll talk about a previous employer whose behavior led me to fantasizing about quitting in a huff... and how I hung in there, took the high road, and ultimately made a graceful exit that salvaged a reference. Likewise, I often tell the story of my first job search out of grad school and how hard it was to turn down an offer that I really didn't want, given that I had no other job leads on the horizon. And I tell them how I ultimately did get my first two real teaching jobs in academia without even having to interview, purely because of how I had proven myself so thoroughly to the professor who was my key reference. Modeling through these personal stories shows students that you really do care and that you have walked in their shoes—even if you're over 40 and perhaps perceived as having one foot in the grave and another on a banana peel!

BUILD STRONG RELATIONSHIPS WITH EMPLOYERS

Most of the educators I interviewed ranked their relationships with employers as a close second to the priority they place on student relationships. But some argue that strong relationships with employers are actually the most important priority of all. The argument is that if you don't have jobs available that are good quality learning experiences for your students, then it really doesn't matter how supportive and nurturing you are in your interactions with students. If they have no place to work, you don't have much of a program.

1. *Customer-Service Mentality*

The first key cited by my interviewees was *having a customer-service mentality with employers*. Some of you will be surprised to find that this is actually a somewhat controversial point with some professionals. "I do NOT provide 'customer service' to anyone; I am an educator," is something that I have heard more than once from professionals. I disagree, and so do many experts that I interviewed. When visiting an employer or talking to one on the phone, I believe that you have to be assessing their needs and figuring out if a co-op or intern can address a need and add value to their organization. As mentioned in Chapter 1, there are many reasons why an employer might hire a co-op; you need to find out which ones, if any, are the motivators for that employer.

Yes, we definitely want employers to see themselves as educational partners—"our educators in the field," as Anita Todd put it when I talked to her. As I indicated in the last chapter, I am not looking for charity. If it's not a win/win relationship, then it's not a healthy relationship at all. Alternatively, I have been on firm visits with colleagues who focused on reciting all the hoops that the employer would need to jump through to have the privilege of hiring our students. This simply makes me cringe.

In contrast, I sometimes tell them that they should think of me as their "unpaid consultant," although I have to admit to them that the term sounds like an oxymoron. Although my job description is primarily to develop co-op jobs with employers and help students obtain them, I encourage employers to contact me any time that they have a question or a need. So some of my employers will call to ask about starting salaries in majors outside of my college or to ask advice about how to best interview candidates or maybe even if I have a part-time candidate that can help. It would be easy to say that all of those things are not my job, but I really like the idea of getting employers to think of me as a solution provider and resource for them.

2. *Employers as Partners in Education*

The second key in building relationships with employers is the aforementioned idea of *thinking of employers as partners in education.* So although we have to acknowledge that employers are customers who only will continue to come to us as suppliers of talent if the benefits outweigh the costs, our next goal is to get them engaged in mentoring the student. Employers might open the door to our students because they are looking for cost-effective, benefit-free labor, but once real people start working for them we hopefully can get them to see that it's both a good business practice and quite enjoyable to mentor a young adult who is smart and eager to learn.

Some employers will have great mechanisms in place for training, setting goals, evaluating, and giving feedback to all employees, including interns. However, you will need to ascertain whether or not this is the case and provide some guidance if employers frankly don't know what they're doing in this regard. You also may need to sell employers on the value of mentoring, emphasizing that they will get more out of students if they develop real relationships with them. Likewise, students need to be coached on how to "manage up" by asking for goals to be reviewed and for performance to be evaluated if it is not forthcoming as desired.

3. *Focus on Win/Win Relationships*

A third key is to *focus on win/win relationships with employers.* One of the great things about our profession is that when things go well, everybody wins. When a student performs at a high level during a work term, the company has received a cost-effective contribution to the bottom line. The student has built his resume and references on top of testing out a field and getting experience. When that happens, you and your program look great. Repeatedly, I have seen students save a company enough money to pay for their whole six-month salary in one fell swoop. Other managers have told me that a co-op did a particular one-month project that justified the students' six-month salary. This is extremely gratifying.

Unfortunately, it can go the other way as well. If a student is underutilized—probably the most common problem that undergrads experience in the workplace—then the student will not learn as much and may complain to classmates about the organization or about the effectiveness of your program. If a student engages in unprofessional behavior at work, then the employer may become dissatisfied and less likely to utilize your program in the future. These chain reactions can be very damaging, so it's important to find a way to monitor your programs to make sure that all parties are relatively happy with how things are going. Field visits are the best way to do that, but checking in via phone or e-mail can help as well. In general, it's human nature for people to avoid conflict and to let negative feelings fester instead of confronting them in a solution-oriented way, so you need to train both students and employers to focus on communication and the win/win goal mentality.

4. *Knowledge is Credibility*

A fourth and final key to a vision of working with employers is that *knowledge is credibility.* When talking to employers, you need to have a good command of your field, whether or not your background is in it. You need to know what they're talking about when they describe trends in the industry as well as specific career paths for students in the majors that you handle. Before visiting an employer, you need to do some homework on their company and industry so you can have an intelligent conversation with them and have some ideas about what types of co-op jobs or internships they might be able to offer. Recently, one of my Supply Chain Management employers came out from the Rocky Mountain region to Boston for on-campus interviews. Given that we had two very successful co-ops working for this organization, I decided it was a good time to probe about expanding into other areas. I knew that the company had 400–500 employees—surely there had to be an IT department, an accounting group, and maybe some other areas that would make sense in light of what I knew about this worldwide distribution company. That was a good conversation piece, and there is an excellent chance will be able to spread our co-op program into other departments before the end of 2009.

I really don't see any way around going out into the field in order to understand employers and build relationships with them. This is especially true when you're new to a program and trying to get a feel for what you've really got in the way of work environments, managerial styles, and what your jobs are really like. Otherwise, you're stuck in your office, reduced to looking at a job description on a piece of paper and telling students, "Well, it seems like this job entails…" rather than being able to tell them what they can expect out there. Likewise, visiting employers can help you share "best practices" with other employers who are trying to begin or improve their own programs.

Most coordinators don't have the kind of workload that would make it plausible to visit all students and employers in a given work term, so it's good to make a prioritized list, organize employers geographically, and find slower times of the year when you can get out to companies. That will give you credibility with the employer because you're tangibly showing your interest in them, just as it will enhance your image with students, who are looking to you for informed expertise on where to work.

MAINTAIN A FOCUS ON CONTINUOUS IMPROVEMENT

One theme that comes up repeatedly is the relentless need to be able and willing to revisit how you run your program in order to maximize efficiency and effectiveness. With every cycle, you need to set goals, put a process in place that you hope will be optimal, and then see how it plays out. One thing that I absolutely hated in this job in my early years was realizing that I had a process flaw when I was in the thick of the busiest time of the year, as I knew I would only confuse students and employers by monkeying with the process at that point. I have seen people try to change a process midstream, but my mindset is that you want to avoid that unless it's a complete impossibility to do otherwise. I just hate being in the position of telling students or employers, "I know that I told you two months ago that you needed to do x and y, but now you really to do steps w and z instead…"

So what do you do instead? You suck it up and get through the cycle at hand, and then you get feedback on what worked and what didn't. Often it will confirm your own nebulous feelings, but not always. What will make things work better next time? Maybe you will need to develop some new handouts for students or employers to explain a process that you found yourself repeating *ad nauseum* during the last cycle. Maybe you'll be more careful about insisting that students complete practice interviews before they go on the real ones. Perhaps you'll tell students that they only have three business days to accept or decline an offer instead of giving them no definite time limit. The realm of possibility is just about infinite, but the key is to really listen to feedback and to not be stubborn about doing things because they've always been done that way or because the processes are convenient for you.

Early in my career, I had the notion that after a few years I would have it all mastered and not need to revisit my process anymore. Think again. The size of my program changed radically almost every cycle for the first ten years in the job, and the mix of employers was constantly in flux. Throw in some generational differences and the impact of technology on the university as well as the workplace, and you can see that the need to revisit how you do the job never completely ends. So you need to keep "tweaking the process," as my colleague Jacki Diani puts it.

Strive for Transparency and Integrity in your Relationships:

As a professional, you need to be exemplary in how you handle your program. Over the years, I've heard stories of coordinators who automatically determined that a specific employer would always get the best available student. Alternatively, I've known coordinators who told students that they would send their resumes to an employer but never did so because they had concerns about that student's ability to perform. Likewise, some professionals have opted to be secretive about pay rates or painted an overly flattering picture of a job or a student in order to fill a position or get a student hired. These are all understandable temptations for a variety of reasons, but I'm convinced that these decisions will come back to haunt you eventually.

In my first year, my wife decided she wanted to hire a co-op from Northeastern. I had no students available, as it was late in the process. So I reached out to some colleagues. Two of them gave me candidates and were honest about why the students were still unemployed. The third colleague passed along a resume and said that the student was great and had the coordinator's "highest recommendation." Largely on the strength of that endorsement, my wife hired the recommended student. Within two weeks, my wife reported that "Kevin" responded to almost any task request by sighing and rolling his eyes. I was concerned and went back to the coordinator who had recommended Kevin, sure that my colleague would be shocked. Instead, I was the one who was shocked when my colleague said, "Well, that's Kevin! But you did a really great thing by helping him get a job. He's going to grow so much from this experience." As you might imagine, the experience taught me that this colleague's recommendations had to be taken with a serious grain of salt.

It's never fun to admit that you made a mistake or to own responsibility when something goes wrong. And when you're transparent with students, employers, and colleagues, you're going to have some uncomfortable conversations in which the truth must be told, however tactfully. But you absolutely want to cultivate a reputation as a truth-teller and a straight-shooter, as that's what leads to lasting long-term relationships. The other day I really praised a student who had beaten out many great candidates for a terrific position, and there were tears of joy in her eyes. It's hard to say, but I think that at least part of the reason she reacted so strongly is that she knows that I'm not a cheerleader who will tell her how great she is regardless of the facts. In fact, the previous year I had given her quite a bit of constructive criticism geared to helping her develop a more accepting attitude towards the emotional ups and downs of a job search. When you are balanced, fair, and transparent with student feedback, they are much more likely to really listen to what you have to say and act on it.

MAINTAIN A BALANCE BETWEEN HAVING A LONG-TERM, BIG-PICTURE VISION WHILE HANDLING THE DAY-TO-DAY ROLLER COASTER

In our profession, it's all too easy to get consumed by the anxiety and urgency that our students and employers sometimes exhibit when interacting with us. Yes, there are times of the year when the focus is on figuring out which fire is most of out control and handling that first. There are always emergencies and deadlines that absolutely must supersede any long-term issues or concerns, and you have to bow to that.

By the same token, though, there are times when you need to step away from the day-to-day frenzy. Even during a busy time of year, there may be times when you need to keep a half-day free on your schedule each week to think about where you are in the process and to step back to make sure that your big-picture goals are being met. Another tactic that I often use is to leave a two-hour window at lunchtime. I might have appointments or walk-in hours from 9–Noon and 2–4:30. Somewhere in that Noon–2:00 range, I am going to dash over to the gym for a quick workout and a shower in lieu of lunch, but that still gives me an hour to see a student or handle a crisis. Last week I had a disgruntled student on the brink of being fired, and I was able to talk the student through the whole thing by talking to him from Noon–12:30, as I had the time free. When you are dealing with a generation that is used to 24/7 accessibility via e-mail and cell phone, you may find it hard to make yourself unavailable from time to time. But it can be valuable both for your vision and for your mental health.

One piece of advice I often give to new colleagues is as follows: "Don't become the anxiety of the student." Boy, was I guilty of that my first few years. I let myself get infected by the anxiety of the students who were worried about getting employed, and I was too emotionally invested in trying to make things happen for them. For a while, I regularly came down with the flu or some other illness right after the busy time of year ended, and I don't think that it was a coincidence. It's important to care about your students, but you need to learn to detach from their stress. Somebody needs to keep a level head during the job search process, and it had better be you.

For the last several years, I've tried very hard to set limits on how much energy I invest. Your "official" working hours—say, 9 till 5 or 8:30 till 4:30—are often pretty meaningless in any organization. In my case, I try hard to make it very rare that I arrive at work before 8:30 a.m., and I also attempt to make 6:00 p.m. my limit in terms of going home to my family. Ideally, I will forego lunch and squeeze in a 30-minute workout on campus in the early afternoon as a good physical and mental health break. I try to not bring work home beyond checking e-mail occasionally or doing related reading at night. Although evening presentations by employers or student emergencies force me to make exceptions at times to my self-imposed rules, I'm convinced that adhering to these plans to the best of my ability helps me maintain positive energy and a healthy sense of detachment amidst the periodic chaos.

Then, in the quieter times of year, I can really step back and consider the big picture of my program as well as work on more ambitious projects, such as this book. This project has resulted in many Sundays on the computer, but I have made a strict rule about Saturdays, when I almost never do anything related to work.

Other professionals handle work/life balance differently. I have colleagues who make a point of leaving much earlier than I do, but they may work on the train going home and/or get on their computer in the evening to catch up on e-mails or administrative tasks. Some people work through lunch to shorten the length of the day without sacrificing productivity. For years my colleague Elizabeth Chilvers found it incredibly effective to reach MIA students by calling during the Super Bowl. Everyone has to find a balance that works for them, but it's important to be self-aware about how much you can handle without compromising your energy, commitment, and health.

Now let's consider what many experienced professionals had to say when I asked them to describe their philosophy, vision, or guiding principles as professionals.

IN THEIR OWN WORDS

PROFESSIONAL PERSPECTIVE #1
"STUDENTS AS PRE-COLLEAGUES"
Bob Tillman, Northeastern University

First off, I was a co-op as an undergrad, and for four years I supervised co-ops. So I had both of those experiences coming in as far as at least what my initial view of this job was. I knew I didn't want someone to just be placed in a job. When I was an employer, I wanted some choice in who I was going to hire. Continuity was really important—making sure as an employer that we had the right students to do the job and we could count on it, and we weren't creating a new job every time we had students coming in.

And then the last thing that I didn't appreciate as much [initially] was having students prepared. When I took over the job and got to handle those issues and make sure that those things happened, at least I had the employer perspective as well as the student perspective. I think the employer perspective at that point was probably more valuable to me. But I also am a firm believer in having a grounding in the field of the students that you're dealing with and having some expectation that you've experienced what they're going to experience in the professional workplace and that you follow the curriculum, you follow the trends in the field, that you have a real good idea of where that field is going on your end. I would find this job to be very difficult to do if I wasn't a civil engineer. Could I do the job? Yeah, I did, when I had architecture students and graphic and media design. Was I as effective in it? No, I wasn't. I could do the mechanics, and I could get students out the door, but it was nowhere near the relationship that I have being a civil engineer.

[My philosophy with running the program now is to] listen to students a lot. Listen to employers a lot. But borrow and beg and steal anything you can from colleagues when it comes to things that work. We don't all have the answers. I think what was always nice was borrowing other people's theories of practice that you may have not seen in your own programs. A good example of this would be when I first started we never let students make appointments. We'd send them postcards telling them when they had to show up. That was awful. What were we teaching these kids? No responsibility—we were managing the whole system, and we're managing it for our needs, not anybody else's.

Another example: I can remember the first time I posted salaries, and I remember the howl from the engineering coordinators. Now, knowledge is good. If we're asking students to learn and part of learning is to determine their worth, their value, to negotiate both their work and salary, why wouldn't you give them the data to do that? But honest to God, you would've thought I'd given up the keys to the vault. I can remember, I just said, "No, I'm doing this. We send it to employers: What's the secret with students?" Well, the earth didn't fall in; the students were fine. They didn't go out and negotiate crazy salaries; they were better informed. And that's been somewhat my philosophy, to be pretty transparent.

I think the last thing when I came in was that students pretty much had no idea which jobs were open. Some students got told that some jobs were open, and some students got told other jobs were open. Some seemed to have "favored nation status," and a lot of stereotypic decisions were being made. A good example is women in construction: "Women can't work in construction, so let's not talk to them about any construction jobs." That's why when I walked into the job, I said, "This is not how we further a relationship." So I started posting all of the jobs, making them all available. We didn't have computers at that time; they were just typed lists. But then when the students started interviewing, they had a pretty good idea: Are there a lot of jobs out there? Is it going to be a tight market? Where are the jobs at? And they responded very appropriately. Again, I think it was an eyeopener for some of my colleagues who kind of liked opening the desk drawer and pulling out jobs for some students. So I think transparency along those lines.

But I think the theme that I would impress upon you is that is that they start as students... but very quickly they're colleagues, and it's not long before they graduate. I think some people miss that aspect of this job. They don't see that we're all in this together. They don't see that everybody's success hinges on everybody else being part of the larger team. When I came in, I saw students being pitted against students, companies being pitted against companies, and down the road, that's a killer. Because somewhere they're going to compare notes, and then you've ruined the relationship. So I think my advice on this end—and it's put in me good stead—is that students are just pre-colleagues. They just don't know it yet.

I find that when students also understand the system that we're looking for everybody's success and not just their little piece of success in this world, I find that they just respond better. I find that they act better; I find that they act more professional. They're much more responsible when they understand that everyone is in this; it's not just getting them a job.

PROFESSIONAL PERSPECTIVE #2
"INDIVIDUALS AND CUSTOMERS"
Anita Todd, University of Cincinnati

On the student side, I think my philosophy is very much one of looking at the students as individuals. We have a mandatory program at UC, so there can be some trappings of rules and regulations within the program. I don't like to use "trappings"—that sounds negative—but students view it like that sometimes. So I think it's important for students to be viewed as individuals and to feel that somebody is seeing their individual desires, interests, and needs and what they're really looking for. So I really try to help them tailor the program to their individual needs within our constraints. So for me it's really important to get to know the students and engage with the students and help them tailor the program to their needs.

From an employer standpoint, I very much look at the employer as a customer. It's hard to have that balance that the student is a customer and the employer is a customer and make sure that everybody is equally happy. We expect the employers to see themselves as partners in education—not just providing a job. I try to make sure that they're provided with the information and the understanding and, in a way, the philosophy that cooperative education is an educational program and that they're the educators in the field for us.

PROFESSIONAL PERSPECTIVE #3
"THE EMPLOYER DRIVES EVERYTHING"
Kirk Patterson, University of Waterloo

Not all colleges are the same, not all the universities are the same, but [when I first started at (Fanshawe] I was responsible for everything from when the student first arrived on campus until they graduated, any time they were on campus. I did the prep classes; I did the postings; I did the evaluations, the visits, et cetera. [Now, working (for University of Waterloo) as a field coordinator, focusing on marketing the program], I go out to introduce myself to employers—and some of them I already know, and some are new to me—and try to say to them "Here's how I like to do things with respect to communication, and if you don't like something, let me know." I do the same with students. I say to my students, "I'm your lifeline to the university. If you don't stay in touch with me, you have no one to blame but yourself."

With employers it's a matter of developing rapport and trying to determine what they want or need in the way of student skills. I'm strong on marketing and strong on public relations. Even when I started co-op, I saw this as "You've got to have the employers. If you don't have the employers, you don't have the students. If you don't have the students, you don't have the faculty." I've had faculty say to me, "You don't have a job if we don't teach." I say, "Excuse me: You don't have a job if you don't have students. Why would they come to the institution if we have a bad reputation for employment upon graduation or during co-op?" You know, your grad rates and co-op rates are going to drop [without good jobs].

So to me, it's the employer that drives everything. Yeah, there's a partnership there; we always talk about it. But the employers are number one in my book followed very closely by the students and then the faculty and everyone underneath that. Because if you don't have employers hiring, what are you going to do? Put 'em out on freebies all over the countryside? Research projects? But to what degree is that beneficial to the student, other than learning to do research?

It's just like any other business, and it was exactly what the speaker [at the 2008 CAFCE Conference] said this morning: service, service, service. I did oddball things and at times got my knuckles rapped by the college. I had no problem sending a bouquet of flowers to an employer if it was some special occasion or buying an employer coffee and donuts for their staff. I didn't always make the school pay for it; it came out of my pocket. Some of my colleagues would say to me, "Why are you spending your money on that?" and I said, "That's the way I want to do it; if I didn't want to spend it, I wouldn't do it." I have no problem with doing things like that or with the PR lunches that we are allowed to do. Hey, employers take you out to lunch, why not take them out to lunch? It doesn't hurt to go out for a lunch with employers to get to know them.

So it's developing the rapport and knowing who they are, what they like, what they don't like, what they like in students, what they don't like in students. Once you know the employers, then you can relate to the students and say, "Look, here are some good jobs!" Even on campus when students come in after a work term and say, "I want to apply to an employer in your area." And I've already been to that employer, and I can say "That's a really good job; you ought to get your app in but study up and find out everything about the company because I do know that company likes students who have studied up and really know what's going on."

PROFESSIONAL PERSPECTIVE #4
"PATIENCE WITH THE PROCESS"
Jacki Diani, Northeastern University

When it comes to having a guiding philosophy in my work with students, I actually have a few principles that I have come to incorporate. First, I practice the learning model that we teach our students: preparation, activity, and reflection. So we—my colleague and I—prepare for the co-op referral cycle just as we ask students to prepare for co-op. We do our homework; we do our research on our employers. We want to know what is going on with them. Are they experiencing financial challenges, or are they launching new initiatives? Who will be seeking students? And we look at our students; what is going on with them? What classes are they currently in and who will be going out on co-op? We ask, do our employer needs match up with the students we have available? So we really prepare.

Once students are placed, we don't just take a deep breath and take a vacation. We sit down and talk about the previous referral process; what went well and what didn't go smoothly. And we literally write things down, like the timing of the interviews was too early, etc. Whatever the issues are, we make a note so going ahead we know what we'll need to adjust. So we absolutely practice that—preparation, activity, reflection. We reflect, and we keep tweaking the process. We ask employers for feedback and students as well. So that's one philosophy we use.

Another philosophy that I incorporate when working with students is to have "patience with the process." The process of securing co-op employment can be stressful for students; it is very important to them to get a co-op and they are busy. They can get very anxious when they're in the process of contacting employers, scheduling interviews, and waiting to hear back from employers about job offers. Their anxiety typically comes from the pace of the employers in responding to them. This is not uncommon and it is completely understandable. We talk to the students about the realities of what the employers have on their plate in addition to interviewing co-op students. For the student, it's one of the most important things that they're dealing with at that moment. Am I going to get an internship? Am I going to get a position come January? And it is important to the employers, but the students have to consider the employer's perspective as well, and realize they have many other issues and responsibilities they are dealing with at the same time they are interviewing the students. The hospitals are a great example; the nurse managers who interview co-ops also work on the units and have a huge staff they manage and daily emergencies and urgencies that arise daily. In the priority of a day, scheduling a co-op interview may be put aside briefly to deal with unanticipated issues that arise. We have to appreciate what the employers have to deal with in their work and be patient with the process.

It is our job to help students learn how to not let the anxiety they are feeling come across negatively to the employers. I tell the students, so they can relate that I often feel the same way they do. Employers are very different; some respond to calls or e-mails immediately while with others, days go by when I don't hear back. Some are very timely and responsive; others are not and that can be very frustrating when I am trying to get answers for the students about job openings. But I don't let them hear my frustration and my negativity because it doesn't benefit anybody in the long run. Our co-op program is built on relationships; in good times and bad, you constantly need to nurture those relationships.

The Human Resources people are gatekeepers for jobs. You're not going to work for them; you just need to work with them to get to the position you'd like. Some recruiters can be difficult to work with and may seem to not want to recruit! But they are the "middle man" in the recruitment process and so very important in terms of gaining access to institutions. Students need to be very professional in dealing with recruiters, even when they may feel they are not being treated great. Bottom line is if you annoy or insult them, it's not going to benefit you in the long run. And it's the same for me: there are times I have had frustrations with recruiters who are not helpful or responsive, but you just have to be very patient and professional with them and eventually it usually pays off.

And I guess the last piece of an overriding philosophy I use with students is a holistic approach to their career. Our students are going into health care, and it can be very stressful. Of course, a lot of environments are stressful; it's not only health care. We want students to work hard and be dedicated to their jobs, but we want balance in their lives. If they're asked constantly to work overtime, they have to be very careful. The work is both very physical and emotional. They're working with people who are very sick, and patients and families who are under tremendous stress. Students often work with patients who are terminally ill and may care for a patient who passes on. In this kind of work, students need time away. When they leave work, they need to walk out the door—go exercise, hang with their friends, do whatever it is. So it's a very holistic approach, and I think that's going to be key for them to be happy in their field, long term. Because people do burn out in this field; our students see professionals who are burned out too early in their career. Maintaining balance in their life is a skill they can learn early on while a student: Work hard when you're at work, but when you leave, clear your head, detach, and go back to work fresh. Don't get burned out.

Now that we have described a sense of the vision and philosophy behind a co-op program, we will delve into the nuts and bolts of how to get your program running on a day-to-day basis. But first you might want to consider some reflection questions that ask you to think about how the content of this chapter relates to your program.

REFLECTION QUESTIONS

1. This chapter discusses how a professional's education and experience informs how they approach their role in a co-op or internship program. How, explicitly, has your background had an impact on how you run your program?

2. How would you describe your style? Are you more people-oriented? Process-oriented? Results-oriented? Are you familiar with your Myers-Briggs type? What are the inherent potential shortcomings of your style or personality type, and what have you done or could you do to overcome them? To what degree do you tend to use your "strong muscles" and ignore the weaker ones, as described in the text?

3. This chapter describes how some educators are irked at talk of providing "customer service" to students and employers, as they see it as denigrating their role as educators. Do you think that educators should focus on providing great customer service, or is that an unfortunate term for describing what it means to be an excellent professional?

4. The "Fundamentals of a Strong Vision" in this chapter include the following:
   • Build strong relationships with students
   • Build strong relationship with employers
   • Maintain a focus on continuous improvement
   • Strive for transparency and integrity in your relationships
   • Maintain a balance between having a long-term, big-picture vision while handling the day-to-day roller coaster

   Which of these are your biggest strengths right now? Where could you improve? How will you try to do that?

5. In his interview excerpt, Bob Tillman discusses the importance of treating students as "pre-colleagues." What specifically are you doing to treat students as pre-colleagues? Are there ways in which you are failing to do this? Why?

6. Kirk Patterson says that the employer drives everything and that employer relationships trump all else when it comes to developing a vision. Do you agree? Regardless, what are ways in which you have gone the extra mile to build or maintain an employer relationship, as Kirk describes in his interview excerpt?

CHAPTER 3

MAKING PRIORITIES

"One's first step in wisdom is to question everything – and one's last is to come to terms with everything."
— *Georg Christoph Lichtenberg*

Vicky Arico, who designed the cover of this book, came up with the great idea of using a juggler to capture the nature of our roles as educators. When I talk to an individual who is considering a career as a cooperative education or internship professional, I often say that there aren't many components of the job that are all that difficult. In my opinion, the biggest challenge in our field is determining what activities are the most worthy of your time. How do you decide what to do each day? For many of us, it's all too easy to spend our time on what we enjoy doing. And many professionals just love to spend time working one-on-one with students. The bad news is that doing so might not always be the best idea. The good news is that there are many ways to utilize various practices and resources to free up more time with students... and to ensure that it's quality time instead of a series of repetitive meetings in which information is simply disseminated.

The irony is that colleagues might be critical if you start putting considerable energy into any number of activities that require an upfront investment of time in the name of saving time down the road. When I was new, my assigned mentor gave the term "mock interview" a whole new meaning: My mentor mocked *me* for doing practice interviews with all of my first-time students! Yes, I was spending an hour with each student to conduct and critique the interview. But I saw so many benefits in terms of education as well as time management. I was working with business students, and business employers often place a high degree of importance on the interview in comparison to some other majors (including that of my mentor).

My students immediately began interviewing better, which meant they obtained jobs faster... and they often were able to get better jobs as well. This inevitably made my job easier, as I didn't have to counsel students through as many failed efforts to get a job—only to try to fix their interview well after it was obviously broken. Getting better jobs for their first co-op made these students even more qualified for subsequent co-ops. Best of all, many employers were often stunned to find that young adults with no corporate experience could come in and pitch themselves strategically for jobs. That enhanced the reputation of the program.

Inevitably, I came to agree with a statement that my colleague Bob Tillman makes in his profile at the end of this chapter. Bob puts considerable energy into working with his freshmen and is engaged in any number of activities that are well beyond his job description. He has had colleagues say, "I don't know how you find the time to do that." His response: "I don't know how you have the time NOT to do it!"

Many professionals get so immersed in the day-to-day, operational elements of their jobs that they become "too busy" to step back and reflect on what they do, how they do it, and why they do it. If they were only to do so, they might find that they could eliminate many labor-intensive activities and enjoy their work more without sacrificing the quality of the educational experience for students. In fact, they might be surprised to find that doing so almost inevitably will improve the experience.

So let's look at some key principles when it comes to prioritizing and managing your time effectively as a professional.

QUESTION EVERYTHING

In her profile at the end of this chapter, Nancy Johnston of Simon Fraser University makes a strong and eloquent case for questioning everything that you do as opposed to blindly accepting the status quo. What do we do? Why do we it? Most importantly, what is the educational impact of what we do? If a process or procedure exists purely to meet the needs of administration or accreditation, can we respectively consider either eliminating it or embedding some educational element into it?

This is simultaneously quite simple but also harder than it sounds. It's very easy to rationalize doing what is comfortable or familiar to you without any real analysis as to whether it's paying off educationally at all. Here are some provocative questions:

Question: Is the process in question helping students learn something that ultimately will help them become more self-aware and capable professionals?

Many organizations are all too good at creating hoops that must be jumped through in order to get things done. Whether these hoops are absolutely necessary or not, they have the potential to turn an educational process into a mind-numbing death march. Always strive to simplify and streamline your process of working with students and employers, always remembering that students are learners and employers are educational partners. Before requiring a form to be signed or a step to be completed, ask yourself: Does this really contribute to learning? If not, do I have to do it? If I do, is there some way I can change it to ensure that it does have some educational payoff?

Just in the writing of this book, I have been finding myself filled with increasing doubts about whether some of my processes are really doing much in the way of learning. As you'll see in Chapter 11, I now wonder if my required small-group reflection seminars are really doing all that much toward making my students better learners or performers. If not, why am I requiring it? Maybe it's because many colleagues also require it, thinking that it was a useful way to reinforce learning. It's also because I have been doing it for a good while and have gotten away from questioning whether it's a good enough practice to continue making it a requirement. One possibility is that the requirement is okay, but I need to find a way to make it better. These are the kinds of questions that educators in our field need to mull again and again.

Question: What do we require or recommend when it comes to students, and is there some long-term indication that these requirements or recommendations are beneficial?

Are you talking to your seniors and alums, asking them to reflect back on their co-op or internship careers? If not, you may have no more than speculation when it comes to whether what you're doing with students is really paying off. Len Glick, an organizational behavior professor in our College of Business Administration, has been using an evaluation tool to see what can be gleaned on this front.

Years ago, I inherited the entrepreneurship program. My predecessor told me that "entrepreneurship students think that they want to work in small companies, but they really don't... They're much better off working in large companies for now to lay the groundwork for starting their own business down the road." I listened but took the statement with a grain of salt. Through talking to students and alums, I ultimately concluded that we needed to develop many jobs with small businesses. When I told aspiring co-ops the nature of these jobs — "The good news is that you'll do everything, but the bad news is that you'll do everything" — I found that they loved the idea of jobs where they would do everything from accounting to marketing, from shipping to clerical work. Some co-ops even started their own businesses, and — as long as I required structure in terms of a business plan with a timeline and deliverables — that turned out to be a good idea as well. Many of those businesses still exist and have grown admirably. But that started with questioning the status quo of pushing those students to work with the big companies that dominate our business co-op program.

Question: Do your students and employers understand why they must do what you're asking them to do?

This is a real pet peeve of mine. I absolutely hate to tell a student and employer that they have to do something because I say so or because it's a requirement. For example, yes, it's a requirement for all Northeastern students to take and pass the one-credit Professional Development for Co-op course in order to be eligible to pursue co-op jobs through the university. That said, the last thing I'm ever going to do is tell students that they need to pass the class simply because it's a rule of our program. They need to pass the class for our co-op faculty to be able to feel comfortable sending their resume out to employers, because doing so is an implicit recommendation of the student. They need to do well in the class because it will radically improve their ability to write a resume, strategically interview, and excel in the workplace for the rest of their careers.

Likewise, I often find it easy to go down the wrong path when a student is talking about waiving one or more co-op assignments, given that co-op is basically a requirement for all of our business students. When a student comes in and asks how many co-ops they have to do, the wrong way to handle it is to pull out the chapter and verse of the college requirements. Usually I'll reframe the question: "Okay, regardless of how many co-ops you might have to do in this program, let's discuss how many co-ops it will make sense for you to do before you graduate?" We then play out the most plausible outcomes of more or less co-ops for that individual. When pushed, the student's real reason is that they are feeling "old" (at 22 or 23!) and believe that they need to graduate as soon as possible. But to do what, exactly, upon graduation? They don't know: They say that they will figure it out when they get there.

This is what I like to call the "finish line syndrome," in which the student is in a hurry to get to the finish line—graduation—but has given no real thought as to what is beyond that finish line. Getting that on the table is a great opportunity to talk about the purpose of cooperative education in the big picture of their education and their lives, but it starts with questions about purpose.

Question: Are we really listening to the feedback of students and employers as well as to our own inner voices?

There are many opportunities to establish meaningful dialogue with students and employers. Periodically my academic counterparts and I pull together graduating seniors to review their whole undergraduate experience. What was really valuable to them as learners in the classroom as well as in their co-op experience? What are we doing right? Where do we need a change in focus—maybe a totally different course or a new sector for co-op experiences? The key with such sessions is to go in with a bunch of questions and follow up only with clarifying questions instead of trying to convince anyone that the status quo is really the best. If you aren't defensive, you'll always learn something valuable from such meetings... and seniors or recent grads aren't necessarily just going to tell you what you want to hear.

At the end of my co-op course, I always ask for extensive feedback and make sure that the class knows that it will have a very direct impact on how the course is taught in future semesters. There are occasional surprises, but I'm more often surprised at how frequently the students will confirm some of my inner doubts and concerns about how things went. If I have the vague feeling that maybe a given section had too much lecture and not enough participation, that concern is almost always verified. This makes the need for change irrefutable.

The same is true with employers. There are various easy-to-use tools such as Survey Monkey that can allow you to get anonymous feedback from groups of employers if you don't have the time or inclination to do so more individually. You can't always address every single concern, but you have to look for themes and trust your constituencies to guide you as you consider better ways to run your program.

Question: Does our program revolve foremost around learning and the needs of students and employers as opposed to less educational and necessary goals, including biases of the institution and/or those running the program?

We all have our preferences as well as superiors with their own goals and philosophies. As much as you can, though, you want to make sure that your program is meeting the educational needs of your students as opposed to your own needs or style.

You might be familiar with the comic strip called "Dilbert" by Scott Adams. One of my favorite strips shows a group around a conference table trying to decide how to handle a business problem. A nerdy looking guy suggests using a nerdy-sounding statistical analysis method, noting that he just happens to be an expert in that method. Dilbert, the computer geek, replies, "No, no, we need to build a computer model." A guy who looks like a thug weighs in: "Bah! We just need to kick some hineys, that's all." It ends with a porcupine sitting at the end of the table: "Listen to me, people! We must stick people with quills! It's the only way!"

To some degree, we all have a tendency to be like the folks around that conference table. The educator who loves structure may tend to convince herself that rules and regulations are the answer to everything. The coordinator who is uncomfortable with technology convinces himself that a CRM system, database, or online teaching tool is more trouble than it's worth. It's suspiciously convenient if every problem that arises has a solution that happens to coincide with our own strengths and preconceived notions. You need to be open to the very real possibility that some solutions may call for a response that is not comfortable or natural to you at all.

CAPITALIZE ON BEST PRACTICES

Several of my interviewees alluded to being careful not to reinvent the wheel when you're considering or reconsidering how to manage your time and run your program in general. You can save considerable time and improve your program significantly by capitalizing on best practices that already exist in the field.

If you're running a small program, you likely need to reach beyond your institution. But even at a relatively big program, it's all too easy to get so caught up with our day-to-day responsibilities that we end up lamenting the failure to share best practices across a university. Either way, let's consider some ways to find out more about what other professionals are doing with their programs.

CONFERENCES AND PROFESSIONAL ASSOCIATIONS

Whether you are a rookie or a wily veteran, conferences can be excellent professional development opportunities. Typically, most conferences last about three days, and there are a variety of activities. Usually there are a few keynote speakers and quite a few concurrent workshops. The nice thing about the concurrent workshops is that you can pick and choose what you would like to attend based on your interests and needs. Most conferences have a handful of themes, such as assessment, behavioral-based interviewing, work-integrated learning, technology, and so forth. Likewise, the workshop topics range from those that are more appropriate for those newer to the field to more advanced topics for veterans.

In my opinion, though, you will get more out of conferences if you view them as something more than opportunities to simply attend the various meals, lectures, and workshops on offer. There are hundreds of fellow professionals at these events, and this is a great opportunity to meet colleagues informally to compare notes on challenges, dilemmas, resources, and ideas. I have many long-standing relationships with professionals that I happened to meet at a conference, and it's had a definite impact on how I run my program.

There are several organizations that have regular or intermittent conferences. The Cooperative Education and Internship Association (CEIA) holds an annual conference for co-op and internship professionals. It usually is held in the spring, and the Association makes an effort to vary the geographical location significantly over the years. All of the major co-op institutions are represented at these conferences as well as dozens of smaller programs. Predictably, you can anticipate large numbers of professionals from the local region in question. Check out http://www.ceiainc.org/ for more information about CEIA, including a variety of professional development programs and other information.

The Canadian Association for Cooperative Education (CAFCE) has a biannual conference;

it is held in "even" years (2008, 2010, etc.). Generally, it is held in June; the next one will be June 20–23, 2010 in Charlottetown, Prince Edward Island. Some professionals in the U.S. may not realize it, but cooperative education has an extremely strong presence north of the border. The world's largest cooperative education program is at the University of Waterloo, and there are quite a few enormous and impressive co-op programs across Canada. As you might expect, most of the attendees hail from Canadian universities, though other nations are represented as well. The CAFCE website is at http://www.cafce.ca, and it includes a variety of resources for professionals.

The World Association of Cooperative Education (WACE) offers a biannual world conference; it is held in "odd" years (2009, 2011, etc.). WACE also holds regular symposia. The locations for both span the globe, literally. As with the other conferences, those who live closest are most likely to attend, but you usually will see attendees from at least four continents. Check out the WACE website at http://www.waceinc.org/ for more information about their events.

There are also the options of various local and regional associations and conferences, too numerous to list exhaustively here. For example, the CEIA is broken up into eight regions, and many of them have one or more smaller conferences per year. These conferences may be less expensive and shorter in duration than the national conferences, and, of course, they may be much easier to reach in terms of time and money.

Another option is to consider conferences relating to your academic specialty. If you need to ramp up or stay current in an academic specialty that is relevant to your program, it might be wise to consider a related conference. There are professional associations in just about every field that you can imagine. Attending these conferences can give you more expertise in the field, which translates to increased credibility with students and employers. Less obviously, such conferences can be a great way to develop jobs, so it's advisable to bring a stack of business cards and some information about your program.

There are other organizations that are less familiar to me, such as the Association for Experiential Education (AEE) and the National Society for Experiential Education (NSEE). You generally will see some presenters from a few of the larger co-op institutions at these conferences, but not too many of them. The workshops tend to cover a very broad range of topics—some quite intriguing and some that are less likely to be of interest to typical co-op and internship professionals, such as sessions on wilderness learning, yoga, and so on.

In all cases, I highly recommend that you carefully scan the conference proceedings to determine if there are enough sessions to make your attendance worthwhile. Most professionals have finite budgets for professional development activities, so you may have to make some choices.

COLLEAGUES

Although I alluded to the value of colleagues in Chapter 1, I should reiterate that reaching out to colleagues is always a good idea. If there are others at your institution engaged in similar work, you can bet that they have some opinions on anything from how to deal with the registrar's office to how to refer a student who is facing a psychological crisis. In the best of all worlds, you would be able to develop jobs for colleagues and vice-versa. Seeking advice from a colleague can be a great time-saving move and a way to improve as a coordinator.

Remember that you don't necessarily have to adopt other's ideas as they are. I sometimes have talked to colleagues at NU or elsewhere and come away deciding that I wanted to do the opposite of something that they were doing! Whenever colleagues ask me for resources—employer FAQs, syllabi, teaching materials, and so forth—I always tell them they are free to use them, modify them subtly or radically, or ignore them altogether. Many of my current practices are a hodgepodge of various ideas, materials, and approaches that I have learned from past and present colleagues. Yet I am often surprised at how relatively uncommon it is for new professionals to pick the brains of possible mentors.

TECHNOLOGY

Although my career in cooperative education started in 1995, it's amazing how much of an impact technology has had on time management. When I started, we had to produce and maintain large binders of job descriptions. They were only available during business hours, and students sometimes had to wait in line to see what jobs were available. All resumes were faxed to employers, and this took countless hours. There was no way for students to schedule appointments electronically, so there was a great deal of back and forth on the phone or via e-mail just to schedule appointments. As for phone messages, most of us just wrote them in notebooks, writing down key names and numbers on Rolodex cards. Heaven help you if you needed to dig up a name or number from one of those notebooks.

Now the landscape has shifted quite dramatically. There are several tools that can be used to make the administrative element considerably less labor-intensive. I can't imagine trying to run a program in this day and age without technology. So let's consider some of the tools that are available to you, how they may be used, and some pitfalls to avoid with each of them.

CUSTOMER RELATIONSHIP MANAGEMENT (CRM) SOFTWARE

Most programs now use some sort of Customer Relationship Management software, also known as a CRM. In a nutshell, organizations use CRMs for an incredible variety of purposes. The common thread is that a CRM gives an organization a way to use technology to manage the storing and processing of information about customers, and doing so in such a way that a variety of system users can enter this data and have access to it.

For the purposes of the professionals reading this book, the most common uses for a CRM may include:

- Maintaining records for students, including data from an academic mainframe as well as placement data, personal notes, citizenship information, etc.

- Allowing a mechanism for students to upload a resume (and, possibly, cover letters, references, portfolios, and so forth)

- Posting job descriptions for students and systems users to access, whether the jobs are posted by the institution or by the employers themselves

- Forwarding resumes to employers

- Running reports on any number of program elements, such as placements, referrals, or breakdowns of job seekers

There are several vendors who make CRM software applications that can be used to automate many administrative processes. Here are the ones I know of, listed alphabetically:

- Decision Academic (formerly DAG)

- JobMine, a University of Waterloo program based on a PeopleSoft framework

- RoboTechnologies, makers of PlacePro

- Simplicity

- The University of Victoria, creators of Mamook

I'm sure there are others. Additionally, there are many professionals who have managed to devise a completely customized software solution, with or without technical assistance from others.

It is beyond the scope of this book to present all the pros and cons of the various options objectively. I do believe it's fair to say that every system has those who swear by it and those who swear at it. That said, here are some key questions to ask if you're considering a CRM or switching from one to another:

1. How user-friendly is the system for students?

   I have heard some vendors claim that their system is totally intuitive and that students and coordinators will require no training whatsoever to be able to use that system. I would be surprised if that's true of any system. It can be very frustrating to have to take time away from more educational responsibilities to troubleshoot student technology issues. Before committing to any off-the-shelf system, you should insist on trying it out as if you were a student. Does it take a bunch of clicks to navigate around the system? Is it very obvious how to rank jobs and apply for them, and is it equally obvious to see what happens once someone does "apply" for a job electronically?

   Given that most systems have their proponents and detractors you might want to get feedback from educators at several institutions—and not just ones that are hand-picked from the vendor—before committing to a system. Writing a message to the CEIA listserv would be one option: At times people have asked about a given system, and there have been some strong pro and con opinions voiced.

2. How accessible is the system?

   Curiously, I have heard of at least one system that shuts down between midnight and 8 a.m. Most people reading this book probably would find that reasonable enough, but the Millennial Generation will be unhappy with any system that's not available 24/7.

3. How easy is the system for professionals to use?

   Outside of cooperative education, SAP generates more revenue than any other CRM vendor in the world. Working closely with Management Information Systems students and employers, I can assure you that the consensus is that SAP systems are extremely powerful and useful… but also very user-unfriendly and difficult to learn. This is a dilemma that is true of many CRM systems. At their very worst, some of them remind me of an old Saturday Night Live fake commercial showing an incredibly powerful wristwatch that requires two people just to get the watch to tell time.

Most CRMs have powerful capabilities, including the ability to produce a great variety of reports. But some of those reports are cumbersome to produce. Once again, I highly recommend that you "test-drive" any CRM for a long time before committing to it. Think about what functionalities you most need, and don't just ask if the system has them: Try them out yourself. See what it entails to search for an employer, post a job, run various reports, and so forth.

Even small issues can be a real nuisance. For example, I often get job descriptions for positions available at a variety of locations around the country. Our system does allow us to post a job's region… but you can only post one region for each job description! So how do I make sure that students viewing jobs by region are sure to find the right jobs? I have to post the identical job description multiple times, forcing many students to get confused when they see what is basically the same job listed as many as five or six times in a row in the system.

Likewise, our system allows students to check a box indicating that they wish to apply for a job. This tends to make students believe that their resume immediately is whisking its way to the employer. But it's not. And students sometimes "apply" for a job and then sit around waiting for something to happen, whereas nothing is going to happen until they come talk to me about the job. Sure, you can train students in how to "beat the system," but this requires time and effort that you'd rather put into real education.

4. Should you consider developing your own system, with or without the help of a CRM software provider?

This is by no means unthinkable. My colleague Bob Tillman developed his own system and still swears by it. However, if you're trying to develop something for even a medium-sized program, building your own model can be a massive undertaking. Yes, you might be able to come up with something that perfectly suits your every need, but unless the developer really knows what he or she is doing, you also could sink a great deal of time and money into such a system and not end up with something that is really workable. So my advice would be to proceed with caution on that front, especially if you have more than a handful of professionals running your program.

Self-inflicted Wounds with CRM Applications

There are some problems that you'll face with systems that have nothing to do with the manufacturer and everything to do with how you and your colleagues use and abuse the system.

Here's a typical problem along these lines. Although our system doesn't allow us to designate multiple geographical regions for one job, we can indeed list multiple majors. This is great, as there definitely are many jobs that we could call "hybrid jobs." Maybe it's a Public Relations job that could be just as appropriate for a Communications major in Arts & Sciences as it would be for a Marketing student in Business Administration. Perhaps it's a job that works for both Supply Chain Management and Industrial Engineering, which can be close cousins.

The trouble arises when an employer or a professional wants to make sure that a given job description is viewed by as many co-op or internship job seekers as possible. Or an employer may insist that they are willing to hire a student of any major. How should we deal with that on the system? Unfortunately, what ends up happening is that some low-level, general jobs are listed for about 50 different majors. So majors in civil engineering or nursing might see a secretarial job listed when they search for their majors only. Understandably, those students end up either scratching their heads—wondering why the job is showing up for their major—or just getting irritated because they have to sift through way too many jobs that have no interest to them at all in order to find the "real" civil engineering or nursing jobs. That's frustrating, and it's absolutely the fault of those who are using and abusing the system.

As far as I'm concerned, a good practice is to post jobs based much more on what the co-op or intern will be doing in the job as opposed to which majors the employer is willing to hire. We have one job on our system that is basically assisting in mental health counseling. The employer is open to any major and wants visibility for the job, so even areas such as accounting and electrical engineering are included on the long list of majors. But a better idea would be to list a small handful of majors that are relevant—human services, psychology, maybe nursing, possibly human resources management—and then making sure that all students interested in jobs in helping professions (regardless of major) can view that job.

Another challenge that is in the hands of the institution and its users as opposed to the software developer is data integrity. This term refers to the fact that multiple users on one system may be able to alter, duplicate, or delete data that other users do NOT want to change in any way. For example, let's say that I work with an HR person in a pharmaceutical company for a corporate finance position. One day the HR person calls me and says that he is no longer the contact for that position; I should change my records to indicate that the hiring manager is the contact. So it would be understandable if I went in to my system and changed the contact information accordingly. But what if that HR contact is still the contact for six other jobs with that employer? Maybe I have just overwritten information that is critical to my colleagues. Thus, it becomes imperative for your system to have some way of reconciling possible conflicts of interest. You need a set of system rules that everyone will abide by—especially if you're in a large program.

There are also situations in which different professionals use the same system in somewhat different ways. Sometimes a student is allowed to merely rank themselves as very interested in a job, and their resume goes out. In others, the student may need to do that and discuss it with their own coordinator. In still other cases, the student might need to go meet with another individual who is the owner of that job. The upshot is students can get confused because everyone is using that system a little differently, and the students' role is always changing.

The only way around these and similar problems that can arise is to have either one person or a committee of people determine how users will use the system. It may be impossible to get a group of strong-minded professionals on the same page, but you need to strive for uniformity if you're going to reap the maximum benefits of a CRM for time management.

E-MAIL: LOTUS NOTES AND OUTLOOK

The prevalence of e-mail and online calendars is another enormous change since I began in cooperative education in 1995. At that time, e-mail was a relatively new phenomenon, and it was used very differently. In some ways, I recall e-mail being rather cumbersome in those days. Amazingly, this was the original e-mail address that I was supposed to put on my business cards:

scott=weighart%faculty%coop@banyan-gateway.neu.edu

As you can imagine, when employers asked for my e-mail address, I would say "Uh, how about if I just send you an e-mail instead, and you can just reply to that?"

In some ways, though, e-mail was much more manageable back then. Because it was relatively new technology, the influx of messages was not so great. Attaching large files and sending to groups was not so easy, so the medium lent itself to simpler messages that often could be answered in a quick paragraph or two.

Nowadays, I often receive over 50 e-mails per day during referral season. We now work with a generation who has been raised on e-mail, so many students will raise extremely complex issues in an e-mail and may expect to conduct all or most of their business with you electronically. I also have heard many colleagues complain that a student will e-mail them, say, at 6:30 p.m. and then follow up with an annoyed e-mail at 7:30 a.m. the next morning, wondering if their advisor received the first e-mail and why they have not yet responded to it!

As with CRM systems and other program management applications, I'm not going to attempt to weigh the pros and cons of Lotus Notes and Outlook. Odds are that you are stuck with whatever e-mail system your institution has adopted, and you may or may not like that system. Regardless, here are some good fundamentals when it comes to using e-mail.

1. *Be timely when responding to e-mails.*

   Most professionals would agree that any e-mail that calls for any response at all should be answered within 24 to 48 hours (or within two business days if a weekend is part of that 48-hour window). Your response may be brief—you may even let the person know that you're going to need more time to reply appropriately—but you do want to acknowledge that message quickly.

2. *Devise a system for organizing your e-mails.*

   All e-mail management systems have the capability of creating folders. This is a great way to keep track of e-mails that are too important to delete over a long period of time but that will be impossible to find unless you organize them somehow. Here are a few of my folder names: Contact info-Northeastern; E-mail templates; Prep Course; Personal; Performance Review; Fall 2009 jobs; Interview/Info Session Rooms; Curriculum Committee; and so forth. These folders help me when, say, I need to remember who I'm supposed to e-mail in the Registrar's Office when a student needs a temporary withdrawal from the university lifted.

3. *Make sure that all of your outgoing e-mails are automatically saved, and manage your "Sent" folder periodically.*

It can be very powerful to be able to refer back to your correspondence with a student or an employer. When a student or parent questions why a job has not been obtained, I can look into that folder and say "I e-mailed John back on August 15, urging him to come in, and he never replied..." Or when a student has a problem blow up on the job, I can scan earlier e-mails to see if there were any warning signs that I should have noticed.

Of course, I often end up with over 200 megabytes of messages. I don't know what my limit is, but I do delete messages periodically that are too old to matter—especially large messages. I tend to hang on to most student and employer messages for at least one year.

4. *Be proactive in educating students on what can and cannot be addressed via e-mails.*

As indicated above, there are students who would be delighted to have your relationship with them revolve around e-mails. But to what degree should you allow that to happen? It's really up to you, and it will depend partly on your style and preferences but also on how easy it is for your students to meet face-to-face with you. My general rule is that anything requiring more than a couple of chunky paragraphs in reply is too complex to be handled via e-mail. However, here are my exceptions:

- Students who are facing challenges or crises at work and who may not be able to talk openly on the phone or meet face-to-face

- Students who are far away from campus—perhaps overseas on Study Abroad—but who are attempting to be proactive by getting a resume critiqued or discussing other important issues

I know that some of my colleagues here and elsewhere—especially at some community colleges with older students who must work or deal with family responsibilities on top of their studies and work experiences—are more willing than I am to use e-mail in more depth. That's absolutely fine, but there are times when you may need to insist on face-to-face meetings. Again, though, it will go over much better if you explain why you require this instead of just telling students that it's a rule. I try to remind them that seeing me in person is a great way for us to maintain a strong relationship and for them to ensure that they are "on my radar screen" when opportunities arise. That seems to resonate. I also like to say that they don't need to see me for every small question or procedural step that arises during a job search, but I do recommend that they see me in person at least once every week or two when they are actively seeking a job.

5. *Use e-mail templates.*

If some of the aforementioned suggestions may appear to be common sense, I would say that using e-mail templates is probably the most underutilized efficiency-minded step you can take with e-mails. Ask yourself the following: "What e-mail messages do I basically re-write again and again because they come up so frequently?" If you are doing that, you are wasting hours and hours each year—even though you might only be wasting five minutes at a time. Instead, consider maintaining a folder of e-mails that you can copy and paste readily—perhaps plugging in a few small fact changes. Here are some e-mails that I send all the time, listed by e-mail subject:

Subject: <u>Appointment cancelled with short notice</u>

Dear _____,

I just wanted you to be aware that when you cancel an appointment in the middle of the night before you have an appointment the following morning, it really doesn't do that much good for your peers or for me. The system "locks" after 4:30 p.m. for the following day's appointments, as this enables me (or any of my colleagues) to know what my day will look like before I leave. So once you cancel, no one else can have that slot. And when you're the first appointment of the day, as you were supposed to be today, this ends up meaning that I'm planning my morning to make sure I get here in time for that first appointment... only to find that I had no need to rush to get here.

I'm sure you see my point. Please don't be cavalier about scheduling and cancelling appointments, especially when it's a busy time of year. The whole morning is booked otherwise, and I'm sure someone would've liked to have that slot. Had you not scheduled it or had cancelled it much earlier yesterday, it would have been better.

Thanks for understanding,

SW

Subject: <u>No-show for appointment</u>

Dear _____,

You scheduled an appointment with me today at 10:30. You were a no-show with no explanation. Please reply as soon as possible to let me know what happened.

If you make appointments, it's important to keep them. Every single appointment slot that I had available today was filled; this means that there were other students who would have loved to have your slot and missed that opportunity. Missing appointments also raises a question about your ability to make commitments and keep them, including interviews scheduled with co-op employers.

In the future, please avoid missing scheduled appointments or cancel them more than 24 hours in advance if necessary.

Thanks, and I hope to see you soon.

SW

Subject: <u>Job lead</u>

Dear _____,

_____ suggested that I get in touch with you regarding our Supply Chain Management co-op program.

I am attaching a SCM Co-op FAQ document for your review. It covers all the basics of our program. In a nutshell, our students are available to work full-time hours for six months at a time. Our next work cycle starts in the beginning of July and goes through most of December; we start interviewing for that work term in mid-March.

Please feel free to give me a call once you've had a chance to review the FAQ. Also note that the FAQ includes a sample job description that you can use as a template in crafting your own.

I look forward to working with you.

Scott

Subject: <u>Reminder message for students finishing a work term</u>

Hi everyone,

Hard to believe it, but your co-op work term is almost over. I hope that you have had a positive experience if I haven't heard from you while you have been away from NU.

I wanted to write with a few quick reminders about wrapping up your co-op experience and doing what you need to do to get credit for co-op:

1. End on a high note -- Even if your experience has not been the best, try to ensure that you leave the job on good terms. Wrap up any loose ends and do whatever you can to make the transition an easy one for your employer and for anyone who assumes your responsibilities. If you're not sure what would be most helpful in the transition, talk to your manager.

2. Remind your manager about completing the evaluation -- It would be a good idea to remind your manager about your evaluation now. Tell your manager that you would like to sit down and discuss the evaluation after he or she has completed it.

3. Meet with your manager to discuss the evaluation -- This is a good learning opportunity; take advantage of it. If you have communicated regularly over the co-op, there should be no surprises. If there are any unpleasant surprises,

though, try to not react emotionally. Ask clarifying questions if need be, but don't argue about the evaluation.

4. You or your manager needs to get the evaluation to me -- This is part of getting credit for co-op. I will want to discuss your evaluation with you as well as your future plans—whether for co-op or for after graduation.

5. Meet with me individually -- If you are around for Summer II, please see me during July or August. In addition to discussing your evaluation with me, students going on co-op again should revise their resumes and bring them to me as soon as possible. Meeting with me individually is also a requirement for getting co-op credit. I will not be around for the first week of July or August, but my calendar will list numerous appointment slots and walk-in hour options for those months.

Thanks, and I look forward to seeing you after the completion of your co-op!

Scott

I have similar e-mail templates for many other frequently arising topics:

- How to view my walk-in hours or schedule an appointment online

- Reminders for employers about an upcoming referral process

- Reflection paper requirements

- Reminders for students on setting goals and getting off to a good start for a new work term

- Suggestions for employers on how to proceed with job interviews and offers once they have received a resume packet

There are many others, but you get the idea. Having such templates will spare you considerable repetitive administrative tasks and free you up for more fun and unique activities.

6. *If possible, use your e-mail/calendar system to enable students to make appointments or view your walk-in hours schedule online.*

One of those "death by 1,000 slices" administrative duties that I just loathe is going back and forth via e-mail to schedule an appointment with a student. Here is the worst-case scenario:

- Student writes to request appointment without specifying a date or time

- Advisor writes back to suggest a specific date and time

- Student replies to say that they have a conflict with that specific date/time and suggests a different specific date and time... which does not work for the advisor

Okay, that's an extreme example, but it's not far off from what can and does happen in some instances. When I get an e-mail requesting an appointment now, I send one of my templates in response:

Dear _____,

I would be happy to meet with you. The most expedient way to determine my availability is to go to myneu.neu.edu and log in. Once you have done so, click on the Co-op/Career Services tab. You will see a link to the Faculty Appointment/Walk-In Calendars. Scroll down to my name, and you will see what I have available.

Note that I typically update my calendar on Thursday afternoon for the subsequent week. So if you are looking to meet with me and seeing nothing available, bear in mind that more availability will be posted by the end of the day Thursday.

That said, if you see nothing that works for you, please e-mail me. Tell me that you checked my availability online and found nothing that works. Then propose a few days and time ranges that would work for you. More often than not, I leave some cushion in my schedule and can accommodate requests.

Thanks, and I look forward to seeing you soon.

SW

There may be better systems than mine, but the key is to get your students to be able to know how things work so you can avoid spending big chunks of time on something as mundane as scheduling meetings. I also try to let them know a few other facts along these lines:

- A hard copy of my weekly schedule is always on my door, so they can drop by and check that out if they are disinclined to look up my availability online.

- Students know that they are free to drop by to see if I'm around and available, but they have to understand that they might not catch me if they do.

- I usually offer both appointments and walk-in hours, as some students like the structure of a planned slot while others enjoy the spontaneity of walk-ins. However, I try to get students to think about the consequences of their choices. If they are coming to walk-in hours during busy season, they may face a long wait, so they should bring some homework or reading material. Likewise, they should know that walk-in hours in the morning are inevitably going to be less crowded than they are in the afternoon. Basically, there are ways to minimize waiting time if that's important to the individual—better to think a little strategically about that rather than continually coming in at 3 p.m. and getting annoyed about a long line.

EXCEL AND ACCESS

Microsoft Excel and Access can be other valuable tools for keeping your program organized. I have even heard of some smaller programs that use these tools to manage all of their job listings and placement information. In fact, I used to use a very simple, self-designed version of Access to track my job referrals, years ago.

Even if you have a more elaborate CRM, I find it helpful to use both Excel and Access for various aspects of running my program. Periodically, I use Excel to try to assess my program. I can have an administrative assistant or work/study student enter data about all of my jobs: company, industry, job type, geographical location, pay rate, whether the job is accessible via public transportation, etc. Then I go in and develop some metrics for my program. Here are some questions that I try to answer:

- What industries are overrepresented and underrepresented among my students' employers? Are we too dependent on one industrial sector? Are there sectors in which we really should have more jobs than we do?

- Do we have enough jobs for students who lack cars? What percentage of jobs am I able to fill that are within a 30-minute drive of Boston? How many can I fill beyond that radius?

- How many jobs did I have available in comparison to the number of job seekers? Do I have a healthy mix in terms of type of job within each major, or do we have too many jobs of one type and not enough of some others? How can I adjust my job development efforts accordingly?

- Do we have enough out-of-state jobs for students interested in that? If not, what are some companies and regions that we should be targeting?

- What is the average pay rate broken out by major? What is the pay range for each major? Given the supply and demand of jobs and job seekers, should we consider striving for higher pay rates, or are we good where we are?

The interesting thing about this type of exercise is that the numbers always end up telling you some surprising facts along with confirming some of your preconceived notions. I feel like I end up with a better overview of my program, which is very handy when talking to students, employers, and administrators. More importantly, I can identify potential vulnerabilities or weaknesses in my program and take action to correct them before a corporate acquisition or recession strikes.

These days I also use Access for a very simple but valuable purpose. I took a four-hour free workshop on campus and learned how to create tables, forms, and queries—nothing fancy, really. But I then designed an extremely basic Access database that I use to write in the key facts from all of my phone calls and voice mails: names, phone numbers, whether the person was an employer (coded as E) or a lead (coded as L), etc.; and a comments field that allows me to write up to 10,000 characters if necessary. Perhaps most importantly, I have a box for each record that is entitled "Action needed?" A check mark is automatically generated in that box, so I know that I haven't taken action on that item until I uncheck that box.

How does this database help me?

- The database becomes an electronic to-do list for me. In the face of dozens of e-mails and voice mails as well as frequent interruptions, the database is something I monitor several times a day to see what remains undone. Sometimes I add items to it that are not related to phone calls at all—just to be sure that I don't forget to do them. When I see a whole screen of blank action boxes, I know I'm caught up.

- The database can be searched almost instantly to dig up facts that could take ages to find in a manual system. I can't tell you how many times an employer has called me looking to hire a co-op, and I have to tell them that a) it's the wrong time of year to attempt to hire someone, b) they are located somewhere that's going to make a co-op hire almost impossible, c) the job sounds really interesting and that they should follow up by sending me a job description, or d) all of the above.

But what ends up happening in these cases? Not infrequently, I have had an employer call me in May looking for a student to work in Portland, Maine. I can't help them at that time, but maybe five or ten months later a student comes in and announces that he or she wants to work in Maine. There's no way I'm going to remember the company or contact name from all those months ago, but I can use the "Find" function in Access and search on "ME" for Maine or maybe even for the 207 area code. Within seconds, I'll find the name and number of that person and be able to make the connection.

Likewise, some of those terrific job leads come from individuals who never end up following up with me as I recommend that they do. So a couple of times a year, I'll run a query that will pull out everyone that I've coded as a lead along with their phone numbers and my comments. Scanning over that query report, I'll find several employers who did end up posting a job and hiring a student. But I'll also see a handful of employers that never did follow up after talking about great opportunities. I call them back, and often I learn that they felt it was too late to hire a co-op or that it just slipped their mind in the face of other priorities. Sometimes that follow-up call leads directly to a new job getting developed. So I am a real believer in finding a way to maintain data on all your job leads and following up on it periodically.

BLACKBOARD

I will discuss Blackboard in greater detail once we get into the chapter on how to teach a preparation course. Suffice to say, though, that Blackboard gives professionals a very handy way to run a course, including posting assignments and readings online, automatically creating a grade book, and so forth. My class is now very close to 100 percent paperless, and that's doing much more than saving trees. It's cutting down on my record-keeping time and freeing me up for other activities while keeping students accountable for meeting deadlines.

PLANNING AND PRIORITIZING

Now let's consider some other fundamentals of making priorities as a professional. These ideas have much less to do with technology and relate more to big-picture planning.

1. Consider establishing relationships with students as early as possible.

At Northeastern, students don't start actively seeking co-op jobs until their sophomore year at the earliest. But there is a growing sense that failing to get involved with our freshmen to some degree represents a missed opportunity. With our business students, we are trying to do more to get them thinking about what they might be able to do during their summer vacation after freshman year that will enable them to hit the ground running when they start their co-op search the following fall or spring semester. We are encouraging them to try to get some relevant work experience, ramp up their computer skills, and maybe even pick up the required textbook for the co-op preparation course to start thinking ahead about their job search. Some have responded well and are way ahead, using the book to come up with a credible first draft of a resume.

As noted earlier in this chapter, Bob Tillman told me how much he does beyond his job description in order to establish relationship with his students. At the end of this chapter, he talks about how he teaches—without pay—a few freshmen sections and advises students on a variety of projects outside of his co-op responsibilities. It's additional work up front, but when it comes time to look for co-op jobs, Bob already knows his students and can go through the job search process much more quickly and painlessly as a result.

2. Understand the cyclical nature of your job and work with it.

Although some professionals have to contend with short work terms on a year-round basis, most of us face an academic year that has different peaks and valleys. As a result, it's important to think about what really has to happen at specific times of year versus what is necessary or even possible at other points of the year.

Firm visits are a great example. For many (but not all) professionals, there is a need to juggle being on campus to work with students and getting out on the road to visit organizations to build and maintain relationships. At my institution, we are placing students to work in six-month, full-time positions that start in January and July. As a result, most of us find it difficult to get out on the road very much between, say, October and early April. Between teaching a weekly class and needing to move students quickly through the preparation and job search processes, there is not much time for whole days of firm visits. Well, you could try to do that, but you might return to 100 e-mails, a dozen voice mails, and a massive crowd at your next walk-in hours.

So you have to think through your goals and how you're going to manage them given the cyclical nature of your job. My colleague, Charlie Bognanni, showed me a grid that he and his accounting colleague put together; it detailed the 20–30 firm visits that they planned to do between early June and early September. The list was based on a small-group discussion of which employers were the highest priority. That may be based on a number of questions worth asking:

- Is this a new employer that has never been visited?

- Is this an employer who regularly hires first-time co-ops who may benefit more from a visit?

- Is the employer a key educational partner, hiring a significant number of students and ensuring that they have a good learning experience?

- Do we think that there are opportunities to grow our co-op program with this employer?

- Is this an employer that has had problems with previous co-ops and therefore might benefit from some extra attention?

- Did the employer struggle to hire students last time, and can we go visit to show them that we value them as a potential educational partner?

- Is the employer in a location that is relatively far from Boston? If so, it might be best to visit them during the summer, when we can afford to be away from the office for a longer period of time. If not, perhaps we can hold off on visiting, figuring we can dash out for a visit at the beginning or end of a work day during busy season.

In addition to ramping up firm visits during quieter times, slower periods are also great opportunities to overhaul your process. Talk with colleagues, students, and employers about what's working and what to change. Develop materials that will save time during your peak times. Attend conferences, do research—there is a long list of possibilities, but the goal is to work toward making the busy times that much easier based on what you do during your slower times.

3. Understand political factors in making priorities.

Political considerations are going to have their impact on what you do and when you do it. If a colleague asks you for some metrics on your program, it may be fine to pull that information together over a period of several weeks. But if your director or provost or president wants that information, you might have to drop everything and turn a report around as soon as possible.

Ideally you would be equally responsive to all parties who need to get information from you, but in reality you often have to decide what balls need to stay in the air versus which ones are going to have to drop for a period of time. Failing to respond quickly to those who have power over your budget and career is something that may be done at your own peril.

4. Don't change your process midstream.

I don't think that everyone would agree with me on this one. Here's the dilemma: Inevitably, you're going to face a situation in which you realize there is a major problem with your process. Maybe it's what you've asked students to do in order for their resumes to go out to employers, or perhaps it's some other requirement that you now realize is superfluous. So what do you do if you're in the thick of one of your busiest times of the year? Do you try to fix it midstream or just accept that you're stuck with it until the next cycle?

There are costs and benefits each way. There is no question that it's very frustrating to keep requiring a step that you know you're going to modify radically or even eliminate. But will it only create more confusion if you tell your students "I know I told you that we were going to do things one way, but now we're going to introduce a totally new different procedure that will be much better."

Personally, I am an adherent to the belief that once you tell people what you're going to do, then you need to stick to that for that cycle to avoid mass confusion, stress, and frustration. The only exception I would make is if something truly catastrophic happens. If I get hit by a bus and am incapacitated during the busiest time of year, obviously that would call for some radical changes for how my group would work with my students. If a colleague suddenly gives two weeks' notice just before interviews begin, then we will have to scramble to deal with the situation. In general, though, you really want to stop and think about how a midstream change will throw off students on top of discombobulating faculty and staff.

Beyond extreme situations like that, though, I am opposed to changing processes and requirements at the most stressful times of year. Years ago, I remember that a new technology was forced on our whole department during the busiest time of the whole academic year. It was close to a disaster. Just switching over to a new application was going to be a challenge and a stressor in any event, but having to ramp up on top of everything else that was going on made it much worse than it could've been. And because it was the first time around with the application, we inevitably found quite a few bugs. Students were baffled on top of handling their usual job search stress. During a calmer time of year that would not have been a big deal, but it was excruciating given everything else that was going on in October.

MAXIMIZE QUALITY OF ONE-ON-ONE TIME

As alluded to earlier in this book, our field attracts many people who love students and are eager to nurture them. That's terrific, but there are many steps you can take to make sure that your one-on-one time with students is great and necessary one-on-one time. Ironically, many professionals are so fond of their students that they fail to take steps that will eliminate more routine and mundane tasks from their meetings with students while creating more time for real one-on-one education. Here are some tips that should enable you to make the most of that precious one-on-one interaction with a student.

1. Delegate and educate.

Sometimes professionals fall into the trap of thinking that "if you want something done right, you've got to do it yourself." If you do have other individuals on your staff who can handle some responsibilities for you, train them to do so. At times, I did all of my practice interviews myself. When my load reached a good size, it became very difficult... but I was able to get funding to hire a graduate student. For several years, I had grad students from various programs—counseling psychology , college student development, and less obvious programs such as engineering—who I trained to do practice interviews. If there wasn't funding, sometimes it was possible to get a student who could have the experience count as a practicum. I have heard of some programs using experienced upperclassmen for this purpose as well.

That's just one example. If you have competent staff, you can train them to assist with all kind of activities: generating reports; forwarding resumes to employers; conducting resume-writing workshops; creating interview schedules, and so on. Obviously, you'll have to be careful about what can and can't be delegated, but there surely are many things that can be passed along. This can free you up considerably.

Yet delegation and education don't only apply to staff members. Sometimes you need to get students to do some of the heavy lifting as well. Years ago, my wife was hired to critique resumes for graduate students at a prominent university. I was rather amazed that the director of that program was willing to pay an outside consultant to basically rewrite resumes for students. Sure, part of our responsibility is to critique resumes, but I don't think we're doing students a favor by taking their resume from 0 to 60 for them. If a student brings in a resume that is based on a Word template or which otherwise indicates that they have not read my book, *Find Your First Professional Job*, I simply tell them that they need to go back to the drawing board and following my step-by-step approach in Chapter 2 before bringing the resume back to me. I try to use a light touch when telling them this: I usually say that I want them to learn how to write a resume now because otherwise they'll be looking me up when they're 47 and planning yet another job change! But I impress upon them that part of the learning process is to learn how to become self-sufficient in a job search, as they won't always have someone like me readily available to them.

The temptation is that it's often much faster to just fix a resume than to teach someone how to fix it. If you write a student's cover letter yourself, you may well end up with a better finished product than if they do most of it themselves. But you're going to bury yourself in work if you don't take the approach of educating students so they can become more independent.

2. Develop time-saving materials.

This is another highly underrated aspect of our profession. One key to my professional existence is the following: If I find myself repeating the same information in more than four or five one-on-one meetings each semester, then I'm missing an opportunity to make my life easier while actually doing a better job.

Here are some questions that I get asked quite frequently:

- What are the most typical co-op jobs and career paths for students interested in Management Information Systems?

- If I'm your student but I want to pursue a job in another area such as marketing, how does that work?

- If I want to develop my own job outside of what Northeastern has available, what should I say to employers to make them want to hire me?

- I'm an employer interested in hiring co-op students in MIS (or Supply Chain Management or General Management). How does that work?

Years ago, I received two calls in a row from potential employers. I was probably on the phone for an hour straight, going through everything about how co-op works: when the work terms start and end; what the typical pay rates are; what factors influence an employer's ability to hire a student; what the typical jobs are; and so forth. After hanging up the phone the second time, I was troubled by a few thoughts. I had just spent an hour with two employers, but what had I accomplished? Did I remember everything that might've been valuable to those employers? Probably not. How much would they remember from my lengthy spiel? Not that much, I guessed. And now they were supposed to follow up with a job description that may or may not bear any relationship to what I really hoped to receive from them.

The next day I came in early and wrote a document called "Frequently Asked Questions About the MIS Co-op Program." If you go to the www.mosaiceyepublishing.com website, you can download this document by clicking on "Learning From Experience" and checking out the free materials to download. As you'll see, it answers all of the usual questions and includes a sample job description with all the information I want to see—including a pay range that I'd like to see!

Now my voice-mail message urges prospective employers to leave their e-mail address. I follow up quickly with an FAQ document instead of having a 30-minute phone conversation. Looking over my aforementioned Access database, I just ran a query and found that I have sent that e-mail to 117 employers who turned up as job leads between January 2006 and July 2008. Some colleagues told me that they didn't have time to create an FAQ for their program, but I figure that it took me about three hours to write the FAQ... and it's saved me 55 hours in the last 2½ years alone! That's over a week of work, and it's inevitably going to be much more fun and interesting work than reciting facts and figures about the program again and again.

The same is true with documents I've developed to address those other questions. If a student wants to know about career paths in their major, I give them a two or three-page document covering them. The document took me a couple of hours to write, and it saves me about 10–15 minutes every time I'm asked the question... which happens at least 15 times per semester.

So as you go through each cycle, try to catch it when you're repeating yourself. Maybe you won't be able to drop everything and develop a document immediately that can be e-mailed or posted on Blackboard, so make a list of possible materials and develop them when the action dies down.

3. Determine what can be done just as effectively in a larger group.

Some activities really have to be done one-on-one. Helping a student finalize a resume, counseling someone through an emotionally challenging situation, and some elements of career counseling really call for one-on-one interaction. Yet there are many ways to be at least as effective with a larger group, such as preparation courses, workshops, and seminars: Whether you have a formal course or an informal workshop or seminar, there is no question that you can teach students a great deal about resume writing, strategic interviewing, and professional behaviors in a group setting. I'll devote a later chapter to prep classes, but on a much simpler level, a one-hour workshop on how to write a resume can save considerable time without sacrificing educational quality. We sometimes offer workshops on "bridging"—making connections between a specific resume and an actual job description—and that can be a helpful activity for students to do in a group, as they can brainstorm creatively to figure out what might work.

Just a few years ago, I came up with a new idea that has worked well. Students in our program are required to sign an agreement form once they obtain a job, and that step has the potential to feel like no more than another bureaucratic hurdle to jump over. So in my one-on-one meetings, I began to deemphasize the signing of the form itself and instead use that meeting as an opportunity to provide closure to the preparation phase of the co-op learning model. I would ask each student the following questions:

- Why is it important for you to do a good job over the next six months? Or, to put it another way, what are the various ways in which you will selfishly benefit by performing well?

- When employers call me due to a problem with a co-op, what is the most common one? Why does that problem arise?

- How often do you think you need to get in touch with me while in co-op?

- Regardless of how often you are required to be in touch, what would be some specific issues that should lead you to get in touch with me immediately?

We also would review the goal-setting process and the evaluation form as well as the steps required for getting credit for co-op. This all would take a good 20 minutes to do it right. Finally I came to my senses and started holding "co-op success factors" meetings for small groups of first-time co-ops. We get a classroom and do all of the above in groups of maybe 10 or 15. Students get to help each other come up with the answers, and I end up doing something that I think is worth doing in about one-tenth of the time it would otherwise require. If preferred, this process also could be done toward the end of a co-op/internship prep class.

MAINTAIN WORK/LIFE BALANCE

When it comes to making priorities, one last topic worth discussing is work/life balance. As we will see in the next chapter, being passionate about the job is one of several elements that differentiate between great professionals in our field and those that are more average. However, you need to make sure that you are not consumed by your job.

In this field, you have to accept that you very rarely are going to be able to go home feeling that everything got done that could've been done in a given day. Sometimes it's quite the opposite: There have been many times when I began to write a response to an e-mail first thing in the morning, only to have one crisis after another arise. Before I knew it, I would be on my way home in the early evening before I realized I never got back to completing the first thing I started that day.

How many hours are too many? That's a very personal issue to work out. It may depend on whether you are single or married as well as whether you have kids or not. Some people seem to thrive on long days, while others burn out—developing psychological or physical health issues due to work-related stress. Another factor is how much freedom your manager allows you in your role. In some work environments, you absolutely have to be in the office by a specific time and not leave until a certain time. Other managers may allow you the freedom to work from home occasionally or to come in late or leave early depending on the time of year or your personal circumstances.

There are also important choices to make about working at home. I have some colleagues who really make a point of leaving fairly early for family reasons, but then they will get on their e-mail later in the evening to get some more things done.

All of that said, you have to try to find a balance that works for you and those close to you. I also recommend setting limits for yourself. For most of the year, I try to take my kids to school in the morning. That results in getting to work around 8:15 or so if I go directly from their school to the office. In lieu of lunch, I usually go to the gym for a 30-minute workout somewhere between Noon and 2 if I can. And then I try very hard to be sure that I am out the door and on my way home by 6 p.m. regardless of how busy it is. Often I'm pushing very hard to answer e-mails and voice mails right up to 6, as I really try to avoid doing work at home. That's time that I want to devote to my family, and I find that having a clean break in the evening makes me feel more energized to come in the next day.

If I periodically am feeling a little burned out, I'll try to come in a little later and leave a little earlier if possible. During the summer months, I'll try to arrange my schedule so I can get a break from student contact each week so I can write or catch up on other big-picture projects. When I go on vacation, I try very hard to make myself completely unavailable via e-mail or voice mail. Then it feels like a real vacation, and I'm much more refreshed. Meanwhile, some of my colleagues are very diligent about checking in frequently when they are away, just in case something difficult arises. There are pros and cons to either approach.

Over my career in various jobs, I have worked with people who were martyrs at work, and they never seemed to be happy. One woman I worked with years ago was chronically short-tempered, often getting sick, unable to quit smoking, and feeling underappreciated at work on top of it all! Yet I'd have to say that she also was not nearly as productive as many of our co-workers, even though she often worked anywhere from 60 to 90 hours per week.

Really, there is no one "right way" when it comes to working in our profession. I have colleagues who get to work much earlier than necessary, enjoying the opportunity to get a head start before the typical college student wakes up. Others come in somewhat later but work through lunch or stay later to avoid a bad rush-hour commute home. Regardless, the key is to do what you need to stay energized over the long haul of your career.

Here's what our experts had to say on the topic of making priorities as an educator:

IN THEIR OWN WORDS

PROFESSIONAL PERSPECTIVE #1
"QUESTION EVERYTHING"
Nancy Johnston, Simon Fraser University

To the extent possible, you want to avail yourself of technologies that make the process easier for all the stakeholders. So if you can get a good customer management database going—we've just moved over to Simplicity—if you're at an institution large enough you can create an enterprise-wide application or buy into one.

That's useful because then you're not doing everything manually, and I know because I was a coordinator "pre-system." We just did everything manually, and once you get beyond a certain critical mass you actually end up with very talented people doing very menial tasks, repeatedly, because the scale of it is so big. You're sending out hundreds of student packages and collating them by hand. It's ridiculous. Any time you can avail yourself of decent, existing technology I think it's best. That way you don't spend years developing some custom system like some schools have and it has damn near crippled them in terms of resources. You utilize what exists—the best of breed—and rework business practices to suit you and the system, that's likely the best way to go.

Then I think you look at what it is you do, and you question everything that has been practiced from an educational standpoint. Just as an exercise ask yourself: So, why do we have them fill out that form? What is that form for? What is the purpose of the form, and what does it have to do with the student's learning? And it's not to say that if it has nothing to do with student learning that it's not a good form. Get really clear on which part of your process you're doing—some of which is very time-consuming because you have to have them fill out the form, and then you have to chase down the person by June 10, and then because they didn't fill it out by June 10, somebody then has to be chasing them down and asking why, and then the follow-up to the chase-down.... So a whole bunch of work happens in co-op sometimes chasing down things that at the root of it all maybe even didn't need to happen, right? Or they happened because administratively it's easier, but if we actually did something different from the admin end it wouldn't necessarily have to involve the other stakeholders.

So I would look at every process that you do from a critical vantage point: Why do we do this? Who is it for? Who does it benefit? Is there a different way? Or is there a way that we can do this operational activity that embeds some learning? So you need to complete a profile, but on it I'm going to have a reflective component that will work on your metacognitive skills. So, yeah, there's an admin piece, but while I've got you and you need to do this, I'm going to take the same form and have a dual purpose to it. Then that's going to allow that form to make sense for the student instead of looking like another hoop that they have to go through for *me*.

So that's one way we started re-looking at our end-of-term reports because students were so chronically dissatisfied with the work report requirements. We tried to look at what it was intended to do: what is the spirit of this requirement? Well, accreditation rules make us do it. Okay, but what's the *intent* of the accreditation? How can we continue to meet the spirit of that but also do something that's more responsive to students' sense of what they'd like or need to be doing, to the context they are in, and to the current times, which is sometimes years after accreditation standards are set. Where do blogs, web pages etc. fit in? You need to stay relevant.

On it goes, but the bottom line is to avail yourself whenever you can of best-practice existing tools. Co-op is a young model of education, but it's a hundred years young, so there's a hundred years of good practice out there. Tune into your local, state, federal, national bodies. Do the conferences; find out what exists. If it's technology, look at best of breed off the shelf. If it's policies and practices; attend conferences.

Nobody's going to be reinventing the core of this wheel. It's kind of basic: You've got to do this; you've got to do this. But then look within your own context and your own organization. Okay, so how are we going to do site visits? Why would we do them this way? What are the learning goals of it? What are the marketing goals of it? What's the cost/benefit ratio from the business perspective? All the different ways of looking at it.

That's a very complex answer, but basically use what's out there and always try to connect back to your key goals.

PROFESSIONAL PERSPECTIVE #2
"18 DIFFERENT WAYS"
Bob Tillman, Northeastern University

I found out a long time ago—I think because I'm an engineer—that I can computerize everything, so I don't have to do things over and over. If I find out I'll need something again and again, I'll use the tools I have. I've written all of my referral materials that go out to students and I give it to them. So I'm a firm believer in giving students a lot of information when they need it. But don't give them a lot of things they don't need; give it to them at the time that they are going to use it and do something with it: Class packs, cover letter guides, resume guides, and interview guides; I have all that. It's all done.

So when I get an upperclassman who comes in and says, "I'm looking for a job for after graduation, and it's out in California..." Fine. I e-mail him a copy of all that material, and we're done. They weren't going to read it when they were sophomores. They didn't see any real urgency. Do I give it to them when they are sophomores? Sure. Some of them actually read it, but I don't have high expectations. Students at that time are more worried about going out in the field and succeeding. There's more of an urgency on that end.

Professionally, whatever you can put together that meets the needs of that student at that time that he or she needs it, great. When it's time to look at companies, I have a completely different handout covering where the jobs are and what they entail. Where they are and what they do. I use a program called 4D, a relational database, and that makes my life so easy. When it comes time for referrals, my clerical overhead is nothing. It's resumes going out the door, cover letters that I want going out the door, salary surveys to employers going out the door—all that stuff—I don't spend a lot of time on it, which leaves me more time with students. We have a really active student chapter of the American Society of Civil Engineers, so I see those students every week with lectures, former grads coming in. We do a community service project. So there are all these connections at different times with most of the students that are in the program.

Let me give you a good example [of how this extra work actually saves time]. I teach two freshman sections. I don't get paid for it; it's truly an overload. I only do it for one reason. I get to make connections with 60 of my civil engineering freshmen and all we have to do is get to know each other. There is no co-op business going on; it's just getting them through freshmen year. When they come in sophomore year I already know them. We've already had a year together. Great! I've got colleagues who say "Oh, I don't have the time..." But I look at it and say I don't know how I'd have the time not to do this. It's two hours a week! Some prep work, some other things... I get to connect them to a student chapter. Those that aren't going to be really socialized into the civil field—I get to have that discussion with them a lot earlier: "You're really talking about a career in business. This isn't where you're going to want to be." It makes life a lot easier.

So that's a good example. Being a chapter advisor is a ton of work, but I get to see kids 18 different ways that I don't see sitting in that chair. I see them working on different projects—going to Florida to work on a steel bridge, going to Maine and building a concrete canoe, building a big community service project. You can see students in a very different light, and they get to see you in a very different light. So I think that is a big advantage with what I have on my end.

PROFESSIONAL PERSPECTIVE #3
"TECHNOLOGY PRIORITIES"
Brenda LeMaster, University of Cincinnati

Before contracting to purchase any software application a program must really think through how they will use the application. I have found that some applications are very good at allowing good management of the activities of our office (placement, referrals, company contact data, etc.) but not very good at providing a usable database to conduct assessment activities. Knowing in advance if your priority is a good transactional application and not necessarily a searchable, historic database is probably a good idea.

PROFESSIONAL PERSPECTIVE #4
"PRE-PROFESSIONAL PREPARATION"
Tamara Pinkas, Lane Community College

We, as a college, let faculty decide for themselves [how to manage their time]. I worked with the colleagues in my discipline to set up a two-credit seminar because I was finding I was doing the same orientation over and over and over again one-on-one, and it was an enormously time-consuming thing. And then the students wouldn't have their resumes prepared, so there would be this big lag time where they'd get their resume instruction individually, and I'd have to wait...

So my colleagues and I talked about "What are the goals for our program? What do we want as outcomes for this program?" And one of them, of course, is employability. So then it makes sense to create several credits of graded pre-professional preparation as part of the training in the two-year degree program. And we call it the Co-op Ed Seminar, but you could call it anything. And that's turned out to be an enormous time saver. Because now I have pre-employment skill development built into the curriculum, and I don't need to have all those one-on-one times when students come and come back and send resume revisions back and forth. It's built in, and it's part of my responsibility, whereas before it was part of my load but not in an organized way. The fact is that a tuition/fee-generating course also helps with my standing in the institution.

PROFESSIONAL PERSPECTIVE #5
"THE BIGGEST ENERGY AND TIME DRAIN"
Jacki Diani, Northeastern University

To me one of the biggest energy and time drains of the past couple years is e-mail. I love e-mail; it has a place and a purpose. It can be very useful and effective; it can also be used for the wrong purposes. Students are incredibly comfortable with technology and e-mail, and they use it a lot.

Every morning when I come in to work, the first thing I do is check my e-mail. The red light on the phone is never blinking—hardly ever because instead you get tons of e-mail. I'll check my e-mail; see what's urgent, what needs an immediate response and what can wait. One of the things I've learned to do when particularly difficult situations are presented by students via e-mail—or a very long e-mail—I respond saying "I've read your e-mail and I think we need to meet and talk face-to-face or talk over the phone." I want the students to understand that certain situations are just not appropriate to engage in a very long e-mail conversation back and forth. Not only does it take too much time, but depending on the situation, sometimes it's just not appropriate to try and solve the issue over e-mail, because you can't clarify things the way that you can in person. It's just not going to work. That's helped me a lot because otherwise you could just end up spending hours responding to e-mails—literally hours.

Our job comes with many interruptions—e-mail, phone calls, student drop-ins—so it can be hard to plan out your day and stick to the schedule. I make a "to-do" list before I leave work for the next day, prioritizing what needs to be done or at least make head-way on. Looking ahead at the calendar and due dates is very important. First thing in the morning, I try to take care of anything urgent and that I can respond to quickly. During the week, I carve out some time to work on projects, research or general program maintenance. When you do this, you need to honor this time: shut the door and say, for example, "I need two hours to work on job development, and I can't be interrupted." I think there is almost no wasted time with employers. Whether phone, e-mail, or in person, you need to be in touch with them consistently.

My job is pretty cyclical; there are times of the year when I am meeting with students daily, while other times the appointments are much lighter and I can be out of the office visiting employers more frequently. If you use your calendar wisely you can make your schedule accordingly and plan ahead when you need to be in the office a lot because students really need to see you. During other periods, you can focus your energy on other things—administrative activities, professional development, and employer development.

REFLECTION QUESTIONS

1. Do you have a mechanism in place that encourages you and your colleagues to question everything that you do in a deep, meaningful way on a regular basis? Whether you do or not, how you can be completely sure that you're doing what's best for your constituencies rather than doing what is comfortable, familiar, and convenient for you?

2. What are some specific ways in which you show students why they must complete various steps, processes, or requirements in your program to ensure that they won't perceive them as pointless wastes of time?

3. Describe a few ways in which you and your colleagues have capitalized on existing best practices, adopting new ways to do your jobs based on what you have read, discussed with other professionals, or learned from attending conferences?

4. Consider how your program is using technology as an educational tool. What is currently most satisfying about how you use technology to save time and enhance the educational experience? In what ways is technology causing frustration to you and your students and detracting from the educational experience? What are your greatest needs when it comes to technological change?

5. What are your beliefs about the usefulness and limitations of e-mails when working with students and employers? What can and can't be done via e-mail? What e-mail templates are you using to save time without compromising on educational quality?

6. What system do you use to keep track of student and employer information so it is readily available when needed? For example, if you needed to dig up a job lead from roughly two years ago, would you be able to do so in seconds?

7. This chapter describes many ways to maximize the quality of one-on-one time with students:
   • Delegate and educate
   • Develop time-saving materials
   • Determine what can be done just as effectively in a larger group

   Can you list ways in which you have done all of the above? Which of these areas has been your greatest strength? What would you like to explore more fully to see if you can free up more quality time for individual students?

CHAPTER 4

STRIVING FOR GREATNESS

"Being busy does not always mean real work. The object of all work is production or accomplishment and to either of these ends there must be forethought, system, planning, intelligence, and honest purpose, as well as perspiration. Seeming to do is not doing."
— *Thomas Alva Edison*

It may take quite a long time—maybe even a few years—for a professional in our field to become competent in the basic nuts and bolts of the job. Not many individuals come into this line of work knowing very much about cooperative education, and every institution is different. As described in the first three chapters, there is much to do simply to ramp up when it comes to getting to know your constituencies and how to develop a basic vision of where you're going as well as the various tools and processes you might opt to use in getting there.

At some point, though, the goal should move from simply getting the job done toward shining as a professional. What does it take to be great? When I asked about 15 experts to tell me what differentiates a great professional from a more typical one in preparing to write this book, numerous themes came up. This chapter is an attempt to synthesize and prioritize those perspectives, as follows.

UNDERSTAND AND FACILITATE LEARNING

Our profession can be perceived as quite simple in some ways. For most of us, our primary responsibility is to ensure that students obtain work experiences. If all of your job seekers are employed in time to start a work term, and there are minimal complaints about you from students or employers, your school's administrators might perceive you as being perfectly successful.

However, most experts believe that you can be extremely competent in the basics of the job—pitching the program to employers, critiquing a resume, and so forth—without being a great professional. The key is to whether you eventually can move beyond your operational responsibilities and become a real educator.

LEARNING THEORY

Although most professionals come to our field with a strong background in a functional area—such as accounting, electrical engineering, physical therapy, etc.—and some also may have excellent experience and/or a degree in counseling, a very small number come into the field with any background at all in experiential learning and its theoretical underpinnings. So delving into the readings of researchers such as Stephen Brookfield, Jerome Bruner, John Dewey, J. H. Flavell, Peter Jarvis, David Kolb, Jean Lave, and Etienne Wenger are good starting points for those aspiring to understand what's really going on when it comes to whether learning is occurring in the world of practice as opposed to in the classroom. If you do so, you'll be digging into a variety of fascinating—and fairly cerebral—subjects. Let's briefly cover some of the most critical ones here.

1. *Historical Perspectives*

As **Nancy Johnston** of Simon Fraser University points out in her thesis, "Conceptions of Curriculum in Cooperative Education: A Framework for Analysis of the Co-op Preparatory Curriculum," the roots of learning theory that are relevant to our field go back as far as Aristotle, who placed an emphasis on practical wisdom. I want to give full credit to Nancy in this chapter, as I need to acknowledge that my brief overview of learning theory here often paraphrases or borrows heavily from her thesis.

In addition to **Aristotle**, another Roman, **Marcus Vitruvius Pollio**, wrote a treatise on architecture that expounded on the concept of blending theory and practice. In her thesis, Johnston notes that Marcus Vitruvius was frequently quoted by **Herman Schneider**, the founding father of cooperative education.

After a long lull, philosopher **Rene Descartes** advanced the cause by generally rejecting the idea that schools should be the primary or only source of education. Some of his ideas—such as the notion that learning is readily transferable from one context to the other are seen as highly dubious by many contemporary theorists, but Descartes definitely saw that experience was how we test our intuition to acquire true knowledge.

2. *Metacognition*

Throughout this book, Nancy Johnston's many quotes often connect implicitly or explicitly to the concept of metacognition, so I want to provide some background here. Metacognition can most simply be thought of as "thinking about thinking," but that doesn't quite capture it. The hope is that knowledge of one's own cognitive processes can lead to an ability to develop self-awareness and therefore an increased ability to alter those thought processes to adapt to new situations. **J. H. Flavell** was the first to use the term, but the roots of it go back to Aristotle and, more recently, **John Locke**.

Locke was one of the first thinkers to suggest that a key to learning is making connections between what we already know and what is to come. So this is an early basis for the link that metacognition theorists make between old and new learning.

Using Locke as a basis, co-op and internship educators should look at better ways to help our student learners make connections from one context to another—whether school to work, work to school, or from an old job experience to a new one. By facilitating the process of making connections, educators can increase the probability that students will be able to transfer skills from one setting to another.

How would this happen in practice? The idea would be to use reflective techniques to get learners to "think about their own thinking" in order to see how two seemingly different problems or situations actually share similar principles or dynamics. The educator helps the learner see the abstract connection, and that helps the learner drawn on those earlier strategies and apply them in a new context.

With this in mind, the co-op/internship professional who believes in this philosophy is going to do whatever is possible to force students to think about what they learn and how they learn it in order to maximize opportunities for knowledge transfer from one context to another. Curiously, the research indicates that knowledge doesn't transfer as readily as we might imagine—even a moderately different context can derail the learner more than you would anticipate, intuitively.

So when you see a superstar student in one term fall on his face in a subsequent term, there are a variety of possible explanations. However, one possible underlying reason that is often overlooked is that the student was unable to draw on the knowledge gained from the first experience and tap into it at the new job. By pulling more of a metacognitive approach into your philosophy, you are very likely going to improve the odds that your students will be more aware of what they learned and how they learned it, increasing their chances of building on it in the future.

3. *Situated Learning*

I have had the pleasure of reading books by **Jean Lave** and **Etienne Wenger** as well as seeing Wenger lecture in person a few times. In reading *Communities of Practice* by Wenger, I was particularly struck by lengthy examples in which the author describes how midwives and weavers in other cultures learn their trade. The gist of those stories is to demonstrate how an individual can grow from novice to expert in a field without any formal education whatsoever—sometimes without any apparent verbal instruction, for that matter. In these instances, there are many examples in which learners begin on the periphery of a profession, taking on tasks that gradually increase in significance while also developing knowledge culled from being part of a community.

The simplified idea is that learning never happens in a vacuum. You can't separate learning from the world in which that learning takes place. Lave and Wenger view knowledge as a cultural and social product, and they challenge the idea that we learn something in one place and then simply apply it elsewhere. This is important, as I think many students and educators initially imagine that they will learn concepts and theories in the classroom and then go out and apply them in a co-op job or internship. While there are instances in which that happens to an extent, such a simplistic view fails to incorporate all of the new learning and flashes of insight that our students undoubtedly experience in an organizational environment.

Another key concept for Lave and Wenger is that learning occurs within a "community of practice." This is described as a collection of individuals who are engaged in a shared enterprise that includes some implicitly or explicitly understood commonalities, such as various beliefs, practices, and norms.

Lave and Wenger also discuss the concept of "legitimate peripheral participation," an abstract but important idea. Here I think it might be helpful to think of an organization as somewhat like a major metropolitan city. Those who are new to it don't arrive with an understanding of what really makes it tick and how to make things happen for themselves within it, but this knowledge gradually develops over time. Where does the knowledge come from? It may come from formal instruction, but more often than not emerges in very complex ways—observing behaviors, overhearing conversations, figuring out how to take advantage of resources and accomplish tasks, navigating through different obstacles, and so forth. Over time, the individual starts to feel like a real member of the organization instead of someone who is on the periphery and not truly engaged in the community beyond a superficial level.

This obviously has relevance for our students. I find that many students are moderately disappointed to learn that most companies don't have formal training programs. They are anxious about how they will learn to be successful at work. While the concept of legitimate peripheral participation may be a bit cerebral for many young adults, I do find it important to prepare students to understand that they will gradually learn a great deal about what it means to be a member of an organizational community if they can observe carefully, seek informal advice while doing tasks, go to lunch and talk to full-time employees about making the transition, and so on. If you can prepare students for the fact that they will start off feeling like an outsider but slowly work their way into the culture—and get them to see that this is actually a big part of the learning available to them—then they should develop a more positive perspective on the transition.

One attractive element of this theory is that learning is much more dynamic than simple observation and learning. It also is a strong argument for students doing jobs that are longer and more substantial in terms of length, number of weekly hours, and intensity of work, as all of those elements would increase the number of opportunities to get closer to the center of the community of practice. In other words, a student working eight hours per week on an unpaid internship is going to have a harder time becoming a full-fledged member of the community than a co-op student who is working full-time hours over several months. Another important idea here is that this theory reminds us that learning is social; others in the learning community play significant roles in the experience.

Understanding situated learning and communities of practice has proven to be very valuable to me as an educator. Many of our students come into a co-op program believing that the learning they will acquire at an organization will be primarily technical in nature—learning how to master a software application, how to reconcile an accounts payable ledger, how to write a news feature for a newspaper, and so forth. I find that students tend to underrate the value of learning by being a member of a community of practice. By doing whatever tasks might be done in a public accounting firm during tax season or in a small physical therapy clinic on a busy Monday morning, a student has the opportunity to observe and absorb many aspects of what it means to be a professional. How does an experienced civil engineer deal with an angry construction foreman? After working in a casual, relaxed software firm, some students may come back and say "That place just wasn't me!" Of course, these are valuable learnings, though not necessarily the ones our students usually expect. While I don't explicitly use terms like "legitimate peripheral participation" or "communities of practices" with my students, I do use my knowledge of this theory to manage expectations and to reframe what constitutes learning before students go on that first co-op job.

4. *Experiential Learning Model*

As Nancy Johnston points out in her thesis, **David Kolb**'s theory is the one that is most familiar in our field. Kolb devised a four-stage model that the learner continually moves through over time. The learner starts with a concrete experience, which is followed by creating a set of observations and reflections about that experience. Next, the learner begins to form abstract generalizations which they later test in new situations. That leads to a new set of concrete experiences, and round and round it goes. You can Google "David Kolb" and "learning styles" to see a visual diagram.

The assumption here is that the cycle is most efficient and effective when the learner has clear goals and a high level of motivation. Some research suggests that the theory holds up when we look at how co-op students use their concrete experiences from the working world and then reflect upon them both on the job and back at school. This leads to new abstract generalizations that they will test out in subsequent co-op jobs or internships. With this in mind, our goal should be to embed opportunities for reflection in our curricula and processes in order to maximize the extent to which students engage in abstract generalization.

One element is reminiscent of the misconception I brought up when describing situated learning theory. Again, the average person who has no connection to our field often believes that co-op involves a) learning a concept or theory in the classroom, and then b) going out to apply that theory in the real world. While this does indeed occur, the cyclical nature of Kolb's theory offers another way of understanding that is often not the case.

Sometimes I ask students about this during a reflection seminar: "To what degree do you feel you learned something in a course and then went out and applied it versus being exposed to something for the first time on co-op and then learning the theory behind it when you returned to classes?" Anecdotally, I would say that slightly more than half of my students have said the latter. I think that Kolb would approve of this chronology.

More importantly, understanding Kolb's theory can be yet another way to gauge your program. Are you providing students with the sort of concrete experiences that are rich and complex enough to lend themselves to real learning? What are you doing to facilitate the observation and reflection process in such a way that will lead to meaningful learning? Given that students are not always great at making the leap from the concrete to the abstract, how are you ensuring that abstract generalization will occur to a sufficient degree, ensuring that students approach their next concrete experience in a way that builds on the previous experience? You could argue that this is another way to think of the knowledge transfer issue that we broached in relation to metacognition.

5. *Reflective Practice*

I was lucky enough to be taking industrial psychology and organizational behavior courses back when **Donald Schön**'s model of reflective practice was new, so I have been familiar with his work for a long while. The situated learning theory that we talked about earlier seems to be a variation on Schön's "knowledge-in-action" approach, as described by Nancy Johnston below.

Schön's model is kindred to Kolb's. In both cases, the learner faces concrete situations and ultimately rethinks their initial perceptions of these situations, resulting in changes in their subsequent beliefs and behaviors. Schön calls this 'reflection in action' and describes learners using a responsive and fluid approach to learning. The learner continually reflects on practice, drawing on prior knowledge and experiences rather than cookie-cutter theories from classrooms or books.

Schön believes that this process cannot be taught, but that it is learnable and coachable. Basically, the learner must engage in the experience and then process it through their interaction. Our students' work experiences give them many chances to undergo the process of learning through reflection in action. However, Schön's theory also implies that a student who participates in co-op is engaged in a different form of higher education that would need to be supported by complementary preparatory and workplace curricula. In other words, we shouldn't assume that learning will just magically occur independent of the educator or institution; we need to create mechanisms to ensure that it happens through our actions.

Some educators in our field would not endorse this viewpoint. Sometimes I think of Schön when I hear co-op/internship professionals complaining bitterly about their institution's efforts to create integration between classroom and workplace. "Integration is something that happens within the mind of the learner!" is the gritted-teeth refrain of some professionals. I don't disagree, but Nancy's point that this form of practical learning needs to be reinforced by the co-op/internship professionals through preparation, activity, and reflection is also a valid one.

To some degree I have Schön in mind when facilitating role plays, as I will describe in great detail when I get to Chapter 8 and discuss teaching preparation classes. While a professional can't simulate a real-world experience, it can be helpful to devise activities that force students to experiment with thinking on their feet in a challenging situation. Last summer I did a training of new hires in a corporate setting, and we ended up with a wonderfully mixed bag of individuals succeeding completely, having mixed results, or falling on their faces in various role plays. Then we debriefed it, and it felt quite vibrant to be able to talk about behavioral choices that different individuals made and how those played out.

This also might be done by giving students rather messy case histories to dissect and discuss. Because work situations are not nice and neat problems to solve, such as a statistical problem in a classroom. They are complicated, and you often lack all the facts. You can't always ascertain the motivations of your co-workers, and the potential consequences of one action versus another are not always foreseeable. In general, getting students to anticipate that their real-world experience is going to be a laboratory of sorts in which they must make constant adjustments and readjustments based on feedback can be useful. It certainly gives students a healthy respect for the learning opportunities at work.

6. Transformative Learning

In her thesis, Nancy Johnston states her belief that the work of **Jack Mezirow** is somewhat overlooked in co-op literature. Mezirow's contribution is in the area of transformative learning. The basic idea here is that an individual who has a powerful experience, positive or negative, has the opportunity to analyze that experience and change perceptions accordingly. Clearly, we see this happen all the time as educators. A student is overjoyed to get a high-paying, challenging job in the field of his choice, only to come away from the experience stunned by a sense of joylessness from a job that he should have loved. An individual coasts through a job happily enough and then is thunderstruck by a dismal evaluation. An intern works at a company when dozens of people are laid off, getting a first-hand view of the emotional impact of such an experience.

All of these experiences are powerful and very likely to have an impact on that student's world view and subsequent career choices, but what do we do with these experiences? As Nancy Johnston notes, "While the co-op model may offer many opportunities for such reflection, most co-op curricula do not encourage or support transformative learning of this nature, either at the personal or societal level."

Instead, "the focus of most co-op programs remains on the employability skills deemed of value to the 'marketplace' and on ensuring that students develop these to the greatest extent possible in order to fulfill market needs. In a sense this turns the selection and determination of the curriculum content over to employers."

This raises a provocative question that will come up repeatedly throughout this book. While it's easy to fall into being expedient as a co-op/internship coordinator, where does our loyalty ultimately lie? Is it to the employers who hire our students? Is it to our institutions, insisting on 100% placement as efficiently as possible, regarding our workloads? Or is it to the students in the form of maximizing their learning as well as their employability? Deciding that one constituency trumps another is fair enough. But if student learning is paramount, then we could do well to think about devising ways to leverage the transformative experiences that our students obviously have.

Additional Readings

Those who want to delve deeper into learning theory will want to consider other sources as well. **John Dewey** was an American philosopher and educational theorist from the first half of the 20th century, and his work on the relationship between education and experience is a theoretical foundation for much of the more recent theories that we've covered already. **Jerome Bruner** is an American psychologist whose work on cognitive learning theory is an important touchstone in our field. His ideas on how categorization is integrally connected to perception, decision-making, and learning are often cited, but I am particularly fond of his work on the importance of narrative thinking. The idea here is that we make our lives and careers into stories to aid our understanding of the world. This was an influence for me when I wrote *Exceeding Expectations*, a book of 70-80 short stories about young professionals.

Stephen Brookfield, who is excerpted in my chapter on "Making Mistakes," is another good researcher to study. Brookfield has done a great deal on critical theory, adult learning, and reflection. Here the idea is to get individuals to see themselves as social creatures and then to encourage them to see how their attitudes, behaviors, and thoughts are affected by the learning context. This self-reflection should change one's perceptions and behaviors over time.

Many of these ideas have forced me to assess and reassess my ways of working with students. Do my processes resonate with what the theorists have to say? My sense is that they probably do, even more than I know. When speaking to Nancy Johnston about a "new" theory that I created about the different stages a student goes through during a six-month work term (more on that later in the book), she was quick to point out that it sounded very much like a concept posited by Jean Lave and Etienne Wenger in their work on situated learning.

Yet whether an educator taps into these theories more implicitly or explicitly, the most intriguing payoff of ramping up on learning theory is that it actually reinforces your own identity as an educator, reminding you that you really have to place that perspective first and foremost in how you run a program. In the face of large workloads and pressures from all constituencies regarding placement numbers, we need all the reminders that we can get that we are not merely placement managers. And if you really are interested in striving for greatness, as this chapter indicates, I don't see how you can ignore the theoretical underpinnings of our profession forever.

In addition to boning up on the aforementioned theories and theorists, note that The Journal of Cooperative Education and Internships has quite a repository of articles and is available online at http://www.ceiainc.org/journal/ and has its archives available electronically for paying CEIA members. Although some articles inevitably will be more substantial or meaningful for you than others, this is a great way to keep tabs on what your counterparts are coming up with in terms of practices and assessment.

My NU colleague Bob Tillman recommends the following co-op articles in particular:

- "Savages In The Fountain: The Co-operative Educator and the University Community" by Ivan Blake. *Journal of Cooperative Education*, Volume XXVIII, Number 1, pp. 6-16. Volume XIX, Number 2, pp. 1-13.

- "Student Outcomes: What Do We Know and How Do We Know It?" by Joyce Fletcher. *Journal of Cooperative Education*, Volume XXVI, Number 1, pp. 26-38.

- "John Dewey and the Future of Cooperative Education" by John Saltmarsh. *Journal of Cooperative Education*, Volume XXVIII, Number 1, pp. 6-16.

- "The Spaces Between: Toward A New Paradigm For Cooperative Education" by Kathleen L. Finn. *Journal of Cooperative Education*, Volume XXXII, Number 2, pp. 36-45.

There's another one that I would recommend:

- "Career Exploration Via Cooperative Education and Lifespan Occupational Choice." By Patricia L. Linn, Jane Ferguson, and Katie Egart. 2004. *Journal of Vocational Behavior*, 65(3), pp. 430-447.

These are just a few of many great articles out there. I also enjoy keeping up with work by **Geraldine Van Gyn** and others out of the University of Victoria in British Columbia, and there have been many great pieces by various people at the University of Waterloo and the University of Cincinnati among other programs.

COUNSELING THEORY

In addition to understanding how students learn, it's very useful to have an understanding of what theories can inform us best on how to counsel our students. For the many educators who come more from a counseling background—I have many colleagues who have degrees in counseling or college student development—you probably can skip over this section. Others may want to linger here or delve further into these areas on their own time.

Let's go over some of the more relevant theories for this book's audience:

1. *John Holland's Typology*

Psychologist **John Holland**'s theory states that individuals are drawn to specific careers because of their personality types along with other factors. Holland basically is saying that we all compare our perceptions of ourselves to perceptions of a range of fields, and this inevitably has a huge impact on our choices of careers. When a student tells you that a certain field is "just not me"—sometimes based on a limited and/or inaccurate perception of what that career path actually is—you might think of that as Holland's typology in action.

Holland identified six different personal style themes with six corresponding occupational environments, which are shown in the table on the next page. Holland's theory has had an enormous impact on our field. In Chapter 7, I will allude to the Strong-Campbell Interest Inventory, which has morphed into two separate tests over the years: the Strong Interest Inventory and the Campbell Interest and Skill Survey (CISS). The Strong Interest Inventory features the Holland's six categories, while the Campbell test has seven analogous themes: influencing, organizing, helping, creating, analyzing, producing, and adventuring.

Theme	Personal Style	Occupational Environment
Realistic	More concrete than abstract; mechanical; may not have social skills	Skill-oriented trades such as mechanics, electricians; more materialistic; less flexible
Investigative	Highly task-oriented; likes math and science; independent; analytical; possibly introverted	Scientific, such as chemist or technician; software developer; research
Artistic	Enjoys self-expression though arts; imaginative, introspective, independent	Creative, including author, painter, musician, editor, critic
Social	More people-oriented; good communicator; interested in service and education	Educational, including teacher, speech pathologist; social welfare, counseling
Enterprising	Likes leadership roles; ambitious, dominating; strong verbally	Managerial (sales manager, personnel director); Sales and marketing
Conventional	Somewhat conservative; in control; fairly social; likes structured tasks; practical	Office worker such as accountant, data analyst, bookkeeper; credit manager

When taking the tests, individuals are asked to agree or disagree to different extents with dozens of statements. The test takes about 30 minutes. When the tests are scored, the results are compared to those of satisfied workers in a few hundred different fields. The test taker gets to see what themes are strongest and weakest for them as well as how their interests correlate with professionals in dozens of occupations.

I took the old Campbell-Strong test back when I was in grad school in 1986. Luckily, I hung on to my test, and I often share it with my undeclared business students. They are fascinated and for good reason. When you look through my results, here were the top matches: college professor, author, minister, clinical psychologist, speech pathologist. I always point out that co-op coordinator was not a possible outcome on the test, but, wow, that cluster of matches is a pretty good forecast of my future. You can't take these tests too literally, of course. I never would've become a minister, for example, but a minister spends a great deal of time counseling people through challenging times and assisting with spiritual growth. What does a speech pathologist do? Basically, they work as educators in a one-on-one setting—much as we often do when counseling students.

A great story turned up in our alumni magazine a few years ago along these lines. An alum wrote in a letter about taking this test at Northeastern. The top match for the then-student? Funeral Director! The letter writer reported that he was mortified, appropriately enough… but the professional reminded him that the test should not be taken as the last word. He then told the student that he did not have to be come a funeral director… but had he ever considered becoming a clergyman? That's exactly what happened. But the last laugh came several years later. The alum was writing the letter about 15 years later, shortly after he took on a new position: head of pastoral grief counseling for his parish!

Obviously, I am a believer in this form of career testing. I wouldn't say that every educator needs to become certified in administering it, but someone at your institution should be.

2. *Myers-Briggs Type Theory*

I've already made some allusions to Myers-Briggs when discussing how personality factors into how an educator opts to run a program, so let's delve a little deeper into this area here. Along with Holland's theory, Myers-Briggs is the most familiar career development theory in our field. This theory draws heavily from the work of Swiss psychologist **Carl Jung**, a contemporary of Sigmund Freud who published *Psychological Types* back in 1921.

Katharine Cook Briggs and her daughter, **Isabel Briggs Myers**, began developing the test during World War II. The initial goal was to help women get integrated into the workforce effectively. Their efforts ultimately led to the creation of the first Myers-Briggs Type Inventory (MBTI) in 1962.

Through a questionnaire, the test yields results regarding four preferences—sometimes called dichotomies—for each individual. It's important to understand that no type is "good" or "bad." The hope is that the test results will give the student and educator a better sense of the person's cumulative type, which may generate some ideas about possible careers.

- Introversion (I) versus Extroversion (E)

This pair requires little explanation. One note, though: For individuals who are on the borderline between the two preferences—which happens pretty often with the MBTI—a deciding question might be "What do you like to do when your energy is low?" If the answer is something along the lines of staying home to read a book, then that might convince you that the person is more of an introvert when stressed. If the individual opts for going out with friends, then that might tip the scale to the extrovert side.

- Sensing (S) versus Intuition (N)

This pair is harder to understand. Basically, a person who prefers sensing is more grounded in the physical world and trusts what is concretely detectable by the five senses. Someone who leans more toward intuiting prefers what is more abstract and theoretical, loving flashes of insight and future possibilities more than the here and now.

My colleague Rose Dimarco is an MBTI expert. In explaining this pair, she described two individuals looking at an elaborately arranged bowl of fruit. Asked to explain what she sees, the sensing person may well name every type of fruit in the bowl and even comment on how ripe the bananas are. The intuiting individual might just shrug and say "It's a bowl of fruit" and leave it at that. That person doesn't want to bother too much with the physical details.

- Thinking (T) versus Feeling (F)

This is another fairly obvious one. Does the individual make decisions more with the head or with the gut? What does he value more, competence or harmony? A thinker is more interested in competence, getting the best results trumps the emotional impact. A feeler favors harmony.

Another Rose Dimarco illustration: Rose describes two female friends who are getting ready to go out for the evening. Friend #1 comes out of her bedroom wearing shoes that don't remotely go with the outfit she is wearing. If Friend #2 is a thinker, she may say, "Oh my God! You're not wearing those shoes, are you? They look awful with that outfit! Go find something that works!" If Friend #2 is a feeler, she may say, "Wow, I really love that blouse, and the necklace complements it beautifully. But you know what? I think that those black shoes that you have would really be the perfect touch to go with everything else..." Note that the outcome can be the same, but the style of getting there can be quite different for a thinker versus a feeler.

- Judging (J) versus Perceiving (P)

This one is less intuitive as well. Basically, a Judging person tends to love structure, details, and orders. Js are people who love to maintain calendars and create lists, crossing off items as they go. Perceiving individuals are big-picture people who favor unstructured situations and who may resent details, order, and process.

When you combine the four pairs of letters, you end up with 16 discrete personality types. That's where the real pay off lies—especially when the person's type is different from your own. A few years ago, I worked with a student who annoyed me because he seemed so blasé about his job search. When I got his MBTI results, I learned that his type was one in which the individual often seems to not care but actually cares very deeply! That definitely changed my attitude toward working with him.

The 16 types can be useful in helping students figure out plausible career matches. Let's say that I was working with an ISFJ, the opposite of my own MBTI type. The test results would tell me that this person is quite interested in working with other people and good at reading them. This individual also should be quite good at creating structure and organization, yet they have a creative side as well. Broadly, some typical careers include interior decorator, designer, nurse, child care, counseling, bookkeeping, and religious activities. But given that my students are all in business, I might try to think of analogous careers in a business context: training, event management, auditing, business analyst, human resource generalist.

Researchers don't all agree on the validity of the MBTI, though most studies are fairly positive. Like the Strong Interest Inventory, you don't necessarily need to obtain a rather expensive MBTI certification. But someone in your university really should have that, especially in this era of increasingly undecided college students.

3. Super's Theories

Donald Super is another big name in counseling theory, and the range of his contributions is fairly sophisticated. He is the first and foremost individual mentioned when counseling textbooks consider the various developmental theories of understanding careers. In other words, there is the sense that some theories focus too much on initial career choice as opposed to how one's life stage can result in changing attitudes toward careers over the course of a lifetime.

The key element of Super's theory is self-concept theory. Super and his associates performed over 50 years of research on this theory. Ultimately, they found that an individual's vocational self-concept results from physical/mental growth, workplace observations, identifying (or failing to identify) with working adults, and other environmental experiences. All of this leads to a sense of what makes an individual see himself as similar to and/or different from others. This self-concept means that a career choice is a means of self-expression.

From this perspective, our role would be to help students to know themselves. Using Super's developmental stages, we would want to consider the age of our students. Those of us with much older students should not be surprised if the self-concept has reached a very different stage that will have implications on career choices. Likewise, we would want to reassure students in the 18-23 age range that it is normal to go through a phase of transitioning from tentative career choices toward more specific ones—something that Super called specification.

Another valuable contribution of Super's is the concept of career maturity. Through a study of ninth-grade boys in New York, Super found that individuals who had a higher degree of this trait—including owning responsibility, planning, and relatively high awareness of the specifics of a preferred career field—were much more likely to be successful as young adults. He found that career maturity was a function of intelligence much more than age.

What is the significance for higher education? Many of my colleagues like to say that past behavior is the best predictor of future behavior. I do take note of students who fail to own responsibility—owning responsibility is one of my "seven keys to professional success" described in my *Exceeding Expectations* book—and who appear to be poor at planning their job search. Super's research seems to prove the point that a student who struggles to demonstrate these qualities while working with an educator may be lacking in career maturity. That would make such a student a higher risk in a workplace, and it would call for educational efforts that will help a student become proficient at planning and taking responsibility for their actions.

4. *Other Counseling Theories*

There are whole textbooks and courses on counseling theory, and I won't attempt to cover the myriad theories. My goal here is to hit some highlights and possibly pique your interest in further study. Suffice to say that there are many other perspectives out there:

- social learning and cognitive theories

- person-in-environment perspective

- other trait and developmental theories

Counseling theories are the basis for career counseling models, including:

- Cognitive Information Processing (CIP) Model

- PEF Analysis

- Trait-and-Factor and Person-Environment-Fit

- Learning Theory of Career Counseling (LTCC)

- Developmental Model

A professional who comes to this field with no background in counseling should consider taking a counseling course or two and studying these concepts more closely.

EMBEDDING EDUCATION INTO PROCESSES

But even for those disinclined to become true scholars of learning theory, there are many simpler ways to be a true educator instead of nothing more than a placement manager. As Nancy Johnston's quotes from the last chapter as well as this chapter illustrate, it's critical to seek ways to build learning opportunities into as many aspects of the student experience as possible. Or, to flip it around, if a process doesn't yield educational dividends, why do it at all? Or why not modify it, at the very least?

There are many trivial but compelling examples. Let's say that a student sends you a mundane e-mail, telling you that the housing department needs proof that the student is doing a co-op far away so she can get her housing deposit refunded. And let's say that e-mail is written as follows:

---

hey scott,

could u let housing know that i will be in nyc for co-op so i can get my $ back?

thx

Although such an e-mail would irritate me—I hate "IM slang"—I would try to conceal my irritation and view this e-mail as an educational opportunity to remind my student that every e-mail sent to me is an opportunity to practice her business correspondence. And my e-mails to her would model what an appropriate e-mail should look like. I have responded in a similar way to other common e-mail errors, such as messages with subjects that simply read "Important" or that say "Mr. Weighart I have a few questions to ask you."

Whether students are filling out forms, arriving late to appointments, doing a great or lousy job in communicating proactively with you, or conducting themselves in exemplary or reprehensible fashion in a preparation course, all of these situations are teaching opportunities for you that can help your students make progress toward being great professionals—if handled correctly.

Although even small elements of interaction are potential grist for the educational mill, let's also consider the bigger picture. Nancy Johnston has done some great research on cooperative education, but not everyone has her qualifications to do serious qualitative and quantitative research. So I asked her what a less experienced or qualified person could do to assess how they were doing as educators. Her answer was compelling:

"The first thing professionals can do for themselves, once they get the bus rolling [in terms of mastering the operational elements of the job], is to say, 'What do I think I want the students to learn from this?' It might be a set of technical skills in the particular discipline. It might be some soft skills, and it might be more generic things like understanding themselves as a learner or being articulate about what they know.

"Then say, 'How do I know if this has happened?' There are multiple places, multiple curricular components where you can introduce any question that you want. I think it is real basic: You do not need a Ph. D. in education; I don't think you need to be reading about transformative learning. I think you need to say, 'My job is this: develop jobs, develop students, and let them run into each other, place them. What do I hope happens on that placement?' You should write down and really ask yourself as the educator 'what do I hope happens?' Then say 'do I have a role in that?' If you don't, then you are purely a placement officer. But if you think you have a role in that, then the next question is 'So what do I do in that role to help make any one of these things happen a little more than they would by chance.'"

Great professionals get away from doing things because "rules are rules" or purely for bureaucratic reasons. Instead they are always looking for ways to milk any interaction for additional opportunities to educate.

INTEGRATION AND REFLECTION

In my opinion, integration is one of the most loaded words in cooperative education. By this, I mean that it is sometimes used in extremely different ways. There are professionals who believe that the integration of theory and practice happens purely in the mind of the learner, and they only use that term to describe those cognitive processes. There are others who refer to integration as the activities that professionals may undertake to facilitate connections between theory and practice, between the classroom and the organizational world.

What gets especially worrisome for me is when administrators start talking about creating a model that will provide "seamless integration" between the classroom and work experiences. That sounds attractive, but it's not plausible. Real-world experiences vary dramatically, as do learners. The path of learning is not always so easy to predict, either. I came into the field expecting that students would learn concepts in the classroom and then go apply them in the organizational world. That obviously does happen, but most of my students say it's even more common to get exposed to something on co-op and then come back to classroom to learn the theory behind it.

In the reflection seminar I conducted the day before writing these words, one student complained that his experience was a great disappointment because he had not really learned key accounting concepts before he did his job, which required strong knowledge of that field. Yet another student felt her co-op was a great success for just the same reason: She began the job knowing nothing about finance, learned a ton, and is now excited to take classes that will reinforce and build on what she learned over her work term.

The other problem with "seamless integration" and with assessing learning in general is that a learner's perspective can change over time. An experience that is perceived as valueless at one point in time may be seen differently after additional experiences alter one's perspective. My favorite along these lines was a student who complained bitterly about his first job in a small-group reflection seminar. "I was basically the marketing bitch," he said, going on to describe the numerous clerical duties that comprised his job. I asked his peers to respond to his statements. One more experienced student spoke up. "My first job was like that, too, and I really hated it," she said. "But in this last job, I had someone who basically did those tasks for me. And you can bet that I treated her a lot differently than I was treated when I was in her shoes." Others weighed in saying some jobs were not enjoyable but that you had to pay your dues to move up—especially in a competitive field.

The complaining student seemed unconvinced. Months later, though, he shocked me. He came in and said that he was going back to that same employer! They had told him that they thought he had demonstrated the ability to handle more challenging responsibilities, and a first-time co-op would be hired to take over his administrative duties. I had to give him credit for hanging in there and coming around to viewing his first experience as a means to a greater end.

In any event, great professionals do need to put energy into making sure that they do what they can to help learners make those connections between theory and practice. One of our law school professors, Brook Baker, knows a great deal about learning theory. He likes to talk about "complementarity" rather than integration. Given how messy and unpredictable experiential learning can be, he thinks we should think in terms of how these experiences can complement classroom activities, and vice-versa. Strong professionals collaborate with academic faculty and administrators to find out what students are learning, where they are learning it, and whether the institution needs to make changes to maximize or improve learning.

Understandably, academic faculty members are not going to want to change their curriculum every time there is a slight blip in the marketplace. Today's favorite software application will be ancient history before our students' careers are over, so we can't expect professors to teach to "flavor of the month" trends in the organizational world. But we can establish dialogues between students, employers, academic faculty, and ourselves to ask many key questions:

- Are students entering the workplace knowing what employers hope and expect that they would know?

- Do our course offerings continue to be relevant in the eyes of our seniors, recent or not so recent alums, and employers?

- What can we reasonably expect employers to provide in the way of training and preparation for a professional workplace, and what should really be the school's responsibility?

- To paraphrase Nancy Johnston, what do all constituencies hope is happening in the way of student learning, and is that actually happening?

Armed with this information, the next challenge would be what to do if there are issues raised by these questions. The easiest thing to do is to rationalize any dissatisfaction that exists. But the path toward greatness might require making some difficult changes in the name of improving educational experiences.

There is much more to say about reflection, and I will say more about it in Chapter 11, which covers the topic. For now, let's just say that there is a wide variety of reflection methods that professionals may choose. But you need to do some sort of reflection at some point in time if you want to say that you're doing all you can to maximize student learning.

BALANCE NEEDS OF CONSTITUENCIES

When I asked the experts about differentiating great professionals from the ordinary ones, another theme that arose was the importance of balancing the needs of the various constituencies that we serve. Perhaps Jacki Diani puts it best when she talks about attending to all elements of the job—not just those that energize you.

The typical professional in our field loves to nurture students. It can become all too easy to spend all of your time in the office, expounding endlessly with a student on a one-on-one basis. You also will receive considerable positive reinforcement from students if you are always available and willing to give them all of your time.

Unless you are in an institution like the University of Waterloo—which has some professionals focusing almost exclusively on student preparation while others put most of their emphasis on employers—you will have to balance your time and energy very carefully. The best professionals recognize that there are times of the year—or maybe even times of each week—when you really need to block off time to contact or visit employers or to catch up on administrative responsibilities. Inevitably, this also means that you will have to manage the expectations of students who may be expecting something close to an instant response in their world of e-mail, cell phones, and BlackBerry devices.

Again, though, the key is to educate students as to why you may not be available constantly in person or via e-mail. I want my students to know that I sometimes need to get out on the road to visit employers or to go to conferences or to write books. Early on during the co-op preparation class, I try to make them aware of my multiple responsibilities. I want them to think of me as their manager, and they should know that every manager that they have throughout their careers will be someone who has many other responsibilities in addition to shepherding them through the role in the organization. I want them to aspire to be more independent, and I want them to see that doing so will benefit them as a professional. That gives an educational slant to the discussion while enabling me to manage their expectations more effectively.

Another constituency that you can't ignore is your institution itself. When you face decisions about how to handle various relationships, sometimes it's helpful to step back and ask yourself which constituency's interests really matter the most. Is it the student or the employers or the institution? A case can be made for any of the three, but developing clarity in your own mind on that question will make it much easier to wrestle with the dilemmas that professionals in our field may face. We'll delve further into that when we get into the chapter on handling "moments of truth."

FORGE STRONG RELATIONSHIPS WITH STUDENTS AND EMPLOYERS

Almost everyone I spoke to talked up how great professionals focus on forging great relationships with students and employers. While students are an obvious focal point for most professionals, Ronnie Porter and Kirk Patterson were quick to remind me that if you don't have good employers with good opportunities, you don't have much of anything. You can have terrific counseling skills and great rapport with students, but if you don't have jobs for them and can't help them do anything about that, you can't be a great educator.

All of that said, what goes into forging these strong relationships? Several subthemes arose in my conversations.

PROVIDING EXCELLENT CUSTOMER SERVICE

As previously discussed, this is actually a controversial topic for those of us in higher education. I have spoken to professionals in our field who get very agitated when you throw around a term such as "customer service." I understand this completely. At first superficial glance, the term seems to pull us away from an educational model and more toward a service-provider mentality. Great customer service is something that we look for from a rental car agency or a waiter, right?

I don't think it's that simple. Yes, education needs to be at the forefront of all that we do. But can you be an excellent educator and still be cognizant of the importance of providing outstanding service to your constituencies so that they perceive value as your internal or external customers? I certainly hope so. I just don't believe that "education" and "customer service" are mutually exclusive elements to have in a program.

With students, providing great customer service or being "student-centered" does not mean giving students whatever they want. It doesn't mean that you have to shrug off obnoxious behavior because "the customer is always right." Quite often, I have students who really want me to say that a certain decision or behavior is okay—maybe reneging on a job offer acceptance or quitting a job because they ran into a problem—and I just can't tell them what they so desperately want to hear. Good customer service doesn't mean sweeping conflicts under the rug, and it doesn't mean that your role is to always advocate for students regardless of what they have done.

That said, professionals do need to provide great customer service in many ways. Here are just a few examples:

- Being careful to ask clarifying questions and avoid jumping to conclusions

- Responding to phone calls and e-mails in a timely manner

- Keeping an educational tone even when frustrated or angry with a student's behavior

- Being stubborn on a student's behalf—not letting a student settle for a mediocre learning experience when a better one is possible, although it is likely to require more work on the professional's part

- Being a sympathetic active listener, allowing students to vent or express feelings—even when you know their concerns aren't that rational

A few of my interviewees talked about treating students as "pre-colleagues" or something similar. I find that concept very helpful. If I always treat an individual student as someone that I ultimately would like to see become a co-op employer, that helps me treat them in a supportive, relationship-building manner. After 13 years in this job, I also actually have seen a former student turn into a manager of co-op students, again and again.

EMPLOYERS AS CUSTOMERS

With employers, there have been times when I have been very dismayed at seeing how some co-op/internship professionals act during meetings that ostensibly are occurring in the hope of turning an organization into an educational partner. I have seen educators basically lay out all the hoops that the employer will need to jump through for the privilege of hiring students from our program. I do think that you need to have a customer-service mentality with employers. Why should they want to hire your students? There are plenty of possible reasons. But as with any potential customer, you'll need to ask questions about what their needs are and figure out if what you can offer them is a match for those needs. Maybe the employer has a short-term need to get a project done or to get coverage for a given job. Perhaps they are just trying to keep their headcount and associated benefit costs down. Or they could be using an internship or co-op program as a way to test out future graduates for full-time offers. Regardless, you need to find out what they want and address that directly. Yes, ultimately you want to get employers to think of themselves as educational partners, and many experts I spoke to used that exact phrase. But first you have to give them compelling reasons as to how students will meet a need that they have.

As with students, it's best to adopt a long-term mentality with employers. Yes, you may have the immediate need to get, say, 90 students employed by September. Most importantly, though, you want to do whatever you can to make sure that students are going to be good fits for those jobs and that they are going to be successful. Doing whatever you can during the preparation process to help students interview well and to prevent problems from arising once employed has a huge payback, and failing to do so can cripple your program. If you look at employers as customers, you have to think about why they're going to want to keep coming back to you for student hires in the future. You want to ensure that you and your students are as "low maintenance" as possible, and you need to be very responsive if there are concerns or issues that arise.

I like to tell employers to think of me as their "unpaid consultant" (however oxymoronic that may sound). I want employers to feel like that they can call or e-mail me anytime to see if I can help them with any questions. What are graduates from our nursing program making? Do I know of anyone who would like a part-time job? Do I have suggestions as to how to hire

Northeastern alums? Can I talk to a son or daughter who is thinking of coming to Northeastern? None of those questions are within the realm of my job description, but I'm going to help out with any of those issues and many more if at all possible. As far as I'm concerned, employers who perceive me as a solution provider are more likely to turn to me for any of their needs. Once you have that kind of relationship, many good jobs end up falling in your lap with little effort

SELLING SKILLS AND CROSS-SELLING

Several of my interviewees reminded me that there are several great counselors who are unable or unwilling to go out and pitch the program to employers. Unless you're in a program in which that responsibility is in someone else's hands, you definitely need to get comfortable pitching the program. Details on how to do so will come later in the book.

Additionally, a great professional doesn't only attempt to develop jobs for his or her own program. Yes, you may only work with students in journalism, English, and communications, but you always want to ask prospective employers about other needs that they may have. Some call this cross-selling. Sometimes I'll go out looking to develop jobs in MIS and Supply Chain Management, but I'll come back with jobs in Finance, Marketing, and even areas like Chemical Engineering and Biology if it's a biotech or pharmaceutical company. Again, the goal is to go beyond your job description and think of the greater good of your institution and all of its students.

CONFRONT DIFFICULT SITUATIONS

Another theme that came up in the interviews was that great professionals are able and willing to confront challenging situations directly and to transform problems into learning opportunities.

One obstacle to overcome is that it's human nature for most of us to try to avoid conflict. Instead of dealing with problems directly, people have a tendency to opt for other reactions:

- Engaging in passive-aggressive behavior, which may include acting resentful, brooding, chronic tardiness, and claiming to forget what one was told

- Shrugging off the situation, figuring it's not worth the trouble

- Pretending that bad behavior never happened

Instead, great professionals in our field need to follow much more positive steps:

- Responding to the problem behavior as soon as possible

- Asking clarifying questions to make sure that the situation is fully understood

- Maintaining an educational tone while addressing the problem behavior

- Treating students as future colleagues as opposed to talking down to them

- Making sure the individual understands all consequences of the behavior

- Being clear on what needs to happen for the relationship to move forward (assuming that that's possible)

- Providing closure to the meeting by summarizing what next steps need to be taken

I like to conclude such meetings by saying something like this to a student: "As far as I'm concerned, this issue is now resolved. If this problem doesn't arise again in the future, I'm never going to raise it again for as long as I work with you. However, if it happens again, then the issue has officially become a disturbing trend, and we would have to revisit it. But otherwise we now have a clean slate."

Chapter 12 will go into much more depth on how to handle specific difficult situations.

DISPLAY PASSION AND COMMITMENT

Another recurring theme from my interviewees was that great professionals need to display many traits: passion, commitment, dedication, and effort are all words that came up. Whatever you want to call it, many experts acknowledged that one differentiator between great and average professionals is that the great ones don't view their role as just a job or a stepping stone to another position. Great professionals have a strong desire to be the best that they can be. Can this be taught? Probably not, but if you do have that passion, there are many ways you can plug that energy into different activities that will allow you to demonstrate your passion to all of your constituencies.

The last chapter covered various ways in which professional development can be pursued, so I won't enumerate them again here. Still, I will linger briefly on how those activities do have an important connection to pursuing greatness.

ENHANCE KNOWLEDGE OF YOUR FIELD

Ramping up your knowledge of the majors that you manage is an important way to build credibility with students and employers as well as enhancing your ability to be great at it. I have seen some professionals come in knowing nothing about, for example, athletic training and proceed to devour as much information as possible to develop mastery of it. You could argue that such an individual will never know as much as a professional who actually had an athletic training degree and/or job experience, but it's certainly possible to become an excellent professional without that background. Taking courses—or at least auditing them—and reading up on your field can help.

Conversely, I also have known professionals who never really bothered to develop expertise on the academic areas that they were handling. This is totally understandable, as it may be daunting for someone with a liberal arts undergrad degree and a master's in counseling to develop a deep understanding of, say, chemical engineering, computer science, or finance. Still, it has to be said that a person who is unwilling and/or unable to ramp up in their field is probably going to have a difficult time being perceived as anything more than competent.

ADDRESS YOUR WEAKNESSES

Your knowledge of the relevant academic disciplines is just one area. If you are a technophobe, you will need to address that in order to utilize the best tools to run your program.

If you shun technology, you're going to have a hard time freeing yourself up enough to get beyond the basics of getting students into jobs. Likewise, someone who is weak on the counseling side may consider getting certified in Myers-Briggs or the Strong Interest Inventory (especially if your job entails working with students who are undecided or undeclared), as these tools can be helpful in guiding students through the more fundamentals parts of the career counseling process. I've also known people who went to selling skills workshops—we hired a consultant here at one time to help all of our business coordinators with that skill when we really needed to focus on job development—and that's another area that may not come naturally to everyone in our field.

Again, you don't have to do all of these things. But if you're interested in being really great in this profession, you need some self-awareness about your developmental needs and to take action to address your weaknesses.

ASSESS AND REFINE PROCESSES

Another differentiator that my interviewees often cited was that great professionals need to assess their programs continually and be open to refining their style and processes. As Nancy Johnston mentioned earlier in the chapter and the book, you need to question everything. Why do we do everything that we do? What are we hoping that students learn through their experiences, and how we can be sure that it's really happening?

This topic is simultaneously simple and profound. It's an easy matter to ask some basic questions about what is actually happening out in work assignments, but what do we do with the responses? Let's say that a student reports that he didn't learn much of anything on a work assignment. If we are being really honest with ourselves, there are several possibilities here:

- The student believes that "learning" purely refer to technical skills that may be valuable toward a future in a specific field, such as physical therapy, civil engineering, etc.

- The student is overlooking all that might have been learned in the way of dealing with co-workers, adapting to an organizational culture, learning to work with a specific manager's idiosyncratic tendencies, and so forth

- The student learned something but does not know to articulate what was learned

- The student really learned nothing of value at all during the experience; it was a complete waste of time

Whether in a group meeting or a one-on-one session, it can be difficult to know what's really going on in such a situation. So you need to avoid getting defensive and try to probe with questions that will show what the student is really saying… without bashing him if it turns out that there legitimately was not much valuable experience gained from the internship or co-op job.

Another tricky factor in assessment is the longitudinal element. Consider the earlier example that I gave about the student who was disgruntled about his marketing job. His subjective assessment of the experience right after he returned to campus was that he had a poor learning experience. With a little perspective from his peers and some time to see how that experience set him up for bigger and better things on subsequent jobs, he ultimately perceived that first job as having much more value than he believed it to have at the time. He eventually became a co-op employer with a strong belief in the value of this form of education.

There is also the issue that one person's great learning experience is another's nightmare experience. I remember having two students sit next to each other in a reflection seminar. They had the same job with the same manager for the same six months. As a learning experience, one rated the job as a 6/10. The other gave it a 10/10! Perhaps unsurprisingly, their reasons were quite similar. The company had just been acquired, and many full-time employees were unhappy and anxious about layoffs. The student who rated the job lower found the negativity to be contagious, while the student who loved the job was able to keep himself emotionally detached from that and found it fascinating to be in the thick of such a major organizational transition.

The moral of these stories is that there are several caveats to bear in mind when assessing your program:

- Over time, you might need to repeatedly ask students questions about what they've learned and whether or not a given experience had value. Asking similar questions during the preparation, activity, and reflection phases may yield varying results and give you some sense of what sort of learning is happening as well as when it is occurring.

- You need to understand why students liked or disliked their experience to understand whether it's a bad job or a bad fit.

- You need to help your students understand everything that we're talking about when we talk about "learning," especially how it transcends the technical elements of a job.

- You might need to probe and coach to help students articulate just what their experience really meant as an educational experience.

- You want to do all this without trying to force students to say what they think you want to hear, so you're not congratulating yourself on "successes" that may or may not exist.

You also might want to consider periodic anonymous surveys of past and present students as well as roundtable discussions with students, alums, employers, and academic faculty to monitor whether or not you are really hitting your educational goals instead of just wanting to believe that you're doing so.

All of that said, here are some good questions to ask as part of assessing learning:

- To what degree did your students improve core skills, such as communication skills, interpersonal skills, computer skills, and ability to work in a team?

- What did students learn that is more directly connected to their field of study, whether human services, journalism, finance, mechanical engineering, etc.?

- What did students learn about themselves in the process: their tendencies as learners, their professional development needs, their strengths, their preferences in terms of industry/culture/managerial style/career direction, and so on?

- What are the outcomes of experiential learning from a variety of perspectives: educational, economic, social, psychological?

A whole book could be written on the topic of assessment itself. This is meant to be a fairly quick overview. If you have the expertise and resources to devise and carry out elaborate research to evaluate cooperative education learning outcomes, then that's a great thing to do. But, if not, this section may give you some guidelines as to some basic steps that all professionals can take. Whatever you do, the key is to be open to the idea that your program could be better than it is, and that not every practice that you intuitively love may have a real payoff in the form of learning. There's nothing wrong with research or assessment that proves that some approach had no impact whatsoever. That just gets you one step closer to a better program.

BUILD INTERNAL ALLIANCES

A last theme that arose in my conversations was the need to build alliances across your college or university. The idea here is that it only will do you so much good to be excellent in a vacuum; you need to make sure that others at your institution understand what you do and why it matters.

In some ways, the rising cost of education might be construed as a positive for professionals in our field. In the United States, experiential learning has gained considerable momentum over the last decade or so. As tuitions increase, more families want to know what the return on their educational investment will be. How will an education lead to a career? Internships and co-ops jobs are a great way for students to test out possible careers early and make transitions if necessary. They also generally lead to a better probability of better jobs and salaries after graduation—quite important given the size of student loans in many cases.

Regardless of this promising development for our field, institutions vary dramatically in the degree to which they believe that experiential learning adds value to the academic enterprise. Colleges and universities are almost always run by individuals who rose in the ranks of the academic faculty, and they almost invariably will see the classroom experience as the core of the institution. Your program might be viewed as a crucial part of the educational experience, or it could be perceived as a fairly trivial enterprise. Perhaps most commonly of all, others at your institution may misunderstand what you do as well as why and how you do it.

What do you do as a result of any of these perceptions? Your basic choices are to try to keep a low profile if you fear becoming a negative target or to try to build some internal alliances at your institution… or maybe both. Either way, the general consensus is that you really want to foster strong relationships with your academic counterparts. You want to make them aware of where your students are working, what they're learning, and what you're hearing from employers about how prepared the institution's students are for the workforce. Attending academic faculty meetings in your college or department can help keep you informed as well as making everyone aware of what's going on in your world.

Sharing metrics from your program may be helpful as well. Passing along the results of an employer survey or a breakdown of information such as placements by industry, organization, major, job level, and so forth may be helpful to your college as they ponder goals in both academics and development.

Another way to build alliances is to talk to academic faculty about having veteran students or employers come to classes in which their perspectives and experiences may add value to a course. I also always try to say yes when I'm asked to provide the names of students who are needed to get involved in orientations, peer mentoring, media interviews, award presentations, case competitions, and so on.

You never know when your institution might undergo a budget crunch, reorganization, change in leadership, or some sort of strategic facelift. When any of these things occurs, you want to make sure that you've done all you can to make sure that you have allies across the institution—people who know that what you're doing adds value to the school.

The last thing that you want to do is take your reputation on campus for granted. You might be doing a great job, and your students and employers may love you... but that may not help you get the resources you need to do the job to the best of your ability. There's no satisfaction with being the best-kept secret on campus, so work toward building strong connections with other departments. The more you are perceived as strategic, organized, and highly educational in focus, the more you will be inclined to get support for your mission.

The remainder of this chapter is devoted to hearing what various experts had to say in response to this question: "In your view, what differentiates an outstanding co-op or internship professional from one who is more average or mediocre?"

IN THEIR OWN WORDS

PROFESSIONAL PERSPECTIVE #1
"HAND ON THE PULSE"
Ronnie Porter, Northeastern University

I think it goes back to really understanding what the work is. The type of person that is highly successful needs to be a person who does have the interest in working with students but also understands and is interested in the employer development piece as well. I've seen people come into co-op coordinator positions because they are primarily interested in working with students, but they don't enjoy doing the employer development piece as much.

I think it comes back to be a problem at some point because as I said: If you don't have good opportunities for students to be in, then you don't have a good program. Getting out on the road, visiting companies, and developing relationships with employers is extremely important. It is also important to know how to manage your time and be able to prioritize and adjust your efforts when it's necessary. If there is a real problem in the economy at one point, you may have to spend more of your time doing one thing than the other.

You've got to be flexible and also continually have your hand on the pulse of your program to really understand its needs and to be able to adjust to changing needs. The ability to do the multitasking that's necessary is crucial to get the job done. Sometimes, I think that's not always the case. I see some people who have great ideas and they theoretically know what students should be doing on the job and whatnot, but I never see them leave their offices. I can't help but wonder how they could possibly have as good relationships with their employers if they do not visit them or they don't have any other ways of interacting with them at professional meetings, etc.

Some coordinators do most of their interactions at professional meetings because they happen to be in a particular field, and they participate in specific professional conferences in the field which most of their employers attend. I think that we need to be visible and we need to know what our students are doing. We need to have a sense of what an environment is like. I think that's the biggest difference between the Northeastern program and some other programs: the Northeastern co-op faculty member is involved in all of the aspects. Therefore they can really advise or guide students in very clear-cut ways because they have been to sites and they know first hand what they are like. They know what the environment is like, and they know what the supervisor is like. They can really help facilitate positive experiences for the students as opposed to a monster.com approach where resumes and job descriptions are loaded on a database and there is no opportunity for personal interaction and education.

The other piece is that we really play an integral role in helping the students integrate the experience. The reflection component of helping with that integration really prepares a student for the next experience whether that be a co-op experience or an after-graduation job search. I think that effective reflection has to include some kind of action plan. It has to be thinking about what happened in the past, and using the information as a springboard for creating actions in the future. That's where I think we play a very important role because students can get the feedback from their experiences and use that information to make good decisions and choices for the future.

PROFESSIONAL PERSPECTIVE #2
"NOT JUST A NUMBER"
Anita Todd, University of Cincinnati

Maybe this sounds fluffy, but I think you really have to love the job. I just found this job that I really love, and I think that shows when I work with my students and with my employers. I may be biased, but I believe I am good at my job. I think I am good because I believe in the power of cooperative education. I know that sounds kind of corny. But I was a co-op student so I saw the benefits as a student. I was a co-op employer, and I saw how valuable it was bringing these students in and what a difference co-op made when converting students to full-time employees. So as an educator, I bring those experiences. I have the understanding of what the student has gone through and what the employer has gone through.

It is really important that the students recognize that you care about them and want them to succeed, that they are not just a number. Unfortunately, I have met advisors that believe they know what is best for their students and do not take into consideration the students' interests or needs. In many cases we do know what is best for our students, but it is important that we recognize that the students are our customers and that they need to feel that they are being served. So I think the big difference is not how successful you are in placing students, but whether the students feel that you have their best interests at heart and that you truly care about their needs and experiences. Students can tell when you care.

There are also more basic things, like being knowledgeable about your field, knowledgeable of your employer base, understanding what skills and experiences your students have that match with what is out there and available. Also, not being afraid to tell your students that they may not meet the criteria for jobs that they are looking to pursue. In Cincinnati, we have some top-notch employers that have an absolute 3.0 requirement, a "nothing below, don't even think about it" type of philosophy. You need to realistically say to your student, "At your level, with your GPA and skills and experiences, these are jobs that are realistically within your view based on my previous experience with these employers." I do not discourage students from shooting for their top company, but I do not want them to limit their choices or have false expectations. They are encouraged to build skills and experiences and work their way up the ladder.

PROFESSIONAL PERSPECTIVE #3
"COMMITMENT AND DEDICATION"
Charlie Bognanni, Northeastern University

This might sound somewhat trivial and somewhat obvious, but I think so much of [being a great professional] has to do commitment and dedication to the program. I think this is true with so many jobs in life. You have to put in the effort; you have to put in the commitment. You have to be devoted to what you're doing, care deeply for the students and for the program, and to put in the time that it takes to help each of the students.

What I've seen as a difference are people who put the time in, are dedicated, devoted, and care deeply about the program versus people who view it as a job, frankly—people who view it just as a position, as a job, it's another stepping stone for something else.

That's number one—dedication and devotion and so forth. And I think the second part of it is the organization. I think you need to have your program organized. I think if you're not organized and you're all over the place and you're just not prepared how to work with your students and with your employers, you can lose control of your program very quickly.

I think at the beginning of each semester you want to sit down and take stock of what you have in terms of students and employers and approach it strategically, preparing accordingly and saying "okay, I need this many jobs, how am I going to do my job development, how am I going to work with my students?" I think if you just walk into each semester blindly and not really with planning, you're going to find halfway through the semester that you're not where you want to be.

And that doesn't mean to say that there aren't going to be some things that are going to happen along the way where you're going to have to modify your plan. Of course that happens. But I think as long as you have a plan you're going to be in much better shape. I think also that learning how to work with students and with employers is a big part of differentiating the average professional versus the very, very good one.

PROFESSIONAL PERSPECTIVE #4
"UNDERSTAND THE HISTORY OF THE PROFESSION"
Brenda LeMaster, University of Cincinnati

I think it is important for any professional in our field to understand the history of the profession, the challenges that have been faced and the disposition of those challenges. Because I come from a co-op perspective, I think it is important for me to know how co-op developed, how it moved out of engineering and into other academic programs, and to know what schools or geographical areas have programs that have significant aspects in common with my program. I should also be familiar with the major research and publications in our field. One could assert that such material is challenging to find but I think that a strong familiarity with the material in the Journal of Cooperative Education and Internships is a very good place to start.

However, the question of striving for greatness is not a simple one to answer because there is no clear profile of a professional in "our field." We have practitioners who span the job title spectrum from clerical to faculty. Over the years I have had many colleagues who focused on the management aspects of running a co-op program (how to encourage students to participate, how to improve relations with employers, how to improve relations with faculty—or the college—or the dean, and how to get respect for the important work we do). I have had as many colleagues who focused on learning and how to measure learning, and how to incorporate this assessment into curriculum and institutional planning. I have had many colleagues who fall between those two extremes. We have one-person and many-person offices and are housed in colleges, departments, career centers, service centers and stand-alone divisions. What unites all of us is the fact that we are educators, regardless of title. We serve students and we must be accountable to our institutions.

Becoming active in professional associations and presenting at conferences and meetings are important ways of growing as a professional, keeping abreast of issues of importance in the field and developing our own community of practice. More programming than I would like is "show and tell," often about aspects of program management or practice that are not new or don't add significantly to the field. However, there are usually one or two presentations that stand out by bringing new ways of thinking or new ways of practice to our attention. Those are the presentations that I look for when I attend a conference.

PROFESSIONAL PERSPECTIVE #5
"MEASURE THE EDUCATION SIDE"
Nancy Johnston, Simon Fraser University

We do parts of assessment well. We assess the mechanics reasonably well, and people who have very tight business processes, they know how many people are in their customer database and they know how many hits it takes for a student to get a job, how many co-postings you need to realize one placement. There are many things that good places measure well on the business process side. I just don't think we measure the education side nearly as well.

There are a lot of statements made about co-op that if you dig deeper there is not a lot that really backs them up. There is a sense that co-op does something, and it empowers students and improves their confidence and employability. There are a few studies you can cite here and there, but I'd love to see something—and I think it's going to have be qualitative research—that just says what people feel they have learned and what they haven't... and if possible, how they think they learned it. You can triangulate it with an employer's perspective. At the end of the day, there's always some subjectivity, but there's always subjectivity around learning. I do not know why when a professor marks something it's [supposed to be] objective. It isn't in most cases—the same level of subjectivity applies to co-op learning.

PROFESSIONAL PERSPECTIVE #6
"FORGE THE STRONGEST RELATIONSHIPS"
Kate McLaughlin, Northeastern University

The best co-op coordinators are the ones who take the time to forge the strongest relationships with their students, and that means finding ways to interact with the students as much as possible in the classroom, one on one, attending club events or, for performing arts students, concerts and plays, and visiting them while on co-op. It means really establishing that personal bond because so much of what determines their success or failure is their comfort level with asking questions and admitting their ignorance and using that as a starting point for learning.

And they're much more inclined to admit their fears and what they don't know with somebody they feel comfortable with, so that one-on-one bond makes a huge difference. The other things—relationships with employers, organization of the program—all of those things matter but not nearly as much.

PROFESSIONAL PERSPECTIVE #7
"A Passion for Co-op"
Mary Kane, Northeastern University

In my experience, two attributes or skills are evident in co-op coordinators that I would say are leaders in the field: passion for cooperative education and excellent communication skills—especially listening skills. Successful coordinators have the ability to transfer that passion to get to know their students, and to be able to challenge them to seek their personal and professional limits. Getting to know your students is a process that takes time. Coordinators can have various techniques and strategies to get to know students, but being a good listener is key. It is the demeanor you have with your students and how open you are when they come to meet with you. You have to be receptive to students when they're in your office because you just never know what's going on behind the face. Sometimes looking at them and being ready to listen, you gain a whole lot that's really going to help you with the relationship with them. Coordinators who are the leaders in developing and maintaining relationships with employers excel because they are good at listening to people. They stop and listen to what employers are saying and really get a sense of what they need and the issues that are important to that particular organization. The mentality of you're there in their house listening to what their needs are, that's what they remember and what strengthens the relationships.

Also, you know it sounds kind of corny, but I do think that some people have more of a passion for co-op. You certainly could do an okay job and have students have great experiences and have them come back, but I think having a passion for this kind of education really does show over the long term in the work people do with their students and employer programs.

PROFESSIONAL PERSPECTIVE #8
"Assessment of Program Effectiveness"
Brenda LeMaster, University of Cincinnati

This is an important question and one that will be answered differently depending on the goals of the individual program. The first step towards any assessment of program effectiveness must be the development of clearly defined program goals. Once these goals are defined it becomes a matter of determining how to measure progress towards accomplishment of these goals. For example: if a program goal is to have every student engage in a work-based learning experience before graduation, a good measure would be tracking the students in the program who have had such an experience. If a program expects students to accomplish specific types of learning outcomes while on those work-based learning experiences, that program will need to articulate those learning goals and then determine how to measure their accomplishment. One of the ways that current practice oriented research can be of help is to suggest ways that other programs have identified and measured their goals.

Now that we have focused on what it takes to strive for greatness, our next chapter will go after some truths that can gleaned from the opposite end of the spectrum: making mistakes.

REFLECTION QUESTIONS

1. What theories of learning and development have most informed your educational philosophy? What theory in this chapter are you most excited about researching further to learn how to integrate it into your educational approach?

2. Can you identify any processes and procedures that might be missed opportunities for embedding learning? Do you have a form or a step that you could modify to get students to reflect on their learning?

3. What do you and/or others at your institution do to facilitate the integration of theory and practice in a meaningful way? What more could you do to make sure that students are learning as much as possible from their combination of classroom and organizational experience?

4. This chapter notes that customer service is a controversial topic in higher education. Do you agree with the idea that a coordinator should portray himself as an "unpaid consultant" who should try to meet employer needs beyond placing students in a job?

5. What have you done in the last year or two to enhance your knowledge as a professional, whether it entails ramping up on an academic discipline, best practices, or on learning theory? How have you addressed your weaknesses as a professional?

6. The chapter mentions how great professionals are constantly assessing and refining their style and processes over time. What do you do to ensure that program assessment happens on a regular basis? What changes have you made in your approach over the last year?

CHAPTER 5

MAKING MISTAKES

"Mistakes... are the portals of discovery."
— *James Joyce*

Years ago, I had the privilege of seeing Stephen Brookfield, an educator who has written extensively on learning and teaching, make a presentation at a conference here in Boston. With his permission, I have added it to the appendix of this chapter. It's a very funny speech about "teaching as whitewater rafting" in which he candidly shares a major mistake that he had made as an educator. You'll be able to read the whole story at the end of this chapter, but the gist of it is that it's all too easy for educators to fall in love with their own preferred teaching methods, even in the face of evidence that their approach is dead wrong. I found Brookfield's speech quite amusing, but it also haunted me for a long while as an educator. Why do I do what I do as an educator? Had I talked myself into believing that my preferred way of running a program was best without having the slightest idea of whether it actually had a positive educational impact on my students? It suddenly seemed entirely possible.

In the same speech, Brookfield also emphasized that mistakes are excellent learning opportunities that should be celebrated. This may seem counterintuitive. It's human nature to cringe at our mistakes. The last thing that most professionals want to do is to draw attention to their shortcomings; we often prefer to sweep them under the rug and not think about them at all. But whether we're talking about co-op and internship professionals or the students that we all counsel, it's crucial to come to perceive mistakes as learning opportunities.

When I interviewed the many professionals quoted in this book, one of the most useful questions that I asked was a behavioral-based question: "Tell me about a specific time that you made a mistake as a professional—preferably one that was instructive to you and led to a realization about a way in which you needed to change to improve. Walk me through the specifics of the mistake as well as what you learned from it."

In addition to Brookfield's story, you'll see many of their verbatim responses to that question at the end of the chapter. As usual, I will summarize and elaborate on the themes of those intriguing replies shortly. First, though, let's consider why mistakes happen and the general categories of mistakes before we delve into those themes.

A BALANCING ACT

One of the greatest challenges for coordinators is the fact that there are several delicate balances in our roles. Working closely with students and employers—yet also accountable to our institution—it can be difficult to determine which responsibility is primary. What do you do when a decision may give a student what he or she wants but may have a negative impact on an employer? How do we balance the pressure of needing to ensure that students need to get jobs within a fairly short period of time versus the fact that we also want these experiences to be as educational as possible? Most programs are stronger at looking at metrics regarding placement and pay than they are at looking at more qualitative outcomes such as educational quality and the transferability of skills from classroom to practice and back to classroom. This creates tensions and dilemmas for professionals.

Likewise, there are balancing acts when it comes to working with students and employers. If your relationships are marked by frequent conflict, this can lead to frustration and withdrawal. But too little conflict is a problem as well. Sometimes you need to be able to have difficult conversations, and many people avoid those due to the fact that they can be unpleasant and risky. Finding the happy medium is the challenge.

Another related balancing act comes into play when counseling students. Given that many professionals just love to nurture students, that trait has the potential to translate into letting students get away with behaviors that are not really acceptable. These can be missed opportunities in professionalizing students. Yet I also have seen professionals who err on the other side of the spectrum. They are tough, demanding, and rigid. They pride themselves on having high standards, but this style also can alienate students and work against building lasting relationships.

AN OVERVIEW OF MISTAKES

Given that my background is in organizational behavior, I often reflect on a credo from the realm of Total Quality Management: Work toward doing the right thing, the right way, the first time. Sounds easy, right? Yet there is a lot of research that indicates that many people in organizations end up doing three other things:

- Doing the right thing the wrong way

- Doing the wrong thing the right way

- Doing the wrong thing the wrong way

What might be examples of these concepts in our field? Doing the right thing the wrong way is a problem of execution. A simple example would be for a professional to insist on critiquing a student's resume before it goes to an employer... but then missing several outright errors. A more complex example would be confronting a student who is consistently late to class... but doing so in an angry, emotional way that escalates the existing conflict as opposed to a more educational, solution-oriented approach.

Doing the wrong thing the right way is more troubling. The problem here is not execution; it's more one of strategy or process. An example might be the professional who does an outstanding job of writing students' resumes for them instead of teaching students how to do it themselves for the rest of their careers. Another example might be the person who does a phenomenal job of explaining all possible career paths in finance in one-on-one meetings with 50 different students. Yes, the educational outcome is fine, but the cost in terms of efficiency and effectiveness can't be ignored. To use a term from economics, you have to consider the "opportunity cost" of what else you could have been doing if you had not spent hours and hours doing something that would have been better handled with written material or in an orientation session or class.

Doing the wrong thing the wrong way is the biggest nightmare of all, as we end up with the potentiating interaction of a bad idea that is then executed poorly. One example might be to decide that you can save a ton of time by not critiquing resumes at all. Instead, you have first-time students work in pairs to critique each other's resumes and then have the resulting resumes go out to employers without any professional review. Given the highly limited experience of students, this is a bad idea that is very likely to be carried out poorly. Another example would be to force students to write reflection papers purely as a means to get credit for their work experience… but to then not bother reading the papers or reacting to them. The strategic error there is the focus on doing things because "rules are rules" as opposed to selling students as to how this is meant to contribute to their learning. The error in execution is reinforcing the "forced march" element of the assignment by not doing anything with the output.

With these ideas as a background, let's go over the themes that arose when I analyzed our experts' reflections on their mistakes.

LOSING SIGHT OF CO-OP AS EDUCATION

This is the flip side of one of the elements that we discussed in the last chapter. Although we all work in higher education, it can be surprisingly easy to get caught up in the day-to-day operational elements of our roles instead of keeping the bigger picture of learning in mind as we run our programs. Here are some symptoms of this theme:

GETTING CAUGHT UP IN URGENCY OF PLACEMENTS

Depending on the institution, there can be a great degree of pressure on professionals to ensure that all students actually obtain jobs. Although you'll feel this pressure from students more than anyone else, you also have to contend with anxious employers who are counting on hiring co-ops or interns to get work done. Likewise, whoever you report to is much more likely to want to know how close you are to 100% placement than, say, the degree to which you are doing whatever you can to ensure that each student ends up in an optimal situation in terms of maximizing learning and growth.

These very real and understandable pressures can lead to some poor judgment calls. It's always a relief when your last student is placed or when a particularly assertive employer hires someone and stops contacting you every few days about making that happen. When a student comes in with an offer for a mediocre job and is unsure about whether to accept it, the easiest thing to do is to just say yes. Complicating the issue is that it often takes at least a few years of experience to know whether a student is selling herself short by accepting a very entry-level job… or whether that student legitimately could get something that's going to be a much better learning opportunity if she is just willing to hold out a little longer and accept the uncertainty of not having a job.

There are many factors that come into play here: the economy, the job market, the student's interviewing skills and general viability as a job candidate, whether the student must get a job or can opt out, and how much time remains before the student's work term is supposed to start.

In the end, the employers need to decide who they want to hire, and students must own the responsibility of whether they should accept. But you're going to be asked for input on these decisions, and I think you do sometimes have a responsibility to recommend to students that they should be a little stubborn and hold out for a better opportunity if it's possible. You need to be honest; sometimes I'll say, "I don't have a crystal ball, but my guess is that there's a good chance you could end up with a more challenging job… if you can handle the anxiety and uncertainty of not knowing where you're going to work for several more weeks. But I think that the worst-case scenario is that you fail to get that more challenging job and then have to accept a job that's no better than this one once we get down to the last few weeks of referrals."

Whatever you do, you want to make sure that you're making recommendations based on what is best for the students' learning as opposed to the convenience of getting students placed and off your plate as fast as possible.

BEING EXPEDIENT INSTEAD OF THOROUGH

This is related to the previous idea. It's great to be efficient, but sometimes you have to ask yourself whether you're doing something simply because it's quick and easy rather than because it's really the best possible way you can get something done.

For a long time, I generally collected student evaluations and looked them over. If there was anything troublesome, I would discuss that with the student in question. But otherwise I spent very little time going over the student's performance with them. I rationalized this quite creatively. First, I told myself that I required small-group reflection seminars for students, so that gave them an opportunity to talk about what they learned. I also told myself that employer evaluations were often very fluffy—many of them didn't say all that much that could be turned into a teaching tool. Lastly, I often would think about how labor-intensive it would be to have a one-on-one meeting with each student after each work term.

What inspired me to change was actually a student survey that specifically asked students whether or not their coordinator actually discussed their evaluation with them. There was no way my numbers were going to be good on that, so I tried to come up with ways that I could minimize the possible negatives of one-on-one post-work meetings. As you'll see in Chapter 11 on reflection, some good outcomes have come of this.

There are many other examples of this idea as well. One problem is what I might call "free-range referrals." There are professionals who basically allow students to apply to whichever jobs they want and however many jobs they want as opposed to having a series of meetings to talk about career goals as well as targeting a small group of specific jobs that are appropriate for the student. Yes, you can run a co-op program in which you simply have students look up jobs in a database, rank the jobs, and then send their resumes to whatever jobs they rank. But then you're more of a placement officer than an educator. The goal should be to give students guidance that will ensure that they have a good sense of how they will get to where they want to go. Some students can do that with minimal guidance, but many cannot.

Another example would relate back to time management. Especially when under stress, educators tend to fall back on activities and processes that are comfortable and familiar to them rather than taking on what may be new and challenging but also with more upside. This is human nature, but it is another way in which we have to guard against being expedient as opposed to being open to something more innovative.

FORCING SQUARE PEGS IN ROUND HOLES

This is another similar concept. One bane of our existence in this field is that you often run into situations in which no one is completely happy. Unless you have a pretty amazing job market—and sometimes even if you do—it's not unusual to reach a point where you have employers crying "Where are the students?" while students are crying "Where are the jobs?" The problem is one of square pegs and round holes. You have plenty of jobs and an ample number of students, but there are not fits between the two.

A tough call is figuring out when it might be a good idea to get a student or employer to think a little more creatively about what would constitute a good fit. However, it's never a good idea to argue hard to get a student or employer to agree to a fit when either party is significantly resistant to it. When you do, the failure of the match is more on your hands than anyone else's.

FIXING MISTAKES INSTEAD OF FACILITATING CHOICES OF OTHERS

Within this category, this is probably the easiest mistake of all to make. The combination of being pressed for time on top of being a true expert in some area makes it very tempting to just do something yourself instead of taking the time it will take to teach a student or employer—or even a colleague—to do something themselves.

There's a Chinese proverb that is relevant here:

"Give a man a fish and you feed him for a day. Teach a man to fish and you feed him for a lifetime."

I still struggle with this one. I can correct a resume very quickly, and there have been times when I have succumbed to the temptation to just revamp a student's resume to get it to an employer as quickly as possible. That's expedient, but I don't think it's a good practice.

Likewise, you can make this type of mistake with students who are facing real dilemmas. Let's say that a student is being treated very unfairly by a manager. It can be very tempting to charge into that workplace and take charge of the situation. But is it your role to do so? I have made the mistake many times of just deciding how a problem was going to be handled, but I try harder now to lay out an understanding of options to students and trying to show them the consequences of various choices that they may opt to make. I think that this is more likely to help empower students and ensure that they learn something about how to own tough decisions instead of having them pulled out of their hands.

AVOIDING CONFLICT

The next theme that arose from the expert interviews was one that could be summarized as avoiding conflict. Like all of the other mistakes we're considering in this chapter, this one is also very understandable. In fact, I'd be very surprised if any experienced coordinator would say that they never have made this mistake. Why is that? Earlier, I mentioned the fact that conflict can be unpleasant. I doubt that anyone got into this field so they could experience conflict on a regular basis.

For me, though, the biggest reason I have made this mistake at times is because dealing with a budding conflict can be unbelievably time-consuming. I have to admit that there have been times when I could see some warning signs of a problem—an e-mail from a student or employer hinting at a problem or maybe even stating it explicitly—and I just shuddered to think of how many other things I needed to get done on that day and how I would have to drop all or most of them to address the problem to the best of my ability. It's much easier to jot a brief e-mail expressing some concern and suggesting a "wait and see" attitude or a simplistic solution. And sometimes you do that, and everything works out okay. But there are times that you really do need to drop everything else that's going on to intervene in a situation at an employer or to have a very long phone conversation with a student or employer who is angry, frustrated, upset, and at a loss as to what to do.

To be successful in this field, you have to be willing to have your agenda go out the window on a certain day. And you have to come around to viewing conflicts as teaching and learning opportunities that should not be avoided because of the discomfort that they cause both parties. As we'll see in Chapter 7 (Counseling Students One-on-One), conflicts can be wonderful turning points in relationships if handled effectively.

Here are some of the subthemes about avoiding conflict that arose in the interviews:

FAILING TO FACE PROBLEMS PROACTIVELY

An employer that I respect heavily at a Fortune 100 company gave me good advice about dealing with bad behavior. You need to address it promptly and directly, and it can be done publicly. Better still, you can handle it proactively. In the preparation class that we all teach at Northeastern, my colleague Bob Tillman announces right off the bat that he may not necessarily comment if a student is text messaging or dozing off in his class… but that he absolutely IS noticing that behavior and factoring it into his perception of that student and his or her readiness for a professional environment.

I believe in providing feedback to students as immediately as possible. Occasionally a student comes into my office with a bit of a chip on his shoulder. Maybe he had a bad experience with other professionals at my university; perhaps his last co-op experience was a real dud. I don't know, but I'm going to ask some questions to find out what's behind the attitude and calmly make students aware of how their presentation of themselves will create negative perceptions in the eyes of others, fairly or unfairly.

Asking questions is often a good way to start. "So far you've really struggled to get every step of the preparation process done on time. Why is that?" Maybe there's a really good reason, maybe not. I won't accept a statement like "I've been really busy" at face value; I'll probe deeper to find out how busy the person really has been.

I actually think you're doing students a favor by pointing out their undesirable behavior and giving them an opportunity to explain it and ultimately correct it. That's part of being an educator, too—getting students to become more aware of the role they play in having others perceive them as they do.

BEING TOO STUDENT-FRIENDLY

As has come up repeatedly in this book, we do a great job of attracting individuals to our profession who want to nurture college students. That's great to a point, but some professionals fall into the trap of avoiding conflict because they are basically sympathetic to students and reluctant to play the role of authority figure.

It's easy to fall into various rationalizations on this front: "I remember how tough it was to be a clueless sophomore…" "I'm sure that this student is just acting this way because he's really stressed out about not having a job yet…" and so forth. While it's important to be empathic and to acknowledge that our students can be under a great deal of stress, that doesn't make it okay for a student to treat you or a colleague rudely or impolitely.

Likewise, thinking of students as customers does not mean we have to buy into the notion that the "customer is always right." I have had students in tears in my office because I wouldn't let them quit a job that they hated or because I didn't allow them to renege on an accepted job offer to get a much higher paying and better job. I have had students who probably were pretty offended when I told them that they weren't good enough to interview for a top job or who were upset when I sided with an employer after hearing all the facts about a dispute.

It's human nature to want to be liked by students, but it's more important to be respected. You have a duty to be truthful and as transparent as possible with students, and sometimes the truth hurts! You can be compassionate in how you deliver tough news or convey unpopular decisions, but sometimes you can't be swayed merely because you're concerned about avoiding conflict or hurting someone's feelings.

BROODING AND LETTING PROBLEMS FESTER

This is another variation on the theme of avoiding conflict. I absolutely hate going home and brooding on a problem from work, and I used to do it much more often than I do now. Yet there is a balance between responding quickly and responding so fast that you end up being overly impulsive and emotional.

When you're feeling that natural reluctance to deal with an issue that requires attention, remind yourself that allowing a long period of time to go by just increases the chances that the undesirable behavior will continue and maybe worsen… and you'll have too much time to stew about it as well.

One key here is to persist in discussing the conflict until it is fully resolved. If it appears that the student is begrudgingly going along with what you say, take the time to probe with questions to get to the bottom of that apparent disgruntlement. This will decrease the chances of having either you or the student brooding unhappily after the meeting.

FAILING TO ADAPT

Curiously, this next theme is almost the opposite of the previous one. If there is a danger in being a little too soft and malleable, there is also the mistake of a rigid, one-size-fits-all approach to working with students. If avoidance of conflict is a likely mistake for those who err on the warm and fuzzy side of the continuum, this error is often made by those who come into the job with strong personalities and a self-determined set of what is right or wrong with little grey area in between. It's great to have a sense of conviction and passion for your job, but there is also something to be said for slowing down and not having a knee-jerk response to problems that arise. This theme resonates with me, as it was one of the greater weaknesses that I needed to address in my first several years in my role.

Here are some subthemes of failing to adapt:

NOT REALLY LISTENING TO STUDENTS/EMPLOYERS

One recurring theme from many of my interviewees was the critical importance of listening closely to students and employers. We all make assumptions about others based on very limited information, and it doesn't always come naturally to lead off with a series of clarifying questions. Obviously, there will never be a consensus when it comes to what works and what doesn't, but here are some thoughts on this subject.

A common mistake is to shrug off repeated grumbles, criticisms, or expressions of frustration… or to rationalize a failure to act on this input for any number of reasons:

- "We've always done it this way."

- "To make that change, I'd have to spend a lot more time [ramping up on technology, developing a new course, attending meetings, correcting papers, etc.]."

- "I really don't know if changing my process would even work."

- "What if my colleagues or supervisor give me a hard time about doing things differently?"

There may be some legitimate reasons why you can't make a change that your students and employers would like to make. You may have workload or budget limitations that preclude some possibilities. Still, a group of students or employers seldom will steer you wrong in terms of process improvement for your program.

Probably one of the greatest missed opportunities for really listening is when visiting employers. I have definitely fallen into the mindset of going out to a company to make a presentation about what co-op is and how it works… only to have someone point out that they are an alum and totally familiar with the basics. So it's often better to go out and ask questions to discern what the organization's needs are and to find out how your program can help. Once you have listened thoroughly, you'll understand what the other party really needs to know. Then you can tailor your own response accordingly.

Active listening requires some patience and persistence. You may need to ask several questions and probe deeper when you get a hint of an issue that is not immediately apparent. But if you do it right, you will have much more efficient and effective meetings, as you will be sure to talk about what the other party really wants to hear.

FORCING YOUR OWN STYLE/PERSONALITY/VALUES ON OTHERS INSTEAD OF ADJUSTING TO DIFFERENT STUDENT STYLES/GOALS/NEEDS

One of the most valuable professional development experiences I had in my earlier years in the field was diversity training. Like many people, I went into the training feeling it would be a waste of time. I felt I was already doing a good job with my diverse students, and I had even taught the topic of diversity in organizational behavior courses. So you can imagine how surprised I was to find the experience useful in unexpected ways. Most interestingly, I believe that the training made me a much better counselor of white male students, let alone anyone of a different background.

A big key of the training was awareness building. It forced me to realize what my style was. As I mentioned in Chapter 2, my Myers-Briggs profile is an ENTP. If that doesn't mean anything to you, I can explain. An ENTP is sometimes referred to as one of any number of types: innovator, inventor, explorer, visionary, etc. Like all of the MBTI types, an ENTP has its possible strengths and weaknesses. On the positive side of the ledger, ENTPs are often thought of as clever, verbally quick, resourceful, and motivated to improve the world. More negatively, ENTPs can be bad at following through on plans and are generally weaker on dealing with structure and details. ENTPs are very logical but not always in touch with their feelings, which may isolate them from others. They also can speak abruptly or intensely when expressing principles.

The diversity training forced me to see that I basically imposed my personality on students and didn't really adapt it to the individual needs of students. Early on, I prided myself on "shooting from the hip" and solving student problems efficiently and effectively. That worked well for some students, but others needed more empathy and compassion. I realized I needed to develop a more feeling style if I was going to be successful in building relationships with students.

It took even longer to figure out that my style actually was impeding my learning opportunities. If a student did something wrong, I was quick to make a tough pronouncement about it—to "tell it like it is" with no room for debate. I have to think that I missed many chances for a real dialogue that would've led to more learning. Although I still try to provide "reality therapy" to students, I have consciously softened my tone and started asking many more questions to get a discussion going about a student's problem behavior. I've found that students seem to feel more willing to share their insights and reflect more deeply on how to change as a result.

There are many different types of students. Some have competitive mentalities and respond well to challenge. Some are strong feelers who value harmony very highly; some are thinkers who place the emphasis on competence. Some love details and structure, while others loathe those elements. To be as effective as you can, you may need to adapt your style and tailor it to different students. Likewise, you need to make students aware of their own styles and how they may need to strengthen areas that don't come naturally to them as well. Sometimes I'll talk with students about my own journey on this front, as it helps them see that we all need to understand our nature and how it may help or hinder us as professionals.

BEING TOO RIGID AND NOT BEING OPEN TO EXCEPTIONS

Due to either the aforementioned personality type issues as well as a fear of being perceived as soft by students, there are professionals who have a very rigid, "rules are rules" mentality when it comes to how they work with students. The most typical rationalization for this style is that it's in the name of having high standards. These people may perceive coordinators who are more flexible as excessively soft marshmallows when it comes to running a program.

This is another trap that I fell into in my early years as a professional. While I did have colleagues who were much more into structure and rules than I ever was, I think that I came across as a tough, intense coordinator who was feared by some students.

I've long since come around to firmly believing that you can have extremely high standards in combination with a calm, unemotional tone. And many of my interviewees indicated that there are times when you need to have a more malleable approach to what you will and won't allow. You don't want to allow exceptions for frivolous reasons, as you always worry about what precedent you might be setting by allow something to occur or not happen. But the consensus is that it's a mistake to be too rigid, as it works against developing long-term relationships with students.

FAILING TO THINK THROUGH CONSEQUENCES

Another category of mistakes that I could see through the interviews was a failure to think through the consequences of one's actions. When dealing with the myriad situations that can arise as a professional, the analogy of a chess match comes to mind. If you take a cursory look at a position in a chessboard, it might lead you to make a move that will eliminate the most pressing and obvious threat or dilemma at hand. But it's important to take a longer look: If you make one move, what will be the impact on the next move? And what about the move after that? You often need to slow down and look at all possible ramifications of any action that you take.

Here are some subthemes of this type of mistake:

PLAYING GOD

One perennial dilemma for professionals in our field is when to "play God" when it comes to playing a role in the placement process. At one time many decades ago, our university's coordinators used to place students in jobs directly as opposed to dealing with a more time-consuming interview process. On the other extreme, there are programs in which professionals have a totally hands-off approach when it comes to determining where students work. They list jobs, let students choose which ones they want to pursue, and then let employers decide whom they want to hire. In between those extremes, many professionals do provide some degree of guidance for students and screening of candidates for employers.

The challenge is just how much to intervene in the process. My interviewees differed on the point of whether or not a professional should play an active role in steering students to specific employers or vice-versa, but there clearly have been some major mistakes made when someone played God without thinking through all of the consequences. It can be very tempting to load the deck to ensure that, say, a student without a car gets the one job you have left that does not require a car while likewise making sure that the student with a car takes the one job that requires a car to get to it. But you generally want to resist tinkering with situations like that.

A few individuals raised the more striking example of allowing a student to renege on an acceptance to take a better offer. Although this was done with the best of intentions, this led to a mess in both cases. One interviewee that I spoke to told me about allowing a student to renege because another employer offered a full scholarship if the student accepted. That sounded nice, but the decision led to losing one of that program's best employers—a company whose name you definitely would recognize—for a solid decade! Suffice to say that you need to proceed with extreme caution when monkeying with the hiring process.

E-MAIL BLUNDERS

A few people mentioned embarrassing situations with e-mail. Recently I revised my *Find Your First Professional Job* book to add a big section on all the things that can go wrong with e-mails. Although that was directed at students, professionals need to watch out for some of the same common blunders:

- Hitting "reply to all" and having a student or employer see something that they weren't meant to see

- Getting into overly long and/or heated exchanges with e-mail instead of handling the situation face-to-face

- Responding to an e-mail impulsively without thinking through the consequences, forgetting that the 'e' in e-mail also stands for everlasting, eternal, embarrassing evidence

I made the "reply to all" mistake just last year. I had exchanged e-mails with a rather entitled student who wanted to know if we had co-op positions in Hawaii and "if so, which islands." Although the e-mail made me feel more like a travel agent than an educator, I responded appropriately. However, a colleague subsequently e-mailed me about the student, and I made a rather sarcastic reference to the student's previous Hawaiian island e-mail. Seconds after I sent the e-mail, I realized that the student was on the cc line! I immediately followed up with an attempt at explaining why I had written what I had, but suffice to say it was a humbling experience.

One of my top students made a memorable mistake. Just like me, she often works with about eight files open simultaneously on her computer, and she pecks away at e-mails while working on spreadsheets and other projects. One day she quickly toggled over to her e-mail and fired off a message. She thought she was writing to her boyfriend, but she actually sent it to her supervisor! The simple message: "Baby, what time is your game on Sunday? I want you all day!"

Her boss thought it was amusing and forwarded it to six or seven colleagues, adding a comment: "I seem to be making quite an impression on my intern!" Those six or seven colleagues forwarded it to several others. By the time I saw it, the e-mail had reached about 70 people in six states!

The upshot was intriguing. Our student was obviously embarrassed and apologized for her poor judgment. I'm sure she will be much more careful about sending off eyebrow-raising messages in the future. But the real interesting part was that her supervisor got in much more trouble than she did. She made a bad move, but it was an accident. He intentionally forwarded her message to others for humor value, which was basically an abuse of power on his part. So he also learned a valuable lesson.

It's surprisingly easy to make some of the above mistakes, so it doesn't hurt to be a little paranoid when it comes to e-mail communication. Always think about how you would feel if an e-mail message became totally public.

ABRUPTLY CHANGING STANDARDS OR PLANS

One of the most painful aspects of my first two years in the field was realizing that my preparation process had a serious flaw when I was in the thick of the busiest time of year. When something is going wrong, the temptation is to fix it immediately. However, that has the potential to make a bad situation worse. I believe that if you've told students and colleagues how a process should work, then you need to stick with that process in the short term. If you suddenly start requiring a new step or procedure, you are likely to confuse people, and—depending on the nature of the change—it may create fairness issues.

For example, I don't think you can suddenly require practice interviews of all students if you're in the middle of interviewing and have allowed some students to move forward without completing that step first. I don't believe it would be a good idea to tell students that they must write cover letters halfway through a given referral period. Likewise, if you've told all students that they don't need a face-to-face appointment to have their resumes go to an employer, I think it's hard to insist on that, weeks later.

Admittedly, this can be painful. In the course of writing this book, I've decided to make my small-group reflection seminars optional. But I had told all students who were coming back recently that they would be required to do this. So now I feel compelled to require this of them one last time. Changing the requirement now probably would just raise questions about my credibility or make some students think that requirements are negotiable. So I'm stuck for now.

There are exceptions to this rule. Major personnel issues may force your hand in terms of how things are done at any given time, for example. But I view mid-stream changes as a last resort.

OVERPROMISE, UNDERDELIVER

Another potential credibility issue is when professionals overpromise and underdeliver. Like most mistakes, the road to hell is paved with good intentions on this one. In wanting to show an employer or student how much you care about them and how willing you are to be helpful, it can get a little tempting to make promises that you might not be able to keep. You need to stay away from guaranteeing any specific sort of outcome for anyone, whether it's successfully hiring a student or getting a job. In fact, some incoming students ask if we "guarantee employment" for our students, given the stature of our program. We always answer that question carefully, indicating that students who do everything that we recommend have a high probability of a successful placement… but that the economy, job market, and employability of the student are major factors.

Likewise, I try to be up front with employers about how realistic their chances are of hiring a student. If the employer is a 45-minute drive from Boston and the job market is strong, I try to make sure they understand right away that they're unlikely to see a high volume of resumes unless the job is something very special. Managing employer expectations up front and getting them prepared for the fact that we may not be able to help them fulfill a need goes a long way to preventing unhappy phone calls to my director when the semester winds down.

The same is true with students. If you are working with a major or industry in which a first-time co-op or intern is going to be doing very entry-level, administrative work, you need to make sure students understand what the job will entail, realistically. You need to prepare them for the fact that a job may have downtime or unchallenging work, and you might have to educate them to help them see the less obvious learning opportunities in such a job—the opportunities to observe, network, adapt to an organizational culture, master simple duties to earn more challenging work, and build a foundation for a more challenging job later on. It's also good to get students ready for the possibility that they may not like their first job; they may even want to change their major after a first work term! If you manage expectations in such a way, then you will help students embrace the full gamut of learning opportunities. If not, students may view some experiences as a total failure simply because the job wasn't that challenging or because it wasn't their ultimate dream job.

WEARING FRUSTRATIONS ON YOUR SLEEVE

Another recurring theme in the interviews can be described as the problem of wearing your frustrations on your sleeve. Again, I am completely sympathetic to this mistake. Many professionals have incredibly challenging workloads, and at certain times of the year the intensity can be unbelievable in many programs. At times I have commented that our finance suite looks like a third-world nation during the peak of referral season; you have to step over densely packed bodies to get to your destination.

In addition to the sheer workload and pace, there is also the factor that we are dealing with young adults. As much as we may love that aspect of our jobs, it also can be an exasperating element as well. There are always going to be a small percentage of students that do incredibly foolish or disappointing things on the job, leading to major headaches. Back on campus, there are always some students who have a highly entitled attitude and who may treat you initially as if you were their administrative assistant. As we'll talk about in the next chapter, we are working with the Millennial Generation—a group that has been characterized as having very high expectations, needing more handholding than their Generation X predecessors, and being so technologically inclined that they expect 24/7 availability from professionals.

When you put all of these elements together, it's easy to understand why a professional might snap at a student or employer or even lose it completely—especially if someone gives you an attitude or treats you inappropriately for whatever reason.

I remember a mistake that I made several years ago. I was working with a pretty demanding student—let's call him Martin. He was a smart guy and a member of our Student Government Association. I had been told that some members of our student government were more likely to complain at some slight injustice, but I hadn't encountered it before Martin.

One day, Martin was scheduled to meet with me for a 10:30 appointment. That time came and went, and he did not show up. Around 10:37, my colleague Elizabeth Chilvers called. She mentioned that Martin had just called her to ask about a job of hers; she wanted to know if he had discussed it with me first. I mentioned that it was funny that she had just heard from Martin, as he was a no-show for an appointment with me. Ten minutes later, Martin called me and said that he was sorry he was running late because his "class had ended late." He wanted to know if it was okay to come by around 11.

I didn't handle it well. I snapped at him, telling him that he had missed his 10:30 appointment with me and as far as I was concerned, he should come to walk-in hours if he wasn't capable of making a commitment and honoring it. This made him angry, and that made me angrier. The upshot was that he went to our group leader to complain about me.

I was a little embarrassed about that. Now someone else's time was getting wasted because I had taken a conflict and escalated it instead of masking my frustration and sticking to the facts. So, in a calmer state of mind, I met with Martin. I apologized for getting angry and calmly explained why I had been frustrated with him. I pointed out that his phone call to my colleague followed by his tale of running late because of class led me to question the legitimacy of his excuse. In retrospect, what I should have done when he called is maintain a neutral, curious tone of voice, and calmly say, "You're running late due to class? I'm confused. Professor Chilvers just called me ten minutes ago to say that you were on the phone with her about a job. So I don't really understand what's going on…"

Assuming he came clean and admitted that he had not been truthful with me, that would have given me an opportunity to remind him about how important it is to maintain credibility in business relationships. We ended up getting to that point eventually, salvaging the situation, but I definitely blew it by wearing my frustrations on my sleeve.

So how can you avoid making a similar mistake? It's not easy, as some situations really do call for a pretty immediate reaction. Still here are some suggestions:

TAKE TIME TO COOL OFF

One expression I like is "strike when the iron is cold." There are times when I receive a maddening e-mail in the midst of a crazy morning, and my knee-jerk response is to send an inflammatory response. Instead, I'll remind myself that I'd be better off delaying my reply until after I go to the gym at lunchtime. Or I might wait overnight if it's been a tough day, and I fear that my response won't be as constructive as it might be when I'm feeling reenergized in the morning.

The same is true when I get a disappointing call from an employer, informing me that a student has been chronically late to work. This drives me nuts, as I dwell heavily on that point in my books for students as well as in my preparation course. It's tempting to call the student up and tell them off, but I have to recognize that I might not be in the best state of mind to communicate with this problem child at the moment. You need to be careful to not assume what is actually happening; keep asking clarifying questions until the truth becomes more apparent. "How do you think the job has been going? Your manager told me that you've been having trouble getting to work. Is that true? What's the issue? How often has this been happening? What steps have you taken to address it?" Eventually you will get a clearer picture of the root cause behind the symptoms, and that will inform you as to how to address the issue in an educational, solution-oriented manner.

Even in a one-on-one meeting, you always have the option to hold off making a final decision if you are worked up about something. If a student comes in the office, tells you he was just fired, and then wants you to send his resume somewhere else immediately, you have every right to say, "I need some time to think this over. I want to talk to my colleagues about this and the employer as well. We'll talk again in a day or two about what the consequences will be."

During this "cool-off period," I also might try to put myself in the other person's shoes. Their behavior toward me may be unacceptable, but odds are that the behavior is a symptom of frustration about something else rather than a personal issue with me. What is my history with this person? What are some alternative explanations that might help me understand what's behind an outburst? I might not have a clue, but thinking this way gets my mind working toward a more solution-oriented approach when I do connect with the student.

WEIGHING CHOICES AND CONSEQUENCES

When you're frustrated and wondering what to do about it, I also find it's helpful to reflect for a while on how to respond most productively. What are my options in dealing with the situation? What do I potentially gain and risk with each of those options? Given that my long-term goals are almost always to keep the focus on the educational aspect of the conflict as well as maintain a relationship with the student as a future colleague, this helps me find the language that will be direct and honest but also constructive and solution-oriented.

When weighing choices, I always try to remember that my behavior toward students is also a model for them to follow—for better or worse. If I get angry, exaggerate the situation, and make assumptions that aren't based on fact, I'm teaching them such reactions are an appropriate way for professionals to handle conflict. Likewise, if I can approach the situation by making sure I have as much information as possible, sticking to the facts, being honest, and working toward a resolution, that sends a different message altogether.

With all of this in mind, I think you'll enjoy reading about some great mistakes from our generous experts.

IN THEIR OWN WORDS

PROFESSIONAL PERSPECTIVE #1
"TEACHING AS WHITEWATER RAFTING"
Stephen Brookfield, University of St. Thomas

One of the things I always did the first day of class was start off my course with a speech that went as follows: "Hi, my name is Stephen. Please call me by my first name; don't call me Dr. Brookfield or Professor, 'cause I like us to be on first-name terms here. I'd like us as much as possible to be coequals. We're moral coequals with maybe a temporary imbalance in amount of expertise, but we're moral coequals. I want to acknowledge that right at the beginning. So please call me by my first name, and I will call you by your first name.

"So it's just great to be a teacher, I'm astonished I get paid for this and it's really such a privilege to come here today and learn from all the rich experiences and lives that you bring to this class. You may feel that you really don't have much experience and knowledge in this area because it seems like a new subject, but—trust me—you know all about this. You can do a lot in this area. It's just that you don't know that you know it. My job is to help your realize how much you already know and how much you can already do.

"Just a couple of things about how I'm going to run this course: Firstly, when you were in high school, probably the thing you were most concerned about was not making a mistake. In my classes, I encourage the making of mistakes because mistakes are the things that we really learn the most from—the richest moments to learn—so when they happen we shouldn't hide them or be ashamed of them and keep them private. We should bring them out into the public domain, tell everybody about them, celebrate them as the instructional friends that they really are. That's what you learn from mistakes; you don't learn as much from successes.

"Just to underscore what I'm talking about, I'm a teacher, but I make mistakes. In fact, in the last three months I've made three basic errors in this area that really helped me understand the system of logic and dynamics better, and it helps make me a better teacher."

Then I end by saying "One final thought: It doesn't matter how carefully I plan this course. Sooner or later, something unexpected and unlooked for is going to happen that will throw everything off. When that unexpected event happens, I don't want you all to look to me to respond to it on my own. As a group of people who bring experience and knowledge to this room, we are going to draw on our combined experience and knowledge to deal with the problem, so we're going to solve it together." So that would be my opening speech. I thank God if everything's good and democratic teacher Carl Rogers is channeling through me.

I was doing work for a book called The Skillful Teacher which came out a while ago. The premise of the book is that skillfulness is not a set of predetermined consequential behaviors. Skillfulness is an ability to get inside a situation to find its internal dynamic and rhythms and then respond to it in an informed way, so skillful teachers constantly research their own classrooms. So I decided to do this. I decided to ask as many of my own students as I could what were the best and worst experiences they'd had with me in the last ten years or so.

So I got to my students and I started hearing this very troubling response. They said, "One of the worst things that happened was when we showed up for the first day of class. You made a speech to us which made us feel very, very nervous and made us feel psychologically inadequate. We left knowing you had a history of making mistakes and you're not actually competent. So that first day when I heard you introduce the class and introduce yourself, I was on the verge of getting out of the class, going down to the registrar's office, and seeing if I could change to another section where I would learn something useful from someone who had something to teach me."

Well, then I have to reason with several of my offshoots about the role of a self-deprecatory initial stance by an educator as a way to deconstruct power relationships. I guess the assumption I was working under was that if I emphasized the experiences of the students and tried to place them on the moral level as me, this would raise their confidence and decrease their anxiety. In fact the opposite was happening. They were being shattered by my obvious lack of basic credibility, and their anxiety had been raised.

Since that time, when I start a new course, I don't make that speech anymore. Instead I try to put myself in the position that my learners are in and see the situation from their point of view. I play a game with myself on the first day of every new course. As I'm walking to teach the class, I'm not the professor, I'm really the student and the course I'm going to take is not a course in whatever it is I'm teaching, but it's a course on whitewater rafting. Because to me that would be the learning experience that is most threatening. I'm not a physical person, but my wife has an annoyingly out-doorsy streak within her personality and is always trying to get me to do outdoor types of things.

So I picture the scene: I'm on a plank in northern Minnesota waiting for our instructor to show up, looking nervously at the raft which is near me. I'm thinking, am I really going to get into this thing bobbing up and down, shouldn't it be static at least here? Then out of the pines, strides our instructor, Svetlana, and she says, "Call me Svety. I'd really like us to be on first-name terms here. I love teaching whitewater rafting. I look forward to it so much; it's a real privilege, and you know why it's a privilege? Because as a teacher I learn so much from you. You bring such a rich experience to this classroom that it's a privilege to get paid for me to be able to access and grow on your experience and knowledge. I know you don't think you can do this, but trust me, you can do whitewater rafting. You already know all about it. You don't know that you know about it, and my job is to make you realize how much you already know."

And then she says, "A couple of things before we get into the boat about how I run this class. First of all, mistakes are something we don't hide. When you make a mistake in the raft, bring it to the attention of everyone. We'll all learn from it and celebrate along with you. Just to underscore the importance of making mistakes, I've made three standard mistakes in the past month which really helped me to understand being a whitewater rafting instructor."

And then she says one final thing. "You know as a teacher, it doesn't matter how carefully you plan everything, sooner or later, something is going to happen that will throw everything off. When that unexpected event happens—we don't know what it is yet—I don't want you all to look to me. We're all going to pool our experiences. So, for example, when we round the bend into the rapids awaiting us there, I want us to form into triads in the raft. Here's some waterproof paper, some waterproof markers, and we'll brainstorm for 30 seconds on dealing with this crisis in our lives. Then we'll come back together as a group and determine the best way to get through the rapids together."

So this is how I prepare for my first day of teaching a class. I try and play this scenario in my mind. One of the most helpful things for my practice of doing this is that I realize something. If I did ever find myself in that situation, if Svety told me, "Trust me, you can do this, it's good for you, it's within your capabilities," I wouldn't believe her.

But I would believe a group of former learners, so if Svety had said, at that first class meeting, listen you can do this, I know you can do it, but I know that at some level you don't think you can, so let me introduce you to someone who I think might convince you that you can do this. And out come three, pathetic, physically inadequate, skinny people. Out they come and she says, "Here are the three successful graduates of the last three classes I've taught, and I'd just like them to tell you how they felt the first evening and to pass on the best advice that they can to you in terms of the shoes that you now occupy."

Let's say that those three people tell me when they came here that they thought there was no way they could do this, but that Svety was a good teacher. "She told us what to do, when to do it, and once we got some basic skills, we were encouraged to experiment with different ways of doing this practice, and look at me, I made it." I would believe that, in a way that I wouldn't believe Svety.

So one of the things I do in my classes –particularly if they're required courses where there's a lot of hostility and resentment on the part of the students—is to start off with a panel of former resistors who come in and talk. Each of them has about five minutes to pass on the best piece of advice they can to the new students about how to survive in this course. And while this happens I leave the room. So the first night of class, I actually walk out on the students.

What I'm interested in is how we apply that particular perspective on criticality to our practices as people who work experientially with learners. It's much harder to look within and adopt a critical practice with our own common familiar practices.

PROFESSIONAL PERSPECTIVE #2
"ASKING ALL THE WRONG QUESTIONS"
Nancy Johnston, Simon Fraser University

One mistake revolves around my personal change from a manager to an educator. About five or six years into my career as a coordinator, I decided to do my Master's. I was beginning to get curious about what happens in the black box of co-op. I know how to develop a job, and I've got a pretty neat little system here for postings and placements. I've got my employer relationships down, and I know how to do my pre and post-preparations with students. But what's really going on here? What am I actually trying to do here? I'm trying to place a student, but I'm really trying to have a student have a wonderful learning opportunity. So I became interested in looking at the nature of learning in co-op. That was actually the title of my master's: "The Nature of Learning in Cooperative Education"—in the sciences, because those were the students I worked with.

So for part of my master's work, I studied two cohorts of three science students who were working in a hospital setting. They were part of a research database collection process, collecting head circumference, bone length, and girths of children between one and five because apparently there wasn't any normative data for that age group. Anyway, these co-op students were out working in a hospital setting, doing kinanthropometry work, measuring little kids. And I studied them and talked to their supervisor and talked to the professor who taught them their kinanthropometry skills before they were hired. I asked them: "What did you learn? How did you learn it? What didn't you learn from? Where did you learn the most? How did that learning interface with your classroom learning?" Because that placement should have had really obvious transfer: They learned how to measure in class, and then they measured in the clinical setting. So that should have been a really clean one.

Long story short: I ended up transcribing all that, looking for themes, coming up with conclusions. What I noticed as I interviewed a fourth-year, about-to-be-graduating student was that she should've been the most articulate, the most knowledgeable, the most thoughtful about her own learning. And she was the worst. She didn't know what she'd learned; she didn't really know how she learned it. She didn't know where she learned better or what her role was in the learning. She really struggled to answer those questions.

So I chatted with the students afterwards, and they said, "I've never been asked those questions. They were really hard to answer." So first I thought, "Oh my God, I've only ever asked these of six people, and I've coached hundreds." And they all told me that those were the most important questions that they'd ever been asked: What did you learn? How did you learn it? How are you going to apply that somewhere down the line?

So the story ends with this one senior student going after her final co-op job. She should've been a shoo-in for the job she applied to because she had already been on another research project, and this was her final co-op so she was also generally experienced. The prospective employer however calls me up and says, "She cannot express in any kind of convincing way how her past skills would be useful in a new context like my research project."

That was the first time I realized I'm asking all the wrong questions for stimulating people's sense of what they know and how they know it, and, oh boy, the most powerful thing of co-op is skills transfer. That's when I began to do the curriculum development in the area of skills transfer and looked at the role of metacognition. So that was a huge learning point, and it came directly out of practice. But not just practicing: Research prompted it, and then when I got the responses that were so disappointing—and then it's corroborated by an employer—I'm like, "Oh my gosh. It's not about kinanthropometry skills or any of that. They can learn those in the classroom. It's more about them understanding the generic skills they need as they move between jobs. That's the difference between a person who's empowered by a co-op experience and a person who just goes from job to job to job in co-op. And we don't do anything systematic to ensure the former versus the latter. So what is it we do that makes people aware of their own learning, aware of themselves as a learner, and aware of how to categorize skills in a way that makes them transferable? You can't just label something a transferable skill; the learner needs to believe it and mobilize it.

That was a real turning point because it started a whole curriculum reform at SFU. Then our bridging online preparatory curriculum came out of that, and the first few chapters of our curriculum is not resume writing or interview skills, it's "How do I learn? What is learning? What are skills? What are tasks? How do I move a skill or task between two different contexts?" It's very theoretical, and the kids are going "What the....? I just want to write a resume!" But for a few, they get it then, and for a few, they get it later. And for another few, they never get it. But at least we're making an attempt. The biggest change was that that was when our staff started to see themselves as educators and not just as program managers or coordinators or administrators.

The irony was that I was considered good at my job! People would have said that I was a great co-ordinator. "She's placed the most of any students in kinesiology; she's diversified the workplaces that they're in. Students love her; the employers are happy." I was by all accounts a really good coordinator, but I was not a really good educator. But nobody was measuring me on that.

PROFESSIONAL PERSPECTIVE # 3
"I THREW OUT ALL THE RULES"
Bob Tillman, Northeastern University

Early on when we used to do this we were on quarters; we had a two-term commitment. And come hell or high water, we would hold students to two-term commitments. I remember forcing students back to a company that in hindsight should've never happened. I should've been more assertive with the company to convey that this was not going to be in the best interest of the student and or the employer. We tended to be more employer-centered at that time, and the employers called the shots.

I think as I grew over time I realized what should've happened. I can remember forcing some students back. That was the wrong move; it was miserable. The students didn't succeed and the company didn't get what they were looking for. I should've been more flexible. But I was trying to honor my colleagues and the employers—again, not looking at the needs of the student. And I had several students that I probably did that with who to this day say, "That bastard! He was taking care of his needs; he was being expedient and he wasn't listening to me." And that was probably true.

[In terms of how I've changed over years of being a coordinator], I threw out all the rules. There aren't any rules. [The style when I began] was very rigid. It was very employer-centered. It was the system I came into. I think it was not having a true understanding of co-op as education. Co-op was looked at as work—having an employer-centered model and handling huge loads. There were things, structure-wise, that today I would look back and say, "God, what was I thinking?" I've always said when we get down to it, if I can't convince a student something is in their best interest and they can't convince me something is in their best interest, we'll say cut the cards. Somebody will win half the time as long as we're both giving a decent amount of effort.

A good example of this is a student who insists on interviewing some place that you know—or at least suspect in the back of your mind—that you're just setting this student up to fail. I've got strong students interviewing; the student is not that strong; the student is insisting, "I want my shot at this company." In the past I would've held the line. Today I'll let that student interview. I'll say, "As long as you understand what you're not doing is interviewing at a company where you have a better chance of getting a job..." And the student is headstrong and, you know, once in a while they get the job. I was wrong; I was wrong. They went out and interviewed; they had some other qualities and convinced an employer to take them over somebody else I would consider to be a sharper, more talented student. It doesn't happen that often, but enough to force you to challenge your view on what you think companies are looking for or your view of that student and how strong they are.

And sometimes you just have to sit back and say I don't have all the answers, I don't know all about this, and sometimes letting the market decide it is great. Now what's the downside? The downside is the student goes out and interviews, doesn't get the job. Meanwhile, jobs that he could've had are no longer available and now guess what? The student is on your doorstep because you can't find them a job. That's the balance, and I think we've all been there on that. I think the other balance is if we could always place students in jobs we wouldn't have square pegs in round holes. And we've all gotten to the end of the term with oversized pegs.

PROFESSIONAL PERSPECTIVE #4
"A Dream Offer"
Charlie Bognanni, Northeastern University

Your timing couldn't be better because I made a major boo-boo—literally about the last month or two—and my two colleagues Beth and Kathy can tell you about it as well. In fact, I probably will share it with my whole group because I think it's an important lesson for other people not to repeat.

We always tell students that once they've accepted a job, it's binding. Don't worry about anything in writing—if a student has verbally accepted a job offer, then it's binding. And one of my colleagues taught me this great analogy that I use when students question that. "How would you like it if an employer hired you but called you back a few days later and said 'You know what? We just saw a better candidate. So we really like you, but we're going to go with the other candidate.' How would you feel about that? You'd be really angry and pretty frustrated."

In any case, we always tell students that. Well, let me tell you something that I did a couple of weeks ago that I now regret. We had a case where a number of students had interviewed at a particular bank for a job, a very good job, and they had narrowed it down to two students, or so the employer told us. He offered the job to a particular student named Sarah. It was Sarah's second choice. She was holding back, waiting to hear from another employer. But after a few days, she hadn't heard back from the other employer, and she had been waiting quite a long time to hear from that other employer. She kept e-mailing them, and we kept e-mailing them and they kept saying that they couldn't make a decision. So she decided she wasn't going to get that job offer and took the job at the bank. The other one was a consumer products company. So she took the job.

Literally a day after she accepted the job at the bank, she walks into my office and says, "You're not going to believe it. I just got a call from the consumer products company, and they offered me the job." To her credit, Sarah said, "This is killing me, but I know what I have to do. I have to stick with the job at the bank, right?" And I said, "Yeah, you really do, Sarah." She said, "I know. I know that's the right thing to do, and I'll do it. I'll live up to that agreement because that's the right thing to do but this is killing me." And I applauded her and I said, "Good for you. I know this is killing you; it bothers me too, but it's the right thing to do." And Sarah walks out of the office. This is absolutely true by the way; I'm not embellishing this at all. This is exactly what happened.

So after she walks out—it might've been the same day or the next day—we wanted feedback on the candidate that wasn't chosen at the bank. If you remember, I told you that we were down to two candidates, right? So my colleague called the employer at the bank and he said the second candidate was terrific, too. "In fact, if Sarah didn't take the job, we would've offered it to Sophia," he said. "We could've gone with either candidate, but we thought Sarah was slightly better, Sophia would've been fine too." This was a voicemail. Click.

My mind started working, and I wish it hadn't, I wish I would have just done nothing, left things alone. But I gathered my two colleagues together and I said, "This may seem like a half-brained, half-cooked, half-baked scheme to you guys, but listen to this. What if we call the bank and said to them, 'Listen, Sarah just got her dream offer, and we know she accepted your job, but how would you feel if she took the other offer, and you could hire Sophia?'" Well, it just so happens that the bank was just being nice to us about Sophia. He really didn't want to hire Sophia. He responded with a voicemail saying, "Well, if Sarah really wants her dream job, go ahead and do it." He didn't say anything about Sophia.

So Sarah did that. He didn't hire Sophia. He was angry. So what we thought was going to be a perfect situation, wasn't. Now Sarah ended up with her dream job, but the employer was a little bit angry. He hired a student from another school. So we knew we needed to do some damage control because I had screwed things up dearly. Fortunately, things worked out. We called the employer. We invited him in and we actually took him to lunch, and he said, "No, I'm not angry at all. I would not want anybody to work for me who really didn't want to be here. I really like Sarah as a person, and I'm glad she got her dream job, and that's fine, and the student I got from the other school is terrific, too, so it will work out and I expect to continue working with you guys and by the way, there were two positions, and the other position is one of your students so that's good." And he claims everything is fine and I think he's okay with it, but, did I screw things up? Absolutely. Will I ever to this again? Never again, and I told my two colleagues if I ever come up with something like this again, tell me to shut up and go back to my office. I violated one of the policies. I stepped in and I tried to make things better for everybody and it didn't work out.

PROFESSIONAL PERSPECTIVE #5
"NOT IN THE HEAT OF THE MOMENT"
Mary Kane, Northeastern University

I think I have changed in a couple of ways. I think as time has gone on I've learned that you definitely don't want to have a conversation with students at the moment that you're upset with them. Because I think you're not as calm, and your anger comes through and that's not really constructive. You can let people know you're disappointed—even angry with their actions, but you need to do it in a way where you're not in the heat of the moment. I think for the role, that's what's really important. So I have worked to make a more concerted effort to give students a chance to speak and then try to really have them walk through what they would do differently.

I think that what I try to do is to really get students to acknowledge what they could've done differently. In the end we can only change our actions and my approach is try to have students look at a situation with what they personally could have done to maybe have a different outcome. What would you have done differently and why should you have done that? I think that's a better approach. The point is to get students to take accountability for their actions and understand that different actions can result in different outcomes.

PROFESSIONAL PERSPECTIVE #6
"THE THOUSANDTH CUSTOMER IN REVERSE"
Kate McLaughlin, Northeastern University

This isn't a mistake so much as a simple part of life. I had a day when I was really frazzled, and I have a rule; if my door is shut and my shades are closed, I'm not available to meet with students. I have it written on my door. If the door is shut, Kate is not available. And that day not only had I had several hours of packed appointments and walk-ins, I had also had several students come by and knock on my door and want to talk to me. This frustrates me because they know the rule and yet they're banging on my door repeatedly because they can hear me in here. They don't just go away.

So I was stressed out and ready to snap at somebody. And a student came by—good student who has done great stuff with me—but he was probably the third or fourth person to bang on my door when it was closed. After this day, I was stressed out. And I opened the door and he started talking, and I snapped at him. He reacted very badly and stomped out of the office. I followed him and tried to apologize, and he just wouldn't talk to me. I felt terrible, but I also knew that this was not entirely my doing. His behavior was completely beyond my control.

So I sat down and I sent him an e-mail, first of all apologizing for snapping at him, but explaining that it had nothing to do with him. It had to do with all of these things that had been happening that day, and I was stressed out and I just needed some time to sit alone and get some work done. He was like the person that was the thousandth customer at the store who gets the balloons except in reverse.

That doesn't make it okay, but this is what being a human being is. We all have times like that. And he and I ended up talking, and it turns out he had been sick and he was feeling really crappy and so emotionally was just not in any way, shape, or form prepared to deal with his teacher snapping at him. It's something that's going to happen. I use that example in class all the time because it's like "Look guys: Whether it's me, your boss, your coworker or the person at the coffee shop, you need to remember that when people are interacting with you it's not just you that's informing the situation. All the other baggage that they've got going on—if they don't feel well, if they had a fight with their girlfriend or boyfriend last night, they couldn't sleep because their baby was up for three hours, whatever it might be—you can't assume that it's just about you or that it's even about you at all. And that giving people the benefit of a doubt will always make a situation easier to handle.

Don't assume that it's all about this person's mad at me or this person's evil as opposed to "Wow, something must be wrong because that's not normal for them." That's one of those things that I had to *learn* to share with my students, because there are things that have happened outside of work here that I've had no problem with sharing. But stuff like that was different. This was my screw-up, and this was with one of my students and I had come to the point where I could share it with them.

REFLECTION QUESTIONS

1. Think about a mistake that you have made as an educator. What led you to making that mistake? What did you learn from it, and how did it change you as an educator?

2. The chapter mentions several ways in which we run the risk of losing sight of education while doing our jobs:
   • Getting caught up in the urgency of placements
   • Being expedient instead of thorough
   • Forcing square pegs in round holes
   • Fixing mistakes instead of facilitating choices of others

   Which of these is the greatest sin for someone in our field? Which is your greatest weakness, and what are some action steps you can take to improve in that area?

3. Another theme in this chapter is avoiding conflict. Describe how you handle conflicts when they arise with students and employers. Can you think of a specific time when you did a particularly good job of this by dealing with conflict assertively and promptly as opposed to being too student-friendly or letting problems fester?

4. As indicated in this chapter, some styles and methods are more effective and appropriate than others when dealing with a variety of students. Describe how you adapt your style when dealing with different personalities, backgrounds, and maturity levels.

5. Typically, some professionals struggle with being too lenient with students, while others are so rigid and strict that they alienate students. What is your natural tendency? What do you do to try to ensure that you have high standards without being the kind of professional that students disrespect or find useless on the one hand or fear, dislike, and want to avoid on the other?

6. How do you handle the issue of not wearing your frustrations on your sleeve? Do you have a conscious strategy that you use when emotions might be getting the better of you?

CHAPTER 6

WORKING WITH TODAY'S STUDENTS

"What nobler employment, or more valuable
to the state, than that of the man who
instructs the rising generation?"
— *Marcus Tullius Cicero*

Before we start to consider how we can help young adults through the processes of preparation, activity, and reflection, it's important to have some perspective on who the students of today really are. From TV shows such as CBS' "60 Minutes" as well as numerous books and articles, you may have heard about the Millennial Generation. You also might have heard colleagues lamenting that times have changed when it comes to students, and—if you've been in the profession long enough—you may or may not have reached that conclusion on your own.

I asked many co-op and internship veterans whether they believe students have changed over the last 15 years or so. As you'll see in the transcribed interviews at the end of this chapter, opinions were mixed on that front. Regardless, I believe it's helpful for all professionals to have an understanding of the admittedly stereotypical view of what it means to be a member of the Millennial Generation.

My goal is not to vilify Millennial Generation students. As you'll see, all generational traits are double-edged swords. Each quality has the potential to surface in a positive or negative way in a given student... if it emerges at all. But being aware of these traits, how they came to be, and ways to minimize the negative impacts of a given characteristic have proven to be very helpful for many professionals. So we will take a careful look at all of that in this chapter.

Before beginning in earnest, I should acknowledge that my colleague Charlie Bognanni played a significant role in writing this chapter.

CHANGING TIMES AT NORTHEASTERN UNIVERSITY

The last decade or so has been an era of significant change for my institution, Northeastern University. We have undergone a conversion from quarters to semesters, and co-op coordinators have been relocated from a central location to the buildings that house their respective academic counterparts. We have continued our transition from what was primarily a commuter school to an institution that draws almost two-thirds of its students from out of state.

Most significantly, in an ongoing quest to become a *U.S. News and World Report* Top 100 university, our administrators have placed a great emphasis on attracting students with better high school grades and higher SAT scores. In 1995, the average combined SAT score for incoming freshman at Northeastern was 951. By the year 2000, it was 1128; in 2007, it was 1251.

In light of these developments, we were not surprised to see gradual but significant changes in the characteristics of the students we counseled in our roles on the cooperative education faculty. Working with undergraduate business students to prepare them for job experiences, we began to notice some developments that ranged from exciting to unsettling. University administrators were a bit giddy over our eyebrow-raising jumps in high school GPAs and SATs. Our former College of Business Administration (CBA) dean at the time predicted that these students were at a whole different level and effectively would "place themselves."

The reality has been much more complicated than he or any of us imagined. Indeed, we now have students who sometimes amaze us with their ambitiousness and self-confidence, their high goals and ability to reach them. Yet we also have seen some unpleasantly surprising trends:

- more students with highly unrealistic expectations for co-op

- an increased level of fickleness when it comes to jobs and job offers

- more high-maintenance parents—some of whom intervene inappropriately

- students who are more demanding of our time and responsiveness

Most interestingly, we have found that a large majority of these students don't "place themselves" by any means. In fact, they are generally more labor-intensive than their predecessors. They challenge us, and that has proved to be a mixed blessing. Our students today are fun, fascinating, interesting as well as sometimes frustrating and needy.

Yet our biggest mistake was to attribute these changes in our students primarily to our evolving priorities as an institution. Although we now may be attracting students who have greater academic potential, many of us came to believe that the changes that we're seeing have less to do with Northeastern and more to do with generational changes that are drawing increased attention in the media. In short, we often felt that our students reflected the transition in college-age students from representing Generation X to the so-called Millennial Generation. Looking to confirm this, I devised a survey for our CBA undergraduates to learn whether their values were consistent with this national trend... or whether students opting for a co-op program would diverge at all from this phenomenon. Before we get to that, though, let's consider the existing research on millennials.

DEFINING AND UNDERSTANDING THE MILLENNIAL GENERATION

Although the book is rather outdated at this point and is limited in its commentary on millenials as employees, *Millennials Rising: The Next Great Generation* by Neil Howe and William Strauss is a useful and entertaining book when it comes to understanding the forces behind generational changes.

The last Baby Boomers were born in 1964. Accordingly, only the most experienced co-op professionals worked with these individuals. In terms of admittedly sweeping generalizations, Baby Boomers have quite an array of characteristics: creative, ambitious, selfish, and judgmental are several mentioned by Howe and Strauss. Coming of age, boomers were more likely to be career-minded workaholics who demanded much of themselves and others. One source noted that boomers "practically invented the 60-hour work week."

With Baby Boomers as parents, Generation X reacted against many of these characteristics. With children devalued by parents who often were preoccupied with their careers, Gen Xers emerged as more skeptical and sarcastic. Where did all that hard work get their parents? These children saw their parents get divorced at a higher rate in the 1970s that at any other time in our history. These kids may have seen mom and/or dad work tons of overtime, only to get laid off during the recession in the early 1980s. As a result, the generation X mentality is more one of trusting yourself rather than organizations or authority figures. According to Howe and Strauss, they grew up "tough and self-reliant."

This trend changed dramatically in the 1980s. Following a decade which Howe and Strauss note was characterized by numerous "evil child" movies (i.e., *The Exorcist, Rosemary's Baby*), 1980s films—including *She's Having A Baby, Three Men and a Baby*, and *Look Who's Talking*—reflected a culture that had come to celebrate children. More people started valuing work-life balance. More families began questioning whether both spouses could be engaged in highly intense jobs without having a negative impact on their children. Individual achievement began to seem less important.

Companies started increasing products, services—and marketing—geared toward children. We began seeing "Baby on Board" signs and hearing about soccer moms, and kids started getting prizes for just participating in sports and activities as opposed to being the best at them. Increasingly, parents stopped leaving their children to fend for themselves or "go out and play" and began scheduling their weeks with ballet, music lessons, gymnastics, swimming, and any number of other activities.

Inevitably, this kind of upbringing has been producing a very different kind of person:

"You might expect this new group of kids to be a bunch of techno-brats—as wowed by the Internet as Boomers are, as obsessed with making dot-com fortunes as the Gen Xers are, and generally spoiled and self-centered from a lifetime of pampering by parents made rich in the roaring '90s. You would be wrong. The millennial teenager appears warm, confident, and upbeat, with little of the moral superiority that characterized the antiestablishment types of the 1960's" (Fortune, 2000). According to Howe and Strauss (2000) among others, millennials are team-oriented, optimistic, practical, and trusting of authority and traditional institutions (Rollin, 1999; Collins, 2000; Howe & Strauss, 2000).

Borrowing liberally from Howe and Strauss as well as numerous other authors on the topic, here are traits that we prefer to use in characterizing millennials:

- *High Expectations:* This term captures what various researchers hint at it when talking about today's college students being "pressured," "achieving," and "confident." Basically, today's generation has very high expectations because they have been told all along that they are special and capable of great things.

- *Preference for Structure:* In the research, you find references to today's college students being "sheltered," "scheduled," and "connected." Between parents planning out much of their activities and technology enabling them to connect readily in a variety of ways, this generation is largely accustomed to high degrees of structure and may be at a loss in situations which lack that structure. In fact, the healthcare industry has already begun looking at steps that healthcare employers will need to take to accommodate the preference for structure in this new generation of workers. Some of them include defining career ladders, establishing thorough orientation programs, and providing mentors to new employees.

- *Highly Technological:* The millennial-era student has grown up with computers, often learning basic computing skills as preschoolers. Today's college students' facility with technology often extends to a strong comfort level with software applications, communication with cellphones, e-mail, instant messaging, and Personal Digital Assistants (PDAs). iPods? On a "60 Minutes" segment on October 3, 2004, one millennial half-joked that they were now "required by law." Many researchers cite data indicating that millennials strongly prefer the computer to the television or telephone. Zemke et al. (2000) stated that "there aren't just three Rs anymore-as in, reading writing and 'rithmetic—there's a fourth: the Internet. And it's as natural as breathing for Generation Next (i.e., millennials)."

- *Highly Attached To Parents:* Other terms that one sees in reference to this characteristic include "special" and "sheltered." The term "helicopter parent" apparently was coined in the early 1990s; it first appeared in a *Newsweek* article on September 9, 1991. This refers to parents who hover over their children—sometimes to the point of offering unwanted assistance to educators. For better and worse, parents are much more engaged in the education of their children—including their adult children who are at college. One might argue that this has already created a closer affinity to family, in general, for these millennials. At Rumson-Fair Haven Regional High School, Stephen says "My only financial goal is to put my kids through college. I worry how much I'll have to make." Adam from Washington and Lee University says, "I would work at a boring job if I could come home to something satisfying" (Fortune 2000).

- *Team-oriented and multicultural:* The research all points to a generation that is more comfortable with "we" than with "I." According to Pickett (2004), Rocky Mountain College Vice President for Student Services Brad Nason points to the fact that today's college students started playing structured team sports as early as age 6. The 2004 movie *Meet The Fockers* has a scene in which a character has numerous ribbons on his bedroom wall. "I didn't know that they made ninth-place ribbons," another character states. This generation often was rewarded for simply participating in team events as opposed to excelling at them. Jane Buckingham, marketing consultant and head of Youth Intelligence in New York, says "Belonging to a group is so important that I caution anyone advertising to this generation against putting a lone individual in an ad" (*Fortune*, 2000).

With respect to competencies, research shows that millennials:

- Work collaboratively, gathering information quickly and sharing it readily (Howe & Strauss, 2000; Tapscott, 1998; Zemke et al., 2000)

- Respect diversity, value multiculturalism, and are resilient (Zemke et al., 2000)

- Converse comfortably and freely on an intellectual plane with adults, and have found that their expressed thoughts are valued much more highly online, where their age cannot be determined (Tapscott, 1998)

- Are brighter than previous generations, scoring 15 points higher in terms of raw intelligence than kids 50 years ago (Greenfield, 1998)

- Have superior written communication skills (Greenfield, 1998; Tapscott, 1998)

Howe and Strauss actually have written another book—the *Recruiting Millennials Handbook*—which teaches employers and military personnel how to capitalize on this new "we" focus in recruiting.

Additionally, this generation is unprecedented in their exposure to diversity. As a result, they often have a relatively high comfort level when confronted with individuals of different race, religion, and sexual orientation.

Interest in millennials has been increasing dramatically, both on campuses and in the media at large. We thought it would be interesting to devise a survey to assess just how "millennial" our business students at Northeastern really are.

SURVEYING BUSINESS STUDENTS

We surveyed students on the first day of our preparation course, "Professional Development For Co-op." This course is a mandatory, one-credit, pass/fail course for all Northeastern students as a prerequisite for co-op. Typically, the course focuses on self-assessment, resume writing, strategic interviewing, and on-the-job performance issues. Business students at NU are required to do co-op, and they typically took COPU101—now retitled CBA103—one semester before they started their first co-op experience.

The survey included 11 "millennial questions" as well as eight questions designed to assess their confidence level in the various subjects taught in the course as well as their expectations about the co-op job search. A total of 197 business students were surveyed. Our primary goal was to better understand who we were really teaching and how to instruct them most effectively. We believed that finding out how "millennial" they were would assist us in adjusting our teaching style accordingly to be most effective with the greatest number of students, recognizing that there will always be individual differences in any group.

With one major exception, we found that our co-op students generally did reflect this national trend of exhibiting values consistent with those ascribed to the Millennial Generation. Here are some highlights of our findings:

- A strong majority (83%) either strongly agreed or somewhat agreed with the notion that their mother or father is their "most important role model."

- There were a broad range of responses regarding students' expectations about their parents calling the school in the event of problems, but 17% of respondents strongly agreed with the statement "I expect my parents to contact the university if I need any support or assistance." Adding in those who somewhat agreed with that statement, we see that almost half of our respondents see this development as possible.

- As expected, students do have a high comfort level with computers and technology. However, we were surprised by the extent to which our students chose computers over TV. Eight-five percent favored the computer, while only 6% preferred TV.

- Reflecting high expectations, a very strong majority (81%) either somewhat agreed or strongly agreed that they should be able to get a great job in the area of their choice for their first co-op.

- Four out of five students either somewhat or strongly agreed with the notion that they have had significant exposure to diversity.

- One key exception that turned up: A solid majority of our respondents indicated that they didn't mind doing low-level work if necessary on the job. About 68% somewhat or strongly agreed with that statement, countering some research that indicates that millennials in the workplace are reluctant to "pay their dues" by doing low-level work.

  We believe that this disparity might reflect a difference in millennials who self-select a program in which full-time cooperative work experience is mandatory as opposed to those who opt against a program in which job experience will be required.

- Roughly 86% of our students somewhat or strongly agreed that they enjoy working in teams.

- About 75% of our students had favorable attitudes toward doing volunteer work or working for organizations that make the world a better place, which seems consistent with the "civic minded" trait of this generation, valuing collective success more than selfish motives.

- Perhaps most remarkably, 89% of our respondents STRONGLY agreed with the statement that "it's important for me to achieve great things in my career and in my life." Although one of our colleagues questioned who would disagree with such a positive statement, we remained struck by just how strong the response was. It might be interesting to refine this question to confirm the strength of this value.

On the whole, we were surprised by the extent to which our survey appeared to confirm the presence of millennial values in our student population.

THE DOUBLE-EDGED SWORD OF MILLENNIAL CHARACTERISTICS

As alluded to earlier, these Millennial Generation characteristics are a mixed blessing for educators who are working with co-ops and interns. Every single one of them has definite benefits and drawbacks. In addition to identifying those here, we offer our recommendations for dealing with millennials most effectively.

POSITIVES OF THE "HIGH EXPECTATIONS" CHARACTERISTIC

In responding to an aspiring fiction writer, author F. Scott Fitzgerald noted that a prospective reader wanted characters that were strong. "After all," Fitzgerald wrote, "you wouldn't be interested in a soldier who is just a little brave."

The same is true when considering the benefits of having high expectations. These students don't want to be just a little successful: They are often very ambitious and goal-oriented. We work with intelligent students who expect to succeed. It's challenging but fun to work with students who have big dreams... and who have the confidence, work ethic, and drive to realize those dreams.

I had one student a few years ago who e-mailed me during his first job search. Although he knew that the process was to see me to discuss the jobs that interested him, he e-mailed me to indicate that he had a really busy schedule that week. Acknowledging that I probably would not generally be willing to do business this way, he also created a spreadsheet ranking the jobs and including his rationale for each selection. I wrote back and told him that I would make an exception to my usual policy, given how much effort and thought he had put in to his way of approaching the problem at hand. This was one of the best examples of a student having high expectations and being willing to go the extra mile to make sure he was doing everything he could to accommodate all the demands on his time.

NEGATIVES OF THE "HIGH EXPECTATIONS" CHARACTERISTIC

While these students can be challenging and fun, they also challenge us because of their relative labor-intensiveness. Having grown up with highly engaged parents—and with technology that encourages immediate feedback 'round the clock—these students expect us to respond immediately and to be available beyond regular hours.

Additionally, some students who have high expectations don't necessarily have realistic expectations. DiGilio & Nelson (*Information Outlook*, 2004) also caution that many millennials seem to expect instant gratification for their efforts. In the absence of stimulation and rewards, job performance could very well suffer. Despite the fact that a given student may be a sophomore with no corporate work experience and average grades, that student may operate under the assumption that he or she should have, say, a position making important marketing decisions for an organization. Likewise, we have students who expect a challenging position with great pay but who are reluctant to look beyond jobs within reach of public transportation in downtown Boston. We spend a great deal of time trying to convince students to consider relocation or at least getting a car to open up options.

Students are more fickle now than they were here ten years ago. In the mid-1990s, Charlie Bognanni told me that a sophomore in accounting would be inclined to accept a job at Deloitte and Touche almost without even asking what the duties would be. These days, we have many students who want to decline their first offer—often a very good offer, as well—simply because "It's my first offer, and I really wanted to get some more offers before deciding."

We also see a degree of what we have termed "pressure paralysis." While some first-time co-op students are knocking on our door months in advance of their first co-op, several others struggle to make time to see us—despite numerous reminders in the prep class. Ironically, our sense is that some students feel that so much is at stake that they become paralyzed when it comes to taking steps toward actually obtaining a job. Similarly, they can become incredibly indecisive when it comes to choosing between multiple offers.

We also worry that having high expectations may lead to making questionable decisions ethically. If living up to their own expectations—not to mention those of their parents—is such a Herculean task, won't some students be tempted to cut corners to get ahead?

RECOMMENDATIONS REGARDING THE "HIGH EXPECTATIONS" CHARACTERISTIC

How can we capitalize on these positives while contending with the drawbacks? We have a few concrete suggestions:

• Push the expectation button: In teaching the preparation course—especially in light of the fact that such classes are sometimes taught as a pass/fail course which students expect to be fairly easy—we find it best to push and challenge students. Sometimes we referred back to the survey itself: "Almost everyone here said that it was important for them to accomplish great things in their career. So our goal is not to have an 'acceptable' resume—you need to know how to write a great resume, and we're going to make sure you know how to do that for the rest of your career."

Recognizing students in class—both for their achievements and, yes, even for just being there—is important; these students have been used to being "special" for most of their lives. I began to take an extra step of bringing a digital camera to class on the first day, taking photos of each student holding up their name card. The next step was to have students fill out 4 x 6 cards with information such as hometown, concentration, career goals, and hobbies. By the second class, I had just about memorized everyone's name and could reel off a few facts about each student. Although this was admittedly labor-intensive, it sent the message that the instructor knew his students and was going to push himself as much as he would push them.

• Use more advanced materials: In a similar way, we have found it wise to raise the bar when working with students. Instead of simply going over interviewing basics, for example, we developed new classroom assignments in which students would have to master relatively advanced concepts. One exercise required that students learn how to respond to a behavioral-based interview. They had to write three to five specific, true stories and then brainstorm to determine which soft skills (i.e., multitasking, customer-service skills) these stories could be used to prove. Stories that were not specific and vivid had to be revised and resubmitted until they did the job. Behavioral-based interviewing—something we never used to consider teaching to "beginners"—turned out to be the most popular aspect of that course.

In speaking to Nancy Johnston of Simon Fraser University, I was intrigued to learn that their curriculum kicked off with a strong emphasis on learning theory, including metacognition. Too cerebral for undergrads? For some, maybe. But I think it's consistent with my notion that millennials tend to respond well when you set a higher bar with expectations.

We also found it was critical to use advanced materials when teaching diversity in class. Students approached the topic with considerable confidence and expressed dissatisfaction in many sections about the handling of diversity: They believed they already knew it all. But one of our colleagues came up with a more advanced exercise that gently showed her class that they did NOT nearly know all that they could know on this topic, and her class rated that subject more highly in their course evaluations.

- Provide reality checks: As the last example indicates, many students today are not necessarily grounded in reality when it comes to perceptions and expectations. We need to be constructively critical when talking to them about their hopes and dreams as well as their abilities. We require all students to do a practice interview—even those who insist that they already know how to interview because they've had many jobs before. These interviews usually turn out to be humbling experiences—good ways to remind students that there is always more to know about any topic.

Likewise, we have provided reality checks to students when it comes to explaining why they aren't qualified to interview for some jobs. With a student who has been adamantly arguing why he deserves to be on the interview schedule of one of our very best employers, for example, we have been known to pull out a resume of a student who is on the schedule so they can see the disparity between their qualifications and those of the bona fide candidate. Additionally, we might pull out a previous employer evaluation to remind the student that they have some key workplace competencies that need improving before a highly desirable job can be pursued.

The key is to temper expectations without crushing them. In giving feedback, laying out steps that they can take in the short run to get to their "big goals" on a future co-op or after graduation can be very helpful.

POSITIVES OF THE "PREFERENCE FOR STRUCTURE" CHARACTERISTIC

On the positive side of the ledger, many millennial-era co-ops are very organized and good at dealing with a highly directive style of management. They are more trusting of authority and less likely to be rebellious. They like undergoing formal training and development, including practice interviews and skill-building courses such as our Professional Development for Co-op course. I think it's fair to say that Gen X students generally were more resistant when it came to such formalized requirements.

If you like using written materials to explain any aspect of your co-op process, these students generally will be receptive to them. Many of our students enjoy my *Find Your First Professional Job* textbook and use it faithfully in preparing for interviews. The book lays out a step-by-step approach for writing resumes as well as a careful dissection of all the most common interview questions and how to handle them. This meticulous breakdown seems to resonate well with this preference for structure.

NEGATIVES OF THE "PREFERENCE FOR STRUCTURE" CHARACTERISTIC

Of course, the majority of organizations do not provide formalized training for co-ops and interns. The figure-it-out-for-yourself nature of many jobs can be more overwhelming and stressful for many of today's students in comparison to their predecessors. After a lifetime of having adults frequently spell out and plan their activities step-by-step, the millennial student-employee sometimes can lack many valuable soft skills: creative thinking; initiative; and the ability to work independently and autonomously all can be lacking. In the world of work, Zemke, Raines, Filipczakk noted that millennials' liabilities include the need for supervision and structure, and inexperience, particularly with handling difficult people issues (p. 144, Literature Review: Factors Affecting the Development of Generation X and Millennials, Denham & Gladbow).

Obviously, these traits are more worrisome in some jobs, fields, and industries than in others. "Creative accounting" may be quite undesirable, for example. But almost any positions have moments that require "out of the box" thinking; millennials generally are more "stay between the lines" thinkers.

RECOMMENDATIONS REGARDING THE "PREFERENCE FOR STRUCTURE" CHARACTERISTIC

We recommend a balance between giving these individuals the structure that they crave while also fostering the ability to adapt to a lack of structure. For example, our co-op prep course is very clear in terms of course requirements and expectations as laid out in the syllabus, but we find that it's also vital to give students some assignments that require unstructured analysis.

One typical homework assignment gives students many specific examples of behavioral-based interviewing (BBI) questions and answers, showing them how a strong BBI answer has to be vivid, detailed, and grounded in a finite time span. Next, they have to come up with their own true stories and brainstorm to identify how they use their stories to prove that they have specific soft skills sought by the interviewer. Although this turned out to be very difficult for some of our sophomores, they ultimately rated this exercise as the most valuable in one of our sections.

One good rule of thumb is to clearly lay out all of the steps and processes involved in the co-op or internship job search. We have found that it's good to schedule a follow-up appointment before the student leaves the office and to summarize next steps as closure for each meeting. This seems to be more important to our students today than for those of yesteryear.

I also am quite transparent about the fact that I will provide quite a bit of hand-holding early in my relationship with these students, but that I am going to wean them off of that need as our relationship develops. In my course, they initially get all sorts of reminders in class and via e-mail, making sure that they know an assignment is due or that they need to come in for a resume critique. By the end of the semester, though, we gradually get to a point where students are expected to be on top of the syllabus and turn things in without any coaxing, cajoling, or threatening. If they have any uncertainties, it's up to them to take the initiative to get assistance.

Lastly, we use the counseling technique of "modeling" to personalize career path uncertainty or to bring to life problem-solving skills. Hearing our own true stories about the unexpected twists in our careers helps them understand that you can only structure your career to some extent: Ironically, you get them to think of change as part of the way of structuring their careers! Spending more time to reassure them that dealing with unstructured situations is a muscle that they need to grow seems to be resonating well so far.

POSITIVES OF THE "HIGHLY TECHNOLOGICAL" CHARACTERISTIC

In a workforce that is graying as Boomers approach retirement age, the workplace values technologically competent employees in a wide array of fields. Millennials' facility with the Internet and numerous software applications is a definite asset in many jobs, as is their ability

128

to master new technologies rapidly—especially given that technological change is a very common trait in the 21st century workplace.

If anything, today's students tend to underestimate just how valuable this facility is. Given that they have been on computers since their preschool years, they take their comfort level with technology for granted. I always try to remind my students that they are likely the most technologically competent generation in the history of the world, and that they will be working with many people who, like me, did not own a computer or use one regularly before reaching adulthood. Of course, the next generation of college students will be even stronger, but students need to be aware of this relative strength and be sure that they capture it on resumes and in interviews if possible.

NEGATIVES OF THE "HIGHLY TECHNOLOGICAL" CHARACTERISTIC

Over the last decade, we have found it necessary to spend much more time cautioning students about the abuse of technology in the workplace. It's not so much that the typical student is trying to "get away with" using Instant Message programs, personal e-mails, Personal Digital Assistants (PDAs), and cellphones at work. It's more that technology has become completely ingrained into their lifestyle. Used to answering their cell phones or using IM while doing their homework, it seems perfectly natural to them that they should keep doing so in the workplace. When you're "constantly connected," it can be a struggle to cut that connection. At a recent Red Sox game attended by my wife, a fan was overheard saying, "Oh shoot, I remembered my BlackBerry!" My wife wondered if she had heard him wrong at first, but then he proceeded to check his e-mail and make numerous phone calls for the next several innings, basically ignoring the game because he couldn't resist that device in his pocket. Obviously, the technology habit can be compellingly compulsive.

An additional issue is that the use of technology in the workplace can be a gray area for co-ops and interns. In some organizational environments, it may be okay to answer the occasional cell phone call, check personal e-mail, or surf the net at lunch or during downtime. In other places, the Internet is strictly off-limits at all times. Learning to figure out workplace norms regarding technology can be tricky.

RECOMMENDATIONS REGARDING THE "HIGHLY TECHNOLOGICAL" CHARACTERISTIC

Using mini-cases, anecdotes, and true horror stories written by our students, we find it useful to bring these dilemmas to life and to have dialogue about what might or might not be professionally acceptable in this area. One mini-case is written by a student who was fired from his job because he received a pornographic cartoon at his work account, and he simply forwarded it on to his school account. Students are sometimes shocked to hear that this sort of transgression could lead to termination. For that matter, some are stunned to learn that organizations have a perfectly legal right to "sniff" any e-mails in search of music files, pornography, or other material that is not work-related. Other stories cover how an impulsively written e-mail can be spread very quickly and basically have an eternal life in cyberspace. Hearing true stories and debating some gray-area scenarios seems to make the issue more real; it puts it on their radar screen.

Likewise, once a first-time co-op accepts a job, we find it helpful to discuss success factors and potential pitfalls for co-ops, focusing on the transition from the student role to the role in which being an employee is primary. As a student—and as a customer of the university—

certain behaviors are acceptable that no longer remain appropriate once the student becomes an employee, a service provider to an organization. Getting students to think of themselves as employees first can be useful here. Lastly, we make sure that students read and re-read the fourth chapter of *Find Your First Professional Job*, which reviews at length what's at stake when students work as co-ops and interns as well as many ways in which they can prevent problems from arising. I recently added about 15 pages on the use and abuse of technology to build awareness on this front.

POSITIVES OF THE "HIGHLY ATTACHED TO PARENTS" CHARACTERISTIC

Quite frequently, today's students come to us with a strong sense of self-confidence, borne of years in which parents' behaviors reminded them of how special they are. One of our Taiwanese students admitted that he was envious of his American peers because of their self-confidence. Growing up, he said that he always was told that he was not smart or capable, and he still has a hard time believing that he is really as good as his co-op coordinator thinks he is.

Our students have a strong support system in their parents, who are more inclined to do what it takes to ensure that they're successful. We hear many stories of students receiving exceptional emotional and financial support from their parents in their quests to live up to the big dreams that they share with their parents. These students are more trusting of adults and authority figures as well.

NEGATIVES OF THE "HIGHLY ATTACHED TO PARENTS" CHARACTERISTIC

This trait inevitably makes some of our students much more labor-intensive. Parents call co-op coordinators much more often than they did ten years ago, sometimes just wanting to understand but also wanting to intervene when a student has been struggling through a job search or in the job itself. We have even had some parents calls employers directly because of a problem at work. These "helicopter parents" aren't always helpful in resolving conflicts; in fact, they become another constituency that must be handled carefully.

Because students value their relationships with parents highly, we have to deal indirectly with "parent experts." A first-time co-op may say, "My dad really thinks I should have an Objective section on my resume..." or "My parents think it's ridiculous that I have to do an entry-level job..." Although some parents can be useful resources, sometimes we have to counter the misperceptions and fallacies that they may have about co-op and careers.

The fact that our students have been "sheltered" and consider themselves "special" can cut both ways as well. Recently we had a student working in a terrific job with one of our most attractive employers, and he blew it by being late on a regular basis. Even worse, this student already had issues in his previous co-op, where he admittedly wasn't a great match for the highly conservative environment but responded by surfing the Internet and showing no initiative. This student's mother was quick to defend his behavior and to attempt to pull strings when he was on thin ice, rather than helping us out by making it clear that his performance needed to be good regardless of whether everything was perfect in his job situation. Our sense was that the student is a nice enough guy but suffering from entitlement issues.

In one of our classes a few years ago, one of our students complained about a behavioral-based interviewer asking her to describe a specific time in which she had encountered and overcome adversity. "I'm 19 years old: I've never had to overcome adversity!" she said.

While it's true that a young adult may have had fewer opportunities to deal with adversity, we also believe that this is more common with the Millennial Generation. With parents who are highly involved—ready to step in and solve problems—and a society that is more likely to reward participation rather than critique it, our present-day students often have had fewer opportunities to contend with life's obstacles on their own. As a result, struggling with the aforementioned behavioral-based interviewing question is the least of their problems! How does such a student deal with making a big mistake at work brought to their attention? How do they know how to handle a difficult co-worker or a problem with too much or too little work? We can't assume that our students necessarily will have the initiative and creativity to be problem solvers, given that they may lack significant experience with that core competency.

RECOMMENDATIONS REGARDING THE "HIGHLY ATTACHED TO PARENTS" CHARACTERISTIC

For starters, we have to acknowledge that parental influence is important to many of our students and can be quite helpful. Yet at times we also need to remind students of the limits and biases of their parents' perspectives. This requires diplomacy. We may say something like "It's great that your parents are so interested in your career and that they want to help you out all they can. However, we also need to remember that your parents aren't the ones with the expertise that can only be derived from helping hundreds of students find the best possible co-op job or internship. I have been down this road many times, and I have a good sense of what jobs are really plausible for you in the marketplace."

It can be helpful to remind students that most workplaces are meritocracies: Those who work hard generally will be rewarded with more responsibility, better references, and a deeper set of skills. These things don't happen magically or unconditionally; they have to be earned: Employees don't get a trophy or a ribbon for just showing up at work.

Lastly, we find it useful to encourage our students to think of us as their supervisors rather than as their parents or professors. What does this mean? If they're going to be late or absent from a co-op class or appointment, we expect advance notice via e-mail or voice mail. We expect them to take the initiative in making sure they understand our expectations and are clear on all steps and processes, as opposed to structuring everything for them or holding their hand throughout a job search or a placement period. Basically, we do this to try to help them be more ready to display the autonomy and initiative that will become more important in the workplace.

POSITIVES OF THE "TEAM-ORIENTED" CHARACTERISTIC

For a long time, our College of Business Administration has required students to work in teams in the classroom—groups that are selected by the professor. The rationale is that employees have to work in groups in organizations, and they usually don't get to pick their co-workers. Today's team-oriented millennial students are much more comfortable with this practice than the wary Generation X students, who had more of a "you can only trust your-self" attitude. So this comfort and competency as team members is a real positive for millennials.

This generation's comfort level with diversity is also unprecedented in our nation's history. Our society has become more diverse, and diversity is discussed much more openly now, giving more visibility to and contact with individuals of different races, religions, and sexual orientations. As such, today's students seem to be readily accepting of the heterogeneous groups that typically comprise organizations.

NEGATIVES OF THE "TEAM-ORIENTED" CHARACTERISTIC

The flip side of being comfortable in teams is that many millennials have difficulty in terms of working independently and taking initiative as an individual. Likewise, even some of our excellent co-ops are surprisingly weak when it comes to self-awareness. In a society that increasingly rewards for participation rather than achievement, our students struggle to understand and articulate their own strengths and weaknesses in comparison to their peers.

Although our students are much more appreciative and accepting of diversity and teamwork, they also may be likely to overrate their understanding of how these issues affect workplaces. In short, they equate exposure to teams and diversity to mastery of the complex issues that may arise in organizations related to these topics.

RECOMMENDATIONS REGARDING THE "TEAM-ORIENTED" CHARACTERISTIC

First, we suggest using tools and techniques that will enhance self-awareness. Using inventories of skills and interests—whether customized or formalized in the form of the Myers-Briggs and Campbell-Strong inventories—can be helpful in understanding how they may differ from their peers. Likewise, classroom exercises in which we show students how to customize their interviewing strategy for a specific job description—contrasting the strategies of different students—can be helpful in building this muscle.

Students also need constructive "truth medicine." We have many students who are prone to either underrating or overrating themselves in the context of available jobs in their field. As amazing as it sounds, you may deal with, say, a sophomore in marketing with no corporate experience who legitimately believes that he or she should be able to get a job making crucial strategic marketing decisions for an organization!

We meet with students individually to make sure that they aren't either selling themselves short or setting themselves up for failure based on the jobs that they wish to pursue. If a student expresses interest in a job that is too advanced, we won't simply say "No;" we'll point out an entry-level or intermediate job that has proven to be a useful prerequisite for the more advanced job. This also helps students understand the individualized nature of career paths.

Finally, we need to recognize that these students are capable of handling relatively advanced concepts when it comes to diversity. One of our colleagues, Mary Kane, simply developed a more challenging diversity exercise that assumed good fundamental knowledge. It's a "Who would you hire?" activity that gives students descriptions of a demographically varied group of job candidates and asks them to determine who should be hired. Generally, subtle (or not so subtle) biases that the students have about age (especially) but also gender and other factors tend to arise, leading to a provocative discussion. This exercise implicitly acknowledged their strength but also showed them that there was still much more to learn.

FURTHER IMPLICATIONS FOR CO-OP AND INTERNSHIP PROFESSIONALS

We believe that our research and experiences indicate that there is a great realm of possibility

132

for co-op and internship professionals who are concerned with maximizing effectiveness with a student population that is ever-changing in its composition. Therefore, we suggest consideration of the following factors as we move forward in understanding of generational differences in our student-employees.

NEED FOR ADDITIONAL RESEARCH ON CO-OP/INTERN POPULATIONS

We would like to see our colleagues at other institutions perform additional research to see how widespread the millennial phenomenon really is. We would be interested in seeing how prevalent millennial attitudes are among co-ops and interns nationally and internationally, given that the existing generational research that we have seen apparently does not pertain to individuals outside the United States. It would be interesting to learn more about whether these trends are true in Canada, given the size and scope of many excellent co-op and internship programs north of the border.

NEED TO MONITOR CHANGING VALUES OF STUDENTS CONTINUALLY

The shifts that we have experienced at Northeastern remind us that we must be vigilant in assessing our changing student populations on an ongoing basis. Through continual surveys and ongoing dialogue with our colleagues here and elsewhere, we can understand whether generational differences are more or less prevalent in various majors or at different institutions.

In terms of monitoring the latest research and publications on the Millennial Generation, we would recommend the following website:

http://lifecourse.com/news/articles.html

This site is affiliated with Howe and Strauss and offers a frequently updated archive of articles on this topic.

PREDICTIONS FOR "MINI-MILLENNIALS"

There is already some research available as well as some prognostication on "mini-millennials"—children born since the year 2000 and who won't even be coming our way until approximately 2018! According to Howe (2000), a new generation comes along about every 22 years. Parker (2005) notes that some of the millennial characteristics already appear to be shifting in intriguing if unsettling ways. For example, the aftermath of 9/11 has increased concern regarding the safety of children. In response, the Japanese city of Osaka and a school in Denmark are using microchips planted in children's clothes or school bags in order to track students' location at all times. Obviously, this is the intersection of our increasingly technological culture as well as the growing desire for parents to structure and control their children's lives.

We predict that efforts such as these ultimately could lead to a backlash, and another generational shift should ensue. Fed up with overly controlling parents, governments, and technologies, the next generation may shift away from being more civic-minded and more adaptive—at least this would be consistent with what Howe and Strauss postulate when they discuss how generations run in cycles. If this does hold true, we would expect that the next generation would be characterized by cautiousness, a "compromising and accommodating" spirit, and a sense of work as a duty. It will be interesting to see how this plays out.

NEED TO CONTINUALLY ADJUST TEACHING TOOLS AND COUNSELING STYLE

Above all, we believe that co-op and internship professionals must not be wedded to using the same teaching tools and counseling style over long periods of time. Our students will continue to change; we also must continue to change our methods appropriately to make sure our students are getting what they need. Ten years ago, we had no co-op prep course, no co-op textbook, and we did relatively little with students to make sure that they understood professional behavior in the workplace.

To survive and succeed, we have made dramatic changes in all of these areas. All Northeastern students now must take the aforementioned co-op prep course before going on co-op for the first time. Efficiently run in groups of 20 to 40 students, these students cover the fundamentals of co-op preparation, including resume-writing, strategic interviewing, and on-the-job performance. We bring in panels of upperclassmen and employers to tell their stories, ease the anxiety over transitioning into the workplace, and model appropriate behaviors for co-ops and interns. Likewise, my co-op textbook has been through about seven or eight iterations over as many years, always attempting to adjust to the ever-changing needs of our students and employers. The chapter that has grown and changed the most has been the on-the-job behavior chapter, as new technologies and complexities have needed to be reflected there.

WORKING WITH GENERATION X STUDENTS

Although most educators will be working with millennials much more than any other generational group, there are definitely many institutions—especially community colleges—that may work with a substantial population of older students. As a result, I think it might be helpful to discuss Generation X students in particular. Understanding this generation is also useful because there are many Gen X managers who are supervising our millennial employees.

GEN X BASICS

Depending on which expert you consult, the cutoff for Gen X in terms of birth year is anywhere from 1961 to 1965 through 1981. So for our purposes here, we're talking about individuals who are close to 30 on the younger end and as old as 44-48 on the older end.

Consider the trends in society when Generation X was growing up:

- More women in the workforce

  These kids often had baby-boomer parents, who often were very focused on careers. With both parents working, we saw the phenomenon of "latch-key kids" for the first time in U.S. history—especially as day care and child care were not as well established as they are now. So kids were left to fend for themselves much more than in the past.

- Significant increase in television viewing

  Somewhat connected to that first point, children began entertaining themselves with television much more. They were the first Sesame Street generation. TV viewing may have turned out to be a substitute for interpersonal relationships in some cases.

- Increase in divorce

  The divorce rate literally doubled in the 1970s. Baby boomers often had different notions about the importance of fidelity, chastity, and commitment in comparison to their predecessors. In general, people became less inclined to stick it out through a bad marriage, partly because women earning a paycheck had more attractive options if the marriage were to fail.

- Difficult economic times, including layoffs

  Children growing up in the 1970s saw some difficult times in North America. High oil prices combined with the high cost of the Vietnam War led to problems in 1973-1975, while another energy crisis and U.S. efforts to control inflation in 1979 led to another recession in 1980-82. The upshot was that Gen X saw their parents sacrificing a great deal for their careers, only to suffer economic difficulties or even lose jobs.

- Post-Watergate and Vietnam, more of a skeptical, cynical perception of authority and apathy toward politics

  This was a great time of disillusionment with authority. The Watergate scandal and Vietnam taught many people that people in charge cannot necessarily be trusted and led people to become more concerned about self-interest. This was also reflected in a sharp decline in church attendance.

Gen X Traits

With the aforementioned developmental influences in mind, there are some stereotypical traits for the Gen X individual—whether we're talking about tendencies of Gen X students or employees. As with our consideration of millennials, all of these traits have the potential to be double-edged swords. With some individuals, the trait might manifest in a purely positive sense, while each one has the potential to be a problem as well.

- "If you want something done right, you've got to do it yourself."

  I like to think of this as the Gen X credo. Given that Xers tend to distrust authority and have been left to their own devices while growing up in some cases, they tend to be relatively self-reliant.

- Skeptical/wary/cynical tendencies

  As you might have inferred from that credo, Xers may have a tendency to be more skeptical, wary, and cynical as opposed to the more trusting, open nature of millennials. This may sound like a more negative quality, but any work team can benefit from someone who has a more critical eye as opposed to being someone who blindly accepts the status quo.

- Values flexibility and freedom, dislikes rigid requirements; likes being "turned loose" to handle work assignments

  Given that the self-reliant, independent Gen X individual is quite comfortable in figuring things out for himself, he often will prefer that at work. Obviously, this could be a real benefit when autonomy and creativity are valued, but it might be a problem in jobs that involve more rules, requirements, and a stricter reporting structure.

- Pragmatic, creative, self-starters

  Just as "thinking out of the box" is often a lamentably poor quality with millennials, that's a strength for many Gen X personalities. They require less hand-holding and training, and they are happier about being kicked into the pool to learn how to swim. Millennials are often disappointed to learn that most employers don't have formal training programs; Gen X employees like it that way!

- More loyal to their career than to a company

  After seeing their parents get kicked to the curb during bad economies, Gen X employees are wary of devoting their heart and soul to an organization. Again, they believe that they need to look out for themselves because no one else may have their best interests at heart. Older employees—boomers and their predecessors—may be frustrated by this tendency and view the Gen X individual as more of a mercenary.

THE GEN X/MILLENNIAL RELATIONSHIP

As you can imagine, the combination of a Gen X manager—or educator—with the millennial employee/student certainly has the potential to be a difficult fit. If we end up with classic examples of each generational type, we may end up with both parties feeling quite frustrated. Consider the possibilities:

- Manager/educator values self-sufficiency and is frustrated by having to spoon-feed instructions, while employee/student feels lost and alienated because of the lack of training/mentoring

- Manager/educator values working independently and autonomously with a more cynical perception of the organization, while employee/student enjoys being a team player who believes in the organization

- Employee/student is very positive and has high but not necessarily realistic expectations, which is bound to irritate the more pragmatic and skeptical manager/educator

Understanding these potential problems and making sure that all parties are aware of generational differences definitely can help minimize frustration in favor of relationships in which everyone is striving to make sure that the other individual is getting what they need.

FINAL THOUGHTS

Although Charlie and I have been working as co-op educators for more than 30 years between us, we believe that we need to continually gauge our approach with students and make adjustments based on their changing needs. Sometimes we may need to overhaul our practices to contend with the evolving nature of our co-op students and interns. If we take the time to learn more about our students' learning styles, values, and attributes—whether further research proves them to be truly "millennial" or otherwise—we will do a better job of providing students with the most effective education possible. In turn, employers need to invest the same level of time learning about these new employees. Organizations need to keep close tabs on young employees as they determine how to best hire, train, and retain professionals.

As a bonus, the process of continually tinkering with and adjusting our approach will keep our own jobs fresh and interesting over the changing years.

IN THEIR OWN WORDS

PROFESSIONAL PERSPECTIVE #1
"THIS GENERATION LOVES TIMETABLES"
Charlie Bognanni, Northeastern University

My style has changed a little bit as the generations have changed. I have found that you absolutely cannot talk down to students; you have to treat them like adults. Now, they're not all adults, and sometimes their behavior won't be manifested as adults. They may still act like children, but they want to be treated as adults. I think you gain their respect and I think you develop a better relationship with them if you treat them as adults and don't speak down to them—don't be didactic; don't preach to them. It typically doesn't work.

I've found that when I meet with students one of the things I say to them is, "Okay, we're going to work together on this. Our goals should be similar. Your goal is to find the best job and my goal is to help you find the best job. So we have similar goals. The plan here is to work together to help you find a terrific coop or internship." I think students appreciate being treated that way, not being told "this is what you have to do; you absolutely need to do this or you're going to be unsuccessful."

So I think that my philosophy is to treat them as adults, treat them with respect. I think most students will respond in a favorable way. I've also found that this is a generation that although they don't want to be preached to, they like to have a strategy. They like to know what's going to happen, so my first meetings with them, both in the classroom and one-on-one, are devoted to what's going to happen this semester. I even tell them to write it down. I give them a timetable, and I'm very clear on it. I say, "Okay, if we do this together and you do everything you're supposed to do, this is going to work out fine." I tell them their resumes are due on this particular day, so for the first couple of weeks of the semester we're going to work on your resume, then interview, then we're going to do some practice interviewing, and that's going to happen between this date and this date. Then interviews are going to start, say, on October 15.

As I'm saying this to students, I always put a positive spin on this whole thing. I tell them this is going to be a fun experience for them because I don't want them thinking they're going into a three-month root canal process and the root canal is going to be on October 1 and the crown is on December 1. This isn't going to be painful. This should be fun if we do it right; you should have a good time doing this. I'm not going to deny that there's going to be some stressful moments, and I tell them that I say there's going to be a period when we hit the middle—and again I'm using the fall semester as an example—when we hit about the middle of October where you're going to be having maybe two or three interviews in one week. You're going to be experiencing midterms; you're going to have a lot of backed-up work at school, and you're going to go crazy. You're going to be very, very busy. But if we do everything right we can get through that period.

So I give them a timetable; I tell them exactly what's going to happen. I say, "If we do this right, ideally, you might have a job by November 1 or maybe November 15 or 30. If it happens on November 1, great. If it happens on December 1, great, if it happens on January 1, that's fine too. The ultimate goal is to help you to get a good job, and every student is different. I say, "Don't believe there is a correlation between good students getting good jobs first and bad students getting bad jobs later because it's not true. Do some of the good students get good jobs first? Absolutely. Do some of the poor students wait till the end? Sure. But I've had excellent students get jobs on December 23 and I've had marginal students get jobs on November 1. So if you don't get a job right away, don't feel badly, don't feel like, "Uh-oh, my roommate got a job, my best friend got a job, my girlfriend got a job, but I don't have one. I must be one of those marginal students."

That's taken me a number of years to get to that point because I think I was much more ad hoc for a while. It's come to the point where I feel like this generation loves timetables. They love to be told "Be here on this day; this is what you're going to do." You know about the whole millennium generation deal, about how their whole lives have been programmed, and I think that you absolutely see it with them when they're 19 years old. They all come in with calendars. Fifteen years ago you tell them be here on October 3, and they'd pull out a piece of paper, a little sticky pad. Now they pull out their calendar, they've got their BlackBerry, they got their cell phone. It's all programmed in.

PROFESSIONAL PERSPECTIVE #2
"ADAPTING WITH TECHNOLOGY"
Anita Todd, University of Cincinnati

[In terms of whether I have adapted my style to work with Millennial Generation students], I'll be perfectly honest, and the answer is no. I will agree that students are more demanding than they used to be. They come in with more specifics about what they want to do. But I don't have a problem with it. I'm glad that they have some direction, that they've done some homework and have some ideas about what they want to do. I find that they are not narrow-minded and are open to other opportunities when they are educated.

I tell my students that "My job is to get you placed, but your job is to get yourself placed." I wonder if it is may be just my way of engaging with the students and the expectations I put on them. I really haven't seen "millennial" issues. UC is a Midwestern city university. We have a very blue-collar student workforce with a good Midwestern work ethic. So maybe it's the type of students we attract or that are attracted to electrical engineering (my student base) or maybe that I'm working more with men than women so I'm only seeing part of the population. I don't know.

I know that today's generation is much more "I want the information now and I want you to be accessible." I use a lot of the technology because that's just me. So my style fits the students. I am always on e-mail. Students know that if they send me an e-mail at 6 o'clock at night, chances are that some time in that evening I will respond. If not, it will be first thing in the morning. I use IM, I am on Facebook. My biggest problem is students are so text based that they send very long questions and want an e-mail response. My response is "Call me or come and see me. This is too long; I can't send a response to this."

PROFESSIONAL PERSPECTIVE #3
"THE SAME BUT DIFFERENT"
Ronnie Porter, Northeastern University

I think the basics are still the same. The method of communication is different. The use of e-mail and cell phones has made communicating with students easier, more timely and more efficient. Access to the Internet provides us with information that is extremely helpful when doing employer development work.

I find that students need a lot more communication than they did in the past, a lot of reminders. We used to send out periodic memos to everybody. Now, information needs to be posted all the time so that students have something to go back to. Sometimes I think they are doing things so quickly and maybe multitasking, so they don't really read, in-depth, the first message that is sent or do not read the entire message. So, therefore we might have to repeat sending communication a few times, but I think the basics are still very similar.

I have always been pretty involved with my students in providing them with information up front in some form—whether it used to be books in the office or whatever. Now, I am thrilled about the new technology and the fact that I can just send out a blanket e-mail to everyone and not have to write out a stack of postcards like I used to do in the old days. Students today seem more particular about the kinds of experiences that they are interested in. I think it's a good thing for them to have information about exactly what they are going to be doing and how this fits in with their career goals.

I think that their expectations maybe are a little higher. I find that they come with much less work experience, so I do have to spend a lot more time on topics relating to some of the "soft skills" that employers are looking for in employees. We discuss etiquette, in terms of communication with employers, follow-up, being reliable, and responsible etc. In my freshman Introduction to College class, I usually ask, "How many people are working part time?" This past year there was one student out of a class of 20 who had a part time job. Whereas 20 years ago there would have been a lot more.

Current students are coming to us with other kinds of skills. Maybe they've done community service or have traveled a little bit more. It's the same, but different. The basic elements of working with students are very similar.

PROFESSIONAL PERSPECTIVE #4
"THEY'RE NOT GOING TO CHANGE"
Bernadette Friedrich, Michigan State University

From an overall perspective, I would say that working with today's students is not vastly different. There are some subtle differences in the way that students interact with us. By that I mean that they may ask for our advice and then also seek it from their parents. In the past, the parents were not a component. I do believe that working with their parents is vastly different than it was ten years ago.

A long time ago, I had one experience when a student was out on his first co-op work assignment. It was probably the end of his freshman year. And his brother who was an engineer called and said, "I don't think it's a good job for my brother, this is why I don't think it's a good job, and I think you should find him another job."

I said, "Look, this is your brother's decision, and it's really his business." And I said, "If your brother's concerned about the position, he should talk to me." Ultimately, the student came in and said, "I love this job; my brother's just being overbearing."

So fine, great, but we get that more and more with parents who really want to know what their students are going to make, what we're doing to help them, and why can't their student get this offer instead of that one. They know his friend got a job at such-and-such. I do think it's different working with parents, and we try to incorporate that into seminars. One thing we bring up is: "Ultimately, this is your decision. You need to seek advice from as many people as are available, but ultimately it's your decision."

I had a student who said, "Would you please call my dad? He's afraid that I'm taking a semester off and I'm never going to go back to school." I'm more than willing to do that. I don't want to make it a career, but the parents are so involved .

I don't think the students are really all that different. It has always been my philosophy to not hold students' hands. There are two schools of thought in the environment I work in. One is definitely a Student Affairs school of thought (nurturing, guiding, assisting), and the other is mine [laughs]—that I really have a job to do. I love students; I love interacting with them. I'll help them out in any way I can, but I'm not going to hold your hand to do it.

I'll tell you a little story about this. I had a student who graduated in the mid to late-1990s—very bright kid who ended up going for a Master's degree at Stanford. Brilliant student—you'd want him on the front of your brochure. He's now working for Hewlett-Packard. He came in to see me a few weeks ago and said, "Oh, I was just on campus so I thought I'd let you know how much you guys helped me." Of course, you love to hear that, but then he said, "I have an interesting story to tell you."

He said, "In the group I work in at H-P, there's a whole bunch of baby boomers—45 and above. They know their ways, and they've been working at H-P forever, and they have a certain mentality. And then there's probably about three or four of us who are in a middle generation—not quite 30 but in that range." And he said, "And now they're hiring a whole bunch of new people, and we have mentors to groups of new hires. The baby boomers are always telling me that I have to interact with the new kids, the millennials, because I can communicate with them better.

"And in meetings, the boomers will say 'Why do they do things this way? Why can't they do this? Why are they service-oriented? Why do they come in and leave?'" He said, "They just complain all the time. And I finally just turned to them and said, 'Look, these are *your* kids! They're your kids. This is not my fault. You created this generation. You need to figure out what happened, and you also need to realize that they're not going to change for you. You need to understand where they are and take it from there. They're not going to change to be more like you.'"

REFLECTION QUESTIONS

1. To what degree do your students seem to fit the characteristics of "millennial" or "Gen X" as described in this chapter?

2. Have you made efforts to change your approach with students based on their generational differences? What have you specifically done to work with your students in a way that will complement their generational tendencies while minimizing the potential pitfalls that those traits also may cause?

3. One key trait of millennials is their high expectations. What have you done to maximize the positives of that trait while also helping students to be more realistic in their expectations? Is there more that you could be doing?

4. Millennials tend to love technology. How do you use technology in teaching and communicating with millennials? To what degree do you insist on face-to-face interaction for certain activities?

5. Reflect on some complaints that your employers have had about your students. In retrospect, can you think of specific examples in which generational differences were a source of friction? What can be done to foster more understanding between managers and employees of different generations?

CHAPTER 7

COUNSELING STUDENTS ONE-ON-ONE

"One cool judgment is worth a thousand hasty counsels. The thing to do is to supply light and not heat."

— *Woodrow Wilson*

Now that we have a generational perspective on working with today's students, let's tighten on our focus on how to counsel students on a one-on-one basis through the preparation process.

Co-op and internship programs vary dramatically when it comes to how professionals work with their students. I have heard of individuals who are responsible for advising as few as a dozen or so job seekers or as many as 300 plus students. Inevitably, such dramatic differences in workload will have an enormous impact on what you attempt to do in groups versus on a one-on-one basis. Workload is also a huge factor in how deep or superficial your relationships turn out to be with students. When I had to help 155 students find six-month jobs starting in January 2000, I couldn't afford to linger too long on the relationship-building process with students; it was more like an assembly line, and education definitely suffered as a result.

Regardless, every professional needs to be able to counsel students on an individual basis. This chapter focuses on the keys to doing so as effectively as possible, and these principles are derived from my own experience as well as that of my many interviewees. I'll begin with some general philosophical principles before moving toward more specific guidelines.

GETTING STUDENTS TO OWN RESPONSIBILITY

Some students may approach the co-op or internship process with an unfortunate preconceived notion about how it's going to work. At the very worst, there will be students who will look at your role as a placement professional. Such a student will believe that their role is passive and that you are there to find a job for them. Actually, that does indeed happen in some programs, for better or worse. Still, some of my colleagues have been justifiably upset when a student treats them more like a travel agent than an educator.

The implicit assumption is that you work for the student. To some degree, of course, this is true. As mentioned earlier in the book, we do need to have a customer-service mentality with students. However, this doesn't mean that the student's role is to tell you what to do, nor is it your role to write a student's resume for them, convince an employer to hire them, and advocate for that student regardless of their behavior.

The ultimate goal is for each student to learn as much as possible through the experience of being a co-op or intern. In the mind of the student, that often means getting a challenging and enjoyable job and learning a great deal about the field of their choice through the direct work experience. However, there are many other crucial learning opportunities that may be less obvious to students:

- Learning how to write a resume, interview for a job, and deal with the ups and downs of a job search, so, once trained, they will know how to handle these steps for the rest of their careers

- Learning keys to professional behavior that are not directly related to their function or major, such as how to deal with a manager and co-workers, how to manage time, how to communicate verbally and in writing, how to handle conflicts, how to earn the opportunity to obtain more and better work, and so forth

- Whether the job itself turns out to be a perfect fit or a bitter disappointment, the student should learn a great deal about themselves, figuring out whether a given career path, industry, major, work environment, or managerial style is a good fit for them

All of that said, I tell my students all the time that success is not magic. When a first-time student hears an upperclassmen student panel talk about their two or three six-month co-op experiences, the rookies are often a little dazzled by these veterans. They can't fathom that they, too, could end up working in great, high-paying jobs by the time they graduate. I have to emphasize that this never happens automatically; it's an incremental, evolutionary process.

However, that process starts with getting students to realize that positive outcomes are not guaranteed. If they have high expectations for themselves—as many Millennial Generation students do—they are going to need to show a great deal of initiative and hard work to make it happen. I tell them that I may be an expert, but my role is to give them advice and assistance. It's a bit like being the coach of an Olympic athlete. I can lay out a training regimen and a game plan, and I can provide a great deal of constructive criticism tailored to the strengths and weaknesses of each individual, but I can't do the event for them.

I am quick to tell students that I *recommend* that they come and see me every week or two during the heat of the job referral process… but I will not *require* them to do so. My attitude is that I'm going to put the vast majority of my time and energy into those who really want it rather than attempting to coax students to do what they have been told again and again that they really should do.

Yet while I *tell* students that their success is all up to them, to some degree I try to *act* as if their success is all up to me. When dealing with students who seem to be paralyzed when it comes to making things happen for themselves in the preparation process, I often will be quite assertive in trying to understand what's going on and what to do about it. Every student is different, and I often wrestle with exactly when and how to address a lackluster approach to the job search process.

Regardless, the goal is to get students to take the ball and run with it. Here are some ideas on how to encourage students to own responsibility through the preparation phase:

- If a student turns in a resume that has little to do with whatever book, handout, or model that you've provided, **don't fix their work for them**. Send them back to the drawing board to take a better stab at doing it right before you provide any specific feedback.

- Make students aware that **they must take the initiative to contact you in advance** if they need to miss an appointment, meeting, class, workshop, or deadline. You shouldn't have to track people down when this type of thing occurs, and failing to communicate about it won't be tolerated in the professional world.

- Provide **guidance but not a definitive mandate** when students face tough judgment calls. I won't tell students that they absolutely must have a more expansive or concise resume. I will help them talk through a few job offers, and I will speak up assertively if I feel that their perception about an offer is inaccurate in some way. In the end, though, the student needs to own such decisions. The student is the one who has to live with the job for several months, and I want to make sure that it's their decision, not mine.

- As Kerry Mahoney from the University of Waterloo told me in her interview (excerpted at the end of this chapter), one intriguing idea is to **never write anything on a student's resume**. Critique the resume, yes, but make the student mark up the resume before going off to make the corrections. That puts the ownership of the process in the student's hands… and also should solve my perennial problem with having students interpret my horrific handwriting!

THE STUDENT WHISPERER

Okay, here is a more unconventional philosophy for your consideration. A few years ago, one of my all-time favorite alums returned to campus to catch up. She asked about how my style of working with students has evolved, and I gave her a detailed example. It involved a student who had frustrated me considerably.

One tradition in my co-op preparation class takes place around the midway point. After reflecting on the weakest performers in the class to date, I often have a conversation with them in my office. Last spring, I had a student who consistently did silly things. He would do the homework but forget to bring it to class, repeatedly. There were various other brain cramps as well. So I gave him this feedback, being sure to use a gentle, teaching tone to counterbalance the tough criticism: "Granted that I don't know you very well, but if someone asked me to characterize you thus far, I would have to say 'Steve is a really nice guy who just can't seem to get his act together.'"

Because of the tone, this opened up a conversation instead of ending it by scolding him. Steve said he thought my comment was fair, but that this was just a one-credit class and therefore not his top priority. "Fair enough," I said. "Sure, it's a one-credit class, and in the grand scheme of things it's really not going to matter whether you get a B+ or a C+. But my real concern is, when you go out there on co-op in a few months, do you want to be known as the guy who drops the ball when it comes to details? Do you want your manager and co-workers to think of you as a likeable guy who's a bit of a space cadet when it comes to getting the little things done?" That got him thinking and seemed to have an impact.

Hearing the story, my alum had a sudden epiphany. "Wow, you're using a 'calm-assertive' style!" she said. "That's just like the Dog Whisperer!"

I had no idea what she was talking about. It turns out that there is a guy on TV named Cesar Millan who has a show on the National Geographic channel called *The Dog Whisperer*. He also has written some related books, starting with *Cesar's Way*. He is an expert on correcting bad dog behavior and—more often than not—doing so by correcting the behavior of their owners, who are almost always the real problem.

Granted, working with students is quite different than working with dog owners and their pets. But after watching the show several times with my family, I'd have to conclude that there are some themes that definitely resonate with counseling students:

1. Use a calm-assertive leadership style. One of Millan's frequent recurring themes is that energy is contagious. If your tone and body language project frustration, anger, fear, or inconsistency, it definitely is an indicator that you are not in control of the situation.

   Your behavior is also a model for your students. Just as a parent who hits a child is teaching their child that physical force is an appropriate response when one is frustrated, disappointed, or angry, a professional who yells or snaps at students is teaching them that is what a professional should do under such circumstances. Conversely, a professional who is direct and honest but who remains calm, assertive, solution-oriented—*especially when faced with someone who is visibly upset or angry*—is providing a good model for their students.

   As stated in Chapter 5, this is easier said than done. I have snapped at students many times and become downright infuriated on occasion. However, I find it to be unbelievably effective and powerful to be very careful to keep my voice calm and neutral, stick strictly to the facts, and to confront disappointing situations by seeking clarity and then trying to move to a solution and closure.

   It's amazing how fast energy can be contagious, positively or negatively. A few months ago, I got very frustrated with an employer on the phone. They had listed a job very late in the process and then gone back and forth about hiring until it was too late to matter. When the job finally got pulled, I know that my subsequent voice mail to my Human Resources contact betrayed my irritation with the company. She actually commented on it when she called me back, and I was annoyed at myself for letting that tone creep into my voice on the phone. It served no purpose, except perhaps to make that person less likely to want to talk to me in the future. So sometimes you really have to bite your tongue or temporarily avoid a conversation until you're ready to be calm and solution-oriented.

2. Maintain a balance of discipline and affection. When it comes to dogs, Cesar Millan talks

about how they need a balance of exercise, discipline, and affection. That's largely true for people as well; we all need balance in our lives. I may have little ability to control whether students are getting exercise, but I think the balance of discipline and affection is very relevant in our field.

Two very common errors in our field are either giving students too much discipline or too much affection. Some professionals are very tough. They are inflexible with students, equating rigidity with having high standards. If this style is used exclusively, the student may perceive the preparation process as a rules-driven 50-mile death march. Professionals using that style run the risk of being perceived as aloof, uncaring, arrogant, and out of touch with their students, who feel that they are forced to jump through hoops because "rules are rules."

On the other extreme, there are those professionals who like to "love bomb" their students. They want so badly for students to like them that they ignore or rationalize bad behavior that should be nipped in the bud. They are so eager to help their students that they often do the students' work for them, fixing mistakes for them instead of empowering the student to take care of business on their own. Overly affectionate coordinators are similar to parents who have an "enabling" style with their children, in which just about anything goes.

Ironically, an overly affectionate style will not make all students like you more. Yes, students do want to work with professionals who genuinely care about them and have their best interests at heart. But students often don't respect professionals who give them nothing but affection. They generally know that they don't walk on water, and they almost always welcome feedback—even if it is strongly worded and pretty thorough when it comes to enumerating negatives—as long as it is presented in a calm style that invites further dialogue instead of abruptly terminating it. That's the tone of a teacher instead of a bureaucrat or mean-spirited boss.

Here is a quick example. Let's say that a student comes in with a resume thrown together with a Microsoft Word template. When you tell him that the resume needs a lot of work, he responds with a rather hostile tone: "Look, I'm happy with the resume the way it is. I don't know why you're trying to force me to follow that stupid example that you gave me. I want it to be like this."

Here are three possible responses:

Discipline-oriented response: "I don't care what you want. We have a format that all students must follow, and there are no exceptions. If you don't like it, you can find your own job. You need to grow up and decide whether you can handle the requirements of this program."

Affection-oriented response: "Hey, there's no need to be upset. I can help you make your resume better. Here, let me show you how I would rewrite that first bullet. And if you don't like what I've done, it's okay for you to have it just the way you want it."

Calm-assertive response: "I'm surprised that you seem to be upset. Look, I can help you find a really good job, but frankly your tone worries me. If your boss on co-op asks you to rework a piece of writing, do you think that it's going to be effective to question whether

147

your boss knows what he or she is doing? Another issue is that your resume is a reflection on me as well as you. There is definitely flexibility as to what your resume looks like, but your resume has too many fundamental problems for me to feel comfortable sending it out as it is. In general, you really need to start showing me that you're able and willing to take direction, so I know that you'll be able to do that when you start the actual job."

These responses are just a small glimpse at the realm of possibility, but hopefully they will give you some sense of the different approaches.

3. Be prompt and persistent when correcting bad behavior. If you're looking to change behavior, it's most powerful when you can address it as soon as it happens. And you have to be prepared for the fact that attempting to correct behavior may make things worse before they get better. So you have to hang in there and not let your frustration level visibly escalate.

Even when you address behavior in a calm-assertive style, you may be disappointed to receive a response that is aggressive, hostile, or defensive. It's crucial to not respond in kind. Instead, sometimes I'll calmly point out that the person's response is not a productive one, and I'll remind them why I'm bringing it up. At times, I can point out that a poor response to criticism on the student's part is an indication that the student needs to work on the crucial skill of hearing disappointing feedback and finding a way to respond to it positively. I will return to that concept shortly with a different slant.

So, as improbable as it may seem, you might find it interesting to check out the methods of the Dog Whisperer!

THE COORDINATOR/STUDENT RELATIONSHIP AS METAPHOR

Another surprisingly useful reference point with my counseling approach is that of Irvin Yalom, a psychiatrist and author. Although some professionals with a counseling background may recognize his name as the father of group psychotherapy and an author of a highly respected textbook on that subject, I have been more influenced by his writings on individual psychotherapy.

Yalom gives us an unusual window into the mind of the psychotherapist in practice. Although I have enjoyed all of his books—a range of provocative fiction as well as non-fiction—I particularly recommend *Love's Executioner & Other Tales of Psychotherapy*. In this book, Yalom describes his therapeutic relationships with several patients; the stories are true but heavily disguised to maintain confidentiality. The author is open about his mistakes, and you really get a sense that psychotherapy is more of an art than a science. That book definitely was one of the inspirations for this book, as you definitely get a sense of how Yalom has wrestled with what it means to be a professional in his field by recounting some of his successes and failures.

In any event, there is one concept of Yalom's that I have found to be highly applicable when counseling students. Yalom talks about how the relationship between therapist and patient can be perceived as a metaphor for other important relationships in the patient's life. If, for example, a patient reacts angrily to constructive criticism or avoids conflict to an unhealthy degree in the therapeutic relationship, that patient is likely to act similarly in other contexts.

NOTING THE SUBTEXT

I think that this is a useful concept when working individually with students. On a superficial level, a student meets with me to discuss career options, have a resume critiqued, and so forth. Simultaneously, though, I often am taking note of the subtext:

- What is the student's typical affect when meeting with me? Is she upbeat and positive? Shy? Distracted? Moody? Sad? Impatient?

- Did the student prepare appropriately for the meeting, indicating an ability and willingness to take direction?

- How does the student respond to feedback, such as a need to overhaul a resume or being confronted with the fact that he was late to an appointment or in getting a task accomplished? Is he open or defensive? Does he seem interested in learning from the feedback or not?

- When asked about job options, what are the student's values? Does she seem to be interested in a challenging learning opportunity, or is she most interested in a job that is convenient to reach, high-paying, or "sexy" in terms of location or industry? If challenge and learning are not primary in importance, I'm going to probe with more questions to determine whether the student's priorities reflect a lack of maturity or realism... or if there is a legitimate reason why those other priorities might trump the level of challenge and learning? For example, a student who needs to make at least $15/hour to have enough funds to keep attending school after the work term certainly has a valid reason for making that the number-one priority.

As Tom Akins and Bernadette Friedrich note in their interview excerpts at the end of this chapter, you sometimes need to read between the lines when counseling students, as the student's *stated* issue or concern may mask the *real* issue. During a job search, a student may come in really down because he doesn't have a job, and he may blame his lack of job experience. From that input, it might be easy to buy into the stated issue and accept the perceived problem as the real problem. But my more immediate reaction would be to think: "Wow, if this student is coming across with such a hangdog style, I'd better make sure that he's not wearing that on his sleeve in interviews!" I also would want to call a few of the interviewers to compare the student's perception to the employer's take on it. Maybe the student has a really bad but correctable glitch in his interview. Perhaps he's getting beaten out by job candidates who have comparable job experience but who are just going the extra mile with research and preparation. Sometimes you need to dig a little deeper to see what else might be going on.

Likewise, some behaviors are *problems*, but others may just be *symptoms* of deeper, underlying issues. For example, a student who chronically "forgets" about deadlines or appointments — or reschedules them repeatedly — might not have her act together when it comes to organizational skills... but it's about as likely that the student is experiencing ambivalence on some level about going out to work. Careful, neutral probing can give you insight as to what is *really* going on, but you'll never find out if you just scold the student because of the behavior.

THE COORDINATOR AS MANAGER

Those are all examples of what might be gleaned from some assessment of *how* a student does business with you. The idea is that the *coordinator is analogous to a manager*. Assuming that you are fairly positive and reasonable, it seems reasonable to believe that a student who demonstrates problematic behaviors with you is much more likely to do so with a future co-op or internship manager in an organizational setting. As such, it can be a great "teachable moment" to use your calm-assertive energy to have a conversation with a student in which you explicitly point out that your relationship with the student is a great opportunity for her to practice the professional behaviors that will help her survive and succeed in the workplace.

One great thing about this approach is that it tends to depersonalize the conflict between the coordinator and the student. If a student fails to show up for a scheduled appointment with me, for example, I *could* choose to make a big deal of the fact that the student failed to meet *my* professional standards. However, there are two reasons why that's the wrong focus:

- My personal standards may or may not coincide with those of future managers, so pleasing me personally is not really a success factor in the workplace.

- Focusing on how the student has failed me personally tends to escalate the conflict, setting us up for a more adversarial relationship rather than taking a more detached, educational perspective.

My emphasis, then, is on encouraging the student to step back and objectively look at the bigger picture of the significance of their one-on-one interaction with me. I want them to see that my concern is not really about me… it's more about what their behavior says about their readiness to deal with a professional manager—maybe one who is too busy or reluctant to give immediate feedback when unhappy with a subordinate's behavior.

When bad behavior persists, sometimes I'll add another element. "We've talked about how your behavior is going to cause you problems in a professional environment," I'll say. "But you're still struggling to solve some of those problems. So now I have a new concern. Pretty soon, employers are going to call me up and ask me whether or not I think you'd be a good job candidate. Obviously, I need to be honest with those managers. I would *love* to be able to tell them that a student of mine is someone I can personally recommend. But speaking as your 'manager on campus,' why should I be excited about recommending you to a manager out in the professional world?"

The light bulb really comes on for many wayward students at that point. They can start to put themselves in my shoes and see how little reason they've given me to be able to be a passionate advocate for them as candidates. That helps us bring our coordinator/student relationship back around to practicing the professional behaviors that will be needed at work.

One occasional objection from students is interesting. When I've pointed out a behavior that would be unacceptable in the workplace, some students say, "Well, this isn't the workplace. Of course, I would never do that in the workplace!"

"Okay," I say. "If so, what makes the behavior okay in this context?" The behavior is generally indefensible, and realizing this can be a good way to get students out of the student/customer mentality and into the employee/service provider mode of thought and behavior.

CONFLICTS AS TEACHING OPPORTUNITIES

In this chapter, I've already alluded to "teachable moments" and "learning opportunities" in the context of coordinator/student counseling relationships. I just want to revisit that topic briefly before we move on to another one. When attempting to correct an undesirable behavior or giving feedback that could be perceived negatively, a great question to ask yourself is "Am I delivering the message with the *tone* of an *educator*?"

It took me years to consciously work on that one. In a moment of exasperation—whether as an educator or a parent—it's so easy to come off as a frustrated disciplinarian. But if you can say to yourself "I am a teacher, and I need to talk like one," this goes a long way to conveying your message in a way that the student will listen and respond to constructively. So often, it's not *what* you say but *how* you say it. An abrupt, brusque tone will result in more expedient conversations, as students will just shut up and shut down. A neutral, calm tone is more likely to get them open up, discuss their reactions, and process the message more effectively.

KEYS TO SUCCESSFUL COUNSELING IN PREPARATION

Now that we've covered some big-picture, philosophical approaches to one-on-one counseling, let's drill in deeper to talk about more specific fundamentals of strong counseling. These are largely based on my interviews with expert professionals.

BUILDING/MAINTAINING RELATIONSHIPS

Most interviewees emphasized how important it is to build and maintain strong relationships with students. The basic idea is that if you don't have a reasonably good relationship, you don't have much of anything. The responsibility obviously falls on both parties, but there are many specific steps you can take to increase the odds of having good relationships with your student population:

1. *Ensure a reasonable frequency of interaction*

   There is a good amount of organizational behavior research indicating that it's difficult to develop cohesive relationships without significant frequency of interaction. In this technological age, you very likely could do all or most of your student interaction without one-on-one contact. Although that can lead to successful placements, it certainly won't lead to a true relationship with students.

   Of course, requiring face-to-face meetings can backfire. I have known of colleagues who made students come in every time they wanted a resume sent to even one additional employer or for some other matter that could've been handled with a quick phone call or e-mail. If you over-rely on one-to-one meetings, students will start to perceive their meetings with you as an onerous, bureaucratic hurdle rather than a meeting with a real educational purpose.

   I usually recommend that students physically come to see me at least once every two weeks during a job search unless there is a compelling reason that cannot happen. Quick questions and logistic details can be handled electronically or on the phone, in-depth conversations about job search strategies, resume and interview feedback, and career counseling call for meeting one-on-one.

2. Build rapport and credibility

Although it may seem frivolous—especially to those professionals who have monster loads—I try very hard to build rapport with students by getting to know them as human beings. I have pretty eclectic interests, and there is almost always something that I can use to connect more personally with a given student: reading, sports, their hometown, skiing, alternative rock, travel, movies, and so forth. Therefore, I like to take a few minutes to try to find a common bond.

After that, the goal is to work toward helping the student see that you have credibility as a professional. This is where all of your effort to ramp up in terms of the economy, job market, industries, and specific organizations really pays off. Likewise, this is one big reason why you want to devote time to data analysis as described in Chapter 1 of the book. If you don't have a pretty ready answer for most of the following questions, students may question how much you can help them:

- How is the job market looking in my major?

- What kind of pay can I reasonably expect as a co-op or intern?

- What kind of job can I realistically try to get, given that I don't have any professional experience?

- What are the career paths in my major, and how will the various co-op or internship options help me toward a given career path?

- What are some good employers for co-ops/interns in my major?

- What are employers generally looking for when they interview students from this program?

You could opt to answer such questions by preparing some sort of FAQ handout if you are concerned about saving time, but I do think it's important to have a pretty good idea of the answers to these questions off the top of your head. It's obviously much more difficult if you're in a program where, say, you are personally responsible for working with *all* business and engineering majors as opposed to dealing with a more narrow population, such as industrial engineering and mechanical engineering or accounting and finance. Still, it really hurts your professional credibility if you don't have a strong grasp of the jobs your students are considering.

Another key to your credibility will lie in your earliest actions with a given student. No matter how much you develop a nice relationship with students, you need to be able to give good advice and direction. Usually, critiquing a resume is one of my earliest steps with a beginning student. Although it's important for the student to have a good resume, how you handle that interaction will say a great deal about your standards and your style. If you take a quick glance at a resume and only fix blatant errors without close scrutiny, that approach will let the student know that your bar is probably pretty low. If you closely inspect a resume and suggest revisions that are in the spirit of having an excellent resume, then you're conveying your expertise as well as a commitment toward excellence.

After critiquing several thousand resumes over the last 13 years, I've found that the errors usually jump out at me pretty quickly. It's pretty satisfying to be able to point out myriad inconsistencies and subtle errors that clearly detract from the resume as a marketing tool, and I often can tell that students are impressed at how meticulous and thorough I am in my editing efforts. In Chapter 9, I'll detail how to handle such a critique. For now, it's enough to reflect on how your early work with a student will set a definite tone for the relationship.

3. *Getting students to stay on your radar screen*

This gets back to the topic of getting students to own responsibility. Whether I'm working with one of my own students or someone who was referred to me by a colleague, I often have students ask me to let them know if a job comes in that fits their interests. Dealing with 80–100 students over the course of a referral cycle, I generally can't do that, and I tell them so. However, I tell students that it's up to them to make sure that they stay on my radar screen.

I literally will say something like this, especially with a student who is not assigned to me specifically: "You seem like a real promising job candidate. And I'm sure I'll remember you for the next week or so. After that, though, it tends to be out of sight, out of mind. If a good job comes through in a few weeks, I might not remember you... or I might just assume that you're all set with a job if you haven't been in touch. So I highly recommend that you touch base once in a while with an update. Drop me an e-mail, stop by during walk-in hours to say hi, whatever."

Last semester I got a call from a student and had to laugh at her response when I clearly didn't recognize her name over the phone. "I'm the student that you described as the 'highly promising psych major with an upbeat personality' when I met with you," she said. "Oh, of course!" I said, laughing.

DISPLAYING EMPATHY

Another theme in my interviews on the counseling topic was the need to display empathy when working with college students. They need to know that you are actively concerned about their welfare and that you have their best interests at heart. So let's break that down into a few subthemes:

1. *It's tough to be a college student.*

When working with students who are under considerable stress or really dealing with a psychological crisis, I often say something that seems to resonate: "It's tough to be a college student, and I think that people often don't acknowledge that. You may have friends or family harping on the fact that this is the happiest time of your life and that it all gets harder later on. I don't believe that!"

I go on to enumerate all of the stressors that college students face:

- Remaining connected to their family but also becoming their own individual

- Living up to the often high expectations of family

- Figuring out what the heck they want to do with their lives

- Dealing with the fact that romantic relationships get more intense and complicated, which can be exciting or problematic

- In some cases, coming to a new or escalated awareness about sexual orientation or gender identity

- Trying to perform reasonably well academically, especially given that college can be fiendishly expensive for many families

- Needing to juggle multiple responsibilities, such as school and work as well as social and extracurricular activities

There is a mythology out there that college life is—or should be—a nonstop party. This is reinforced by peers who are much more likely to share experiences that reflect positively on themselves as opposed to psychological, social, and emotional scars. All of this can make a stressed-out college student feel quite isolated when dealing with difficulties beyond the more acceptable anxieties of papers and exams. It's important that you acknowledge some of these stressors, especially when dealing with students who are struggling in any number of ways.

2. *Use active listening skills*

Although you want students to treat you in a respectful, professional manner, you also need to give them the opportunity to express their emotions. It can be healthy for a student to vent. Let's say a student prepared really hard for an interview, only to end up meeting with a dreaded "non-stop talker" who gave them little opportunity to share their considerable research. You need to let them talk about that and acknowledge their frustration.

Active listening also means that you may want to paraphrase what a student has said to you in order to make sure that you understand what's been said… and to make clear that you really did hear them! Asking clarifying questions to be sure you *really* understand helps as well.

Even if the difficulties and frustrations seem somewhat irrational to you, it's important to acknowledge those feelings. It's a little hard for me to relate to someone who is terrified of getting lost when driving to a job interview, but I have to be sure that I don't belittle that and instead offer a variety of solutions that will decrease the student's anxiety level.

3. *Try to avoid being judgmental*

No one likes to think of themselves as judgmental, but it's human nature to have a knee-jerk reaction to values, attitudes, and lifestyle that differ from your own. When such a situation arises, you sometimes need to avoid getting preachy and opt for a more pragmatic approach.

I had quite a surprise last year. A student came back from co-op, and he'd had a successful experience. This was somewhat of a surprise, as I'd had to confront the student repeatedly during the preparation process. He had great difficulty following through on any number of tasks and assignments that I'd set out for him. I did work with him but made clear that he needed to pull it together and earn a good evaluation, or it would jeopardize my willingness to work with him in the future.

When he came back to school, we discussed his evaluation and reflected calmly on his difficulties with me in the fall. He admitted to me that the real issue all along had been that he was a "total pothead," and he finally was coming to terms with how much it was dominating his life. All of his close friendships revolved around getting high. More recently, he had been diagnosed as having attention-deficit disorder, and a professional was urging that he go on medication for that. He was resisting, as he felt it was important to stop smoking pot for a good while so he could begin to understand who he really was without being on *any* drug, legal or otherwise.

I tried to listen a lot and be sympathetic. I made no effort to push him on any decision; we had more of an objective discussion of how smoking pot might have had an impact on his short-term memory and organizational skills. I tried to make clear that this was not a moral issue to me. However, there are pragmatic consequences of being high much of the time, and his ADD diagnosis added yet another variable to the mix. My sense was that he was coming to terms with the fact that marijuana had become too much of a focal point in his life, and he needed to make a change. I think we both came away from the conversation feeling good about our trust and the fact that we were working together for the student's benefit. He ultimately decided to take a medical leave, and I'm hopeful that he will come back with a much better sense of who he is and find a productive alternative to his drug use.

4. *Don't impose YOUR goals on students*

This is a somewhat tricky point. You do want to have high standards, and you can do a great deal to encourage your students to make that a goal for themselves as well. However, you have to be careful about confusing your own values and preferences with what may or may not be in a student's best interest.

For example, my own philosophy is that a person in his college years and into early adulthood should be willing to make considerable sacrifices to further his career. A young professional should be willing to work long hours, relocate to an unglamorous city, or endure a long and unpleasant commute. But not every student would agree with me on that. In fact—as noted in the last chapter—many young adults today are placing a higher premium on work/life balance, and some absolutely will not want to work in a job that requires, say, a 60-hour work week.

In that situation, I would try to talk through such a decision, reminding a student that it might be worth their while to make some concessions in the name of maximizing their degree of learning. But ultimately, the student is the one who has to do the job for the duration of the work term. These days I am less likely to do some arm-twisting to convince a student to take a job that feels like an uncomfortable fit. Just a few weeks ago, I received an accidental phone call from a student who was in the midst of arguing with his girlfriend. I felt obliged to tell him that this had happened, so he could be sure it didn't happen to him again in the future.

When we next talked about his upcoming co-op job search, he said, "Well, I know that you're aware that I'm having some relationship problems right now. As a result, I really don't want to consider a job out of state." We had talked about some terrific opportunities around the country that would be great matches for him, but I was quick to say that I really didn't want him to do anything unless he could do it wholeheartedly.

Likewise, sometimes I am rather amused when a student describes their dream job to me. Not infrequently, the job sounds like a dreadful job to me—something I would never want to do at any salary. Less dramatically, I can recall an instance when a third-time co-op really wanted a job that I had always viewed as an entry-level position. I was mystified, but some questioning led me to believe that this young woman completely understood what the job entailed and was very attracted by it. I held my tongue about the fact that only sophomores had ever handled the job, and she accepted it. Not only did she do her co-op job in that role, she accepted the same job after graduation. As far as I know, she may still be in it.

Thus, it's important to remember that beauty is very much in the eye of the beholder when it comes to any number of things in life, including jobs and careers. You have to be careful to not let your own biases affect someone else's decisions.

TRANSPARENCY

Another theme that various experts mentioned was transparency. I'm sure that this might be considered a quasi-controversial idea by some. In a basic sense, though, most professionals agree that you need to have a basically open process. I am aware of programs, past and present, in which students have been quietly earmarked for certain jobs or employers as opposed to having open competition for jobs. Now, there may be times when it makes sense to screen out candidates for a job that is a poor fit. But I have heard stories of a long-since retired business coordinator who made sure that a certain firm always got the best available student in his major.

Let's consider some other elements of transparency:

1. *Honesty*

It may sound like pure common sense to say that you should be honest with students, but all professionals know that sense can be surprisingly uncommon. It's not so much a question of lying to students as withholding the truth at times. I have known of situations in which I strongly suspected that a coordinator never actually sent a given student's resume out for a job after saying that they would do so. Alternatively, there is the option of holding off on sending a resume until it's too late to matter.

Often this kind of situation arises because of a desire to avoid overt conflict. Some students are upset with me or my colleagues when we tell them that their qualifications aren't strong enough to justify sending out their resume for a specific job. From the student's perspective, why not send out resumes to all jobs that interest the student? Well, I'm really not doing my employer any favors by sending, say, 30 resumes when they only want to hire one student. Nor am I making the employer's life easier by forcing them to read 20 resumes carefully to figure out what I already know—that there are about seven candidates who are head and shoulders above the rest. The flip side is that I have to break some unpleasant news to students on this front, and a few don't take it well.

Honesty also includes giving difficult feedback. When I have to tell a female student that wearing a lacy, low-cut camisole top with her suit is *not* a good idea for a job interview (regardless of what some women's magazines seem to say), it's an awkward conversation for both of us. Still, it's a conversation that has to happen. Likewise, students sometimes get defensive or grumpy when I give them immediate feedback on the impression they're making on me in my office, but I always try to frame it by telling them that I'm just trying to be totally honest in my feedback. I want them to know that my praise, when given, is real and not just a blind cheerleading quality. When praise and criticism are both doled out as they are earned, students tend to take both the positive and negative feedback to heart.

2. *Confidentiality*

There are a few limits on transparency. Maintaining coordinator/student confidentiality also can be trickier than it sounds. As Tamara Pinkas indicates in her transcribed comments at the end of this chapter, you have to be careful how much you disclose to an employer about a student. An employer who hires a student often has much more day-to-day interaction with that student than you ever will have. As a result, an employer eventually may pass along whatever you had to say about that student, so you'd better think about that before passing along any critical comments!

Confidentiality is also a concern when it comes to sharing information about one student with another. Students have the right to share whatever information they like with other students, but that doesn't make it okay for you to do so. It can seem innocuous to let a student know who else is interviewing for a job or who did or didn't receive a job offer, but offhand comments on those topics could backfire occasionally.

Probably the biggest key is being very careful about passing along information that is truly private. These days, you will learn about students with ADD, ADHD, dyslexia, eating disorders, psychological issues, pregnancy-related issues, and many other possible sensitive topics. You have to be very careful about what goes into your notes, especially if they are in a public journal on a CRM system. You also need to watch out what you say to other professionals, as the student may not want other coordinators or academic faculty to be aware of what was shared with you.

3. *Knowing your limitations*

That last point relates directly to this one. A good professional is not afraid to talk about difficult personal issues, such as the aforementioned physical, psychological, and learning issues. Over the years, I had students who have told me about eating disorders, suicidal tendencies, dysfunctional family dynamics, and even a student who worried that he was so frustrated in his job that he feared he might physically hurt a co-worker. While you need to be able to be a good listener in these situations, you also need to know when you are out of your league.

I have been working for a few years with a student who is chronically depressed and who often comes to me to share her struggles. I do try to give her some perspective and encouragement, but the first priority was to ensure that she was seeing a professional psychotherapist. At times, I've been able to have an impact with her. When she complained that no antidepressant medication worked for her, I was able to point out that she had mentioned drinking alcohol regularly. How could she know if the medication was really working if she was still drinking? Alcohol is a central nervous system depressant, and it very well could cancel out or impair the positive effects of her medication. She probably had heard that from a psychiatrist before, but hearing it from me seemed to make the difference. However, I also know that I am not qualified to be her primary therapist, and I constantly defer to those experts when she discusses her ongoing issues. Many questions have come up that are beyond my expertise.

As a result, you have to become aware of what resources are available to your students when they need a referral to another professional. Is there some sort of disability resource center on your campus? Where do students go when they need psychological counseling, including emergency services if they are suicidal? What is your recourse within the university if a student breaks the law or the code of conduct at school or work? On a more mundane level, are there individuals who are trained to administer tests such as Myers-Briggs or the Strong Interest Inventory if you don't have that training? How about a language center that can help international students improve their English-speaking skills? In general, you need to be transparent with students and admit when you don't have the answers and when they therefore need to meet with someone else.

One last point here with limitations: There is nothing wrong with saying "I don't know, but I'll find out" to a student. Or: "I'm not sure how I want to handle this; I want to think it over and/or discuss it with a colleague." Even if it's purely a co-op/internship issue that does not call for an outside reference, it's better to take your time and get the answer right.

MANAGING EXPECTATIONS

A big theme in counseling students is in managing expectations. As mentioned in the previous chapter, today's students often prefer a high degree of structure, and they also may have lofty expectations. That's a challenging combination. Both traits call for an emphasis on making sure that students know what's going to happen, when it will happen, and, most importantly, why it happens.

1. *Educate about objectives*

Students often need clear, structured objectives combined with an understanding of what educational purpose the action serves. Without that explanation, students end up perceiving the structure as an irritating, pointless series of bureaucratic hoops and hurdles that must be circumvented or begrudgingly completed. It's important to not confuse *compliance* with *commitment*. Just because you're successfully forcing a student to do something does not mean that he or she has bought into the value of it.

A good example comes up in mandatory programs. Quite often, a student comes in and questions how many co-ops they have to do. I can answer that question in terms of rules and regulations, but it's far more important to talk about how many work terms make sense for that student to do in terms of their educational goals. I'm often quick to point out that it would be easy for me to say fewer co-ops is better—hey, one less student for me to handle!—but that I prefer to look at the long-term welfare of the student. If the student has a great job offer after one co-op, maybe one is enough. If they don't have one after two co-ops, then doing a third is probably a much better idea than graduating first and worrying about a full-time job later.

Practice interviews are another good example. We require them for all first-time business students. It's rare that students grouse about the requirement, but, if they do, it's best to downplay the fact that they're required and to focus more on why they really want to do this activity and put considerable energy into doing it as well as possible in order to obtain the optimal job.

2. *"Action-oriented advising"*

In her interview with me, Kerry Mahoney talked about "action-oriented advising." Charlie Bognanni doesn't use that term but takes a similar approach. The idea is that every meeting with a student ends with a clear description of what action the student needs to take next to keep the ball rolling with the job search process. Charlie likes to have students book their next appointment before they leave the current one, and he finds that students really like to know exactly how long it should be before they come back and what they need to do in the meantime.

3. *Raising and lowering student expectations as needed*

At the CEIA Conference in Myrtle Beach in 2008, I saw two professionals from the University of Cincinnati do a presentation on preparing students to interview. One metric that emerged confirmed my own experience when it came to doing practice interviews:

- About 75 percent of the students came into the practice interview feeling very nervous, insecure, and lacking in confidence when it came to interviewing

- About 25 percent of the students came into the process with an inappropriately high degree of confidence in their own ability to interview

The upshot of the practice interview was that the process resulted in a cohort of students that all had about the same level of confidence in their ability to interview. The less confident interviewees came away with a heightened sense of their ability to handle a job interview, and the overconfident group tempered their expectations after a useful reality check.

You'll see quite a few of students on both sides of this spectrum, and not just when it comes to interviewing. There are many students who see no reason why they can't work in the most challenging jobs at our most competitive employers despite average grades and no professional experience. More frequently, there are students who truly fear that no one will want to hire them despite the fact that they have outstanding transferable skills and some very meaningful (if non-professional) work experience. Accordingly, sometimes you need to help students get their goals aligned with the possibilities.

One tactic that I sometimes use is sharing "before and after resumes." I have some alums who started off very modestly and ended up in amazing jobs. Sometimes I'll show a "before" resume—featuring nothing more than retail or low-level administrative jobs—and then show the "after" resume, which indicates the progression of learning experiences that culminated in a great job after graduation. That can help a fearful student see that her resume may be modest, but that others have started in her shoes and moved on to greatness. By the same token, a student who can't understand why he didn't get an interview may get the message if he takes a look at the resume of a student who was hired during a past term.

GETTING STUDENTS TO SEE THE BIG PICTURE

This is another key that various professionals have raised with me in my many conversations. In general, it can be hard for students to see beyond the day or week at hand in favor of a longer-term view. Let's consider a couple of specific ideas here.

1. *Patience with the process*

My colleague Jacki Diani likes to talk to students about "patience with the process," as she discusses on pages 32 and 33 at the end of Chapter 2. The gist of it is that students often have a hard time getting outside of their own perspective—especially in the heat of a job search. Jacki has to remind students that the co-op hiring process may be all-important to the student but that the employer may have many other bigger priorities on their plate. Students today are accustomed to the 24/7 convenience of cell phones and the Internet, so this may be an adjustment.

A big problem to watch out for in the preparation process is what I call panic mode. In my co-op preparation class—which will be the focus of the next chapter—we sometimes discuss job search scenarios. Here's one that is especially interesting:

"It's November 5, and you get an offer for a very entry-level position doing general office work. You are lukewarm about accepting the offer, but the fact is that you have no corporate experience, no other interviews scheduled, and no other possible offers at this point. You need to start work on January 2. What do you do?"

Much to my surprise, more than half of my students often say that they would accept the offer. Given the job market for my students, this is not an offer I'd like them to accept—not that early in the semester, at least. Still, it gives us the opportunity to talk this through, and I can reinforce the idea that they really should not accept an offer without discussing it with me first unless they are very excited about the job in question.

I think the underlying issue here is that students sometimes take situations at face value. With this scenario, they look at it and say, "Well, it seems like I have no choice but to accept the job," given that there is nothing on the immediate horizon. In response, I like to remind them that it's like getting married: If you want to get married really badly, you can get married really badly!

Another way I frame it is to ask students what they would prefer. If they accept such a job, they have the security of knowing that they have a job pretty early in the job search process. That alleviates some fear and anxiety, to be sure. However, the possible cost is that they may end up with a job that they will master in two weeks and then be relatively bored over the next five and a half months. Alternatively, I'll ask, are they willing to suffer through the job search for another month or two in exchange for a more enjoyable and challenging six-month work term? In the big picture, it can be really worthwhile.

2. *Choices and consequences*

This last example tees up the next subtheme. After doing this job for a few years, I found myself gravitating away from a more directive style to a more educational approach that emphasized building a student's awareness of the available *choices* in a given situation as

160

well as the range of positive and negative *consequences* to each choice.

One example would be in critiquing a resume. Certainly you will come across unequivocal errors that really must be corrected. There also may be aesthetic issues that I will insist on fixing, as the look of the resume will affect an employer's perception of my program based on what I allow. Thirdly, there may be some formatting or content issues that I insist on to give the resumes some degree of consistency, making them easier for employers to read through quickly. Some examples might be how the student's major and concentration(s) are listed, and insisting that a graduation date is included as well as a computer skills section.

Beyond that, though, I try my best to make students aware of the fact that much of a resume is more art than science. Should a resume be relatively terse and objective—a "just the facts" approach? Or should it be more expansive, highlighting accomplishments and transferable skills in order to "sell" the candidate more assertively to an employer? My own personal bias is toward the latter approach, but I don't require that of my students. I make them aware of why some of my colleagues and employers favor the more concise approach. Ultimately, the student needs to decide what resume really fits their own values and goals best.

Another good example might be in what jobs a given student is allowed to pursue. In my immediate group, we only let students pursue about six or seven jobs simultaneously. The idea is that we don't want students to fling their resume at dozens of jobs at once. We want them to target a handful of jobs, forcing them to make priorities. This way, employers are only receiving the resumes of students who have a legitimate interest in working for them as opposed to being used to satisfy a student's minor curiosity or to assuage a student's fear about getting a job.

A student could insist on picking nothing but "reach" jobs if they choose, but they would have to hear me talk through the pros and cons of such a move. It could lead to a better job, but some great entry-level jobs might come and go in the meantime. Are they willing to live with that? If so, I'm okay with it.

Whenever a student is not sure of what to do—accepting a job offer, getting rid of a nose ring before interviewing, whatever—it's always good to suspend your own opinion to some degree and focus more on the choices and consequences of the various alternatives.

FLEXIBILITY

A good professional develops a program with goals, objectives, and standards. There may be rules and regulations. Over time, you tend to develop a standard way of counseling students. That said, there are times when you need to throw your usual approach out the window and make a major adjustment to meet a need.

1. *Handling surprises*

You never know what issue will come up next in our roles. I often say that this is not a great role for someone who loves a predictable, structured day, as there are often major surprises. When counseling students, you may have to reinvent your process—sometimes dramatically—to get a desired result.

I had a student a few years ago who told me that she was really worried about interviewing. I went into my usual spiel, acknowledging the normalcy of those feelings and how our usual process of reading my book, discussing the topic in class, and undergoing a practice interview would help her learn to harness her nervous energy and use it positively.

The student was adamant, though, that her problem was way beyond the usual butterflies that almost everyone feels. She did a good job of communicating to me that she was *not* talking about a slight case of jitters; it was a deep-seated, paralyzing fear. Once I really got the fact that we were talking about an outright phobia as opposed to a bad case of nerves, I really dug deep into my bag of tricks to try to help her.

Wow, we really did just about everything you could imagine. I questioned her to get some better understanding of how the phobia had developed. I confided in her about some of my own experiences that required me to deal with fears and how I handled them. I shared some self-hypnosis techniques that I've learned—basically a relaxation exercise in which the individual learns how to first focus on breathing and then turn their mental energy to focus on external stimuli as opposed to rampant, negative internal thoughts.

We then did multiple practice interviews with a variety of interviewers. At one point, I asked her if she could see anything positive that would arise in an interview. She said that the one thing she actually enjoyed was when people grilled her about company information, as that pulled the focus off of her. Although that surprised me, I went with that feeling and tried to help her build an interview strategy that she could feel was more of a test of *what she knew* rather than *who she was*.

She finally came to her first "real" interview, still feeling very scared but determined that she was not going to give in to her fear. Coincidentally, her first interview turned out to be for the job she wanted most. That worried me, as it raised the bar. I wished she could have had a lower-stakes interview for the first real one. But my worries were misplaced. The very first question, oddly, was "What do you know about our company?" That was just the kind of question she had wanted, and she dove into it enthusiastically and then held her own through the more personal questions. She got the job and ended up doing all of her co-ops with that employer before accepting a job with them after graduation. So the final punch line is that the most fearful student I ever worked with on interviewing ended up with a batting average of 1.000 during her co-op career!

2. *There's a first time for everything.*

Over a decade into this job, it's refreshing to know that there are still new ways to do things… if you can only be open to being flexible. One great example came up a few years ago. I had a student who wanted to do something very, very different for her resume. This didn't surprise me, as the student is a very charismatic, strong-minded young woman. Still, here's a question for any professional: Would you allow a student to have her resume use a landscape format? In other words, this student wanted her resume to appear with the words running from left to right on the *longer* side of the paper! On top of that, she had a quote running across the top of it. It certainly was most unusual.

After my initial reaction of surprise, I resorted to my usual "choices and consequences" approach. Was the student willing to accept that the resume definitely would turn off some professionals? It might send the message that the student was a rebel who was a little too independent-minded to fit in at an organization. Yet it also had the potential to be perceived as a creative way to market herself. But was she ready to have employers grill her about the resume and possibly be openly critical about it during the interview?

The more we discussed it, it sunk in for me. *This resume would be a disaster for most students, but it's perfect for Genna. She's determined, and she's going to make this work.* And it did. Not everyone liked the resume, and it probably cost her some interviews and jobs, but it also created considerable intrigue. She was ready to field questions about it, and she did so very effectively.

The amusing footnote here is that Genna graduated last spring, and I saw her at a reception. What were her plans for after graduation? Predictably, they were unconventional. She had met the owner of a bar on Wall Street, and she had agreed to become a bartender there. All kinds of powerful people came into the bar, and the plan was for her to build relationships with them when they did, ultimately leveraging that into a fast-track position at a prominent investment firm. I had to smile. "That would be an awful move for most people, but I'm sure it will work for you," I said.

Likewise, I've made exceptions on any number of policies, and it often works out well. You have to be careful—you have to be fair about it and not interpret flexibility as letting standards go out the window. The bottom line is that you want to treat students *fairly*... but that doesn't always mean that you treat them *equally*.

HANDLING CONFLICTS

As we delved into this topic earlier in this chapter as well as in Chapter 5, I won't linger on it again here. But the interviewees often noted that handling conflicts in a calm, honest, solution-oriented manner is an important part of the counseling process.

MODELING

I touched on this slightly in the earlier example of my student with an interviewing phobia, but it's worth expanding on here. One powerful counseling tactic is to model the appropriate behavior for your students. There are a few different angles to consider here:

1. *Show students the right behavior instead of just telling them about it.*

   As a somewhat closeted fiction writer, I can tell you that an age-old axiom in that field is "show, don't tell." In fiction, the point is that it's much more powerful and convincing to *see* a character display a given trait in action as opposed to having the author *tell* you that the character has that quality. For example, a narrator could tell you that a character is heartless, but it's far more powerful to have that character check his watch repeatedly during a family member's funeral.

   The same is true when advising students. Talk all you like about the importance of keeping appointments and being on time, but failing to do so yourself will undermine that completely. On the more positive side of the ledger, demonstrating intellectual curiosity, an upbeat attitude, a solution-oriented style, and genuine caring for others will help your advisees get a better feel about what professional behavior looks like in practice.

2. Delve into your own professional experiences to show empathy and strategies that may illuminate the right course of action for a student.

I will return to this idea when we get to Chapter 10, which is on assisting students when they are actually in the midst of a work experience, but it also comes to play in the preparation process. Not infrequently, I will share my own stories about job searches when helping students manage the ups and downs of their experience.

For the student who struggles with a resume because their experiences are all over the place, I can bring up a similar problem that I had during the job search that led me to Northeastern. I had done some writing, teaching, consulting, and management work, so I feared that my resume would come off as a hodgepodge. That had the potential of making me look like an eclectic and interesting person, but it also made me look way too broad and scattered to fit a specific job slot. So I devised three different resumes—one with an educator focus, one with more of a corporate management focus, and one as more of a creative consultant. All of the same jobs were on each version, but I was able to slant the language for each job to focus one of those three themes as was appropriate. Sharing that with students can help them see the possibility of multiple resumes, including how much extra work it is to prepare them and keep track of which employer is getting which version.

Another example comes with the student who gets a job offer that they don't really want. I had that happen right out of grad school. It was the summer, and the job market was slow. I got offered a job and was not that excited about it, but I knew that it could be months before I got another. Initially, I told the employer that I would need a salary beyond their pay range, figuring that would kill it right there. To my surprise, they agreed to give me the pay figure that I wanted… but they also asked if I really wanted the job. It was excruciating, but I had to say no. It was the best decision with the benefit of hindsight, but it was not easy.

There are many other stories that I share. The one about what I went through to prepare for my interview at Northeastern is a popular one. I talk about the number of people I called who had some connection with the university, only to come up with no really helpful inside information. Finally, I remembered that I had a former student from Boston University who was doing her master's at Northeastern. Through a practicum, she knew a woman who knew the coordinator role as well as everyone on the committee. I called her up and asked if we could meet, and then I pumped her for information. She was able to give me some really good guesses as to what the interview would entail, including the probability of a sexual harassment scenario. That made total sense, but I had never thought about how I would handle such a case. When it arose in the interview, though, I had a game plan. Later I heard that some members on my hiring committee thought that I had a script for the interview. I didn't feel quite *that* prepared, honestly, but it was fun to go into the interview armed with more knowledge than the interviewers would expect of me. This is a memorable way to get students to see what the realm of possibility really is when it comes to researching a job.

3. *Be open to sharing personal experiences with students.*

As the years have gone by, I've become much more inclined to share more personal information as well. It's important to note that a professional can't do this for his or her own selfish benefit: You're there to counsel the student, not vice versa. However, I've come to believe that I have a moral responsibility to be open about some of my own personal struggles when I'm dealing with any human being who is experiencing something similar.

As a result, I sometimes have told students the story of the second semester of my junior year, which was the darkest time of my college career and one of the most difficult periods of my life. I don't go into the details of what happened, as they aren't that important. I focus more on how difficult it was and what I did to get through that time. Likewise, I have been known to open up about various personal challenges if I am working with a student who really would benefit from knowing that someone has been in their shoes and, over time, found a variety of ways to get through a difficult stretch. Hearing that makes a troubled student feel less isolated, and, inevitably, it forges a more special connection between us.

How much sharing is too much? That's a personal decision. When you share personal information, you have to know that it may not remain confidential. A student may not be able to resist the temptation to share a juicy detail with a peer. You have to think about how okay you are with that before you decide how much you're willing to share. That said, I have to say—and a few of my interviewees agreed with me when it came up in passing—that I have yet to be burned by sharing something personal. That doesn't mean that I recommend sharing anything and everything, but there definitely can be a place for modeling in this way to some degree, depending on your comfort level.

COUNSELING STUDENTS WITH DIFFERENT BACKGROUNDS

By now, it should be clear that counseling any student presents potential challenges. That is all the more true when working with students whose backgrounds present a whole other set of issues and concerns. So let's consider a few of those populations now.

INTERNATIONAL STUDENTS

Given the strength of other currencies and economies against the dollar and the U.S. economy, many institutions are resorting to a higher percentage of international students in their undergrad population. This has a definite impact on professionals, but it also can be a highly unpredictable one. Let's go over some considerations here:

1. *Citizenship Issues*

   You absolutely need to know every student's citizenship status:

   - U.S. citizen – This will have no negative impact on a student's job search.

   - Permanent Resident – This status means that the individual has a green card and ultimately may obtain citizenship. Permanent Residents may not be eligible for some co-op jobs or internships, particularly with government agencies or defense contractors who work closely with the government. However, the good news is that permanent residents can be hired after graduation without needing H-1 sponsorship.

   - F-1 and J-1 visas – These are the most typical visas that international students receive—especially the F-1. Typically, an F-1 student must be in this country for several months before they can begin paid work, unless it's on campus. A J-1 student often can start work much sooner. F-1 and J-1 students have to be aware of how much they work. For example, it's usually not in their best interest to work part-time hours year-round; they should not do co-op or an internship for any more time than they are in classes.

One key with F-1 and J-1 students is keeping close tabs on how many *weeks* they work. This is an odd but important concept. As of the writing of this book, my understanding is that all international students can work no more than 52 weeks before graduation if they are to remain eligible for Optional Practical Training (OPT). If they remain eligible for OPT, they can work for an additional 12 months in the U.S. after graduation before they either need sponsorship to continue or to leave the country.

The catch is that there is no real difference between a student who works one day or a handful of hours per week versus the student who works 40 hours per week. *Either way, it still counts as one full week.* So it's very important that international students think long and hard about when they start and end work, and staying on to work part-time hours after working full-time for four or six months is generally not advisable.

In addition to not being legally eligible for some jobs, there are many employers who either refuse to interview students unless they are citizens or permanent residents, or they will interview them but view them as less desirable hires. This is true for many of the employers who have co-op and internship programs almost exclusively because this is a great way to have a "mutual trial period" for future full-time hires. Why hire a co-op or intern if they aren't readily eligible for post-grad hiring? That's the logic. Yes, the company could attempt to sponsor the student for an H-1 visa. But in addition to costing some money, the bigger issue is that the U.S. government only gives out so many H-1 visas annually. Another factor is that there is a good deal of paperwork for the employer to complete. Basically, the employer has to *prove* that they were unable to hire a U.S. citizen or Permanent Resident for the job in question. That's a hassle, and there's no question that getting sponsored is rarely an easy task for most international students… but the more they get experience through your program, the more they improve their chances to whatever extent possible.

2. *Language Issues*

Once beyond the visa issue, another possible concern is language issues. Working with international students, you'll have every imaginable level of English proficiency. There are students whose English is so great that you may forget that they aren't U.S. citizens—something you don't want to overlook for the aforementioned reasons. Some students have strong accents and initially are difficult to understand, but otherwise their English is really fine. Then there will be students whose spoken English is weak but who have good comprehension—not an unusual combination at all. Lastly, there are students who have very serious issues with both speaking and comprehending English.

A variety of approaches can be useful with this range of challenges:

■ If there is a language center on campus, find out if a student can get assistance—especially with spoken English.

Students with strong accents who are initially difficult to understand may scare off potential employers. Likewise, students who understand well but speak rather poorly may raise a flag with interviewers. Either way, it's good to coach students in how to talk about their English skills during a job interview. I often encourage students to raise the matter directly, perhaps in response to the typical question about weaknesses:

"Although my understanding of English is quite strong, one of my weaknesses is that my spoken English is not yet at the same level of my comprehension. This sometimes can make people think that I understand less than I do. However, I've found that, over time, people I work closely with do get used to my accent. And I'm working hard on improving my English. I'm sure that being in this work environment every day will help me get better, so I don't think it would keep me from doing a good job for you."

- Sometimes I've found it effective to give an employer a proactive heads-up before a student with a significant language issue interviews for a job. With an e-mail or phone call, I might let them know my honest impression of the student's language ability. I find that this tends to lower employer's expectations for the interview; frequently, the feedback is that the student's English was better than they had anticipated from my comments. It also helps my credibility with the employer, as I'm being forthcoming about a student's weakness.

- More than I did in my earlier years—when I often just felt frustrated at how language issues impaired an international student's job options—I try hard to show empathy over language issues and to suggest other coping mechanisms. I'm quick to recount my own experiences of speaking French in Paris and Montreal; I know just how tiring it is to try to communicate intelligently in another language as opposed to just asking for directions or commenting on the weather!

  When meeting one-on-one with an international student, I will correct speaking errors. I recommend that they carry a notebook at work to jot down unfamiliar words and idioms, so they can look them up at night to expand their vocabulary.

  I have seen many students with really tough language issues, and they often struggle—especially with a first job search. Poor language skills *will* rule out some jobs—particularly ones involving significant telephone work—but persistence and a strong work ethic ultimately will trump this weakness.

3. *Cultural Issues*

Cultural issues are often the trickiest of all to identify and handle when working with international students. There are students who speak great English but who were raised in very different cultural environments. Others may not have such great English, but they are from a culture that is not so radically different from a North American mindset. Another challenge is that students come from a ton of different countries, and it's impossible to be familiar with each country's general philosophy on, say, interviewing.

In some cultures, it is considered downright inappropriate for a job candidate to tout or sell themselves during a job interview. After years of being raised to believe that self-promotion is not a desirable trait, a student often will be less able and willing to sell themselves aggressively in the "American" style. This is not an issue for all international students, but you definitely need to be proactive in handling it.

So what to do? The first thing to do is to probe to seek clarification in order to build your awareness. With my Japanese students, I often say, "I know that some people in your culture are uncomfortable when it comes to talking up their strengths in a job interview. Are you that way, or not?" Sometimes the answer is yes; sometimes it's no.

Other times, I may or may not bring up the possibility of this conflict, but students—American-born and otherwise—may bring up their discomfort on this front. These students *loathe* the idea of going into an interview and saying, "I have terrific interpersonal skills, and my work ethic is outstanding." It just feels completely unnatural to many students, and that's especially understandable when one grows up in a culture that de-emphasizes individual accomplishments. One Japanese proverb: "The nail that sticks up gets hammered down." I really don't want to force a student to do something that goes so much against the grain of their cultural identity.

The trick is that you simultaneously need to respect and appreciate a student's cultural differences while helping them adapt to seeking a job and working in what may be a radically different culture. Ellen Zold, a former colleague of mine at Northeastern who worked extensively with our international students, taught me a good way around this dilemma. Instead of taking a "you're in America now" attitude and forcing students to sell themselves hard, I suggest a happy medium. Instead of:

- "I have outstanding interpersonal skills"

How about:

- "I love working with people."

Instead of:

- "I have a terrific work ethic."

Let's try:

- "I really enjoy working hard."

You get the idea. Students find this to be much more comfortable, and it still does the job of conveying some important strengths, albeit more indirectly.

Cultural differences also can be a major factor in how international students perceive potential jobs. I have worked with many international students who are hell-bent on working for a Fortune 100 or 500 employer—a corporation that will have name recognition and possibly even job opportunities somewhere close to home. While that is not necessarily a bad idea, we don't want any student to be developing tunnel vision during their job search. When students insist that they will only consider a big-name company, I might say, "So would you rather be doing filing and faxing at Microsoft than an intense and challenging job that directly relates to your major at Shlabotnik Enterprises?" (I'm sure no one catches the subtle reference to Charlie Brown's favorite baseball player, the fictional Joe Shlabotnik.) I would go on to make the point that we want to focus on obtaining the best possible learning experience; maybe it's at a company that no one has ever heard of. This is especially true for the international student who will have multiple opportunities to work before graduation.

STUDENTS WITH DISABILITIES

For older professionals, it's easy to equate the term "disability" with physical impairment, such as people who are in wheelchairs or who have significant issues with vision or hearing. While you very likely will work with students who fall into those categories on occasion, you are going to work with many more students whose disabilities are less obvious.

As noted in the previous chapter, this is the "special" generation, a term with a double meaning. For our purposes here, it means that students today are the most diagnosed generation ever. As a result, we are much more aware of students who identify themselves as have attention-deficit disorder (ADD), which is now more frequently known as attention-deficit hyperactivity disorder (ADHD). Fortunately, this condition has lost much of its stigma in recent years. It doesn't hurt that many great people in history—Thomas Edison, Albert Einstein, and Walt Disney—are now believed by some experts to have had the disorder. In terms of the present day, Olympian Michael Phelps talks openly about his ADD, as has singer Justin Timberlake and carpenter Ty Pennington (host of Extreme Makeover: Home Edition) among many others.

As a result, students are much more likely to disclose to you that they have any number of disabilities. Over the years, I have worked with students who have any number of issues: partial or complete paralysis of the legs, an artificial leg, anorexia, dyslexia, ADHD, panic disorder, chronic or acute depression, deafness, and so on.

Ronnie Porter is our resident expert in disabilities at Northeastern, so I would say that her words on the subject are more authoritative on this topic than mine could ever be. You'll find them in the transcribed interviews section at the end of this chapter, but here are the highlights:

- Do some outreach with professionals on campus to emphasize that people with disabilities are encouraged to participate in your co-op or internship program

- Assuming you have a disability resource center on campus, reach out and form partnerships with them to attract people with disabilities to your program and to ensure their success

- Thoroughly assess the ability and skills of students as individuals and make determinations as to what jobs are possible with "reasonable accommodation"

This last point is critical. Employers may shudder to imagine the cost of reasonable accommodation—and it's undoubtedly a nebulous term—but generally we're not talking about a major expense. In some cases, a reasonable accommodation may not cost anything at all; it may be just a matter of changing a policy or some relatively minor rearrangement of a work space.

Most of my students with disabilities were not identifiable as such until they disclosed this fact to me. I have a few students with ADHD right now, and I have regular contact with a great person in our Disability Resource Center. She checks in frequently to see if our mutual students are actually meeting with me, completing work on time, and doing what they need to do to move forward. With one student, she was able to tell me that the student had been diagnosed quite recently and thus had a great deal of learning to do in terms of coping mechanisms. That led us to decide to defer the student's first co-op in order to focus on that priority, and I'm confident that will increase his ultimate likelihood of success. Knowing his diagnosis also forced me to rethink my perceptions of him. I had originally assumed he was disorganized and unmotivated, but now I know why he was coming off that way. This gives me hope that getting support and assistance will help him figure out what he needs to do to come across more professionally. We'll see how it goes.

It's not easy for many disabled individuals to get appropriate jobs. The Americans with Disabilities Act (ADA) was well-intentioned, but, according to Ronnie, did not come with a budget. This makes "reasonable accommodations" quite expensive, prohibitively so for smaller employers. Employers are confused about the rules, and one upshot is that organizations may be more reluctant to hire people with disabilities. Basically, this is a population that can be challenging but very rewarding to assist. The long-term payoff for society is substantial if we can ensure as many people with disabilities as possible are integrated into our labor force.

KEYS THROUGH THE PREPARATION PROCESS

Now we've covered an overview of counseling with a good degree of thoroughness, let's walk through what you need to be doing with students during the preparation process, step by step:

1. *Gather information*

   When working with a new student, you'll want to gather some key information and have it readily accessible, whether in a manual file, spreadsheet, database, Blackboard, or a CRM:

   - Hometown

   - Major

   - Short-term and long-term goals

   - Citizenship status

   - Transportation/willingness to commute

   - Willingness to relocate

   - Breadth or narrowness of focus when it comes to considering jobs

   I want to have all of this information readily available each time I meet with the student individually. At a glance, I want to be able to remind myself of these essentials so we don't have to waste time covering the same ground. I'll never remember all of these facts for 70–90 students, so I need a system where I can have them on hand quickly.

2. *Build rapport*

   I covered this earlier. Ideally, you want to have a little time early in the relationship to get to know the student as a human being.

3. *Use diagnostic tools, if necessary*

If your population is primarily students who have a very clear career direction—such a civil engineering or physical therapy—you probably can jump ahead quickly to the next item on the list. I currently work with three populations of business majors: management information systems, supply chain management, and undeclared students. As you might guess, the first two groups are pretty straightforward to handle. The undeclared students, however, consist of a) students who are considering two or three concentrations to some degree but are paralyzed when it comes to picking one and b) students who have little or no clue at all as to what they want to do on co-op or in the classroom.

This is a trend in higher education these days. There are various books on undecided college students, and institutions have wrestled with ways to help students explore areas of study while working toward a degree. At best, a co-op or internship work term can be a huge asset in helping a student toward a decision. But how do you help a student figure out what they should do for a job without having them review hundreds of jobs in dozens of majors?

One option is to use formal diagnostic tools. In earlier chapters, I've described the Myers-Briggs Type Indicator (MBTI), the Campbell Interest and Skill Survey (CISS), and the Strong Interest Inventory. I'm not certified to give either test, but I often refer students to our Career Services group if they are truly at sea when it comes to a career choice. As described in detail in Chapter 4, I also pull out my own testing materials from 20-odd years ago—back when the Strong-Campbell Interest Inventory was in vogue. Students get a little excited about the possibilities when I model for them in this way.

Yet there is also the option of doing much more informal diagnostic work to help a student home in on a field or some more narrow element of their major. As Bernadette Friedrich said in her interview (transcribed at the end of this chapter), it can be as simple as asking students "what do you like to do?" Her examples relate to engineering, but I could apply them just as easily to, say, marketing. Do you like to crunch numbers and analyze them? Are you good with computers? Then market research might be plausible. Can you handle a bit of an emotional roller-coaster? Do you have good verbal communicate skills? Can you deal with rejection? Do you like tangible feedback for your performance? If so, sales could be an option. Do you have good writing and speaking skills? Can you work in a team? Maybe public relations could work.

Not infrequently, students pick a major without having an in-depth understanding of what the range of career options might be within their field. An accounting major could hate a tax job but love an audit position. A psychology major might love working with developmentally disabled children but find that a research lab is a bad fit. Understanding the various branches of your field and understanding what sort of person would love—or hate—each job type will help quite a bit as you steer students toward one job type or another.

4. *Develop a game plan for the job search*

These conversations lead directly to a game plan for a job search. I really would hate to be a coordinator who just said, "Check out the jobs online, rank the ones you like, and we'll send your resume to them." What does each student really hope to learn in their co-op job? How challenging a job can we realistically hope that the student can obtain to maximize their learning? What is our fallback plan if we are unsuccessful in getting one of the most desirable jobs? These are some questions I like to discuss early in the referral process.

There is strong educational potential in the simple process of sifting through a variety of jobs. With my undeclared majors, I worry much less about whether they are applying to jobs in marketing or supply chain management and much more about whether the student is applying for jobs that fit their general preferences in a job. Right now, I'm working with an undeclared student who has no idea what she wants in terms of a business concentration, but her MBTI results clearly indicate that she needs to be in a highly people-oriented job with a high degree of structure. So her game plan is to target job descriptions with those elements as opposed to a given concentration. She is looking at jobs such as HR generalist, recruiter, event manager, salesperson, trainer, and public relations assistant.

Another student might be torn between, say, Finance and Marketing. In that case, I'd encourage the student to set a goal of pursuing jobs in both fields and remaining open to accepting a job in either area. I would recommend that the student decide on the basis of challenge and learning opportunity rather than major, company name, and so forth.

Yet another student might have more of a Plan A and Plan B. Plan A is to see if they can get a highly competitive job in networking at Cisco, a leader in telecommunications. If that doesn't work out, Plan B could be to get an advanced job in PC/LAN support that will build networking experience and tee them up for that more desired job for the next cycle. Regardless, it's good to start off with some sense of what we're trying to accomplish and what might or might not be possible in the job search.

5. *Set expectations for the preparation process*

Although I personally resist hard and fast deadlines, students need to understand what they need to do and when they need to do it over the course of the job search. I try to keep it simple:

- Have an initial meeting with me within the first two weeks of the semester

- Get your resume approved within the first three weeks of the semester

- After your resume is approved, schedule and complete your practice interview

- If the student needs to develop their own job, give them advice on how to do so, including how to market the program to an employer and what constitutes a job that would qualify for credit

- Otherwise, rank a large number of jobs online, and print out your 10–12 favorite jobs, ranked in order of preference.

- Bring in that batch of job descriptions at least a week or two before the first round of resumes goes to employers; we'll discuss your choices and reach an agreement on about six or seven jobs to pursue initially.

- See what happens for 11–14 days, then come in again to discuss next steps. If you have active interest from, say, two of those six or seven jobs, then we'll consider applying to four or five additional jobs. The goal is to pursue no more than about six or seven jobs at one time; as jobs are ruled out by you or companies, we can bring the number back up.

- Stay in touch and maintain consistent contact until you get a job.

- If you're ever unsure about what to do, contact me immediately.

- Once you get a job offer, you have three business days to make a decision.

- Once you accept a job offer, you don't interview anymore, and you can't renege on your offer if a more desirable one comes along.

- Attend a co-op success factors meeting to provide closure to the preparation process once you obtain a job.

That's my process in a nutshell. In the interviews at the end of the chapter, Kate McLaughlin expands on student-developed jobs. Other coordinators and programs will vary considerably. The point is not exactly how you do it, but that you are clear with students on what you're doing and why you do it as you do.

6. *Help students prepare resumes and interviews*

The next two chapters will have much more on how to do this.

7. *Get feedback from employers*

It's a great idea to get feedback from employers during the interview process. Employers are our educational partners, and you need to emphasize how interview feedback can be a valuable teaching tool for our aspiring young professionals. Not all employers will be willing to disclose specifics about individuals. Some fear legal consequence, and others are just not good at articulating why one candidate is better than other. "She just seemed like a better fit for the job" is one comment I've heard all too often.

Still, you have to try to get any feedback you can. We seem to do best when employers come on campus to interview. At the end of the day, I can sit down with pen and paper to record any comments. Whether an individual did something especially impressive or disappointing, this gives me an opportunity to make the interview a teachable moment for the student.

That said, you do need to filter and interpret the feedback at times. Before I pass along feedback—especially negative feedback—I'll often ask the student to give me *their* feedback on how the interview went first. If the employer slams a student simply for being inexperienced, I'm going to soften that criticism considerably. In general, I'm going to try to take whatever the feedback may be and translate it into an educational message for the student. The upshot could be "You did a great job; you just got beaten out by a more experienced candidate. Just keep doing what you're doing." Or it could be "The interviewer had the impression that you really didn't want the job, based on the fact that your answers were really short as well as the fact that you didn't ask questions. Did you want the job?" As with every interaction, the goal is to have honest communication that will facilitate learning and improvement.

Sometimes you do need to remind students that most interviewers are by no means experts in interviewing. It can be very frustrating for students to deal with interviewers who never shut up but never ask questions, or interviewers who ask only a few fuzzy questions and don't seem to know what they're doing. Likewise, interviewers don't always hire the best candidate for a job. All you can do is try to make sure that the student doesn't carry any frustration with one interview or interviewer into the next one.

8. *Manage the emotional roller coaster*

For many students—or for any job seeker, actually—a job search can be a real emotional roller coaster. On one day, you might be sky-high when you find out that you have an interview that you didn't expect to get. Four days later, you might be down in the dumps when you were beaten out for the job and now have nothing else on the horizon. When you're looking for a job over a period of time, it's easy to take rejection personally as opposed to accepting the fact that someone else might just be a better fit for a job. It can be very stressful. One first-time student was in tears in my office three times during the first three weeks of the job search, and nothing unusually bad had even happened!

This is where someone really needs to stay calm, and it had better be you! Here are some statements I'll repeat frequently during the peak of referral season:

- "There have been many times over the years when a student struggled to even get one interview in the first month of referrals, only to end up with two or three offers in a couple of days later in the semester."

- "If you're still looking for a job late in the process, your resume is going to start looking much better to employers. Right now your resume compares unfavorably to the more experienced students, but most of them will be hired within a month. At that point, employers will look at your non-professional job experience with a more open mind. If you remain unhired long enough, eventually you'll become the best candidate still looking. And if that happens, all of a sudden you're first in line for some great jobs that always come in late in the hiring process. It's what I call King or Queen of the Mountain—hang around long enough and you may well end up on top."

- "No matter how discouraged you might feel now, you always have to act as if you're 90–95 percent of the way toward getting a job. It might just take one more interview, one more burst of positive energy to get a great position. But if you start going into interviews showing your frustration, it won't happen for you."

- "I know this has been hard for you. But, believe me, I'd rather have you suffer a little longer through the job search process instead of getting any old job quickly... and then suffering through six long months of an unchallenging job."

- "If you get beaten out by a superior candidate, you have to tip your cap to that individual. But don't ever let yourself get outworked in your preparation for an interview. Your goal is always to be able to walk out of an interview knowing in your heart that you did as much as you realistically could to get the job. Everything else is outside of your control, and you have to try to let all of that go."

- "Yeah, it's difficult now, and I know it feels like it's taking forever, but when you look in the rearview mirror at this job search from the vantage point of having a great job, the amount of time and effort you put into getting it will seem negligible."

There are many others, but you get the idea.

Another way to keep students from freaking out during job referrals is to give them some time to digest and reflect on information before plowing ahead at different moments in the job search. As Tamara Pinkas says in her transcribed interview segment, coming up shortly, sometimes it can be good to build in a little lag time so a student can mull whether they really want to pursue a really good job that may have low pay and a tough commute. I have found that true with students when it comes to relocation. Often I'll bring up a job in California or Washington, and the student will have a knee-jerk negative reaction to moving 3,000 miles away. I've learned to just say "That's fine. Let me just give you a little more information, and get back to me within a few days if you're interested." It's not all that unusual to come in the next morning to get a voice mail: "I don't know what I was thinking! Of course I'd be interested in that job. I just had never thought about moving, and it threw me when you brought it up."

Better still, I now try to get students thinking about relocation way in advance to lower their resistance when the time comes. The point is that people may need time to adjust their expectations and decide if they're game for something outside of their comfort zone.

9. *Advise on job offers, as needed*

As the job search process progresses, a common question often arises: "I just got an offer. Should I accept it?" Some professionals refuse to get involved, insisting that the student take full responsibility for the decision. I agree that the student needs to own the decision, but I do think a professional can help a student talk through the decision.

If there are multiple job offers, I have a coined a term that has proven to be useful. I like to talk about "dealmakers and tiebreakers." Students often get bogged down with the quantity and variety of factors in the decision, befuddling themselves as they weigh pay, commuting distance, job quality, work environment, and company reputation. It can be helpful to simplify things by talking about what *should*, generally, be the dealmakers in this decision. I would do this by asking these questions:

- Which job will you enjoy doing the most, day in and day out?

- Which job will be the best learning experience?

- Which job will be most challenging?

- Which position has the greatest potential for growth?

- Which position will put you on a trajectory toward your next job or toward your long-term career goals?

If the student has little positive to say in response to most of these questions, then that raises serious questions as to whether the job should be accepted. However, if the individual has more than one offer and finds that their answers to the dealmaker questions still leave

175

them deadlocked, *then* I suggest that we go to the tiebreaker questions:

- How well does each job pay?

- What work environment did you prefer?

- What commute is easier?

- Which co-workers or supervisor did you prefer?

These questions are not pulled from the air; they hearken back to my days of teaching Frederick Herzberg's theory of motivation in my Organizational Behavior course. In research that was generally supported empirically, Herzberg found that the following factors generally lead to job satisfaction: the work itself, achievement, recognition, growth, responsibility, and advancement. Other factors—the so-called "hygiene factors"—can lead to dissatisfaction if they are negative but only lead to a *lack of dissatisfaction* if they are present: work environment, relationship with supervisor, pay, company policies, and relationships with co-workers. In other words, if you have great pay and a nice work environment, you will not necessarily feel motivated as a result; at best, these elements can help you avoid dissatisfaction. An analogy can be made to personal hygiene: If it's good, no one notices it. But if it's bad, it's a problem!

So my advice is that unless those hygiene factors seem to be highly unsatisfactory, it's best to only think of those as tiebreakers when it comes to accepting an offer. Thus if you're choosing between two equally good jobs in terms of the work itself, the learning opportunity, and so forth, you might take a longer look at the pay and how you feel about the organizational culture and work environment. There can be exceptions—there are students who believe that they can't afford to turn down a significantly higher-paying job in favor of one that all agree would be a better learning experience—but obviously we want to discourage that kind of choice where possible.

Students can be overly swayed by pay rates and snazzy work environments, so I think it's helpful for them to hear this perspective. After that, though, it's basically up to them. The only exception would be if I feel a student's perception of a job is inaccurate. If a student has the impression that a job will be highly challenging, and I see it otherwise, I will probe to find out what their basis is for that perception. Or if they are underestimating the learning opportunity in a job, I might weigh in on that front. Usually, though, letting the student talk through the pros and cons of each job offer makes it pretty obvious to both of us which one is best.

The situation is a little different if there is only one job offer. I am pretty stubborn and really hate to see a student accept a job if they are lukewarm about the offer. However, I always try to give the student my best guess as to whether or not they are likely to get a better offer at some point down the road if they decline the one that they have. Sometimes I'll give two or three scenarios as to what could happen in the weeks to come, adding the caveat that I'm operating under the assumption that the energy that they put into a job search continues in strength and consistency.

Overall, I sometimes feel that students are overly fickle, dragging their feet with a really good offer in hand. This may come from students equating the process with applying for colleges, when you have the luxury of applying to a half-dozen or more schools and letting all the results come in before you make a commitment. The business world doesn't operate that way, though, so we don't let students sit on offers for more than three business days. The last thing we want to see is a student hanging onto an offer "just in case" for a few weeks before declining... at which point every other candidate who interviewed is long gone.

More often, though, my experience is that students get panicky and are more inclined to accept a relatively weak offer early because they don't know what the forthcoming weeks will bring. Although that's nicely expedient for the professional, I think we have a moral responsibility to let a student know if he is selling himself short. No one has a crystal ball, but time and experience will give you a good feel for what is legitimately plausible for a given candidate.

10. *Providing closure to the job search process*

Eventually, we hope, every student who goes through the process as recommended will get a job. What next? I think it's appropriate to have some sort of closure step, whether it's a final one-on-one meeting or a small group session. In Chapter 3, I talked about my co-op success factors meetings as a time-saving and educational step for my first-time students. Revisiting that now, we cover these questions:

- Why is it important for you to do a good job over the next six months? Or, to put it another way, what are the various ways in which you will selfishly benefit by performing well?

- When employers call me due to a problem with a co-op, what is the most common one? Why does that problem arise?

- How often do you think you need to get in touch with me while in co-op?

- Regardless of how often you are required to be in touch, what would be some specific issues that should lead you to get in touch with me immediately?

That may be more elaborate than what you might choose to do. But I do think it's good to bring the preparation process to a formal close, and this is an opportunity to reinforce some important points as opposed to simply having a student come into my office to fill out a form before disappearing for six months.

To reinforce the information in this admittedly ambitious chapter, let's see what our group of experts had to say about counseling students during the preparation process.

IN THEIR OWN WORDS

PROFESSIONAL PERSPECTIVE #1
"PRESENTING ISSUES VERSUS REAL ISSUES"
Kerry Mahoney, University of Waterloo

When advising a student it is important to try to get a complete understanding of where the student is coming from as sometimes the presenting issue is not the real issue. Establish rapport with the student, and then ask some deeper questions. Maybe they've come to you with their resume, but the reason they're struggling with selling themselves via their resume is that they're feeling that they're not in the right academic program.

The following example may illustrate this point. One day I was job shadowing one of our field coordinators who was doing student site visits (I do this occasionally to ensure our co-op preparation course is mirroring what's really going on for students out there on their work terms). One of the engineering students we visited was working at a law firm. I thought that this was curious. As it turns out, this student was doing some work around patents.

This student's story was very interesting—her mother was an engineering alum from UW, as was her father, and her fiancé who was a current engineering student. So this student had been having all sorts of doubts about her program and her work terms reflected that. One of her other work terms had been teaching engineering concepts to children but it was the teaching that interested her. All of her work terms were on the periphery of engineering—related enough to engineering that we could give her credit but not really engineering heavy. The real issue was that she did not want to be in engineering; in fact, she didn't want to touch it with a ten-foot pole. She had made an educational decision for all the wrong reasons and now she was trying to follow through and make the best of a difficult situation. She felt like she was too far into her program to start over. We began a conversation that day about what she really would love to do—she ended up applying to a faculty of education and she helped me out by telling her story to other students.

The takeaway from this is to be prepared for the conversation to go someplace unexpected. Try to determine where the student is at and look for the body language and what they're not saying. I'm not suggesting you go out of your way to uncover problems where there aren't any, but be receptive to going off your path of "I want to cover these five things in this session."

One other piece for me is "know what you don't know" and make referrals when it makes sense. Our coordinators are hired with a whole bunch of different skill sets in mind. They need to be salespeople out there developing brand new jobs. They need to be relationship builders to maintain and grow the current pool. They have to be problem solvers. And they need to counsel students. Some have lots of education and experience in that area and others have less. Knowing what you don't know and being able to refer to others is important. In the case of this engineering student, Career Services staff would likely be in the best position to work with the student around reconsidering academic and career plans and determining how best to balance personal and family desires.

PROFESSIONAL PERSPECTIVE #2
"THIS IS HOW YOU LOOK"
Kate McLaughlin, Northeastern University

[Counseling during the job search process] depends on how far along your program is in terms of whether you actually have jobs that they can apply for or if you're at a point where you really don't have anything to offer them. In that case, what you need to offer them is "this is how you look; this is how you do a job hunt." That's something that I do with my students—explaining to them how to approach companies. What are the pros and cons of approaching a company directly? What are the differences between approaching a big company directly and a little tiny company? What are the different reactions they're going to get? And then walking them through okay, you've sent out your resume and your cover letter to these folks, when do you follow up? How often do you follow up?

When you finally start getting calls and interviews, how are those going? Who's sending out the thank-you notes afterward? Are you still pursuing other leads? The decision-making process—you have an offer, but it's really this other company that you really want to work for. Do you accept it, or do you wait? You need to talk them through that process. This is actually where meeting with them frequently is actually more valuable than any other time because this is the scary part. They're used to being able to sign up for classes, and they know what they're doing. Here a lot of it is out of their control, so one of the easiest ways to feel like you've got some semblance of control is to be continually sending your resume out to new places. Because until somebody offers you a job and you accept it, you should be looking. You may find the job that's exactly what you want tomorrow, and it's a job you didn't know existed yesterday.

Doing that helps them understand how to do these things when they no longer have the luxury of career services or a co-op database full of jobs to consider. If they do have that luxury now, get them to understand the difference of applying for a job through an institution versus on their own. Understand that employers have needs and frankly may not care about you. You are nobody to them until they decide that you are the right person for the job. You have to come in and show them that you would have value to the company. Until then you're just a name, and nobody knows whether you've got great potential or no potential. They don't know, and you have to get to the point where they care. Remember, they don't care right now. They're not your parents; they're not your teachers. So that's where actually more of the handholding happens. I describe my job sometimes as half holding their hand and half kicking their butt, and kicking their butt happens earlier on. Holding their hand tends to happen later. Because if they haven't taken advantage of the butt-kicking early on, they don't get to the handholding part.

PROFESSIONAL PERSPECTIVE #3
"WHAT DO YOU LIKE TO DO?"
Bernadette Friedrich, Michigan State University

In a field like engineering, we have really broad majors—mechanical engineering, electrical engineering, chemical engineering—so we have to get a student to understand that there's not going to be a job title that says "Mechanical Engineer." So how can they best figure out what they want to do, especially if they don't have any experience? We work with students; we do some broad-based stuff, but much of it is one-on-one. We ask: "What do you like to do? Do you like to take things apart? Do you like to create things that are different? Do you like to work by yourself or do you prefer to be in more of a group environment?" All engineers work in teams, but if you're a design engineer, you probably spend more time thinking and creating—whereas manufacturing is figuring out problems, efficiency, and process.

We are trying to get the student to look at "What do I like to do?" They don't know the meaning of "process engineer" or "quality engineer." Our goal is to steer them into things that they like, to talk to them about what they like to do and what they don't like to do. We want to get them to understand a little bit more about where they want to be when they graduate. Our ultimate goal is to have the student get the best job upon graduation—the best job for them personally. They'll say, "Well, I'm a mechanical engineer, and I'll work anywhere." Yeah, but are you going to be happy anywhere? Do you like to take things apart? Because that's different from designing things. Do you like to fix stuff? And so we try to get them to focus on those aspects of the career.

PROFESSIONAL PERSPECTIVE #4
"WHAT THEIR HEART IS SAYING"
Tom Akins, Georgia Institute of Technology

Of course the most important thing is communication skills. I've had situations come up with some of our own employees where I said "You need to improve your communications skills" and they thought that I meant, well, I need to speak better. No, that's not what I'm talking about. They need to improve their communications skills by listening more, and I think that's probably one of the worst things that maybe we do as co-op advisors.

Listen to what they're really saying as far as their desires and what they believe that they need as far as their education and their career concerns. Listen to what they're saying, and then don't always make snap decisions on a particular student because we have to understand that these are young people who are not coming from the same basis of knowledge that we have in most cases. They're very limited in experience, unless they've had some family members that have maybe exposed them to some things. A lot of students that come in they don't realize what's out there, and it's constantly changing, of course, particularly in engineering and the technology fields. So we need to listen to what they're saying and then sometimes compare it to experiences we may have had with other students or maybe our own personal experiences. But keep in mind that the students today are a lot different from us. Maybe they've been exposed to more things than we had been at that age, but they're not as different as we may think. They're still facing similar challenges that all of us have faced when we were that age. We had just started to school and were trying to figure out what we wanted to do. The key thing I think, though, is listening to what they have to say and not only just verbally. Sometimes you have to read between the lines as to what they really want to do. Maybe more of what their heart is saying to you than what their voice is saying to you.

I can remember one particular example. I had a young man who was in electrical engineering. He was doing fine. He had no academic problems, and he could do well on his job. He came in and told me: "I can do the work; I can do the academic portion in the classroom. I'm just not excited about it." And I said, "What do you want to do?" He says, "Well, my dad says I need to ..." I said, "Oh no, no, what do you want to do?" He said, "Well, I talked to my dad and he advised me ..." And I said, "No, no, no." I asked him three times: "What do you want to do?" He said, "Well, I don't know." And I said, "When are you the happiest? When are you most content?" He says, "Well, actually I have a band, and I really enjoy when we're playing music and we're entertaining people and people are happy." So I said: "Okay. Why don't you see if you can pursue something in the music field?" And he said, "Well, I don't know..." Long story made somewhat short, he wound up changing from electrical engineering to a business management type major here and then went on to work in the business end of the music field. And he was much happier. Because that's where his heart and his passion was. It wasn't that intellectually or intelligence-wise he couldn't handle electrical engineering but his real passion, where his heart was, was in this whole music field.

Just understand that: Try to get the students to understand they need to do not necessarily what their parents want them to do or what their parents think they should do, but they really need to find something they have a passion for and follow that. So I think that's what I'm saying when I say you need to listen to what their heart's saying, too. Where's their passion?

PROFESSIONAL PERSPECTIVE #5
"LAG TIME"
Tamara Pinkas, Lane Community College

My writing students work for some publications, including a women's literary journal that's out of Corvallis, Oregon which is 45 miles from my college. It's a big commitment for a student to drive an hour to their co-op twice a week or three times a week. So what I do is I always have a lag time. The students meet with me, and we talk about their co-op. Then I have them do some research and come back. Because I find that if I try to set up an internship the minute they walk in the room and seem excited, they get caught up in my interest and my excitement, and it doesn't give them the time they need to reflect on whether this is the right thing for them—the timing, the cost, the drive, dealing with family issues like children or whatever their commitments are.

So I wouldn't say it's efficient, but it's a very important psychological step to make them go away and think about it. I have them communicate with me within a week to confirm that this is something that they want to do. I've found that over the years if I don't do that, then students somehow disappear. They say they'll follow through, and then they don't. So then you end up with a site that's all excited about a student because you've made the contact. Then you try to get a hold of the student, and they won't call you back because they feel badly and have decided not to do it. It's a better system for making sure that there is a commitment especially when dealing with students who are not required to do an internship as part of their program. It's a buy-in step—time to be very clear that this is what they want.

PROFESSIONAL PERSPECTIVE #6
"RULES ARE MEANT TO GUIDE, NOT INHIBIT"
Nancy Johnston, Simon Fraser University

The whole counseling side is where the real emergent opportunities for learning are. Some coordinators, the excellent ones, see that. They see their role and opportunities as educators. When they see all the resume mistakes, the missing of due dates, the lack of applying to jobs, they realize that there is a punitive approach they can take or an educational approach to these problems. A lot of people who are more operations-oriented will opt for the punitive. "Hey, you needed to have this work report in by January 10, and you didn't, it is ten percent off now. I need it in by January 12 or your grade turns to an F."

A true educator would ask, "So what's happening? Why did this not get in on time? Is it the topic? What would have been more useful or engaging for you to write about? Now that we are back on track, I will give you until such-and-such a date to produce this because it is something more in sync with what your learning goals were for the work term." It is an entirely different way to approach non-compliance issues. When you move from an administrator/manager mentality in which you make sure the rules are followed, and then you move into making sure every educational opportunity that you can is exploited, you do the job completely differently. You read completely different books: You're not reading *The One-Minute Manager*, you're reading about transformative learning. You just have a whole different orientation and world view. I realize that many of us have to walk somewhere in the middle, but more coordinators, in my mind, tend to walk as administrators and managers.

But I firmly believe we're educators. Rules are meant to guide. They are never meant, in my mind, to inhibit. When they start to just be inhibiting, or punitive, then they have lost their purpose. They're actually meant to guide growth or whatever your goal is.

PROFESSIONAL PERSPECTIVE #7
"ENCOURAGE STUDENTS WITH DISABILITIES"
Ronnie Porter, Northeastern University

I think the important thing is really to be able to assess the skills and interests of the students as individuals. It becomes very important that we have a clear understanding of particular job descriptions and responsibilities. It is critical that we know exactly what the tasks of the job are. Having a disability may have no functional impact on a student's chosen career. Some people may be able to do the job but need a reasonable accommodation. For purposes of assessing whether they can perform the primary job functions—the clarity of the job description becomes very important.

I would say that we need to know the students very well; we need to be able to look at a job and help them determine whether they have the skills or not to do the job with or without reasonable accommodation. We need to encourage students with disabilities from the very beginning to participate in co-op and internship programs. I would encourage co-op coordinators, career services professionals, etc. to do some kind of outreach with the disability resource center on the campus. Ask if you can participate in new student orientations to let students with disabilities know about the program. Let them know that they're welcome—really encourage them to participate. Recent literature has reported that employment for people with disabilities has actually declined since the passage of the Americans with Disabilities Act. Work experience matters in terms of gaining access to the world of work and has an impact on future earnings.

There are two major reasons [for the recent trend of increased unemployment for disabled individuals]. From the research that I have read, one is that the reasonable accommodation mandate came without a budget. So it really has been kind of a backlash in some ways. Though the ADA was written to be very broad and inclusive, the interpretation of who is disabled under the law and what a reasonable accommodation is is very narrow. There is a great deal of confusion because decisions on whether an individual has a disability are made on a case-by-case situation. Appellate courts in different regions have made conflicting decisions for similar cases, which has led to much confusion and little consistency. The confusion may have led to the hiring of fewer individuals with disabilities to avoid what they may see as some potential problems down the road. It's much more difficult to prove discrimination at the hiring stage than it is at the promotion stage or other steps in the personnel process. The second thing is that at the same time that the ADA was passed, the Social Security Administration liberalized the eligibility requirements. In difficult economic times particularly people who are lower wage earners may opt to get onto the disability rolls who may have otherwise participated in the labor market because it might be more financially advantageous.

As the economy has changed from a manufacturing to a service-based economy, the growth in new types of jobs require a more highly educated workforce. That's why it's critical to encourage students with disabilities to further their education. The research that I did also pointed out that experience really matters, so I think I would translate that to the work that we do. Getting as much experience as you can matters. It also really matters if your job is related to your field of study—that has an impact on earnings. I think that we really need to spend time sharing that information with people who are working on the front lines with students with disabilities. We need to collaborate much more to facilitate opportunities for students with disabilities, provide information to them regarding these opportunities, and encourage them to take advantage of them. We need to promote further collaboration between professionals in college disability resource centers and those in co-op and experiential programs. While some colleges and universities have made efforts in this area some have not. It is important that in addition to getting support for getting through the academics, students need to be encouraged to participate in experiential programs to enable them to be more competitive. If students with disabilities are not in a position to gain access to the labor market despite having a college education and can't take their rightful place in our economy, then we will have failed. It is critical that people who work with co-op programs, internships, any kind of experiential education do the outreach to their colleagues in disabled student development and vice versa so that they really work together for the benefit of the students.

There is a young man I worked with who had a stroke when he was 12. As a result, he had some physical weakness on one side of his body and can't use one arm. He wanted to come to Northeastern, but his parents were really concerned about him going to a large school in a big city, and made him go to a small college outside Boston. He ended up going to a small college that didn't have public transportation, and he was miserable for two years. They finally allowed him to transfer here to Northeastern.

He was a political science major, very interested in policy and also quite an accomplished athlete. He was on the paralympic soccer team and did an internship working on a research project, he helped develop an awareness course, and he also did some programming, and was able to combine several of his interests. After that, he did a paid internship available through and worked for one of the Representatives in the State House.

We talked about some of the skills he wanted to develop. He wanted to develop his leadership skills so he applied to be an orientation leader one summer. By the time he graduated he really had a very well-rounded resume that described some very good skills in terms of research, programming, public policy, communication and he had had the opportunity to network. It only took him a couple months to find a job. He was able to move into a job in a field that he chose based on the internships and co-ops that provided him with the experience that he needed.

PROFESSIONAL PERSPECTIVE #8
"COUNSELING INTERNATIONAL STUDENTS"
Marie Sacino, LaGuardia Community College

LaGuardia students come from all over the world. Among the 15,169 students in academic programs, there are 156 countries represented and 118 different languages spoken; 58 percent of our students are foreign-born. To create a sense of connection and community, we work in groups and teams in our classes. This alleviates some of the isolation that our international students may feel as well as prepares all students for teamwork in their upcoming internship assignments. Student groups make presentations to classes on chapter assignments, reading, and special topics. Group work begins straightaway in our professional advancement courses; students may also be assigned to work in pairs on projects and research. As the course concludes, students begin to make individual presentations on book assignments and on their ePortfolios. One of the things that we try to do is to remove that sense of isolation that many students feel by providing opportunities for students to speak in small groups as we know that they are not ready to speak in a large classroom setting. Another very important area is establishing rapport with our students. We need to provide encouragement and support to our international students so that they begin to feel confident and capable to complete an internship assignment. One of the great things about our internship program is that it is the only way an international student can have an opportunity to work in a paid internship assignment. But, we do need to counsel them in special ways. That might mean telling them that their English is in a developmental stage. It's going to take some time as well as some strategies to continue to improve. And, that might mean suggestions, such as, "you need to speak up in the classroom more" and "you need to practice English more outside of the classroom—at home, with friends." We work with communication skills a great deal in our classes. Students are constantly working on their speaking and listening skills by making presentations in a group, as a pair, or individually. It's a good strategy for scaffolding communication skills in our courses.

Additionally, we ask students to keep a journal of new vocabulary as they read articles, listen to podcasts, or watch the evening news hour. If they are reading a biography or autobiography in class, they're preparing and presenting a PowerPoint on their critique. Being in New York City with its tremendous diversity, we find that our international students do quite well in terms of their internship assignments. They can really compete with our American students equally as long as they have a strong intellectual background and are doing well in their classes. The international students are particularly appreciative of all of the work that we do in the internship program. They know that the internship is the only way that they can work in New York City and that it might take a little more time and energy in finding the right placement. One of the things that we need to do is to show them that there is a transition from one culture to another. So, we have to help the students to be able to make a transition from one culture to another as well as from being a student to being an intern.

PROFESSIONAL PERSPECTIVE #9
"A DIAMOND IN THE ROUGH"
Tamara Pinkas, Lane Community College

It was very early in my career, and I was working with welfare moms. They were being forced to do a clerical training so they could find a job and get off welfare. They came with fairly negative attitudes about education as well as negative feelings about governmental systems. So there was a lot of negativity.

Over the course of the six months' training, at the very end they did a co-op to prove themselves and get hired. I was setting up an internship for one of the students and the employer asked me about her. I used this exact phrase: "I think she's a diamond in the rough. That's what I think she is. She's great. But I think she needs some polishing." Which I see as a very positive statement. It says volumes about my estimation of this student.

The student does her internship and I go to do the site visit. I always have the student walk out to the car with me because that allows some private time for the students to say something they would never say in front of a supervisor and within earshot of anybody. It's a common technique I use for privacy at the workplace. As the student and I are walking out, she says to me: "You know, my supervisor told me that terrible thing you said about me—that I was a diamond in the rough."

I was just taken aback. I said, "You are aware of what that means?" and I explained the meaning of that phrase. She said "No, I thought you were being really negative about me, I thought you were saying bad things about me." And the lesson–the takeaway–for me was to be very careful about 1) what I say to supervisors, and 2) when I say things, I also make sure I say them to students so that there is never any chance for this surprise, where a student can misinterpret something that I say because the supervisor didn't bother to explain it.

I just don't want anybody to get triangulated or have any kind of negative experiences as that poor student did. She obviously labored for weeks and weeks with this belief that I thought she was a terrible person. I felt awful and I never wanted to do it again. So I've always practiced that from then forward. I'm much more circumspect about what I tell employers, and I'm very careful to be sure the students know what I said to them. I call them or I e-mail them to say "Here's what I told the employer about you."

REFLECTION QUESTIONS

1. The early part of this chapter focuses on getting students to own responsibility instead of doing work for them. What have you done to increase your students' self-sufficiency without compromising your responsibilities as an educator?

2. In the section entitled "The Student Whisperer," I emphasize the importance of using calm-assertive energy with students as opposed to projecting irritation, frustration, impatience, or anger. How would you characterize the energy you project toward students? Does that change when a student frustrates or angers you?

3. In citing the work of psychiatrist Irvin Yalom, I talk about how the educator/student relationship is a metaphor for the student's future manager/employee relationship. Can you think of a specific time when you were able to use a student's problem or shortcoming as a way to show them how it could translate into being an issue in the workplace? In general, do you embrace the idea of the educator as manager? Why or why not?

4. What specific steps have you taken to ensure that your relationships with students are positive and productive? Have you had to work on being either too much of a rules-oriented disciplinarian or too much of a student-hugging buddy in order to reach a more balanced style?

5. This chapter talks about how modeling from one's own experiences can be a valuable tool for educators. To what degree do you share your own experiences? What limits would you set on whether a professional should share personal stories?

6. If you work with international students, how do you ensure that your style with them is as effective as possible? Would you agree that we sometimes need to treat students differently in order to treat them fairly, or should we emphasize equality in how we work with students who have individual differences?

7. The author offers many statements he makes when helping students to manage the "emotional roller coaster." Which statements resonated with you the most? Are there substantially different ones that you have found to be valuable?

CHAPTER 8

TEACHING STUDENTS IN GROUPS

"A teacher is one who makes himself
progressively unnecessary."
— *Thomas Carruthers*

A professional's workload will have a huge impact on the time available to work one-on-one with students. However, teaching students in groups is not only possible for everyone, it's highly recommended for all but the very smallest programs. If anything, teaching students in groups is probably an underutilized tool at many programs. Why is that? One reason is the recurring theme of professionals enjoying their one-on-one time with students. Another is that professionals may find it impossible to get their institution to approve a course for credit.

The most amazing excuse I've heard over the years is from professionals who "don't have time" to teach students in groups. This mystifies me: If you have time to teach something 25 times to 25 individual students, you must have time to teach it *once* to 25 students!

Likewise, the other arguments about working with students in groups are pretty easy to dismiss. You prefer working with students one-on-one? That's great. Use a group session to milk the obvious advantages of a classroom setting. You have the opportunity to disseminate the same information to a big group in one shot, ranging from lecture material to announcements. You can engage students in group discussion and facilitate collaboration in small-group work, including role plays. Best of all, covering many issues in a large group inevitably will improve the quantity *and* quality of your one-on-one meetings, which can be tailored much more to the individual needs of that student.

As for the lament about not being able to teach a course for credit, well, who says that students need to get credit for large-group work? Before we had a mandatory co-op preparation course at Northeastern University, many of us conducted resume-writing and interviewing workshops or orientation sessions in which mechanics of the job search process were covered.

I don't want to try to get into the full gamut of possibilities here, but this chapter and the appended interview transcripts allude to many of them: workshops, orientations, one-credit courses, three-credit courses, and so forth. Obviously, having a course for credit does give some legitimacy to your efforts, and you may be able to assign more homework in a class for credit without as much squawking as you'd find in a non-credit workshop. Regardless, there is always a way to work with students in groups, and I can't imagine doing otherwise for at least some elements of running a program—unless you are working with, say, five or ten students and have plenty of time.

For the sake of simplicity, I am going to refer to teaching a class throughout this chapter. I will run through a pretty broad range of possible topics, approaches, and specific exercises. Ultimately, you may very well decide that you don't want to cover all of these topics in a group setting or that you want to approach group work quite differently. By all means, feel free to adopt, adapt, or reject any ideas here if you have something that works better for you and your program.

POSSIBLE CONTENT AREAS

As Mary Kane discusses in her end-of-chapter interview excerpt, there is a division between the two primary topic areas for a course. There are many topics that relate to the *preparation* phase of getting ready for the workplace. In fact, many students come in to our Professional Development for Co-op course believing that this is the sole purpose of the class. It's not all that unusual for students to ask if they need to keep coming to the class once they get a job!

Au contraire: A big chunk of our course covers professional behavior in the workplace—the *activity* phase of the co-op learning model, and there is some attention devoted to the *reflection* phase as well. Students often have a hard time seeing beyond the immediate issue of getting the job, so we've had to work to get them to understand how crucial it is to understand how to make the transition from classroom to professional setting.

Through my interviews and conversations over the years with individuals at various programs, here are some typical topics that programs may opt to cover in a course or in other group settings:

- assessing students' values, perceptions, and areas of intellectual curiosity

- the nature of learning, including theories such as metacognition

- career development and career paths

- understanding transferable skills

- resume-writing

- strategic interviewing

- the job search process

- professional behavior, including ethics, diversity, and sexual harassment

- reflection

COURSE MATERIALS

I have to admit that I'm biased when it comes to discussing books that one might use when teaching preparation courses or workshops. I'm the author of two books that are used at Northeastern University as well as many other programs around the U.S. and Canada. I will discuss those books, but I also will try hard to give you some objective information about other options as well.

There are tons of books out there that might be used for this purpose. I'm honestly not familiar with many of them, but there are many that cover all the bases without getting into great depth. If you're going to use someone else's book, I think it's best to go with something written with co-ops and internships in mind as well as with an author who has expertise in our professions.

In general, there may be other good options that I have not come across, but I generally think that you're likely to be best off with one of three options:

1. *Use an existing textbook written by a co-op or internship professional from another institution.*

   To the best of my knowledge, there are only two such books available. One is called *Introduction to Professional Practice: Centennial Edition*. The author is listed as the University of Cincinnati Division of Professional Practice. This textbook covers most of the aforementioned course topics, and it also includes material on the history of cooperative education as well as delving into diversity, organizational behavior, and some other areas. It's a 367-page book published by McGraw-Hill. According to the publisher, the suggested retail price is $73.13 as of December 2008, but the price may vary by bookstore. You should be able to obtain a complimentary copy at this URL:

   http://www.mhprofessional.com/product.php?isbn=0073194603

   My primary course book is called *Find Your First Professional Job: A Guide For Co-ops, Interns, and Full-Time Job Seekers*. My book doesn't attempt to cover the history of co-op or some of the other topics raised in the UC book, but it has relatively deep material on resume-writing, interviewing, and professional behavior in the workplace. It's a 237-page book published by Mosaic Eye Publishing. The suggested retail price is $24.95 as of December 2008, but this may vary by bookstore as well. My book is basically self-published; I've turned down a few opportunities to have someone else publish it because it's been an effective way for me to keep the price down. As such, complimentary copies are not available, but discounts are available for educators. Go to this website to learn more about the book:

   http://www.mosaiceyepublishing.com/

   Click on "Contact Us" to request information about educator discounts on this and my other book, which I'll mention shortly.

   The advantage of using an existing textbook is that you don't have to reinvent the wheel; you can use what someone else has developed. You can opt to have students read the whole book or assign chapters selectively if you have a more or less ambitious plan for your course or group work. As for which book you might use, I'd suggest getting both books and seeing what you think of the content, style, and value of each for your purposes. I think it would be fair to say that the UC book is broader in scope than my book, but mine delves deeper into topics such as interviewing.

The biggest disadvantage of using an existing book is that it is not customized to the specific needs of your program. So let's look at the next two options:

2. *Develop your own course materials and use those.*

This is perhaps the most common practice in the profession, and there are two primary benefits to "growing your own" materials. First, you can create something that is 100 percent customized to your students and your program. Given how idiosyncratic most programs are—especially when it comes to the job search process—this is significant. Another advantage is cost. Most home-grown materials are photocopied, and they often can be duplicated and sold through a campus photocopying center at a reasonable cost to students—just like any other course packet. Alternatively, you could put all of the information online.

The downside of the do-it-yourself approach is that—and I speak from experience when I say this—writing substantial course materials is quite labor intensive. By putting your energy into that, you run that risk of reinventing the wheel. My book has been through at least seven or eight significant revisions over the last decade or so, and UC's Centennial Edition obviously represents a ton of work as well. If you're in a big program, maybe you'll have a few people who can collaborate on such a project if they have the time, energy, and expertise to do so. Otherwise, you'll have to ask yourself whether you're better off having something quite specific but also potentially lacking in comprehensiveness.

3. *Work with the creator of one of the existing textbooks to develop a customized version for your student population.*

I know that the University of Cincinnati has publicized their willingness to adapt their book for other programs, and I have two works-in-progress going with educators right now who want to adapt *Find Your First Professional Job*. This could be a good option, but it likely is only plausible if you have a relatively large program or if you are teaming up with a few other programs. I can't speak for UC, but my opinion is that such a project is not likely to be feasible unless the resulting book is guaranteed of selling a minimum of 500 books per year. Even then, the cost of such a customized book could vary substantially depending on how many books would be sold on a regular basis. This is simply the nature of the publishing industry. Printing 1,000 books at a time may be expensive, but printing 2,500 books does not result in anywhere near as big of a cost increase as you might imagine. So it would be difficult to customize a book that will sell only a few hundred a year, though not impossible depending on the price of the book to students.

In any event, if you have a program that is fairly large, and you like some but not all of the content of the aforementioned books, this may be an option worth pursuing.

Whatever you decide to do with a primary textbook, I think you want to end up with something that gives students a wealth of information while saving yourself considerable time. I also strongly believe that students learn best when presented with information in a variety of ways. Knowledge transfer is most likely to occur when it's reinforced repeatedly and in diverse ways. With interviews, for example, my students *read* about how to do them in a book and answer chapter review questions on the topic. Then they *hear* about them in a lecture and *experiment* with interviews with some homework assignments and in-class activities that I'll describe in this chapter. Then they'll *do* a full practice interview as a dress rehearsal, getting extensive feedback. By the time they go out for their first interview, they have had ample opportunity to learn about interviewing through a variety of approaches. Good course materials may not get your students from "0 to 60" when it comes to writing a resume or interviewing for a job, but if they can get the student from 0 to 30 or 40, you've just saved yourself a ton of work.

ANCILLARY BOOKS

I think that having course materials that focus on the fundamentals of resume-writing, interviewing, and professional behavior is essential. But you may or may not want to consider additional reading materials as well.

A few years ago I felt frustrated because our students seemed to be stumbling more than we would like when it came to professional behavior in the workplace. Eventually, though, I tried to put myself in the shoes of the students. Yes, I would tell them to "own responsibility" or to "go the extra mile" at work… but these are abstract concepts for many young adults.

The upshot was that I decided to write a book of true stories about and for young professionals—both success stories and horror stories, organized thematically. The hope was that students would read the 75-80 stories in the book and say to themselves, "Oh, so *that's* what it *really* means to stay positive at work" (or any number of other qualities).

The book is called *Exceeding Expectations: Mastering The Seven Keys To Professional Success.* Many of my colleagues and I use it as a supplementary textbook in the course. We have small and large-group discussions of the stories as cases, and the book leads in to some major writing assignments as well. Now that I've used it for a few years, I've found it interesting to have students come back from a work term and report that they faced a situation that was analogous or even identical to a story in the book. One student's boss offered him alcoholic drink tickets at a company Christmas party, although the student was underage. Remembering a similar story with disastrous consequences from *Exceeding Expectations*, my student handed the tickets back to his boss. At his final review, the manager said that the student showed better judgment than he had as a supervisor.

That's just what I hoped for when writing the book. When faced with a difficult co-worker, a seemingly bad or boring job, or an opportunity to slack off, I hope that the stories will come back to mind and help students through the tough stretches.

In addition to my book, I have heard of professionals using other career-related books such as *What Color Is Your Parachute?* by Richard Nelson Bolles and even some more tangentially related books along the lines of *Tuesdays with Morrie* by Mitch Albom. A book like that might be more appropriate if you are interested in delving into values and priorities with students as opposed to more directly relevant texts. Yet another option would be to assign an ancillary book that is highly appropriate for a specific major. If I had a class that had nothing but marketing and entrepreneurship students, for example, I probably would assign *Purple Cow* by Seth Godin, a very entertaining book that describes niche marketing and how conventional advertising is going the way of the dinosaur in this era.

TEACHING PHILOSOPHY

The next consideration in running a course is teaching philosophy. Yes, you need to teach the operational nuts and bolts of how your program works, but you also have an opportunity to turn your class into a truly educational experience on a number of levels. As such, I'll walk you through my own teaching philosophy for the Professional Development for Co-op course:

1. *Think of yourself as manager, not instructor.*

   To maximize learning, I encourage students to think of me as a manager rather than as an instructor. I don't want to be called "Professor" or Mr. Weighart, as the first-name basis is fine at work. In general, the expectations are similar to a good workplace:

   - If you're going to be late or absent, I don't need a note from the health center to prove anything. But you do need to call or e-mail me in advance to let me know what's going on.

   - Student "employees" need to seek assistance proactively and to come to "work" ready to participate and produce.

   - Feedback will be prompt, honest, and thorough.

   - There is no "curve" for grading; it's a meritocracy, and I'm open to having the whole class perform at a high or low level

   - Expectations and goals are laid out in a "realistic job preview." I am very transparent about the fact that there will be a heavy workload early in the semester, while later in the semester there will be stretches in which you mainly need to show up for class and participate.

2. *Push the high expectations button.*

   In Chapter 6, I talked about the high expectations that many of today's students have. That's a button that I push early and often in the course. I tell students that the bad news is that my course might be the most demanding in the university... but that students often say that their friends come to them for interviewing advice by the end of the semester. If you want to accomplish great things, then it's going to require some time and energy. The time is now.

3. *Students do need "reality therapy."*

   Likewise, Chapter 6 talked about how today's students may lack self-awareness when it comes to understanding their strengths and weaknesses. As a result, they desperately need honest feedback from you, both positive and negative. So all work in the class is judged not on the basis of "It is what it is." I will not hesitate to give a perfect score on any assignment if I can't come up with any way the student could do better. But I also give a low score and tons of constructive criticism if the work isn't up to par. Early in the semester, I emphasize that the grading in the course is totally based on the quality of the work—not trying to build up or tear down anyone's ego. I don't try to guess why an assignment turned out badly; I just write down what's wrong with it. I rarely get complaints about grades, and students often like getting thorough feedback.

Likewise, a student's behavior in class may give hints as to how ready they are to function effectively in a professional atmosphere. I like to have conversations about such issues to find out what's really going on: "Gee, it seems like you just can't get to class on time. What's the story with that?" "You know what? I'd have to say that right now your level of performance is dead last in a class of 37 students. Why are you struggling so much?" I try to be calm and inquisitive, and I make sure that the student knows that I'm not branding them forever as a malcontent or problem child. Usually a good conversation results that gives the student some reality therapy while giving me some insight into their behavior.

4. *Give students a high degree of structure at first, but then wean them off of that need.*

Again, we're dealing with Millennial Generation students. If they're young, they may be used to having someone walk them through activities. That's nice, but it often won't occur in the professional world. So I tell them openly that I'll hold their hand early in the class with plenty of e-mail reminders and the like, but by the end of the semester I will adapt a more purely delegating style of leadership. By the last class, students should know that it's up to them to read the syllabus, know the deadlines, and raise questions if they need assistance.

5. *Integrate technology into teaching.*

I'll delve into this more deeply later in this chapter. Basically, though, this is a technology-friendly generation, and technology also can be a great labor-saving mechanism. Take advantage of it.

6. *Think "edutainment."*

Yes, I'm an educator, but I also realize that I need to keep students engaged so they don't tune out the message. As you'll see later in this chapter, I've devised many exercises that are meant to be fun and entertaining as well as provocative and informative. I also pepper every lecture with war stories on the topic, including many from *Exceeding Expectations*.

For example, my colleague Bob Tillman likes to pose a provocative question: "How would you act differently if you knew that you were being videotaped all day, every day at work?" As a thoughtful exercise, this makes for a good conversation. But the final punch line is that Bob once had a couple of students who decided to consummate their relationship in a company conference room… only to find out later that they *were* being videotaped! That's a memorable story, and it reinforces the original idea.

7. *To grade or not to grade?*

This is a judgment call, and we have perennial debates about it in our business co-op group at Northeastern. We used to do the class on a pass/fail basis. Now we have letter grades, A through F. Some people are happy that we changed, and others adamantly believe that we should change back.

Pass/fail grading keeps things simple for instructors and students. Why put a ton of energy into grading work if the class is one-credit or no-credit? The point of the course or seminar is to make sure students become reasonably good at writing a resume, interviewing, and understanding what is takes to be a professional. As long as students learn these elements, do we really need to have gradations of difference in the degree to which they've mastered these elements? Pass/fail grading also means that you are unlikely to have much haggling with students over grades—unless the debate is whether or not the person has passed the course.

Using letter grades is a way of saying that differences in performance level *do* matter. In other words, the goal is not merely to be adequate; we want students to aspire to be top performers. Having letter grades will encourage some students to do better work and to be sure to get work in on time. With pass/fail grading, there sometimes is an increase in the need for "meter maid management," in which you have to coax students to turn in assignments and to do really good work as opposed to just enough to get credit.

8. *Get other people into the classroom.*

Although you can do a multiple-credit course with no assistance, it can be very valuable to have some occasional guest speakers. Bring in an employer—or even a panel of employers—to share *their* perspectives on resumes, interviews, and professional behavior. If you have an on-campus expert on sexual harassment, diversity, or legal issues, that can be powerful.

I especially like to bring in upperclassmen as a student panel for a day, and sometimes I supplement that with a shorter visit by an alum or an individual student. Tom Akins talks about this at the end of this chapter as well. It always amuses me when a group of upperclassmen makes points that I've been making all semester, only to have them come across as if the students are hearing those ideas for the first time! Students are going to listen to and believe peers in a way that they won't quite ever do with an instructor.

9. *Get thorough feedback and act on it.*

I start each semester with a strong vision of where I want the course to go. But I also have to keep my ears open to see what the class wants and needs as well. Given that our course is concurrent with the job search, I'll leave some wiggle room in the classes that come at the peak of the referral process. During those weeks, I'll often start the class with a "bull session" in which students can ask me the questions that have some real urgency.

These bull sessions are quite unpredictable. Sometimes there are no questions, and we are on to the day's regularly scheduled programming within a minute or two. On other days, we may have a quite extemporaneous class for up to 45 minutes. With questions about drug testing, background checks, off-the-wall interview questions, and job offers, everything is fair game, and the resulting conversations can be extremely lively.

Likewise, I make a big deal about getting very comprehensive surveys completed at the end of the course. I take this feedback very seriously and at times have revamped the course dramatically as a result of comments that either confirmed my nebulous concerns or that surprised me altogether. It's all too easy to shrug off comments that reflect negatively on your teaching style, as that feels a bit personal. But I think that a majority opinion—or even an opinion by a small handful of students—has never steered me wrong.

SETTING THE TONE

One of my pet peeves as a college student was the fact that the first day of class was often a waste of time. A professor comes in, introduces himself, hands out the syllabus, then reads it aloud for the benefit of those who may be illiterate… and that's it! See you next class. What a missed opportunity!

My class only meets once a week, so I really don't have that luxury—not that I would do it under any circumstances. I like to think of the first day as "the crucial first class." Your choices for that first day will say everything about how high or low your standards are, how excited you are to work with your students, and how engaging and challenging the classroom experience is going to be.

So here's how my first day goes:

1. *Take digital photos of all students*

   I arrive early with a digital camera and start taking photos of students holding up their name cards under their chins. Combined with some personal information that I'll obtain via index cards or a Blackboard survey, this will help me memorize everyone's name and basic background by week two. It also says more than I ever could about the fact that I know and care who they are.

2. *Do the "Munze Exercise."*

   My former colleague Bill Munze came up with this one. One problem on day one is that students inevitably drift in late. They may have had trouble finding the room, or they may be used to professors who don't care if they're late rather than a manager who expects his workers to get to work on time. Regardless, I love starting off the first class right on time with an activity that won't be compromised by the fact that a third of the class will be arriving five, ten, 15 minutes late. This exercise is perfect for that.

   I simply ask students "What questions do you have about co-op? What are the questions that you'd like to learn how to answer by the end of the semester?" I ask for a student to be a scribe on paper while I write the questions on the blackboard, breaking them into three unlabeled categories: preparation, activity, and reflection.

   This exercise tells me where my new group is in terms of what they want to know, and I can revisit the questions during the semester to make sure we answer all of them eventually. At the very last class, I can turn the tables and have *them* answer all of those questions to reinforce the semester's learning.

3. *Do a survey.*

   I don't do a survey with every first class, but sometimes it's been helpful. I often do a Likert scale survey with statements that require the student to strongly agree, agree, neither agree nor disagree, disagree, or strongly disagree. Here are some typical statements:

   - It is important for me to accomplish great things in my career and in my life.

- I believe that I should be able to get a great first job, even if I don't have prior professional work experience.

- I am nervous about going on co-op.

- I am confident in my ability to interview well for a job.

As you can see, there are some statements geared to learning how "millennial" my students are, but there are also some meant to help me assess a "before and after" degree of confidence in terms of the preparation process. Doing surveys like this occasionally can be eye-opening.

4. *Go over course goals and policies.*

I like to hold off on course policies until I know that everyone has actually arrived, as that's the most important part of the day. This is where I'll introduce the idea of the class being run by a manager as opposed to a lecturer or instructor. I'll see if they can figure out what that means, and they'll usually figure out at least some of it. Ultimately, I'll make sure we've covered all of the policies on attendance, tardiness, assignments, grading, and so forth. A common theme is that "co-op success is not magic." Students can accomplish great things, but it will require time, patience, and energy.

As you'll see in Bob Tillman's interview excerpt at chapter's end, this is also the time to remind students of what else is at stake. If you're working with your own students, you might want to remind them that you'd love to be able to recommend them highly for jobs… but you can only do so if they give you good reasons to do so through their assignments, their in-class behavior, and in one-on-one meetings. As Bob indicates, bad behavior may or may not result in a comment… but it's always noticed.

RESUME WRITING

As the course progresses, the focus turns to writing resumes. A good question to ask your class: "How many of you are confident that you have experience that will be relevant to a professional employer?" Most of my students come into the class excited but scared because they believe they lack any relevant experience. I tell them a couple of things:

- Most employers I meet tell me that technical skills and experience are great, but that transferable skills—communication skills, motivation, ability to learn, etc.—trump technical skills.

- Even students who have never worked in a professional environment are often surprised to realize how many skills they bring to the table.

I reinforce the latter point with a Skills Identification Worksheet from the back of the *Find Your First Professional Job* textbook. Students are asked to check off each skill that they've demonstrated in a variety of contexts: school, work, or extracurricular activities. Almost everyone is surprised to discover that they have literally dozens of skills that will be valuable in the eyes of professional employers. This builds confidence and sets us up for work on resumes.

TEACHING ABOUT RESUMES

Here are some fundamentals that are useful to bear in mind when teaching a group how to write resumes:

- Count on the book or course packet when it comes to basics of formatting and sections such as education, computer skills, and interests. Why waste valuable class time going over material that is objective and fairly obvious?

- Warn students about how everyone is an expert when it comes to resumes. I wish I had a dollar for everyone who told me that they did something dumb on a resume because a friend or relative told them that it was a good idea.

- Beware of the "Superstitious Dance." If someone with 17 bullets for each job description gets hired, they may believe that all those bullets were the reason they got hired. But sometimes people get hired *in spite* of something very wrong on their resume. So students should be wary of anyone who tells them that they *have* to have an objective on their resume, a bullet format, or whatever, as this is likely more of a superstition than a fact.

- Discuss the more controversial points of resumes. A perennial debate is whether job seekers should highlight accomplishments and spell out transferable skills to spin a resume versus having more concise and objective job descriptions. My belief is that it's best to walk through the choices and consequences of each approach in class, and then let students decide.

- Devote the most time to helping a few students craft their job descriptions, step by step. This is the trickiest aspect of learning to write a resume, by far, so I will devote most of a resume-writing class or workshop to this process. I will ask: "Who has had a job that they did really well but that has no direct professional relevance to what they want to do for co-op?" Once I get a volunteer, we'll set up the heading for the job description on the board as follows:

Amalgamated Industries   Denver, CO
Administrative Assistant   May-Aug. 2005

Then we'll build the job description step-by-step, a process that is also laid out in *Find Your First Professional Job*. We start by capturing the simple tasks that will form the basis of three or four bullets. We may add a clause to open the first bullet to make it more of a topic sentence: "Working at a small electronics manufacturer...." Then we'll add some qualitative and quantitative details. Next I'll ask the student if there were any accomplishments of note in the job that might capture *how* he did the job as well as *what* he did at work. Then I might broach the idea of grafting a few transferable skill phrases onto the job description, if the student wants to do so. What would his boss say is his best quality or trait? What kind of person would you look for if you were to replace yourself?

Sometimes other class members chip in a word or phrase if the student and I are struggling to come up with something. I also will ask the student if he definitely can back up any skill he claims to have. Basically, after we do two or three of these on the board, people seem to get it. By the next class, everyone turns in a completed resume.

Another option that I use is a follow-up exercise in which students work in small groups, competing to see who can find the most errors on two "bad resumes" that I've created. This gives them an opportunity to see the value of having multiple eyes on a resume. When the first draft of resumes are turned in, I might get permission to photocopy a couple of them or to show them on screen through a computer and projector. Then I'll critique the resume for all to see. With these activities, I'm trying to get everyone to hone their editorial eye as well as to reinforce how much an experienced eye can discern.

INTERVIEWING

I have a good exercise to kick off the topic of interviewing with students. Here are the instructions.

1. Get out a pen and piece of paper.

2. I will read a list of about 15 one-syllable words. At the end, I will say "Go ahead." At that point, pick up your pen and write down every word you can remember. Don't worry about remembering them in order.

3. I slowly read the list of words:

   Chair
   Flag
   Sink
   Hat
   Pen
   Truck
   Bird
   Nail
   Dust
   Sign
   Key
   Belt
   Phone
   Rug

4. Then I read the list a second time: "As I say each word, raise your hand if it's one that you remembered."

5. "Notice how many people raise their hands as I read each word."

6. "Why do you think I start my instruction about interviewing by doing this exercise?"

What generally happens is that almost everyone remembers the beginning and end of the list, but the recall rate drops off precipitously in the middle. This is a psychological phenomenon called primacy-recency effect. As some students eventually will realize, the idea is that the interviewer probably will have the strongest memory of the beginning and the end of the interview. An unfortunate coincidence is that these areas happen also to be the two weakest areas of the interview. So I ask students why *that* is the case, leading us into a conversation on various key topics:

- utilizing nervous energy effectively

- dealing with fuzzy, vague open-ended questions that often begin an interview

- Q & A at the end of the interview as well as closing the interview.

I like to lecture on interview questions with an Oprah Winfrey-style approach, complete with an Oprah-esque title: "Questions Students Hate… and Learning to Love Them." Students are urged to share the questions they fear and loathe, and we walk through how to turn them around.

BRIDGING EXERCISE

I have two powerful but labor-intensive assignments that I give each semester, though I readily admit that I could not pull these off with a group that is larger than 40 students. The first is a bridging exercise, which works as follows:

1. The student picks a specific job description.

2. The student must "bridge" from their resume to the job description, writing a "Tell Me About Yourself" answer that marries skills and experiences to specific employer needs for that job.

3. The student must *support* two of their strategic selling points with behavioral-based stories, *proving* that they are not conveniently blowing smoke when it comes to the aforementioned strategy.

Here is a great answer to "Tell Me About Yourself" for a Supply Chain Management student who wanted to show that she was a good fit for a logistical job at EF Education:

"I am very pleased to be interviewing for this job today because I believe my combination of skills would be very useful here at EF. I know this job requires great communication skills. Through my experience working for The Cedarvale Syrup Company, I resolved customer problems over the phone. I also have some useful leadership and coordination skills from working as an activities specialist at a small summer camp.

"I know a strong initiative is necessary in this position as well. Whether it's tackling over 80 orders in an hour waitressing or coordinating a Christmas sales rush of gift boxes, I know how to take the initiative and get a task done."

That student then supported her claim about resolving customer problems with the following behavioral-based story. I have broken the story into segments so I can showcase the elements of a good BBI story:

- Overview:

  "While I was working at The Cedarvale Maple Syrup Co., a small family-owned farm and store, I had to deal with a lot of customers over the phone regarding their orders. This was mostly due to the fact that 80 percent of Cedarvale's business was by mail and during the busy holiday season.

■ Defining a specific conflict or problem:

"On one of these busy nights in December, the 20th to be exact, I received a phone call from a customer in California. She was desperate to place a last minute order for a family member also in California. Now, being located in New York and doing our order shipments through UPS, five days is necessary to guarantee a shipment to California.

■ Intensifying the conflict:

"Needless to say, the woman wanted the package delivered by Christmas. I had to tell her truthfully that our last pick-up for that day had already left and if I sent her order out tomorrow (the 21st) I couldn't guarantee it to arrive there by Christmas. She sounded completely crushed when I told her this news. Then suddenly I thought of a plan.

■ Resolving the conflict:

"I asked her if I could call her back within the hour as I was going to speak to UPS regarding her situation. I told UPS the name of our driver, and they gave me his cell phone number after hearing my situation. I called him, and he was only about ten minutes away finishing his route and was happy to stop back quickly! I was so excited to be able to tell the customer her order could now be guaranteed delivery by Christmas!"

--Isabelle Wiles, NU Class of 2011

BEHAVIORAL-BASED INTERVIEWING ASSIGNMENT

After getting feedback on their bridging assignment, students have the opportunity to take another shot at writing BBI stories. Although many interviews don't require BBI answers, I like my students to have about five stories ready to use, as they are such a great way to prove strategic points vividly and believably. Candidates can't use conveniently "scripted" answers with BBI. These stories also can tap into areas outside of work, which may assist less experienced candidates. This approach also helps students truly believe that they *do* have relevant experiences and skills that may transfer into a professional setting.

So here's what happens next in the class:

■ The best supporting BBI stories are compiled and shared with class if authors give permission.

■ We show how each story *was* used to prove one skill but *could* be used to prove at least three skills.

■ Students then must write three *more* specific stories, listing at least three soft skills that each story could be used to prove.

After those two exercises, students have a great sense of how to strategize for an interview along with an arsenal of supporting proof. Sometimes they only use one story in a given interview, and sometimes they have a completely behavioral-based interview in which they are very happy to have five ready-made stories.

There are other approaches. Some professionals ask students to prepare a "60-second commercial" in which the candidate must articulate, rather generally, who they are and what they have to offer. This is a great exercise if your students are going to a job fair or in other situations that call for a less specific pitch. Other coordinators may require students to develop cover letters. I have information on that in my book, but most of us at NU don't require that in our referral process.

Another in-class activity is one in which I will turn the tables and have a student be the interviewer while I model how to ask questions of an interviewer at the end of the interview. Very expediently, I can show students what to ask, how to react to the answer in a way that reinforces key points, and how to transition from job-related questions to next-step questions before ending the interview. This is always a powerful and effective demonstration.

Here are a few summarizing themes on interview Q&A, which is so often a missed opportunity:

- Urge students to "take control of the ball."

- Ask questions that reflect research and force the employer to imagine you in the job.

- Ask questions that show positive values:

- "What can I do between now and the start of this internship to hit the ground running?"

- "What can I do to be considered a terrific performer in comparison to someone who is more average?"

- Always close by asking about next steps in the hiring process and by summarizing your strengths

Lastly, I may opt to do some *Find Your First Professional Job* scenarios on interviewing, such as the following:

- Interviewing Scenario: "You accept a job offer from Pandolfo Hospital in October and feel pleased to have a job. Two weeks later, though, you get a surprise offer from The Drury Rehabilitation Center that had interviewed you in early May; you had given up on getting an offer from them, but now they are offering you more money, an easier commute, and a better job than the one at Pandolfo. What do you do, and why?"

  Working in small groups, students have the opportunity to compare notes on values and perceptions, and I can follow up with my perspective when we debrief.

JOB SEARCH

Most of a class or workshop will entail laying out the processes and timeline of the job search at your institution and answering questions about those areas. But you also can include a small-group element by devising scenarios. I have a bunch of them in the back of *Find Your First Professional Job*. Earlier in this book, I mentioned one involving students' tendency to panic and accept a mediocre job early in the process. Here is another typical one:

You get two job offers, and you're struggling with which one to accept. Job A has really nice people and a great work environment, and the commute is about 15 minutes. The job itself seems kind of easy; you're not sure if you would learn very much. In contrast, job B would be very stressful and fast-paced. You'll be thrown in the deep end of the pool to sink or swim. It's also a 50 to 60-minute commute. But you would learn much more in this job, as it's much more challenging. Which job would you accept? Would a big pay difference change your mind?

PROFESSIONAL BEHAVIOR IN THE WORKPLACE

As mentioned earlier, this is the most difficult topic to teach in a prep course. Students tend to underestimate their ability to get a job, but they also frequently *overestimate* their ability to make the adjustment from campus to a professional environment. You need to engage students with interactive teaching methods as opposed to purely lecturing them on all of the possible pitfalls, as that runs the risk of coming across as preachy and condescending. So here are a few useful activities that I can recommend.

THE CHAUFFEUR EXERCISE

This one came to me at 4 a.m., several hours before teaching a class a couple of years ago. I decided to give it a shot, and it worked great… and it takes no more than 15 minutes.

Here's what you say to your group:

"Imagine this situation *really* happening to you: The more you imagine it to be real and respond accordingly, the more powerful it will be. Okay? Let's say that you have no car and no money to buy one. However, you get offered a job that is located a 45-minute drive south of campus. The route is intense during rush hour on the highway. However, I have some great news: The employer has agreed to provide you with a chauffeur! He is 17, just got his license, has never driven on the highway, but is enthusiastic, confident, and eager to learn.

"Take a few minutes to jot down a few thoughts in response to these two questions:

1. What is your emotional reaction to the thought of having this chauffeur drive you to and from your new job every day?

2. Regardless of your emotional reaction, how would you approach dealing with the chauffeur if you had no choice but to make the situation work?"

Here are some typical responses to question #1:

- "I would be terrified! I know what a bad driver I was at 17."

- "Would I really have to take this job and deal with such an inexperienced person?"

- "I would be psyched! I hate driving, and I would be thrilled to not have to deal with it."

- "I guess I would be a little wary, but I'd try to keep an open mind and see if the kid knows what he's doing or not."

Here are some usual answers to question #2:

- "When he showed up the first day, I would tell him 'I'm driving—get into the passenger's seat!'"

- "I think I would start off by having him show me that he can drive in a big, empty parking lot, and then maybe move on to back roads before working our way up to the highway."

- "I would sit in the back seat and read the newspaper, ignoring the driver altogether."

The conversation usually gets pretty humorous. Then I ask, "Okay, why do you think I started off our discussion of professional behavior with this exercise?" As you might have guessed, it's meant to be an analogy. The first time I did it, I happened to have a senior in the room with me. After hearing their responses, he couldn't resist jumping in: "All of those reactions that you described are ways that I've been treated at some point or another over three co-ops! There will be people who will be terrified that you're going to make some terrible mistake, and there are those who ignore you completely and let you do what you want. There are those who will try to show you the ropes and who will give you more responsibility... if you earn it. You're going to encounter all of those attitudes!"

I then tell students that when they're feeling disappointed about how some full-time workers react when they start their new jobs, they should remember how they felt, emotionally, when doing this exercise.

TRANSITIONING FROM STUDENT TO EMPLOYEE

This is another helpful exercise. I know that Bob Tillman does something very similar in his class.

- Working in small groups, write down the ways in which the roles of students and employees are *similar* and then how they are *different*.

- Another option: Have students work in small groups and imagine themselves as managers. Then, brainstorm about ways in which a new hire could make life *more difficult* for you and your co-workers as well as *less difficult* for you.

- Another idea is to have a debate on the following statement: "A student with great grades is much more likely to perform well at work than a student with poor grades."

That debate can be surprisingly provocative. Good students like to think that their good grades are evidence of their ability to do well on a job, and weaker students are quick to point out many reasons why a person might not have such good grades but could be a great employee. After the debate goes on for a while, I ask if anyone knows about correlation coefficients. Business students usually know that a +1.0 is a perfect positive correlation, -1.0 is a perfect negative correlation, and that 0.0 means that there is no correlation whatsoever.

I ask them to guess what the research indicates on this question, and almost everyone guesses that there is much more of a correlation than there is actually is. Most studies I have seen have shown a positive correlation, but only about .12 to .18. That really gets the goat of the smartest students, but it enables me to get the point I want to reach: Basically, everyone starts co-op with pretty close to an equal opportunity to succeed. Good grades might help you get a better job, as many employers don't know or believe that research. But by no means am I assuming that a student with a 3.8 is going to perform better than someone with a 2.5. I tell them quite honestly that I've had a student with a 4.0 get fired, and I recently had a student barely graduate who received a standing ovation on her last day of work on Wall Street.

USING CASE STUDIES

The UC book has numerous case studies. Naturally, I use the scenarios from *Find Your First Professional Job* and mini-cases from *Exceeding Expectations* in my class. For the latter, I provide an Instructor's Guide offering "case clusters" that facilitate small-group discussion by theme: paying dues; "sexy" jobs; what differentiates great performers from average ones; and so on. *Find Your First Professional Job* also has very short professional behavior scenarios. Whether or not using my book interests you, nothing prevents you from developing your own cases, whether they are disguised fact or completely fiction. I think disguised fact is better, as students often love to hear what *really* happened in the actual scenario.

Here are some typical case studies, boiled down to their simplest details:

- An intern is bored a few weeks into a job that is supposed to last several months, and she wants to quit. The job is as advertised, but she has realized that this field is not for her. There is also a good deal of downtime. Should she be allowed to quit? Why or why not?

- A co-op gets into a romantic relationship with a co-worker. The happy couple insists that they are completely professional at work, but other workers complain that the two of them often bicker about non-work issues. The co-op says that this is not true; others are simply jealous of the relationship. What do you think is going on? Are there situations in which a romantic relationship at work could be considered acceptable, or not? Why?

- A female student walks into her manager's office and sees a pornographic image on the manager's computer. The manager quickly hits "ALT-TAB" and is clearly embarrassed about what has happened. Yet this happens again several days later. Could this be considered to be sexual harassment?

Case studies give students a chance to debate issues in small groups, which they usually enjoy—especially if the topics are as juicy as a couple of the ones above. I like giving students the opportunity to see if they can work together to come to the "right" answer on these instead of just telling them. Sometimes they nail these, and other times I have to show them a side of the issue that they hadn't considered. This can be effective in driving home the point that they may not know as much as they think they do about professional behavior. True stories about their slightly older peers also give a greater emotional impact to the topic at hand.

ROLE PLAY DAY

Role plays can be tacked on to any workshop or class to help bring a point to life, but I like to have a whole day in class devoted to them. They can be a great way to enliven and engage a class, as long as you allow ample time for participants to study roles and get in character.

Role plays are another great way to underscore that professional behavior is nowhere near as simple or easy as students might imagine. One of my favorite role plays is called "The First

Meeting." The premise is that a student is extremely bored in the early stages of their work term. When I used to just ask a classroom of students how they would handle such a situation, the response invariably would be: "Well, I'd just talk to my manager about it and find a diplomatic way to let them know I want more work." That sounds easy enough, but choosing the exact words is often not so easy.

In the role play, the student's role is to emphasize the monotony of the job and casually let drop that the student sometimes surfs the 'net because there is so little to do. The manager's role indicates that the manager has a pretty neutral view of the student. The manager is told that they should hammer the student if words like "bored," "frustrated," or "unhappy" are used. If the tone is negative and whining, the manager is advised to rant a little bit about the student's Internet use and their unrealistic expectations about getting challenging work immediately. If the student uses positive and solution-oriented language, the manager is told to be more conciliatory in response.

If you have several groups doing the role play, some will do it really well and others won't. Debriefing the role play, you can go over what approaches were most and least effective. The goal is often to remind students that their perspective is limited and that it's good to imagine what their response would be if they were in another party's shoes.

I have another really popular role play called "The Twin Terrors." In this one, the intern needs to get the assistance of two full-time administrative assistants who are jaded veterans of the professional world. Although they are on the bottom in terms of legitimate power in the organization, this pair is very intimidating. They are highly sarcastic and more interested in chatting than helping an intern—especially if he or she doesn't find a way to create some rapport as opposed to attempting to give them marching orders. The result is usually pretty hilarious in the classroom.

You can e-mail me at s.weighart@neu.edu if you'd like these role plays as well as others in addition to a complete annotated syllabus that I use for my course. For now, I'm just trying to give you some options to show how you can get beyond the pitfall of simply lecturing students in favor of engaging them with interactive material.

USING TECHNOLOGY

The interview excerpts from Kerry Mahoney and Marie Sacino at the end of this chapter will show you some creative ways in which technology can play a major role in group preparation activities. As Kerry describes, the University of Waterloo has a mostly online course, and it's fascinating to see how the largest co-op program in the world prepares its students. Marie discusses ePortfolios among other technological elements used at LaGuardia Community College. For my part, I will focus more on how I use Blackboard, a commonly available classroom teaching application.

USING BLACKBOARD

In April 2007, I had no Blackboard page whatsoever. When I gave my usual end-of-class survey, one comment hit me hard: "Good class, but why no Blackboard page? Get into the 21st century, Scott!" I had to agree with that blunt appraisal. I had meant to do something on that front for a few years but needed a bit of a slap in the face to get me going.

By September, I had a rudimentary Blackboard presence. I had my syllabus and contact information on the site, and I occasionally put some background reading materials up there. I figured it would be a good idea to have a message board, as students would be familiar with that. Instead, it turned out to be pulling teeth to get anyone to use the message board! In general, it felt like Blackboard wasn't adding much value. Should I get rid of it?

Then I noticed a letter to the editor of our student newspaper. A former student of mine had become an environmental advocate, and she talked about how more classes should go paperless altogether. That got me thinking. Maybe I just needed to go all-out to make Blackboard work for me. I talked to a business professor named Mike Zack about his experiences of teaching a paperless class. When I told him about the failure of the message boards, he laughed and said, "That's because message boards don't really work for students." He had tried them and found little interest as well. But he had enjoyed great success with everything else.

I adopted many of his principles and created some new ones of my own:

- Students fill out a Blackboard survey to help me get to know them, including contact info, hometown, career goals, musical preferences, and "unusual facts."

- All assignments are now created in Blackboard, and students submit them online via the application.

- "Course Materials" include samples of great work by previous students

- All grading is done on Blackboard. I have created Word documents that are basically answer banks. Instead of hand-writing similar responses on dozens of papers, I can copy and paste the responses from Word into Blackboard, tweaking the boilerplate text if needed.

- I use a digital voice recorder to record each class, broken into segments of no more than 20-30 minutes each. These are posted on Blackboard under a "Podcasts" tab. Students who miss a class listen to the podcast and write a one-page summary of the missed class, just so I know that they're on top of the material. Others can review key topics through the podcast, which is in Windows Media Audio (WMA) format.

PROS OF PAPERLESS CLASS

In Fall of 2007, I had my class vote on whether the class should go entirely paperless. About two-thirds of the class favored it. At the end of Spring 2008, the class voted on whether I should keep doing the paperless class. To my surprise, the vote was 28-2.

There are several benefits to going paperless:

- It removes any doubt about when or if assignments were completed. Without Blackboard, it often was a pain to figure out who had not turned something in. I would have to see what was in the pile turned in during class and then check my e-mail to be sure that it didn't come in that way. Now I can see in seconds what's in and what's missing.

- Grading is faster, more thorough, and more fair because of the ability to copy and paste answers. Given that I no longer have to rewrite similar feedback again and again—with my simply terrible handwriting—I find that it's easier to provide more detailed responses with less effort... and to ensure that I'm giving similar points to answers of similar quality.

- I no longer need to devise make-up assignments for missed classes. I used to spend time each week coming up with activities that would helps students prove to me that they understood that week's topic. Now it's almost automatic, and everyone knows what to do. As Kerry Mahoney notes with respect to Waterloo's online course, students also like to be able to revisit material from class on occasion. With a regular, unrecorded lecture, that's not possible.

- Blackboard also provides some inherent organization for the student and the grader. When you create an assignment online, Blackboard automatically adds it to a grade book. Students know that all grades and comments are in there, as are course materials for those who are prone to losing track of syllabi and other handouts.

CONS OF PAPERLESS CLASS

All of that said, there are some definite negatives to running a paperless class. I wouldn't say that I'm a technical guru, but I am pretty comfortable with learning how to use a software application. Those who are technophobes may not be so comfortable with relying so heavily on an application.

There are other cons, too:

- Although going paperless has saved me considerable time when correcting papers, it definitely increases instructor's amount of "screen time" in terms of computer usage. I do almost all of my grading at home. Given how much of my day entails looking at a computer monitor, it's somewhat demoralizing to go home and get back on a desktop or laptop during weekends and evenings.

- The amount of clicks and alt-tab toggles to open files and copy/paste text definitely gets tedious. It takes a fair amount of navigation to go into a student's homework assignment, click to open a file, and tell my computer that's it's okay to open the file. Then I have to read the assignment and click back and forth between the answer key in Word to copy and paste and the comments section in Blackboard, and so on. Doing it once is nothing. Doing it with 30-40 students gets tiresome.

- A few students dislike the lack of hard copies and may need some coaching on using the system. There have been few gripes about the paperless class, but some students just don't like it. I need to do a better job of reminding students that they can print out documents posted on Blackboard if they prefer hard copies. Blackboard is fairly intuitive, but a few students also run into occasional problems with submitting work online. Students need to be told to submit via e-mail if they have difficulty.

- Occasional technical glitches can be disconcerting. I'm still a relative novice with Blackboard, but Mike Zack has mentioned that there are periodic updates to the application, meaning that you have to relearn how to do certain tasks. Sometimes it's not clear why a student is having trouble submitting an assignment. I also had a pretty bad near-miss with one glitch last semester. In my electronic grade book, I manually created columns to track attendance by class, noting problems with tardiness, absences without advance notice, etc.

The problem arose in a surprising way. My class started at 1:50 p.m. If a student was late, I would note the time of arrival in the grade book: 1:58, 2:03, etc. That seemed fine as the semester progressed, but something funny happened when I began to look at final grades. Blackboard automatically sums students' point totals for you on all assignments, which is handy. But I had one student who had a chronic tardiness problem. I was quite surprised to see that she had ended up with something like 95 points for the course, as she was by no means an A student. It turned out that Blackboard thought I was giving her, say, 1.58 or 2.03 points for each incidence of tardiness! I had to change all of those times to a letter (L) to solve that problem!

Now that I've given you some sense of the realm of possibility when it comes to preparation work in groups, let's see what some professionals have to say about the topic.

IN THEIR OWN WORDS

PROFESSIONAL PERSPECTIVE #1
"REALISTIC EXPECTATIONS"
Tom Akins, Georgia Institute of Technology

We don't have a formal class that they sign up for that appears on their transcript, but before they begin interviewing, sign up for any interviews, or be referred to any employers, we have a series of orientation meetings they have to attend. They're mandatory.

They cover procedural aspects of things that we do in the office, but also we try to cover how you should act on the job, professionalism, safety on the job, what you can expect when you go out on your first day, and what you can expect hopefully when you go for your return term, as our students typically go back to the same employer for their co-op career unless they change majors or their career goals take a major shift.

I guess the main thing is really to help them to understand and have more realistic expectations of what's going to happen. We will bring in some employers to give them an idea, and we'll also use some of our upperclass students to come in who have been out at work. Because *we* can tell them, but if you bring a *student* in there or even an outside employer they tend to carry more weight than we do. So we try to do that. Mainly we want to get their expectations to be more realistic and to help them feel comfortable when they report for that first day.

PROFESSIONAL PERSPECTIVE #2
"TRIGGER A DIFFERENT LEARNING"
Mary Kane, Northeastern University

I think there are definitely certain key things that are very, very important as far as the preparation process goes. I do think in lots of ways people learn best from each other, so I try to encourage group activities and group discussions. Sometimes that can be a struggle. I have seen over the years that structure and clear directions help facilitate group discussions. (Letting students know you will want one person to record, one to report out, etc.) The other important aspect is to be able to connect back the group activity to its importance in the professional preparation process. Activities are not done simply to have activities, but to start to build awareness in students of their role in their career and professional development. The coursework is one element that will be enhanced with employer evaluations, reflection, and further self-assessment.

I have begun to take advantage of students being millennials and seeking the advice of their parents. A new assignment I have introduced in my Professional Development class is the interview I have them do with a professional. I tell them to pick a professional who's been working for at least five years and to ask them what was their biggest adjustment when they went into the workplace for the first time. Then I asked them to ask them about informal rewards: What did people get rewarded for? What got people in trouble? Then I asked the students to summarize what the impact is going to be on them. It's great; we go around the room, and they share with me the different situations. Some things never change: stories include the impact of not figuring out how long the commute was going to be; what happens when people who they worked with partied too much; and if you work really hard, you will eventually get rewarded. If you deal with the grunt work in the beginning, that's how you get more responsibility.

I'd say 90% of them choose to interview their parents. Many times this is the first time they have seen their parents from this perspective and are able to identify firsthand what some of the challenges will be when they start working. I think they gain a lot from that. When they talk to someone whose opinion they respect, and they can connect that to what they're doing, the learning is tremendous.

PROFESSIONAL PERSPECTIVE #3
"YOU'RE BEING VIDEOTAPED"
Bob Tillman, Northeastern University

Early on in the prep class, one thing I say is "let's have an understanding that we're going to be working together for the next 3-3.5 years. When you sit in class and I can see you're not paying attention, and I can see you have your cell phone out under the table or you're having a side conversation or you're doing a crossword in the back row, please don't ever make the mistake that I didn't see that just because I didn't call on you and make a judgment about you... Because I did.

"If it bothered me enough, I might pull you aside after class, and I'll tell you to knock it off. If I see it again, it's going to have some impact when we do business later on down the road. A lot of the time it's not commented on, but it is noticed." I am one of the only teachers that teach the civil engineering freshmen section, and student services faculty teach the other sections. They always talk about how unruly the students are, but I've never had that problem. If you set the tone, it will carry over into co-op. If you can't show up and function and pay attention, you're not going to make it out there. If you can't take care of your own issues, how are you going to take care of millions of dollars of work? It's not going to happen.

I think I set the class up by talking about what are the expectations of work: assignments being turned it; timeliness; taking pride in your work; listening to what is required. I try to mirror what will be happening when they are working. That seems to be pretty effective.

[To explain why I've had classes imagine how they might act differently if they were videotaped constantly at work], it was an ethicist view of the world. It only hits some people if they think they are going to be watched and there will be repercussions for their actions. They act very differently than if they weren't being watched, but if they're going to be watched and evaluated they'll act differently. If you have two different modes of acting, there's a problem. That's because you don't know when that switch is ever going to be flipped. In class I say, "You're being video-taped; you just don't know it. The data is being collected, but you just think you're clever enough that nobody is seeing it. They are.

"Pretend for a minute that you're being sued. You're in a courtroom, and all of your work is being projected on a big board for the world to see how you solved this problem. How do you want your work to look? That happens a lot in our business [of civil engineering]: the Minnesota bridge collapse, the Central Artery [Tunnel Project, in which a partial collapse led to a death], and several companies went out of business.

"If you're acting differently because you thought somebody was watching, you need to start examining your actions. Most importantly, what's the issue? What is it that you think is going on when everybody around you is producing and you're not?"

PROFESSIONAL PERSPECTIVE #4
"A TIMED COURSE ONLINE"
Kerry Mahoney, University of Waterloo

The online course that we have is a combination of career preparation pieces (e.g., resume writing, interviewing, job search, on-the-job conduct) and co-op process pieces (e.g., how to apply to jobs, dealing with interview conflicts).

Our course is "real time" alongside the co-op process, with weekly materials and deadlines for submissions. While the course is online, we have a one-hour, face-to-face kickoff to set expectations and let the students know that there are human beings to support them.

Students are enrolled in this preparation course as they go through the process of applying for jobs so the course is very real. We don't just give them the theory of resume writing; they need to apply that theory now because they must use their resume to apply to jobs. Likewise, the interview piece is timed to be just slightly ahead of when students will be involved in the interview process.

There are various reasons we take an online approach. The first is that we have a large number of students to get through the process so an individual or small group meeting approach is just not possible. We have over 11,000 students; this means that in a fall term, there are between 2,500–3,000 students in the online co-op prep course.

Secondly, we believe in online education. Having materials online helps us to ensure that each student has the same kind of experience and receives the same messages. We've done large group face-to-face sessions in the past, but they were really just lectures. Resume writing is a good example—it is difficult to make the topic interactive in a large group but our online materials include activities that are more engaging.

This is not to say that online is best in every case. Having students practice interview responses in person would be better. However, co-op students at UW can supplement their online co-op preparation course with in-person workshops and individual advisement offered through Career Services.

A bit more detail on the online approach we take: students read resources and then complete activities (about 50 activities across the 10 or 12 weeks of the first co-op prep course). Some of these are "marked" by the online system; students submit and receive some generic feedback. Four others are marked by TAs using staff-prepared rubrics. The first is the resume. The second is responses to typical interview questions. The third is the self-introduction (for use in developing jobs) and the fourth is on-the-job scenarios. In the latter, we outline a situation that could happen on the job and we ask students "How could the student have avoided this situation? What should they do now that this has happened?"

Student course evaluations are quite positive. They like that they can revisit the information and they like the discussion boards.

Another aspect that works for us is that staff can review student submissions and provide individual coaching—because of our numbers, we only do this later in the term with students who have not yet secured employment.

We are lucky to have faculty support for all of this. This course is one in a series (others are taken when students are on their work terms) of required (credit/no-credit) courses intended to help students reflect on their co-op experience and improve their employability skills. Topics of the other courses include: communication, team-building, reflection, and report writing.

PROFESSIONAL PERSPECTIVE #5
"ePORTFOLIOS IN A PREP CLASS"
Marie Sacino, LaGuardia Community College

Originally, years ago, we had something we called "Co-op Prep" and then we had something which was called "Gateway to the Workplace," and we found that it wasn't enough. It wasn't enough preparation. It wasn't exactly what we wanted to do; we wanted to do career development. Then we developed a course called Fundamentals of Professional Advancement, which is a three-credit course. It runs for the entire 12-week session, 30 hours, and it's a comprehensive course on understanding yourself, understanding your interests and your skills and your values. And part of that course is the ePortfolio development. So to give you an idea: if I were teaching CEP 121—or FPA as we sometimes call it—and I have, for instance, a Tuesday and Thursday schedule, I would be meeting with my class Tuesday for two hours and I would be in a "smart classroom" so we have the opportunity to use the Internet.

Sometimes we would be working in a lab doing Myers-Briggs or doing Interest and Skills Surveys or reading things from the *Wall Street Journal*. We have a textbook as well and some of the exercises from the text are online, so it's really using a lot of online materials in addition to textbooks. But on that Thursday I would be meeting with my students for just one hour. In that second hour on Tuesday they would have a course, which is taught by the staff from the Center for Teaching and Learning and the students would be learning the technical skills to put together a career ePortfolio.

So we're responsible for the content, and these ePortfolio consultants are responsible for technical tasks, such as how to download a template, how to work with Netscape Composer, how to resize an image—the kinds of things that many of us may know how to do, but that are not our forté, not exactly what we want to teach.

On the ePortfolio, students create a variety of different pages and the first one is: About Me. We've used the *New York Times* column, "The Boss." We have students read a lot of those in terms of someone's career construction, their identity, what their childhood was like, how they developed an interest in chemistry or business or whatever the particular discipline might be and who their role models were and what kinds of activities they liked to engage in as a child and how they decided to go to a particular college, what was their family like, and so on.

We read a lot of these articles and then we ask them to work with their About Me in the same format as "The Boss." So, they also have a textbox where they put their favorite book or something that they can't live without (which is generally their cell phone), their dream vacation, their dream career. So it gives a little bit of creativity as opposed to something which is just text. And they don't talk about their boyfriend or their fiancées or video games. It's basically career-oriented. It's not MySpace. There are times when we have to tell the students "That picture is terrific, but it's not appropriate for this." So there's a lot of that going on, but we find that there's a deeper learning. It takes students awhile; it takes them maybe a month to get it crafted correctly, and we don't want them starting out with "My name is Joe. I come from Brooklyn." Rather, "As a child I always had an interest in books and that's what's led me to become a teacher of children. I have an interest in literacy, and these are some of my favorite books." They might talk about the courses that they're taking that are meaningful to them and that matter when they go out on their internship—courses that they want to apply on the first internship.

They're basically giving something about their identity, what courses they want put into practice on the internship. We do have an education program and our interns go out in the field, so they talk about wanting to be fourth-grade teachers or they talk about wanting to work in a program like the dual-immersion program. They would be doing the same whether it's computers, Web design, or network security. So they're really talking about what their interests are and what kind of internship they'd like to engage in.

Technologically, we work with Blackboard. The students have an ePortfolio link on the Blackboard site and we use Netscape Navigator. The Center for Teaching and Learning has developed templates for the students, so the students have an intro page where they can put an image of something that they think will engage the reader and say "Welcome to my ePortfolio. Here you'll find my resume, some of my reflections, some of my coursework." The Welcome page is the first page, which is an Intro, and then About Me, which I've just described. And then they'll have Courses and Projects, which is really important. So if I've got an Education student, they might have examples of lesson plans they've developed.

So if they go to an employer, they might even take this ePortfolio, place it on a CD, and during the interview they might say: "During the course of my program at LaGuardia, I've been able to develop an ePortfolio, and I know that you might not have a lot of time but I can leave my CD with you. If you have an opportunity, you can take a look at some of the lesson plans that I've developed." Some of our employers have been blown away by that, and they tell me that it shows so much initiative. They've created this ePortfolio and they're already hired because their employer is very, very impressed that they have this. Of course, they generally look at it at some point in time, but just bringing that along and having a conversation about what they've done is really, really impressive to the employers.

REFLECTION QUESTIONS

1. What are the most effective ways in which you work with students in groups right now? What opportunities do you have to try new ways of working with students in groups without compromising on educational quality?

2. Are there ways in which you act as the manager of your students as opposed to purely their instructor? Do you like the concept? Why, or why not?

3. The chapter discusses the debate between pass/fail grading and letter grading for co-op preparation courses. Considering the pros and cons of each, what do you think is the better idea?

4. I describe any number of creative exercises that could be used in a preparation class, such as the Munze exercise, the primacy/recency effect exercise, "The Chauffeur," and various role plays. Which are you most eager to try? What's the most creative exercises you've devised for working with students in groups?

5. Another idea here is conducting a "paperless class" via Blackboard. Is this something you would consider trying? Why, or why not?

6. Some of the interviewed experts talk about conducting online courses and having students create ePortfolios among other things. Do you see you and your program moving toward a greater use of technology to deliver information to students in groups? What do you see as the pros and cons of going in that direction?

CHAPTER 9

CRITIQUING RESUMES AND INTERVIEWS

"Like all great minds Eugène wished to owe his success to nothing but his own merit. But his temperament was preeminently southern; so that when he came to carry them out his resolutions were bound to be affected by the hesitations that seize young people when they find themselves on the open sea, anxious to exert their strength but not knowing in which direction to steer, nor how to trim their sail to catch the wind."

— Honoré de Balzac, <u>Old Goriot</u>

Being able to critique resumes and practice interviews are very valuable skills for a professional. Yet the difficulty of doing so as effectively as possible may be underrated. While the student has the ultimate responsibility for having an error-free resume, he or she generally has not developed an editorial eye to pick out errors. When you're new to the profession, this may or may not come naturally to you, either. So this chapter is devoted to helping you understand what goes into critiquing a resume, breaking down the critique into a step-by-step process.

While professionals almost always review resumes, programs vary considerably when it comes to practice interviews. Many Northeastern students are required to complete a practice interview. More often, practice interviews are optional in co-op and internship programs. Depending on workload, your program may do very few mock interviews. Still, I think it's very important to be able to understand what the most common errors are when it comes to student interviews. Even if you do few or no practice interviews, the material in this chapter should help you know what to look for and how to help a student who struggles with actual interviews.

CRITIQUING RESUMES

Let's start off with resumes. For me, a fundamental philosophy that I have when it comes to approving a resume is that a "good enough" resume is not good enough! In the co-op class, I tell students about a consulting firm that I once knew. Their head of HR has been known to circle errors on a cover letter and resume, sending them back to an applicant with a note indicating that the candidate's standards are not high enough for the firm. Some students find this harsh. I tend to think that it's very kind of the firm to point out these errors. Most companies simply wouldn't call the candidate, who might always wonder why.

More to the point, I remind students just how powerful a first impression can be. If they're interested in a rock band, but the first song they hear from that group seems awful to them, how much more of a chance do they give to that group? If they are on a first date, wouldn't an obnoxious statement or behavior in the opening minutes loom large?

I like to talk about "sympathy with the interviewer." I want students to put themselves in the interviewer's shoes. Imagine having a really busy day and only having maybe 10-20 minutes to review a big stack of resumes. You don't know anyone personally, and you're trying to pick four or five people to interview based on 15-20 resumes. Wouldn't you be inclined to remove someone from consideration pretty quickly if you caught a blatant typo or spelling error? Or even if the resume just looked shoddy based on the formatting?

Fairly or not, the employer often assumes that a resume represents your best possible work. What you don't want to have happen is for the employer to think "If this is the best, I'd hate to see the rest."

So where do you come in as a professional? Your responsibility is to make sure that each student understands what is at stake with a resume. Then you need to provide them with some good samples and helpful hints on how to produce a good resume—whether you use one of the books mentioned in the last chapter or your own materials. More than anything, though, you need to maintain high standards when it comes to critiquing the resume. Given that a resume critique might be your first opportunity to provide meaningful and constructive criticism to the student, your approach will set the tone for future interactions. If you are able to catch significant errors and provide wise counsel in terms of the choices and consequences of various inclusions and omissions from the resume, then the student will be more inclined to view you as a credible expert. If you are unwilling to settle for a resume that is merely error-free and bland, then it helps get the student into the mentality of striving for excellence instead of getting by.

Conversely, if you give the resume a quick once-over and shrug off questions that a student has about the resume, you send the message that you're more interested in being expedient than being excellent. I have heard of students who told me that their advisor never even looked at their resume and that the only feedback they received was by pairing off for peer reviews in a preparation class! That's just unthinkable to me. And it's not even self-serving in terms of expediency: A student with a crummy resume is often going to have a tougher time getting a job. So it's sad to imagine that a professional doesn't have time to give a student's resume a proper review... but that there apparently *is* time to keep meeting with that student repeatedly throughout the weeks and months of a mysteriously unsuccessful job search.

You always want to give students the impression that a great resume is completely up to their efforts and that they are responsible for catching errors. Still, it really angers me when I miss an error, however small. After doing this for 13 years, errors *usually* jump off the page at me. But occasionally I miss them, presumably because I let myself become rushed when things get hectic. So more than anything, be ready to *slow down* and do it right!

PERENNIAL QUESTIONS WITH RESUMES

There is about as much art as science when it comes to writing a resume. As noted in the last chapter, there are many disagreements among professionals as to what should be on a resume and how it should be written. I will go into more detail on several bones of contentions here. Many of these dilemmas are also wrestled with in my *Find Your First Professional Job* textbook.

1. *Should students have an Objectives section?*

It's not uncommon to see an Objectives section just below a candidate's name and contact information. But is this wise? I would never want to say never, but my opinion is that 90% of the time it's a waste of space. The problem is that the stated objective usually says nothing, or it says too much.

Here's an example of an objective that says nothing:

"To obtain an internship in a corporate environment that will help me learn and grow as a professional."

Well, I would *hope* that this would be your objective! This is incredibly vague, and it states the obvious. The alternative would be to be a bit *too* specific:

"To obtain a position in Tax with a fast-paced, Big Four accounting firm that will lead to a job after graduation."

That's okay if you're only going to apply to one of those Big Four firms. Are you going to have to change or eliminate that wording if you apply somewhere else? You'd better. Incredibly, I have seen resumes of people applying to our university with objectives indicating that the person wanted to be in the corporate world! Alternatively, I have seen this objective: "To work as part of the cooperative education faculty at Northeastern University." Did this person really think we would say "Wow, what a coincidence! That's just the position we're looking to fill!"?

The exception to the rule could be if the candidate's resume gives off a false impression about that person's job search goals. For example, let's say that a student did two internships in software development, but now wants to obtain a management job in technology. One possibility would be to write an objective that clues us in to the change of direction:

"To broaden myself beyond hands-on technical work by obtaining a position on the analytical, managerial side of technology."

2. *Should there be a Summary of Skills?*

It's not unusual these days to see a resume begin with some sort of summary of skills or qualifications, including bullets along these lines:

- Outstanding communicator with strong interpersonal skills

- Self-starter with previous professional experience in communications

I'm not a proponent of this approach. When interviewing candidates, I certainly wouldn't disqualify a candidate who used this approach... but I personally don't think it adds enough value to justify the use of space. One problem is that these sections often cite transferable skills that the candidate supposedly brings to the table. But as they aren't connected to anything specific, there is no way of knowing whether the claims are valid. A second problem is that this potentially creates a problem of repetition. If the person above really does have previous experience that is relevant, they are going to show me that in the Experience section. So why tell me twice when space is precious?

The only exception I can think of might be if I were to have a student who literally has never held a job. That's rare and a painful challenge. Even then, my tendency is to have the students write up some classroom projects or extracurricular activities as if they were jobs. That's not optimal either, but we have to have *something* on a resume. If doing that still left us with some glaring white space, I might be open to some sort of skill summary. Still, I think what I would really want to do is urge the student to volunteer somewhere immediately, so we could have *some* sort of job to add to the resume!

3. *Is it okay to have more than one page?*

This is a pretty common question, and students typically expect a yes or no answer. To be fair, this one is more debatable. I know professionals who think that a student should *always* have a one-page resume. For that matter, there are employers who believe that every professional should have no more than one page—even a candidate with over a decade of experience! The rationale is that business communication needs to be concise and that no one has the time to read a long-winded resume.

My experience is that a strong majority of students who ask whether they should have something more than a one-page resume actually should *not* do so. However, I would never say "My policy is that all students should have a one-page resume." Rather, the key question is: "Is the student effectively penalizing himself and hindering his ability to put his best foot forward as a candidate by cutting his resume down to one page?" If the answer is yes, then I allow the student to have a two-page resume. For example, I have worked with several students who started their own computer consulting businesses at age 16 on top of holding some other technical jobs. They have great job experience and an impressively large set of computer skills to capture on the resume. In those cases, I think it would be punitive of me to demand a one-page resume.

As Tamara Pinkas points out in her comments at the end of this chapter, there are many professionals who believe that a two-page resume can be justifiable. This is especially true when you are working with older students who may have a decade or more of job experience worth capturing on a resume. Not everyone would agree even there, but I personally would not want to shortchange that individual by absolutely forcing her to leave valuable experience off of the resume.

When dealing with younger students, though, I have found that the answer *usually* should be no when it comes to a multiple-page resume. When someone hands me a two-page resume, I often notice that the individual has opted to include anywhere from four to eight previous jobs. Almost invariably, there are several jobs that have no professional relevance. Sometimes there are multiple retail or administrative jobs with comparable duties. It's not uncommon for a student to believe that she must include every last job she's held. She doesn't need to do so, of course, nor does she need to include only her most recent jobs. Generally, I want my students to focus on two to four previous jobs, including only those that are most relevant to the impending job search. If they have a few directly related jobs, then it's easy to choose. If none of their many jobs are obviously connected to their major, then it becomes a tougher call. Here are some questions I might ask in helping them decide which jobs to cover:

- Which supervisor will give you the best reference?

- Which job had the highest level of responsibility?

- Which job did you hold the longest?

- Which job required skills that will transfer most readily to what you want to do on co-op?

The last question is especially provocative and interesting, but students might need help to understand possible connections. My employers who hire PC support co-ops often like to see customer-service experience, so a retail or restaurant job might be better to include than a job as a groundskeeper. An accounting employer might be more interested in someone's experience as a cashier or a waitress as opposed to someone who had a sales assistant role in a department store. Someone interested in hiring for an early childhood education role might be more impressed by a lifeguard position than that cashier role. So helping a student target a few jobs to highlight can start to get students thinking about how their knowledge and experience from one venue might be transferable to a professional context.

One last note here: If you *do* allow students to have a two-page resume, I highly recommend that you have them use a footer on each page, such as this: "Michael Ablove resume – Page 1 of 2." When resumes are e-mailed as is so often the case these days, the employer may overlook the fact that a resume has two pages or become confused if the pages become separated.

4. *Is it better to "spin" the resume by emphasizing transferable skills and accomplishments, or is a more objective "just the facts" approach better?*

By a wide margin, this is the biggest bone of contention of all. Using my *Find Your First Professional Job* textbook as an example, I can say quite honestly that there are professionals who have told me that my material on integrating transferable skills into job descriptions is the very favorite part of the whole book. Yet there are others who would say that the same material is what they *dislike* most in the book!

The biggest headache that I've had with the book has been trying to make everyone happy on this front. In the most recent edition of the book, I bent over backwards to lay out the arguments for and against a more expansive and subjective resume versus a more concise and objective approach. I will attempt to summarize these arguments here.

Those who prefer a more concise, objective, "just the facts" approach emphasize the following points:

- Employers are too busy to wade through a flowery, verbose resume; you may only have 60 seconds or less to convince the employer to interview you, so respect their time and stick to the simple facts about your background.

- Those who attempt to build up, say, a waitressing job by stressing transferable skills and accomplishments are attempting to "dress up a pig," and may be perceived as attempting to "BS" the prospective employer, affecting the candidate's credibility.

- The resume's purpose is to obtain an interview, not to give the employer a sales pitch. Candidates should save their selling for an interview.

Those who favor a more expansive, subjective, "selling" approach would counter with these arguments:

- Most co-op and internship employers are most interested in a person's transferable skills—work ethic, ability to work in a team, ability to multitask, and so forth—because technical skills can be learned, but personality traits are difficult to change. Thus, transferable skills should be included on a resume.

- If your past experience is not directly relevant, then you need to show the employer how your work as, say, a waiter or lifeguard might have helped you develop competencies that can translate to their professional environment.

- Why should someone care about non-related experience? They won't—unless you focus on *accomplishments* in each job as opposed to simply listing *duties*.

- It's all well and good to say that a candidate should save the selling for the job interview... but what if they don't get the interview because the resume is bland and doesn't really market the person for the role?

Whichever set of arguments is more persuasive, there are obvious pitfalls to each approach. Personally, I favor the more expansive approach in which a student pitches themselves and includes accomplishments and transferable skills—though the latter are less critical when the student has directly relevant experience. Still, I have to be careful: Can the student really support a claim that he makes about having a given soft skill? Is he exaggerating his responsibilities, accomplishments, and importance? Are his descriptions too verbose and flowery? These are definite concerns, and I have to make sure that the student doesn't overdo any of these elements.

Likewise, if I work with a student who favors a more simple, objective approach, I probably still would suggest that the student try to consider whether she has some objective and preferably quantifiable accomplishments, such as including how much money a cashier handled on a daily basis, how many tables a waiter handled simultaneously, and whether the individual received any awards or recognition for performance.

For yet another perspective on this debate, I really like what Anita Todd has to say in her comments at the end of this chapter. She finds it useful to remind students that transferable skills can be *explicit* or *implicit* in a resume, but that they definitely should be one or the other. At the minimum, the employer should be able to *infer* that the candidate has some specific skills as opposed to simply knowing that various duties were accomplished.

There is not a consensus among employers, so either style is bound to satisfy some employers and disappoint others. It can vary by industry, function, and region, so I'd recommend talking to employers to find out what *your* employers value in a resume as opposed to going on your own preferences and assumptions.

Lastly, I think that students should be allowed to decide what resume approach is really "them" and go with that. In the book and in my course, I lay out the pros and cons of each philosophy. Some students come in and say, "It makes me uncomfortable to have a resume that touts how great I am—that's just not my style." The student has to live with their resume's impact more than I do, so I absolutely would allow that. But it bothers me when I meet students who were very eager to create a resume that would assertively market themselves, only to have a professional tell them that is not allowed. You have every right to refuse to send out a resume that has errors or which reflects poorly on your program due to issues with its tone or appearance. But some issues are definitely judgment calls—say your piece and then cheerfully allow students to choose as they will.

5. *Is there a way around the reverse chronological order rule?*

This is another common question, and the answer on this one is an emphatic yes. It's not uncommon for a student to have a pretty menial part-time job to make money while in school. But certainly we'd rather not lead the Experience section with a waitressing job if someone had a terrific internship or paid position while in high school.

The easy solution is to have one section called "Related Experience" and another called "Other Work Experience" below it.

6. *Can a student have multiple resumes?*

Sometimes students like the idea of having more than one resume, and this might be sensible. For example, if someone is a Music Industry major with a business minor, it might be appealing to have one resume that emphasizes the former and another that focuses on the latter. In Chapter 7, I described how I've done this myself during a job search.

Should you allow that? Ideally, yes, but it might depend on what system you use to send out resumes. If your system allows students to post multiple resumes and designate different ones for different jobs, then I see no problem with it. But if you have to keep track of which resume is going where, then this could become a nightmare.

7. *How can we make sure we are doing justice to computer skills?*

The Computer Skills section also has its potential pitfalls. Professionals are wise to be wary of students who exaggerate their computer skills, making it seem as if they have significant experience with an application when they don't.

While this does occur, I find it's much more common for students to sell themselves short in this section. Amusingly, students often tend to believe that experience doesn't count unless it's obtained in a classroom or in a professional job. So I often will run these questions by my class when we talk about resumes:

- Have you ever built a website?

- Have you done any informal troubleshooting of computer problems for friends and family, such as setting up a wireless network, upgrading memory, building a computer, or debugging a computer?

It's surprising how often I come across people who have created a website or built a computer but failed to mention those skills on a resume. Likewise, there are students who are afraid to list a software application because they're afraid of exaggerating their skills. Although that's a good instinct, it can create a missed opportunity. Not including Excel or Access at all will tell a prospective employer that you have zero experience with those important applications. If you really don't, that's fine. If you have some experience, though, you should use phrases like "Proficient with...," "Familiar with...," "Exposure to...," or "Currently learning..." to delineate your degree of knowledge.

8. *Should we bother to include interests?*

I've met employers who have said, "Who cares if someone enjoys cross-country skiing? Why include interests and hobbies at all?" Others have said, "I am absolutely astonished when a job candidate doesn't include a brief Interests section."

So what should you recommend? Although I would never say that an Interests section is anywhere near the most important element on a resume, I am a proponent of including one. Here is the rationale:

- If you're a job candidate, what would you prefer as a first question in your interview? "Why should we hire you for this job?" or "I see you're interested in running. Tell me about that." Not infrequently, interviewers will ask about an interest to break the ice and set the candidate at ease to start the interview.

- Interests humanize a job candidate, making the job seeker more of a person rather than merely a list of qualifications and experience.

- Interests are an opportunity to build rapport between an employer and job seeker, especially if there is a shared interest or one that is intriguing to discuss.

- If the candidate has a career-related interest that they cannot convey elsewhere on the resume, this is an opportunity to do so.

As always, there is an opportunity for Interests to go awry. Too often, they are bland and predictable—music, reading, and sports—rather than sharp and specific: folk rock, contemporary short fiction, and college lacrosse. Even worse, you need to make sure students avoid controversial or questionable interests, such as hunting, nightclubs, and socializing. Students also need to be able to talk with some authority about *anything* on their resume, so if they list current events or American literature, they'd better be ready to talk about what's been in the news as well as a few favorite authors and novels.

GENERAL POINTERS WITH RESUMES

Next, let's walk through the actual process by which a student creates, modifies, and finalizes a resume, noting what you need to do each step of the way.

1. *Consider developing an evaluation rubric.*

   At the end of this chapter, Tamara Pinkas describes a rubric that she has created to evaluate resumes. This is an efficient and effective way to give students general feedback. Very quickly, you can identify a specific resume's strengths and problem areas. The student then knows where to focus the revision effort without you spending an inordinate amount of time copyediting a resume that may not be ready for that. I like to take only one extra-close look at a resume, and a rubric definitely can help. I haven't included the whole rubric here for space reasons, but I'm sure that Tamara or I could provide hers to you if you're interested in using or modifying it.

2. *Provide models.*

   You're setting yourself up for an extremely labor-intensive process if you don't provide students with some guidelines for writing a resume, including some samples of what a first resume could and should look like. Obviously, I have the *Find Your First Professional Job* book for that, but you always can create a small packet with your own guidelines and sample resumes if you prefer. My book has a step-by-step approach to creating a resume, and students that follow it carefully are usually well on their way to having a resume. Then you can focus on the fine-tuning and error-spotting instead of the grunt work of formatting.

   Regardless of how you go about it, you need to provide some examples unless you really want to fix fundamental errors again and again. Your examples can vary—personally, I am not hung up on specifics regarding font, bullets versus a paragraph format, margins, and so on—or not, if you think there is something to be gained by that.

3. *Make the student own the responsibility of writing and critiquing their own resume.*

   Several years ago, a renowned university hired my wife to critique the resumes of all grad students in a specific program. The student turned the resume in, and the department sent my wife a parcel of resumes to mark up and fix. You could call this amazing customer service, but I would call it a disservice to students and a waste of resources.

   Students need to learn to write and revise their own resumes. As Kerry Mahoney mentions earlier in the book, one idea is to not even write on the student's resume when you're critiquing it—let the student write down exactly what should be done next. When a student asks me to write a job description for her, I try to respond with a bit of humor. "I could do this for you, but if I do, I think you'll be looking me up for every job search for the rest of your career!" If a student hands me a resume that is based on a Word template or is obviously thrown together quickly with little regard to what I've discussed in the course or in the book, I basically will send them back to the drawing board. My job is not to turn a lump of coal into a diamond; my role is to take the rough diamond and polish it, making sure it looks just right.

If a student is obviously putting in the effort but is struggling with the job description, I might walk them through it with more hand-holding than usual. Still, I try hard to resist the urge to do it for them, even though this would be much faster. Better to invest more time up front to teach them how to do it once and for all.

4. *Look over aesthetics.*

Once I have the resume in hand and can see that it has the basic elements it needs per the book and classroom discussion, I try to resist jumping into a line-by-line critique in favor of a more holistic perspective. Here are the questions that I'm asking myself:

- Is the print readable?

In attempting to squeeze as much as possible onto one page, many students will decrease the point size of their font to the extent that the resume is annoyingly difficult to read. I often will use a bit of humor when commenting on this as well, reminding them that many employers might be at that age when their arms are no longer long enough to be able to read small print. I'm not quite there myself, but I'm sure that that point is not far off. The last thing a job seeker needs is for the employer's first reaction to be one of annoyance.

One other concern is with font. Personally, I find it a little boring if all resumes are in Times New Roman, the default font in Microsoft Word. I encourage students to use other fonts, such as Garamond or Palatino. But students need to make sure that they don't get too wild with fonts. You need something professional. It's also worth noting that sans serif fonts such as Arial and Helvetica can be good for headings, but serif fonts are generally considered more readable when you're dealing with an extended section of prose. I don't know if that matters too much on a resume, but, if asked, I recommend using a serif font. For those who don't know, a serif font's letters have little hats on top of letters:

This is serif font (Palatino Linotype).
This is a sans-serif font (Arial).

- Does the resume utilize space effectively?

A resume should have a sense of visual balance: I don't want to see text crammed on every inch of the paper with little spacing and minimal margins, but I don't want to see a vast desert of white space, either. Another issue is when text is heavy on one side of the page versus another, such as this:

XYZ Industries, Boston, MA, May – June 2007
Production Assistant

This would look much more balanced as follows:

XYZ Industries	Boston, MA
Production Assistant	May – June 2007

Students are prone to forget that they can alter margins and point sizes to make things fit. It's optimal to have the resume fill the page without looking crammed.

- Does the resume have some visual variety to it?

It's not wrong to have a whole resume in one point size or in nothing but plain text, but the end result will be a resume that it is not as visually compelling as it might be. I generally suggest that the candidate's name be somewhat larger than anything else on the resume, and in boldface text. Section headers should be next largest—smaller than the name but larger than the body text—and also in bold text. Next, why not use bold text for all organization names and italic text for job titles?

There are other elements that can be used as well: diamonds or squares in the place of conventional bullets, underlining to underscore a break between sections, and so forth. Such formatting can get out of hand, but it's more common to see too little variety rather than too much.

5. *Make sure the resume has an internal logic to it.*

There are many ways in which a resume might be organized, but you want to make sure that students have consistent logic that they follow through the resume. For example, resume writers could opt to list job duties in chronological order to capture a sequence of events, or they could choose to list them in order of importance or impressiveness. Either way is defensible, but students should have a rationale in mind as opposed to dumping their thoughts out randomly. A good question to ask: "Why did you choose to put your bullets (or sentences in a paragraph format) in this order?" There should be a logical reason.

6. *Watch out for deadly inconsistencies.*

For many style points on a resume, the answer on how to do something is that "it really doesn't matter." Does bulleted text need to end with a period? Does there need to be a blank line between a section heading and the next line? Should we write out full state names or use abbreviations? Should the section headers be centered or flush left? Should text be indented or not?

I really don't care what a student does on any of the above. However, I will be an absolute stickler to make sure that they do it the same way in every instance, as inconsistencies will betray a lack of attention to detail.

One typical problem is a job listed as, say, March 2007-Present. If the student is still doing the job, the verbs should be in the present tense:

- Show strong customer-service skills when waiting on up to six tables simultaneously.

- Obtain dessert orders from roughly 40% of tables by using suggestive-selling skills.

Likewise, all verbs should be in the past tense if the student is no longer doing the job.

7. Probe with clarifying questions.

Once I've looked at some of the big-picture formatting issues, I would delve into asking a bunch of questions to make sure everything is accurate and as inclusive as it should be:

- Is this your updated address, phone number, and e-mail address?

- Is your GPA up to date?

- Do you have a secondary concentration or minor?

- Are there any clubs or other activities you do on campus?

When it comes to the most crucial part of the resume—the job description itself—I will linger on some pertinent questions if key details are lacking:

- What kind of business is this company in? I might suggest starting the first bullet with a descriptive clause if that's not as obvious as something like Pizza Hut or Target: "Working at a small electronics manufacturer..." or "Working at a start-up business specializing in upscale travel..."

- Did you do a good job in this position? Some resumes say a great deal about what the person did, but not how they did the job. As noted earlier, it's debatable as to whether this is necessary. Still, I prefer to ask the student whether there are any accomplishments for which they earned recognition, or if there are some quantitative details that would convey some sense of the scope of their responsibility.

- If I were to ask your manager to characterize you, what would he or she say? This might help identify a couple of transferable skills that we might want to weave into the resume, implicitly or explicitly. If the student is stumped, a similar question would be "If you were to hire someone to replace yourself, what qualities would you be seeking in that candidate?"

- Did you display skills that might have some relevance to an employer in your prospective field? If the student is going to be seeking a marketing or communications job, I might probe to see if they had opportunities to show an ability to communicate orally or in writing in a job. If they were an engineering student, I might try to delve into jobs that showed analytical skills or an ability to improve processes. This also helps the student think more about knowledge transfer—how their skills will translate from one context to another. This can facilitate and enhance learning.

Recently I had a Supply Chain Management student who wanted to do a co-op in logistics. His best job was working in a sandwich shop on campus. When we delved deeply into that job, it turned out that he approached that menial job like a true logistics professional. Every day, he had to make plans relating to inventory and production while making about 200 sandwiches daily. Without any hyperbole, this translated very nicely into his resume and interviews.

One caveat: I never encourage students to make a job something other than what it was. If the answer to "Did you do a good job?" is something like "It was just a job; I can't say that

I'm especially proud of my performance," then I'm not going to try to pretend that the student was a terrific employee. More frequently, students believe that their non-professional jobs will be irrelevant to future employers, and they shrug off terrific accomplishments as "no big deal." So it does take some persistent probing to figure out if the student is selling herself short or if the job truly was nothing special.

8. *Discuss choices and consequences.*

I've alluded to this earlier in terms of the general philosophy of selling yourself on a resume versus a more terse and objective approach. Yet there are other types of choices and consequences on a resume as well. Should you list a job that was a great experience... but one where your reference may or may not be stellar? What if you have some terrific experience in leading some campus club that relates to politics, religion, sexual orientation, and so on? I don't see my role as telling students that they should or shouldn't include some information, but I do feel compelled to let them know the benefits and risks of disclosing personal information on a resume.

This can be very tricky. Years ago, my former colleague Bill Sloane worked with an older student who was a Vietnam War veteran. The student absolutely insisted on disclosing his issues with post-traumatic stress disorder as well as the 15-20 jobs he had held over the years—even though many of those jobs were extremely short-lived. Beyond correcting errors, there was not much that Bill could do but to make sure the student was fully aware of the consequences of those choices in an attempt to get him to reconsider what should go on his resume.

9. *Learn how to catch errors.*

I doubt that any co-op or internship program gives applicants a copyediting test, though sometimes I think it would be a good idea to give a potential coordinator a really bad resume and see if they can spot all the errors. It's fair to say that some professionals have a more natural talent than others when it comes to editing and proofreading resumes. Whether it comes naturally to you or not, there is always room for improvement. Here are some common errors; keep your eyes peeled for them:

■ Misspelled headings

It's pretty funny how often you'll see words such as Experience and Interests misspelled. They obviously aren't hard words to spell; the problem is that the eye tends to skip right over headings instead of scrutinizing them. So I often will make a point to read all the headings right after I check out the overall aesthetic look of the resume.

■ Abbreviation abuse

Maybe I'm getting old, but sometimes it seems as if the art of abbreviation has gone out of style. It's not unusual to see the following

44 Scotland St   33 Amory Ave
Pittsburgh, PA.   Aug – Dec 2005

Obviously, these are all incorrect. All states should be abbreviated with their two-letter postal abbreviation, which never has a period at the end. Otherwise, students should always use periods when abbreviating words, and use of abbreviations generally should be limited to the aforementioned examples.

- Spelling errors

While it would be impossible to enumerate all the ways in which words may be misspelled on a resume, here are at least some of the most common spelling errors that I see:

Wrong	Right
activites	activities
preformed	performed
costumer	customer
defiantly	definitely
Deans List	Dean's List
National Honors Society	National Honor Society
experence, or expereince	experience
intrests	interests
relevent	relevant
Power Point	PowerPoint
aid (as in the job title)	aide
Bachelor of Art	Bachelor of Arts
recieve	receive
inquires (as noun)	inquiries
lead (as past tense)	led

To be fair, I see "definitely" written as "defiantly" more often in cover letters and e-mails than on resumes. With resumes, a common problem with aid, inquires, lead, costumer, defiantly, and preformed is that these are all words; a spell-checking program will not view them as errors. You might want to Google the phrase "spell-checker poem" if you want something amusing to print out for students on this point. I would include it here, but I have no idea about its copyright. The gist of it is that someone wrote a poem in which there are tons of spelling errors that no spell-checking program will catch. It's pretty funny.

- Capitalization and punctuation errors

Many people—students or otherwise—appear to be confounded by the difference between common nouns and proper nouns. While a noun is a person, place, or thing, a proper noun refers to a specific and potentially unique entity.—the actual name of an individual, an organization, a product, a job title, or so forth.

Here are some common nouns and proper nouns that may turn up on resumes:

Common nouns	Proper Nouns
computer	Administrative Assistant
customer	Dean's List
business	Varsity Basketball
inventory	Mosaic Eye Publishing
products	Sales Assistant
clients	Hiking Club
projects	Bachelor of Science

As for punctuation, the two most common problems are missing commas and difficulties with possessive nouns. With the former, you often can infer where a comma should go by either a) reading the sentence aloud and seeing where a natural pause occurs, and/or b) making sure that a comma goes right before the primary verb in a complex sentence:

Missing Commas:

- When working in a team displayed positive attitude while painting house
- Answered phone calls directing them to other employees efficiently

Correct Use of Commas:

- When working in a team, displayed positive attitude while painting house
- Answered phone calls, directing them to other employees efficiently

With possessive nouns, you sometimes don't know where the apostrophe should go unless you ask the student to clarify. Consider these two:

- Answered customers questions efficiently
- Assisted with co-workers training needs

In both cases, we can say with certainty that something is wrong. But we would have to ask the individual how many customers or co-workers they are talking about in each case. If we're talking about answering the questions of multiple customers and the training needs of a single co-worker, we would apostrophize as follows:

- Answered customers' questions efficiently
- Assisted with co-worker's training needs

One last pet peeve with apostrophes is how people write up years on resumes:

Wrong	Right
Aug. 04 – Feb. 05	Aug. 2004 – Feb. 2005
May '00 – January '01	May 2000 – January 2001
'90's or 1990's	1990s (unless it's used as a possessive)

In general, it's pretty common to see a misplaced apostrophe.

- Hyphenation errors

At the risk of showing off my obsessive-compulsive disorder, I can't resist talking about hyphenation errors. In a previous incarnation, I was a medical writer. When writing about a drug that treats HIV, I had to write about T cells quite frequently. The upshot was that I was forced to learn when and how to hyphenate words and phrases to avoid going completely insane when doing a project. I had to know when to write about T cells as opposed to T-cell receptors or T-cell activation.

The basic principle is that a phrase that is acting as a noun or a verb is generally not hyphenated, but a phrase acting as an adjective is hyphenated. Here are some examples of correct hyphenation that might turn up on resumes.

Displayed excellent customer-service skills when…
Provided excellent customer service when…
Handled time-sensitive tasks…
Managed computer-related responsibilities…
Showed strong time-management skills…
Showed ability to handle time management…
Displayed results-oriented approach when…
Proved to be results oriented when…

CRITIQUING AN ACTUAL RESUME

Let's take a stab at critiquing an actual resume. I have disguised the student's name, contact info, and a few other identifying characteristics, but this is otherwise a 100% real resume sent my way by my colleague, Linnea Basu, who characterized this as a pretty typical first-time co-op resume. The resume is on the next page.

First, I print out the resume to look at a hard copy as a whole, aesthetically. It's much harder to critique a resume onscreen. My first concern is that Steven has crammed too much text onto one page, leading him to use a point size which is too small. There are no spaces between sections, schools, and jobs. In Word, I can see that it's Book Antiqua, 10 point. That combination gives the page a dense, cramped effect that may put off a potential interviewer.

You can't really tell a student that a specific point is too small; 11 or 12 point can be too small or too large depending on the font. However, 10 point is usually too small. So right off the bat I'm going to point that out and say that we will need to condense or eliminate something here. My initial thought would be to get rid of the second activity or condense it somehow. Another idea would be to combine Skills and Interests (funny how he is using the label "Personal" here—I would change that) to save another line or two.

The next thing that is bugging me is how the city and state data is crammed next to the organization names. Let's suggest spreading those out like so:

CALLERY SCHOOL   *Worcester, MA*
Assistant Lacrosse Coach   *May-June 2007*

Another aesthetic detail: The resume mysteriously changes font in the last couple of sections. Checking electronically, I see that it moved from Book Antiqua to Times New Roman. Steven probably did that accidentally.

Next I would ask my usual questions about verifying personal data. Assuming that this was correct, I would move on to the education section. Students move frequently and sometimes fail to update their addresses and phone numbers. The month and year of graduation are included, but I would like to move them down one line. That will let us slide Boston, MA over to the right, and it also will put the graduation date on the same line as the degree; that makes sense. I think I would put a semi-colon after the GPA and move up the Dean's List info by one line to save a little more space, though I could also put "Honors:" in front of Dean's List. Along the same line, I would put "Activities:" in front of "Peer Tutor for Financial Management." Not only is that a good idea, it is also a consistency issue, given that Steven uses that heading in the high school section.

Steven B. Trigg

44 West Eton St., Apt. 5 │ Boston, MA 02116 │ (508) 321-0000 │ Email: trigg.s@neu.edu

EDUCATION

NORTHEASTERN UNIVERSITY – *Boston, MA*   *May 2010*

Candidate for Bachelor of Science in Economics
GPA: 3.27/4.0
Dean's List: 2008
Peer Tutor for Financial Management
Relevant Courses: Financial Management, Financial Accounting and Reporting, Money and Banking, Statistics, Macroeconomic Theory, Principles of Macroeconomics, Principles of Microeconomics

CALLERY SCHOOL – *Worcester, MA*   *June 2005*

Graduated with High Honors
New England Prep Lacrosse All-Star and Callery Lacrosse Sportsmanship Award
Activities: Varsity Lacrosse (Captain), Varsity Soccer (Captain), Volunteer for C.A.R.E

PROFESSIONAL EXPERIENCE

BASU TECHNOLOGIES INC. – *Millbury, MA*   *July-August 2007 & 2004*

Maintenance
- Performed site maintenance projects at a gas compression tube manufacturing company
- Worked with a team painting buildings and machinery
- Installed equipment such as guard rails and inventory shelves
- Asked to return in a following summer

CALLERY SCHOOL – *Worcester, MA*   *May-June 2007*

Assistant Lacrosse Coach
- Coached the Callery School men's lacrosse team by running drills during practice with the offensive team
- Gave advice and suggestions to offensive players on how to improve their performance
- Responsible for subbing players during games and giving game-time advice
- Ensured accuracy of players' statistics by communicating with the record keepers

BOUDREAU GARDENS – *Centreville, MA*   *July-August 2006*

Landscape Designer
- Worked with a team planting and maintaining gardens as well as building landscape construction projects
- Communicated with clients and company owner to develop preliminary plans for garden and construction projects
- Helped company owner plant a first place installation at the Newport Flower Show

ACTIVITIES

C.A.R.E
- Mentored two children with mental disabilities during the Fall and Spring over three years throughout high school
- Met Saturdays and participated with C.A.R.E buddy in indoor and outdoor games and arts and crafts

CENTRAL MASS STATE LACROSSE TEAM
- Played for the central Massachusetts lacrosse team in the Bay State Summer Games for two seasons
- Won both silver and bronze medals

SKILLS

Computer: proficient in Excel, Microsoft Word, and PowerPoint
Languages: intermediate Spanish

PERSONAL

Enjoy skiing, playing guitar and physical fitness

The high school info is in pretty good shape. I would move the "June 2005" date down a line to match what we did above, and I see that Steven has left the final period off of C.A.R.E. as well.

Now we go to the Experience section. At this point, I would question Steven about whether or not he was any good at these jobs. With the exception of the last bullets on the first and third jobs, there is not much of a sense of accomplishment in these three jobs. So I would want to discuss whether or not he really wants a resume that simply lists his duties rather than delving into achievements and character traits that he brought to these jobs. I also might see if there are some quantitative details we might add, though I wouldn't push too hard on that. There are some good qualitative details and some decent action verbs here.

Next I would scrutinize the wording of each bullet. Steven seems to be rather allergic to commas. So I would change the first job's second bullet as follows:

• Worked with a team, painting buildings and machinery

Otherwise it seems like he's working with a "team painting"! With the last bullet in that job, "Asked to return in a following summer" is an odd phrasing. Admittedly, this is a tricky situation since he returned to the employer three years later. Let's change it to "Asked to return in a subsequent summer."

For the Callery School job, let's initial cap Men's Lacrosse, as that's a proper noun. In the third bullet, let's get rid of that all-too-ubiquitous resume phrase, "Responsible for," in favor of a good action verb. After all, the individual was responsible for everything that they did on the whole resume, no? So how about this:

• Handled player substitutions during games and gave game-time advice

The next job description's first bullet has another missing comma problem—this time between "team" and "planting." The third bullet is also missing a hyphen in "first-place installation."

When we move on to the Activities section, we see that Steven repeatedly fails to put the last period into the C.A.R.E. acronym. Well, at least he's consistent! The lack of spacing between the various activities also increases the cramped feeling of the resume.

As noted earlier, I might ditch that last activity. But if we keep it, let's get rid of the word "both" in that second bullet. Otherwise, it seems as if he might've won TWO silver medals as well as a bronze.

Lastly, I've already mentioned changing the font in the Skills and Personal section, which we will rename as Interests. I also would initial cap Proficient and Intermediate, as those are the first words after the colon on the two successive lines. The interests themselves are fine, but I might eliminate the word "Enjoy" and ask Steven if he has any career-related interests, such as the stock market, investments, or reading *The Wall Street Journal*.

Now we have a better looking resume. The only problem is that we still have problems with space. When I insert blank lines between all sections and increase the point size to 11, I end up going onto the next page by about eight lines. So what are our options?

CONDUCTING AND CRITIQUING PRACTICE INTERVIEWS

Now let's turn our attention to conducting and critiquing practice interviews—a good skill for every professional to know, whether or not you engage in this activity regularly. I have done at least 300 of them over the years, but I rarely do them anymore. Fortunately, we have assistants who handle this step. Still, I regularly train people to handle all aspects of practice interviews, and I coach students on interview strategy on a continual basis during every interview cycle.

One fundamental is that it's relatively easy to tell if an interview is good or bad, but it takes more time and practice to be able to discern exactly how good or bad the interview is versus how good it could be. Likewise, most people need experience to be able to pinpoint why an interview is not as good as it could be and how to best articulate constructive criticism. So let's walk through the whole process.

BEFORE THE INTERVIEW

Some important steps need to happen before the big day even arrives. Here are some ways to ensure that you get the most bang for your buck with the practice interview.

- Make sure that students understand interviewing fundamentals before the practice interview. This may sound like stating the obvious. However, in our zeal to have everyone complete a practice interview in a limited period of time early in the semester, we've sometimes had students do the mock interview before they read about interviewing in the book or learned about it in the class. The upshot was that those students needed much more coaching on fundamentals than they would've needed otherwise. You have only so much time to do one-on-one work with students, so you'd much rather fine-tune a pretty good interview as opposed to overhauling a disastrous one.

- Have students select a specific job description with a specific company. No real interview is going to occur in a vacuum. So we require students to pick out an actual job description in advance—preferably one that is a "reach" job as opposed to a job for which they are very obviously qualified. The student e-mails the job description to the interviewer at least a day before, so the interviewer can prepare a few questions that are unique to that job description.

  Make sure students understand that they have to use the job description to research the company and job and to prepare strategically for the interview. I always tell students that the interviewer only has about 30 minutes at most to critique their interview. If she has to use that time to fix basic, glaring errors, then she will do so. Obviously, we'd much rather have her take a good interview and make it great. The more the interviewee prepares, the more likely they are to be able to work on subtle improvements.

- Make the practice interview a full dress rehearsal. Students need to understand how to dress for an interview. We do a full dress rehearsal. Part of it is to make it a realistic experience, but it also gives an opportunity to nip fashion issues in the bud: low-cut blouses, garish ties, white socks with dress shoes, questionable piercings, and so on.

DURING THE INTERVIEW

The practice interview is scheduled in advance. If the interviewee arrives late to the practice interview, I usually zing them with a strong opening question: "In this job, we're looking for someone who is reliable and dependable. Given that you showed up ten minutes late for this interview, why should I assume that you have those qualities?" Obviously, there is no really good answer to that question. Attempting to answer it and confronting that question is a good opportunity to learn what will go through an interviewer's mind if you're late—whether or not such a direct question is asked about the tardiness.

Otherwise, here are some recommendations for the interview itself:

- Prepare 8-10 questions, but be ready to diverge from the script. When you're new at doing this, it's a good idea to have a rough plan of what you're going to ask. I don't bother with that anymore, but you don't want to underestimate how difficult it is to conduct one of these interviews if you haven't done it before. Simultaneously, you are attempting to:

  - Ask questions

  - Think about what to ask next

  - Evaluate the quality of each response and whether to ask a follow-up question

  - Take notes

  - Be relatively cordial

  That's some serious multitasking! Having a game plan for your questions is a good idea.

- Take notes. You don't have to write everything down, but I still need to write down notes for every answer as well as a few evaluative comments to jog my memory for the critique. Sometimes I'll write a check mark for a good moment, or I'll draw a small flag to remind myself about a particularly bad glitch.

- Don't be afraid to take time to collect your thoughts. There's nothing wrong with allowing for some silence while you jot down some thoughts or think through what you'd like to ask next.

- If you have a video camera or webcam available to you, this can be a powerful way to show students their strengths and weaknesses—especially with nonverbal elements.

- Probe with follow-up questions, especially if an answer raises a flag. If a student's answer raises a concern in your mind—which I refer to as a flag—I think it's best to let them know about your concern by asking a follow-up question. Let's say that we ask a student what he liked least about a previous job as a grocery bagger, and he says that it was that it was very monotonous. If he was applying for a job as a software tester, I might point out that there is a good deal of repetition in the job. Will that be a problem?

  Such a question might be considered a little impolite. But I think it accomplishes a few goals: When you voice your concern immediately, the student can see how his previous answer led directly to a problem that needs to be addressed. It also gives the student an opportunity to address the concern, rather than having it linger in the interviewer's mind. Afterwards, I often will point out that I did the student a favor by alerting him to a flag and giving him a chance to do something about it.

■ Ask a variety of questions. Students will encounter all kinds of interview styles: interrogative, behavioral-based, warm and friendly, vague and fuzzy, and so on. This will help you make a more effective critique. Here are some categories of questions and some examples of each:

Open-ended questions:

· Tell me about yourself.

· What are your strengths?

· What is your greatest accomplishment?

· What do you see yourself doing in ten years?

Specific/behavioral-based questions:

· Why do you think you would be a good match for this job?

· You mentioned your ability to learn quickly: Can you give me a very specific example of a time when you demonstrated that?

· Tell me about a specific time when you had to handle a really challenging situation with a customer. Walk me through the details of it, including your thoughts, emotions, and actions, as well as the ultimate outcome.

Negative questions:

· What's your biggest weakness?

· What did you like least about your job with _____?

· How are you grades? (assuming you see no GPA listed on the resume)

Questions unique to the job description:

· As you know, we're looking for someone who can work with Symantec Ghost. What do you know about that application?

· What you do understand about market segmentation?

· You probably know that we're a third-party logistics firm. Explain what your understanding of that is.

· As you know, we're looking for someone with good computer skills. I see that you describe yourself as "proficient in Excel." So tell me how you would take a column of 1,000 numbers and multiply all of them by, say, .05 in one swoop.

Questions that reveal how much research the candidate did:

- What do you know about our organization, beyond what you read on the job description?

- I can see that you've never worked with SAP, a preferred skill for an applicant for this job. What do you know about it?

A question about interests:

- I see you're interested in skiing. Tell me about that.

Also give the candidate an opportunity to ask questions at the end of the interview. Answer the questions to the best of your ability, but don't worry if your answers are accurate. If the interviewee has no questions or doesn't know how to make the transition from asking questions to closing the interview by asking about next steps and summarizing their strengths, I usually will allow an awkward silence for several seconds, and then I'll make a very awkward statement. "Well, I don't have any more questions, so, um, if you don't have any more questions, well…. I guess… that's it." This is a little excruciating, but enduring that awkwardness will help me make a point about how the interviewee needs to "control the ball" effectively at the interview's close.

SELF-EVALUATION

Our practice interviews seldom take more than 15 minutes. Sometimes five or six questions are enough to get a sense for what the interviewee is doing well or poorly, but sometimes it takes a few more. After the interview ends, I usually tell the interviewee that the primary goal of the practice interview is to teach students to interview better for jobs. But a secondary goal is for students to be able to reflect on their own interviewing performance and to build objective self-awareness of their strengths and weaknesses. After all, that's a quality that I want them to be valuing as they go into the job itself.

Therefore, I give the student five or ten minutes to critique themselves. I ask them to rate themselves on a scale of 1 to 10, with 1 being a disastrous interview and 10 being a terrific one. I often add that I want them to rate their performance in the interview as opposed to rating themselves as a job candidate or as a human being. This is a way to remind the student that any criticism is not personal, it's behavioral.

While they are doing a rating, this gives me an opportunity to organize the notes for my own critique. I will write an overall score, and then I'll write a list of positives and negatives. I will try to prioritize them and talk about the most important ones first.

Then I will listen as the interviewee tells me their self-rating and evaluation. This is always interesting. There are students with very bad interviews who are quite good at dissecting them effectively, and there are those who have an unbelievably inaccurate sense of how they did, whether they did poorly or well. Either way, this will merit some comment on self-awareness. Sometimes I will ask clarifying questions to be sure I'm clear on their self-perception.

One very human tendency is for students to be incredibly eager to discuss their weaknesses. That's okay, but be sure that they find some strengths and discuss them first if at all possible.

THE CRITIQUE: Helpful Hints

Here are some tactics that I find quite helpful when critiquing the interview.

1. *Start off with positives.*

No matter how weak the interview is, find some positives, even if that only means punctuality, attire, or continuing to try despite butchering some questions. The goal is to make sure the interviewee knows what's going right so they can be sure to replicate those qualities in the future. You want to give students a sense that they have some sort of foundation that they can build on.

2. *Focus on finding themes*

Try to get beyond the details and assess the problem rather than its symptoms. It's easy to get caught up in a question-by-question critique, but it's much more useful to track the problems to their sources. I created a handout for *Find Your First Professional Job*, listing the most common problems in order of frequency as well as suggestions as to how to address them. You can see that on the next page.

Let's go into a little more detail with each theme:

A. Being *"interviewer-dependent"* is a term of my own invention, so I should elaborate. The idea here to some degree is the old saying: "Ask a stupid question, get a stupid answer." Many students have a tendency to mirror the interviewer. So when the interviewer asks a sharp, specific question, they provide a sharp, specific response. But when asked a vague, general, open-ended question, the typical response is an all too vague answer.

Students typically *hate* open-ended questions. They usually just don't know what to do with them, so they fumble around and recite their major, hometown, interests, and so forth—all of which are obvious on the resume. You need to coach students to *not* be interviewer-dependent; they should provide a sharp, specific answer to an open-ended question. "Tell me about yourself" is giving students the option to decide *what* to tell. So why shouldn't a student talk about why they are a good match for the job? If the employer asked because they wanted to know more about the student's hobbies, then he or she can follow up with a more specific question to that effect.

B. *Lacking a strategy* is also a common error and strongly linked to the aforementioned inability to deal with open-ended questions. I want every student to come into each interview with three specific reasons why they are a good match for the job at hand, and I want them to seize the first reasonable opportunity to put those reasons on the table. After all, some chatty interviewers may only ask one or two questions, total. Obviously, if the first question relates to one of your interests, you're not going to launch your strategy. But any open-ended question about you, your strengths, and your background is a good enough reason to talk strategically.

When students fail to interview strategically, I'll often ask them if they did indeed prepare a strategy with three or four planks. Occasionally, they did prepare one and failed to articulate

COMMON INTERVIEW PROBLEMS AND HOW TO SOLVE THEM

PROBLEM		SOLUTION	
A.	Being "interviewer dependent" (Quality of your interview depends on quality of interviewer)	A.	▪ Answer general questions with specifics ▪ Use specific stories and examples ▪ Make interview a "conversation with purpose"
B.	Lacking a strategy	B.	▪ Write down three reasons why YOU should be hired for THIS specific job ▪ Discuss these reasons ASAP in interview
C.	Inadequate research	C.	▪ Prepare as if your life depended on it ▪ Weave your research into answers and questions
D.	Answers aren't helpful	D.	▪ Always tie answers to company's needs on job description
E.	Negative nervous energy	E.	▪ Preparation ▪ Practice ▪ Putting energy into presentation ▪ Maintaining external focus
F.	Weak opening and/or closing	F.	▪ Don't rehash resume ▪ Articulate strategy early ▪ Prepare ten good questions ▪ Bridge to Close
G.	Getting stuck; blanking out	G.	▪ Ask clarifying question ▪ Don't be afraid to pause ▪ Use note page (carefully)
H.	Raising flags for interviewer	H.	▪ Preparation ▪ Focus on positives, always ▪ If negatives must be discussed, choose ones that won't hurt you
I.	Insensitivity to interviewer: ▪ Talking too fast ▪ Lack of "active listening" ▪ Digressing from the point	I.	▪ Practice speaking style ▪ Pause, especially after key points ▪ Respond to verbal/non-verbal cues ▪ Stick to what he or she needs to know

it, but more often the student never even thought about it. Sometimes you may need to help them understand what experiences and traits may differentiate them from other candidates. Students overlook obvious strategic opportunities, such as a strong GPA, which can be cited as proof of an ability to learn quickly. Likewise, a former waiter may not realize that such a job may give him an opportunity to talk about multitasking and customer service. So some coaching here may be needed.

C. Inadequate research is also common. Even among job seekers who are a decade or two removed from college, I'm often surprised at how little research many job seekers do. Just recently we interviewed for a new co-op faculty position, and one candidate obviously had no real idea of what the job was. Others have asked questions that could've been answered with a two-minute look at our website. Relatively few people get beyond the job description at all.

I like to ask an admittedly melodramatic question during some critiques: "If your life depended on getting this job, how might you have prepared differently?" Whether or not they know the answer to this question, I can highlight many much overlooked options:

- Asking me for the name of a current or former co-op who could be contacted in order to ask about the job, the environment, the manager… and maybe even what to anticipate at the interview!

- If it's a company that has a retail presence or that sells consumer products, why not try out the products yourself, if possible?

- If there is any term on the job description that you don't understand, your goal should be to research enough so you can have an intelligent conversation about anything that might come up in the interview.

- Researching a company through their website or Google is not a bad idea to understand the purpose of the job, but don't waste time memorizing quasi-relevant facts like annual revenues, how many mutual funds the company runs, and so on.

D. If one's *answers are not bad but aren't helpful,* then the issue is that the interviewee is forgetting that almost every question is really the same question: "Why should we hire *you* for *this* specific job?" Even a question such as "What do you see yourself doing in ten years?" is no different. Often the interviewer *really* wants to know "Why do you want to do this job *now* in light of what you want to do in the future?" I have seen students fail to get a job with a high tech company because the student said that their long-term goal was to be a consultant. The high tech employer figured that they weren't interested in training students for six months so they could go work as consultants; they wanted to hire people who were interested in working in high tech in the long run.

E. *Negative nervous energy* is a common problem, compounded by the fact that many students will have family and friends encouraging them to "relax" before the interview. This is both unfair and unrealistic. Interviewees need to embrace their nervousness and transform it into projecting enthusiasm, excitement, and passion. But this can be easier said than done.

You can diagnose negative nervous energy from a variety of symptoms:

- Some people tend to speak much faster than usual and also may rush into answering questions instead of reflecting on a response first.

- Other people will do the opposite: They will get very uptight and become very terse. Often such a person has rather frozen body language as well.

- Non-verbal communication also can betray negative nervous energy: shaking hands, wild hand gestures, clicking a pen, fiddling with clothes, and so forth.

- Using words such as "like" and "you know" an incredible number of times in almost every sentence.

You need to bring all of the above to the interviewee's attention, as it may be unconscious. Students may need some assurance that it's okay to have a few seconds of silence. Others may need additional practice.

F. *A weak opening and/or closing* are also quite common. The open-ended questions up front are problematic for students, while anxious students might blow off the opportunity to ask questions altogether, basically because they don't know how to take charge of the interview and perhaps are just eager for it to end.

G. *Getting stuck or blanking out* is another common fear, and sometimes it does happen. Fortunately, this is an easy fix. Such students should be encouraged to use a notes page. I have a great sample notes page in *Find Your First Professional Job*. The notes page is just one page, and it is written or typed in large print so it can be read with a quick glance. The notes pages includes just enough words to remind students about their strategic points, stories that support those points, key research facts, some great questions for the end of the interview, and some blank space for writing down notes.

Much to my amusement, students are amazed to find that this is permissible. They seem to think that it's cheating. I remind them that much has to do with their attitude about it. If they act defensive or sneaky about looking over their notes, it will come off poorly. If asked directly about what they are looking at, they can say, "I like to be organized, so I prepared some notes as reminders of what I wanted to be sure to cover during our meeting today." If you're okay with that, the employer will be, too. Lastly, I tell students that notes are basically a safety net. If you never need to look at them, great. Ironically, once you have them in place, you probably are less likely to need them.

H. I've talked already about *raising flags for the interviewer*—making a statement that is worrisome to the interviewer. This is usually a symptom of poor preparation or negative nervous energy. The student either hasn't thought through how his response might be interpreted negatively, or she blurted something out quickly because of nerves. More prep and a more careful pace will help here.

I. One last recurring theme is *insensitivity to the interviewer*. This might include talking too fast, as the interviewer will not be able to keep up with you. But it also could mean that you aren't really listening to the questions or picking up on an employer concern. Here's a good example: If a student doesn't hand me a resume as soon as the interview begins, I won't ask for one directly. Instead, I might act like I'm looking around my desk while saying, "I'm trying to remember where you worked previously from your resume. Can you remind me?" If the student is really paying attention, he'll immediately ask if I'd like another copy of the resume. If not—probably because they are focusing more internally on their own nervousness—then they will just answer the question.

You want students to pick up on verbal and non-verbal cues. If the practice interviewee is giving a very long-winded, digressing response, I might intentionally start glancing at my watch, heaving sighs, and so on. I'd just like to see if they can pick up on the hints and start becoming more concise.

3. *Make sure the interviewee understands how to make improvements.*

It's not enough to spell out the students' strengths and weaknesses and send them on their merry way. You need to be sure that they really understand how to improve in addition to what they need to improve.

There are several questions you can ask to assess whether they know what it's going to take:

- Given that you didn't really articulate a strategy, can you tell me three or four reasons why they should hire YOU to do THIS job?

- Can you give me an example to support each of these reasons, using specific stories to bring them to life?

- If you wanted to go all out in research and preparation, what could you do differently?

- Can you think of a question that you (the interviewee) could ask that would reflect a job candidate who is REALLY interested in getting this job?

If the candidate is stumped on questions like these, you may need to discuss these points in greater detail. You might ask them to go write up answers to a few of these questions and then run them by you, just to make sure they're on the right track.

4. *If there is a glaring weakness, have the student try to apply your advice right away.*

After hearing the critique, the interviewee can be encouraged to take another stab at a question they bombed on, or at speaking with a volume, pace, or energy level that is new to them.

5. *Model a great answer for the student.*

This is always powerful. If a student had no strategy and ended up with a weak answer for something like "Tell me about yourself," I might take a minute to pull together a strategy that would work for him for that job and then show them what it might sound like: "I'm excited to be here today, because I know that you're looking for a self-starter with good computer skills who can work in a team environment. My experience as a landscaper definitely required initiative, as we often started really early on weekends. Yet we also had to work in a team. As for computer skills, I'm getting stronger all the time by using Excel in my business classes."

I often model the Q&A section as well, as described in Chapter 8.

6. *Give an honest score.*

This may sound harsh, but my average score on a practice interview is probably about a 3/10 or 4/10. I don't give everyone a poor score. It's not too unusual to give out a 7 or 8, and I think I have given maybe two 10 scores out of 300+ practice interviews. Still, there's no question that your score makes a statement. I give a 10 when I can't think of anything that I would want the person to do differently. An 8 or 9 would mean that there are a few subtle tweaks that are advisable: Maybe the interviewee asked only a question or two, and they weren't smart questions. Or perhaps the person stumbled on a specific question or two but otherwise is doing great. Someone who gets a five or six might've had a pretty good interview over all, but they may have bombed totally on one or two major elements, such as having a strategy or dealing with negative questions.

So what would result in that typical score of 3 or 4? Well, if you didn't have a strategy, and you couldn't tell any good behavioral-based stories to prove that you have some desirable qualities, and you also asked no questions or one or two bad ones, then I would say that you have glaring deficiencies in all three key areas of the interview. Even if you got through the interview and had a few other good answers, I want to make the point that there is a long way between where you are and where I want you to be.

I do have to make sure that the student doesn't get too down about a low score. I tell them quite honestly that I have seen someone go from a low to a high score very quickly if they take the criticism to heart and act on it. It's not a personal judgment; it's a performance appraisal... and it's subject to change if the performance changes.

7. *Try to customize your criticism to the needs and abilities of that individual.*

Given that you can't fundamentally change an individual's personality, try to offer solutions that may be uniquely plausible for him or her. For example, some students are just not the kind of people who are great at projecting energy and enthusiasm. If a student has a difficult time projecting enthusiasm with his voice, have him at least make statements that reflect an enthusiastic attitude. If a person has major problems with her interview, don't overwhelm her by noting every little error that she made. Give her two or three major things to focus on. I may even try to incent the student by telling her that her practice interview might be a 3/10 right now, but fixing two or three key elements could lift it to a 7/10 in a hurry.

8. *Keep a written record of all comments*

Lastly, keep a record of your comments as well as those of the students, as it is a good teaching tool to pull out and review after they have had one or two "real" interviews. Using a formal evaluation sheet that you complete and students can take with them is another really good idea.

CRITIQUING COVER LETTERS

Cover letters are quite a different medium from interviews, but the mistakes are often similar. Here are the elements that I'm looking for in a good cover letter:

- A brief mention of how the applicant became aware of the job opportunity

- A well-articulated, strategic sense of why the applicant is a good match for that specific job, including a few connections between past experiences and the job

- A closing that summarizes those strategic strengths and explains how the candidate can be contacted via e-mail or by phone

- A letter that is absolutely impeccable in terms of spelling, grammar, typos, and formatting

This all appears to be pretty simple, but often something goes wrong. The most common error is to write a generic cover letter touting general strengths instead of marrying one's strengths to a particular job. Sometimes this is unavoidable; there are situations in which a candidate writes a cover letter to a company without knowing what positions are available. However, it's inexcusable to send out a generic cover letter when pursuing a specific job. Whatever the intention, the tacit message to the employer is "I can't be bothered to write a letter that conveys why I would be good for your job; that's just too labor-intensive." The employer could be forgiven for believing such a candidate is flinging her resume at 50 jobs, hoping that something sticks.

Yes, it's quite labor intensive to customize each cover letter that you write. But you don't need to start from scratch each time; many elements can be quite similar from one cover letter to the next. The key is to ensure that the strategic element is carefully considered. If the person has a quality that could be perceived as a weakness, the cover letter might even be able to quell that concern to some degree.

One of the best cover letters I ever saw was by Kim Eldred, a former co-op colleague of mine. When she applied, I looked over her resume. She hadn't been out of school all that long, so her job experience was limited. Most of it was in a student affairs role at a university, and I didn't see the relevance of that. However, her cover letter showed that she had thought long and hard about why she would be a good match for our posted finance co-op faculty role. She was able to show that there were some significant parallels between her student affairs experience and our job, and there was more of an understanding of financial services than I would've expected from the resume. The cover letter got her in the door for an interview. That was a good thing, as she proceeded to have one of the best job interviews I'd ever seen.

Too often, the cover letter rehashes the resume and adds little or nothing else in the way of strategically marrying the candidate to the job at hand. Like the interview, the cover letter is the link between the resume and the job description. A little extra effort can go a long way to getting an interview… and a job.

IN THEIR OWN WORDS

PROFESSIONAL PERSPECTIVE #1
"GO AHEAD, RIP MY RESUME TO SHREDS"
Kirk Patterson, University of Waterloo

I used to start off using my resume. I used to put it up on the overhead and use that. That way I was able to get students to question my choices—Why did you say this? Why did you put that in?—as opposed to using a standard student's resume or one of those out of a textbook. Every now and then if I had the opportunity and I saw a really great one, I would get permission from the student and I would use their resume, but in general I used mine. That was my approach to it—throw mine up there, let them look at it and tear it to shreds.

I would point out how I was highlighting my skills, what I was best at, and why I felt I was an appropriate candidate for a position—in my case applying for the position as the co-op consultant. So here's what I put down on my resume, here's where I've put in my strengths, here's where I put in my weaknesses, and also near the end all of my interests. The difference between the student and me is I have 20 years of experience and I'm trying to fit 20 years into two pages whereas you're only trying to get one page because you only have a couple of years to offer. But whether it's one page or two pages, it still has to catch the eye of the employer. And I'd go through that and I'd let them look at it and ask some questions. Why would you say you have this skill? How is the employer supposed to know? And I'd say that's a good question, an employer would have to decide through their interviews whether or not what I put down there was a valid comment about myself.

They may test me by asking me examples. Can you demonstrate how and where you developed this skill, give us an example of what you did in that job? So I tell them when you put your resume together and you tell them you did this, this, and this, hopefully you have the material to back it up because if you don't you're just giving a bad impression of yourself.

A lot of times students wouldn't give themselves credit, especially those who didn't have jobs in high school, or just did babysitting. I tell them they don't have to put it down as babysitting; there are other ways of doing it. I've told them, "Well, I was a babysitter for five years. I took over my sister's business because she couldn't cope with a couple of large families. For me that was great—learning how to deal with problem children and also develop the patience for dealing with that area. I even had it on my resume when I was in college. I didn't have a problem putting it down because I had to develop coping skills."

And that was a big thing, especially as I was moving into the legal field. You had to be able to cope with angry clients, annoyed lawyers, belligerent staff of some kind, there was always some area where you had to cope, so those skills are very important. I don't care if you worked at a McDonald's or a Harvey's, shining shoes, everything is important. And I always tell students before you bring me your resume you put everything down on it. I don't care if it's a 20-page resume, I want to see everything about you, then we'll sit down and design a resume that fits you. You're going to do the work, but I'll help you. And that's where you go through and edit out the unnecessary jobs or develop a creative name to describe what you were: child care provider, public service advocate.

Getting the resume down to a page or two pages, that's the easiest part of the whole critique. It's just the matter of getting the information on there such that it catches the eye of the employer. Don't be afraid to use bold print here and there, or quotations, or whatever, but definitely highlight anything and explain to them why it's essential to have the babysitting skills, the customer-service skills from McDonald's and everything else. I have farm students from rural Ontario who will say, "I have no job. I went to school five days a week, and for five years I was busy milking cows every morning." I say, "That's the most important job you had; that's the biggest selling feature." They look at me and they go, "Well, how can that be a selling feature?" I say, "Let's go over a few things. What time did you have to get up for milking, 5:00, 5:30, every day right? And then what would you do?"

"Well I'd milk and clean up and then go in the house, clean myself up, eat breakfast, and then catch the bus. And what would happen at night? Come home, do my homework, do the evening milking, and go to bed." I say, "You kept a schedule. You were able to juggle your home skills on the farm and your school skills." It wasn't uncommon for them to be involved in extracurricular activities. A big one for them over city kids is that a bunch of them used to belong to the Junior Farmers or whatever. I would say, "That shows organization skills, it shows commitment to family, it shows commitment to your school, and that says a lot about you." There are a lot of employers who will say to a young applicant, "if you can do all that, and still produce grades, I want to give you a shot."

PROFESSIONAL PERSPECTIVE #2
"WAS THERE ANYTHING ELSE?"
Linnea Basu, Northeastern University

Certainly everyone has their own stylistic preferences when it comes to resumes. Here are a few of mine.

I really prefer a bullet format over paragraphs, because it's easier to read. To my knowledge, the paragraph format is a little more dated. I used paragraphs when I was in college, but I feel like bullets are more 21st century. But I suppose that a pro of the paragraph form is that you can fit more in.

When I see bullets starting with "Worked...", it drives me nuts!! To me, it's just not a strong enough action verb. So in the sample resume that's used in this chapter, I told the student to change one of the bullets from "Worked with a team painting buildings and machinery" to "Painted buildings and machines, working with a team". But perhaps this goes back to the argument about task/fact-based resumes vs. skill-based resumes.

When I work with students one-on-one, one of the questions I always try to ask is, "Was there anything else you wanted to put on your resume but didn't because you didn't have room?" I'm amazed at what people leave off their first drafts because they don't think it's important, particularly when it comes to school activities. For a sophomore in particular, the strong leadership role that they took running a club in high school may be much more meaningful than a retail job they did for two months. I just met with a student this week who told me she spent almost ten hours per week during high school on one of her activities, but yet she barely mentioned it in her Activities section. The work she did for this organization gave her a ton of transferable skills, but I think it would have been glossed over completely if we hadn't fleshed it out on her resume.

The interview section of this chapter mentions "lack of a strategy" as one of the most common mistakes. For me, the biggest mistake students make is that they do not show enough sincere interest in the job or employer. One of the things I've been telling my students is to find something about the job or employer they can get excited about, as it will make it much easier for them to show sincere interest in the interview. Even students who do well at selling themselves seem to forget that employers want to hire students that sincerely want to work for them!

PROFESSIONAL PERSPECTIVE #3
"THE RESUME AS MOVIE TRAILER"
Anita Todd, University of Cincinnati

When I teach resume writing to students, I use the example of a movie trailer. When you go to a movie and you see the trailer, it gets you interested and excited and you want to see more. You never see the bad parts of a movie in the trailer, only the best parts. A resume should be similar. You want a resume to get a recruiter excited and interested in you and want to see and hear more. You only present your best possible self on your resume.

My first step in teaching resume writing is to have students find job descriptions or some other listing of qualities and skills sought by employers. From individual assignments, we pull together a master list of items employers are seeking in candidates from practical and soft skills to personality traits (honesty, integrity, etc.). I give a copy of a list to my students and tell them that either explicitly or implicitly their resume needs to show they somehow possess skills on this list. This is a great way to get students to think about transferable skills. For example, how can a student show that a fast-food job was a valuable experience? If they had perfect attendance, that shows reliability. Were they given management, training, opening or closing duties? Was their cash box always balanced? This shows responsibility. I try to challenge them to think about how to describe their work experiences to show these skills. I also try to encourage students to think about the work they have done and the results of the work and be sure to include important results in the descriptions. If as a result of their work they saved time or money or made some other tangible contribution, this needs to be noted. If their work had purpose, note the purpose so it is evident why the work was important.

Describing work experience is probably the most difficult part of a resume for students to write.

I also have one comment about cover letters that I wanted to share. As part of a long ago abandoned MBA program, I took a Business Communications course. The professor was outstanding and this course had a huge impact my writing style. The professor wrote the book for the course and in the section on cover letters he recommended that you ask for an interview and designate a follow-up time. This seems very awkward and forward to include (to me), but his point is that if you specifically ask a question it begs an answer. If you tell someone you will follow up on your application in two weeks, then they will probably act on it in some way in anticipation of your follow up. He would suggest something like the following be included:

Can we set up an interview? I can be reached at XXXX or XXX to schedule a mutually agreeable time. If I do not hear back from you by Sept. 21, I will follow up with you regarding the status of my resume.

I am not sure if I agree with this, but I thought it was interesting to consider.

PROFESSIONAL PERSPECTIVE #4
"A QUICK AND DIRTY PRACTICE INTERVIEW"
Nancy Chiang, University of Waterloo

This is a quick and dirty way to deal with a high number of students. Students are given a sample job description to prepare for the interview and a list of five questions that will be asked of all students:

- What do you know about our company? (To see if they'd done company research)

- What do you understand are the attributes required to be successful on this job? (To see if they understand the job description and the role)

- Why do you feel you are a good fit?

- Give them a situation and ask them what they would do.

- Ask them something from their resume and ask them to talk about it—could be the program they're in, could be their hobby

Then we ask them if they have any questions for the interviewer. The interview will last a total of 20 minutes: 15 minutes for the interaction, five minutes for feedback on their answers, their delivery, their demeanour, their dress code, their handshake, and so on.

This has worked really well, and students are really appreciative of hearing the feedback!

PROFESSIONAL PERSPECTIVE #5
"A RESUME EVALUATION RUBRIC"
Tamara Pinkas, Lane Community College

I have created a rubric that I use for evaluating and critiquing resumes. It's in table format, and it's a three-page document. There are seven rows—the seven areas that we are evaluating:

- Immediate Impression

- Heading

- Objective

- Format & Style

- Content

- Word Choice

- Spelling & Punctuation

For each of the seven categories, there are four columns representing how far along the resume is in terms of each component:

- Beginning

- Developing

- Accomplished

- Exemplary

There is a short description for what it means for a resume to be, say, Developing for each of the seven components. For example, the description of "Developing" for "Heading" is as follows:

- Information is incomplete; may be missing mailing address, phone and/or e-mail

- Font size is too small

- E-mail address is provocative, cute, macho, or a nickname

When I initially lecture about resumes I discuss this rubric and hand it out. After students have had the chance to revise their resume several times based on feedback from their peers, they turn in a copy to me. I evaluate the resume by attaching the rubric on which I have circled all appropriate feedback and given them an overall evaluation: Exemplary, Accomplished, Developing, or Beginning. I then give students the opportunity to revise their resume several more times until it is due at the end of the term inside their portfolio where I evaluate it once again using the rubric.

The beauty of this system is that it is a very fast way to evaluate each resume and provides very specific feedback without needing to write lots of notes to each student. If I see something that's not on the rubric, I write a note to the student. If I think it is of value, I add it to the rubric.

Another thing I'd like to see in your resume chapter is an acknowledgment that many professionals think a two-page resume can be effective, especially when the individual has many years of job experience prior to his/her recent education. Obviously, a two-page resume must be carefully crafted so that the most important information is on the first page. At a CEIA conference many years ago, there was a panel of four or five important employers talking about hiring students. When asked the question about how many pages should a resume be, one employer responded: "That is the wrong question. The question should be 'What information does the individual need to provide the employer to help that employer choose the individual for an interview?'" The employer went on to say that he liked two pages when it aided him in making the "Who should I interview?" decision.

PROFESSIONAL PERSPECTIVE #6
"SOMEONE WHO DOES NOT KNOW THEM WELL"
Kirk Patterson, University of Waterloo

When it comes to practice interviews, I have conducted them with my students, and I have come up with a couple of ideas that suit them pretty well. You've got to create a very similar situation to what they might be up against. They will be up against someone who does not know them well and who needs to find out what they can do in an interview. So we take turns critiquing each other's students from time to time. It can be helpful that way. When you feel close to the students, you might give them a break or maybe help them out too much. You may let something slide when you should jump on his case and ask why did you do this or why did you do that? That is the first thing I recommend to co-op people—get a partner to work with. Do practice interviews with students with whom no relationship has evolved so you won't cut them too much slack. Secondly, make sure you get a real job description, even if you have to borrow one from an employer.

I found the biggest plus was asking employers if they would do mock interviews. I think there is more benefit to that. During my co-op classes, I always have a number of well-devoted human resources professionals that used to do mock interviews. This is what I say to the students. "Look, I've got employers coming in. All I am going to say is they are going to interview you. Yes, it's a mock interview. On the flip side of it, if you think you are going to apply to this employer, you may want to consider that and volunteer for this. Yes, you will be doing it in front of your classmates. Yes, they are going to critique you. On the flip side of this, the employers will be thinking about you when you do apply for that job. We used to run those because I had a two-hour class. I run at least three critiques in a two-hour lecture. You get to know your employers. If you've got a great employer, they are going to be more than willing to help you out on this. We set up an office right in the lecture theater. It wasn't hard to get students once they realized what was in it for them—the fact that they may end up securing a possible interview for the real job later on.

REFLECTION QUESTIONS

1. This chapter discusses using rubrics and models to make the resume critiquing process more efficient. What tools and tactics do you use to avoid having to spend a great deal of time building a resume from the ground up? What could you improve in this area?

2. Professionals often disagree about whether a resume should have a terse, objective, "just the facts" style or more of a selling and subjective approach that implicitly or explicitly incorporates transferable skills. Where do you stand on this debate?

3. I talk about "choices and consequences" in terms of what a student opts to include on a resume. Are there limits to what you would allow a student to include on a resume? What would be total deal-breakers for you—aspects of a resume that would force you to tell a student that you are not willing to send the resume out unless it is revised?

4. What do you currently do to ensure that students know how to interview effectively for a job? Are there approaches here that you might be able to incorporate into your arsenal of preparation methods?

5. What are the most common interview problems that your students seem to have when they go on job interviews? What are you doing to address those, and what else could you do, based on what you've read here?

6. In her comments at the end of the chapter, Anita Todd describes how she tells her students to think of the resume as the movie trailer. Do you have analogies that you use to help students understand what purpose a resume should serve? In your mind, what is the role of a resume?

CHAPTER 10

Maximizing Student Learning On The Job

"One must learn by doing the thing; for though you think you know it, you have no certainty until you try."

— Sophocles

Obviously, the preparation phase is a critical one for students and educators. If a student is unable to obtain a meaningful job, there is little opportunity for learning. Yet sometimes it seems as if the activity phase doesn't get the attention that it deserves. There are a few reasons for this. One is a case of "out of sight, out of mind." Once a given student gets a job, she may no longer be on your doorstep or contacting you by phone or e-mail to seek your counsel. Meanwhile, the next wave of job seekers likely will start demanding your attention once the previous batch is out at work, so it's very easy to focus on the next preparation process rather than on those who are out in the field.

Another issue is division of labor and workload. At the University of Waterloo, there are several educators whose primary role is to get out in the field to meet with students at work as well as their employers. However, that's more of the exception than the rule. At many institutions, educators are responsible for *all* phases of the co-op learning model. While there are advantages to the various divisions of labor, one reality for those who do everything is that it can be quite difficult to get out in the field as much as would be optimal. Still, there are steps that can be taken before and during a work term that will help prevent problems as well as enhancing learning opportunities.

FEAR IS A MAN'S BEST FRIEND

There's a song I like by John Cale — a former member of the highly influential Velvet Underground — called "Fear Is A Man's Best Friend." If you'll overlook the gender-specific nature of that song title, perhaps you can think of this as a useful starting point for students about to begin a work term. My experience is that many students start their first professional job with a significant level of fear or anxiety. No matter how much you share success stories about past interns or co-ops who had terrific careers despite having absolutely minimal job experience, I think it's hard for students to believe that on an emotional level—at least until they have been in that professional job for quite a while.

I opt to acknowledge the fear and anxiety rather than pooh-poohing it or shrugging it off. I tell students the truth: Unless it's completely paralyzing, a degree of fear and anxiety is a *positive* sign as far as I'm concerned. It means that the student *cares* deeply about succeeding. There have been many great athletes, authors, artists, and inventors who were wracked by doubt and insecurity. The key is to be able to harness that energy and use it to drive yourself to a higher level of performance. I frankly tell students that I worry much more about students who get into their jobs with a carefree, super-confident mentality. Those students may do just fine, but they also may be underestimating the transition and what it will take to be successful.

When dealing with fearful students, I try to reassure them that this is a normal reaction to a significant transition and that, if anything, it's a positive sign. I also tell them that the stress of a job search or the first few weeks of a job are never as bad when viewed from the rearview mirror as they are when they are in the moment.

THE NEVER-ENDING QUEST FOR IMPROVEMENT

Another mentality that I try to foster with students is some awareness of and excitement about the fact that learning never ends. When I was fresh out of grad school back in the late 1980s, I was a part-time lecturer in Organizational Behavior at Boston University. I vividly remember one student who came to my office hours to complain about the C+ she received on her first paper. "I already know everything there is to know about this subject," she said. Although many students came into the class believing that OB as a discipline was mostly common sense, her arrogance really surprised me. I put one hand on my desk and the other high above my head, and then I said, "So if total ignorance of this field is *down here* and total knowledge if *up here*, then you're saying that you're already up here at this level?" I hadn't misunderstood—that was exactly what she had meant.

"That surprises me," I said. "I teach this course, but I feel like my knowledge level is around *here*," I added, putting my hand around one-fourth of the way from total ignorance toward total knowledge. Later, I was amused to find out that this student had a C+ average in all of her classes! I wonder if she thought that all of her professors just failed to perceive her brilliance.

I tell students this story and also will add that I've been doing this job for over 13 years, but I am not remotely satisfied with how I'm doing. I'm very good at some elements of my job but still have much to learn in several aspects. But, I tell students, this is what keeps my job interesting. I really don't know if I could be happy doing a job in which I knew everything and had nothing left to master.

The other point on this front is that just about every field or subject is considerably deeper than you might imagine. One of my favorite self-coined expressions is a bit like a Zen proverb: "Once you've realized how little you know, then you've made great progress as a learner." That might be a bit cerebral for some young adults, but it's an important concept. Your job might include some deceptively simple tasks. What is the purpose of the task? How does it fit into the big picture of the organization? Understanding elements like these are important when it comes to knowing how to excel.

I have a few good anecdotes that illustrate how large the realm of possibility can be when it comes to learning. A few years ago, one of my students was asked to handle a mundane task—setting up a meeting to discuss the next step of a significant change within his department. Ten minutes after starting to make a list of contacts, the student went back to his boss. "Why are we having this meeting next week?" the student said. "Shouldn't we wait till after that other meeting that happens later this month? If we don't know the outcome of that meeting, we can't have this one... And why didn't we invite the head of Market Data Services?" As you might guess, the student got an outstanding evaluation. A big part of it was his lack of complacency—his ability to think beyond the task at hand and to focus on being the best he could be by understanding the big picture of what his group was starting to accomplish.

More recently, I had an interesting conversation with an employer. He described some real frustrations that he had with his first co-op. He found the student to have an inflated sense of his own worth, and the student also had a habit of taking credit for his manager's work while blaming him for anything bad that happened. Just when I started getting really worried about the future of my relationship with this manager, though, he was quick to rave about his newly hired co-op. "I was astonished by something Zach did last week. He had only been here about eight business days. We have a small office, and Zach sits right next to me. One day he was doing some work on his computer, while I pitched a proposal to a client visiting the office. Just when I reached a point when I realized I was about to need a certain visual aid, Zach just handed it to me without any comment. That absolutely floored me."

That's what happens when a student goes into a job with the mentality of striving to master the job, realizing that perfection will never be attained. Encouraging students to shoot that high—and making them aware that the realm of possibility is much greater than they often imagine—is essential.

AN OUNCE OF PREVENTION

We've talked about getting students ready for the activity phase as part of the preparation phase. In my books, in the class, and in personal meetings, I talk frequently about how it's great to solve problems but far better to prevent them from arising altogether.

What preventative measures can you take once the job has begun? There are a few key alternatives. One is to e-mail all students who are working periodically with various reminders. Another is to choose your site visits strategically.

E-MAILS TO STUDENTS

Here are the group e-mails that my students usually receive:

1. *A message sent shortly before the work term.* This message will remind students to set personal and professional goals for the work term after discussing them with their manager. I remind them that they can get in touch with me during the work term and that they absolutely should get in touch if faced with various specific problems: too little work, too much work, pay issues, problems with their supervisor and co-workers, sexual harassment, etc.

2. *A message sent after the first week or two of the work term.* At this point, I mainly will remind them to set goals and write them down, though I also let them know that they should feel free to get in touch.

3. *A message sent around the midpoint of the work term.* Now I will remind students that they are about halfway through the work term. What have they learned so far? Learning can be technical or non-technical, and it also can come in the form of a new sense of self-awareness: Which kind of learning has dominated thus far? If the manager has not reached out to do a midpoint review, the student should "manage up" and request a brief, informal meeting with his or her manager to find out exactly how well they are doing and whether they need to do anything differently. This will minimize the possibility of unpleasant surprises when the final review comes, broaching the subject when there is still ample opportunity to make amends.

4. *A message sent in the last few weeks of the work term.* At this point, I will focus on the importance of finishing on a high note, whether or not they have loved their job. When it comes to the evaluation and future references, managers and co-workers will be swayed much more by how the student performed during the last few weeks than anything else. You want to make sure that the student runs hard to the finish line instead of letting up as the job winds down. In this e-mail, I also would remind the student to ask for their final evaluation and to discuss it with their manager. I would wrap up with reminders about what they need to do to get credit for co-op on their transcript.

5. *A few messages sent in the weeks after the work term ends.* Once students are back on campus, the e-mails will focus on reminding them about what they need to do to get credit for co-op as well as what they need to do to get ready for their next job search.

PRIORITIZING EMPLOYER VISITS

The other preventative measure that I take is to prioritize my firm visits. I can't possibly visit every student at every employer, so I often decide which ones to visit by asking myself the following questions:

- Where do I have a first-time student working for a first-time employer?

- Do I have a particular employer that has had previous problems with a student and that really needs to have a success this time?

- Are there students who accepted jobs that struck me as potentially problematic?

- Are there students or employers whose history makes me worry that problems are more likely?

- Have any students or employers contacted me with nebulous or specific concerns?

The answers to these questions often steer me to visiting one employer over another. When I do, it's not all that unusual to find the seed of a problem—sometimes a surprising one. That gives me the opportunity to intervene before it escalates.

PHASES OF DEVELOPMENT FOR CO-OPS AND INTERNS

A few years ago, I was looking for a way to help my students develop realistic expectations for their work term. Based on years of talking to students over various points of their jobs, I came up with a model that seems to resonate well with students. I can't claim that it's scientific, but it does seem to be helpful in that students can start to anticipate the dynamic nature of each work term.

ORIENTATION

Orientation is my name for the first phase of an internship or co-op job. It may begin before the official start date if the student gets some training or has an opportunity to meet people before the job actually begins. It can continue for several weeks after the start date. The orientation phase may or may not include formal or informal training. Some employers will devote several days to training, in which students learn specific skills and/or background information about the company. In other cases, the student shadows a full-time employee. Probably the most common beginning of all is having the student thrown right into doing a task, though it often is something quite simple. Simultaneously, the student has much to learn about the organization. Some of these learnings are relatively mundane: What is the best way to commute to work? Where are the restrooms? What are the best places to eat lunch? Other questions can be critical and even profound: What are the *real* rules about when you should be getting to work and leaving at the end of the day? How long a lunch is really okay? What is the smartest way to dress? Who really has power in the organization, regardless of job titles?

There are some common themes for the orientation phase, and students should be made aware of them:

- *Underutilization* – Students often get frustrated during this phase. It's a difficult time. A new hire is usually dying to prove that she can be a great contributor in her role, but the opportunity to contribute significantly is often not immediate. And those first tasks may be quite menial, especially for a first-time intern or co-op. I often tell students the following: "It's not as if your manager is necessarily assuming that you're an idiot until you prove otherwise. They just need to check out your skills—and maybe your attitude—by giving you fairly easy, low-level work at first. Do it efficiently and effectively—and with a positive attitude—and you're likely to get more and better work sooner or later.

- *Feeling overwhelmed* – If the student is *not* underutilized, there is a pretty good chance that they'll face the opposite problem. We certainly want students to get a challenging job. In my case, I often remind students that a six-month work term is a long time; feeling overwhelmed in the early going is probably a good indicator that they aren't going to be bored. Still, it's stressful. Depending on the organization, there can be tons of acronyms to decode as well as any number of projects and tasks that need to be understood and mastered. It's normal to feel pretty stupid in the early going. After all, you're brand new, and you've just jumped on a moving train. It will take a while to learn where that train has been, where it's going, and how you're going to help it get there.

Here are some key coping skills to emphasize during the orientation phase:

- *Patience:* Before the job begins—and after it's begun, if necessary—I often tell students that patience is a priority when starting their job. It's hard to be a superstar in the first few weeks; and students need to accept that. Millennial Generation students are not always great at dealing with adversity. With some young adults, there is a tendency to reach the first nominal hurdle and view it as an insurmountable obstacle. So you need to make sure students know that the opening weeks may be tough. The employer might need to figure out how to best integrate the student into their organization and assess their ability to contribute, and the student has a ton to learn about how that specific organization operates. So both parties need to hang in there during that initial settling period.

- *Staying positive and seeing the big picture:* Students sometimes engage in "doomsaying" during the orientation phase. When given low-level work for the first week, they may extrapolate from that and assume that they've accepted a job that's far below their competency level. If a manager doesn't give them much time, they may conclude that the manager doesn't care about nurturing them, making success impossible. Likewise, being assigned an unpleasant task may lead them to conclude that this company, industry, or major is not for them. As a result, it's important for students to be told to try to assume the best of situations and to understand the bigger picture of their work term. No one should expect to enjoy every hour of their job. Doing all tasks as positively and effectively as possible is very likely to lead to bigger and better things, though it may take some trust and faith to see that.

NAVIGATION

Navigation is my term for the second phase of a co-op work term. After students figure out the basics of how to do their job, deal with their boss, and know their way around the work environment, the next step is usually one of figuring out more about their co-workers and people beyond their immediate group, whether they are more distant employees or customers or vendors. This phase often starts a few weeks into a work term and can continue for a couple of months, potentially.

I first noticed this phase when visiting students at Microsoft. They were about six weeks into six-month jobs. Here are the themes that emerged in those conversations as well at other organizations subsequently:

- *Learning how to obtain assistance:* A student in this phase might say, "I basically know how to do the job at this point, but I'm still trying to figure out who to turn to when my boss is unavailable." In most work environments, there are people who can answer questions and provide additional work if necessary. However, it takes some time to figure who is able and willing to do so, as well as who the *best* resources are in those situations.

- *Circumventing obstacles:* After feeling stumped by obstacles in the orientation phase, students now start figuring out how to get around them. Many organizations have employees who are useless, or worse! There are also annoying processes that may lead a new hire to spin his wheels completely or waste an inordinate amount of time, at best. Determining how to get things done, regardless, is a priority during this phase.

Here are some keys to getting through this phase successfully:

- *Being assertive:* Many students experience a real dilemma at this point. On the one hand, if they ask a lot of questions about how to do things or geared toward understanding the big picture, they may come across as being annoying or stupid. But if they don't ask those questions, they remain ignorant. It's good to coach students on ways to assert themselves with questions. Some ideas include:

- Keeping a notebook or Word file with questions, so the student can save up questions and get several answered at once instead of asking for assistance every 15-20 minutes

- Trying to reach out to a variety of co-workers if possible, both to get to know more people and to not be a burden to one person

- Attempting to pick up on cues as to how busy a person is, so the student can time questions well

- *Being persistent:* When attempting to navigate a complex organization, an individual is going to reach some dead ends and unanticipated obstacles. Therefore, it's important that students display persistence. If underutilized, the student may need to keep reaching out to different individuals in a positive way. If one person doesn't have work to do, then maybe someone else will. The best performers don't shrug it off if they don't get a desired result; they keep after it.

MASTERY

Developing a sense of *mastery* in a job may take anywhere from a few weeks to a number of years depending on the complexity of the role. This can be a very exciting time for a young professional. Years ago, I had a very difficult job at Gillette. The role required the co-op to learn an incredible amount of jargon that was totally unique to that role. I used to tell students that the job was analogous to moving to Moscow with no knowledge of Russian and then being completely immersed in the language. They were going to suffer mightily for a few months, then—often quite suddenly—they would be able to speak the language of that job.

Here are the themes of this phase:

- *Significantly increased levels of competence and confidence:* At this point, students need considerably less hand-holding. As they become more *able* to do the job, they also are likely to become more *willing* to do the job. They often feel more of a sense of purpose and accomplishment. Sometimes this phase also can lead to *overconfidence*, as expressed by the saying "a little knowledge is a dangerous thing."

- *Readiness to consider future career path:* You can try to talk to a student about future jobs early in a work term, but they generally aren't ready. Once the student has that sense of really knowing what it takes to do the job at hand, it can be good timing to reflect on what they've learned, whether they like this job, and what might come next.

With this theme, here are the keys for getting through this phase:

- *Guard against overconfidence and complacency:* Over the years, I've visited students around the midway point, and most of them are confident and comfortable by then. But I always try to check in with their managers to see if everyone is on the same page. It's not all that unusual to find a student who *thinks* he's doing a good job, only to learn that the manager doesn't see it that way. I'll discuss how to deal with that disparity later in this chapter, but, in general, it's a good idea to make sure that students maintain some sense of humility.

This is another reason why I like to talk about the immensity of possibility before students go out on co-op. If you get people to buy into the notion that there always will be more to know, they are less likely to rest on their laurels.

- *Don't let thoughts of the next job detract from the current job:* Given that most of us pitch our programs as great ways to test out careers, there are students who view career exploration as the whole purpose of co-op. If a student has that mindset, it's all too easy to feel that all is lost if the job proves that the student is on the wrong career path. Alternatively, some students may like their job but lose focus eventually because they are already focusing on what they *really* want to do on their next job. I try to remind students that if they are definitely moving on to a different job or organization in the future, then it's even *more* important to keep focused on the current job to ensure a great evaluation and reference for that future, better job.

EXCELLENCE

I make a distinction between *mastery* and *excellence*, though one could argue that the terms are interchangeable. To me, an individual can master how to do a job without necessarily being any more than adequate at it. Think of being a waitress: You might know how to seat people, take orders, bring food out when it's ready, calculate a check, and so on, and we could say that you've mastered the various elements about doing the occupation. But there still could be a great deal missing. Even in a fairly simple job like that, there are countless nuances of service that might lead a customer to give anything from no tip at all to a 25-30% tip.

The same is true in all professional jobs. Every field—every role, even—has its elements that separate out the great performers from their average or mediocre counterparts. For our students, they may not reach this phase for months, if they reach it at all. Here are some themes of this phase:

- *Actively seeking development opportunities:* Performers who are interested in excellence are persistent in attempting to exploit development opportunities. It might be a matter of getting some constructive criticism during a performance review and assertively acting on that, or it might be learning from a mistake—whether or not it was a mistake that you made. Just as easily, it could be something that springs purely from a positive desire to find a way to do the job better—potentially redefining how a job or task is done. Either way, it requires a refusal to be satisfied and an ability to do the basic job efficiently and effectively while looking beyond those duties.

- *Attempting to leave a legacy:* When I've visited Microsoft co-ops in the second half of their work term, they often have talked about "hitting a home run" or "leaving a legacy" when they finish their job. The premise is that no one else can tell you what you will need to do to reach that goal; the individual contributor knows her job best, and only she is in a position to determine what the best possible way would be to add value to a project. The hope is that the intern can figure that out and accomplish something that will remain in place long after she returns to campus. This will benefit the employer and the student dramatically.

Here are some keys for getting through this phase:

- *Think big:* Today's students do tend to have great expectations. In the preparation process,

I like to have them meet some experienced students who *were* able to accomplish great things. This can help students see that a) it's not that easy, and b) it's by no means impossible.

- *Encourage students to question everything... carefully:* Of course, I don't want students to shoot down a company's business process at every turn, as that could backfire in a big way. Yet I do want them to believe that they should look for opportunities to make things better wherever they work by paying attention to how tasks are done and thinking about how processes may be improved.

With their great technological skills, this generation may be able to automate some cumbersome processes, for example. One of my business students just returned for co-op, and I asked him his top accomplishment. He was able to revamp a website to make a delivery process much less labor-intensive for his successor. It started with him questioning a process and patiently working on it until he found a better way. Too often, employees at all levels of experience are too quick to accept the status quo. People are handed a job description, and they let that define precisely what they should do; anything outside of that is "not my job." But great performers always wonder if there is a better way, and they welcome additional responsibilities.

CLOSURE

However long the job lasts, it almost inevitably will end. Whether the experience was fantastic or arduous, there is much more at stake in the last few weeks than many students realize. I have seen students do a terrific job for over five months, only to blow it in the last few weeks. It may be a case of mentally checking out while staying on the payroll, or perhaps the student abruptly asks to quit the job early for a longer vacation—leaving the employer in the lurch.

Conversely, I have seen students who struggled early in their co-op, but who really came through when needed in the last few weeks. In evaluations and references, employers will put more weight on how well the student performed during the last month than at any other time during the work term. So this phase truly represents an opportunity for students.

Here are the themes for this phase:

- *Making the transition from employee back to student:* If the student is in an alternating program, it's all too easy to start focusing energy on getting back to campus or the classroom. Even in a parallel program, the intern may start to look forward to being able to focus purely on the classroom or on other activities. Either way, there is a potential for distraction during the waning days of the work term.

- *Seeing beyond the finish line:* In the classroom, it's not uncommon for students to have the mentality that they are done forever with a subject once a final exam or term paper is completed. That may be a fallacy in the classroom, but it can be a disaster in the workplace. A student who views himself as done forever with a given company or supervisor is being incredibly short-sighted. It's a good idea to remind students that they want to emerge from their job with *multiple* references. After all, their immediate manager may move on to another job: Is there anyone else who can vouch for them during their next few job searches?

Here are the keys for completing the closure phase successfully:

- *Take a long-term, relationship-oriented approach to moving on:* Students should be advised to leave their work in great shape for a successor. Writing a manual for the next co-op student is one idea, as is offering to train a new hire. Making sure that computer files and hard-copy materials are well-organized is also critical, as a good reputation can dissipate quickly if the student's replacement can't make heads or tails of past projects. So attempting to wrap up tasks or to leave foolproof instructions behind is a great idea.

- *Finish on a high note:* The most obvious recommendation is to work hard up till the last hour of the last day. Less obviously, I have seen students do some really smart things at the end of their work terms—getting a few greeting cards for people who were especially helpful to them, going around to say thanks and goodbye to colleagues, making sure to tell people to call them if they have questions about any of their work, asking people for business cards so they can stay in touch, and so forth. None of these steps require a great deal of effort, but they can make a lasting impression.

There can be surprising opportunities for students who run hard to the finish line. Just a few weeks ago, I met with a student who had just finished her first co-op job. By the midway point, she knew that the job was not a good long-term fit for her, but she didn't let that affect her performance in the slightest. During her very last week, she was supposed to have the opportunity to sit in on a critical planning meeting, at which her group had to prepare a presentation that would be highly visible throughout the company. In the middle of the night before the meeting, her immediate boss had to take his toddler son to the hospital. Suddenly, my student had to step in for her manager. Fortunately, she was on top of all the details and able to lay out everyone's responsibilities—just as her manager had wanted things to go. It turned out to be the highlight of the whole six-month term and a major accomplishment to discuss with future employers.

We then talked about her game plan for managing the relationship in the months to come. Seeing beyond the finish line also means planning to stay in touch periodically with a call, e-mail, or visit. I suggested that she writes an e-mail three or four times a year just to let people know how she's doing and how her career is progressing. That will set the stage for future references and maybe even some personal networking for a job with that employer or another one.

HANDLING STUDENT PROBLEMS AT WORK

If I have 80 students working at one time, odds are that 80-90 percent of them will have no significant problems. If that leaves anywhere from eight to 16 students who have problems, those issues will vary dramatically as well. Many students will have a minor issue that can be resolved easily. Others have a more significant problem, but one that resolves fairly easily. But there are always a few really tough situations, and occasionally a student gets fired. If I have 160 students going out each year, probably one or two will get fired. That's not a huge number, but it's almost always painful. Let's go into some of the underlying challenges with handling problems students have in their jobs.

PERCEPTION VERSUS REALITY

This is an important concept for educators—and students—to understand. Sometimes the reality of a student problem is clear and unambiguous. For example, the student is chronically late to work, and the employer has been direct in addressing it… but the behavior hasn't changed enough. While this is still a problem, at least both parties are on the same page.

A more challenging issue is when the employer and the student have substantially different perceptions of what is really going on. Let's say that an employer underutilizes a student, giving them only two hours of work for an eight-hour day for whatever reason. The student does the work, and his boss is at a meeting when he finishes. So he shrugs his shoulders and surfs the Internet until lunchtime. A few co-workers notice, and they mention it to his boss. Maybe the boss doesn't feel like confronting the student, so he doesn't. But when the student shows up a few minutes after 9:00 the next day—just as he had every other day—the manager makes a note of it. And so it goes.

Perception of performance is often a domino effect. I try to make sure student employees understand that this can be positive or negative, and it's not necessarily fair or accurate either way. An employee who shows up early every day may start to be perceived as a good employee, even though she is less productive and accurate than her counterpart who comes in right on the dot at 9:00. Someone who makes careless spelling errors in an e-mail might be thought to have poor attention to detail on all tasks, whereas that person might just be a poor speller who is extremely methodical in other ways.

The worst thing that can happen is to get branded as a problem employee at work. A significant error or display of a bad attitude will put everyone on the lookout for corroboration of that early evidence, while minor issues will get overlooked if the employee has a reputation as being strong.

When students are upset and confused as to why they are viewed so negatively—or held to a different standard than their co-workers—this can be a good concept to discuss with them. Better still, you want to make sure they understand this through your preparation efforts.

COORDINATOR AS LAWYER AND JUDGE

This is another tricky aspect of the co-op/internship professional's role. Students tend to assume that our job is to be their advocate, come hell or high water. Employers may expect us to respect the fact that they are the ultimate customer, while administrators expect that their needs are the priority. Nancy Johnston of Simon Fraser University refers to this scenario as the "coordinator dance." To whom does your ultimate responsibility lie? Being clear on that can help.

Still, it's not always clear-cut for me. Sometimes, I've flat out told students the following: "You might think of me as your lawyer, and to some degree I am… but I also have to be your judge at times." Odd as it sounds, it can be possible to be both. We have a mandatory co-op program in our College of Business Administration, and students occasionally want to opt out of co-op. To me, coming to Northeastern and not doing co-op is kind of like going to Paris without eating anywhere but McDonald's, and I might point that out to the student. Still, I might try to wear both the lawyer hat and the judge hat with the student. As his judge, I'll tell him why I think his request is likely to fail and why I think it's a terrible idea. But as his lawyer, I'll try to educate him both on what he would gain educationally by going on co-op, *and* explain the best way to try to get the requirement waived if he is determined to do so.

In some situations, I am determined to be more purely a judge. That sometimes disappoints both the employer and the student, as both parties might expect me to take them at their word. However, I've learned the hard way that you're best off asking a ton of clarifying questions before reaching any final conclusions. In March 2008, a student e-mailed me saying that he wanted to quit his job. He had obtained a position with a new employer who had promised he would be doing equipment installations around the country. This seemingly had gone well for several weeks—I received a glowing e-mail from the student around the third week of employment—but now the employer had decided that he would be doing no more travel. Instead, he was stuck in the home office doing phone support for nine or ten hours a day.

To be honest, I was a little suspicious of this employer. Run by a charismatic entrepreneur, I had worried whether he had pulled a "bait and switch" tactic—promising glamorous work and then pulling that off the table once the job began. But I decided I'd better probe to see what was going on. I asked the student what the rationale had been for pulling him off the road. He told me that the owner didn't have enough field work for all of the students that had been hired and that it was more of a priority to get engineering students out there rather than business students. Also, the company's financial situation had changed, and my student was told that he was needed in the office.

All of this supported the student's case that he had been more or less duped and should be allowed to quit the job. However, I didn't want to make a judgment without hearing from the defense! It took a while for the owner to get back to me, but he had a very different story. He told me that my student had proved to be a real pain in the butt out in the field. No one wanted to work with him because of his attitude and inappropriate sense of humor. "Did you tell him that was why you were moving him to the office?" I asked, figuring that the answer would be no. But the student had been told just that!

By the time I had that conversation, the student had backed off of his threats to quit, as he had found a niche in helping the company's CFO. However, when he returned to campus, we had a long, intense conversation about his "selective omission" of the facts when he was hoping I would authorize his resignation. I told him that it really affected my ability to trust him in the future and that he really needed to be thoroughly honest if he wanted to build lasting business relationships. He didn't seem to get it at first. I had to repeat the points several times and finally told him that I was doing him a favor by being totally transparent about my feelings about his behavior; someone else in my shoes might have just privately decided that they were never going to work with this guy again and to never lift a finger to help him in the future. That seemed to sink in. I think that the fact that I used an educational tone when making some very critical statements had an impact on him.

In general, here are some good reminders when attempting to figure out what is *really* going on when faced with inconsistent stories from a student and employer:

1. *Consider your previous history with each party, but otherwise try to assume nothing.*

In my view, a coordinator's job is not to defend a student regardless of the facts or to take the attitude that the employer is always right. But if you have prior experience with the student or employer, you might take that into account to some degree. If an employer has had no problems with five previous interns and suddenly is raising questions about their current student, then I would look at that differently than I would if prior students had complained about the employer. Likewise, if my personal history with a given student is great, I might be inclined to trust their perceptions a little more than I might otherwise. Still, you have to be careful about making assumptions. I've had students who I think very highly of who have screwed up at work, and I've also had employers who disappointed me greatly by not handling a situation as well as I would've expected, based on my history with them.

2. *Hear both sides of the story.*

It's very easy to knee-jerk when you get a phone call or e-mail from an unhappy employer. When you hear that a student has been falling asleep at her desk, for example, it's very tempting to leave an angry voice mail or send a scathing e-mail. By the same token, when a student complains that an employer promised him a great job but then seemingly pulled a bait and switch, you might be tempted to give that employer a piece of your mind.

Instead, slow down and be sure to hear both sides of the story. Ask plenty of clarifying questions, being sure to keep the tone neutral. If an employer is complaining that the student is asleep at his desk, there are a few obvious questions—most of which apply to any number of other situations:

- When did this first happen?

- How many times has it happened?

- Have you discussed the situation with the student? If so, what explanation did the student give?

- Have you explained the consequences of this behavior happening in the future?

3. *Differentiate between problems and symptoms.*

Sometimes there is a difference between symptoms and problems. Maybe a student is surfing the Internet when she should be working. Okay, we need to address that. But I don't want to tell the student to knock it off; I want to understand why it happened. Does the student have issues with asking for additional work? Is she making the assumption that it's okay to check her personal e-mail, as long as she comes in earlier or later? Is she angry about being given menial work and responding with passive-aggressive behavior? Anything is possible, but I'll be able to give better advice if I know what's behind the behavior.

4. *Respect confidentiality.*

You need to be really careful about this. Sometimes a student or employer may vent to you about the other party, saying things that they would never say if the three of you were sitting down together. For that matter, one party or the other may have a need to vent to you, but they may not want *any* hint of their feelings made known to others in the office.

As a result, you need to proceed with great caution. Momentarily, I'll talk about how to coach students through problems, but sometimes a coordinator does need to intervene. If I do, I want to be very sure that I'm not sharing any information that one party does not want the other person to hear. When a student needs direct intervention, sometimes I'll suggest that I call or come in and initially "play dumb" with the employer, simply asking, "How's it been going with Anne?" and seeing what the employer's perception is of the situation. If an employer is quick to acknowledge that Anne is underutilized and he know that needs to be addressed, then I simply can reinforce that as a wise course of action. If he seems unaware of any problem, I might go back to the student and suggest that we approach the matter more directly. But I don't want to disclose anything against anyone's wishes; the only exception would be if someone's personal safety were in jeopardy.

5. *Once clear on the situation, recommend an action plan.*

You may never feel that you're 100 percent sure of what's actually happening. I think it's rare (though not unheard of) for an employer or student to lie to you about what's happened, but perceptions can vary significantly. I also have found that it's rare for a problem to be 100 percent the result of a student's behavior or to be employer's fault entirely. Most often, both parties have contributed something to the problem, and hopefully there is something that can serve as a learning experience for each party.

Still, at some point, you have to come to your best conclusion as to what's been happening and move away from analyzing it and toward some sort of action plan. If a student has committed a major transgression—most often theft, falsifying time sheets, engaging in an illegal activity at work, or blatant sexual harassment—then immediate termination is usually appropriate. For more minor but ongoing problems—tardiness, unexcused absences, excessive use of the Internet, performance errors, and so on—then the usual course of action would be a verbal warning followed by a written warning, and then termination.

With students, I find it best to focus on a concrete plan to change behaviors. I think it's a mistake to deal with students who can't get to work due to oversleeping by simply letting them assure you that they will "try harder" to get to work on time. What does that mean? I'd like to understand why it's happening and what behavioral change they're going to make to ensure that they overcome this issue. Whether it's going to bed early, moving their alarm clock across the room, leaving the house 30 minutes earlier to allow for commuting delays, or all of the above, I'd like to know that concrete steps are being taken to make success that much more probable.

On the employer's side, my sense is that, if anything, most employers are way too lenient when it comes to accepting the unacceptable. They may be annoyed at various student behaviors, but they fail to confront them because the person is "just a student" or because they don't want to get the student in trouble with the school. I always tell employers that I want students to be treated the way any new hire would be treated—no better, no worse. And most of my students really don't want special treatment either. Frankly, termination is the best thing that ever happened to some of my students. It was the wake-up call that they needed to understand that they really do have a problem in the workplace.

THE MOST COMMON STUDENT COMPLAINTS

When you get an e-mail or phone call in which a student lets you know that they are having a problem at work, the vast majority of complaints fall into these categories:

1. *The student is underutilized and/or not challenged.*

This is probably the most common complaint, especially in the first several weeks of the job. Sometimes it can be a matter of just taking a wait-and-see approach if it's very early in the job. You want to find out what, if anything, the student has done to seek out additional work in a positive, solution-oriented manner. Also, are there people besides the manager who might have work to do? Have they been given any reason for the relative dearth of work? Most often, coaching the student on how to reach out assertively seems to work. I will let the student try that for a while and encourage them to follow up if the problem doesn't resolve within a reasonable amount of time.

2. *The job description is not as advertised.*

This can be a serious concern, but you have to take this one with a grain of salt. Again, you need to probe to find out *why* the job is not as it was promised to be. There are only a few possibilities:

- The student hasn't yet shown the ability to handle some key aspects of the job.

- Some time between hiring the student and the start date, the employer's needs changed significantly for some reason, perhaps temporarily or perhaps not.

- The employer intentionally or quasi-intentionally misled the student, luring him to accept a mediocre job because she needs the help.

I have seen all three of these situations occur, but I would never want to make an assumption about what's going on. More often than not, the situation is a temporary problem, either due to the student's current ability level or because the student was needed to assist on a task that was more urgent than the stated job description.

Students do need to understand that everything doesn't go according to plan and that they may have to do some unanticipated, uninteresting work. On the other hand, employers need to make every effort to live up to their promises and to communicate effectively when plans change, so there is a minimum of misunderstanding.

3. *The student hates the job itself.*

This is a different kind of concern. Sometimes a student accepts a job, knowing full well what the job is… only to find out at some point that they really can't stand it. A somewhat similar situation would be a student accepting a job with only a vague understanding of what the job really entails. Either way, you may hear from an unhappy student who wants to quit.

I won't go into great detail on this one, as it's one of the "moments of truth" we will discuss in Chapter 12. Obviously, though, you're going to be less sympathetic with the student who accepted a job without showing due diligence in advance to make sure they really knew what they were getting into.

Either way, the quick answer is that quitting should not be the first resort. In some cases, it shouldn't even be the last resort. But we'll revisit this in Chapter 12.

4. *The manager or co-workers are a problem.*

This is not uncommon, either, but the issues can vary dramatically. Here are the most common complaints with this theme:

- The manager is nice but has a laissez-faire approach, failing to give the student work, direction, advice, feedback, etc.

- The manager is great in many ways but is rarely available to the student, leaving them lost.

- The manager is harsh, critical, unfair—you name it.

- Co-workers are hostile, condescending, indifferent, unhelpful, verbally abusive, etc.

Obviously, co-worker problems are much easier to solve IF the student has a good manager. Problems with the manager are inherently trickier, especially given the imbalance of power between student and manager. If the manager's biggest issue is unavailability and unhelpfulness, I probably would coach the student on how to have a conversation with the manager or with co-workers to obtain more direction. If the manager is hostile and negative, I might be more inclined to obtain the student's permission to get in touch with the manager to get some insight into the behavior. If I had an HR contact that I trusted, I might try to get the student's permission to broach the issue with that individual. As always, I want to understand what's really going on before jumping to conclusions. The manager might have other stressors affecting his behavior, or maybe the student has done something to evoke the ire of others in the workplace. We need to find out.

5. *The student is being sexually harassed or discriminated against.*

It's absolutely crucial for educators to understand the different forms of sexual harassment from a legal and managerial standpoint. When you're new to the field, you might think of sexual harassment taking the form of, say, a manager offering a raise or promotion—or denying the same—to an employee in return for sexual favors. While this is a blatant example of sexual harassment, I've never heard of it happening to a co-op or intern. In contrast, more subtle forms of harassment are much more common.

Here are the two key types of sexual harassment:

A. Hostile environment

Everyone has a right to feel comfortable at work, regardless of gender, sexual orientation, religion, age, or disability. Everyone should be able to do their jobs without having to deal with any number of behaviors on the part of a manager or co-workers. Students are often surprised to learn that there is much more to harassment than an unwanted, direct sexual proposition. The following behaviors all could be considered to be sexual harassment in a court of law:

- Making sexual comments or jokes, including material passed along via e-mail

- Having pornographic content visible on one's computer screen or hung up on a wall

- Making sexist comments

- Commenting on someone else's personal appearance, favorably or unfavorably

- Putting pressure on someone to keep quiet about the harassment of another employee

- Inappropriate staring or touching, including hugging

Of course, there are other considerations when it comes to a hostile environment:

- Frequency

- Severity

- Whether the action was physically threatening

- Whether the action affected someone's job performance

- The degree to which it affected the target's psychological well-being

- Whether the perpetrator held a power advantage over the individual, such as a supervisor/subordinate relationship

Students sometimes get a little freaked out when they start to understand the realm of possibility here. I tell a few stories to accentuate the point. Apparently we have a professor on campus who was at the student center in broad daylight, sitting at a table with several students, both male and female. The professor is a vocal fan of the New York Yankees, and it came up during this very informal meeting. One thing led to another, and a male student said an insulting thing about the Yankees—something you would hear all the time at Fenway Park. Everyone laughed, and the professor responded with a two-word insult. There was no profanity in his reply, but it certainly had a sexual connotation to it—yet, again, you would hear such verbiage all the time at the ballpark. Again, most of the group laughed in response.

But a female student at the table was offended, and she reported it to our Affirmative Action team. As far as I know, the professor was not punished, but he was warned that he really can't say things like that.

My students are often a little incredulous to hear that this situation led to a complaint. Recently, I had colleagues tell me that they did an exercise about behavior that might be deemed offensive, and *no one* in a class of 30 students expressed any problem with a hypothetical situation in which a co-worker is playing music that prominently features sexual language, profanity, etc. These examples reflect the fact that students need to understand that "offensive" is very much in the eye of the beholder. Personally, I am not offended very easily, but it's hard to be sure about whether or not various comments or jokes might be offensive to my colleagues. In fact, it may take *years* to really get to know someone at work well enough to know what you can and can't say. So you have to err very much on the side of caution.

B. Quid pro quo

You could consider this to be the more stereotypical form of sexual harassment. Literally, *quid pro quo* means "this for that." A supervisor might promise a raise, a promotion, or more beneficial work in return for sexual favors. Alternatively, those opportunities might be withheld for a failure to reciprocate romantic or sexual interest, or an employee could be punished with a demotion or less attractive work because of declining a sexual relationship.

Basically, though, there are three simple categories here:

- Unwelcome sexual advances

- Requests for sexual favors

- Other verbal or physical conduct of a sexual nature

Handling allegations of sexual harassment is a relatively rare occurrence—I've had about a dozen cases of varying degrees of seriousness over 13 years in the field—but quite a tricky one as well. I will go into detail on this in Chapter 12.

6. *There is an unanticipated change to handle.*

Organizations are dynamic. Companies get acquired; managers quit. Projects fall through; groups are reorganized. This is obviously extremely stressful for everyone—sometimes even more for full-time employees than for co-ops or interns. Students know that their jobs are temporary, and their livelihood is not necessarily at stake at work. On the other hand, students may lack the maturity and experience to roll with changes and adapt accordingly.

Just a few days ago, I heard that one of my employers is on the brink of firing a student. It's basically a performance issue; the student just seems overwhelmed. Yet another aspect that is really exacerbating the situation is the fact that the student was hired by one manager who left for another opportunity before the student even began her work term. When her new manager has attempted to critique her performance, the student repeatedly has become upset and said, "You weren't supposed to be my manager!" This is not helping, and it reflects a lack of maturity.

It's good to encourage students to reach out to you if they are anxious about a change. Sometimes the change is either pretty innocuous or actually a positive, but the student may have a hard time seeing that at first. Other times the change legitimately is going to have a negative impact on the student's work experience. Find out all the facts before you buy into the student's anxiety about the situation.

MAXIMIZING STUDENT LEARNING

So in the face of all of the above, what can we do to maximize student learning at work and to best assist students when problems do arise? All of the following steps should help:

1. *Encourage or require students to set learning goals.*

It's advisable to get students thinking about what they want and hope to learn during their work term. How they come up with goals could vary quite a bit, but ideally the educator and manager would have some input here. The goals could range dramatically; here are a few possibilities to give you some sense of the realm of possibility:

- To become proficient at using MS-Excel

- To adapt successfully to a corporate environment and earn a great evaluation

- To work on my assertiveness by actively seeking out additional work and constructive criticism

- To develop a better organizational system to keep track of all tasks, projects, and deliverables

- To network interpersonally in order to come away with at least four strong personal references

- To obtain an understanding of how the company works internally

You also might see some that are quite specific to a major or industry. Here are some actual ones from my business students:

- Learn how compliance ties into logistics as well as its effect on logistics departments such as planning, transportation, etc.

- Learn the necessary steps to troubleshoot a PC in order to diagnose an issue and find the correct path to a solution

- Manage the monthly brokerage report, running all necessary calculations with limited supervision and striving to improve and automate the existing report to a greater degree each month

- Lead at least one conference call with 5-10 analysts, setting up the call while briefing others on pertinent information

- To obtain at least one certification related to computer networking

Although not always easy or possible, it's great if at least some goals can be specific and quantifiable. A goal-setting activity helps ensure that everyone's expectations are on the same page and gives some way for students to know what they are trying to accomplish as well as what a manager can measure them against. Megan Brodie of the University of Guelph talks about teaching SMART goals: specific, measurable, action-oriented, realistic, and time-targeted.

2. Prepare students for less obvious forms of learning.

Shakespeare said that "the course of true love never did run smooth." Quite often, the same is true for learning. Without guidance, students may expect that the goal of experiential learning is to learn the nuts and bolts of an occupation. A computer science major eagerly anticipates the opportunity to obtain real-world experience in software development with C++. A journalism major might aspire to get out in the field to interview citizens for news stories. We certainly want students to get meaningful, challenging jobs in their fields. Yet students who are fixated on that goal may be prone to overlook some other forms of learning that are every bit as important.

Over the last few months, I've been asking my students what they were proudest of learning on co-op... and *how* they learned it. Here are some of the actual responses, as captured in my notes:

- Feels really good about developing project management skills.

- Found that she really preferred doing projects over weekly reports/tasks. Really liked having goals to work toward, leading toward mini-presentations.

- Proudest of using this experience to figure out where she did and didn't want to go—had ample opportunity to do career testing in this position.

- In terms of learning, feels really good about what he learned about how investment management works—how bonds work, how they invest in things. His ability to articulate that to a trainee was the moment where his learning really hit him.

- Proudest of how he was an "experiment" in terms of having no experience; had to ask a lot of questions the first month and never felt that he would be good at it, but ultimately mastered the job.

As you can see, the nature of learning was quite varied, even among a fairly narrow group of students when it comes to major. Here are some important learning achievements that students tend to underrate:

- Effectively dealing with a difficult manager or co-worker

- Having to learn about the complexities of a new field/industry/organization from scratch

- Figuring out how to turn a mediocre job into a good one

- Being able to get a great evaluation in a job that they don't enjoy or even truly dislike

- Managing time and improving organizational skills

- Handling criticism appropriately

- Learning to adapt to varying corporate cultures

- Figuring out when it's a good time to assert oneself to offer an idea, seek more work, or express concern about a project… and when it's not such a good idea.

- Determining how to be sociable at work in a way that is appropriate to that particular environment

- Managing money if they are earning a significant amount for the first time

There are infinite other possibilities, of course. The key, though, is that reminding students of some of these less obvious forms of learning can make all the difference between a student quitting a job and a student who learns something very powerful at work.

A few years ago, I had a student who was very concerned about her status at work. After her first two months of co-op had gone well, her sense was that her supervisor had become dissatisfied with her. The manager had ignored her for several weeks and was abrupt with her on the rare occasions in which they directly interacted. So the student e-mailed me and asked for help, fearing that she was on her way to getting a bad evaluation.

The challenge was that I obviously had no idea as to what was *really* going on in that job. Of course, I could've called the manager to ask directly about my student's performance, but I thought it was a good opportunity for some of that unanticipated learning. So I reminded the student that we really don't know if there is a problem here or not. More than anything, I told her that the worst thing she could do was to start *acting* as if she were a poor performer merely because she believes that her manager may have that perception of her. I told her that there could be any number of other explanations for the manager's behavior. I suggested that she have a conversation with her manager at some opportune moment when the manager seemed less preoccupied. When doing so, the key would be to not assume the worst. I told her to stay positive and focus on asking clarifying questions when meeting with the manager: What do you think of my job performance thus far? Is there anything I can do to improve? I wanted to make sure that she kept her questions—and tone—neutral.

Well, she was able to do everything I asked of her. It took a few more weeks to have a sit-down meeting, but her manager responded by filling her in on her own challenges. The manager had been under considerable pressure from *her* boss, and she knew that she had not been very helpful or supportive to my student in recent weeks. In fact, she was *delighted* with the student's performance! My student was relieved, naturally, but she also learned some powerful, albeit unanticipated, lessons about making assumptions and testing them before acting based on those assumptions.

In that situation, I was trying to reframe the situation for the student to get her to see where the learning opportunity had arisen. Sometimes I talk about *degree of difficulty* with students at this point, as if it were a gymnastics routine at the Olympics. A job with a "high degree of difficulty" is most readily thought of as a job consisting of difficult tasks. But it just as easily could be defined as a job that is hard for any number of other reasons—a demanding boss, a hostile co-worker, a very negative work environment, a complete lack of feedback, or even because there is a dearth of work! I remind students of this all the time: A typical co-op or intern can do a great job in a position that they love, but a *great* co-op or intern can do a great job *despite* the fact that they don't love the job, the boss, the company, or the work environment. Getting students to focus on the varied forms of learning can help them embrace these situations and rise above them.

3. *Manage expectations.*

When I met individually last summer with all of my co-ops who worked from January through June, I was happiest about the fact that many students discovered that their job was not a great fit… but that discovery generally had no impact on their performance or evaluation. While this is a credit to these individuals, I think it is also partly attributable to managing expectations. Before and during a work experience, I try to remind students of the following:

- You probably will have some low-level, menial tasks to do at some point.

- You likely won't enjoy every element of your job.

- You might discover that your company or industry or major is not for you.

It's helpful for students to be reminded that all is not lost in these instances; it's all part of the learning process.

4. *Make sure that they know when to contact you.*

There are different schools of thought on how often there should be contact between student and educator during a work term. Some educators require a certain number of calls or e-mails, while others may have assignments due during a work term. The argument there is that it's important to keep students feeling connected to the university and that they are given some structure that will facilitate learning.

I don't have a problem with that, but personally I am much closer to the opposite end of the spectrum. I've literally had students say to me: "No offense, Scott, but when I'm on co-op, I want to forget about the university as much as possible and immerse myself in being a professional." I find it hard to argue with the student who wants to go that route, so I don't require students to contact me on a regular basis—much to the surprise of many of them. If students want to feel connected to the school and contact me regularly, that's great. It's just not mandatory.

However, I am emphatic about letting students know that there are several scenarios that really mandate contacting me, whether they prefer to or not:

- If the student has been warned about termination or actually been fired

- If they are a victim of abusive behavior, including sexual harassment or discrimination

- If the job description was not as advertised

- If they are underutilized at work

- If the pay is less than promised

- If they are having any other problems that are difficult to discuss with a supervisor

One of the biggest disappointments in my job is when a student finishes a work term and only then tells me about one of the above problems. "I didn't think it would make a difference" is the usual explanation. Maybe not, but I sure would've liked an opportunity to try. And once the job is over, we can only do a post-mortem; we can't do emergency surgery.

5. *Coach students rather than solving problems.*

Given that many educators see themselves as nurturers to college students, there is sometimes a tendency to intervene excessively when a student faces a crisis or dilemma at work. A student who seemingly is being treated unfairly can bring out the paternal or maternal tendencies that many of us have, and sometimes it's hard to resist charging into a work environment to try to right a wrong.

It may seem counterintuitive at first, but we may be doing students a disservice if we are too quick to intervene. If we look at navigating difficulties in the workplace as a learning opportunity for students, then why should we take that away from them?

Unless the situation is extreme—or unless the student's own efforts to address a situation have not been successful—your better bet is to try to coach students through a difficulty. In that role, you can be *extremely* valuable to the student. In addition to being older and more experienced, you are not immersed in the situation; you are not as emotionally invested in the outcome. As such, you can remind them to try to stay unemotional and solution-oriented at a time when they might be tempted to lash out verbally at a manager.

Tamara Pinkas's lengthy story at the end of this chapter is a great example of the myriad steps that a professional can take in coaching a student through a challenging situation at work. She wisely uses role playing to give a student an opportunity to articulate himself appropriately when dealing with a very challenging supervisor, for example.

In addition to role plays, this is another opportunity to use modeling skills as a counselor. When dealing with agitated students, I often tell the story of how frustrated I was in a previous job and how I fantasized about telling off the boss, quitting in a blaze of glory. After more consideration—and a great talk with my mentor—I ended up giving my notice, but I did so in a way that smoothed my relationship with my supervisor dramatically. I gave her plenty of options and showed that my goal was definitely not to leave the company in the lurch. That led to a positive conversation about how to make an optimal transition, and I'm sure it made all the difference between getting a very good reference and a dicey one.

6. Urge students to weigh the consequences of all choices carefully, especially when upset.

This is just an extension of the previous thought. When leaving a job, you always want to look back at your behavior proudly. Maybe you worked with incredibly cynical, unhappy, conniving people. Perhaps you toil alongside people who have made an art of doing as little as possible while still drawing a paycheck. Is that you? Do you want to become one of those people? Are you so weak-willed that your standards will lower to the lowest common denominator around you? I hope not.

7. Try to get students to see things from the employer's perspective.

For a young adult, it can be all too easy to fall into the trap of thinking that everything at work revolves around him. If an employer is grumpy or brusque, the student may believe that it's a commentary on her performance—which may or may not be the case. As Jacki Diani indicates in her transcribed comments later in this chapter, you want to make sure that the student can put himself in the shoes of the employer. What other priorities and pressures does your manager face, professionally or personally? If you were that manager, how could a young, inexperienced employee be most helpful to you? This is not easy, but it can be helpful for students to step outside of their own limited perspective at times.

Let's see what our team of experts had to say about professional behavior in the workplace.

IN THEIR OWN WORDS

PROFESSIONAL PERSPECTIVE #1
"AN EMPLOYER WHO YELLS"
Tamara Pinkas, Lane Community College

I have an employer who yells. I didn't know that the first time I sent a student to him, and the student came to my office just as upset as could be. The supervisor had said things like: "if you don't learn to work faster, you're never going to be successful in this career, and we're going to have to fire you." I mean, really nasty/abusive language. So here is the student standing outside my office yelling at me about how upset he was to the extent that my boss came down the hall and stood nearby. She was worried about my safety.

First of all, my desire was to help that student calm down. I wanted to get him to a place where I could clearly understand what had happened and to see if this was salvageable. I always go for the win/win because this is a very small town I live in, and we can never afford to have unhappy students and unhappy employers. So the goal is to salvage it, to see what we can do.

How did I calm the student down? Well, this is a while back so let me think. I think what I do with everyone is first I just let them talk until there's a clear stopping point, even if they're loud. I let them come to a place where they actually stop. And then I try to say in the quietest, calmest voice I can, "I really want to hear more about what you have to say; it seems like it's very important to you. Can you please come in and sit down? I'd like to hear more." So I want them to know that I care about what they're saying, and I try to get it into a place where my behavior is making them calmer. I also am letting them know I'm not going to be fighting them; I'm not going to be pushing back in any way. I think of it as sort of like Tai Chi: the energy's coming at me and I just want to flow with it, allow it to come — like what you would you do with an arm movement – sort of capture it in your arm and slowly move it and ground it.

So the student sat down in my office. I said, "Now please, can you share with me step by step your sense of what happened, how this came to be." It was within the first week that the student was there. You know, students frequently make mistakes and aren't very fast because they're just coming out of classes; they don't have that professional speed that you often develop with software. I tried to find out if the student thought there was some legitimacy to the employer's comments, and the student said, "Yes. I think I am not very fast yet, but I don't deserve to be treated this way." Of course, I agreed that that wasn't appropriate. Then what I always do with students is talk to them about what would they like to see happen next. Always the goal is "How can we salvage this? How can we make it so that you can get the experience you need and be able to walk away when you're done, feeling like you can get a good evaluation from this employer. Because that's very important to you and the employer."

So we talked at length about whether it would be appropriate for me to call and make an appointment, or did the student feel like he could handle it himself? I asked the student if he wanted to practice what he might say. I thought some role playing could be valuable because I want students to learn to talk to the employers about work issues. I believe it is part of their professional

276

preparation to learn to deal with difficulty in interpersonal relationships at work. In this case the student decided that he was going to do it himself, and we did some role playing. I pretended to be the supervisor; he was the student. He could talk about how he felt when talked to in that way and what he wanted from the relationship with the employer. He actually did it, and he called me up so excited that it went well. He reported that the employer listened to what he had to say, didn't get defensive, didn't yell again.

We had talked a lot about the idea that when people are yelling, don't yell back. You stay focused; you stay calm. You're clear on your message. You have a message; the message is: I want to work here, I feel like I have a lot to learn, I feel like you have a lot to offer, and I think we could have a really good working relationship, and what I would prefer is that when you have concerns, that we can discuss that in a calm, professional way. The student did do that.

It turns out the student stayed there, got hired on part-time while he continued school. When he was no longer an intern, he would stop by my office regularly so I could hear what was going on. The company is run by a husband and wife and it turned out that this student became part of the family. He got to be very close with them because he could make it through the yelling.

It was a crucible for them: The family had to storm because it could form. It was like team building. It was a classic team-building sequence. So I asked the student: "Did that ever happen again?" He said, "Absolutely it did, but once we had made it through the first time I was able to continue to remind him that I wanted a different relationship, that I didn't take it personally because I realized it wasn't me. He was just a yeller."

PROFESSIONAL PERSPECTIVE #2
"A CASE-BY-CASE BASIS"
Charlie Bognanni, Northeastern University

Everything has to be considered on a case-by-case basis. In over 18 years of doing this, I've seen cases where the student will complain about the job, and the employer will complain about the student. When it's all said and done, I find that the student was probably justified in complaining about the job, it really wasn't a very good job; the employer had embellished the job description. But I've had a lot of other cases where the employer was really telling me more the truth. The student was lazy, and the student wasn't really doing what she should be doing. The student was rationalizing about her poor performance by saying the job really wasn't working out well.

To get to the bottom of these situations, I think it requires probing and asking a lot of good questions. I always ask the students if the job is living up to the job description. Is what you're doing what you were told you were supposed to be doing? I think that's critical. If the job is consistent with its description, then I don't have a heck of a lot of sympathy for the student who is unhappy with it. I'd say, "Well, maybe it's unfortunate that you're not as challenged as you would like, but frankly that's the job you accepted. You knew it when you accepted it."

If it's not, then that's when you go and talk to the employer and you say, "Well, the student's telling me that she's really not doing what the job description says." Here's the important part: The employer's going to tell me why. It may be a case where initially they thought the student would be able to handle the job but for whatever reason concluded that the student just isn't capable of doing those tasks. "She just doesn't have the skills; she's frankly a disappointment to us." So that's a case where you go back to the student and say, "Well, it sounds like it's more of a performance issue than a job description issue." You talk to the student about why and so forth.

Obviously, you want everyone to be happy. You want the student to walk away saying, "Okay, now I'm feeling a little more challenged." Sometimes that happens. I'll give you an example. We had a case a year ago where we had a very, very good student at a health care organization, and I couldn't understand why she was unhappy. We had worked with the company before and everything had been fine, so we were kind of confused — a very good student, a very good employer. Something's happening here. We went down to visit the employer and spoke to the HR person. She disclosed to us confidentially that the student was working for a manager who traditionally had not supervised co-op students. Frankly, she said he was not a good manager, and that's why the student was unhappy.

This turned out to be a good situation because they moved the student to a different department. They moved her under a new supervisor, and it all worked out. It doesn't always happen that way. So I think for the purposes of your training as you start this profession, I would say approach situations on a case-by-case basis. Don't go in with preconceived notions about the student's always at fault if the employer's complaining. If you're one of these student advocates, don't go in thinking, "ah, these darn employers, they take advantage of kids and they embellish job descriptions." You really need to go on an open mind. I think you have to go in as a judge, hearing both sides and trying to see which is the best way to get the desired outcome.

PROFESSIONAL PERSPECTIVE #3
"DAY ONE"
Nancy Chiang, University of Waterloo

I have a very interesting example. I had a student who was very experienced. He was on his sixth and final work term, so he's not a young guy. He wanted to work on a trading floor — the stock market and all that — just to see what it's like. He had been warned already that this is a very demanding area and how you have to work long hours and this and that. And he said "Yeah, that's OK." Then he went on the job. Day one, he called me on campus and said "I want to quit." And I say, "Oh, why?" Of course this turned out to be a really long discussion.

I had to be really calm with him — even-keeled — though of course my feeling was "Oh my God." That's how I felt. So I said, "I think we need to have a long discussion. We need to talk about this, and I cannot talk to you now and you're at work and you can't — you need to take an hour to talk to me. So let's set up some time to talk tonight" because I was in Waterloo and he was in Toronto. That night, I called him and I talked to him for almost two hours. I let him vent, because he must have a lot of reasons why he wants to quit on day one. So I let him vent: "How do you feel? What happened today?" And then I asked him, "Okay, why did you want this job? Tell me what your objective was and how it matches or doesn't match what you experienced today."

I did point out to him that "I think I did tell you that this is a very demanding job." He said, "I heard you, but I couldn't imagine how demanding it is. I don't think I can do it." I didn't want to say "you have to do this; you have to do that" and so I sympathized. I said, "I've listened to how you feel. You wanted to get a sense of what it's like. You've only been there one day. Do you really feel that in one day you will really get the entire sense of how it feels? Let me tell you how previous students felt about this job. You are not the first one who felt this way. And I can tell you, today's the worst day. From now on, it will be easier. Because you will get used to it, and then maybe you will like it, maybe you won't like it."

I reminded him of the benefits of being on the job. It's a chance to explore. Secondly, if you are able to put on your resume that you have worked in this kind of environment and you can handle it, you can handle anything and it means a lot on your resume. We went around and around and around and talked about the same things over and over. At the end he promised me that he would try another week. I said, "Okay, try another week. See how it goes. If you really can't do it, I will talk to the employer because there's no point in keeping you here if you feel this way about the job. We have a rule that once a student has accepted the job, they cannot quit. If they quit, they generally get a failed work term. I understand where you're coming from. It's quite early in the term. But give it a try, another week. Call me."

I didn't hear from him after one week and I thought: "I'd better go and visit this student early. I don't know what's going on." We usually don't visit in the first month. Right at the beginning of the second month, I went in and did a visit. "How is it going now?" "Oh," he said, "I got used to it now." I didn't want to disturb him any more so I asked him about what he's been learning and covered the usual things. And then, guess what, at the end of the term, he contacted me and he said, "I plan to go to graduate school." "Oh, good," I said. "What kind of graduate school do you want to do?" He was in an engineering program, so I asked him if he wanted to continue to do engineering. He said, "No, actually, I want to go and study finance. I want to continue to pursue this direction in my career." I said, "Now that you tell me this, then I want to ask you: you remember what you told me on day one, eh?"

And he did remember and then he said "It's not so bad after all; you just have to get used to it." He ended up finding it very challenging and interesting, so he wanted to do graduate school so he can learn more and be able to pursue a finance career. The last I heard, actually he didn't go to graduate school. The company offered him a chance to go back full-time, and he went back full-time. So that was really interesting, after day one.

PROFESSIONAL PERSPECTIVE #4
"STEP OUT OF YOUR SHOES"
Jacki Diani, Northeastern University

I've learned that there are two sides to every story. Sometimes students find themselves in a position or setting for co-op that they don't like and are not enjoying. When this happens, I usually hear from the student. Not that I don't ever get them from the employer but usually it's the student saying "I'm unhappy; I have a problem." It's often via e-mail, and the first thing I do is say "Let me know when you're available so we can talk and not dissect this over e-mail."

Often right off the bat, I say to the student "I'm really sorry. I could tell from your e-mail that you're unhappy and frustrated. I'm sorry to hear that. So why don't you tell me the story from the beginning. When you started co-op, how did it go? Just give me an overview of how things started and how they developed." During the conversation, I'll periodically stop them to ask clarifying and reflective questions like: "How did you feel then? What did you do next? How did you respond when X happened?" When the student's issues involve challenges with their manager, I will ask, "What do you think the manager was thinking at that time?" Or, "What else might your manager have been dealing with at that time?" I try to get them to step out of their shoes and look at the situation from a different angle, from the perspective of their manager. It can be difficult, but in these situations it is important to try and be objective about what is going on; assessing the situation from different angles will help accomplish that. It is not always apparent to students exactly what their supervisor is dealing with beyond what the student sees them doing, but the reality is the supervisor probably has a lot going on the student is not aware of. If the student is upset because their supervisor promised them an opportunity to do something and it hasn't happened, there is likely a good reason for it, not just that the manager doesn't care. They may be overwhelmed at the moment, dealing with issues the student wouldn't know about: political issues within the organization, staffing problems, and perhaps their own personal issues. They could be going through a divorce; they could have a sick child at home they are worried about. I do not tell the student I am excusing the behavior, necessarily, but let's think about the situation from another perspective and that often sheds light on things. I'll say, "Some day when you are in a supervisory position, you would want your staff to try and see things from your point of view."

When a student is unhappy while in a co-op or internship, deciding what to do can be complicated. I'll say to the students: "Right now you just want to get through this co-op and maybe you'll look back on it and say 'Glad I'm not there anymore.' But you want to finish the experience with your head held high and hopefully with a decent evaluation so let's try to end on a high note." I often encourage them to meet with their supervisor, even though that may involve a not-so-pleasant conversation with them, but it is very important to ask them for their feedback and for the student to sit there and take it. In-person conversations, especially when things have been challenging, are crucial. First, no one is perfect, so receiving feedback is critical to a student's development. Second, during these conversations, students can clarify things; they can say, 'That wasn't my intent; somebody misinterpreted my actions. But I now understand why you were so upset when you heard I did that. This is hard for me to hear, but this is helpful feedback so I won't repeat this mistake in the future." The manager will appreciate the student addressing these difficult issues head-on and discussing them in a professional manner. I guarantee it will help improve the relationship between the supervisor and student.

Lastly, when talking with students, I sometimes say "Think back to co-op class. We never said all these co-ops were going to be perfect. Co-op positions are in real-work settings, which are often complicated and can be very challenging. It's often the more difficult situations that you learn the most from. As a nursing co-op, you may discover you do not like working in the Emergency Department. You thought you were going to love being there, but you've discovered you don't enjoy working in this type of environment. This is such a valuable thing to learn before you graduate. If you hadn't spent six months there, you would likely not know that this setting is not a good fit for you, and may have even sought a full-time position after graduation in it. I always try to get them to see that even despite a difficult situation there's something that you take away from it.

REFLECTION QUESTIONS

1. What preventative measures do you take *before* your students go out on co-op in order to maximize learning and prevent problems from arising altogether?

2. This chapter identifies numerous phases of development over the course of a work term for a co-op or intern: orientation, navigation, mastery, excellence, and closure. Which phase seems to cause the most problems for your students? Are there adjustments that you might make in the preparation process to help students avoid or overcome those difficulties?

3. This chapter describes the challenge of the educator serving as the lawyer and the judge, determining the truth when an employer and student have conflicting perceptions about a situation. How do you or would you handle such situations, step by step?

4. What are the most common complaints or concerns that students in your program have about their work experiences? What does that tell you about your program and what you need to address with either students or employers?

5. How do you educate students about sexual harassment before they go out in the workplace, including the concepts of quid pro quo and a hostile environment?

6. What do you do to prepare students for the fact that some forms of learning in the workplace may be unanticipated and less obvious, ensuring that they maximize the educational opportunity of each work term?

CHAPTER 11

MANAGING REFLECTION PROCESSES

"Life is a ticklish business; I have resolved to spend it in reflecting upon it."
— *Arthur Schopenhauer*

Although I asked experts to respond to a variety of challenging questions in the process of compiling ideas for this book, the topic that turned out to be the most fascinating of all turned out to be the reflection process. While I fully expected to encounter a sense of doubt on this front, I was amazed at how many experienced educators indicated that they honestly felt frustrated and disappointed on this front. Very few people seemed confident that what they were doing really works well with students.

Perhaps I shouldn't have been surprised. After all, I have felt much the same way over the last decade. Yes, I've conducted small-group reflection seminars quite faithfully, and some of them have been terrific. I've used other reflection tools, such as journals, papers, and one-on-one meetings. Again, these approaches have yielded great results at times, but I can't say that I've been remotely satisfied with my ability to obtain consistently great results.

That said, I would have to say that researching and pulling together this chapter has led me to some exciting new perspectives on reflection, and I'm already starting to see a change for the better after applying some concepts that my interviewees shared with me. So I hope that this chapter will be an especially provocative and useful one—even for very experienced educators.

CAUSES OF DISSATISFACTION

So why does the very mention of the reflection component lead to such figurative weeping and wailing and gnashing of teeth among educators? There are several legitimate reasons.

1. *Confusion about the timing of reflection.*

As mentioned earlier in the book, the co-op learning model breaks the process into three discrete stages. Preparation, activity, and reflection are thought of as before, during, and after the work term, respectively. While this is a conveniently simple paradigm, it sets up students and educators to think of reflection as something that one only does *after* a given experience. While this obviously occurs, this way of thinking can lead to sequester reflection. Perhaps unconsciously, we start to think of reflection as something that happens in a one-hour group meeting or a 30-minute one-on-one discussion after the student returns to campus. In researching this topic, I've come around to thinking that this might be the root of all or much of the evil when it comes to the pitfalls or reflection.

As you'll see in Nancy Johnston's interview excerpt at the end of this chapter, it's very helpful to consider that reflection is not a timed activity; it's a way of learning. If you think of it that way, there are opportunities to facilitate and encourage reflection all through the preparation and activity phases in addition to whatever might be done after the work period ends. We'll delve more into this idea later in this chapter.

2. *Whose needs are we meeting?*

In another interview excerpt at chapter's end, you'll see Bob Tillman's approach is quite different from Nancy Johnston's in terms of the nuts and bolts. However, I would say that Bob and Nancy are very much on the same page in the most important sense. They both tend to question whose needs we are meeting when we insist that students go through a variety of hoops and hurdles to get credit for co-op.

My term for this reflection dilemma is the "forced march." Bob talks about a former colleague who students *loathed* because of his insistence on requiring any number of checklist requirements to be fulfilled. Bob argues that you need to consider when students are most ready to reflect on their experience. Rather than forcing small-group meetings to happen, he believes that students in his admittedly insular major are going to share their experiences with their peers without his intervention. If an early work experience raises questions that they want to discuss, he absolutely will do that. Otherwise, Bob is wary of forcing undergrads to reflect, finding that the timing is best when students are close to graduation and truly ready to think back on their cumulative experiences.

Regardless of how reflection activities are handled, the idea here would be to think less of what you would find most expedient as an educator and think more about what will enable your students to maximize their learning.

3. *Reflection is valuable but often woefully inadequate.*

In one form or another, this is the most common lament that I hear from my fellow educators. There is this sense that reflection feels like a forced march for educators—not just students. In her interview, Mary Kane said that about only two out of ten of her small-group seminars seemed to be really productive and useful, and others often agreed with her sense of the batting average.

With small groups, I often ended up saying to myself, "This is okay, but I'm really just scratching the surface instead of mining the rich ore of learning." Typically, many of us at Northeastern have required students to do one small-group meeting of no more than 75 minutes. Often I would end up feeling that we had just started to get thinking about the more provocative topics of learning, and time would be up!

It's not just the format. Papers and journals are often richer and deeper, but they often have an autopilot feel or a rather contrived sense of the student telling you what she thinks you want to hear rather than what was actually learned.

4. *Handled poorly, reflection has the potential to make co-op and internship professionals feel more like meter maids and less like educators.*

Given how much that we all have to do in our roles, it ultimately becomes distressingly easy to reduce our jobs to a series of bureaucratic tasks that need to be completed. That includes, say, creating a spreadsheet to track who has turned in an evaluation, who has attended a reflection seminar, and so on. In the clutter of forms to fill out, e-mails to answer, large loads of students to handle, and requirements to tick off, I fear that we run the risk of losing sight of education. As Marie Sacino indicates in her interview excerpt at the end of this chapter, sometimes you need to acknowledge that you've got it wrong and that you need to overhaul your process to obtain a truly educational outcome. It's only natural for educators to resist sweeping changes in favor of the status quo, as it's so time-consuming. However, focusing on change and improvement is a great way to avoid that trap of being more of a meter maid—the kind of professional that views the program as a series of rules and regulations to enforce, focusing on minor infractions rather than the more important issues, such as real learning.

These are some of the challenges that we need to overcome, regardless of what mechanisms we use to facilitate reflection. With these in mind, let's consider those mechanisms in greater detail.

TYPES OF REFLECTION

Let's consider the pros and cons of various types of reflection, discussed roughly in order of the popularity of the method:

SMALL-GROUP SEMINARS

When I use the word "reflection," most educators probably immediately conjure the image of a group of anywhere from five to 20 students in a classroom after the students return to campus. Many people at Northeastern hold these seminars; usually they are one-time meetings of no more than 75 minutes in length.

The focus usually begins with students briefly sharing the basic facts of their work terms. I limit my seminars to a maximum of 15 students, as it's hard to have much real dialogue with a larger group than that. Before I have students share, I might check in to make sure that they understand *why* we are doing the reflection seminar. I might say, "I know that the cynical answer to that question is that you don't get a grade for co-op unless you go to the reflection seminar. But why do you think that we often do require it? What do we think the benefits of reflection are?"

Generally, students will be quick to say that this is an opportunity to compare notes with their peers. That's legitimate, but I also tell them that my most important goal is to get them to think about what they really learned on co-op and how it connects up with their classroom learning. I also counsel them that they need to be cautious about accepting their peers' opinions about a given job. I like to tell them that I once had two students at the same job with the same manager for the same work term. One person said that the job was a 10/10 as a work experience, while his peer rated it as a 6/10! In that case, the company was in the process of being acquired during the students' work term. One student said that his role gave him a fascinating perspective on organizational transition, while the other student found that the anxiety and fear of the full-time employees was contagious, poisoning the environment for her.

It's important to understand that one person's dream job is another's nightmare. Another example I use with my students is how different people perceive PC support jobs. We could have two students with the same manager and job. Student A reports, "Don't ever do PC support! It's really a frustrating job because there are constant interruptions, and you're dealing with clueless and upset end users all the time. They take out their frustration on you, and I hated that!" Then Student B might say, "PC support is a great experience! It's a terrific job because you always have a variety of tasks to do. New issues arise all the time, and the day goes by fast as you juggle what to do first. You learn a lot about prioritizing. End users sometimes are frustrated and ignorant about technology, but they are so appreciative when you can resolve their problem—and often it's a very quick fix. I also met a lot of people across the organization, as I was helping people in all functions. I highly recommend this job."

Once students understand that all perceptions are subjective, I would go on to ask them to cover the basics about themselves and their jobs in about 90 seconds or so. I ask them to share:

- Their first name and major/concentration

- Where they worked and what they did, describing their role in terms that any grandparent would understand

- Their rating of their job from 1 to 10, with 10 being a terrific learning experience and 1 being a disaster

- A brief rationale as to why this job was a good, bad, or mixed learning experience

The rest of the group is encouraged to ask questions if they want to know more. I try to make clear that this session is more for their benefit than mine, so they should be presenting to the room instead of to me. As they go around the room, I will try to see what themes arise. If possible, I will try to follow up if a provocative theme arises.

Sometimes you get lucky, and an amazing dialogue results. Back in Chapter 4, you might recall that I had a student who complained that he was the "marketing bitch" for his job and how that led to a healthy conversation in which more experienced students showed him how his entry-level job could be a highly relevant stepping stone.

I remember another great one that I facilitated with a group of entrepreneurship and small business management concentrators. One student described his experience as follows: "I worked at a small restaurant in the Back Bay. It was an okay experience, but I was frustrated because the manager was really secretive about the financial side of the business—something that I had hoped to learn about in this experience. Eventually I figured out the reason: He was almost definitely underreporting his revenues so he could avoid paying taxes on his profits as much as possible. But I guess that's what you've got to do to make it as an entrepreneur."

I was dying to jump in and react to that student's statement—especially that last comment. Instead, I tried to stay in the role of a neutral facilitator. "Okay. What reactions do the rest of you have to that?"

Almost immediately, a student spoke up. "I come from a family that has run a business for several generations now. My grandfather had that same attitude, and he ended up going to jail."

There was an audible gasp in the room, and the student went on to describe how his grandfather served time for tax evasion. This led to a rather intense and provocative discussion of the pressures that entrepreneurs face and how entrepreneurs make their own rules—sometimes at their own peril. I loved it, mainly because the students managed to reach some great conclusions on their own rather than having me pontificate on it all.

After some review of common themes, I often will ask another question or two to keep the conversation going. Here are some that I have asked over the years:

- At Northeastern, you take classes in your major, and you take liberal arts classes. You also go out on co-op repeatedly. To what degree does knowledge from one area transfer over into another area?

  There is often a silence in the room as they attempt to digest that one, so I might have to probe deeper with more questions. "Are there things that you've learned to some degree in the classroom, only to have your understanding of those subjects change while at work? Are there things that you learned at work that changed how you approach classes as a student? And the $64,000 question: Do you think it's possible that taking a liberal arts class that has nothing to do with your major—say, botany or art history—actually could help make you a better professional?"

  Usually students start to make connections. Ideally, they can identify a course or two that maybe proved to have more or less relevance once they worked in the field. Interestingly, professionals who expect that students will report that they learned in the classroom and then applied that learning at work are by no means the overwhelming majority. Quite often, students will report that they first learned about something at work and then learned the theory behind it in a class after the fact.

  That question about the connection of something like art history to a successful career in business or engineering is the toughest of all for most students. They often will answer by saying "Well, liberal arts classes broaden you." To which I'll say, "Okay, but so what?" They'll then say, "Well, if you know something about art history, I guess it would make you a more interesting person. It would give you something to talk about at lunch..." But, of course, I'm not talking about being a good lunch date.

  Sometimes I'll then remind them of the preparation process: "Remember when we worked on your first resume, and all you had for job experience was your job as a waiter or a lifeguard? How did we deal with that on your resume?"

Given that I encourage first-timers to discuss transferable skills on their resume when they have no relevant job experience, they'll start to pick up on where I'm going with this question. I want them to at least consider the possibility that a well-taught, well-learned liberal arts class might be an opportunity to improve any number of skills that will transfer to workplace success: analytical skills, writing skills, presentation skills, time management, perhaps working in a team, and, more than anything, *learning how to learn*.

I also might follow up with another thought to model another perspective for them. "At the risk of sounding like I'm 1,000 years old, I also want you to consider that it's very hard to predict what classes ultimately might matter over the course of your career. When I was a freshman, I took a biology course, purely to fulfill a natural sciences requirement. For reasons unclear to me now, I did not sign up for the bunny course for non-majors; I selected the prerequisite for all nursing and physical therapy majors. So the class turned out to be my hardest by a long shot. I worked incredibly hard and still got the lowest grade of any of my courses that semester.

"I often wondered why I did that to myself. Little did I know that 11 years later I would be hired to be a medical writer and project writer for a pharmaceutical sales training company. When we got a new project—developing sales training materials for a new vaccine, contraceptive, or other drug—I was expected to ramp up on the science within a week and start producing a reader-friendly set of educational materials, becoming the company's resident expert on gynecology and immunology in the process. And you'd better believe I was really happy to have that foundation of biology from way back when!"

- If you attended another school in the area—Boston University or UMass, for example—you would take very similar courses. The biggest difference here at NU is that you also go out and work two or three six-month work terms. How do you think that being in a program like this has changed you as a person and professional?

This question was inspired by a conversation that I once had with learning theorist Etienne Wenger, who has written some provocative books on experiential learning, such as *Communities of Practice*. Wenger talked about how experiential learning gives the individual an opportunity to navigate a sense of their identity through the experience. That is maybe a little cerebral for the typical undergrad, so I have tried to simplify it. To what degree does an individual undergo an experience and conclude, *"This just isn't ME"* or perhaps "This experience really told me something about what's important to me and what direction I need to go in subsequently."

I have used this question quite often recently, and it usually leads to some useful reflection. Often students talk about how their friends at other institutions once made fun of them for being in a five-year program that requires work. Now those friends are approaching graduation and have no experience and no idea about how to write a resume or interview for a job.

Sometimes students talk about how much their sense of purpose and ability to perform in the classroom has improved after being on co-op. Asked why, some attribute it to the discipline gained by simply needing to wake up early and show up ready to work for eight hours every day. Others needed to get a taste of the professional world and how it operates in order to understand why some classes were not a waste of time after all.

Another theme is that students often comment on an increased sense of confidence and clarity about their career direction through experiential learning. They often reflect on how expensive education is these days and how fortunate they feel to have had the opportunity to realize early on that they are or aren't on the right track.

Just before this book went to print, I heard some especially great responses to this question. One woman said the following, more or less: "I now feel really aware of the fact that college students generally live in such a *bubble*. We're surrounded by people our age who have our own values and interests. It's very insular. Going on co-op is kind of like having my mom come to visit my apartment at school. When she comes, there are certain things that I don't want her to see and that I put away. It's like that when you go on co-op. You need to put away certain sides of yourself and also learn to relate to people who are in very different life situations." I picked up on the bubble theme and ended up using it quite a bit through subsequent reflection activities as well as reporting that back to my first-time students in my current preparation class.

A day later, another student used the analogy of the "latchkey kid" when describing how co-op has forced him to grow up faster than some of his friends. In other words, he has had to become more self-reliant and autonomous ahead of schedule, just like an eighth-grade student who comes home to an empty house after school. That led to a great conversation about the pros and cons of that status—for example, a co-op student might experience more stress due to being less sheltered at the age of 19 or 20.

- What did you learn during your work term that had nothing to do with being an accountant (or whatever occupation)?

Unless you prepare them otherwise (which I'd recommend), students often go into a job thinking that the only important learning will be something directly related to their major. Getting them to think beyond that is important, as I've discussed in other parts of the book. So in a small group, I do like to get people talking about other learnings, such as integrating yourself into an organization, figuring out the unwritten rules, getting yourself organized, dealing with your manager and co-workers, and so on.

- What did you learn about what it takes to be a good manager from your experience?

This is an easy topic, as everyone will have an opinion about their manager. Whether they thought highly of their manager or not, there are always lessons to be learned about how the student can become a good manager in the future.

Small-group reflection seminars have the advantage of being fairly efficient. You can facilitate learning in a group, and, ideally, students will be able to learn from each other. If you can roll with the group's themes, comments, and energy instead of imposing too much structure on these meetings, you can have some really positive interactions that will get students to compare their learning to their peers.

At worst, this type of reflection is a forced march, and you get the feeling that no one wants to be there. You don't have enough time to go into depth, and you end up having the sense that it was a superficial activity more geared to being able to claim that you actually do *something* to encourage learning after a work experience.

ONE-ON-ONE MEETINGS

Whether one-on-one meetings between students and educators are a formal requirement or more *ad hoc* in nature, they certainly are a common way in which students might reflect with coordinators.

For years I did very little one-on-one when it came to reflection. One wake-up call came when we did a student assessment on all co-op coordinators. One question specifically asked if the students had discussed their evaluations with their coordinators. Generally, I wasn't doing that—mainly because so many evaluations say very little. Still, I thought I would give that a try.

So now I always go through the evaluation in the student's presence—sometimes very quickly if the employer's comments were minimal or generic. If there is something more educational, we'll linger on that. Regardless, we'll then move the conversation to a more detailed discussion. The questions I ask have morphed considerably over the last year or so. I won't go through the whole evolution, but I must say that writing this book has led me to make some changes. I just keeping hearing Nancy Johnston's voice in my head, reminding me to tighten my focus on learning!

Likewise, Ronnie Porter's interview excerpt at the end of this chapter reminds us to get students to focus on what they learned and how it is going to be helpful. She wants it to result in an action step. As you'll see, this is consistent with my approach.

Right now, here are the questions I have been asking in my one-one-one meetings:

1. *"In my view, there are three different general types of learning that happen during a work term. There is technical learning—learning how to use Excel more thoroughly, mastering fundamentals of cost accounting, learning to fix a computer, and so on. There is non-technical learning—adapting to an organizational culture, learning how and when to assert yourself, how to deal with a difficult boss or co-worker, etc. Then there is self-awareness learning—getting a better sense of who you are and what you like and dislike in terms of a career direction, a work environment, degree of task structure, and so forth. Thinking about those general categories, what would you say were your most valuable learnings during this work term?"*

So far the responses to this long-winded question have been quite satisfying and interesting. It might be worthwhile to do a study with a variety of majors over time to be able to say anything definitive about it, but I've seen some interesting trends so far:

- It's often fascinating to hear students' perceptions about what represented "valuable learning." In a few back-to-back meetings one afternoon, I had students express amazement about the interdependency of employee roles at work. They had learned how their success or failure on a given task had a domino effect on others in the organization, and it struck them as something profound and powerful in comparison to the experience of being a student in a classroom.

- While employers often value technical learning, students seem to cite non-technical learning or a self-awareness insight as most valuable, more often than not. Just yesterday, a student told me that his manager raved about his ability to master knowledge of products quickly. "He would've said that that was my most valuable learning, but I didn't see it that way at all. What was most valuable to me was that I learned that I really don't like a very casual and informal work environment. That was a complete surprise to me and very interesting." So that was a nice moment of self-awareness. Pressed for other learnings, that student placed the next highest value on learning how to handle working a 50-hour work week, getting up early every day, and working on many weekends as well. That's obviously more of a non-technical learning. The more technical elements were less compelling, as he's not interested in staying in that industry.

- Students who disliked their jobs most often talk about self-awareness learning first. "More than anything, what I learned is that I really don't want to work for a big company," some students say.

That's a valid learning, but my response there is what I call my "n=1" story. If a student has a bad experience at a company, he may come back to me and announce that he learned that he hates marketing… or that he hates a large company…. or something similar. At times, I've responded with a story.

A few years ago, my son woke up complaining about severe pain in his ear. It was a Sunday morning, so I had to drive him quite a distance out to the suburbs to see a doctor. After a long wait, the pediatrician saw him. Using an instrument, the doctor looked in my son's ear for about five or ten seconds before announcing that there was no infection. He told me that there was nothing to be done but give it time.

I felt mildly frustrated at the amount of time it had taken to make this office visit happen. "You know," I said to the doctor. "Sometimes I think I should just get one of those instruments and look in my kids' ears myself. It would save a lot of time."

The physician was unfazed. "You *could* do that," he said. "The problem is that you would be trying to make a conclusion on an *n* of 1. I can look at an ear for ten seconds and tell if it's infected, but I'm making a judgment based on an *n* of maybe 10,000 to 15,000. Sometimes an ear looks infected when it's not, and vice versa. It's easy to tell, but only when you have considerable experience."

Sometimes I'll make a different analogy with students: "Let's say you have a friend who dates a varsity athlete, and that person turns out to be a conceited, self-important, mean-spirited individual. After breaking up with that person, your friend says to you, 'I am NEVER going out with an athlete again! They are conceited jerks!' What would you make of that?"

Obviously, I am trying to caution students against over-generalizing from their limited experiences. If a student hated her job, there are various possibilities:

- The student is in the wrong field altogether and should change majors.

- The student is the right field but was in the wrong type of job within that field.

- The student is in the right type of job in the right field, but a mismatch with a manager, co-workers, organizational culture, or working environment may be affecting her perceptions about whether she was really in the right job or field.

It can take careful and persistent probing to get to the bottom of what's really going on in these situations, but it's important to get beyond the face value of what the student is saying.

There is another reason why I like to ask that question about most valuable learnings. If I'm going to be working with that student again in the future, I want to get her thinking about what she should articulate about her previous experience when revising her resume. In Chapter 9, I talked about my philosophy with regard to writing resumes. Given that I prefer to see students going beyond duties to include accomplishments, I often suggest that they allude to some of those valuable learning points that we discussed. If their most powerful learning was learning how to plan ahead and improve their efficiency, I'd like them to refer to that on the resume.

Of course, if their primary learning was that they hate finance or that they need to avoid bosses who are quick to take credit for other people's success while blaming others for their mistakes, then we might not include *that* on the resume. Still, I like how the reflection conversation becomes a touchstone for the next job search.

2. What, specifically, would you say was your top accomplishment in this job—whether it was a specific project or task or perhaps how you handled an especially difficult day or week or situation?

This is the second question that I tend to ask now. Predictably, most students struggle to come up with a quick answer. That's okay, as it helps me prove another point that I like making in this meeting. Students need to start thinking about how their accomplishments in one role are going to result in knowledge transfer to their next job. Yet not too many people are great at pulling these off the top of their head. By asking this question, I'm hoping to get the student to start thinking about possible behavioral-based interviewing stories that they may be able to use in their next round of interviews. This reinforces a concept that we worked on way back when in the preparation course, which might as well have happened a decade ago as far as most students are concerned.

If we linger on that question, the student should have the seeds for at least one good BBI story. Depending on the nature of the accomplishment, it may end up on the resume as well. I would encourage—but not require—the student to consider writing out two or three specific stories from this recent job that they may be able to use in their next interviews. I also like this question because I'll sometimes hear some amazing stories that can be shared with other students when sharing models of great professional behavior.

3. Even if your manager believes that you walk on water, there are always ways you can improve as a professional. What would you say are the areas you most need to work on when you return to the workplace?

If there are needs identified by the supervisor, I might ask whether or not the student believes that the manager's criticism is valid. Regardless, I'm most interested in the student's self-perceptions on this front.

Sometimes it's helpful to probe a little deeper when you hear the response:

- Why do you think that you struggle with that?

- What do you think is the underlying reason for that weakness?

I've asked a few hundred students this question over the last couple of years. By a wide margin, these are the two themes that have arisen the most:

A. Lack of assertiveness

This is a very understandable concern for a co-op or intern. Any new employee in an organization often fears drawing attention to themselves for the wrong reasons, and that can translate into failing to obtain attention for the right reasons.

Students articulate this theme in a variety of ways:

- "I struggled with deciding when it was okay to ask questions; I didn't want to interrupt my boss or look stupid."

- "I got so mad at myself because sometimes I had good ideas in meetings, but I was afraid to share them… only to have someone else bring up the same idea and get a ton of praise for it!"

- "I don't think I was always great about reaching out for more work when I definitely could've taken on a higher level of challenge."

In response, I try to acknowledge the very positive intentions that underlie this developmental need. Then I talk about setting a goal for their next job. It might be concentrating on taking "reasonable risks" when pitching an idea, or it could be giving students some strategies when it comes to asking questions: saving up questions rather than asking every few minutes; navigating the organization to figure out more than one person that they can go to with questions, and so on.

B. Nagging doubts about organizational skills

This self-identified developmental need has been more surprising to me. Sometimes a student will have an impeccable evaluation, but you'll still hear statements like this:

- "They thought I was great, but on my end I know that sometimes things slipped through the cracks."

- "When I was asked to keep track of a bunch of projects or deliverables with different timelines, I struggled to stay on top of everything."

- "I think I need a better system to manage my time."

Perhaps these concerns are less surprising upon reflection. These are students who are moving from classrooms that usually have highly structured tasks and deliverables with specific deadlines. In the workplace, students encounter much less structure, and deadlines may not be fixed. Projects don't fit into the tidy structure of an academic term, and they may have a history that began ages before the student's start date and that will not end until well after the student's employment ends.

Complicating that is the fact that all professionals are generally deluged with a variety of communications: e-mails, phone calls, verbal instructions, written directives, and meetings. That's relatively complicated, and most academic institutions do little if anything to prepare students when it comes to organizational skills.

Now that I've identified this as a common developmental need, I'm beginning to try to address it in the preparation course. In the meantime, I try to give the students some thoughts on how to hone their organizational skills. This is tricky, as everyone is a little different. We talk about different organizational systems that might work. I might share my Access database (described in Chapter 3) as an example of an electronic system, but I also would talk about using calendars, to-do lists, and so forth. Ultimately, a student needs to devise a system that works; I mainly want to build awareness of the need and get the student thinking about how they might address it.

After dealing with those three questions and any tangential questions they raise, I feel ready to turn the page and start talking about goals for the next job search, revising the resume, and everything else that goes into the forthcoming preparation process.

FORMAL CLASSROOM INTEGRATION

Now we start to get to less common forms of reflection. There are a few programs that devote whole courses to reflection. Whether taught by co-op faculty, academic faculty, or both, these courses are much more in-depth ways to extract the learning from the work experience. Obviously, any program that has the luxury of doing this could go a very long way indeed to ensuring that reflection is extremely rich and robust. Over the course of weeks, you could walk through myriad elements of the workplace: organizational culture, leadership, motivation, group dynamics, power and politics, ethics, and diversity to name a few. Likewise, you could drill much deeper into self-awareness, non-technical learning, and career development. In Northeastern's Bouve College of Health Sciences, we have had some great courses where this has happened.

Another option is to try to build many of these elements into a required course rather than inventing a reflection course—especially as there may not be space in a curriculum for the latter. For my business students, organizational behavior is a mandatory course, and students can't take it until they've done at least one co-op. The professors use the co-op experiences as fodder for classroom discussion. I've taught this course myself and can attest that it's much easier to teach, say, Hersey-Blanchard situational leadership theory to a group of students who have had a mixed bag of good and lousy managers in corporate settings as opposed to students who have never had a professional job.

There are other situations in which technical elements of student experience can be capitalized on by a resourceful professor. I always tell people that a Northeastern professor has to be able to handle the fact that they sometimes will teach students who know more than they do about some element of a course that they are teaching. After all, a student who has just worked six months in telecommunications at Cisco Systems or Raytheon is going to be much more current on networking than a professor who may be several years removed from similar exposure, at best. But if the professor is not too insecure, it's possible to use that knowledge in class.

Another option would be to make connections between your employers and your academic faculty. Many professors love having an expert come in to discuss the real-world applications of theories discussed in class. Anything you can do to facilitate these relationships can pay off in terms of job development as well as learning, as it enhances the idea of the employer as educational partner.

How formal integration happens will vary dramatically by major, course, and professor. Many prerequisite courses are harder to connect to the real world, and a history of philosophy course wouldn't exactly lend itself to anything a student did on an internship in all probability. But collaborating with academic faculty to bring the real world into the classroom is a win/win in many situations.

JOURNALS AND PAPERS

Some educators will recommend or require that students keep a journal throughout a work term, whether electronically or in hard copy. The journal could be highly structured with specific topics or questions to address that would be relevant at various points of the work term. There could be assigned questions as follows:

- Before Day One: Write about your expectations, hopes, and concerns about the work term. What do you hope to learn from the job?

- After Week One: How was your stress level this week? Did you come up with a strategy for finding out facts that you need to know without feeling like you were becoming a nuisance?

- After Week Two: How would you characterize your organization's culture? What "unwritten rules" have you picked up on so far?

You could go on through the work term that way if you chose. One great thing about journals is that most people don't notice how their attitudes and opinions evolve over time. Capturing reactions at a variety of intervals over the course of a work term—and then reflecting back on them at the end of the term—can be eye-opening if the writer has taken the task seriously.

Another option is to have students write a reflection paper at the end of the work term, generally of some minimum length (often at least three or four pages, maybe more). In this case, you'd want to give students some guidance as to questions that they should address. Otherwise, a reflection paper can be nothing more than a plot summary of the work term with no real reflection in it! You can imagine: "First, they had me learn how to do a mailing. Then I also helped out with some data entry on a market research project. After that..." Obviously, we're not as interested in what they did as what they learned and how they learned.

When I assign reflection papers to those who have been unable or unwilling to attend a mandatory small-group seminar, I tend to have them answer the aforementioned small-group questions. One reason I do this is that I really don't want the paper to feel like punishment for those who failed to attend the group meeting. That type of paper tends to read like someone who is writing "I will not miss all of the reflection seminars next year" 300 times on a blackboard.

That leads me to comment on the biggest negative of journals and papers. Because they are perceived as somewhat similar to writing a paper for class, there is that element of forced march to some of these papers. There is also the fear that students will attempt to write what they think you are hoping to hear rather than what they did or didn't learn. Stephen Brookfield has discussed this in some of his writings and speeches. He talks about how students should feel free to express negative thoughts in a journal, such as the fact that a given task was not satisfying or did not result in learning, without feeling that they will be punished or criticized for that honest admission.

This can be tricky, though. It's not always easy for the student or for you to know whether:

a) The student legitimately didn't learn anything from an experience.

b) The student did learn something valuable but is failing to perceive a less obvious form of learning, such as developing a new awareness of what they like or dislike

c) The student did learn something important but may not come around to realizing that until they have additional experiences that transform this experience from the perspective of the rearview mirror.

So I think you need to tread carefully when critiquing a journal or paper that is negative—or in having a knee-jerk reaction to negative reflections in general. I think it can be worthwhile to probe deeper to find out if there really were any forms of learning without twisting the student's arm to see it that way.

When you're discussing learning one-on-one with a student, I do feel that there is less of a tendency for the student to "manufacture" some sort of learning for your benefit. On the other hand, some learners do extremely well with written reflection and go into much more depth than you'd ever get from a small-group seminar or even a one-on-one meeting. As such, these reflection tools are good ones to utilize in at least some situations. Personally, I use them quite often when a student is doing a very independent co-op, such as starting their own business or working very independently from supervision in some other way.

ONLINE ASSESSMENTS, PORTFOLIOS, AND SEMINARS

This is probably the most dramatic change in reflection over the last decade. As programs and their students have become more reliant on technology, it makes sense that more programs are dabbling with ways to enhance reflection with online options. Some customer relationship management (CRM) systems have ways for students to assess their own learning online. We've had some educators experiment with concurrent reflection methods in which students exchange ideas over a message board, with the educator facilitating the discussion of ideas.

I know that my colleague Kate McLaughlin uses Blackboard to do midpoint reflections with her students. I'll talk about that more shortly. At the end of this chapter, Marie Sacino discusses how LaGuardia Community College recently moved to an online reflection course. As you'll see, this was a very ambitious undertaking, involving writing activities, podcasts, and discussion of books and newspaper articles. It sounds exhaustive and exhausting, and Marie generously shares the pros and cons to date. Ronnie Porter also refers to electronic portfolios. Just as LaGuardia Community College uses ePortfolios in their preparation process, they can be used just as readily for a student to capture their learning with a multimedia format. This might be an especially obvious option for students in areas such as art, graphic design, web design, journalism, and civil engineering, but with some creativity there are ways that a portfolio could be used for other areas as well.

Online reflection has its advantages. Today's students are likely to be comfortable with this medium, and it can be a great way to work with students in groups without needing to get everyone together physically. For reflection during a work term, that can be invaluable, but it also can be handy after the work period. One major positive is its efficiency.

On the negative side, developing such systems can be costly, time-consuming, and labor-intensive. My colleagues who facilitated message-board discussions said that it was great but that the time commitment was driving them crazy. System problems can be a pain, as can training students, faculty, and staff to utilize the system without difficulty. At worst, systems can pull you further away from education, as you're spending too much time on the technology itself. At best, the technology can enable a more multidimensional, convenient, and efficient group dialogue.

TOWARD A MORE HOLISTIC APPROACH

Researching and writing this chapter has brought me around to a more holistic approach to managing the student reflection process. It really starts with the preparation process. As Nancy Johnston indicates, we need to embed reflection into all elements of our activities with students, so it starts right away. Through preparation classes and individual meetings, we need to get students thinking about what they want to learn and how they will best be able to learn. We also can make them aware of the different phases of co-op (as described in Chapter 10) as well as those areas that previous students have found challenging, such as asserting themselves at work and devising an organizational system. By helping students anticipate opportunities and challenges to come, we will be doing what we can to make sure that their learning is not derailed by many typical pitfalls. Working with students on how to set goals is also important here.

The activity period also has many opportunities for enhancing the reflection process. As Jacki Diani indicated in her interview, we do need to reach out to students at a variety of times to make sure that learning is progressing as we hope. Checking in with e-mails at various points (as described in Chapter 10) is a good way to alert students to different themes that might be arising at different stages as well as letting them know that we are available if they need assistance.

That said, some educators go beyond sporadic e-mails during the activity phase. Other educators will hold classes either virtually or in the classroom during the work term. If the students are working full-time, then these classes usually are held in the early evening.

As mentioned on the last page, Kate McLaughlin uses Blackboard to do a midpoint review, using a central Blackboard site that her students can access during her co-op preparation course. Then, during the work term, Kate follows up with an e-mail asking students to submit a Mid Co-op Report via Blackboard. The reports include company name, an informal description of the work, whether or not the students likes the job, and what they are learning. They are also asked to identify a challenge that they overcame or an accomplished they achieved as a co-op. Lastly, they say whether they would recommend the job for others.

All of this is in a discussion board format, so students have the opportunity to read their peers' reports and comment on them. This is a program requirement for Kate's students, so everyone participates. She has found that students generally enjoy sharing information this way. After co-op, Kate sets up chat rooms on the same Blackboard site and preassigns five or six students to a small group. Within each group, students must read everyone else's Mid Co-op Reports and prepare an "experience-specific" question for each of their peers in the small group. Kate tells me that this leads to far deeper, richer conversations than students otherwise would have within the finite time of the typical reflection period. Kate also has a prep class assignment in which students read Mid Co-op Reports going back several years. Students have to identify three reports that they found to be particularly interesting and informative, and they have to explain why. This gives students a sneak preview of co-op life, and they may adjust expectations accordingly.

All of Kate's innovations here are great examples of how to overcome the fundamental problem of reflection—namely, buying into the illusion that all reflection activities must happen after the work term. You definitely can make magic happen with various forms of reflection, but it's a process best spread out over all phases of the co-op learning model: preparation, activity, and what we perhaps misleadingly refer to as the "reflection" phase.

There are some real advantages to getting students to reflect during the work term:

- You can tailor the content to the phases of the work term.

  We had a pilot program a few years ago in which co-op students met once a month during the six-month work term. I was asked to provide some questions to kick off a discussion, and the idea was to tailor these queries toward themes that likely would be arising for the students at that particular phase in the work term. At the one-month mark, we asked students to reflect on what they had discovered to be the unwritten rules of their specific work environments, for example. At two months, the focus shifted toward some discussion of how students were dealing with navigating their organizations—learning how to overcome obstacles, get assistance, and so on. Later, we could ask students to start thinking about how they could exceed expectations now that they had mastered their basic duties. As a result, the conversations generally had real relevance at any given point.

- You can help students make timely adjustments, preventing problems and enhancing learning.

  A great frustration with post-work term activities is that you often learn too late that a student failed to address a problem or missed an opportunity to learn. With significant efforts toward concurrent reflection, students can learn from you and each other about strides that may be taken immediately to improve a situation. That's obviously a major plus.

  However, there are some very real problems with concurrent reflection as well. It can be very labor-intensive to do it right. You're spending a great deal of time monitoring message boards or facilitating classroom conversations after normal working hours. Meeting face to face also may be quite difficult if students are working in far-flung locations. If you require such activities, some students may resent the fact that they have additional "work" to do after a long day, and they may not like any activities that pull their focus away from immersing themselves in the role of employee. Still, such activities can be intriguing to try as an educator.

After the activity period, there is something to be said for Bob Tillman's notion of giving students what they need when they need it. You might need to talk to students—especially seniors—to ask what reflection activities proved to be most helpful to them as well as what changes should be made. If you do require reflection processes to be completed throughout a student's career, you have to ensure that students really understand *why* they are doing those steps as opposed to viewing them as a forced march. I think that either a highly structured or unstructured approach to reflection could work. The more important factor is whether you are able to convey to students that the objective is to make sure students are really thinking about what they're learning and how they're learning it as opposed to focusing on getting credit for their work or not. Marie Sacino talks about competencies; Nancy Johnston uses the terminology of knowledge transfer. The nomenclature is perhaps a bit overrated. Whatever you do, you want to make sure that students are really engaged in the process and that you're not just convincing yourself that something is worthwhile because it works for you and makes sense to you. Getting feedback regularly and over time will help you understand if you're on the right track.

So what is the upshot for me? For the next cycle, I plan to discontinue small-group reflection seminars as a requirement, though I am leaning toward doing a few optional ones. Usually the first couple of seminars attract the most eager students, and the discussion is best. The stragglers are usually the ones who are coming because they have to do so, and the conversation is never good.

Otherwise, I'm going to try harder to get students thinking about what and how they learn throughout all of my interactions with them. I think I need to do more to get out of the trap of treating reflection as a post-work activity only. To some degree, I've been doing that implicitly, but there's no reason why it can't be more explicit.

In general, I think that educators can overcome the rather defeatist attitude that seems to prevail around reflection. A good analogy might lie in how interviewing might be taught. A few people can read about interviewing and immediately get it. Some people may need to read about and hear about it in a lecture, while others won't get it unless they do a written assignment about it. Then again, almost anyone would benefit by actually doing a practice interview, right? Even then, getting some coaching and feedback after some real interviews would reinforce that great variety of previous learnings on the topic.

Why not think of reflection the same way? A few students will need no help whatsoever when it comes to having a thorough understanding of what they learned, how they learned it, and how it might translate into something that can be tapped in a future experience. Every learner is different, though. Some will get it by reading about it, while others need to write about it or discuss it with peers, formally or informally. Yet almost anyone will get that much more out of it if an educator can get them to articulate their learning verbally and in writing on a resume.

What will be the right formula for your students? That's for you to determine over time by experimenting, listening, and learning. There is a very rich variety of techniques to explore. If you can see the enormous realm of possibility when it comes to reflection opportunities—understanding what can be done over months and years instead of viewing reflection as something that will or will not happen in a one-hour post-work session—then you are well on your way to learning just how satisfying and important these activities can be for educators and their students.

On that note, let's see what our experts had to say on the topic of reflection.

IN THEIR OWN WORDS

PROFESSIONAL PERSPECTIVE #1
"TWO OUT OF TEN"
Mary Kane, Northeastern University

I have recently changed how I conduct reflection. In the past I would offer small group reflections (15 students), but I was frustrated with the outcome. I would usually offer about ten reflections and maybe two were great in terms of what I was getting out of it and what the students were getting out of it. In the other sessions, I felt students were just going through the motions. So I now have a multi-level approach. I ask them to write a short paper on the areas or things that I think are important. I have found that I get much richer information this way. I then meet with them individually as I would anyway before they go out on their next experience. I also provide all my returning students with a list of their peers that includes student name, company, and position of their most recent co-op and contact e-mail. I encourage students to reach out to students who have worked at companies they are curious about. This has received great feedback from students. I get important information that I need by reading their paper, reviewing their employer and self-assessment, and students get an opportunity to reach out to other students to learn about other co-op positions and companies. This activity also showed me how industrious students can be. Many use the list once interviews for the next cycle start. Students will reach out and contact a previous co-op to help them better prepare and understand the co-op position.

I think refection is really personal. I don't know if everyone coming back after the first experience has had time to process it and really get it. If you are doing the goal setting and really talking about the experience and helping them get ready for the next one, I think you're accomplishing what you want them to accomplish because the reflection takes place in them and not you, the coordinator.

PROFESSIONAL PERSPECTIVE #2
"REACH OUT TO EVERY STUDENT"
Jacki Diani, Northeastern University

In addition to meeting with each student after their co-op is complete, I reach out to every student during co-op. A couple months into the co-op, I e-mail them to check in and see how things are going, so it is a concurrent or "reflection in action" approach. I don't just ask, "How are you doing?" I'll ask a few specific questions, like how their orientation went, how the staff is to work with, and how they like working with that particular patient population. A lot of times—not always—students respond: "I love it! Everything's great!" and they talk about what they are learning and liking about the position, so there's not much to worry about. But for those students who are running into some bumps in the road, they will respond and talk about those issues and their concerns. Depending on what their concerns are, I can respond via e-mail with suggestions and encouragement, and ask them to check back with me to give me an update. Or, I'll decide to give them a call or suggest that we meet in person to talk things over and strategize how to approach the issues they are facing in the workplace. The goal is to help the students learn how to approach and solve issues in the workplace, not to do it for them.

I think concurrent reflection is very valuable, because while they're still in the co-op they can think about "What is happening here? What could I turn around? What could I tap into that I'm not tapping into over the next two months to help me?" or something like that. When facing difficulties during co-op, I don't want the students to mentally "check out" and say "just get me through this." I want them to make every effort to turn things around and end on a positive note.

Additionally, we do reflection individually when the students return to school from co-op, to reflect on the co-op generally, as well as review the co-op evaluation. During this time, we are able to discuss their supervisor's comments on their performance and let the student talk openly about whether they agree or disagree with them. I might say, "Your supervisor said 'this.' What do you think she meant by that?" and use that to prompt the student to think back about the co-op and what they are taking from it. Together, the concurrent and post reflection seems to work well.

PROFESSIONAL PERSPECTIVE #3
"ALL DONE ELECTRONICALLY"
Ronnie Porter, Northeastern University

Reflection is something I'm struggling with also. I find it very difficult to schedule reflection seminars because of the differences in students' schedules. The only common times that students have free are during activities periods and we can't require that they participate in formalized programs during those times.

As a result, we have been using an individual approach to reflection. Students must complete an online self assessment and they and their supervisors participate in an online performance evaluation process as well. It is expected that students and employers will meet to discuss the evaluation prior to the students' return to school. When students return to school they meet with their co-op coordinator and using the self assessment and employer evaluation as a base, have a reflection meeting.

A basic question that we discuss is: "What did you learn, and how is this going to be helpful in your future plans?" I think that effective reflection has to be looking back but also looking forward as to how this information is going to be utilized. There has to be some kind of action step to be able to take it to the next level for it to really be effective.

I am currently engaged in a project with a college student development professor in which we are analyzing the data from the self-assessments and the employer evaluations to see what emerging themes there are. Using student development theory, we are trying to interpret the information to help us to develop some guided reflection tools. I think that that's the next step in bringing this to another level and enriching the reflection process.

We have developed a rubric to assess student learning both academically and experientially. Students and expert reviewers assess pieces of student work to document students' proficiencies in meeting curriculum objectives as well as levels of proficiency. When students place a piece of work into the rubric they must also do a reflection to explain how and why they have given the work a particular rating. We are hoping to eventually integrate this into the new electronic portfolio system, and have it be an ongoing tool and practice.

PROFESSIONAL PERSPECTIVE #4
"RETHINKING THE INTERNSHIP SEMINAR EXPERIENCE"
Marie Sacino, LaGuardia Community College

Writing is another way that students can really hash out what's going on and what actually happened in the situation: How did I react? Should I have been more responsive and thought about something before I reacted to it in my situation? This is experimental, this is brand new, we've only tried it this first time around, but we've found that students have been more engaged by using a seminar in this kind of a format.

Our hybrid and online seminars are very creative and non-traditional in that they don't use a particular critical reflection book. They use articles from the *New York Times*, they use podcasts, they use videos, they use movies, and they use first chapters from books. In our traditional on-campus seminars, about 25 students come to class and they sit in a room. Some may be actually engaged in the reflective seminar and some may not. In the online classes, students must participate in order to be recognized and in order to get a grade. For many students, this type of seminar has increased their engagement with the faculty member as well as with other students.

I guess there are six sessions and they're two-hour sessions, but they're conducted online and they're asynchronous. For instance, the students might be given a particular article to read from *The New York Times* and everybody has to log into that and give their comments about how it might relate to their internships. So clearly they're not being asked a question that's directly about the article but rather how this article has an impact on what you do on your particular job. There's one article that I think we've used in a number of classes, which is by the *Freakonomics* authors [Steven D. Levitt and Stephen J. Dubner]. They wrote an article called "A Star is Made." I don't know if you're familiar with it, but it's a good one. [You can read it online by Googling "A Star Is Made" along with the term Freakonomics.] This article talks about the idea that talent is overrated; it's more a matter of practice and dedication and passion for what you do than being born with a particular skill or talent.

Extrapolating from that, we can talk about how success in an internship doesn't just come. You don't just go into the door and become this star performer; it does take a lot of practice. The instructors will ask a student "How does that relate to you and your learning and to your experience?" The student can respond in a number of ways. Professor Susan Sanchirico will say: "You can create a podcast about this instead of actually doing the writing." And our students are pretty technical in this Millennial Generation, so there are a number of ways they can do this. There's an actual number they can dial into; there's some software that they can use to create a podcast.

Or instead of reading something they could go to a podcast of Thomas Friedman of *The New York Times* and hear him talk about the economy or jobs, and students will talk about how that might reflect on their own learning experience or what's happening in their career field, whether it be accounting or computer science or travel and tourism. How does that have some relevance to what's happening on their internship? So we're finding that that seminar has been more meaningful and students are more engaged in doing that kind of work.

PROFESSIONAL PERSPECTIVE #5
"DIFFERENT THINGS AT DIFFERENT TIMES"
Bob Tillman, Northeastern University

I think we need to define what the expectations are of a profession. A lot of times—particularly in some of the fields that may be a little more wide open—students don't view it as a profession in the sense that they don't understand what are the trappings of a profession, what are the identities, what are the languages, what are the norms, what are the expectations. They're there, and I think in some of those fields we just have to spend a little more time connecting the classroom aspect that they may know to what they're going to experience. But a lot can happen when they come back after the first time—helping them pull that together in a sense that they understand that they are part of a larger system, that there really are some professional expectations and identity.

They've never experienced the identity piece; they've never seen it. But after they go out and work the first time, when you say Financial Analyst or you say Practicing Nurse or Physical Therapist, whatever the field is, it should be grounded a little more. They should have some exposure as to what it means to be part of that group. "What's the identity of that group? Do I fit that identity?"

[As far as actually engaging in reflection activities goes,] I just talk to them. There doesn't seem to be a problem on this end. I think in the old days you sent for students and said "Here's your appointment." Well, everyone tried to get everything done in 20 minutes. And then they would spend 10 minutes writing notes about what was said and most of the time it was so they could come back and say "Well, last time we met you said this and you told me this." That's nonsense. That's not a discussion that's going on. Sometimes it was an interrogation, hell, at best an interview.

But I may get different things done at different times with students, and part of it is recognizing when they want to spend some time. If I see a student early on and three, four, or five times, that's not unusual. Some students don't want to do a lot of sharing. Things are going great—their identities, their needs, etc. Well, don't spend a lot of time on that because it's not going to be worthwhile with that student at that time. Maybe later on they'll want to connect, after they've had a little more chance to think and talk with other students and see some trends: Did this happen to you? Are you seeing this where you're working? Is this a trend that's going on with your company? You work for a small company; I notice small companies are struggling now, did you have that same experience?

But I think it's also knowing the students that you're dealing with, what stage they're in as they go through their education. Let's face it, it's a lot easier to have those conversations with students who have been out a couple of times. You've developed a relationship with them; you've developed some trust. You know a lot more about them so that when you see things that don't fit or things that might look a little different, it's a little easier to bring it up.

When you're dealing with sophomores who you're putting out for the first time that have never worked, now, that's not probably going to be time well spent because you're asking to have discussions about things that haven't happened, that they've never experienced. They come back the first time, and you still don't have a lot of trust. I mean, it's still pretty new. And it's over time that I find that that happens best. I also find that I'll have discussions with juniors and seniors about stuff that happened sophomore year because now it's starting to connect. Now they're starting to connect the dots, now they're starting to see some patterns as to how things went, now they're much more ready to have that discussion.

We pretty well know that if you're really going to do reflection, do it at the end—way at the end. If you really want meaningful reflection, then that's the theory of co-op: It's sequential, one builds on the other, so build on it when they're all done. Five years out, people are going to have much better discussions about their co-op than when they were in that moment, when they haven't had time to process. You bring students back that have worked for six months, and we're on tight deadlines, so a lot of times you're trying to get some other things done: "Who am I looking for jobs for? Where are you going to be? What geography?" You try and get all those things out of the way, the mechanics, so at least you know what the game plan is, then it's a little easier to go back and have a discussion, but the students have had more time because they've talked to each other now. So the informal network has already taken over, they've already started sharing: "What did you do on co-op? How did you like that?" Students do that all the time.

I remember when I was an undergrad, we shared a lot about co-op that was never shared with a co-op coordinator. It just didn't happen, either timing and/or process. But I find now that when you can see kids three, four, and five times, it's a little easier to get some of that out of them. They've already had a chance to debrief with their peer group: peer reflection—informal not the forced march—I think starts to get these things going.

Whose program is it? Whose needs are we meeting? Because in most of those cases, we're meeting coordinator needs, not learning needs, not student needs. So who cares? I don't. Some students want to do that. It's recognized. They want to go over their evaluation line by line, while others look and say "no need." Okay. This is your program; this is your learning. We may not do it at that time; we may do it later. Well, let's do it when you're ready, not because it's my need at this point and Goddamn it I've got a checklist and we're going to finish the checklist. I worked with a colleague that did that, and the students loathed him for that. I shared a program, and I could see it firsthand. The kids dreaded coming in and going through the forced march and being grilled. It was meeting his needs; it wasn't meeting the needs at that time of that student.

Now that's not to say that we do everything just because the students want it, but recognize when the learning is taking place, when the sharing is taking place, and what are we doing the reflection for. Not my original idea, but reflecting in, on, and for are three very separate processes of reflection. Each time you're talking to a student, you need to understand: Which piece of it am I dealing with? And when are they ready to do their piece, to do that part of their learning that's going to have meaning to them? Because if you do it in other times it's just not going to happen. I don't do group work. Tried it. We did the forced march here in engineering—not successful. A lot of students don't want to share as part of a group. They will go through the process, but they resent it. It's not hitting where we want to hit. Some students will do a great amount of sharing and some students will do very, very little. They have no needs; that's not what they're here for.

PROFESSIONAL PERSPECTIVE #6
"DEVELOPING METACOGNITION"
Nancy Johnston, Simon Fraser University

Let me preface it by saying I don't think reflection is necessarily a timed activity, I think it's a way of learning. It happens as we experience things; it doesn't necessarily have to happen after the work experience. If you ascribe to Schönean notions of reflection in and on practice [referring to learning theorist Donald Schön], where he explores how people learn through practice, then what you have to do is to actually embed reflection early on in students' ways of being in co-op, as a part of them understanding that that's how they learn.

Reflection is an opportunity to step back from positive incidents, negative incidents, troubling things, problems, and reflect back and reflect forward on what was learned, what was generalizable. So I think the fact that you're doing something on reflection is good right then and there, as the event is happening. We're also trying to contextualize it in the bigger picture. We like to conceptualize reflection as an activity that helps develop metacognition, which means your ability to think about thinking. Then students understand that the reason they're trying to think about thinking is because if they don't, their chances of transferring any skill or task or problem-solving approach that they've learned from one context to another that's slightly different or very different, is low.

So they understand: "I need to be reflective because that's how I learn. Thinking about an event forces me to recall any previous thinking or actions that might be similar as well as to consider any future activities where similar strategies might prove useful. When I think about previous thinking and when I think about future thinking, research shows that just that activity alone ups my chances for successful transfer when things don't look exactly the same."

When things are the same, people are generally smart enough to go "Hey, that's kind of like the other!" and they move their mental framework over or they use the exact process they used to solve the "problem" the previous time. But when things are slightly different—and it's unbelievable, they only have to be slightly different—people don't tend to scaffold unless they physically, explicitly make themselves. Now once you begin to think like this, you then no longer have to do it explicitly, it just becomes part of how you learn. That's why I say that we raise reflection to an explicit nature because some people don't always do it or they don't understand why they do it or they think of a specific technique and negate it. "It was journaling; I'm not a person who likes to write things down." We're just giving a technique here for learning. There are myriad ways you can encourage reflection, and we at SFU encourage it from the very beginning by saying why we're encouraging it and making it explicit and linking it to metacognitive development and skills transfer. So there's something in it for you as a learner; it's not just a hoop to jump through or a report to fill out. Then on almost every form or activity or place that we drive students to, we have a reflective piece. "Hey, we'd like you to submit a profile at the end of your work term. Shoot us a picture of yourself, we're going to put it on our online community. There will be a picture of you, and it goes like this: What's the company, what did you do, what did you learn from what you did?"

It's always embedded in almost everything we do. When they're in their web CT preparatory course, there's a little learning icon we have—I think it's a person with thought bubbles or something coming out of their head—and it'll be a reflection exercise. They know we're forcing them to work on this skill. If they've listened like we hope they have—(and probably half of them haven't!)—they understand why. And then eventually we stop and just assume reflection. So when you come back for a group debrief, we might ask one behavioral-based question: "Tell us about a problem you had and how you solved it." We'll go around the room with 17 people, all different workplaces, completely different problems, and then we'll go "What kind of general themes arose here?"

So this is the metacognitive piece, right? Now we're trying to think about our thinking and engaging in general solution-finding that we share. Literally, we would say "So your problem in a physio office and the way you solved that is very similar to this person here that was in a woodworking mill. So now you're looking at transfer—always pounding that home. And what did you do as a learner—the self direction piece. So we try to embed reflection in this larger sense on transfer and then give people the skills to do it and understand why we're pushing it all the time.

With their work reports, there's a little page on reflection. The poor guys—every single place they get asked "So why?" It's annoying, right? It's like being that parent who responds to questions from their kids by saying, "Well, think about it. How do you think that should be?" And after a while they're like, "Just tell me!!" Because students are busy and they're stressed, and they just want you to tell them. And so we annoy them by not telling them and making them think. And in the end, mostly, they say "Thank you that was useful but, geez, it was painful at times!"

REFLECTION QUESTIONS

1. How satisfied are you with your current methods of conducting reflection? What are your biggest sources of frustration or dissatisfaction with reflection right now?

2. One theme of this chapter is that it might be useful to think of reflection as something ongoing through all phases of the co-op learning cycle rather than looking at it as a discrete event that will happen in a short meeting after a work term. What opportunities do you see to increase the probability that students will reflect on their learning at various points during their academic careers?

3. This chapter described various specific ways to handle one-on-one meetings and small-group sessions during and after a work term. What idea are you most tempted to try in your program, and why?

4. Advantages and drawbacks to reflecting *during* a work term were described in this chapter. What are you currently doing to connect with students while they are actively working? If you were to add something to the mix, what might you do to enhance connection and learning to the work term?

5. Bob Tillman favors holding off on reflection until students are ready and eager to talk about their experiences, while Nancy Johnston prefers an approach in which students are required to reflect on their learning experiences throughout their academic career. Which argument is more persuasive to you, and why?

CHAPTER 12

HANDLING MOMENTS OF TRUTH

*"The truth is that our finest moments
are most likely to occur when we are
feeling deeply uncomfortable, unhappy, or
unfulfilled. For it is only in such moments,
propelled by our discomfort, that we are
likely to step out of our ruts and start
searching for different ways or truer answers."*
— *M. Scott Peck*

A great variety of personality types comprise the ranks of co-op and internship educators. Still, I always tell those who are interested in working in this field that they have to be able to deal with many unstructured days and grey-area scenarios. If you are in this field long enough, you might start to think that you've heard it all. To name a select few, here are some of the more bizarre and challenging situations I've had to handle over 13+ years:

- A student who was fired from an out-of-state job that provided free lodging, who then balked at moving out after his termination

- A student who was accused of making out with her boyfriend while waiting for a job interview near an unattended receptionist desk

- An employer who asked a student to drive him to his laser eye surgery and then asked her on the way home if she'd consider dating a man in his forties, later claiming that it was the sedative that led to his inappropriate question

- A student who had a co-worker refuse to give him help and who then proceeded to compare his relationship with the student to America's dependency on the Middle East for oil, culminating in the employee intentionally spilling coffee on the co-op's procedure sheet to accentuate his point

■ Here is an excerpt from a memorable e-mail from an international student:

"I am really sitting on duck eggs. No wonder why the previous kid left, and that has been a long stay for him indeed. I am really considering my situation but it is close to unbearable all that humiliation. My name is Excuse Me for a week or so. My boss even does not bother to remember my first name and this is a problem when she's introducing me, to three people so far though. And of course there is NO communication even though we sit across each other. I will do my best here in the following weeks, but I do not see myself learning anything since there is no communication and that makes the whole co-op experience with her impossible."

On any given day, an educator's beautiful plans go right out the window because of an un-anticipated problem that suddenly surfaces. When that happens, you often can see most of your morning or afternoon go up in smoke, and you have to be able to accept that. Granted, the aforementioned issues are some of the stranger ones that I've seen, and you likely won't see anything that is identical. But I promise you that sooner or later—and probably sooner—you're going to need to handle situations that are grey, emotional, and not likely to respond to a quick fix.

The structure of this chapter is different from all of the others in *Learning From Experience*. When I interviewed the various experts for this book, I asked each of them to reply to at least one out of five different true scenarios that my colleagues and I have faced over the years. Some are fairly common, and others are rather atypical. Either way, there is much expert advice in this chapter that can be applied to similar or analogous situations.

You'll also notice that our experts are not always on the same page with every scenario. In some cases, the responses contradict each other. I also think that this is useful, as some of these are definite judgment calls as opposed to situations in which there is one unequivocally right answer.

One other note: I have used many of these scenarios when interviewing prospective co-op co-ordinators. When I do, I'm not hung up on whether the individual ultimately would choose to do what I would do in that situation. I'm more interested in their thought process: Can they quickly understand how a course of action will affect *all* parties in the situation? Do they get the fact that these can be deceptively complex situations with long-term consequences, or do they see them as quick fixes? Some of the best interviews I've seen were with people who clearly relished the scenarios and asked great clarifying questions before describing what they might do as well as the pros and cons of the different alternatives.

With all this in mind, let's jump into the scenarios. We'll present each scenario, followed by our expert responses, and then I'll add my own reflections... including what really happened, where appropriate.

SCENARIO #1 – QUITTING TIME?

A sophomore nursing student calls you during the second week of a six-month co-op job. She complains that she hates the job and wants to quit. You ask questions and determine that the job is basically what it was advertised to be: It's a "hospital sitter" job, where the student's role is to keep an eye on a patient in the ICU, being sure to call for assistance if the patient pulls out his or her tubes. "All I do is sit there all day, watching someone who is completely out of it. I'm not learning anything—I want to quit!" How would you handle this situation or something similar in your field?

RESPONSE #1 – TOM AKINS, GEORGIA INSTITUTE OF TECHNOLOGY

If you're saying that the company is delivering what it said it would be, our stance in a situation like that would be pretty firm—if you're not counting any extenuating circumstances. We would say to a student—and we have done this—you need to remain there for the rest of this particular term and work out the term. Then when you come back, we'll talk about what we need to do about meeting your goals and your career interests because obviously you're not interested in this. And maybe it'll improve over the term.

We also give them a suggestion to either go to their supervisor or if they have a mentor there—obviously some employers have mentors that are not the supervisor—and talk to them about how maybe you're interested in something different, and maybe you can work in a different area when you come back. But for right now, this term, you need to remain in that job and continue to do the best you can in that situation because we feel that that is also part of the learning process. You've committed to something, and the ethical thing to do—the honorable thing to do—is to meet your commitment by working this particular term in that job and do the very best that you can.

If the student says "Well, no I'm just going to quit," that's like withdrawing from school as far as Georgia Tech is concerned. If you quit your job in the middle of a work term, you've essentially withdrawn from school and that's the way it shows up on your transcript.

One exception would be if there were some unresolvable personal issues. We have seen that before, where it's just an unbearable situation for that particular individual. I can remember one particular situation. It was a young lady who was having to close up an operation late at night and it was in, let's say, a less-than-desirable area of town. We were very, very concerned about her safety, and so we went to the company and told them: "You need to make some changes here or we're going to pull her out." They actually did make some changes, but anything that's going to put the student's safety in jeopardy, something like that, we would certainly pull them out of there.

Or if it's just an unbearable personal conflict that they have with their supervisor and it's just not going to get any better and we've counseled with them, we've tried to get them to stick it out, but if they can't do it, yeah, we'll give them permission to hang it up. Another situation I can think of from over the years was when a student wasn't even being paid. They were supposed to be paid. "I've been here a month and they keep telling me they're going to pay me." It might've been a small start-up company, they had these great aspirations but they just weren't having the cash flow coming, and they said "Well, we can't pay you." And we did tell that student, "Yeah, you can quit. If they're not going to pay you, you can just get out of there. They promised they'd pay you, and they're not paying you." So that's another kind of situation that I can think of that has happened to us, more than once I think.

RESPONSE #2 – TAMARA PINKAS, LANE COMMUNITY COLLEGE

What I often tell my students is that the first two, three weeks of a job often is terribly boring. It's true. And I've had co-ops in clerical work and drafting and writing. I've done it in so many different ways over my years, and I have a lot of experience across many career paths: physical therapy, you name it. Anyway, what I tell students is "Remember, I told you the first couple weeks would be like this because here's what's happening. Remember we talked about it: One of the things that's happening during these first two weeks is they're looking at your attitude, they're looking at your willingness to do mundane things and do them cheerfully and willingly and to make the best of the situation. So you're in that first two or three weeks where you're under the microscope and they're seeing what else they will give you later on. So if you are unhappy and moody, then that's going to come through. They'll be unlikely to give you more interesting things to do because they don't think that you have the right attitude."

So your attitude is the issue at the beginning of every internship. I also talk to them about what have they taken responsibility for with their learning. What's around? Are they looking at the patient charts? Are they taking advantage of learning things that are in that environment? Are they going beyond the job description—which is to sit and watch—but what could they take advantage of? Do they take the opportunity on their breaks to speak with other nurses about what they like about their work, what they don't like about their work and learn more, to ask questions about how things are organized?

They can't do it every minute of the day, yes, but learning—there's a lot to be learned even when one is doing something that isn't all that exciting. So I push them to think about it: What are some learning opportunities that you might be able to take advantage of in this fairly routine kind of a job? And then I also talk to them about how long the job will last. Typically for most of them it's a term, so whether it's a quarter or a semester, it has a very fixed end date. We talk about how if you take advantage of everything you can learn, you're not going to be there forever. This isn't the job of your life; this is really to get you in and get some contacts, to meet people and learn more about this environment. So you can do anything for three months or six months. Even if it's not the most exciting thing in the world, you can walk out the other end with some good relationships with nurses so you can come back and work with them later in a much more skilled capacity. You also need to realize that there's more that you can be learning that you may not be taking advantage of. Then, of course, if I were a nursing instructor, I would know what those things would be so I would be able to work with the student to develop them.

RESPONSE #3 – JACKI DIANI, NORTHEASTERN UNIVERSITY

Immediately I would respond and acknowledge how she's feeling. A big mistake would be to say "You know, the job is as advertised, you took it, you're committed to it, so that's that." Right off the bat I would say "I can hear how upset you are; this obviously is a frustrating situation. It sounds like you were expecting more. What's your schedule because I'd really like to sit down and talk with you about this in person?" If the student's local, there's no reason we can't find a time to meet. They can come to my office or I can go to their worksite and maybe we can meet for coffee on their break. If possible, I want to meet in person; it usually results in a much more productive conversation. If not, I'd choose a phone call over using e-mail to discuss the situation. Once we meet, I would start by going back to the beginning, "Tell me about when you interviewed for this position. Who did you interview with? What did they tell you about the job? Do you work with this person or has someone else taken over?" It is important to go over the details regarding how the student came to accept this position, and what their expectations were at the time and what they currently are.

There are so many factors that could play into a situation like this. Perhaps a student was lukewarm about a job but decided to take it, thinking that once he is in it, he can change the position. Or, she took a position without really learning the details of the job. After reviewing things, if it comes down to "it (position) is what it is and that's the job," I would talk to them about honoring a commitment made. "You made a commitment. You wouldn't feel so good if two weeks into your job the employer said 'we don't really want you anymore.' Thinking about it from another perspective can be helpful.

Additionally, while talking with the student I will ask lots of questions about the position and setting in which they work, and drill deeper into what's possible with the job itself. "Tell me about the patients that you're sitting with. Why do they need a patient sitter? What's wrong with them? What are their medical issues and what is so serious about these conditions?" Get the student talking, and as they talk say "I'm hearing you describe medical situations and psychotic situations. Listening to you describe these patients, I can tell you have already learned a lot!"

Additionally, I would be likely to talk with them about what they can take advantage of at work outside of the position. For example, "As an employee of X hospital, what can you take advantage of over the next few months to add to your experience there? Can you set up informational interviews? Can you attend some in-services while you're there at the hospital? What areas of nursing are you interested in? Psych? Emergency nursing? What resources can we tap into?" My goal would be, if possible, to see how to not only enhance the position they are in, but the overall experience of working for this employer. What ideas does the student have regarding what they could offer to do to make the position more challenging or interesting? Beyond their role, what opportunities exist in the workplace that they can tap into and learn new things? I would want to try to strategize about that. Lastly, we need to keep on the table the ethical situation; she made a commitment, so let's honor the commitment and discuss how we can be pro-active and make the most of this experience.

Students sometimes forget that as an employee of many organizations you have access to in-services and speakers and lunchtime seminars and maybe even picking up some shifts in another area. So that position that you're not thrilled with is a foot in the door to other things—meeting other people—and I can help you with that. We have alums there, we've got managers, and maybe I could help you set up three informational interviews so you'll meet people for your next co-op.

REFLECTIONS ON "QUITTING TIME?"

This is one of the most common scenarios you'll face in one form or another. Note that all three experts agree that the student needs to understand the importance of honoring the commitment. Additionally, you can see how cleverly these professionals work on expanding the perceptions that these students have about what the realm of possibility is with this situation. As described earlier in the book, students can be too linear and narrow in focusing on the tasks themselves rather than the other learning opportunities in a professional situation. For that matter, they may be underestimating what is learnable in the job itself.

My experience is that it's quite possible to talk students through these situations and to coach them to be more aware of the educational payoff of such jobs as well as reinforce the ethical element of maintaining a commitment. In this case, I might also be tempted to remind the student that a first-time nursing co-op is actually limited in how much she is legally allowed to do in a hospital setting. That's another way of saying what Tamara's saying—the job is not forever, and it's a building block for future experiences... but only if the student gets through the whole work term so she can put the job on her resume and put her manager and others on her reference list.

I had an analogous situation this spring. A student that I like very much came to see me; she was just past the halfway point of her six-month co-op job. She told me that the main thing that she had learned was that she hated her job and her company's industry. She had fully intended to stick it out for six months, but an unbelievable opportunity had arisen. In December, she had visited Israel and fell in love with Jerusalem. Now she had been offered a "once in a lifetime" opportunity to do a seven-week fellowship at low cost in Jerusalem.

With tears in her eyes, she asked me if I would let her quit the job. She said she had performed well and that she was pretty sure that the employer would not be upset if she quit. In response, I did the following:

- Using a calm, neutral, assertive tone, I told her how sorry I was that the job had not been a great fit for her.

- I told her that I couldn't put a gun to her head and force her to stay in the job. That was going to be her decision.

- However, I told her that I would not be able to give her credit for working a six-month work term if she was only going to work for four months. She asked why not, especially if the employer was okay with it. I told her that I wasn't sure that the employer would definitely be okay with it. Sometimes employers will say yes to a request even when they aren't happy about what a student is doing. How would this affect my relationship with the employer going forward? And would it be fair for me to give her credit for working four months while other students had been told that they had to work for six months? So I saw it as an equity issue as well as one with long-term consequences. There was also the fact that there were still learning opportunities in the current job, and she acknowledged that it would be nice to complete her Six Sigma quality training. We talked about other steps she could take to improve the quality of the job.

- I also told her that saying no to this fellowship was not equivalent to saying no to Israel forever. "You obviously are very passionate about Israel right now," I said. "I can't imagine that you're not going to get back over there—hopefully for much more than seven weeks. So this fellowship opportunity might be fleeting, but if you have that itch to go to Israel, I'm confident that you're going to find a way to scratch it before too long."

- Then I raised another point. I told her that we'd had a great relationship. But if she reneged on the commitment she'd made to working a full six months, it raised the question for me as to whether I could trust her to honor a six-month co-op next January. She immediately looked shocked. "You're saying that you wouldn't work with me for the next placement cycle if I quit this job?" she said. "I didn't say that," I replied. "I honestly don't know what I would do. If it came down to it, I guess it would depend on just how upset the employer would be after the dust settled. But I'm just trying to be very transparent in telling you that I definitely would question my ability to trust you in the future if you jump ship now."

- Although the student had attempted to make a strong case—and gone through much of my tissue box in the process—she sighed at that point. "Yeah, I guess I knew that you were going to say all that," she said. This was true—everything I had said was consistent with what she had learned in the preparation process. Still, it was different for her—as it is for many students—when the situation is at hand. So it was good for her to talk about it.

- She told me that she was going to think about it for a few days. I told her that was absolutely fine and simply asked her to let me know her decision. I felt that I had said my piece and made my case for what I thought was the right decision. Now it was time to back off and let her own the decision without any additional pressure.

She stayed in the job, as I expected. When we did our debriefing afterwards, she was really proud that she hung in there and felt good about maintaining her commitment. She did receive her Six Sigma certification, which was a highlight. The upshot is that she has a strong evaluation, good references, and better skills for her next job.

I ended up using that situation weeks later when we were hiring a new finance co-op coordinator, and it was really interesting to hear what candidates had to say about whether the student should be allowed to quit or not and how either decision would affect the coordinator's future relationship with the student and the employer.

SCENARIO #2 – "IS THIS SEXUAL HARASSMENT?"

You have just received an e-mail from a female student who is out on an internship and now reports that she is uncomfortable about her situation at work. She is one of three interns in her office. A few weeks ago, her male supervisor offered her the opportunity to work overtime at 1½ times her pay rate, and she was thrilled to get the chance to make more money. But now she feels "a little weird" about it. She has noticed that the other two interns have not been asked to work overtime and doesn't know why. Then, last week, her supervisor mentioned that it was getting dark out and that he really should drive her home. This happened a few nights in a row. Then, yesterday, her supervisor said that she has done such a great job that he really wants to take her out to dinner to show his appreciation for her hard work. Nothing has "happened," but she feels uncomfortable about the situation. Now she is coming to you and wants to know what she should do. How would you handle the situation?

RESPONSE #1 – TAMARA PINKAS, LANE COMMUNITY COLLEGE

Well, I agree with her: She should be uncomfortable!

When I sign up my students for co-op, they've already heard from me once about their options with regard to harassment and discrimination; it's part of my syllabus. We're going for the win-win; eliminating the problem while salvaging the internship whenever possible. I want to validate her and her behavior by coming to me when she's noticing things that are interfering with her ability to learn. So I want to make sure that any student—male or female—when they do step forward, they really hear that I appreciate that that's the right thing to do.

So then we talk about what she would like to have happen. What's the outcome she would like? In a scenario like that one, typically the student would say: "Well, I like my supervisor, I like the work, I appreciate the overtime, but I feel this supervisor is going beyond my comfort level. I don't really want to go to dinner with him, and I don't think I want to have any personal relationship, so I want to communicate that." So I talk to the student about some options.

I offer the opportunity to role play to give students the chance to practice what they want to say. I tell students that if they absolutely don't feel comfortable doing it, then that's something that I can participate in, but I'm always encouraging the students to do it themselves because that's empowering. I'm very interested in students feeling able to deal with workplace issues themselves with support. I don't insist, but I would say that 99.9% of the time I'm very effective at helping the students pick a solution to a situation like this where they themselves take the initiative. They can write a letter or a note or speak with the supervisor in front of someone else so that there's a witness. That makes them comfortable and not feeling like they're behind closed doors in an office where the power situation isn't comfortable for them.

I encourage them to be very clear about what they want to say, but to do it in such a way that they're not accusing the supervisor of anything because nothing's happened so far. Just say "I'm not comfortable having dinner with you. I think it's very kind, and I appreciate that you think that I'm doing a good job but that just feels like it's moving in the area of a more personal relationship. I'd like to keep this very professional. I do really like working for you, and I think I'd like to continue as long as that's an option." So I'd practice with the student because a lot of times students are so uncomfortable and have never had to confront this. They don't really know what to say.

I often tell students that if they need to or want to they can always use me as the scapegoat, if you will. They can say, "My instructor at the college has told us that we should never do that, that it's really inappropriate." If they feel that they have to use that excuse, I give them permission to do that. "We've talked a lot about professionalism in the workplace and we were told that during our internship it was very important to keep separate that sort of behavior."

I try to develop four or five options that will work for them and we talk about the advantages and disadvantages of each option. "What do you think will work? Why does that one feel right? Do you want to practice it? Do you want to go home and think about it and then come back and practice it? Do you want to call me right before? How can I give the most support to you?" And then if it looks as though they're not able to handle it, sometimes I'll bring in a counseling staff member. Every program has counselors and advisors and sometimes that's appropriate. I've only had that happen once where that worked out to be the best solution, but I take advantage of whatever is going to be best for the student in terms of trying to work that out. I want students to know that we want them to feel like they got a great experience, being very positive about their learning and having the employer feel positive about them and the college.

RESPONSE #2 – KATE MCLAUGHLIN, NORTHEASTERN UNIVERSITY

Well, because there's been nothing explicit here, the first thing that I would do is try to help the student by recognizing that you could have a legitimate issue that this guy is making the moves on you. But he could just be someone who is genuinely concerned about your walking home after dark and is genuinely appreciative of you, so try not to jump to conclusions... but definitely keep your eyes open.

The other thing is look for ways out of the situation that allow you to gracefully avoid it. If you're working late on a regular basis, then figure out ways for you to get home where you're not walking in the dark—a friend's coming to pick you up, or better yet your boyfriend. That's always a great way to deflect those sorts of things. If you can say "You know what? I need the exercise while I walk to the subway, and then I've got a whole bunch of reading I've got to do on the train. I really appreciate this but I'm not at all worried."

Because as a woman you have instincts, you pick up on vibes, but they're not always correct. You don't want to misjudge someone, but you also want to keep yourself out of trouble. And one of the things that I have found from my own personal experience is that the more independent I behave and the more I utilize humor to convey that, the less I find myself in situations where I'm feeling like somebody has control over me.

An example of using humor would be this. He says, "You know, I'd love to take you to dinner." I might say, "That would be wonderful, but I'm on a diet and restaurants are just completely off my list right now. The servings are enormous and the temptation is just too much." Personalize it in a way that is maybe self-deprecating, sometimes that's an easier way to go about it. But take the focus off of the two of you. Another idea: "That would be really cool except that I've got this big beach vacation coming up with my boyfriend, and I really want to fit in my bathing suit. Restaurants? I just can't do them."

Then there are more explicit situations. I once had a situation where I was at a conference with a presenter I worked with for a long time. I was wearing a skirt that I would no longer wear because frankly I was in my twenties. I could pull it off then, and now I can't. But the male presenter walked into the booth, and we sit down, we start talking. This is a guy I've worked with for years. He's like, "You know what? You have really great legs." I said, "Thank you" and immediately changed the subject. Whatever's going on there, just deflect the situation and move on to a different subject. Because the more you communicate that you're either not interested or you see what's going on and you're not going to let it happen, the more likely they'll stop trying.

Humor is a great tool because it changes the situation generally without hurting feelings. What you really want to avoid the most is if this guy is hitting on her is getting to that point where he gets explicit—either tries something or says something and she has to actually turn him down. You want to avoid that because then it's a point of no return. Here you can pull back.

The thing I'd also do is ask her to look at other hints. Does he ever call you nicknames? If the guy has ever called you "kiddo," you're completely safe. When I was 20, 21, I had a couple different bosses that would call me kiddo. And they were definitely paternalistic, but it was completely harmless. I was 20, and it annoyed me because I wanted to be seen as a grownup, but, at the same time, it was completely non-threatening. Here we have a guy who if he's married, he has kids, if he's got a daughter, this could be the paternal instinct kicking in. We don't know.

Don't assume the worst—just keep your eyes open because most people are good people. There's the Anne Frank quote: "I still believe underneath it all people are really good at heart." Make that assumption. But remember that sometimes people do things that aren't so good at heart. It's human nature that people are attracted to each other. But it's very unprofessional for someone in that position to try and take advantage of it. So if the guy is attracted to you, well, that's too bad for him.

REFLECTIONS ON "IS THIS SEXUAL HARASSMENT?"

The respondents clearly understood the delicate nature of the situation, given that we can't tell the manager's true intentions here. I was very interested to see how the idea of using humor came up as a tactic; that's something that hadn't occurred to me, but it makes sense.

I also was interested to see that the focus was much more on coaching the student as opposed to jumping in to intervene directly. This is actually a controversial point. I know that some professionals believe that educators should always make the company's human resources manager aware of any case of sexual harassment. The argument is that if the company is not aware of it, officially, then we don't know if the perpetrator has a history of this behavior. There is also a legal point that is troubling here: If a professional is aware that unequivocal sexual harassment is going on but does not report it to anyone, could legal action be taken against the university?

This is worrisome. Still, my philosophy on sexual harassment is a little different, and not everyone will agree with it. I think that if we're dealing with an individual who is feeling vulnerable and powerless, then I want to empower that individual. If I intervene directly and broach the matter with HR against the student's wishes, then I may be increasing her sense of vulnerability and powerlessness.

Instead, my inclination is to start off with plenty of questions to get a sense of how serious the situation is. If I were to believe that the student's safety was in jeopardy, I might indeed get HR involved—even against the student's wishes. I definitely would contact our university's Affirmative Action specialist to make sure I have clued in someone who knows the legal aspects better than I do. Generally, though, I would be more inclined to define the realm of possibility for the student and allow the victim to choose what happens next. On one extreme, we could do nothing and see what happens, trying to avoid the individual. If the behavior was mild and/or the work term was almost over, then some students might opt for that. On the other extreme, the student or I could go to HR and file an official complaint.

There also are many options in between. As suggested by my fellow educators, coaching the student on how to deflect the behavior indirectly or confront it more directly is a definite option and a less extreme one than filing a report.

If the behavior strikes me as less ambiguous in terms of constituting harassment, I would make a stronger case for reporting it to the powers that be at the company. The biggest argument for doing so is that we are making other co-ops, interns, and full-time employees more vulnerable if we sit on our hands. That said, I am personally very reluctant to force a student to report the behavior or to do so myself. For me, the analogy would be a case of rape. Would I encourage an individual to report an attack? Absolutely. But I believe that the decision should be owned entirely by the individual.

It's very natural that a student will fear the consequences of reporting sexual harassment. The victim may fear that the perpetrator may seek revenge or that the company will punish them indirectly for being a "whistle blower." This is by no means the norm, but I can never promise a student that there will be no negative consequences to reporting such behavior.

A few years ago, I had a student report a manager's sexual harassment. Without going into a very long story, the upshot was that the employer's lawyer investigated the matter for several weeks and ultimately the manager was terminated. However, the lawyer also claimed that my student had performance issues—something that no manager had raised with her before. The lawyer also lied to me directly, telling me that my student was moved to another department because of workload issues, when another person in HR had told me that this was not remotely true... and every manager and intern with any connection to the situation corroborated that! Most disturbingly, my student was fired a few months later. The lawyer claimed to have information indicating that the student had been falsifying her time sheets. It was all very suspicious, to say the least.

I had another situation around the same time that was different. My student was called in by HR to ask if she could corroborate a full-time employee's complaint of sexual harassment by their mutual manager. My student could indeed corroborate the complaint, as she had received some appalling e-mail propositions herself, but she was anxious about accusing her manager, given that he had the power to decide whether she would receive a full-time offer. She told HR as much but then did cooperate. The manager was forced to take a short, unpaid leave of absence, and my student was told she would now report to a new manager—who happened to be her old manager's best friend. When she pointed out that this was not acceptable, she was told in so many words to shut up and get back to work. We finally got a better outcome, but it took weeks and weeks to get the company to do the right thing.

Again, most organizations will take complaints of sexual harassment seriously and deal with them appropriately, just as you would wish of any educational partner. Occasionally, though, companies will take steps to cover themselves legally by discrediting individuals who report such behavior. It's important to know that this can happen. In any event, sexual harassment cases are extremely emotional and exhausting. As for how to handle specific situations, you should talk to any Affirmative Action specialists and/or legal counsel at your institution before determining how to proceed.

SCENARIO #3 – "A TRANSSEXUAL STUDENT'S RESUME"

A coordinator in our criminal justice co-op program came to me years ago with a dilemma. A student of his had presented a resume to him, and it prominently featured information as follows: "Vice President of Boston Transgender Student Association, Treasurer of Bisexual Student Association" as well as "job experience" that was basically fundraising for these causes. There was almost nothing on the resume that had anything whatsoever to do with criminal justice. The coordinator felt paralyzed by the situation. He wasn't sure about what advice he should give to the student. Should he insist that those items be removed from the resume, given that they could be fatal to a job search in a relatively conservative field? What would your advice to this colleague be?

RESPONSE #1 – KERRY MAHONEY, UNIVERSITY OF WATERLOO

The key for me is that the student needs to make the decision about what to include on his or her resume. But it is our job to advise students about the potential impact of what they may choose to include. Any reference to sexual orientation needs to be carefully considered; the same applies to religious or political affiliations. While it may not be fair, including such information could be used by an employer to discriminate against the student.

I advise students to deal with this resume dilemma by listing the experience in a generic way. In this case, rather than indicating they were Vice President of the Transgender Student Association, they might just say they were Vice President of a University of XXX Student Association but not name it. Then, include all of the great experience they gained using accomplishment-oriented bullet points.

It is also wise to query the student as to how they feel about listing the experience as above. Maybe they wouldn't want to work for an employer who would view their experience negatively. The risk of getting fewer interviews may be mitigated by the knowledge that at least the interviews that they get are with employers that may be more welcoming.

Ultimately, it is a personal decision for the student to make. Interestingly, had you asked me this ten years ago, I think I'd have given a more definitive "don't do it" reply. Now my advice is: "It's a choice—here is the upside and here is the downside." We all evolve.

RESPONSE #2 – CHARLIE BOGNANNI, NORTHEASTERN UNIVERSITY

I'd say in all of these cases it's very important not to impose your beliefs or your values on a student because it's very easy to do that. I'll give you an example. I happen to be a Democrat; I'm a liberal. I had a student last year who was part of some Republican group and had it all over his resume—had it under student groups, volunteered for some local politician who is Republican. I even think one of his interests was listed as Republican politics—I mean it was all over the resume. What I said to the student is "Okay, let's look at the positive things here. You're involved; you're active. I think that's a good thing. But be careful about being too blatant about your beliefs or background, whether political, religious, sexual orientation, whatever, because they could be perceived differently by an employer."

Unless obviously there's something blatantly wrong—errors on the resume, terrible format—I will say to the student "It's your resume; it's your choice, and if you feel strongly about putting that on your resume, that's fine. Understand that there may be an employer out there who's going to screen you out—not interview you, not hire you, and never tell you it's because of that information on your resume—but you might not get the job. Obviously, it's illegal not to hire a student based on sexual orientation or religious beliefs or whatever, but you may have an employer who does that.

I think it's similar to when students come in with a nose ring or a tongue stud. I had a student this past year whose hair was pretty long, and he had a little bit of a beard. Now I happen to work in a field that's very professional—I'm in accounting—and it's certainly become less conservative, but it's still a fairly conservative profession. The student's name was Dylan—his parents named him after Bob Dylan—and I said, "Dylan, it's your choice. I know you like to have your hair a little long and to have a little bit of a beard. Are there going to be some employers who may decide not to hire you because of that? There could be. But that's absolutely your choice." He compromised—trimmed the hair a little bit, and beard was neater. He still had the beard, and he did end up getting a good job with a very good employer who would probably be perceived by the outside world as being a fairly conservative company, but he got the job. But he knew going into it that he might be facing some problems.

You need to treat students as adults. I often say "This isn't high school where we're going to tell you what to wear. You're in college; you're an adult. You need to make these decisions. Understand the consequences, understand the ramifications of your actions so that if three months from now you've been on ten interviews and you don't have a job, and you get the sense that's what it was, fine. But we talked about that, didn't we?"

RESPONSE #3 – ANITA TODD, UNIVERSITY OF CINCINNATI

My personal philosophy on a resume is that you do not want to put anything on a resume that could potentially get you de-selected as a candidate and you want to include items that will get you selected. In the case of this student's resume, it appears the student did not include items that should be there and included some items that could get the student discriminated from a job. So my first piece of advice is to find items that should be included on the resume that relate to criminal justice. Work with the student to focus most importantly on these items. Next, I believe in being very honest with the student about what their choices are of inclusion on a resume and what the consequences may be. The student has to decide what they consider de-selection. If a student is transgendered and their philosophy is "I don't want a company that does not accept me for who I am," then the items should be on their resume and the student should recognize there are going to be some companies that will not choose them for this reason, but the ones who do may be the companies in which the student will feel most comfortable. It might take the student's employer pool down, but if they are okay with that, then it is their personal choice.

But if the student knows they really want to get a job and are not that concerned about their identity, then I would recommend to that student to eliminate some of those things or to tone it down so that it is not their full identity—just something else they do. Today, you never know what is going to offend somebody or affect somebody's decision. I will see things like Young Republicans and Young Democrats, and you have to tell students that someone might discriminate against them because of their political views. If you do not want to get in fights over dinner, you do not talk about religion or politics. Same thing on a resume, you do not want it to create controversy.

Fundamentally, the student has to make the decision; it is their resume. But I need to make sure they recognize all the ramifications of their resume choices. If I presented those choices and they decide, knowing the options, then that is okay. I have done my job.

REFLECTIONS ON "A Transsexual Student's Resume"

This one actually happened many years ago. My advice was generally consistent with what you've just read; I told my colleague that he should focus on making sure that this student understood the options and the positive and negative consequences of each. I think I laid it out pretty specifically. There definitely are some positives to including that information. By being forthcoming about being transgender, the student could go into the work environment knowing that this was a known and accepted fact up front. And if the student had felt closeted in terms of sexual orientation and identity over much of a lifetime, maybe the student would have a strong need to be totally open about it now.

On the negative side, though, you might run into outright discrimination, as others have indicated. However, I think I would worry even more about a manager who looks at the resume and thinks, "You know, I could really care less whether this person is straight, gay, bi, celibate, whatever... But what troubles me is that this resume seems more intent on making a statement on that front as opposed to trying to convince me that they have the skills we need in a candidate!" So I think that there a few ways that such a resume could backfire, even if it's not a blatant case of discrimination.

At the same time, I would have to acknowledge that there are pros and cons to omitting or obscuring that information. Yes, the student might be more likely to get an interview or an offer, but it could create an awkward moment at an interview or in the early days of a job. To not acknowledge this at all might seem to be a lack of transparency, and I think even a liberal employer might be distracted when meeting the student, depending on where they're at with the process of changing gender.

In the end, though, I agree wholeheartedly that professionals are sometimes too quick to tell students what can and can't be on a resume. With the exception of fixing outright errors or putting my foot down because a resume has formatting inconsistencies or just plain looks bad, I am reluctant to tell a student that they can't make their own judgment calls on resumes.

This is also one of those cases that you may never encounter during your whole career. I still wanted to include it because you definitely are going to be dealing with analogous situations with resumes, job offer decisions, and so forth.

SCENARIO #4 – "A SECOND CHANCE?"

Last year I dealt with a student who had received a so-so review from his first co-op. He got a job far outside of Boston for his second co-op. Within a few weeks, he was abruptly fired from the job. The employer said that he frequently missed work for "quasi-legitimate reasons:" various illnesses, car problems, and so forth. He also seemed uninterested in doing much at work. I talked to the student, who seemingly was stunned by the termination. He acknowledged the frequent absences and said that he'd just had really bad luck. He also said that there really wasn't much work to do at the job. I called the employer back, and they acknowledged that this was true: "We don't really give co-ops much work to do; we just think it's nice if we pay them well, but we don't expect to get much out of them."

The student very badly wanted me to help him find another job. I talked to two colleagues about whether I should do so. They said that they wouldn't because past behavior was the best predictor of future behavior. I agreed to some extent but also felt that the employer was partly responsible by hiring a student that they didn't really need. Would you give the student a second chance?

RESPONSE #1 – KIRK PATTERSON, UNIVERSITY OF WATERLOO

They all make mistakes; that's my belief. I have that right now—a student who was just dismissed last week. "I'm better than his full-time employee," the student told me, so he has no concept why he was being fired. I've worked with students and had that situation with a student where it's a grey area, but what I used to say to them is "Look, you've been dismissed. I have the authority (during my College tenure) to put the co-op as complete or incomplete on the transcript, and that's my final call. I can be overruled by the Dean, but it's my decision."

And I say "Okay, here's the deal. I honestly shouldn't be working with you because if that employer does give you an F on the transcript or on the evaluation form, it will have to go through. If they just release you as marginal, fine, but in the interim if you want to work, get out there and start looking. I'm not going to put you in the system until you prove yourself. I can't put you back into the pool. But I'll support you: I'll give you tools to go look for a job. I'll approve a job if it works in your area, but you are on your own, and if I see one slip-up, you're cooked."

And I have done that, I've seen exactly as you've said, getting fired was probably the best thing that happened. It turned them right around and they went on and performed fantastically. They learned from their mistakes. We've all done that. And that's why I can relate to it. I made my mistakes, too, and if I hadn't had an employer back me up and give me a second chance, I don't know where I'd be today either. We all have to learn, and should we penalize them to the nth degree? Some of us are from the school of hard knocks and may want to but we have to think what is best for all concerned. I think it's a judgment call. It really is. You know your students, you know everyone you're working with, and if you know your employer you can always go back and talk to the employer and say, "Well, was it just not a match? Do you think the student really deserves a second chance? Or what?" I've even had an employer take back a student and say "We'll give him one more shot here. I'll hold off giving him his termination; we'll give him three more weeks to turn around, but he's going to be expected to produce."

RESPONSE #2 – KATE MCLAUGHLIN, NORTHEASTERN UNIVERSITY

Well to me this is a tremendous opportunity. You can take this student and really help him learn a lot from this whole thing. First of all, I would work with him. However in doing so, I would be laying down a lot more structure. To let him know that he screwed up. And that if I trust him to go out and work with another employer, he'd have to not only do a decent job but do an outstanding job. Getting sick, having car trouble, these are excuses.

You need to do everything you can to keep from getting sick. I talk about that in my class. "You guys are in a horrible situation. You live in the dorms; everyone eats junk and you're exposed to every bug that comes through town. Get yourself healthy. Don't go out and stay out all night before work because you actually need sleep. You lose opportunities when you're out sick." You let him know that if you put your neck out for him, if he screws up again, he's done. Give him a second chance but lay it down hard. And be clear with the employers that he could have simply had a string of bad luck. But he didn't handle it well. You're going to provide some guidance to him in how to handle that sort of thing. But you need them to not only provide a job that has solid structure, but also high expectations. Because this sort of student is one that really needs to know that they expect you to really perform at the same level as all of your co-workers. And that you're not expected to do less just because you're the co-op student. The higher the expectations, generally the greater the results.

So I would give the kid a second chance, but I would provide some serious structure. Probably say, "Okay, I want you checking in with me every two weeks. What's going on? Are you getting to work on time every day? Have you had any days where you've had to take off? What have you been doing? I would require them to check in every two weeks, and it might not be for the rest of the co-op. It might just be for the next month or two. Certainly that would work for us, but those are the students that very often benefit the most. If they're still talking to you after something like that happened, that's a good sign because many of the students that I've had get fired from their jobs, they generally vanish. Then there's no opportunity for them to learn.

RESPONSE #3 – CHARLIE BOGNANNI, NORTHEASTERN UNIVERSITY

I'm going to be honest with you. I'm probably not the best person to talk to about this because I probably give too many students second or third chances which I shouldn't do, and I've been burnt—twice this year. I had two students who didn't get fired, but both got very poor evaluations and were on the brink of getting fired. In both cases, I kind of took their word for it that there were extenuating circumstances and so forth. They're both on co-op as we speak, and both are not doing well.

Literally I got a call two days ago; one of them is on the brink of being fired. Same thing as before—the tiredness, the attendance, the whole thing. The other guy was more an issue of effort. This is an interesting case: smart guy, no question that he can do the work, lack of effort. There was not enough on his evaluation for me to say I can't place you again. But I know enough people in this organization that it's a flag. He said to me, "No, no, it's the culture of the organization; it wasn't right for me. Trust me." Well, guess what. I saw the employer recently, and there are about six students working there. The employer says, "Everybody's doing great except for Brad." What was it about Brad? Just effort and commitment. In the accounting profession, everybody's expected to work Saturdays. I think he's worked one Saturday in the past four months. There's always an excuse as to why he can't do it.

Let me give you more of a sort of general answer. I think you give a second chance if it's a student on their first co-op, and they weren't fired for anything that was horrific: you know, stealing money, falsifying a time sheet. Nine out of ten times, it's standard behavioral stuff: attendance, tardiness. I tend to give that person a second chance, and I think most people in our profession would. You talk to them, you work with them. You tell them that this can't happen again. You tell them what the consequences are. And there are students who rebound and do very well; we've all had success stories like that.

It's true that past behavior often is an indicator of future behavior. It usually is, but I would also argue that we've all had cases where students turn it around. I had a case just a couple of years ago, a student didn't do well on his co-op when he worked at a very conservative financial institution. It was a completely conservative culture—suit and tie every day, whereas you could wear jeans at his first job. And he really struggled, almost got fired. On his next co-op, I had real reservations about it. In fact on his third coop, I had to recommend him for an overseas job. He said the issue was the culture; he said he was a laid-back kind of guy. So I recommended him for the overseas position, and he did a great job. So I was glad I gave him a recommendation because I would have felt badly if I didn't. It's a case-by-case situation, it really is.

RESPONSE #4 – BERNADETTE FRIEDRICH, MICHIGAN STATE UNIVERSITY

I would without a doubt give the student a second chance. As I was listening to you tell the story and what your colleagues said, I was like "What? Our whole point here is to teach the students." If you don't pass a class, you have the opportunity to take it over. We have all made mistakes. I would put the fear of God or whatever power I had into the student and say, "I'm putting my job on the line; I'm putting my reputation on the line. I know that this company in the past has had great experiences for students. They've had lots of opportunities, and I'm looking at your evaluation. You weren't so hot the first time around, and now you've messed this up. Whatever the experience that you may have had there, instead of not going to work, you should've called me and said, 'You know what, they're not giving me enough work to do.'" That's something we talk to students about—if you're not getting a good experience, if you're making copies, you need to tell me. Make this an experience for the student. "This is it; this is your last chance. Here's an opportunity for you, this is an employer that we've worked with before and don't screw it up or we won't be helping you."

I had an employer tell me that if we allowed a student to have another experience that they wouldn't work with us anymore. "I just want you to tell me that you're not going to let this student work for another employer because then how do I know that I'm not just getting someone who's like this?" An engineering student worked for a power company, did work that was related, not probably our strongest co-op experience—tracking lines and doing a lot of documenting for this experience. He had worked for the company for three semesters, and had received great evaluations each semester.

For his last semester, he was supposed to hand in his badge, his all-weather gear, and whatever else he had from the company. For some reason, during the last week of work, stuff happened —car trouble—and he didn't turn it in. When they contacted him, he couldn't find it. He had a new car and he didn't move all his stuff out of the old car, the whole convoluted story. The company was very, very upset. They were really concerned about their ID badge; they came in and had a sit-down with us and with my supervisor, who was the director of the program at the time. They wanted to just talk it out and tell us their concerns, and we listened politely to all those things and the employer really said, "I want to know that you won't give this student another opportunity."

Much to the displeasure of my supervisor, I said, "I will help this student. He's had great evaluations, you've done nothing but praise his work, you've paid him, you brought him back for three semesters. He made one mistake and that's questionable at the end of the experience, and you're telling him that he should never have another shot at a job? The whole point of this is a learning experience and I think the student has learned a tremendous lesson in this." The student was stressed out about it. They were quite upset. We did ultimately place other students with that company, but my concern was I'm not going to criticize this one student for basically one mistake.

REFLECTIONS ON SCENARIO #4

This scenario is especially intriguing because I also have presented it in my prep class and asked students what they would do if they were in my shoes as co-op coordinator. It makes for a terrific case study, as it turns out. I give them an extended version of what happened, and I ask the students to assess what percentage of the blame belongs with the employer versus the student. Last time I did this, there was an amazing disparity of opinion. Some thought that the fault was as much as 90 percent on the student's end of it, while others thought it was as little as 20 percent.

Then I ask them what they would do if they were in my shoes in terms of giving them a second chance. Almost invariably, they would do just that. Then I tell them what actually happened.

I did just about everything described here. Kate McLaughlin's response is pretty close to how I handled it. I made sure that I conveyed that he definitely was at least partially responsible for the situation. I thought he had shown bad judgment and communicated poorly about his illnesses, and when we dug into the car troubles his explanations were pretty lame to me. So I kind of read him the riot act and even frankly told him that I was going against the advice of two colleagues by giving him a second chance.

So he got another job through one of my colleagues, a first-time employer. It was much closer to Boston, and they definitely had challenging work. So I knew we had addressed two legitimate problems that he had faced in the first job. Well, within three weeks, we started getting complaints from the employer. It was basically the same stuff—a spotty record with regard to attendance and punctuality, and a mediocre level of performance. I was furious and sent a pretty scathing e-mail. As before, he seemed very surprised and claimed that his new boss had not communicated to him about these concerns. I very adamantly reminded him that *I* had communicated to him very clearly on these matters.

In this case, the employer really didn't want to fire the student. They needed the labor! But the litany of excuses became unbearable. He left work at 3 p.m. one day because he said he needed to renew his license. I looked online and saw that the Department of Motor Vehicles was open till 7 p.m. that night. When I mentioned this to the student, he replied, irritably, "Well, I didn't know that!" To which I said, "Well, I did, because I took 60 seconds to look it up online." He also asked for Patriot's Day off (a holiday for some but not all Massachusetts organizations) so he could watch the Boston Marathon with his sister, and he got his hackles up when I suggested that this was a bad idea given that his absenteeism rate was about 20 percent.

The final straw was when he called in sick with an alleged case of conjunctivitis before a Monday morning planning meeting. The employer said, "I just never know if he's going to be here or not, so it gets hard to allocate work to him, not knowing if it will get done." We lost the employer as a result. The student asked for a *third* chance in the fall, and I declined. To his credit, he found his own job and performed well. We had a good, unemotional talk about it a couple of months ago, and it was clear to me that he had grown up a great deal. I told him that I'd often wondered if I'd done the right thing and if I could've done anything more that would've helped him see the light and avoid termination. He seemed to feel badly that I was thinking along those lines. He just said that he was going through some things in his life at that point that would've made it impossible for him to be a successful worker, and he apologized for the harm his actions had caused the university.

I tell students this story because I do want them to understand that getting referred out to employers is a *privilege* and not a *right*. And I want them to see that these are judgment calls, and it's easy to be wrong. I just hope that they see that a coordinator who opts against referring a student out to an employer really isn't trying to be punitive; he's trying to think of the big picture. If I have another problem with this employer, will I lose the position permanently? It's easy to say that every student should get every chance to pursue any job, but what about future students? Is it fair for innumerable students to *not* get an opportunity to do a great job at a great company because the coordinator knowingly referred out a risky student and then, lo and behold, the person was a disaster?

Yet the final punch line is that I probably will continue to give a second chance in the future to students who have had similar issues. It will depend on the circumstances, of course, and maybe I'll do some things differently. Maybe taking a little more time after the termination would've helped. Maybe I could've required him to show up at my office every day at 8:30 for a week or two, just to make sure he actually could do that. Perhaps probing deeper to attempt to surface the underlying personal problems would've helped. I still can't shrug it off. Yes, it was the student's responsibility, but I still feel haunted by what I might've done differently.

SCENARIO #5 – "PLAYING GOD"

Several years ago, I got a call from a new employer with an exciting opportunity. A well-known firm was offering well-paid, challenging jobs in Florida with free housing in furnished condos. They also were paying for round-trip airfares—one per month over the work term! The only catch was that they were calling in early December, wanting students for early January. I had only eight or nine students available, and only one or two of them were people who had done everything right in the preparation process. The others had not impressed me during the job search process, and their lack of proactive, responsible behavior made me wonder if they could be trusted to go to Florida and do a good job.

It was evident to me that if we had a student or two go down and succeed, then this relationship could expand significantly over time. But I also worried that if they ended up hiring five or six co-ops and had substantial problems with two or three of them, then that relationship might get derailed. So what would you do? Would you refer all candidates and let the cards fall where they may—more of a "free market" approach—or would you "play God" and determine that only some students' resumes should be sent? To what degree would you make recommendations to the employer regarding who they should hire?

RESPONSE #1 – NANCY JOHNSTON, SIMON FRASER UNIVERSITY

That's the coordinator dance, right? Because you're an advocate for all three stakeholders. The institution: Are the students going to represent us well? The student: Should I minimize their opportunities? And the employer: Do I want to send them a doofus and not be able to place with them again? So you've got these tensions that chronically exist within co-op. One thing I would say is a really useful exercise to help begin to understand how to respond in those situations that have tension is to understand who's your number-one customer. Yes, co-op can't work without any of the three. They're all important. But who, at the end of the day, if everything were equal, would you defer to? That alone will help you in any of these kinds of situations.

Here at Simon Fraser, we've decided that it's the student. Don't get me wrong: Employers should think it's them; the institution should think it's the institution, and the student should feel it's them. Actually, the student probably thinks it's not them in many cases! They think we advocate for employers. But at the end of the day, you'd say, "Okay, what's the best for these students? Well, these three deserve it. I'm going to send them down no holds barred, and I'm going to say to the employer, 'These three are strong students; we think that they can meet your needs.' The other six, it isn't best to send them down there because they're going to get blown out of the water, or they're going to go down and have a negative experience. And then we're going to be in a situation that I could've foreseen but didn't mitigate."

So I personally—ideally, if I had time—would've e-mailed those five or six students and said "Here's an employer opportunity. My concerns with your resume and your behavior during the job search are as follows. Please indicate if you have a strong interest in this and how you would respond to my concerns." This is if you had a perfect world, right? You probably can't even find some of them. And probably half of them would self-eliminate by not answering and proving that they aren't responsive, so boom, gone. And the others you would send down with a little note to the employer saying "Here's my second-round group. I have some concerns about these candidates, but the students have assured me, etc. Have a look; be critical." That's the perfect world, but that's the world where the student interest comes first.

If you said, "Well, we're a private-sector institution; we've got really strong bonds with community; we're hooked into the development office, and industry comes first..." then you send your three, and you tell them "I've got six others, but they're not good enough for you." Right? And if the institution is the most important stakeholder, then you place as many darn students as you can. You'd send all ten and hope that they hire eight, and pray to God that the five problematic ones that you sent don't screw up, but at least you've got your placement numbers up for the semester, and sadly often that's the only thing an institution measures.

So it's interesting. When we get stuck as coordinators with these dilemmas, it really helps as a coordinator to be clear on the culture of where you work. What's my number-one priority?

[In response to the fact that some professionals would opt instead for a more "free-market" philosophy in which all candidates are sent out], I would say that if you were running a placement agency, then that would be completely accurate. So I would say to someone with that viewpoint, "Why don't you just have a placement agency about two miles off your campus, unencumbered by all this educational crap? Why don't you? It would be way cheaper. What is your role? What is the role that you play in a free-market value post-secondary?" Because if you just free-market value take anyone who comes your way and send them out, you're simply the mechanics. You're simply the nuts and bolts. You're a placement agency. Learning occurs, at best, by happenstance.

RESPONSE #2 – RONNIE PORTER, NORTHEASTERN UNIVERSITY

Sometimes as educators we are in those situations and we have to make decisions based on what we think is best. Having a well-run program is a balancing act. We need to first and foremost meet the needs of our students. However, in order to maintain good opportunities for our students we need to be responsive to the needs of our employer partners. One of the benefits of knowing the students that we work with is that we have greater insight into what their interests, strengths, and abilities are. Knowing the employers and having a good understanding of the companies and job descriptions can enable us to facilitate good experiences for both students and employers. Some employers expect that we will prescreen candidates for them while others prefer to do it themselves. Sometimes in order to make everything work there is a little bit more of a matching process, and I don't see anything wrong with that. Obviously it's a case-by-case situation. I would never want to run a whole program like that but for certain situations we do need to make judgment calls as professionals.

As co-op coordinators we have to see the big picture and how to make it all work as well as it can for, first and foremost, the students and also for the employers. We do have to make decisions that we think are best as we go along to have a good, strong program. Employers trust us and it is important that we provide them with appropriate candidates. We have to make decisions as we go along. Sometimes we're going to be right and sometimes we're not going be right. I think over time with experience you're probably right more than you're not right because you have a sense of things through your experiences.

RESPONSE #3 – BRENDA LeMASTER, UNIVERSITY OF CINCINNATI

The older I get the less comfortable I am with "playing God." In this scenario, I would start with making sure the potential employer knew that I considered the opportunity one that could be a mutually beneficial long-term partnership. I would let the employer know exactly where we were in the placement process and when the ideal time to begin the placement/interview process would be for future reference. I would share the resumes of those students who were eligible— regardless of whether or not I was entirely comfortable with all of them—and make it clear to the employer that I could recommend those students I knew well.

I would also let the employer know that if we were unable to fill all open slots for the upcoming term I would work very hard to fill them for the next term. I would emphasize again the long-term nature of our developing partnership. As a note, I have had many similar situations over the years and as often as not what sounds like an amazing opportunity often disappears after a short-term need is met.

RESPONSE #4 – CHARLIE BOGNANNI, NORTHEASTERN UNIVERSITY

That is a really good question because I do struggle with this. I guess I don't subscribe to either philosophy completely; I guess I'm somewhere in between. I probably lean a little more toward the free market one; I lean more to letting things take shape, letting things happen on their own.

I don't deny there are times where I maybe get a little involved and I try to tweak things a bit to make them happen if I think it's going to help both student and the employer. I think the only time I'll get involved there is if I know something about the students and their past that I think can help the employer make the right decision. For example, if I knew a student did not get a very good evaluation at the previous job versus a student that did, and the employer asked me what I knew about their backgrounds, I'm going to offer that. I'm going to share that, but again in general I think I try to make the employers make the decision. I prefer not to get too involved in that; I don't necessarily think that's my role to be quite honest with you. I think my role is to guide the students and help the students.

But have I done it? Sure, I'm sure I've done it at times, and I know that there are coordinators that do that, and that's not to say they're not successful; they are. But as a new coordinator in this profession I would say go into it without a preconceived notion of which way you're going to operate and see kind of on a case-by-case basis which works better and which makes you feel better. I don't think I'd step back and say this is absolutely the way you want to operate, but I would say in general try not to play God. I don't think that works.

REFLECTIONS ON "PLAYING GOD"

This scenario proved to be the most controversial, to some degree. There are professionals who are very reluctant to put their fingers into these situations, and there are others who think that this is absolutely justifiable and that a free-market approach is more akin to acting as a placement agency. Yet in reflecting on these responses, I think there is more similarity than difference. While playing a more active role in the selection process clearly makes some people uncomfortable, it appears that just about everybody does play God to some degree.

The difference seems to lie in how you do that. On one extreme, there is the completely transparent, explicit approach as espoused by Nancy Johnston. All parties are clear on who is being referred out and who isn't, what students are strongly recommended and which ones aren't. On the other end of the spectrum, there are coordinators who want to be subtle about it, knowing and maybe even hoping that the employer might pick up on your positive comments or having your silence speak volumes.

I think that there is a balance. On the one hand, I do want students and employers to own the responsibility for their decisions. After all, they are the ones that are really forced to live with the decision for up to six months of full-time work in some co-op programs. I wouldn't want to twist anyone's arm to hire a candidate or to accept an offer. On the other hand, I think my program is going to suffer if I turn a blind eye to the whole process, allowing any student to apply for any job instead of counseling them to determine whether the job really meets their educational goals and is a good fit for both parties. If a student ends up in a job that is far too difficult or too easy—or if the student's personality is just a lousy fit with the culture—then it's a lose/lose proposition. So unlike some of my colleagues, I have been known to talk students out of accepting an offer for a job that, to me, is too entry level.

One irony here is that there are two very different ways for a professional to fall into the trap of being more of a placement professional than an educator. On one extreme, there is the way we used to do it decades ago at Northeastern: coordinators basically developed jobs and literally placed students into them in lieu of an interviewing process. It was fast and convenient, a very expedient system, really. But it denied the student the opportunity to have the learning experience of interviewing for jobs and making decisions about offers, and inevitably there were equity issues.

Yet I also would have to say that any program that merely lists a ton of jobs in a database and then lets students apply for whichever ones they choose without any real discussion or screening process is no less of a placement professional than the person who dictates where every single student works. That's more akin to computer dating than education, as far as I'm concerned. Yes, students would still have the experience of going on interviews and so forth, and it probably is much less expensive and labor-intensive than a program in which coordinators play a more active counseling role, but you can't say much more about that approach in terms of positives. Could education still occur in such a program? Sure, but many students tend to underrate or overrate their ability to get a job of a certain level. Some employers won't hire an overqualified candidate, but others have no qualms about hiring an experienced person who is not going to be challenged. So personally, I don't want to be in the business of determining precisely who works where.... but a completely laissez-faire approach makes me just as uncomfortable—maybe even more so.

REFLECTION QUESTIONS

1. Reflect on some of the toughest specific "moments of truth" that you have faced as a professional thus far. Looking back, what were the lessons learned from those experiences?

2. Having to deal with a student who wants to quit is one of the more common moments of truth that educators in our profession have to face. What would be the characteristics of a situation in which you *would* give your blessing to let a student quit a job without negative consequences from you or your institution?

3. Sexual harassment is obviously one of the most difficult situations we may have to face as professionals. How would you deal with a student who definitely was being sexually harassed but did not want to address it or have you get involved? Would you address it with the employer, even if the student didn't want you to do so?

4. Beyond blatant typos, errors, untruths, and horrible formatting, are there things that you would not allow a student to include on his or her resume? Are there other elements that you only would allow to include after some dialogue about the risks of doing so?

5. What are some specific behaviors or situations in which you no longer would be willing to give a student an additional chance as a co-op or intern?

6. There is some debate about the degree to which professionals should "play God." To what degree should educators play a role in determining who hires who? What would constitute playing too small or too great a role in hiring decisions?

CHAPTER 13

DEVELOPING EMPLOYER RELATIONSHIPS

*"The question is, then, do we try to make
things easy on ourselves or do we try to make
things easy on our customers, whoever they
may be?"*

— *Niccolo Machiavelli*

The nature of developing employer relationships is going to differ considerably from one program to the next. At Northeastern, we are fortunate to be a highly known commodity, especially in our region. We also have a very large alumni base, and we're based in a major metropolitan area. As a result, we probably get more job leads from employers calling us than what might be the case if we were a smaller school outside of a city with a lower profile in cooperative education.

Likewise, the economy and the size of an educator's workload will have a huge impact on the characteristics of your relationships with employers. During the great economy that we enjoyed in the late 1990s, I was able to develop many great jobs by simply answering the phone. After 9/11, most of us were digging through old job leads, reaching out to alums, and even cold-calling employers in some cases. Similarly, I had only about 30 students for my first referral period in 1995, so I was able to get out to 15–20 companies in my first month on the job. But when I maxed out at 155 students in January 2000, it was almost impossible to get out on the road for several months at a time. Now I have a ton of employers—more jobs than students usually—so I have to be very selective about which employers to visit and what types of jobs to develop.

Regardless, there are some fundamentals that all co-op and internship educators should know about job development. Bearing in mind that everyone's situation is different, let's review some keys to building great relationships with new employers.

MAKING TIME TO GET ON THE ROAD

There are many professionals who say that they just don't have time to visit employers. While I want to be sensitive to the staggering workloads that some professionals in our field endure—and there is no question that a heavy load is going to make it very hard to get out with any regularity—I take the attitude that you really can't afford to *not* get out on the road.

When you have not visited an employer, it's so much harder to counsel students through possible job options. For me, it's always a downer when a student brings me a job description for a company that I have never visited, asking me what the job or organization is really like. I'm reduced to studying that job description and saying, "Well, it *seems* like this type of job is *probably*…." instead of being able to give the student much more helpful information: "When you go into this place, it's deceptively quiet. You barely hear a peep, yet you still get the vibe that people are very, very focused. It's also pretty formal—you would never see a guy without a tie, even when they're crawling around to fix a computer. But I also got the sense that it's work hard, play hard: People often stay till 7 or later, but then they go out together, too."

I also say that ten minutes of time at a firm visit is usually worth more than one hour of trying to understand the job over the phone. You can get a pretty quick read on all kinds of things: manager style, attire, work environment, pace, appropriateness of space for a student employee, ease of commute, and so on.

As I'll discuss in greater detail later, there are so many good (and often unexpected) things that happen from just showing up. The fact that you made the time to just be there says a great deal to the employer about your feelings about their importance as an educational partner. When you're out there, the employer gets the opportunity to view you as a real human being as opposed to some name on an e-mail or over the phone. That starts to form a connection that will have a much greater chance of surviving the ups and down that inevitably happen in the organizational world. My colleague Elizabeth Chilvers often mentions how many recessions she has gone through in her decades as a coordinator. Having good personal relationships won't make those downturns effortless, but it can soften the impact dramatically.

One of the best pieces of advice I received as a new coordinator was to visit companies early and often. My colleagues told me that as time goes by, there are many forces that end up making you feel more tethered to campus—committee work, teaching activities, student expectations, and so on. I'm glad that I managed to get a few dozen visits under my belt early. As I talked about earlier in the book, this changed some misconceptions I had about jobs and employers, and it helped me create a vision for my program. It also made a statement to existing employers about my interest in having a real relationship with them… and some of them had felt neglected.

It might be helpful to view your firm visits as an investment of time. Yes, they take valuable time away from other activities up front, and you do need to be judicious about who to visit and when to visit them. But ultimately, a strong emphasis on visiting employers ends up saving you an unbelievable amount of time and trouble over the long haul. You are improving your ability to make sure students are choosing the most appropriate jobs to pursue, while also helping employers understand how to best hire and mentor young professionals.

Here's another way to think of it: If you feel that you *don't* have time to get out on the road at all, you have to ask yourself if you think you *do* have time to deal with students who are unhappy in their jobs or employers who are unhappy with their students, including all the negative consequences that are going to result from mismatches. Even one really bad match can scuttle your relationship with an employer permanently and sour a student on you and your program. Conversely, getting out on the road on a regular basis is going to do wonders for your level of expertise regarding employers and industry, and this will have a very positive impact on your credibility as a resource to students as well as employers.

The very worst case can arise during a bad economy. Students are going to be anxious, and they will want to meet with you more frequently. But the ultimate irony is if you are sitting in your office—available to students on a regular basis, yes—and all you can do is tell students that you don't have jobs for them. If you lack adequate jobs in terms of quantity or quality, then the best counseling in the world will still be relatively useless. Sometimes you just have to get out on the road to make things happen.

QUALIFYING LEADS

In the next chapter, I'll be talking in depth about how to prioritize your visits to existing employers. One key difference, though, between prospective employers and active employers is that it's almost never a bad idea to visit a company who has hired one of your students. However, setting up a meeting with a potential employer is more of a judgment call. In my early days, I was much quicker to say yes when just about any employer called and asked me to come out to do a pitch for the co-op program. Likewise, it was not unusual for me to cold-call an attractive company to set up a meeting, regardless of whether there was definite interest in our program.

Now there are some questions that I would want to have answered before charging out into the field to attempt to develop a new relationship. In sales lingo, I want to "qualify my leads" before investing time and energy in the pitch. So here is what I would want to know:

- Is the employer aware that Northeastern is primarily looking for jobs that are paid, full-time, six-month positions? Do they know what the approximate pay range is for the field(s) in question?

- Does this employer seem to have the types of jobs that would add something that we need to our mix of offerings for students?

- Is the employer located somewhere that will be accessible to a reasonable number of our students?

While these aren't the only questions that will matter when determining if the employer is suitable for the program, they are probably good enough when attempting to ascertain if an initial meeting is worthwhile. These questions probably seem pretty obvious, but they need to be asked and/or weighed. In my program, there is not much point going to visit an employer who absolutely cannot pay at least $12–14/hour, depending on the job and location. If they can only hire a student for 20 hours per week, then that's a deal breaker for most of our business students (though maybe not for someone interested in music industry or some other "sexy" fields outside of business). If it's a summer-only program, then that's generally not a fit either. Best to find out before you spend a half-day spinning your wheels.

Job type and location are vital to consider as well. Right now I have an unbelievable number of PC support jobs, so I would be hesitant to go out of my way to develop more through firm visits. Just the same, jobs that are more than 45 minutes from Boston are going to be a tough sell unless the position is really something extraordinary as a learning opportunity and/or in terms of pay.

The same consideration is multiplied when we go outside of Massachusetts in our program. As longs as the jobs are of good quality, we can usually drum up interest in companies located in Florida, California, Seattle, Chicago, Denver, and Dallas, and I've had really good luck with a new employer in the Salt Lake City region due to the national parks and skiing. Conversely, it often takes a *really* good job to get students interested in positions in Hartford, New Jersey, and Pennsylvania (unless we're talking about Philadelphia), and sometimes great job quality won't even help. There are exceptions—some students want to live at home to save money—but jobs can be hard to fill if they aren't in glamorous locations.

To be fair, this may be truer for schools like ours that are located in an attractive place for young people. Our Admissions Department does a great job of selling students on how great it is to go to school in Boston, which is teeming with college students. Naturally, many students want to continue to work within striking distance of Boston while on co-op. For co-op/internship programs located in suburban or rural areas, there may be almost no choice when it comes to relocating for a full-time co-op job or internship. When that's the case, moving to Hartford might seem as good as anywhere, and relocation is more likely to be accepted as an inevitability.

Once we get into that fateful first meeting, we can start going into additional questions. Will the employer be a suitable educational partner? Will they give the student meaningful work? Are they appropriate mentors and managers who will help students maximize learning? These are important questions, but they can wait until that face-to-face meeting as long as you've decided that it's worth a visit.

SPEAKING THE LANGUAGES

Ronnie Porter brought up an interesting theme in her interview. As you'll see at the end of the chapter, she talks about how co-op/internship professionals really need to use the language of educators as well as the language of the field or industry. If you're talking like an educator, your conversations are going to include some discussion of how the student's experience is going to tie into the academic curriculum and develop competencies that are going to complement what is being learned in the classroom.

Just the same, you need to be able to communicate with employers by speaking *their* language as well. You might need to ramp up in a given field through taking courses, reading up at night, talking to academic faculty, and so on. Having conversations with veteran students about what they actually have done can be very valuable. While you can't become an expert in all areas in which your students might work, you need to have a thorough understanding of the jobs in your field. What personality type is a good fit for each category of job? To what degree is the job collaborative or independent in nature? Structured or unstructured? Complex or simple? There is often some jargon or lingo to learn.

More specifically—as Nancy Chiang points out at the end of the chapter—you need to do your homework before going on a firm visit. What does the organization do? Who are their probable customers or competitors? Do they have a history of working with anyone in your institution? If you have a job description in advance, you'll want to study that carefully, perhaps looking up some unfamiliar terms and preparing some questions you might have about the job.

THE EMPLOYER AS EDUCATIONAL PARTNER

This theme was raised constantly in my interviews. Just about every expert I interviewed emphasized how important it is to think of the employer as a customer and particularly as an educational partner. This sounds good, but what does it really mean? There are many considerations here:

ENGAGE THE EMPLOYER IN DISCUSSION OF INTEGRATED LEARNING

How is this job going to tie into the academic curriculum? What learning opportunities will be available to the student? What behavioral competencies might be developed that could transfer into the classroom or into other professional roles in the future? These are all questions worth asking.

As Jacki Diani indicates in her interview, some of my colleagues have managed to get employers involved in changing curricula at the university. Over time, I have seen various individuals reach out to employers and conclude that we need to make changes in what we are teaching. After talking to some of my key employers, the Management Information Systems faculty began to ensure that a discussion of the software development life cycle is embedded in almost every MIS course. Employers develop a good sense of what our students bring to the table and what they are lacking; the institution needs to reflect on that and decide whether changes should be made.

TAKE A LONG-TERM VIEW

In any given work term, your institution needs you to get students placed in jobs. The pressure on you certainly will relent when everyone has some sort of a job. As a result, it's very tempting to make that happen as expediently as possible. I have seen professionals give unequivocally positive recommendations for students who did not deserve them, and I have heard students complain about coordinators who pushed them to accept a menial job against their better judgment. Sometimes that student probably was not going to get a better offer and needed to come to terms with that unpleasant fact, but I also have seen many cases of students who almost definitely could've obtained a better job if the coordinator could've been a little more stubborn on their behalf.

Doing the right thing is not as easy as it sounds. Any number of times, I have struggled between what is easy and expedient and readily possible versus what is difficult and inconvenient and maybe not even plausible. Years ago, I had a student with really poor English, and it took him months to get his first job. When he came back to discuss it, he immediately said that he wanted to go back to that job. Knowing that he would be in for another really tough job search due to his English—and that he would be on my doorstep all semester as a result—I'm sure I winced internally before telling him the truth: "You need to go after a more challenging job. That was a good job, but it was entry-level. You need to challenge yourself more."

What helps is taking the long-term view. Let's say that I have a student who is having a tough time getting a "real" business job—something substantial in marketing, information technology, or supply chain management. The reason that he's not getting anywhere is that he lacks any meaningful job experience. When that student gets an offer to be an administrative assistant, it solves the immediate problem. Yet I end up envisioning the next co-op cycle, and I know it's going to be the same issue all over again—a struggle to get a decent job because the student *still* lacks meaningful experience! So my motto with students has become: "Better to suffer for three months through a job search to have a good job for six months rather than obtaining a job in one month that's going to be a lousy learning experience for six months."

The same is true with employers. When you have a new employer, you might be able to twist their arm to hire three students instead of one. But if you try to force round pegs into square holes while filling those three jobs, they may end up having one good co-op and two bad ones. With that batting average, they may not come back for another term. Meanwhile, if they hire one student who is a great fit, then they might be eager to hire two students next time.

You always have the problem of ensuring that students get meaningful jobs. But it's not the responsibility of a given employer to solve that problem for you—particularly if it comes down to hiring someone who is a questionable fit. The trick is to try to develop a range of jobs that will match the range of abilities, skills, and interests that your varied group of students will be seeking. You do your best, but you don't want to force things to happen.

So what do you do with students whose track record is poor? Sometimes I have flat-out told students that I'm going to limit the jobs that they can pursue. With some jobs, I'm not willing to take a major risk based on the company's importance or my history with that employer. There are other employers whose record is as questionable as the students, and there are positions that are just hard to fill due to their location and pay. It can require some tact, but sometimes I think it's reasonable to set some limits on jobs that a student can pursue.

In the last chapter, professionals debated about "playing God." Every professional has to make decisions about how much to screen resumes or steer candidates to or away from a given employer. I always give *some* guidance to *all* students as to what jobs they should pursue, and that takes care of most potential mismatches. At times, I do take a more active role in determining which candidates get serious consideration, and not every educator agrees with me on that front. To me, it comes down to where your priority lies. Intervening to make sure that students and employers are good matches for each other just makes a great deal of sense to me, especially when taking a long-term view.

Some may say that being student-centered means that a student gets to pursue any job that they want. But if that student is a disaster, here are the very possible consequences:

■ That student has a discouraging, disappointing experience.

■ That employer decides that your program has lousy students and doesn't list the job ever again.

■ An untold number of students who *would* be great matches for that job never get the opportunity to work for that employer in the future.

I would concede that this is tricky business. I could decide that a given student is a problem who can't cut it with a given employer... and I might be wrong. If a student is persistent in wanting to pursue a given job after I've told them they can't, I certainly will hear them out and sometimes change my mind. Still, I don't believe that any student should be allowed to pursue any opportunity, regardless of their previous history or qualifications.

VIEW THE COORDINATOR ROLE AS THAT OF AN UNPAID CONSULTANT

I often tell employers that they should think me of as their unpaid consultant, though I have to acknowledge that the term sounds like an oxymoron! One of my pet peeves—and one that Kirk Patterson of the University of Waterloo echoed in his interview—is when I hear of employers calling in with a good question and getting shuffled around the university in search of an answer. Another qualm I have is when I hear of educators who strictly adhere to their job description when working with employers. In other words, their only real contact with employers is to get students official jobs for official work terms.

If you think of yourself as an unpaid consultant to employers, then there is a whole range of activities you could find yourself doing:

- Reaching out to recent alums to see if they need a full-time job to help an employer fill a position

- Finding out salary information for recent grads, even if it's outside of the majors that you handle

- Connecting an employer with an expert on the academic faculty for help with an issue or to develop a case study about the company, benefiting students as well as the organization

- Even if you don't generally help students find part-time work, you might help an employer with an immediate need by finding a student who could use some money and/or experience

This last bullet merits further comment, as I've had some colleagues tell me flat-out that this is not their job. Well, they're right. This is not remotely part of the job description, and it does create some extra work. My rationale is as follows:

- I always want employers to be thinking of me first when they have an employment need; I want to be thought of as a solution provider.

- Getting the first employee into an organization—or into a new job at an existing employer—is often the biggest challenge, and I hate to pass up an opportunity to do so.

- When placing students on a part-time basis, I can be selective about who I send, ensuring that a new employer has a very positive first experience with our program.

This approach has had amazing results at times. A few years ago, an employer called with an immediate need in mid-October. The simplest thing to do would've been to say that the next co-op term begins in January and to start interviewing soon for that. Instead, I announced the job to my preparation class, and a promising sophomore was interested. Although she was really less experienced than the employer might've hoped, I worked with the student on the strategy for the interview: She could emphasize the fact that she could work for three months part-time, then six months full-time... and then another six months part-time. So in return for training an inexperienced person, the employer could have her around for over a year! That piqued the manager's interest. He not only hired her—she stayed on for all three six-month co-ops and is still working there. Yet maybe the manager would've gone in another direction altogether if I hadn't been willing to think outside the job description. Since then, he hired a second co-op who also became a full-time employee.

Then, in early November 2008, he called me to let me know that he needed to let two experienced people go due to the financial crisis... but that he also had cut a deal to hire two additional co-ops to replace them at much lower cost! And when the economy gets better, he hopes to be able to hire these two on a full-time basis. All this started with that decision to think out of the box and help an employer with an immediate part-time need.

There are innumerable ways in which you might approach the role of unpaid consultant. The key is to develop a mentality of helping the employer rather than treating companies as if you are doing them a favor by allowing them to hire your students. As Nancy Chiang mentioned in her interview at the end of Chapter 14, employers have said to her that "you have more industry knowledge than we do!" If you are getting out to many companies, you have your finger on the pulse of who's hiring and for what types of jobs. You get to see the best practices of other employers when it comes to marketing a position, interviewing, and mentoring students, and you can share those innovative ideas with other employers.

All of these steps can be a little extra work up front, but they can reap great dividends in the long haul. The more energy you invest in creating a sense of an educational partnership, the more likely you are to have a strong program that can withstand an occasional performance problem or economic downturn.

DEVELOPING LEADS

It's certainly convenient when a job lead comes in over the phone or via an e-mail request. If the organizational community is familiar with your institution—and if the economy is reasonably good—you sometimes have the blessing of developing great new jobs with minimal effort. That's not always the case, though, so let's consider some other important avenues for job leads.

ALUMNI OUTREACH

Some colleges and universities have unbelievably great data on alums, while others are abysmal. In an ideal world, you will be able to get contact information broken out by state, major, and even by employer! At the very worst, your alumni relations group will hoard what information they have, or they won't have much of any at all. Find out what information you can get, and don't hesitate to reach out to alumni to see if they might be able to use a co-op or intern.

Alumni often make for some of the best educational partners—especially if they were co-ops or interns themselves. They don't have to be sold on what an inexperienced but energetic young professional can add to an organization, and they are more likely to be sensitive to the fact that this is an educational experience as opposed to no more than free or cheap labor.

JOB BOARDS

While I don't often go to www.monster.com, www.careerbuilder.com, or similar job sites, sometimes checking out job listings can be a useful exercise. Surprisingly, www.craigslist.com has become a great source for job listings as well; many of my seniors seeking full-time jobs tell me that they've had more luck there than with any other job board.

Typically, I don't go to job boards to try to scoop up a specific, existing job. Many of these boards are looking for people who have more experience than my students, and most listings are for full-time, permanent employees rather than a co-op term. So it's a low-percentage possibility that I'll find a match for my students. What I'm really seeking, though, is a sense for which companies clearly are in a hiring mode as well as what types of jobs they are listing. This might give me a sense of what employer might be ripe to approach about a co-op program, selling it as a way to ultimately circumvent using job boards altogether.

This is especially helpful when I'm trying to break into a new region. Years ago, I had an employer that often hired 10–15 co-ops at a time down in Tampa, Florida. Planning a visit, I thought it made sense to check out what other major employers were hiring in the region. I contacted four employers, and I managed to set up a presentation with a major corporation in nearby St. Petersburg on my next visit to Tampa. This led to a new program and a few hires.

GOOGLE AND OTHER INFORMATION SOURCES

It's important to be on top of the major employers in any regions where your students might work. In my neck of the woods, *The Boston Globe* publishes an annual business section that breaks down the top employers according to any number of useful parameters: number of employees, market capitalization, growth over the last year, industry, etc. I always check out that section with a critical eye: What companies are in growth mode and might be open to hiring our students? What companies really *should* be one of my employers, and why hasn't that happened? Depending on my needs, I might reach out to Human Resources to see if they're interested in learning more about our program. If I've chosen well, it's not unusual to find a receptive contact—maybe even an employer who has been meaning to get in touch.

Even without a helpful local newspaper, there is a wealth of options online these days. Just now I decided to Google the words "Denver largest employers" to see what I could find. Within seconds, I was scanning www.careerinfonet.org, which has a nice list of the 50 largest employers in Colorado, including their city and number of employees. Right away I was startled to see that Allstate Insurance has 17,000 employees in Colorado Springs—far more than any other employer in the state. There is also a surprising number of hospitals and medical centers on the list, and a few big high-tech employers in IBM and Hewlett-Packard. All of this might give me some starting points if I were looking to get a toehold in that region.

CAPITALIZING ON STUDENT-DEVELOPED JOBS

This is an easy and effective way to build additional opportunities. Whether or not your institution develops numerous jobs for students, there will always be students who develop their own jobs for all sorts of reasons. Maybe they have a personal connection to an employer, or perhaps they wanted jobs that fell outside of your usual offerings in terms of industry, job type, or geographical location. Regardless, following up by visiting that student in the field is a great way to build on an initial connection.

Just recently, one of my first-timers developed a job with a really interesting start-up company within public transportation of our campus. Ironically, that student did only a so-so job—something that came up in a conversation that I had with them a few months into his work term. The upshot of that dialogue was that the employer decided that they needed a more experienced student and were willing to pay very well to make that happen. They hired through me the second time around, and this second hire was offered a full-time job within the company after graduation. He also has been asked to supervise incoming co-ops, so that has been a great success all the way around.

EXPLOITING FACULTY CONNECTIONS

Depending on your field, the academic faculty in your institution may have considerable connections to industry. Cultivating a good relationship with relevant professors—giving them lists of where students are working and what they're doing; inviting an employer to be a classroom guest—definitely can lead to other employers that you may not have reached otherwise. I know one professor who consults with a large engineering firm, and he personally reviews the resumes for the two co-op jobs that this company now fills.

BUILDING DIRECTORIES

Whenever you go out to visit a company, it's a good idea to take a few extra minutes in the lobby to review the building directory if there is more than one tenant. Who else has space in the building? Offhand, do any of those organizations look plausible? Sometimes I wrap up a visit to one employer by asking if they know anyone in other companies in the building. Even if they don't, occasionally I'll try a cold call to see if I can talk to someone in HR who might have an interest. Given that I'm already in the building, the downside is low.

I had a good reminder about why this is a good practice back in September 2008. I made a long overdue visit to a company in Andover, a good 30–40 minutes north of Boston. I was right on time and thus took just a quick glance at the directory before turning around and heading toward the stairs for the second floor. Then I stopped in my tracks, remembering that I hadn't really studied the directory. Walking back for a brief scan, I was shocked to find an employer who used to hire from me a couple of years ago—right on the same floor as the new employer! After my scheduled visit, I caught up with my old contact. Just by luck, he told me that there was a new HR person in place who was interested in getting new co-ops around the country. He introduced me, and we're now talking about jobs around the country.

Of course, the best ways to develop new jobs are by maintaining the old ones properly and cross-selling at existing employers to get jobs outside of the majors they currently hire. We'll discuss that later on.

WHAT TO BRING ON A FIRM VISIT

Once you've lined up a company to visit and done some research on that organization, there are various materials that you'll want to at least consider bringing with you when you go out in the field:

- *Business Cards* – This one is pretty obvious. You'll want to have plenty of business cards with you, as you never know how many potential managers you'll meet who may want to contact you.

- *Marketing Materials* – Whether it's a slick, full-color handout about your program or something you've written up and printed out in Word, it's good to have a piece that talks about what makes your program special. I often hand out a simple one-page piece on Northeastern letterhead in which the benefits of hiring a co-op or intern (to be discussed shortly) are enumerated.

- *FAQ Document* – Earlier in the book, I talked about how an FAQ document can be a valuable timesaver when responding to employer inquiries about your program. If I haven't e-mailed this out already, I would bring this with me to the interview. As described before, the FAQ covers the nuts and bolts of how the hiring process works: timelines, typical jobs, factors in successfully hiring a student, pay ranges, employer responsibilities, a sample job description, etc. All of this keeps the employer from having to take notes extensively when you meet.

- *Employer Handbook* – We also have a mass-produced employer handbook. I'm up front in telling employers that it's not exactly the most riveting reading, but it does cover many rules and regulations that the employer may need to know when it comes to termination, withholding federal and state income taxes, and so forth.

- *Sample Job Descriptions and Resumes* – Employers aren't always great at developing job descriptions. Often their descriptions are too short and vague, omitting information that will be important to students. Alternatively, many descriptions are detailed, but they fail to give the student a qualitative sense of why they might or might not like the job at hand. Sharing a few successful job descriptions can save you quite a bit of back and forth with employers when they are creating new jobs. Make sure that each sample job description includes all elements that make for a good job description: company information; a job title; a job description that specifies what the student will do and what they might learn; a list of required or preferred qualifications; a pay range; and some information about hours and location. I also make sure that my sample job descriptions feature the kind of pay range that I would prefer to see, and I try to emphasize preferred qualifications rather than requirements.

I also like to bring at least three sample resumes to a new employer. This can be a quick and easy way to illustrate our three levels of students: sophomores, middlers, and juniors. The sophomore resume often has no corporate experience on it. These samples give me an opportunity to discuss how we can meet a range of employer needs as well as to highlight why some students have more earning power than others.

- *Academic Curriculum* – Employers may or may not have much interest in what classes students are taking toward their degree. Regardless, it's a good idea to share this. At the very least, it underscores the idea that the student's work term is meant to be an educational experience as opposed to no more than a job for money. At best, it can lead into a conversation about how the job might dovetail with a student's academic experiences, giving the employer ideas as to how to help the student optimize the work term as a form of learning.

- *Giveaways* – There is no end to the myriad promotional items that a coordinator might give away to an employer, usually with the university logo brandished across them. Over the years, I've been able to give away calendars, coffee mugs, pens, calculators, business card holders, T-shirts, bumper stickers, pens, umbrellas, and even blankets. Some of these things may seem like cheesy trinkets, but they can be useful bits of advertising for your program. These items build a little goodwill, but, most importantly, they can serve as useful visual reminders of your program around the employer's office.

Typically, the budget is limited for such items, so you may need to pick and choose who gets the really good stuff. Still, it's good to see if you can get some funding to purchase various small items, as it can go a long way.

BUILDING RAPPORT

Once at the employer, the most common mistake is to leap right into a sales pitch or presentation about your program. Don't worry—there will be time enough to cover that territory. The more immediate priority is to build rapport with whoever you meet, remembering always that you're trying to create a relationship.

In his interview, Waterloo's Kirk Patterson talks about how a professional needs to open his eyes and be genuinely interested in the employer as a person. He notes that he's always checking out framed diplomas and degrees, as he might be able to build a conversation around that. Similarly, I often like to pick up on interests from the manager's office. If I see some hockey memorabilia, I might mention that I write for U.S. College Hockey Online as a paid hobby of sorts. There are many other hints that might be worth picking up on: a skiing trail map; a Red Sox calendar; a Dilbert cartoon; a novel; a copy of *The Seven Habits of Highly Effective People*; an art print by Gauguin or Van Gogh—I probably would comment on any of these things and see if it leads to a friendly chat before we get down to business.

The next step is one that Tom Akins of Georgia Tech emphasized in his interview. Even when the conversation moves toward a possible relationship between institution and employer, it's critical to ask questions and listen at great length. Here are a few questions you might ask to learn what you'll need to know about the organization:

- How would you describe the culture of your organization?

- What kind of person most enjoys working for your organization?

- What challenges is your organization facing in the months to come?

- What are your greatest needs right now as a manager?

- Do you have any special projects in the pipeline right now?

- How do you think a co-op or intern might be able to help you?

- What would you like to know about how our program works?

- What questions do you have for me?

You really run the danger of going off on the wrong tangent if you don't check in with the employer about what they really are hoping to get out of your meeting. I've made that mistake a few times—explaining how the program works, only to find out that I'm dealing with an alum who knows all of that and has a completely different agenda in mind.

A few years ago, an employer asked me to come down for a visit. It sounded pretty informal—I was told that another manager was interested in hiring a co-op—but I brought extra employer materials just in case. It turned out to be a bit of an ambush. As soon as I arrived, I was ushered into a meeting with the company's CIO and his honchos. I had been all ready to do more of a sales pitch and struggled to get out of that mindset. I asked the CIO how I could be helpful to him, and he promptly launched into an interrogation regarding why I had been sending them so many fewer resumes than usual. Obviously, I had to just go with that, and my careful plans were readily abandoned in favor of a totally extemporaneous give-and-take on the job market and the economy. Basically, it was a good reminder of the importance of asking questions and thinking on your feet to ensure that you have the kind of dialogue that the employer needs to have with you.

BENEFITS OF HIRING CO-OPS AND INTERNS

As I've mentioned before, the day that I have to tell an employer that they should hire a co-op out of the goodness of their heart is the day that I want to get out of this field. If we are going to have strong relationships with employers, we need to focus on what they are going to get out of having our students working for them. I touched on many of these briefly earlier in the book, but it's well worth expanding on them here. If you start off by asking questions to ascertain why the employer is interested in hiring a co-op or intern, you probably will hear at least one of the reasons below. *After* hearing out the employer, it's a good idea to make sure they are aware of the benefits that they did *not* mention, as this may help the employer see new ways that your program can be utilized most effectively. Here are the various reasons employers usually will raise when asked why they hire our students.

THEY ARE SEEKING COST-EFFECTIVE RESOURCES FOR GETTING WORK DONE.

Basically, co-op and internship wages are a reflection of wages for full-time employees. A good way to think of the money equation is that each $1/hour is equal to roughly $2,000 in salary on an annual basis. In other words, a co-op student who makes $15/hour would be making the same on an hourly basis as a full-time employee who makes $30,000 per year (without taking benefits into consideration). Understanding the math here should be helpful in giving you a ballpark of what students should be making in most fields. If you are working with engineers who are going to make an average of $50,000 after graduation, then that would be equivalent to $25/hour. But given that your students have yet to graduate, they probably would be making somewhat less than that. In that example, I would imagine that the high end of co-op or internship wages might be around $20–22/hour for a student who has done multiple work terms and is approaching graduation, while an inexperienced student might be more in the $15–17/hour range.

If the example were taken from a field in which salaries are lower—such as early childhood education—we would see lower co-op wages, naturally. Given that starting salaries might be in the $31–33K range, I seriously doubt that many co-ops would make more than about $13–14/hour at best. I just tested that theory by checking out our jobs database, and a quick scan of pay rates showed several jobs at $9–10/hour and a few at $10–13/hour. So that theory seems to hold up.

Regardless, a big reason that employers like to hire co-ops and interns is because it is a good value. They are rarely making more of a commitment than four or six months, and the budget for each position is rarely more than $20,000—even for a six-month, full-time co-op position in one of the more lucrative fields. That's a good value for employers, especially when you consider the alternatives. The vast majority of our students want to work hard to build experience, get a good reference, and possibly obtain a job after graduation. Thus, they are going to be more motivated than a temp, whose goal is more likely to be financial. Meanwhile, they are less expensive and less of a commitment than a full-time hire, while being able to do the same level of work in many cases. So financially, this is a winning equation for employers.

THEY ARE CONCERNED ABOUT THE HIGH COST OF BENEFITS AND LIKE THE IDEA OF CO-OPS OR INTERNS AS BENEFIT-FREE LABOR.

Even without looking at benefit costs, we've shown that our students are a good deal financially. However, you might be surprised at just how good a deal they really are when we go a step further and consider what employers have to pay a full-time employee for benefits. According to June 2008 statistics from the U.S. Bureau of Labor Statistics, the cost of wages and salaries were at an average of $19.85/hour for hours worked that month. The cost of benefits amounted to $8.63/hour on top of wages and salaries. For state and government agencies, the cost of benefits came to an eye-popping figure of $13.11/hour!

Obviously, these are very substantial costs. Why so high? Remember that they include the cost of health, life, and disability insurance as well as legally required benefits such as Social Security, Medicare, Unemployment Insurance, and Workers' Compensation. When you add other elements—vacations, holidays, sick leave, personal days, retirement plans such as 401K or 403(b) options, overtime pay, and so on, you can see how all of this can add up.

So when an employer is mulling whether they should hire a full-time employee for $40,000/year versus a co-op student who is making exactly that amount on an hourly basis (assuming a generous $20/hour figure), the extrinsic compensation still favors hiring a co-op by a wide margin. If that employee makes $40K, the salary reflects only about 70% of what it will cost the employer. So that employer would be paying almost $57,500 in total compensation for that employee making "only" $40K! That amounts to something like $28.75/hour, and a co-op making anywhere from $17–20/hour starts looking better and better.

One buzzword that you may hear from an employer on this front is "headcount." Managers talking about pressures to keep headcount down are basically being told that they need to find ways around having full-time hires in order to a) keep benefit costs down, and b) minimize a long-term commitment when it comes to budgeting for human resources. This does NOT mean that the employer can't hire your students. In fact, your students might be a great solution for someone facing this mandate. Keep an ear open for that.

WHEN THE ECONOMY IS UNPREDICTABLE, CO-OPS OR INTERNS ALLOW THEM A WAY TO GET WORK DONE WITHOUT MAKING A LONG-TERM COMMITMENT TO A RESOURCE THAT MAY NOT BE NEEDED IN THE FUTURE.

I've always felt that this is a highly underrated benefit for educators to tout when talking to employers. It's easy for an educator to assume that economic downturns and periods of great economic uncertainty are going to bode poorly for co-op and internship programs. In the face of a severe economic crisis—such as what we saw after 9/11—there is no question that our programs will suffer accordingly. Yet it's also true that we sometimes can seize opportunities when the economy is dicey. When things are shaky—as they are as I write these words—I always try to make this statement when talking to prospective employers: "Obviously, we're in a time of economic uncertainty right now. No one knows what's going to happen. But if you have work that needs to get done, and you're unsure about what the future holds, a co-op can be a great solution. Co-ops are a *hedge* against economic uncertainty."

I might go on to explain this if necessary. Let's say that an employer is feeling wary of making a commitment to a full-time, permanent hire. The employer worries that this person may have to be laid off if the economic picture gets worse. That's unpleasant and costly, as the employer is liable to pay unemployment for the laid-off hire. In contrast, a co-op is generally going to be hired for no more than six months. If the economy picks up during the months to come, the employer can hire a full-time employee or additional co-ops. If business gets worse, they simply can opt against hiring another co-op without having to lay off someone and provide unemployment compensation.

A CO-OP OR INTERNSHIP PROGRAM IS A GREAT MUTUAL TRIAL PERIOD TO HELP EMPLOYERS AND STUDENTS FIGURE OUT IF THEY ARE A GOOD MATCH FOR EACH OTHER AFTER GRADUATION.

In a variety of ways, it's extremely costly to hire the wrong individual. If someone needs to be fired, it's extremely stressful and time-consuming for those involved. Often an employee has to be given repeated warnings and counseling, both in an effort to rehabilitate the problem employee as well as to minimize the risk of a lawsuit if the employee is ultimately terminated. After that, there are additional costs in having to hire a replacement.

Another issue is that interviews and other selection tools are not necessarily highly scientific predictors of job success. I have seen a number of studies suggesting that there is only a modest positive correlation between success in conventional interviews and success as an employee. Likewise, education level, resumes, and reference checks are not as good at predicting success as most employers believe. Some methods—behavioral-based interviewing, work samples, and some (but not all) mental ability tests—seem to be better predictors, but they are all far from flawless.

The bottom line is that it's very hard to tell if someone will be a good employee on the basis of a resume, a 30-minute interview, and a few references. Conversely, an internship can be thought of as an extended interview. The student's performance over time will tell the employer more than an interview ever could about their attitude, dependability, and ability to learn and perform effectively. If the employer is paying any attention at all, it should be easy to develop a sense of the employee's strengths and developmental needs. Likewise, the student will learn a great deal that will help in ascertaining whether the job and/or company are a good long-term fit. Does the student like the work itself? Is the culture comfortable? A student who has worked in a given environment is more likely to stick around for a while if she does indeed accept a job after graduation. This is a definitive positive for employers. In fact, many employers are frank in admitting that they would not hire co-ops or interns at all if not for the opportunity to audition them for full-time roles.

CO-OPS AND INTERNS ARE A GREAT WAY TO DEAL WITH TEMPORARY OR CYCLICAL NEEDS.

Besides financial considerations, there are many other reasons why an employer might favor hiring a co-op or intern. As you might imagine, many of our accounting employers hire very heavily for our January–June work term while hiring few if any co-ops for the July–December cycle because of tax season. Other employers may have needs that are seasonal, fitting nicely the on-again, off-again nature of most co-op/intern programs.

In other instances, students are hired because of a personnel issue, such as the need for coverage during a maternity leave or a similar reason. Another reason can be some sort of organizational transition. Several years ago, I had one student doing IT work downtown for a financial services employer. While visiting, I learned that the company planned to move their whole company—a few thousand people—to a new building a few blocks away. Thinking of all the work that would go into moving thousands of computers and servers, I suggested that the employer hire several IT co-ops for the upcoming cycle that would include the critical time of the move. They hired four co-ops, and those students were able to get some great experience. But the real surprise came months later: The employer found that they really *liked* having four co-ops, and they have kept hiring that number or more ever since! So sometimes a seemingly temporary need can open the door for expanding your program.

STUDENTS ADD VALUE TO THE ORGANIZATION.

I wouldn't want an employer to hire a student unless there was meaningful work for the student to do at that organization. Students themselves often underestimate what they bring to the table. Our students:

- Bring fresh ideas to the workplace

- Have a great deal at stake in terms of resume and references, and their motivation level reflects this.

- Often are more technologically savvy and comfortable than older employees in the workplace

- Can offer a more objective perspective on job tasks and processes, as they are not as immersed in the corporate culture

- Sometimes pay for themselves, literally

Kirk Patterson of Waterloo touches on this point at the end of this chapter. I have seen it happen as well. Occasionally a student has refined a process or discovered and fixed a problem, saving the company so much money that they literally paid for themselves in one swoop.

YOU AND THE UNIVERSITY ARE THERE TO HELP WITH PROBLEMS AND TO PARTNER IN OTHER WAYS.

As Tom Akins points out in his interview excerpt in this chapter, another good selling point is that the educator is there to help if any problems arise. If a student employee is having issues with tardiness or work ethic—or if the employer is struggling with how to best interview, mentor, discipline, or evaluate the student—the educator can bring considerable expertise to the situation and take a potential problem off the employer's plate. The fact that the educator can offer an objective view may be helpful if there are conflicts between the two parties. In general, the educator really can make life easier for the employer, as long as the educator approaches the relationship with that mentality.

As noted earlier, the university also can be an educational partner with the employer and engage in many other activities that facilitate a deeper and more mutually beneficial relationship between organization and institution. Consulting projects, research connections, guest lectures—there are quite a few ways to bring the real world onto campus while making students more aware of organizations as possible future employers.

SELLING THE PROGRAM

So you've gone to the employer and done a good job of asking questions about needs as well as listening carefully to what the employer has to say. Now you have your opportunity to make your pitch in response. Obviously, you're going to touch on the aforementioned benefits of the program. Additionally, there are a few more subtle points worth mentioning.

CROSS-SELLING VERSUS TUNNEL VISION

While some educators may work with students across all majors, most work with only a portion of their university's students. At some programs—including ours at Northeastern—educators work with a very narrow slice of the pie educationally. This has the great advantage of cultivating a culture in which the educator can become a real expert on the job market for accounting, nursing, industrial engineering, and so forth, but it also can lead educators to develop tunnel vision while on firm visits.

This is understandable. When I'm visiting a company, my primary focus is on paying close attention to any hint of a possible job in management information systems or supply chain management. More recently, I started working with our undeclared business students, and I find myself getting a little excited when I hear an employer describe a fairly broad job that would give a student exposure to a variety of business functions—perfect for the student who could benefit from a taste of two or three areas during one work term.

However, I also try to remind myself to probe for areas that are outside of my immediate area of responsibility. After all, just about any organization should have hiring needs beyond what my students are interested in doing. While our system doesn't directly reward coordinators for cross-selling by talking up what else our program can do beyond one's immediate area of responsibility, it's definitely important. By doing so, you're being a better colleague and doing a greater service to that employer. This is especially true when you're talking to a human resources professional as opposed to a manager who has a more narrow focus. Maybe one functional area was your ticket to get into that organization to sell your program, but capitalize on that entrée into the organization. So be sure to ask if other groups have needs, and be ready to elaborate on what other programs do co-ops and internships at your school.

NAME-DROPPING

"Name-dropping" is a term that generally has negative connotations. If you'd rather think of it as "modeling," feel free. Either way, there is something to be said for sharing what other employers hire your students as well as why they do so and how they make it work most effectively. When a company hears that other prominent employers are using your program, it can legitimize your program—especially if it's small and struggling to get a toehold in your region. Hearing *why* these companies hire your students may add credence to the program benefits that you're attempting to tout. Learning about *how* a good employer goes about hiring, mentoring, and evaluating students is also a way for some of the best practices to filter down to other organizations.

For years, I would tell employers what a veteran HR professional at Gillette had told me when we got into a conversation about why Gillette valued our students. "We figure that if we hire ten co-ops from Northeastern, nine of them are going to work out great—and at a reasonable cost in terms of budget," she had said. "And if we end up hiring even three out of those nine after graduation, then that's a pretty good batting average there as always." She went on to emphasize that Gillette could hire great candidates from dozens of schools in the Boston area, as we have an amazing concentration of excellent academic institutions. "The problem is that it's so hard to know how good someone is from a half-hour interview. And if we hire the wrong person, we can't just fire them; we have to coach them to death."

By "coach them to death," this person meant that Gillette had to schedule repeated coaching meetings before terminating a problem employee. After several weeks of meetings and documentation, the upshot almost always was termination. Obviously, the whole process was something that the company wanted to avoid altogether.

You'll notice that nothing in this anecdote is all that new based on the ideas presented earlier in this chapter. Yet there is something more compelling about hearing those selling points presented through the vantage point of a real person at a prominent employer. Likewise, if an employer asks about how the interviewing process will work, I might say, "Well, one thing that Covidien has found to be really effective is to try to conduct all their interviews within the first official week that interviews begin. They come on campus and actually make offers on the phone before they leave for the day; they've learned that it's definitely a 'snooze and lose' hiring process."

HANDLING OBJECTIONS

For professionals in sales, there are whole workshops and books on handling objections that customers raise in the selling process. While most people reading this book are not primarily salespeople, it's important to be aware that you do have many techniques to use when employers raise objections:

1. **The About-Face** – Here you acknowledge a concern and incorporate it into your response, trying to flip it around:

   Employer: "I don't know about hiring a co-op. I just think that the burden of training someone every six months is going to be too much of a hassle for us."

   Coordinator: "You're right; there is definitely an investment that needs to be made in training any new hire. But our employers are often surprised to find how quickly our students can learn, given how smart and motivated they are. Also, a really smart thing that many employers do is to have the current co-op take the responsibility of training the incoming co-op before they start. Many co-ops actually will write a manual that future co-ops can follow and update, and quite a few employers will ask the second co-op to overlap with the first one if possible so they can take that training burden off your plate."

2. **The Big Picture** – In this case, you help the employer keep an objection in perspective by urging them to take a broader view of what really matters:

   Employer: "How would it work if a student needs to get fired or disciplined in some way? I would hate to have to fire a student."

Coordinator: "The quick answer is that students can be fired just like any other employee. We definitely would not want a student to get special treatment just because they are young and inexperienced. That said, bear in mind that terminations are extremely rare. I often have about 75 students working during each six-month term, and it's unusual for me to have more than one student fired per year. I would help you through the process if it came up, but it's pretty unlikely to be a significant problem for you. Remember, many students picked our school because they *want* to work hard!"

3. **The Creative Solution** – With this approach, you try to think outside of the box to get your program off the ground with a new employer. The idea here is to get the relationship started however you can, and worry about having it translate to a regular position later.

Employer: "We're a start-up operation, and I don't think we can afford a full-time co-op just yet… and our need is immediate, while it sounds like your next cycle is several months away."

Coordinator: "There are a few other ways I might be able to help you. I often have some really experienced students who do their co-ops out of state and then want part-time work locally when they're back on campus. I might be able to come up with a really good candidate who can work 10–15 hours per week for you over the next few months if that helps… or I could see if there is a freshman who would work some unpaid hours in the hope of getting some professional experience on his or her resume."

4. **The Hurdle** – Here you deal with an objection by acknowledging that there may be some hurdle to overcome if a hiring is going to occur…and then suggesting a solution:

Employer: "I don't know if a co-op will work out for us. I just don't think that a student would have enough technical background for this job."

Coordinator: "I see. Okay, then, I have a proposal. Why don't you pull together a job description, and we'll post it and see what students express interest. Take a look at their resumes and bring some in for interviews. If you don't find someone who can cut it, you have no obligation to hire anyone at all."

5. **The Perception Reconfiguration** – Sometimes an employer has a negative perception about some aspect of the program, and you need to address that directly before perception be comes reality in their mind:

Employer: "I just don't think that we can afford to pay $15/hour for an intern."

Coordinator: "That's interesting. Many employers tell me that the reason they hire co-ops is because it's so cost-effective. Many of our students do the same work as full-time employees, and certainly you'd have to pay much more than the equivalent of $15/hour to have a full-time person do the same work. Temps and contractors are more expensive on an hourly basis, too. So if you have work that needs to get done, I think that you'd have a hard time finding a more cost-effective option than our program—especially given the rising cost of benefits for full-time employees."

351

6. The Probe – Sometimes the objection is nebulous. You just get the vibe that the employer is reaching some sort of internal conclusion that the program is not a fit. At that point, you may want to reach out in a neutral, non-defensive way to learn more about what's going on.

> **Coordinator**: "It seems like you are a little hesitant about moving forward with this program. I was wondering if you could tell me why you seem unsure about hiring a co-op."

There are other approaches that could work as well. My main goal here is to get you thinking about the fact that you want to listen carefully to employer objections. Don't get deflated by them; address them directly and unemotionally to see if the employer's concern is definitely a deal breaker or not.

APPARENT FAILURES

There is one last point I'd like to make about attempting to develop employer relationships. This one comes from a summer job that I had a very long time ago. During my college years, I found it tough to get a job to make some money while on break from school. The best I could do was getting a job selling cookware to young women in their homes—almost on a door-to-door basis. It was a very challenging job, as you actually could end up losing money on a weekly basis if you didn't make sales. The fact that I had never done more than boil water or use a toaster-oven didn't help!

Although I wouldn't want to do it again, I learned some valuable lessons from being a salesman. One especially valuable one was this: If you fail to close a sale, then fail with class. It's very disappointing to put on a good sales presentation, tailoring it to your audience carefully, listening to objections, responding to them appropriately… and then have the customer opt against it. Regardless, you want to make sure that your disappointment and frustration is not apparent.

While a high-road approach is smart for all forms of sales, it's especially crucial for co-op and internship professionals. Remember, our goal is long-term relationship building. It's not at all unusual for a new relationship to take six months, one year, or longer to get off the ground. Sometimes a large company needs to submit a requisition to hire a student several months in advance, or the company's fiscal year doesn't dovetail well with the timing of hiring that first co-op.

I've also had situations where a terrific job was posted, and it led to an outpouring of interest from students… only to have the employer call me up weeks later to let me know that they no longer have budget for the position or that it fell through for some other reason. No doubt that I've cringed or winced sharply on the other end of the phone, but I try my hardest to remain upbeat with the tone and content of my response: "That's too bad, but I understand completely. As you saw from the number of resumes I forwarded, your position definitely resonated with our students. I'm very confident that we'll be able to get a great relationship off the ground in the future. By all means give me a call if anything changes in the weeks to come, and let's be sure to follow up for the next work term."

The last thing I want is for an employer to be reluctant to deal with me in the future because he fears that I will get angry or sarcastic if things just don't work out. If that difficult news is handled gracefully, it can be an opportunity for the employer to see that you are an attractive business partner in the future.

IN THEIR OWN WORDS

PROFESSIONAL PERSPECTIVE #1
"FIELD DAY"
Nancy Chiang and Kirk Patterson, University of Waterloo

Nancy Chiang (NC): "I would first do a little bit of research about that employer, so that I know what the business is. So I can try to guess what their needs might be. And I would also check on our system and see if they have participated before, or if they have people in the company, but in a different department, that are already hiring from us. Then, when I get out there, we have a method. We don't necessarily start to go there and talk, talk, talk, but we ask them a series of questions in order to further find out what they are looking for. So we ask questions about the business. What new projects are coming up? Have they hired co-ops before? What are their reasons for doing it or not doing it?"

Kirk Patterson (KP): "Are they having ongoing problems with full-time employees? Are there human resource issues that can be addressed by using co-op students in lieu of going out into the unemployed work force to hire? You know, maternity leaves come up. You have to look at every angle."

NC: "So we know why they are interested, and where their needs really are. Then we can do the selling. We have a lot of case scenarios that we can share with them... There is also a list of benefits that we can use to handle all kinds of objections."

KP: "From a cost point of view, a big benefit is recruiting. Why not use a co-op instead of having to recruit and have to run ads in the *Globe and Mail* [a Canadian newspaper] all the time? Why not set up a permanent co-op position? If you want to argue the financial side, I always say do a cost-benefit analysis. What's it going to cost you to hire someone full time with benefits, when you can know you can have an ongoing co-op student there—who, yeah, may eventually become that full-time employee—but you've always got that bowl of talent that you can draw on. You may use that connection immediately, or it may be ten years later that you come across that same student who was an employee of yours who's got more work experience. Say they're with IBM, and you've got a software company. You might say, 'Hey, I want that employee.'"

NC: "And then I would also bring some sample job descriptions for the company... I would say, 'This is an example of what other companies are doing, and this is what students can do for you.' Or I'd bring some sample student resumes. And then they take a look and they see, 'Oh, these people could work for me.' You really want to sell them on the benefits."

KP: "And along with selling that, you can also pitch to them the cash advantage to it. Because you can bring up situations where students have saved the company money or made them money. I saw that many times in the business field where students were able to either do a marketing plan or come up with another idea and say, 'Well, why are you doing it this way instead of that way?' Or you're in a manufacturing area and someone says 'Why aren't you doing it this way?' and you're going 'Oh! I never even thought of it.' So you end up in the long run saving money or the cost of that student through what they've been able to save the company.

"When I go into an office, I walk in, I see who they are. But the first thing I do is check out the bookcase, if there is one. I check out the diplomas, degrees, what is on the wall. I check out his or her desk, and then I come from a personal angle first. I like doing the personal thing, trying to find something common. I'm a Rotarian. I see a Rotarian button on them; we've got something to talk about right away. And, knock on wood, I have more success that way rather than doing the hard sell or just going in and trying to pitch the program and why they should do it, and not taking a personal interest in them."

PROFESSIONAL PERSPECTIVE #2
"THE EMPLOYER AS EDUCATIONAL PARTNER"
Ronnie Porter, Northeastern University

Although not all co-op coordinators in the profession are in faculty positions, it is important that we think of ourselves as educators. The language we use is important and should be reflective of that. We are talking about student development; we are talking about learning; we are talking about curriculum and integrated learning. We recognize that employers have a job to be done, but we want them to be able to use the teachable moments to help students learn and develop. It is important that co-op professionals either have a background in the field or make the effort to become knowledgeable about the major fields of study of the students that we work with as well as potential occupations. Co-op professionals should have knowledge and familiarity with the labor market both regionally and nationally.

It is important to do the necessary research in preparation for company visits and/or discussions with employers. For example, when doing employer development work in the biotechnology industry, I ask questions about how long a company has been in business, what the basic philosophy is, what kinds of diseases are they developing drugs or treatments for, who the clientele is, etc. It takes time and effort. But, when we go out there, we need to be seen as professionals who are knowledgeable. We bring employers on board as partners to assist in the education of our students. A former dean of co-op referred to employers as "our faculty in the field."

It is important that we pay attention to the language that we use when working with employers. When we talk about integrated learning to help students integrate the critical concepts and skills that they learn in class with what they do in the field. Employers in our program participate in an online performance evaluation to provide feedback to students on their development and accomplishments in the work place. We want students to set goals that are realistic that are going to meet their needs as well as the needs of their employers. The next step that we would like to take is to share the rubric that we developed so that they are aware of the curriculum objectives and goals.

We want them to be familiar with what kinds of things that students are learning at the university including critical thinking, understanding of critical concepts and skills, proficiency in the laboratory, and professional behavior and ethics. If employers have a better understanding of the educational goals of the program they can help to provide opportunities in their companies to enable students to further develop their skills, on co-op, in addition to what they do in the classroom.

PROFESSIONAL PERSPECTIVE #3
"How Can We Help You?"
Tom Akins, Georgia Tech

My viewpoint on that has always been, and continues to be, you don't want to go out there and start telling the employer when you visit them what this program can do, and talk about how great our program is. I believe what we need to do when we visit an employer as an educational institution is to say, "You're the employer; you tell me: What are your needs? How can we help you meet your needs?" And you tell me what your needs are, how you think we can help fulfill them, and then I can tell you what we're able to do. And I think somewhere we can come to an agreement of how we can build a relationship.

It goes back to relationships. I firmly believe that we have to listen to what the employer has to say, and find out what their critical needs are. Then we can say, "Look, I know right away we can handle this particular need because of this program and we can do this. Now this other need that you have over here, I'm not sure but I can put you in touch with somebody on campus or I can check on some things and I'll call you back and let you know." So I think the first thing I would tell someone who is first going out is, "Why don't you just sit and listen to what they have to say? And if they have some issues, try to address some of those issues, and treat those as opportunities for us to try to help out that employer and meet whatever needs that they have."

And if there comes a point when we can't meet a specific need that they have, then there might be another school and I tell employers, "Don't rely on Georgia Tech to furnish all of your manpower or co-op student needs." Because we really believe that a healthy program within an employer is going to involve a lot of other schools. So if they want somebody, say, for six months at a time, I'll say "Maybe you ought to go to Drexel, where the students are working for a longer period of time." And give them an option, you know, help them out. Because the employer, they're trying to meet their needs. And if you can help them meet their needs, then they're going to be happy.

The biggest selling point, to me, is that you're able to create a pool of candidates for potential long-term employees in the next two or three years, whenever they get their degrees and graduate. This is first of all what you're doing, and it really is a win-win situation for you because you get to look at these employees over a longer period of time. It's like a two or three year-long interview. You get to see them actually work and produce, and you can measure not only the quantity of their output but the quality of their output as a potential employee. And, it's obviously a winning situation for the students because they get the work experience, plus feedback from the employers as to how they can improve performances on the job. That's the main thing.

I also like to let the employer know that they're a partner with us, that we're not just going to leave them out there high and dry, as in you hire a student and then we're going to leave you. No, if you have an issue or a situation or problem, we're also here to help you as an employer, not only for the student. We're an advocate for the student also, but we're here in addition to really help the employer and let them know that they're a partner in providing this method of education for the students.

And we also try to let them know that another selling point is, if you're hiring co-op students, that gives you an entry into the campus. In other words, at Georgia Tech, if you're hiring our co-op students—and a lot of relationships have been built this way, sometimes I don't think our office gets enough credit—but the next thing you know, you've got someone who is looking for some

355

help on something. So what we do, we direct them to a faculty member here who is maybe doing research in that area, or someone at our research institute who can enable them and this company to maybe work through this situation, or give them some consulting advice.

We've had equipment donations to the school, and it all came about because initially we had a co-op student working for that employer. By hiring a student, in many cases it really is the first step toward a really complete partnership where this employer can avail themselves of not only the students –let's just say low-cost employment can help there—but also have access to a huge range of technical and other types of expertise just from the faculty and others on our campus.

PROFESSIONAL PERSPECTIVE #4
"EMBRACING FEEDBACK"
Jacki Diani, Northeastern University

I think being honest with employers is critical. We've changed our curriculum in nursing, and it's changed our preparation for co-op. We proactively went out and talked to as many people as we could about the changes so that they wouldn't be surprised. In meeting with them we could explain the changes, why we made the changes, answer their questions, and address their concerns. We also asked for feedback. It helped us in our transition to a new curriculum to be proactive with employers rather than sending students out and having them say, "You didn't tell me you dropped this course!" They were prepared and they understood the changes; this helped them and the students.

This week I had a conversation with a recruiter who relayed a story from a manager who didn't have something nice to say about the changes we made in our program. I responded that I respect her feedback and will be sure to include it in our ongoing evaluation of the program. She (the manager) is an experienced person, and we need to take all feedback we receive, not just the positive feedback. I said to the recruiter, "We've received a lot of good feedback, we've received some mixed feedback, but it's all important and we want it all. Any negative feedback we get, we need it, and we'd be happy to talk with the manager in more detail about her concerns about the changes in the program." It can be hard to receive criticism; who likes to get that? But we need to listen to their concerns and see if we can address them, and they will appreciate the effort. In the long term it helps the success of the program.

PROFESSIONAL PERSPECTIVE #5
"FIND THE ANSWER"
Kirk Patterson, University of Waterloo

I always tell my employers, "Look, if I don't know the answers, I'll find the answer, or find someone that can tell you." I refuse to turn away phone calls because I don't like being bounced around myself. When I was based at the college [as opposed to out in the field], because I was in the business division, I got every phone call for everything. And a lot of it was not co-op related. But you know, I ended up getting some leads out of those calls, because even though I was talking to someone because of something else, I wrote down some information and bingo.

If you couch your language properly with employers and the students you're visiting, and you do them a good deed, it's going to come back in spades. I've seen it with myself—the number of referrals I've got out of it, comments I've received, getting phone calls from far ends of the world from people I've never even known. When you trace it down and ask, "How'd you get hold of my name?" the answer is, "Well, someone said you were able to help them out with a student." Sometimes I'll hear them out and say, "Well, it's not my bailiwick, but yes, I can help you out."

REFLECTION QUESTIONS

1. What do you think would be a good goal for your program in terms of the number of firm visits you go on as an individual over the course of each year?

2. What do you currently do to cultivate relationships in which employers view themselves as educational partners with your institution? What else could you do?

3. This chapter talks about how educators might want to think of themselves as "unpaid consultants" to employers. What are you willing to do to go beyond your job description to build a relationship with an employer? Was there anything in the chapter that struck you as going too far?

4. What have you found to be the best way to develop leads when attempting to bring new employers into your program? Were there other methods mentioned in this chapter that you would like to try?

5. This chapter emphasized the importance of asking questions when meeting with employers and actively listening to the answers. What would you say are the three most important questions that you would want to ask a prospective employer to better understand their organization?

6. Many benefits to hiring co-ops were cited in this chapter. Which ones seem to be the most powerful selling points for your employers?

CHAPTER 14

MAINTAINING EMPLOYER RELATIONSHIPS

"Nothing great is created suddenly, any more than a bunch of grapes or a fig. If you tell me that you desire a fig, I answer you that there must be time. Let it first blossom, then bear fruit, then ripen."

— *Epictetus*

Once you have succeeded in getting organizations to hire your students, the next step is to make sure that you're doing everything in your power to make them true educational partners. When you have a company in the fold, it's easy to take them for granted by minimizing your contact with them. Even worse, some educators make the mistake of creating any number of bureaucratic hoops and hurdles that employers will have to navigate for the privilege of being allowed to hire and mentor that program's students.

There are definitely some balancing acts when it comes to relationships with employers. We want to provide employers with good customer service and make life easier for them, but not at the expense of appreciating that an educational partnership is going to require some time and energy for all parties. We need to respect the fact that employers aren't hiring students out of the goodness of their hearts; they need students to be human resources that can help fulfill organizational goals. Yet we also want to ensure that they remember that these young, temporary employees are students and learners—not just cheap labor.

Maintaining a strong relationship of any sort requires communication, time, flexibility, and commitment. In this chapter, we'll discuss how to ensure your relationships with employers are strong enough to survive the challenges that inevitably will occur.

PRIORITIZING EMPLOYER VISITS

As Charlie Bognanni indicates in his interview excerpt at the end of this chapter, you need to invest some time in planning your firm visits. Part of that is time of year. Unless you are at a program like the University of Waterloo—where some professionals are primarily devoted to working with employers in the field—you just aren't going to be able to get out on the road at certain points in the school year. Even when you do have the time, it's highly likely that you won't be able to come anywhere close to visiting ALL of your students during a given work term. I actually tried to do it once in my early days, and I got out and saw about 40 of 60+ students. It was a great goal but basically impossible to fulfill without neglecting other critical responsibilities.

So now you have to ask yourself some questions so you can prioritize whom to visit. I reviewed these back in Chapter 3, but it's worth mentioning them again here:

- Is this a new employer that has never been visited?

- Is this an employer who regularly hires first-time co-ops and who thus may benefit more from a visit, in case there are problems that we can catch early?

- Is the employer a key educational partner, hiring a significant number of students and ensuring that they have a good learning experience?

- Do we think that there are opportunities to grow our co-op program with this employer?

- Is this an employer that has had problems with previous co-ops and therefore might benefit from and appreciate some extra attention?

- Did the employer struggle to hire students recently, and can we go visit to show them that we value them as a potential educational partner?

- Is the employer in a location that is relatively far from the university? If so, it might be best to visit them during the summer, when we can afford to be away from the office for a longer period of time. If not, perhaps we can hold off on visiting, figuring we can dash out for a visit at the beginning or end of a work day during busy season.

After mulling these questions, I'll then see if I have some geographical clusters of employers. For example, I really wanted to get to an employer about 45 minutes south of Boston a few weeks ago, so I dug through my database and found an employer 15 minutes away from that one. I was able to get over there easily and check in with three more students.

Another key when prioritizing is that not all employers are created equal! If I have an employer that seems to have a huge upside for hiring, I might visit that employer four to six times in a year, while not getting to another even once during that time frame. In other cases, I might never get to a distant employer who has hired sporadically over several years.

Ideally—meaning that if you have ample time and budget—you would get out and visit every single employer that hires on a regular basis. Maybe you won't be able to go out and vet every new organization, and it has taken me a few years and several hiring cycles before I've managed to make it out to see some employers, but you have everything to gain by making sure to get out there sooner or later. Visiting current employers will enhance your credibility when counseling students, and it will make a definite statement to the employer about how much you value their relationship. As we'll see, this is also the easiest and most productive way to develop new jobs.

GENERAL PRINCIPLES OF MAINTAINING EMPLOYER RELATIONSHIPS

There are several factors that differentiate educators who do a great job of maintaining employer relationships versus those that fail to do so. As you can see below, almost all of them revolve around communication and effort.

1. *Be proactive*

For the most part, your contacts have plenty of things to worry about besides their relationship with co-op and internship programs. Timely e-mails and phone calls are important ways to remind them about updating job descriptions, conducting interviews, and making offers during the preparation process. Communicating to them about setting learning goals, giving periodic feedback, understanding what is or is not acceptable when it comes to professional behavior, and completing a final evaluation will lead to fewer unpleasant surprises during the activity phase.

It's important to remember that managers vary dramatically when it comes to the degree of training and skill that they bring to their roles. How do managers become managers in many organizations? Often the person who is best at performing as an individual contributor is suddenly given responsibility for managing a team of contributors. Does that mean that they will be good at doing so? Not necessarily. As a result, you may need to provide some tactful advice as to how to conduct interviews, give feedback, address problems—basically any or all of someone's managerial responsibilities.

It can be a good idea to feel out a manager as to whether they would welcome input from you on any of these fronts. Yes, it may result in more work for you up front, but imagine how much time you might save when it comes to dealing with a conflict that could have been prevented with a more proactive approach.

2. *Be responsive*

Nothing says that you're uninterested more clearly than failing to respond to an employer's phone call or e-mail. An important goal is to attempt to get back to an employer by the next business day. This is easier said than done at peak times of year—just yesterday (November 10), I sent out 79 e-mails to students, employers, and colleagues as well as 13 resume packets to employers!

But being responsive means much more than just getting back to people. It also means following up thoroughly and thoughtfully when an issue arises, whether it's an employer who is frustrated by a lack of applicants for a job, a manager who calls with a quibble or major gripe about a current employee, or whatever it may be. Over time, you want to cultivate a reputation as someone who responds to concerns in an empathetic, honest, and solution-oriented manner whenever possible. That professional style will make people seek you out in the future.

3. Make life easier for the employer

Why would an employer contact me if I'm going to make their life more difficult? They would have to want my students *really* badly to put up with me if I provided them with an obstacle course of requirements to complete. Conversely, there are many ways in which an educator can make life easier for employers. I have heard people whine about some of these being "labor-intensive." Yes, these steps can take time and effort, but not nearly as much as having to develop new employers from scratch. Here are some steps that many (but not all) employers will appreciate if you can offer these services:

• Screening resumes

At Northeastern, we pride ourselves in being a "high touch" program. There is a good deal of one-on-one interaction between students and coordinators to ensure that we have candidates pursuing educationally appropriate positions.

That said, this is also a service to those that hire our students. Most employers don't want to see 25 resumes for one position. They don't want to slog through dozens of overqualified and underqualified candidates to find the handful of prospective hires who are needles in the haystack. And they don't want to call a student to arrange an interview, only to learn (or infer) that the student has done a "resume fling," sending out resumes for a few dozen positions to see what sticks rather than targeting a small handful of jobs that truly interest them and are plausible matches.

• Scheduling on-campus interviews

We tend to take care of the scheduling of on-campus interviews for employers who come to Northeastern to determine who to hire. Occasionally, we'll do the scheduling for interviews at the employer site as well. Again, this takes a little time, but if the employer is investing the time and money to come on campus, it seems like the least we can do.

• Helping employers with interviewing

If students come back from interviews and report that the interviewer really didn't ask them any questions, I try to follow up to see if that manager could use a little assistance. I have taught any number of employers how to use behavioral-based interviewing methods. This will help them do a better job of selecting the right people for any kind of job, let alone co-op positions.

• Helping employers in marketing their program

Many employers truly wish to be great educational partners but don't know how to go about it. There are a number of ways in which an educator can help an organization to market themselves better while also enriching the educational payoff of the relationship. This may include showing employers how to write a more thorough, realistic job description. Another idea might be getting employers as guests in academic classes, which serves the dual purpose of bringing the real world into the classroom while building student awareness of the employer's job opportunities. There are many other mechanisms for helping employers become better known with potential co-ops and interns: guest appearances at student clubs; job fairs; co-op prep class panels; focus groups; and so forth.

4. *Be aware of the balancing acts*

I alluded to this earlier in the chapter. Yes, we want to make things easy for employers, but we don't want to sacrifice education in the spirit of being as purely expedient as possible. How do you balance that? I think that you always have to ask yourself why you are requiring an employer to do any paperwork, survey, or form that you ask them to complete. Are you getting good information that you actually use? If so, does the employer understand the purpose of the activity, or is it just perceived as a useless nuisance? If the task is not too onerous and the employer has been educated as to how it is contributing to learning, it should be fine... but you don't want to take that perception for granted.

Other balancing acts come into play when it comes to the hiring of students. Your institution may pressure you to get everyone placed as soon as possible. That's a very real pressure, but pushing for placements that are not good educational matches is going to be a very short-sighted strategy. Likewise, some students and employers will pressure you at times as to what the final outcome should be. Many students are quite ready to accept whatever job you recommend, while some employers would love you to make the hiring decision for them.

As we talked about in the material earlier in the book on playing God, this is an area where you need to proceed with caution. On the one hand, I think it's a cop-out to refuse to give either party any assistance whatsoever in processing the decision. Having employers talk through what their thought process is with different candidates—and correcting them if their insights seem to be off target—is perfectly legitimate. Yet I'm reluctant to state bluntly that a manager should hire candidate X over candidate Y, as I'm not the one who will need to live with that decision every business day for six months.

The happy medium would be to offer an additional perspective while leaving the final call to the manager. I might say something like this: "If you think that it would be better to hire someone who has experience, you might go with Juan Mario. He has done a co-op already, and I think he would get up to speed quickly as a result. But if you want someone who has more upside over the long run, you might want to lean more toward Jill. She lacks Juan Mario's experience and might have a tougher adjustment over the first month or so, but she has a 3.8 GPA and is definitely going to be great once she gets more professional seasoning."

5. *Manage expectations*

You always have to be careful about what you tell an employer you or your students can do. I think that the concept of "under-promise and over-deliver" is a good one. If I have a student with real issues speaking English, I often will alert the manager to that before the interview. I actually view this as being in the candidate's best interest—just in the way that political "spin doctors" try to lower expectations before a presidential debate. Often a manager will call me back and say, "Gee, his English was much better than I had expected."

The same applies when you get a new job description in. If the job is in a tough-to-reach location or looks unlikely to appeal to candidates for any number of reasons, I will try to alert the employer to these issues right away. If we end up coming up with a handful of great candidates, it's a pleasant surprise. If not, the employer knew that this was a possibility and may have hedged their bets by exploring other options in addition to our program. Either way, you're fostering a better relationship based on transparency and honesty.

6. Get feedback

It's important to find out how you're doing and to have open dialogue about it. Raytheon has been one of my best employers in this regard. They often stage an "outbrief" event toward the end of the work term where students will report out on their experience while coordinators can talk informally with managers. Better still, I always have a face-to-face meeting with my Raytheon contact at the end of each referral period, and we share very honest information about how we're all doing and what could be done better. How much of an impact did the information session have? How timely were the interviews and offers? How good a job did we do of communicating about candidates? What was the student feedback about the online application process? When you're not in the heat of the moment, there is more openness when it comes to weighing in on process improvement.

There are other options besides face-to-face meetings. You can do online surveys, whether anonymous or not. Anonymous surveys may give you more honest feedback, but they have the disadvantage that anonymity brings as well. It's hard to know how to fix a relationship if you're not sure which one is broken! So you have to consider that when determining how to get feedback.

Above all, you have to resist the natural tendency to get defensive when you hear negative feedback. Maybe you can make a change to deal with a concern, and maybe you can't. But you need to acknowledge differing opinions and focus on understanding rather than placing a priority on showing why you're right when you may just perceive things differently.

FIRM VISITS WITH CURRENT EMPLOYERS

Whether you are able to get to four employers per year or 40, it's important to understand the many benefits of visiting organizations who are already hiring your students as well as all the little things that you should be doing whenever you're going out on a purported "job maintenance firm visit."

1. The value of just showing up

Woody Allen was famously quoted as stating that 80 percent of life is just showing up. While there are no metrics on such a statement, there is no question that there is real validity to this for educators in the field. Yes, there will be times when a snazzy sales pitch or a clever handling of an objection will result in a new job, but just as often it happens because you simply made yourself visible.

A good example arose a few years ago. Long after I had met the VP of a big company downtown, I stopped in to check in on the latest batch of co-ops. The VP happened to spot me in a hallway and flagged me down. "Hey, do you guys have marketing students who do co-ops?" "Sure," I said. "Wow, that's great—let me pull together and get you a job description. We could use someone." That was that, and four students have had that job over the last two years. When you're on the radar screen of the decision-makers in an organization, good things happen. You'll see another example of this in the Nancy Chiang/Kirk Patterson transcript at the end of this chapter.

2. *The stated reason for your visit*

Although you may indeed get some good jobs just by showing up, it's much easier to get in the front door by saying that you're coming down to check in on the current co-op or intern. Unless someone calls me to tell me explicitly that they want me to come in and talk about new opportunities, I never mention job development when I'm scheduling a visit to an existing employer. But it's always on my mind.

So the initial priority is to come in and talk to the student and his or her manager. Once you ascertain that all is well (or address anything that merits discussion), then you can probe informally through conversation to find out how the company is doing. What challenges are anticipated for the coming year? At worst, you'll probably get some information that will be useful for future applicants and employees to know. At best, you might find out that there are some ways in which your program might branch out.

3. *Nipping problems in the bud*

As we've discussed earlier, it's human nature to avoid conflict. On top of that, managers are busy! When you go out, you may well find that a manager has some small or significant gripe about a student's attitude or performance, but the manager has not found the time to address it. Likewise, you may talk to a student who is concerned or unhappy but who has not brought that to your attention before.

For these reasons, going out in the field is the way to address problems before they've grown and possibly created irreconcilable issues. For this reason, I always try to get some private time with the manager and student, so either party has the opportunity to give me a candid appraisal of how things are going. Tamara Pinkas of Lane Community College tells me that she often asks the student to walk out to her car with her as one way to ensure that students have an opportunity to share information confidentially if necessary. If there is a problem, you can coach the concerned party on how to broach the issue in a solution-oriented way. In some cases, I may even mediate the issue. If you can convey that you are an objective person who is looking for a win/win solution, then your advice may carry some weight. All too often, employers are reluctant to call students out on behavior that they would not tolerate in full-time employees. Why? Because they are "just students." If this comes up, I can emphasize that I want any student to be treated no differently than any full-time employee.

Similarly, students are reluctant to bring up concerns with employers. They worry—not without reason—that they may be labeled as malcontents or whiners, and they know full well that they have relatively little power in their relationship with their boss. When I hear about this reluctance, this gives me the opportunity to acknowledge that they do need to proceed with caution when voicing concerns. But these situations also represent valuable learning opportunities, and they can be powerful experiences if handled correctly. Whether it's a case of being underutilized or having to deal with an unpleasant co-worker or supervisor, this is probably not the last time that the issue will arise in the course of the student's career. We then can talk about the kind of tone and language to use to address an issue as well as whether the concern is significant enough to address at all.

It's important to remember that the student basically IS your institution in that workplace, especially if that student is the first hire for that company. You can talk all you like about how great your program is, and you can do a fabulous job of building rapport with your contacts.

But if the student bombs, it's all for naught. Visiting students greatly decreases your chances of losing relationships when problems escalate without getting handled responsively.

4. *The student as job developer*

Simply by performing well, your current student is probably a better job developer than you ever will be. There are many organizations that started off with just one hire. Eventually, conversations start happening in workplaces. Managers talk about where they obtained their great, cost-effective resource, and the next thing you know that company hires two co-ops, then three, and on it goes. I have several employers that started with one co-op and ended up with as many as 15.

With this in mind, anything you can do before, during, or after each work term to increase your students' probability of success is a good idea. We've talked about much of this earlier, so I won't belabor it here. But the point worth reiterating is to make sure that students realize that all is not lost if the job or company or field is not the right match for them in the long run. Building awareness of how much learning happens outside of technical skills is crucial.

One other point here: Students also can be literal job developers as well. When I interviewed Kirk Patterson from the University of Waterloo, he talked about his students who opt to develop their own jobs. He always asks them to bring back business cards, Chamber of Commerce directories, and so forth. We do the same thing. If a student develops their own job, we try to roll it over with our current jobs. In fact, one of my best new jobs was developed by a student whose father was friends with one of the principals. I talk all the time about how I hope students will let me know if they hear from friends and relatives about hiring needs.

5. *Checking with the employer to ask what's in the pipeline*

While ostensibly just making conversation, I often like to ask managers what challenges they anticipate for the year to come. What's in the pipeline—any new projects, developments, or trends that are of interest? Sometimes you'll learn about a maternity leave or a temporary project that will dovetail well with your program's flexibility and relatively short-term level of commitment.

A few years ago, this kind of probing revealed that a big employer of mine in downtown Boston was going to be moving 2,000 employees to a new office building a few blocks away. Knowing that they had only been hiring one PC support co-op, I immediately suggested that they hire three or four for the six-month term that included the move. After all, there would be a ton of work when it came to moving desktop computers, reconnecting networks, replacing outdated equipment, and so on. The company liked the idea and hired four co-ops. But the real payoff came six months later: When their move ended, they found that they really *liked* having four co-ops in terms of cost, productivity, attitude, and flexibility. They have hired at least four ever work term since!

6. *Making the employer aware of timelines*

Visiting employers is a great way to reinforce important timelines. You can remind both student and manager about the advisability of a midpoint review, and you can get them both thinking about revising the job description if you're going to be requesting that soon by e-mail. Seeing you in person will reinforce the importance of being on top of these timelines.

7. *Being alert to hints*

Sometimes you will be able to pick up on relatively subtle issues by visiting a company—nuances that you would never catch over the phone or via e-mail. Maybe it's a sense that the employer seems a little exasperated when listening to the student describe what they're doing. Perhaps the student's desk looks like total chaos, and everyone around them has everything in order. This can lead to opportunities to probe a little more deeply to see if there is any cause for concern.

Recently an out-of-state employer surprised me by bringing the current co-op with them for their on-campus interviews. I had known for quite a while that the co-op was unhappy because she had been badly underutilized. She had been saying all the right things to me on the phone, but her facial expression when she visited worried me. She just seemed to be wearing her frustration on her face, and this was on a day when she had the treat of being flown up to Boston for interviews! Since then, I have tried to take extra care to remind her to stay as visibly positive as possible for the duration of her co-op, even though her situation is difficult.

8. *Being the answer person*

Visiting companies gives you a great opportunity to reinforce your image as the "unpaid consultant" I described earlier. I make sure my employers know that it's fair game to ask me questions about best practices, hiring trends, starting salaries, whatever. I want them to look forward to my visits, and any excuse for them to call me is a good way for me to ensure that I am still on their radar screen.

9. *Reinforcing student learning*

Although this part of the book focuses more on employers, it's worth noting that job maintenance visits are great ways to see how students are faring as learners out there in the organizational world. So when I sit down with them privately, I certainly will ask them how things are going in general… but I also will want to talk about what they've been learning, how that matches up with what they expected to learn, and how their self-awareness has changed—especially when it comes to what they now think they want to do for their next job.

When talking to students, I also will ask questions related to the different phases of the work term that I discussed in Chapter 10: orientation, navigation, mastery, excellence, etc. More than anything, I'll make sure they have the opportunity to ask me any questions that they may have.

10. *Payoffs of strengthening relationships*

Sometimes you will not walk out of a building with a definite sense of having accomplished something tangible during your firm visit. It's not at all unusual to find that the student is doing fine and that the status quo will continue with no job development resulting. Still, it's hard to quantify just what your job maintenance visits might be doing for your program.

Sometimes you'll get no immediate interest when it comes to expanding your program, but you might get a call weeks later on that front. Another consideration is that managers change roles, moving on to a new department or a new organization. As described by Nancy Chiang and Kirk Patterson later in this chapter, this is a great way for your program to spread quite organically. However, it's much more likely to happen if you have something more than an e-mail and phone relationship with that transient manager.

Another factor is that economic times are always subject to change. If times are bad, you obviously want your program to be the last thing that gets cut and the first resource that the company will turn to when they are ready to grow once again. Without strong personal relationships, this becomes much more of a long shot.

ENHANCING THE EMPLOYER PARTNERSHIP

I alluded to some of these ideas earlier in the chapter when talking about how to help employers market their company to students. While this is important, the ultimate goal is to enhance and cement a true partnership between important employers and the institution. All of these ideas are ways to increase the employer's investment of time, money, emotion, and energy into your program.

ON-CAMPUS INFORMATION SESSIONS AND INTERVIEWS

We often have our larger employers put on information sessions to promote their co-op programs. These are held in the early evening or during student activity periods when no classes are scheduled on weekdays. The information sessions can be a great way to make students more aware of companies that they might overlook in a database of job descriptions.

However, the info sessions can backfire, too. If you do them, remember these keys:

- Tactfully remind companies that info sessions can be a 50-mile death march if they are long-winded, one-sided lectures with an overemphasis on company history and organization charts.

- Conversely, suggest that a good session gives a brief overview of the company before focusing on specific job opportunities that will be available to students.

- Making sessions interactive is always good. Ideally, getting current or former co-ops to discuss their experiences and/or answer questions on a student panel adds interest and credibility.

- In most cases, a good goal is to have the formal session last no more than about 45 minutes, with about 15 minutes for Q&A. This is especially true if your program has many info sessions; students will just stop coming if they are too much of a time commitment and/or if sessions persist in being too long with too little value.

- Providing refreshments, free product, or some sort of giveaway can add interest. With product, my marketing colleague Erin Callery always says that students are more interested in a company with a product that they can touch. So we often have employers giving away everything from shampoo to software.

- Some coordinators give extra-credit points in their co-op prep class to students who attend info sessions and write short reports about what they learned. This fills seats and gives students an additional incentive to learn more about employers they might not otherwise consider.

On-campus interviews are a real missed opportunity for many institutions. I have heard from employers who no longer go to some other schools because of how they were treated while "guests" on campus. Some of the typical complaints:

- No screening of resumes, resulting in many interviews that were obviously a waste of time.

- Poor interviewing facilities, including thrown-together spaces on a basketball court with no real privacy and with noise proving to be a problem.

- Poor scheduling, resulting in, say, an 8:00 a.m. interview followed by a two-hour "break" and/or interviews spread widely across a very long day with no concern for the employer's convenience.

- No one greeting them at the beginning of the day or meeting with them at the end of the day to get feedback on candidates.

- No food or refreshments readily available, free or otherwise.

The space issue can be a real challenge. We need a lot of space for interviewing, but we need it primarily for roughly five months out of the year. As a result, we always have other people on campus ogling our interview rooms, wanting to convert them to offices. We do whatever we can to make sure that we keep that space for employers, as it's absolutely critical if you expect to satisfy out-of-state employers.

I can imagine that some programs may feel that they just don't have the resources to avoid some of those aforementioned complaints. To me, it's so much less expensive to satisfy those employers who are willing to beat a path to your campus than it is trying to drum up new organizations from scratch. When companies come in for the first time and are wowed by the preparation of your students, the professionalism of your faculty and staff, and the comfort and convenience of your facilities, then they are definitely going to put your school higher on the list when it comes to prioritizing schools for future visits.

JOB FAIRS

Most colleges and universities have some sort of job fair, usually run by Career Services. Often we have very large career fairs at Northeastern. The primary focus is usually on full-time hires, but we have many employers who find that this is a great way to promote their co-op opportunities as well. On the student side, I usually tell my co-ops that while the career fair is more geared to seniors, it can be a great way for them to get out there and work on a 30-second commercial about themselves with relatively little downside.

How about a co-op or internship job fair? It definitely can be done, though we don't do them as often. Most often, we have had ones that have a more narrow focus, such as a special expo for Computer Science or Accounting co-op employers.

These events can be a great deal of work for the institution. They also can create some messy situations. We have had students who have been deemed ineligible for co-op but have managed to get themselves an interview or a job by showing up uninvited for one of these fairs. So you might want to have a few caveats in mind for employers, but job fairs are another way to help build partnerships with companies.

369

CLASSROOM INVOLVEMENT

If you're interested in doing something to foster true integration of the classroom and the workplace, consider bringing together some of your best managers with some academic faculty who might want to bring a real-world element to the classroom. For example, I was able to assist a business professor by connecting him with a company that does cutting-edge work in "word of mouth" marketing, and a company expert came in and showed the class one of the hottest trends in industry. That was exciting for everyone involved, and it underscored a few points of emphasis:

- It's great to remind employers that they are educators and not just managers, as this can carry over into how they manage co-ops and interns.

- It reminds the classroom professors that they need to keep their class topical and relevant, especially when teaching students who are fairly sophisticated in terms of their exposure to contemporary organizations.

- It reminds the co-op professional and the academic professor that they are both striving to educate the student, albeit from different angles.

Employers can be brought in as part of panels, prep classes, student clubs, or to address special areas of expertise that may go beyond the knowledge of the professor. If employers are game, they can get very involved on campus. Everyone can win when that happens.

CASE COMPETITIONS

Organizations wishing to make a bigger commitment may sponsor a case study or business proposal competition. Every year, we have a large company sponsor our Introduction to Business class. Students are asked to generate business ideas for that company—generally someone with a retail presence—and the best teams earn the opportunity to present their pitches to a panel of executives from that company. The best teams often have amazing ideas—ways to make the company more green or to capitalize more effectively on technology are not unusual—and the company generates great interest in their co-op jobs. I'm sure that the publicity doesn't hurt their retail sales and brand awareness, either.

COMMUNICATING WITH EMPLOYERS

Of course, it's not always possible to get employers to come to you or to get out on the road to visit them. When that happens, we are left with phone calls, voice mails, e-mail, and snail mail. At this point, I think I almost never use snail mail to communicate with employers. Sometimes we mail out calendars or Christmas cards to employers, but I can't think of any other instance in which I would send physical mail to employers anymore.

When weighing whether to use e-mail or the phone, I'll make every effort to defer to what works best with a given employer. There are some employers who attempt to avoid the phone at all costs, while others just can't be reached unless you pick up the phone.

Generally, though, I prefer the phone if I am dealing with any issue that is relatively complicated or that has the potential to involve an emotional exchange. As I've discussed in earlier chapters on working with students, the one-sided nature of e-mails leaves them very open to be misinterpreted or for minor issues to get escalated. I recently made that mistake with an employer who e-mailed me to complain about getting resumes of students with GPAs below 3.0. The right thing to do would have been to pick up the phone and talk through the employer's concern. Instead, I wrote back and suggested that it would be a good idea for the employer to be open to students with lower GPAs. After all, there is no scientific evidence suggesting that there is anything more than a mild positive correlation between GPA and job performance. The employer responded with a heated e-mail about how his organization only wants to hire the "best and the brightest," and that they have a corporate HR mandate to not hire anyone below a 3.0 GPA. I have to think that I could have adjusted my message and prevented some sore feelings if it had been a phone conversation.

That said, e-mail can be a great way to maximize efficiency without compromising much in terms of the quality of your message in many instances. Back in Chapter 3, I discussed how handy it is to keep a file or folder of e-mail templates to disseminate information. These can be used to remind employers about turning in job descriptions, how to proceed after receiving a packet of resumes, setting goals with new hires, doing midpoint evaluations, and so on. If done properly, these group e-mails can seem quite personal, too.

TROUBLESHOOTING PROBLEMS

In Chapter 10, we discussed the most common student complaints that typically arise when co-ops or interns are working. Here we will focus more on employer complaints. That said, it's important to emphasize that it's quite rare to come across a problem that is 100% the fault of the employer or the student. Sure, that does happen—you will have the student who gets fired for some outrageous—even illegal—behavior. And then there are employers who engage in highly unethical behavior, too. In my experience, though, usually both parties played at least *some* role in creating the problem. I'll follow up on that when we discuss troubleshooting tips, but first let's consider the most common employer.

COMMON EMPLOYER COMPLAINTS

Every educator hates to get a phone call or an e-mail from an unhappy employer. "We're having a problem with our student," they will tell you. You take a deep breath and try to keep your tone neutral, hoping it's not something horrific. "I'm sorry to hear that," you'll say. "What's the concern?"

Usually it's one of the following:

1. *The student is frequently late or absent, sometimes without notification.*

I talked about this earlier in this book. This is maddening, as it obviously doesn't take a genius to get to work on time. And in my case, I feel like they've read what I've had to say about that in my *Find Your First Professional Job* and *Exceeding Expectations* books on top of hearing me talk about at length in class and in the co-op success factors meeting. Still, it happens.

When this comes up, you'll want to get some data from the employer. How often has this occurred? Exactly how late has the student arrived? What reason did they give, if any? Has the employer discussed the issue with the student and laid out possible consequences?

2. *The student is abusing technology.*

When I started as a co-op coordinator in 1995, I rarely heard about issues with technology. With the last edition of my *Find Your First Professional Job* book, though, I added about 15 pages of material on e-mail etiquette. As we discussed in Chapter 6, today's students have an extremely comfortable relationship with technology, and they are not always good at setting boundaries for themselves with their computers, cell phones, and PDAs at work.

The magnitude of the problem here can vary dramatically. The complaint may be something relatively minor, such as a tendency to surf the Internet instead of asking for more work. Excessive checking of e-mails and sports scores is another issue, as is heavy use of a cell phone or BlackBerry. More seriously, there are technology abuses that can lead to instant termination, such as downloading pornographic videos.

Here you'll also want to focus on gathering as many facts as possible so you can determine whether this is a minor peccadillo or a major transgression.

3. *The student has other professional behavior issues.*

There are many possibilities here. The most common one might be attire. Students get many mixed messages about appropriate workplace attire. If you don't address this issue proactively in your preparation activities—and even if you do—you may be getting more phone calls than you would like about cleavage, piercings, blue jeans, and T-shirts. Now that "business casual" is commonplace as the official office attire mandate, we find that students may push the "casual" side of that envelope. Even worse, there are students who interpret the more casual attire as a cue to take a more casual approach to the job itself.

Other office etiquette issues also come up periodically. Excessive socializing, inappropriate humor, taking an excessively long lunch, printing out schoolwork on the office printer—these all can be issues. We had a student fired a few years ago because he had printed out an Organizational Behavior paper at work. Well, it wasn't just that it was schoolwork; it was actually an assignment where he had to critique his manager's leadership style!

Sometimes we have had problems when a company hired a large number of students from our program. The students formed a clique at work instead of integrating themselves with the full-time employees, and this created an "us and them" mentality that didn't serve anyone well. We now try to advise students at our largest employers that they should make a real effort to have lunch with full-time people and not cling to their peers from school.

Another disappointing issue is when an employer calls to say that her exemplary co-op suddenly became a problem when the co-op term ended and the student began a part-time schedule. This comes back to the concept of failing to "under-promise and over-deliver." Some students ambitiously promise to work 25–30 hours per week when in classes, and then they find they can't handle it. So they ask if they can cut their hours to 22, then 18, then 15, and the manager gets exasperated. Alternatively, the student changes their schedule every week as their academic workload waxes and wanes; ultimately, no one at the company has any idea if the student will be in or out on any given day.

Obviously, these issues are best dealt with by taking steps to prevent them from arising altogether. However, we will deal with steps in addressing them shortly.

4. *The student has attitude issues.*

This can take many forms. The student may have the "instant messiah" syndrome in which they expect to be given high-level responsibilities immediately, regardless of their experience level. Along the same lines, another theme is that co-ops or interns—especially the millennials that I described in Chapter 6—have really not experienced a meritocracy before. They don't understand that the ticket to earning better work is by doing whatever you're asked to do really well and coming back eager for more.

Some co-ops or interns also forget the saying that if a job was nothing but fun, then they probably wouldn't have to pay you to do it. Others may become disillusioned when they discover that the job or field is not to their liking, and they respond by going through the motions. Similarly, some students simply do as they're told but make no effort to go beyond the job description. Whether such a person is content to be adequate or lacks the creativity or drive to see beyond the literal duties of the job is a good question—one worth probing as you look into that sort of issue.

5. *The student needs too much hand-holding and direction.*

This certainly sounds like another of the Millennial Generation complaints that I discussed in Chapter 6, and it's compounded if the manager has that self-sufficient Generation X mentality.

When you dig into this one, you might find that both parties are unhappy. The manager wants the employee to get off their duff to figure things out or to ask questions if necessary—or to maybe ask less questions in some cases—while the employee is disgruntled because of what he or she perceives as inadequate training or mentoring.

6. *The student just can't do the job.*

Given that my students often obtain technically challenging jobs in which they must learn new skills, I feared that this would be a common complaint. However, I have only had one or two students let go over 13+ years because of incompetence, and one of those was more of an English language issue that should've been sorted out during the job interview.

Occasionally, though, a manager will call and express frustration about someone's inability to catch on. At times, we definitely have had managers alter the job description to make it something that the student could handle without problems.

TROUBLESHOOTING TIPS

The first challenge when you get an employer complaint is to not get swept up in the emotions of it. If it's a serious problem, I often can visualize my ambitious plans for the next half-day exploding instantly. I have to let go of any frustration, anxiety, and disappointment that I may feel about this unexpected difficulty, as it will prevent me from handling it as effectively as possible. With that in mind, let's walk through some general pointers on dealing with employer complaints or concerns.

1. *Assume nothing.*

There is always a tendency to take the side of the person who is calling you to complain, and this is probably even more the case when it's an employer calling to voice displeasure with a student. After all, the employer is almost always going to be closer to your age than the student, and he or she is in a position of power. And while you hopefully think of both the student and the employer as your customers, many coordinators are more anxious about the loss of an employer relationship than they are about a disgruntled student.

Regardless, it's important to try to assume nothing when you start to gather facts about a problem between a student and employer. One slight exception would be that inevitably you're going to mull your history with each party. If you have a great relationship with the employer, and this is the first student that has evoked a concern or complaint after several successes, this bears consideration. Likewise, if the student has always been exemplary while your history with the employer is limited or mixed, you might be less inclined to take the employer's grousing at face value. Still, every situation is a new one, and there is always the possibility that someone will surprise and disappoint you. And as stated earlier, it's rare to find a situation that is purely the fault of one party.

2. Stay calm, objective, and neutral in tone.

When you get a complaint, there is a pretty good range of possibility in terms of the employer's tone. They may be a little amused, totally neutral, somewhat frustrated, or quite angry. The key is to avoid getting defensive or angry on your end. It's important to let the individual know that you're sorry that they're having an issue and to show eagerness to learn more about the nature of the problem. But you want to come across as calm, intellectually curious, objective, open, and solution-oriented.

Without coming out and saying it, I want my tone to say "Let's get all the facts so we can work toward solving this problem together." In terms of words, my initial focus after acknowledging that there is an issue is going to be on asking clarifying questions. Exactly what happened? When did it happen? How has it been handled thus far? How can I be most helpful in determining what happens next? I want to ask those questions before I judge any behavior or suggest any next steps.

3. Maintain confidentiality, "playing dumb" if necessary.

In these situations, you often end up privy to some strong statements that an employer or student may say to you in confidence. Sometimes either party will call you or e-mail you with a specific and seemingly legitimate complaint, stated in very strong terms. Whether the statement is accurate or not, you have to be careful about what you repeat to the other party. Will it escalate the conflict between the two? Will sharing the information help effect a solution? Would the individual be okay with repeating that to the other party, or was it a case of that person just needing to vent before a more constructive tone can be taken? These are critical considerations. As with the Hippocratic Oath, your motto here should be, "First, do no harm."

Sometimes I will "play dumb" in my quest to find out what's honestly going on in a situation. Even when I know that one party is livid about the other's behavior, I might approach that other person as if I had no idea about this. If a student is angry because the employer never gives him meaningful work—but is afraid about broaching the issue—I might call the employer and say, "I just thought I'd call and check in on how things have been working out with Jeff so far."

This serves several useful purposes:

- I don't have to disclose that Jeff contacted me to complain about the employer, as that may affect how the employer treats Jeff going forward.

- Given that I only have Jeff's perception to go on, this gives me the opportunity to hear what the manager's honest perception is—without making the manager defensive or angry by making accusations that may be unfair.

- After hearing the manager's perception of the situation, it leaves many options available to me: a) going back to the student and suggesting a course of action based on the manager's sense of what's going on; b) telling the student that I think it might be helpful for me to come in for a visit to deal with the issue more directly; or c) getting the student's permission to go back to the manager at some point to broach the concern more directly if the student is uncomfortable doing so.

So I increase my options by approaching the conflict in this neutral manner. Regardless, I do think you have to be very careful about confidentiality. Although you want to be as transparent as possible, it's always good to get permission before sharing someone's concerns, and you should let them know exactly how you will characterize those concerns.

4. *Ask clarifying questions of both parties, reserving judgment until you've heard both sides of the story.*

Not infrequently, a disgruntled employer or student will push you to respond quickly to a problem. The employer tells you that a student is a poor performer and wants your blessing to fire the student. The student tells a tale of woe and seeks permission to quit a job that they have portrayed as intolerable. In an effort to resolve the situation as they see fit, either party may push for the most expedient solution. In order to get you to side with them, either party might selectively omit some key details. Less nefariously—and more commonly—there is the simple truth that different individuals always perceive situations differently. A person may truly believe that she has been wronged or short-changed, and she may conveniently blame the other party. That doesn't necessarily mean that her perceptions are accurate.

As a result, you need to slow things down—especially when there are conflicting perceptions. There are very few conflicts between employer and student that mandate immediate action. If someone's physical safety or psychological well-being is at risk in a significant way, then getting the student out of that work environment—at least temporarily and perhaps permanently—may be advisable. However, this is very rarely the case. More often, conflicts call for someone with a level head to keep asking questions of both parties until some sort of reasonable conclusion can be reached.

Here are some good clarifying questions for students, stated very generally:

- What was your understanding of what the job was supposed to be? What was that understanding based on? Was everyone on the same page with their expectations?

- When did the problem in question seem to emerge? Why did it emerge? How was it handled then? What was the response to how it was handled?

- What ideally would you like to see happen now? How can I help make that happen?

This last bullet point merits further comment. At times I have been stumped as to what to do with a student in crisis. Just a few years ago, I had a student who was in the thick of a very unpleasant sexual harassment situation. HR had asked her to corroborate a complaint of a female co-worker. She did the right thing by doing so, but the company then attempted to sweep it under the rug. I was really upset and not sure how to proceed, given that the company had essentially failed her. So I just asked her how I could be of most assistance to her under the circumstances.

To my surprise, she was totally clear on that. "I need you to reaffirm that I did the right thing by going to HR and to remind me that I'm a strong person who is going to get through this tough time." "I can do that!" I said, and we were back on track. We hung on there and finally found a sympathetic ear at the company, and all turned out well.

5. *Remind everyone that quitting/firing should not be the first resort, generally.*

As I've stated, very few people relish conflict. When absolutely forced to deal with it, people want to get it over with as soon as possible. Managers often take too long to nip a small problem like tardiness in the bud, and by the time they opt to deal with it, they may want to let the student go without even a warning. On the other side, students—especially Millennial Generation students, who stereotypically have a lower frustration threshold—often have little experience dealing with adversity. What happened when they didn't like their activities (swimming, piano, ballet, and so on) during high school? In some cases, they were allowed to bail as soon as it became less fun. Whether or not you think that's fair, I definitely have seen many students who get to that first hurdle at work and go, "Wow, that's high!" They want to walk away from the hurdle instead of figuring out how they are going to get over or around it.

So we need to remind employers and students that firing or quitting should not be a first resort unless something extremely awful has happened. A student caught falsifying a time sheet or stealing company property should be let go immediately. A student should not be punished for quitting a job if the employer unequivocally makes sexual advances or puts the student in physical jeopardy. Again, though, these scenarios almost never happen, and those who push for an immediate firing or abrupt resignation generally need to be talked off the ledge while you sift through the facts and search for a solution.

6. *Focus on win/win solutions. For the student and employer, the problem is a learning opportunity. Remind everyone of what is lost by terminating the relationship and what can be gained by salvaging and improving it.*

Regardless of whether the employer and/or the student believe that you automatically will side with them, you want to focus on win/win solutions. The simple fact is that a premature ending to the work term will be costly to all parties. The employer will lose the cost-effective resource that they expected to have on hand for a full work term, and there may be no obvious option when it comes to picking up that slack. The student may lose credit for their work term, and how are they going to learn anything at all if they're unemployed? And if both student and employer lose, that's going to affect you, too. The employer may be leery of working with you in the future, while you might be wary of trusting that student or organization when the next go-round starts.

I like to remind both parties of the following:

- We all have everything to gain by making this relationship work.

- We all have an opportunity to learn something valuable by addressing a conflict in a solution-oriented manner and seeing what can be done to make the situation workable.

- Even if the situation ultimately doesn't work out, we all want to look back at the experience and feel good about how we handled it. Conversely, if we are disappointed in the actions of another party, we are not going to be satisfied in the long run if our response was to sink to their level.

- While it's not unprecedented to see a problem that is 100% the fault of one party, this is rare. Usually both parties have contributed to the problem, or one party has exacerbated a problem that the other created.

- The nature of learning is unpredictable. We don't always get what we expect when we set out to learn something. The more we can embrace the learning opportunity—however unpleasant—the more we are likely to benefit.

TROUBLESHOOTING STORIES

Let's walk through two specific troubleshooting situations to see how these principles might play out in some real-life situations. These are both true stories, though I will alter the names and identifying principles to maintain confidentiality.

THE TIME SHEET ACCUSATION

One morning, my HR contact at Shumbata Products—a Fortune 100 company and employer of many Northeastern students—called me up. She was very angry. She informed me that they had just fired Dmitri Popov, one of my co-ops. "He has been falsifying time sheets for the last few months. His manager became suspicious, and we started keeping track of when he got to work and left. Consistently, he's been working around 40 hours per week and submitting time sheets indicating that he worked 55–60 hours per week."

In a heated tone, my contact asked me what I would do to ensure that he was punished appropriately for his actions. I told her that I first would need to talk to Dmitri before I could say anything about what next steps might occur. She was livid! "I've already *told* you what happened!" she said. "We want to know how Northeastern is going to respond to this." I told her that I just needed to gather all the information before any decision could be made and that I would follow up with her. She remained dissatisfied, but that was my final word for the moment.

Then I spoke to Dmitri. Interestingly, he denied any wrongdoing and wanted me to send his resume out to another employer as soon as possible! Like my contact at Shumbata, Dmitri was very dissatisfied when I told him that we weren't going to do anything of the kind until I had gathered enough information to decide what would be an appropriate next step.

So I did my best to assume nothing and starting hitting Dmitri with clarifying questions. Dmitri insisted that he was innocent and that he had been set up by a co-worker who disliked him. His story sounded a little shaky to me, but it wasn't totally implausible. So I just kept asking him clarifying questions. "Why would someone want to set you up?" He claimed that an African-American employee had told him that he didn't like Russians coming to the U.S.A. and taking jobs away from Americans. Although the racist comment irked me, I let it pass for the moment in favor of more questions. "Okay, so you're admitting that you got paid for hours that you didn't work. Didn't you notice that on your paychecks?" He said that he hadn't. He was using automatic deposit; he said that he checked the first one or two but hadn't looked at his account since then. He added that this was an account that he set aside for tuition, so he never looked at it.

I saw my opportunity. "I've got a great idea," I said. "Let's prove your innocence. You admit that you were paid money that you didn't earn. So tomorrow, I want you to bring in a cashier's check made out to the company to compensate them for the money that you were paid, erroneously." He said okay, but I could tell from his lack of enthusiasm that the money was not there. Within a day, he changed his tune. He said that though he was not guilty of the offense, he was willing to *say* that he was guilty if it led to a less severe penalty. Based on that and the failure to repay the employer immediately, I then turned the case over to our Judicial Affairs group. He was suspended and not allowed to return until he repaid several thousand dollars to the employer. Although I was saddened about the whole development, I felt good about the fact that I had resisted the urge to act until I had sufficient facts. Best of all, while my contact at Shumbata initially had a "told you so" reaction when I told her that I had sufficient proof of the student's wrongdoing, she was shocked to hear that I had been able to recoup the money, as they had written off that possibility altogether.

MARKING TIME

This story arose while writing this book. In September 2008, an employer of mine called. He is an NU alum and has had about eight to ten co-ops work for him over the last four years or so. While he had no previous complaints about co-ops, he said that he was sorry to say that he thought he was going to have to fire a co-op for the first time.

I asked for the details. "Kevin" had been working for the company since July. There had been any number of issues since then. The biggest complaint was that Kevin was almost always a little late to work, and he had a tendency to take long lunches without making up the time at the end of the day. On top of that, he was a slow, unproductive worker who was prone to errors. Had they talked to Kevin about these issues? Yes, they had, and the manager concluded that it was probably a hopeless case. I asked if I could speak with Kevin before anything was decided.

I took a few minutes to cool down. Knowing the manager and knowing Kevin, my sense was that Kevin was *probably* more to blame here. He was an okay guy, but his social skills and judgment had seemed somewhat questionable in my previous dealings with him. However, I knew that reaming him out on the phone was only going to escalate the problem. So I went with my usual plan of asking how things were going in a neutral way.

He felt that things were going okay, but his biggest problem was that he had written the job off. After discovering early on that he didn't like the company, the field, or the job, he became very disgruntled. "So you've basically just ended up viewing yourself as marking time until the six months is up?" I said, and he agreed that this was an accurate assessment.

Curiously, he seemed oblivious to how unhappy the employer really was. When I asked him if he had been told about any concerns, he mentioned the tardiness issue but shrugged that off as well as other problems. At that point, I told him that he was at risk of losing his job. To my surprise, he said, "That would be fine with me! I'm not getting anything out of this anyway."

That was a turning point of sorts for me. I could see that the *real* issue here was that Kevin was one of those students who decide that all is lost once they realize that the job or career path is not for them. This is sad, as obviously this is only a small piece of the possible learning for any co-op or intern. So I tried to reframe his situation. For him, he had a great challenge and learning opportunity in front of him. Could he turn around a negative perception that the employer has about him? I told him that a typical performer excels in a job that he loves, but the great performer finds a way to excel regardless of the task, the manager, or the professor.

And there were also a ton of learning opportunities that he was overlooking: How do I diplomatically ask for more and better work? How do I perform in such a way that shows that I deserve such work? How do I collaborate with a manager and co-workers who have different priorities, values, and personalities? There are so many learning opportunities that are available regardless of how one feels about the job itself.

He was a little intrigued but not thoroughly convinced. I then played out the other scenario. He could quit, or he could be fired. If that happened, the failure to get co-op credit would be the least of his problems. What would he do for the next three months that would represent real learning? How would he explain the gap on his resume and transcript to a future employer? If he got fired, he was going to have a tough time deciding whether this job should go on his resume. I also reminded him that even if things ultimately did not work out, he would want to be able to look back at his behavior and feel that he took the high road by doing all he could to salvage the relationship.

While I left him to think all that over, I got back to the employer and told him that I had encouraged Kevin to turn around his performance and make the most of the learning opportunity. I didn't share Kevin's complaints about the employer, but I did say that I had gotten the sense that maybe Kevin didn't have much training up front. The manager admitted that he had been traveling a lot when Kevin started and that he believed that the problems could have been addressed much more expediently if he had been around to train Kevin and address issues as soon as they arose.

I think we all came away feeling a little humbled. I certainly felt that I had not done enough in advance with Kevin to prepare him for how to be open to the idea that all is not lost if he didn't like the job. Kevin cooled down and bought into the fact that there was something to gain by making his turnaround the top learning goal for the rest of the work term. And the employer got a reality check when it came to acculturating a co-op into his small work team.

As I write this, it's November 16. Last month, the manager told me that Kevin was trying much harder to make it work, and the company was responding in kind. Kevin still has five weeks to go, but I'm hopeful he'll make it.

UPDATE on December 19: Looks like Kevin survived the six months! I can hardly wait to meet with him next month to find out if he truly managed to turn around such a tough situation.

CUTTING TIES WITH EMPLOYERS

There is one last topic to handle, and it's an unpleasant one. How does an educator determine when an employer is not going to be appropriate as an educational partner? This is always a judgment call, and it's not necessarily an easy one. In an ideal world, we would have the luxury of only working with employers who are wonderful mentors. It would be great if every employer embraced the idea of setting goals and doing thorough evaluations at various points of a work term. Likewise, it would be great if we could only work with employers who pay top dollar and offer challenging, meaningful work with the opportunity to take on more and better work if the student shows the ability to handle that.

Realistically, though, you may have to accept the fact that not every employer is going to be the optimal educational partner. This is especially true when the economy or job market is hurting. For years, I kept working with one manager downtown despite the fact that he was a rigid, overly demanding manager. He fooled me for a while—he was so deferential whenever I spoke to him or met with him! And when the first student complained that he was stern and unreasonable, it was easy to chalk that up as a he said/she said situation. Sometimes there is just a bad fit between a given employee and manager, right?

But that kept happening. Unfortunately, the economy was bad at the time, and I didn't feel like I could just get rid of the job. So I started being honest with potential applicants, telling them that the manager had a reputation as being a difficult guy. Could they handle that? Some couldn't, and I didn't press the point. Others did okay with him, though I felt better for forewarning them. Still, I ultimately decided that it just was not a healthy learning environment, and I was relieved when the employer decided not to hire. If that had not happened I definitely would have ended the relationship with that employer regardless.

So what are some good reasons to cut ties with an employer or to avoid starting a relationship with an organization?

1. *The employer is unable or unwilling to compensate a student fairly.*

This statement absolutely requires further explanation. Some industries and fields pay much more than others, whether we're talking about full-time employees or temporary co-ops and interns. There are some "sexy" fields in which a student must work for little or nothing in order to get a toehold in that industry. Also, a full-time co-op working for four or six months probably merits higher pay than, say, an intern who is working 15 hours per week for one semester.

Still, you need to be vigilant to ensure that students aren't being exploited. I fear that an employer who is paying little or nothing for a resource will not necessarily have the incentive to provide the individual with meaningful work. Left unmanaged by the educator, the employer could do whatever they want. The educator needs to be sure that the manager is providing a real learning experience replete with feedback. This is true with paid positions, too, but I think it is more likely to take care of itself than what we see with unpaid positions.

At Northeastern, we also are very leery of jobs that are wholly or mostly commission-based. Again, the problem is that the exploitation potential is high. The student can be lured into accepting a job that theoretically could pay off in a big way, but the risk is totally on the student's shoulders—not the employer's. If the student sells a lot, great—the employer makes good money, and so does the student. If the student sells so little that they can't even pay their expenses, what difference does it make to the employer?

With such employers, I usually will propose that they pay the student a somewhat low hourly rate—at least $10/hour—with performance-based bonuses on top of that. If the employer is not willing to do that, then I can't see posting the job under my name on our system.

2. *The employer treats students unfairly.*

Obviously, any employer that asks students to do unreasonable tasks or who treats them as no more than cheap labor is a suspect partner for you. Years ago, we had an employer who sent in a job description that literally started the list of duties as follows:

> 1. Get the doughnuts each morning.

Did we really need to go beyond that first item? Sure, our students may have to do menial work—and sometimes quite a bit of it depending on their previous experience as well as their career path—but we don't need employers who view students as flunkies who exist purely to do low-level work that is repugnant to everyone else in the office.

An even greater concern is outright discrimination. A work environment that is rife with sexist, racist, homophobic attitudes—whether directed at our students or not—is not going to be a healthy learning atmosphere for any student. You need to be very leery of any employer who insists on hiring an employee of a specific gender or race. I've heard of employers who said, "We just don't think a woman would be comfortable on this team." If that's the case, is it really the kind of place that would be beneficial to the growth and development of a male student?

A trickier example would be the employer who calls up and says that they want to fill a position with a "diversity candidate." This is usually code for "African-American or Hispanic." While it's great for our employers to do whatever they can to promote a diverse workforce, it is wise to be a little wary of employers who don't want to consider candidates unless they are minorities.

In that case, my response would be to encourage the employer to use the job description to emphasize the fact that they value diversity and are open to hiring candidates of all backgrounds. But I can't list a job that is available to some students and not others based on gender, race, religion, etc.

3. *The employer does not appreciate the fact that the student is a learner.*

This is the hardest statement of all to prove. There are employers who provide great learning experiences for students, though they do a lousy job of setting formal goals, training/mentoring their young employees, and writing up evaluations. There are the opposite cases, in which the job itself is basic or limited, but the student learns a lot because of the efforts of an attentive and understanding manager.

Sometimes, though, there is just not much going for a job at all. The student is not challenged, has a great deal of downtime, is left to their own devices by the manager, and is not really learning much beyond the fact that they don't like the job.

Even with all of those negatives, though, you can't necessarily jettison that job. Depending on your program, you sometimes *need* to have low-level jobs, as there are students who are just not qualified for something more advanced. I hate to see students accept jobs with certain employers in our program, yet I know that we definitely need to have a good number of such jobs available. For students with minimal experience, low grades, poor interviewing skills, possibly poor English, we have to take what we can get—especially if we are dealing with a dicey economy.

More than anything, I'm on the lookout for employers who push to hire our best and brightest students but then fail to give them any real challenge or learning. After getting extremely frustrated with an employer who did this to my best students repeatedly, I finally gave one of them permission to quit after weeks and weeks of trying to improve the situation. The employer took it to heart and overhauled their program, and now they offer what might be my best learning experience of all.

4. *The employer's behavior is unprofessional.*

I have seen many employers engage in behavior that we would not accept in our students. While some situations call for further dialogue and investigation, they definitely call for terminating a program if matters cannot be addressed to your satisfaction.

An organization that tacitly allows sexual harassment in any form—even after it's been brought to their attention—may get axed from your list. Employers who engage in unethical behavior—rescinding an offer in favor of a better candidate who came along later, for example—are not going to be good models for your students. I had one entrepreneur who asked a student to do personal favors for him, and that was an early indicator of a general lack of awareness about professional boundaries. One manager borrowed a substantial amount of money from one of my students. The company discovered it before I did and terminated the manager, so that one took care of itself.

Most recently, a student reported that a new employer gave her an extremely hard time after she politely declined his co-op job offer. He grilled her on why she declined and made several sarcastic statements about her decision. This is obviously a flag for me. I can address the situation by making sure that he knows that a student is not compelled to accept any offer made to them, but it raises the question of whether I want to do business with this person, regardless. If you went on a first date with someone who had a temper tantrum over some minor disagreement, would you not assume that you're seeing only the tip of the iceberg when it comes to bad behavior?

In one of the excerpts that follow, Tom Akins says that his criteria are that a position should be "paid, planned, and progressive." All good relationships need to result in all parties gaining some benefit from them and being willing to put some energy into them to make them work as well as they can. If you have a relationship with an employer that has substantially more costs than benefits—and it seems clear that it will be difficult or impossible to change that fact—then you need to cut ties amicably and focus your energy on more productive relationships.

IN THEIR OWN WORDS

PROFESSIONAL PERSPECTIVE #1
"STRATEGIC JOB MAINTENANCE"
Charlie Bognanni, Northeastern University

Well, I think it's only been in the last maybe five or six years that I've stepped back and approached job maintenance more strategically. Let's use the fall semester as an example. Now I step back in May and strategically look at the fall semester and say "How do I want that semester to go" rather than just waking up on September 5th and reacting to a bunch of students coming in and employers getting in touch. I've really started to be more strategic about this in terms of timing and looking at where do I want to be in October? Where do I want to be in November? What do I want to do?

So what I recommend to you is to look at the full semester and set some goals for yourself. So let's say you have 60 students, for the sake of an example. You want to take a look at those 60 students and you want to break them down by class year. How many students do you want to place? How many students are sophomores, first-timers, juniors, etc.? What types of positions are they likely to be interested in?

You want to do that first; you want to take a look at that. And if you have access to the information, it probably wouldn't be a bad idea to look at the GPAs of students. I work with accounting students, and employers value GPAs highly. So what am I likely to see this semester? Am I going to have a lot of high-quality students?

For example, this past spring semester my colleague had a lot of very marginal students she had to place. We don't know why; it just happened this way. She had at least 10–15 students with very low GPAs. So we sat down and we took a look at that, and we kind of adapted our strategy a little bit. We realized that we were going to have to get some what we would call marginal positions for these students. These students are not going to be able to apply for high-caliber jobs and as a result we decided to look for some positions we felt were more appropriate for them and we did that. We started doing some job development and we talked to some employers. So you have to look at who you have for that particular semester and the caliber. That's one thing. You want to take a look at what you have for existing employers.

Now, if you're brand new to a program, you may be walking into a program where someone's going to hand you some jobs, some employers. That's fine. You might walk into the program with nothing. Hopefully you don't because if you have 60 students and zero employers that's going to be tough for you. So let's assume you have at least something. You again want to take a look at how many jobs you have, what types of jobs do you have, where are the employers, and start saying, "Do I have enough? Do I not have enough? Where am I going to need jobs? Where are the gaps, geographically? Do I have the right number of jobs?"

If you see gaps, the best bet is to start with current or recent employers. They already understand how your program works, and they probably have had good experiences with your students.

383

Checking in with the ones who will help meet your needs can be the easiest solution. Selectively visiting those employers and asking about upcoming needs can directly lead to new jobs for the upcoming work term.

Then let's think about the students—that's one other thing we've been doing the last few years. We usually send an e-mail out to the students at the beginning of the semester asking them geographically where they're interested in working. If it's the fall semester, we do that back in August. We need to know early on: Are we looking at 60 students who all need to be in Boston? Are we looking at 40 who want to be in Boston, ten who want to be in New York, and another ten who want to be scattered all over the country and all over the world? Do we have a dozen who are flexible and just want the best job, wherever it's located?

That's important as you start planning your job maintenance strategies. My colleague and I have modified our strategy depending upon where students want to be. I remember about three years ago, we sent the e-mail out and out of maybe 80 students, I couldn't believe it, I think we had one or two that wanted to be in New York and everybody else wanted to be in Boston. I had never seen that before. So we immediately said we don't need a lot of jobs in New York and we did not spend a lot of time talking to our New York employers because we knew we would probably have a difficult time filling jobs there. Conversely, about a year later, we had about 15 or 20 students who wanted to go to New York and as a result we started visiting more students who were currently on co-op with New York companies. In fact my colleague went down to New York and tried to develop more jobs. So you need to get a kind of geographic distribution as well of where you think your students want to work, and industry as well, if they know, a lot of students won't know, the sophomores may not know, but if they do then that's better.

PROFESSIONAL PERSPECTIVE #2
"TAKE A REAL INTEREST"
Nancy Chiang and Kirk Patterson, University of Waterloo

NANCY CHIANG (NC): Usually, I set up a firm visit through the student. I will ask the student, who is your manager? I would normally meet with each student for about half an hour and try to schedule the manager for about 15 minutes. I get the scoop from the student, so I don't need to take up too much of the manager's time. I don't like to ask for a half-hour of a busy manager's time. So we'll book 15 minutes, and they could end up talking to us for longer than that, and that would be fine. The excuse is to get feedback about the student's performance.

They can talk about the student, but at the same time we can ask them a lot of other questions about opportunities. Do they have leads? Do they have any issues or concerns about the way things are going? And we can nip things in the bud if there are problems. I do find that I can be doing a visit and I can get leads in surprising ways. There could be someone else walking past, and the manager says "Oh, this is the coordinator from Waterloo." That passerby says, "Oh! We need to talk to you later!" We get a lot of leads that way.

And employers move around. They might move to another department, and they start hiring co-ops there. Or they leave the company, and go somewhere else, and they will be contacting us. I find that it is really, really important to maintain that group of loyal employers, and wherever they go, they will be growing our business for us.

KIRK PATTERSON (KP): And that is easily done by sending congratulatory notes if you know when they move on. But when you go into a company, you've got to be prepared to look at the whole picture of the company and think "Okay, fine, you're only hiring engineering students here. But what are you doing in your accounting department? Or what are you doing in your shipping department?" It's all in learning how to speak to them. It's Group Dynamics 101. It's learning to be social with them, and to be genuine, to take a real interest in their company.

I can honestly say, in all my time with co-op, there is not one company I haven't learned something from. It's like going to school every day. And that's what I tell the students. I've had students say "Well, why would you do this?" and I say, "It's interesting. I've found out something about you. And you've found out something about me. I found out something about this company that I had no idea...." One advantage we have at Waterloo is that we have those two teams—one on campus and one in the field—and we're the ones who are out on the road.

NC: I used to teach, too, and I find that now that I've done both, I always tell the students that I'm learning so much. When I'm doing firm visits, I hear so much about what is happening out there. And when we talk to the employers, sometimes they will actually comment that "You have more industry knowledge than we do!"

Another thing that we do during the visit, we ask not only the employers for leads, we ask the students as well. I always tell the students, "You are my spy here." So I ask them "Who is hiring? What are the other groups here?"

PROFESSIONAL PERSPECTIVE #3
"PAID, PLANNED, AND PROGRESSIVE"
Tom Akins, Georgia Institute of Technology

It was a restaurant business. And, actually, the difficult part was that one of the co-founders is a Georgia Tech alumnus. In any event, they wanted some of our management students to learn to be operators of the restaurant units. Which is a great idea—bring them in, let them work there and get some of the administrative work, maybe work in the office for a while? Anyway, what it wound up being is these students were basically working in these restaurants cooking food, waiting on people, bussing tables, and working about 80 hours a week. And this is all they ever did. So we went to the employer and we asked them, "Are they ever going to be able to move into the business area, work in the corporate offices for a term?" And they said, "Well yes, that's our plan." Anyway, that went on for about two years and we never saw any movement in that area. It was somewhat painful, but we had to tell them that we were going to terminate our relationship with them, and we were no longer going to recommend students to them. It's been somewhat unfortunate. They have taken students as interns, but not as co-ops anymore. They could not commit to a training program that would involve moving the students around and getting a better view of the company and how it works not only at the retail level but as far as the corporate end of it was concerned.

Assessing the educational value of the job was exactly the basis that we used to approach them. We said, "Look, this is an educational program and we can understand certainly the student working at the retail outlet for a term, because I think it's actually important to know how that operates, and the nitty-gritty of that. But you're just hiring them as cheap labor, to work there and to handle these outlets. This is not the intent of the program." The intent of the program, and we all agree, is it's part of their educational process. It's a method of education. And they are not learning. The 3 Ps we use in co-op are "Paid, Planned, and Progressive," and that job was close to only two of those. Although it was paid, it wasn't planned or progressive. We had an amicable separation; they just realized they were not going to be able to meet the needs of the co-op program, and it was not the right program for them, because they were not going to be able to do what they thought they were going to do. And it's fine, we're okay with them now. We have some interns that go with them from time to time, but not co-ops.

PROFESSIONAL PERSPECTIVE #4
"THE RULES HAVE CHANGED"
Marie Sacino, LaGuardia Community College

I can talk about a situation with an employer. A very large and very important employer and I had a group of about 10–15 students working on a financial mapping project. A very important project, and very team based, very well coordinated. The lead supervisor was somewhat young and her attitude towards work was "As long as you get it done, if you come in at 9:30 rather than 9:00 that's okay... If you need to stay a little bit late or skip lunch..." She was very flexible, very casual, even in so far as how students dressed—not so much jeans or anything, but every day was kind of casual, and every day was a casual Friday.

In the midst of this financial mapping project, the lead supervisor got called away to work on something else. Suddenly, my group of 10–15 students who were not worrying about the subway being delayed, or having a leisurely breakfast, or reading the newspaper—whatever they were doing—they get a supervisor who is wonderful, but who has been with the company about 30–35 years. This manager was from the old school: "If you're supposed to be here at 9:00, that means 8:50." Suddenly I've got these students who are acting as if they're still working for that prior supervisor. So I get a phone call. "What is going on here? And what are you going to do about this?"

I was really concerned, because this is one of our major accounts. This is a person we've worked with since 1997, and this is a long-term relationship that we've had with them. Suddenly this person who has given wonderful opportunities to students all throughout the years is unhappy, and this employer pays for our community college students to complete their degrees at other schools, such as NYU or anywhere they want to go. I'm getting quite anxious because what am I going to do? And this woman is also very strong, she's not talking to me in a diplomatic friendly way.

What I did was get the e-mails of all the students working down there, and I told the manager that basically I was on my way. With an employer like this, and with all our employers, we want to be responsive because we feel they go out on a limb for us, taking these students that are very inexperienced, and helping them to learn and to grow and to mentor them.

Basically what I asked the manager to do was give me maybe an hour, and I took my classroom down there, and I set them up in a conference room, and I told the students some of the concerns. The manager had sent me an e-mail with this long list of concerns that she had, and most of them were that the students were coming in late, they weren't dressing appropriately, they weren't responding appropriately, they were just kind of very laid back. You know, if it doesn't get done today, it'll get done tomorrow. So we sat in a conference room, and I went over all of the concerns. And we also went over what it's like to work for one supervisor, and what it's like to work for another. And we've got to now put on another face, put on another hat, and it's a new day with new expectations. If you want to continue to work here, this is the ballgame you're going to be in, and these are the rules you have to follow.

Some of the students were frustrated. "The rules have suddenly changed, and now we're in trouble." I said, "If you want to continue to work here and have a successful internship, and if you want to possibly have the opportunity to become a permanent employee here, and want this to be successful, you have to choose whether you want to be in the game." It's kind of like, "It is what it is, and I can't have any whiners here, and I can't have someone that's going to say 'I want to go back to the old supervisor.'"

"This is a new day. If you want to be in the game, fine, if you want to check out of the game and this isn't the right internship for you, you can let me know that right now." I really had to be forceful with them, and say it is what it is, and this is what you had with one supervisor, that's how someone wants to run the show, and this is someone else. So now you're going to have to step up to the plate and be in this new game. And yes, it's going to be a little bit challenging for you, but this is the way it has to be. And I saw some of them nodding their heads because this is a highly paid internship—one of the top-salaried internships.

I tried to get them to think of it almost like you're working with a new company. These are the changes, and this is what you have to adapt to. And the changes were not that drastic, it was just more structured. You were working somewhere that was less structured and more flexible, but now you work for this person who comes in at 7:00 in the morning. She wants you there at 9:00, because at 9:00 she's ready to roll, so you've got to be at your desk and ready to go by 8:45, because she's going to be there. And this is a supervisor who works from 7:00 in the morning until 8:00 at night, so the nature of the person is totally different. So you're going to have to step up and this can be a good challenge.

I came in a second time. The supervisor came in after I talked to them for about an hour. And basically she said, she thought they were doing a good job, but that there were changes and that there are always bumps in the road when there is a change in supervision. I guess she gave them a little bit of a pep talk, and she really wanted this to work out. So the outcome was successful; the students did respond. The large majority did change and did do as they were supposed to do. I don't know if they were all happy about it, but it really was a successful outcome. But it really meant taking my classroom, holding a class at the site, and saying "This is what's going on, these are the concerns, and this is how we have to address them." And I think that really worked. But it was really challenging.

REFLECTION QUESTIONS

1. How do you prioritize when it comes to determining which employers you should visit first?

2. To what degree does your referral process include determining which resumes end up going to one job rather than another? Whether you are heavily involved or more laissez-faire, what is your rationale for your approach?

3. Name three specific things that you do that are designed to make life easier for your employers.

4. This chapter describes a variety of ways to get employers engaged in activities on campus. Beyond simply having students work in their jobs, what other ways do you encourage employers to be educational partners with your institution?

5. What are the most common complaints that employers make about your students? What steps can you take to prevent or minimize the possibility of these concerns arising in the future?

6. Considering the step-by-step process of handling conflicts between students and employers included in the chapter, what do you think is the most crucial step for an employer to take if a conflict is going to be resolved successfully?

7. The chapter includes several stories about troubleshooting conflicts between employers and students. What is your best example of a time when you able to resolve such a conflict successfully?

EPILOGUE

TOWARD FLUENCY

"A successful career will no longer be about promotion. It will be about mastery."
— *Michael Hammer*

Many years ago, I decided I would attempt to write a novel. Writing had always come fairly easily to me, and I had an idea that seemed plausible. I had taken no courses in fiction writing and read no books about the craft of writing a novel. That didn't seem to deter me. No doubt I had some things to learn, but I figured I could learn from experience.

For several months I labored away in solitude, writing maybe nine or ten chapters of a novel. I was thinking of calling it *Marzipan Skin*. It was fun and exciting, and I figured out some useful techniques. However, there were a few significant downsides. For one, I learned purely from trial and error. Sometimes I would write a whole chapter before realizing that it was superfluous. Even more often, I had a nebulous sense that there might be some sort of problem, but I was reluctant to address it. For one thing, it was tough to face revisions because it would force me to accept that I had wasted a great deal of time the first time around. Plus, I generally didn't know what to do to address the shortcoming. For example, the dialogue sections seemed laborious, but I didn't know how to fix that. The reader needed to know what the characters were saying to each other, but it seemed like I had to include long conversations to set up the handful of key exchanges. Also, my peripheral characters were lively and real, but somehow the main characters were harder to capture.

Worst of all, I really didn't know if the whole thing was remotely good. I showed it to a few people who like to read, and they thought it was strong. But in my heart of hearts, I knew that the average person was blown away at the idea that someone they knew might write a novel. So they weren't objective, and they weren't experts. Hearing their praise was nice for my ego, perhaps, but it didn't really mean anything.

Finally I signed up for a short story writing course at the Harvard University Extension School. While the crux of the class was to write fiction, we spent the early weeks going over the *theory* behind the writing of fiction. Simultaneously, we studied passages from many classics in order to learn various tricks of the trade. Although my novel-in-progress never saw the light of day in that course, I suddenly had many clear insights as to what was wrong with it:

- For starters, it was probably a dumb idea to set out to write a novel. My instructor pointed out that a writer could write one 200-page novel or 20 ten-page stories. By necessity, the novel will need to have the same style and tone all the way through. In contrast, she assured us that our 20th story could be radically different from—and probably much better than—our first.

- My novel had way too much "setting of the stage" and not nearly enough conflict to hook the reader in the beginning. When I reexamined the novel, I realized that the first three chapters would need to be scrapped. Chapter 4 was when the action *really* started.

- I had many silly superstitions as to what I should and shouldn't be doing to become a writer of contemporary fiction. I had not been *reading* much contemporary fiction, fearing that it might lead me to copy someone else's style. In the class, I was quickly set straight about that. I needed to be doing just the opposite, seeing what had been done out there to see where fiction was at and where it was going.

- My novel was missing the benefit of innumerable tricks of the trade—many easy-to-learn techniques that would make my writing fresher and more vivid while also economizing on language. I learned how techniques like indirect discourse and narrative summary could solve my previously nebulous difficulty with dialogue. I discovered that many of my adverbs were dead weight and needed to be eliminated or changed so that they would *really* modify my verbs. I found out that there were clever ways to convey physical description, mood, and personality with subtle use of language—showing the reader instead of telling them.

All of this was intriguing and useful, but I finally had to produce my first short story for the class. I worked really hard on it and thought I had done a good job of coming up with a very plot-driven story that had some humor. When the time came for my critique, I had some butterflies but felt hopeful.

The story was ripped apart by the class and the instructor. It wasn't cruel—they were just telling me what was wrong with it. Still, I went home a little depressed. But by the next day I was determined to prove everyone wrong with a new story. Within a few weeks, I had written an all-new story—making sure that I didn't make the same mistakes again. Back we went to the critique.

This one was panned again. I had succeeded in not making the same mistakes but made a bunch of new ones instead. It was very deflating. Writing had always been so easy, and now it was suddenly hard. But there was nothing to do but let the criticism sink in and continue to work as hard as I could in reading and critiquing my classmates' stories. They had many failures, too, but there was always something to learn as the group of us discussed a story, always being sure to persist until we had gotten to the bottom of what was working and what wasn't.

In the meantime, I was now immersed in books like *On Becoming A Novelist* and *The Art of Fiction* by John Gardner, learning more about writing theory. The concepts of conflict, emotional distance, high and low language, verisimilitude, narrative points of view, transitions, sensory detail, and so forth gradually took hold. When I came to one of the last classes with a third short story, it felt like a moment of truth. I was more nervous than ever. I remember thinking that I believed it was a good story. But what if I was wrong about that? Then I would have to conclude that I was really lost.

Our instructor has always said that we shouldn't have hurt feelings if she slammed our stories. She said that she wanted it to mean something when she told us that we had written something good and that we had produced something publishable. She was right. When she told me that night that I had produced a publishable story, it was extremely vindicating. It had been a hard-earned victory.

From there, I ended up joining a writing group with two of my classmates. We worked together for a few years, and all of us have published books subsequently. Eventually, I took another fiction writing course at Harvard with a different instructor. By the end of that course, our instructor needed to be hospitalized. She told me that I was the best fiction critic she had ever taught, and she asked me to step up and teach the class in her absence. Obviously, a great deal had changed since I had made my fledgling attempt to write a novel without any assistance.

THE STUDENT AS WORK-IN-PROGRESS

Why do I tell this story now? Reflecting on the writing of this book over the last six months, I see some definite parallels between my attempts to become a fiction writer and in the journeys that our students make as "works-in-progress" toward becoming successful professionals. In either case, the goal is for the individual to internalize and synthesize a surprisingly complex array of theory and practice, the latter of which includes the myriad behaviors, strategies, and techniques that lead to success. These are absorbed tacitly through observation and participation in various communities of practice, and they also may be discussed explicitly through interaction with workplace professionals, academic faculty, and co-op/internship educators.

Our hope is that these learners may start with the perspective of the novice but that they gradually build competence and confidence as they develop a progressive sense of mastery of the professional realm. In many ways, they are akin to the learners of any language. With the right combination of instruction and immersion, we can be startled at how quickly they move toward fluency.

While producing *Learning From Experience*, I have had to think a great deal about our roles as co-op and internship educators. To what degree is it our responsibility to ensure that students are moving as efficiently and effectively as possible toward becoming "fluent" professionals? How much of an impact do we have on what students learn?

I'm not sure if we'll ever have a definitive answer to those questions. For a long while, though, I have adhered to a fundamental belief about my students. While I can't prove its validity, it has resonated positively when I've broached it with colleagues. It goes as follows:

- There is a small group of students—maybe five percent—who would be incredibly success-ful as co-op or interns *even if there was no one in my role whatsoever*. In other words, these students have enough initiative to develop their own jobs or figure out an appropriate learning experience by combing through a database. Once they get into the job itself, they will figure out how to maximize their learning. When they return to the classroom, they readily will be able to make connections between the real world and their coursework. In short, they probably don't really need an educator's assistance.

- There is another small fraction of students—again, maybe five percent or so—who are most likely to struggle mightily through a co-op job or internship experience *regardless of whatever superhuman efforts that an educator might undertake to ensure their success*. The problem may be one of intelligence, attitude, personality, or language, or it may be some combination of those elements. Regardless, there is definitely a subset of students that are likely to struggle to get a job, keep a job, or learn anything from a job. Maybe they will have difficulties with *all* of those areas.

- That said, the vast majority of students—about 90 percent if you've done the math here—are in neither category. Most students have the ability to be very successful and to learn a great deal through their experiences of working with an educator who is assisting them through the preparation, activity, and reflection elements of the co-op learning model. Before we get too excited, though, let's remember that this majority is full of students who also could do very *poorly* in their real-world experiences. Even worse, the typical student might go through a co-op or internship program without learning anything that can be transferred into some other context in the future.

This is all true with just about any learning experience that you might imagine. Let's reconsider my fiction writing experiences. Yes, there are successful writers out there who never had formal training, never studied theory, and never received significant mentoring. Those individuals are "naturals," people who were just able to figure it out working independently or close to it.

Sad to say, I was not one of those rare birds as a fiction writer, as you could tell. Even with writing in general, I have to give significant credit to Joe Grover, my English teacher in 11th grade at Wooster School. For a whole school year, I was in his "Term Paper" course. Believe me, when you meet every day and spend an entire week or more on concepts such as library research, topic sentences, thesis statements, outlines, and even how to *title* a piece of writing, you've got a skill set that will carry you through life!

So I was not hopeless. I was in that 90 percent. I had some basic intelligence, and I certainly put a great deal of time and energy into writing over the years. But I can't say that I would've been able to make several great leaps forward without a combination of real-world opportunity along with the mentoring of an educator.

LEARNING ROADBLOCKS

I believe that this is just as true for the students that I now work with as a co-op coordinator. Unfortunately, there are many ways in which a well-intentioned educator gets derailed when attempting to provide that mentoring. When interviewing 17 educators and incorporating their words into this book, many tensions came up repeatedly. As professionals, many of us are struggling with any number of issues that came up at various points in this book—reflection, playing God with referrals, and so forth. Yet the biggest challenge of all is keeping a focus on education and learning as opposed to becoming little more than a placement manager.

There are frankly several forces working against an emphasis on learning. The biggest one is workload. I have met educators who tell me that they are asked to place 200+ students in a variety of majors for a given work term. While I wouldn't want to wave the white flag at the thought of educating that many students, there is no question that such a workload would force me to rely more heavily on large-group methods than I think would be optimal. Educators in this situation need to do whatever they can to build awareness on their campuses about what can and can't be done in the face of daunting workloads. Coming up with an educational vision and spelling out what resources you will need to make it a reality may fall on deaf ears, but it's well worth trying if you have an enormous workload. If the institution can see how better educated students are going to translate into higher-paid and more satisfied graduates, maybe the long-term benefits in terms of fundraising could offset the higher cost of a more educational approach.

Even when educators have workloads that are more manageable, there are still forces working against learning. Another challenge is simply mastering the operational issues of the job. As Nancy Johnston and others alluded to in their transcripts earlier in the book, this role is not quite like any other job out there in the academic world. It may well take a minimum of a year or two for a professional to feel that they have a handle on the nuts and bolts of the job—a CRM system used to list jobs and send out resumes; the timing of a referral process; a better sense of what students, employers, and your institution really want and need from you. It's hard to focus on maximizing learning when you are trying to get through an intense referral process with everyone placed.

Speaking of which, another issue is that most of our institutions, employers, and even our students are putting pressure on us to focus our energy on making sure that students get jobs and employers fill their jobs—preferably as expediently as possible. This is a pressure that probably will not go away, even after you reach the point of having the operational elements under control.

This pressure to place is understandable, as I've said earlier in the book, but you don't want to be infected by all of this anxiety to the point where it makes you lose sight of education. I have to admit that I have been a little haunted by one of Nancy Johnston's quotes earlier in the book. Like her, I think many people would've said that I was a good co-op coordinator in my early years. I had 100 percent placement, and I was pulling more students into my concentration. Employers and students respected me, and there were few complaints. Yet, like Nancy, I can't say that I was doing anywhere near to what I could be doing to ensure that students were really learning as much as possible. I didn't really prepare students for the range of possibility that is out there when it comes to learning opportunities, and I wasn't really getting them to reflect on their learning by going through it all in depth afterwards.

Were my students learning? Sure. Getting back to my own formula, there were those five percent who would've succeeded regardless. Of that 90 percent, there is no doubt that most of them were avoiding significant problems and that some unknown percentage of them were really learning something out there. Better still, I'm sure that many were able to bring that information back to the classroom and into future jobs.

Left to their own devices—or with some minimal assistance—there is no doubt that many students can and will learn. The tougher question is how many of them will learn and if *any* of them will be able to maximize their learning without the assistance of an educator who is engaged in ensuring that the student understands that every element of the co-op/internship experience is a learning opportunity. This includes writing a resume, learning interviewing skills, sifting through and weighing job possibilities, deciding what job to accept, getting the most out of the job itself, and making a successful transition back to classes as well as into a future job experience. For that matter, it can even include tasks as mundane as filling out a form or exchanging e-mails.

The more that we remind ourselves that we are all educators *all* of the time, the more we will exploit those opportunities. If we are talking to students with the voice and attitude of educators on a consistent basis, they are much more likely to see themselves as learners instead of no more than job candidates.

KNOWLEDGE TRANSFER IN ACTION

Nancy Johnston also offered another of the more haunting ideas in this book. She talked about the tricky nature of knowledge transfer. As a reminder, the research shows that transferring knowledge from one context to another is much trickier in practice than most of us would assume. Just as I found it was difficult to make the transition from being a "good writer" to producing publishable contemporary short fiction, most individuals struggle to take knowledge from one context and put it to practical use in a new situation. The especially interesting and unsettling element of this is that this is true *even when the two situations are relatively similar*. It makes sense that a student may struggle to see how her waitressing experience does indeed have some transferability to a corporate sales position. But the really mind-blowing fact is that the same student also may find it extremely difficult to build on that experience when she moves into a public relations role on a subsequent co-op.

This is very disturbing, really. But if you've been in the field for a while and think it over, you already know that it's true without seeing any data or research. We've all had students who were superstars in one context and then bombed in a seemingly similar job. And we've all had students who improved their performance dramatically when given a second chance. The hard question here: What can we do as educators to ensure that students are able to become more aware of what they've already learned and how that can inform what they think, feel, and do in a future context?

My initial goal in writing this book was to create a resource that would be especially useful to newer professionals in the field. But given how much I've learned and altered my style and processes as a result of this undertaking, I am reminded that professional development is a never-ending journey for all of us. After digesting my conversations with Nancy and others over the summer, I've taken knowledge transfer as my challenge throughout the ongoing fall semester. I find myself revisiting many of my age-old processes and procedures to see if there are better ways that I can assist students in understanding what they already knew, what they've learned, and how it will translate to a present or future context.

As you read about in Chapter 11, I already feel like I've revamped my one-on-one meeting with students *after* their work term, and I've found that this intensified focus on learning has paid dividends already. But what about the preparation and activity phases? Well, here are a few stories that I hope will show how knowledge transfer can be facilitated.

A few weeks ago, I did a practice interview with a first-time co-op student that I'll call Nathan, a starter on our Varsity Soccer team at Northeastern. We had just hired a new Student Services assistant, so I had her sit in on the interview and subsequent critique. Nathan had an okay practice interview, slightly above average. However, my assistant and I were surprised when

Nathan critiqued himself. He told us that he couldn't believe how nervous he was when he walked into the room. His heart was pounding like crazy. He hadn't anticipated that, and it really threw him off.

My assistant and I looked at each other. I had just asked her to critique his performance before he came back in the room, and she hadn't picked up on any negative nervous energy. Neither had I—it wasn't apparent at all. So we were surprised, but I went after that comment.

"Why were you nervous?" I asked. He couldn't articulate it, and I had to keep asking the question in different ways. Finally, I went more with a behavioral question, asking him, "What was going through your head when you were sitting outside the office, waiting for the practice interview?"

"I was thinking about how I'm not remotely qualified for this job," he said. "All I have going for me is that I have a good GPA. I've put so much energy into soccer that the only job I have on my resume is a caddy at a country club. So I was really stressing out about the fact that I don't have any related experience for this role."

"That was really helpful," I said. "But tell me something. I know that you're a really good soccer player. When you're warming up before a game and getting mentally prepared, what are you thinking about? Are you thinking about how the guys on the other team are probably faster and stronger than you?"

"Of course not," he said. "I'm thinking just the opposite—that I'm faster and more skilled than they are."

"Okay," I said. "What else do you do to get in the right mindset before a game?"

"I visualize myself being in the right places, doing the right things—being alert, being in position, executing the game plan," he said. "And I visualize times in the past when I've played really well."

"Exactly," I said. "So here's what I think is going on with you. You came into this practice interview today believing that you had no experience to tap, but you completely overlooked the fact that you *already* know how to get yourself in the ideal frame of mind for a job interview! I know that this is a new and different setting for you, but I really want you to prepare for your first real interview by tapping into that terrific experience you have with getting yourself to be ready for a soccer game."

That seemed to resonate really well, and it also set the stage for talking about his perceptions about his "meaningless" high school job as a caddy. Okay, it's not a professional job experience, and it's not obviously transferable to a job in the financial services industry. But what does it take to be a good caddy? You are in a subservient position, and you have to be able to take direction respectfully and responsively. You need to be able to deal with a variety of personalities and keep a positive attitude—even when people may be frustrated or acting in a condescending manner. There are definitely going to be times in co-op when those experiences are going to have some relevance. But many individuals are quick to negate or overlook what was learned in other contexts, so I thought it was important to make sure he understood that his caddy job had at least some value. What I hope will happen for Nathan is that he will start to become better able to make *other* connections on his own in the future.

Another situation arose this semester. I have a student that I'll refer to as Isaac here. Isaac had a great evaluation from his first co-op employer and is currently doing his six-month co-op job. Not long ago, I was startled to receive the following e-mail from Isaac:

Hi Scott,

I had some questions regarding my current co-op situation. I am currently working for [name of company] as a finance co-op. I am having some issues with working here and I do not know what to do.

The work I am assigned to do is fine. The problem is the environment I am working in and the way management treats me. Many times I feel offended by the way my manager treats me. I do not feel I am being treated like an employee and many times get the "cold shoulder" when I need help with my work or have questions. There were no standard set of procedures or any directions on how to do my work so I kind of had to teach myself. I don't have a problem with that because that's kind of how it was on my last co-op. But whenever I do have questions, my manager shrugs me off and when the work is due I get all the heat if I missed something or if I made a mistake.

I feel disrespected every time I speak with my manager by her condescending tone and attitude towards me. Even today she closed her office door in my face while I was asking her a question about work. Prior to this there have been several instances where I felt very disrespected and insulted (I can specifically describe them).

I know I should have contacted you and told you earlier about this but I thought I was going to be able to tough it out. However I am honestly miserable working here and feel bad about myself when I leave every day. I don't know how much I can take. Is there any way I can find another co-op? Or is it too late? Please let me know what my options are.

Thank You,

Isaac

When you receive an e-mail like this, it's very easy to fall into the trap of taking the situation at face value. Although I wasn't initially sure about how I might most effectively deal with Isaac's situation, one thing I definitely was *not* going to do was to get into any kind of discussion about whether or not it's too late to find a job elsewhere. The *real* questions for me were as follows:

- Is the situation really as bad as it seems, or is Isaac making it appear to be less salvageable than it really is because he's taking the manager's behavior personally?

- How can I most effectively get Isaac to realize that we want to explore ways to overcome these challenges instead of being like a runner who wants to quit a race just because there are some hurdles?

- How can I get Isaac to see this as a learning opportunity instead of nothing more than a pain in the butt?

I looked back on my journal notes from when we had met one-on-one to talk about what he had learned in his previous co-op. Although Isaac had a great experience, it was an extremely challenging one, too. He worked alongside union workers who treated him with a great deal of contempt at first. He had told me that his top accomplishment in that job was pulling strings with the union workers to bring them around toward having a decent working relationship with him.

Suddenly it occurred to me that Isaac was so immersed in the emotions of his current job that he was forgetting how much he already knew about dealing with difficult people! Once again, that persistent idea of knowledge transfer came to mind. Knowing that I had the advantage of being emotionally removed from the situation and thus relatively objective about his tussles with his manager, I wrote the following e-mail back to him in an attempt to get him to reframe his perceptions about the problem at hand:

Isaac,

Thanks for getting in touch. I'm really sorry to hear that you're having a difficult time at your job.

I think my initial goal here is for you to give me a more specific idea of what's going on. I do think it would be helpful if you could describe perhaps the two or three most unpleasant situations that arose. As much as you can, just describe the facts of exactly what happened, step by step. That will give us a little better sense of what's going on and hopefully a better idea of what to do about it.

To answer your question, I don't think it would be advisable to even consider quitting the job at this point. You are in a difficult situation, but there are any number of steps that might be taken to make things better. After we learn more about some key events from your perspective, I may opt to get in touch with the employer or maybe even visit the company to get a better sense of what's going on from their perspective. That may give us more of an explanation as to why this happening as well as what might be done about it.

In reading your e-mail, though, I found myself remembering what you told me about working at your first co-op. I know that you had to deal with some very difficult union workers, and it took real perseverance to get results in the face of adversity. I think that you're facing a different kind of challenge here, but, likewise, this also represents an opportunity to find a way to overcome having to deal with a challenging personality. We can never predict what sort of learning opportunity will arise for a student on co-op. While I'm sure you would prefer to not have to deal with this challenge, this could translate into one of your top accomplishments by the end of this work term. That's what happened last time, right?

In the meantime, remember this: However you are treated, try to not wear your

---

frustration on your sleeve. Remind yourself at all times that you want to look back at your time in this job and feel proud of the fact that you did not respond to negative behavior with that same kind of negative energy. Also, remember that this individual's treatment of you may have nothing to do with YOU whatsoever! It could be due to personal issues, job stress, etc. So try your best to not take it personally, even if the behavior is offensive to you.

Quitting a job is never a "first resort" when difficulties arise. We want to make sure we do all we can to understand what's happening and try to fix the relationship. It's possible that a point could be reached where we feel like the situation is hopeless, but many steps would have to happen before we reach the conclusions.

I hope this helps, and please reply with more information and any questions.

Thanks,

Scott

I was delighted to see Isaac's response:

Scott,

After reading your e-mail, I've decided to try to actually resolve this with my manager and try to talk to her about these issues and find solutions to them. I'll try to see this as just another challenge and try to get through it.

I'll keep you guys updated on how things go.

Thank You.

A few weeks went by. Then I got a call from Isaac. "I have big news," he said. Uh-oh, I thought. I feared that his manager didn't take kindly to his efforts to resolve the conflict and that she had him fired him. So imagine my surprise when Isaac told me that his *boss* had been fired. In fact, he had just been asked to assume many of her responsibilities. In retrospect, he had realized that the negative behavior that had been directed toward him had perhaps been a reflection of other political issues that his manager had faced at the company… and it seemed possible that her negativity may have been a factor in her termination as well.

There are many interesting considerations to ponder here:

1. Learning is unpredictable

First, it's important to remind students that learning is unpredictable. In my preparation class last week, I told Isaac's story to my students. I wanted to remind them that most of their learning will not be captured on the job description of the position that they accepted. In fact, there are times when they will become what I call a "reluctant expert" on one of the less enjoyable aspects of becoming a professional. To some degree I'm reminded of a saying that my kids were told at preschool in the face of small injustices about who was allowed to do one activity over another on a given day: "You get what you get, and you don't get upset."

That's easier said than done, naturally. How do you deal with a co-worker who blames you for his mistakes or takes credit for your accomplishments? What do you do if sexual harassment affects you at work, directly or indirectly? How do you raise a concern about being underutilized without being branded as a malcontent? These are critical skills to learn, and you need to be ready to embrace these learning opportunities if necessary without getting bogged down in your bad luck.

2. Real learning isn't always easy.

Isaac obviously didn't hope to have a boss that made him feel badly about himself. Who would? I'm sure that he still wishes that he had a great boss and that he enjoyed going to work every day for six months. But here's a provocative question: Would he have learned more if that were the case? It's impossible to say, and the question warrants research, but my own experience with students tells me that a relatively negative job experience often results in more powerful learning than an experience that is neutral or moderately positive.

This isn't always a good thing. A student who has a negative job experience often will overgeneralize from it, becoming all too ready to conclude that *all* jobs in that same field or industry or with organizations of similar size will be poor choices in the future. Handled appropriately by the educator, though, the learner can come away with deeper convictions about what really matters as well as keenly enhanced self-awareness.

Even in very positive learning experiences, real learning usually doesn't come easily. A few years ago, I had a student at Microsoft who felt completely overwhelmed and lost through the first six or seven weeks. His perception was that he wasn't moving toward fluency at all; he felt like a fast-moving train was rushing by him and that he would never be able to jump aboard. Fortunately, he went to his manager and told him that he would do whatever it takes to overcome this enormous challenge. Together they worked out an action plan, and the student ended up with a full-time offer by the end of six months.

A CHALLENGE FOR EDUCATORS

As indicated in the introduction, the title of *Learning From Experience* is intended to have a double meaning. As such, everything that I've said about students in this epilogue also can be applied to us as educators. We face roadblocks of time, energy, money, and resources that will make it more difficult for us to become the best professionals we can possibly be. Like our students, we may struggle to take what we have learned from our education, reading, and job experiences and apply that learning to our roles as co-op and internship professionals.

Likewise, our learning as educators is unpredictable and sometimes difficult. Just the other day, one of my colleagues had a company rescind three co-op offers—several weeks after the students had accepted—because of the economic crisis. She had never had an employer rescind an offer and was stunned. How should she respond? She was disappointed and upset on behalf of the students but also struggling with how to respond to the employer. Given the nature of the economy, she knew that it was not a frivolous move by the employer. How could she communicate with them appropriately and assertively? What realistically could or should be done at this point? It won't be easy, but she will learn some valuable if unpleasant lessons that should help her in the future.

Meanwhile, I am dealing with a first-time co-op student and not sure how to proceed. He has been a no-show for two appointments with one of my colleagues, and, in general, he has been extremely inconsistent in his behavior. I have had to address various issues with him. He is smart and has shown flashes of brilliance, but he also has sent me some unprofessional e-mails—including a very pushy message in which he wrote on a Monday asking why I hadn't sent out his resume yet after we had discussed doing so "last week." I checked my notes and confirmed that we had met on Friday—just ONE business day before—and now he was implying that I had slacked off by not sending his resume out immediately.

I took a long while and reflected on similar situations that had happened in the past before meeting with him. It would be much easier if I was positive that he would do a bad job on co-op. I don't really know that for sure, but I decided to tap into similar experiences in the past. I brought him in, and we had a tough conversation about why he couldn't get his act together. It wasn't fun or easy, but I tried to channel my calm-assertive energy while working with him to dissect what had gone wrong and what might be done about it. I gave him some options, and we'll see if he can turn it around. It's another of those grey-area cases, and I can't begin to predict whether my intervention will be successful. Even after 13 ½ years in this job, I still wrestle with situations like these.

I don't think that will ever end. Just as almost all of us go through our whole lives without understanding a surprisingly high percentage of words in an English dictionary, I believe that all of us are learners who never reach the final destination as we continue to move toward absolute fluency as professionals. The goal is to never stop making progress in that direction.

So here is my final challenge for you as an educator. What are you going to do in the next year to move closer toward fluency as a co-op or internship professional? Were there learning theories earlier in the book that you are going to delve into more deeply, maybe reading about metacognition or communities of practice? Will you attend a conference or two—not just to attend some workshops but also to enjoy dialogues with professionals who, like you, are striving to find a better way to educate students? Are there ideas or practices from this book that have challenged your notions about some element of what you do and that you are now eager to address? I hope so.

Although I suspect that few of us reflect on it, all of us working in the world of cooperative education and internships comprise a community of practice. In this book, you have heard just 18 voices in addition to mine. There are many other experts out there, and I truly believe that everyone has something to share whether the educator is a wily veteran or a newcomer to the field. What do you have to offer? While I hope that our words in this book will help you in your personal journey toward fluency, I also want to urge you to join the chorus.

SELECTED BIBLIOGRAPHY

BOOKS

Albom, Mitch. *Tuesdays with Morrie*. New York: Broadway Books, 2002.

Balzac, Honore de. *Old Goriot*. New York: W.W. Norton, 1994.

Bolles, Richard Nelson. *What Color Is Your Parachute?* Berkeley, CA: Ten Speed Press, 1971-.

Epictetus. *The Art of Living*. New York: HarperCollins, 1995.

Gardner, John. *On Becoming A Novelist*. New York: Harper & Row, 1983.

Gardner, John. *The Art of Fiction*. New York: A. Knopf: Distributed by Random House, 1984.

Godin, Seth. *Purple Cow*. New York: Portfolio, 2003.

Howe, Neil and Strauss, William. *Millennials Rising: The Next Great Generation*. New York: Vintage Books, 2000.

Jung, Carl Gustav. *Psychological Types*. Princeton, N.J. : Princeton University Press, 1976.

Lave, Jean and Wenger, Etienne. *Situated Learning: Legitimate Peripheral Participation*. Cambridge [England]; New York: Cambridge University Press, 1991.

Levitt, Steven D. and Dubner, Stephen J. *Freakonomics: A Rogue Economist Explores the Hidden Side of Everything*. New York: William Morrow, 2006.

Millan, Cesar. *Cesar's Way*. New York: Harmony Books, 2006.

University of Cincinnati Division of Professional Practice. *Introduction to Professional Practice: Centennial Edition*. New York: McGraw-Hill, 2005.

Weighart, Scott. *Find Your First Professional Job: A Guide for Co-ops, Interns, and Full-Time Job Seekers*. 3rd ed. Brookline, MA: Mosaic Eye Publishing, 2007.

Weighart, Scott. *Exceeding Expectations: Mastering the Seven Keys to Professional Success.* Brookline, MA: Mosaic Eye Publishing, 2006.

Wenger, Etienne. *Communities of Practice: Learning, Meaning, and Identity.* Cambridge [England]; New York: Cambridge University Press, 1998.

Yalom, Irvin. *Love's Executioner & Other Tales of Psychotherapy.* New York: Basic Books, 1989.

PAPERS

Davidge-Johnston, Nancy. "Conceptions of Curriculum in Cooperative Education: A Framework for Analysis of the Co-op Preparatory Curriculum." Ph.D. dissertation, Simon Fraser University, 2007.

WEBSITES

Canadian Association for Cooperative Education: http://www.cafce.ca

Cooperative Education and Internship Association: http://www.ceiainc.org

Information about Millennial Generation: http://lifecourse.com/news/articles.html

Journal of Cooperative Education and Internships: http://www.ceiainc.org/journal/

Journal of Vocational Behavior: http://www.elsevier.com/locate/jvb

Mosaic Eye Publishing: http://mosaiceyepublishing.com

Survey Monkey: http://www.surveymonkey.com

Univ. of Cincinnati textbook: http://www.mhprofessional.com/product.php?isbn=0073194603

World Association of Cooperative Education: http://www.waceinc.org

INDEX

4D relational database 61

A

academic faculty 2–3, 9, 11, 15, 16, 79, 86, 87, 88, 157, 294, 295, 336, 339, 342, 370, 391
Access, Microsoft 3, 51, 52, 57, 139, 222, 294
Adams, Scott 38
Akins, Tom 14–15, 149, 180–181, 194, 208, 311, 344, 348, 355, 382, 385–386
Albom, Mitch 191
Aristotle 66
assessment 11–12, 15, 17, 39, 61, 72, 85–87, 91–92, 290
Association for Experiential Education 40

B

Baby Boomers 121
Balzac, Honoré de 215
Basu, Linnea 230, 233, 247
behavioral-based interviewing 39, 128, 131, 200, 292, 347, 362
best practices 39–52
Blackboard 52, 57, 170, 195, 205–208, 212, 296–298
Blake, Ivan 72
Bognanni, Charlie 2, 6, 53, 90, 114–115, 119, 125, 137, 159, 277–278, 320, 323–324, 328–329, 360, 383–384
Bolles, Richard Nelson 191
Boston University 2, 18, 164, 254, 288
bridging exercise 199
Briggs, Katharine Cook 74
Brodie, Megan 271
Brookfield, Stephen 66, 71, 95, 109–112, 295
Bruner, Jerome 66, 71
Buzan, Tony v

C

CAFCE. *See* Canadian Association for Cooperative Education
Cale, John 253

Callery, Erin 368
Campbell Interest and Skill Survey 73, 171
Canadian Association for Cooperative Education 39
Carroll, Lewis 1
Carruthers, Thomas 187
CEIA. *See* Cooperative Education and Internship Association
chauffeur exercise 202
Chiang, Nancy 248–249, 278, 336, 340, 353–354, 364, 367, 384–385
Chilvers, Elizabeth 29, 107, 334
Cicero, Marcus Tullius 119
Cincinnati, University of 30, 61, 72, 89, 90, 92, 138, 159, 189, 190, 247, 320, 328, 401
closure 261
conflict management 83, 100–101, 107–109, 151, 163–165, 373–382
coordinator
  as lawyer and judge 263–266
  as manager of students 148–150
  as unpaid consultant 24, 82, 94, 339, 340, 367
  firm visits 6, 7, 21, 24, 53–54, 256, 334, 336, 349, 358, 360, 385
counseling
  calm-assertive style 145–148
  coordinator/student relationship as metaphor 148
  flexibility 161
  getting students to own responsibility 143
  getting students to see the big picture 160
  handling conflicts 163
  keys through the preparation process 170
  keys to successful counseling in preparation 151
  modeling 163
  students with different backgrounds 165
  students with disabilities 169
  the student whisperer 145
cover letters
  critiquing 244–245
CRM. *See* customer relationship management software
customer relationship management software 39, 41–44

D

Decision Academic software 42
Descartes, Rene 66
Dewey, John 66, 71, 72
Diani, Jacki 2, 6, 15, 27, 32–33, 62–63, 80, 160, 275, 279–280, 297, 300–301, 312–313, 337, 356
Dilbert 38, 344
Dimarco, Rose 75
Dog Whisperer, The 146
Dubner, Stephen J. 302

E

e-mail
    abuse of 268
    as problem management tool 45–50
    blunders 105–106
    errors in 105, 263
    templates 45–50, 64, 212, 371
    to students 255
Edison, Thomas Alva 65
Egart, Katie 72
Eldred, Kim 245
employers
    as customers 30–31
    as educational partners 337–340, 368–370
    benefits of hiring co-ops/interns 7, 345–349
    common complaints 371–373
    cutting ties with 380–382
    developing leads 335–336, 340–342
    program assessment 6–7
    relationships with 24–26, 81–83, 361–364
    selling to 349–352
    troubleshooting problems 371–382
Epictetus 359
ePortfolios 211–212
Exceeding Expectations 71, 76, 191, 193, 204, 371, 402, 408
Excel, Microsoft 3, 4, 51, 222, 231, 234, 237, 243, 270, 290

F

Ferguson, Jane 72
Find Your First Professional Job 56, 105, 127, 130, 189, 190, 196–197, 201, 204, 217, 219, 223, 239, 242, 371, 372, 401, 408

Finn, Kathleen L. 72
firm visits
    building rapport 344–345
    prioritizing 360–361
    what to bring 342–344
    with current employers 364–368
Flavell, J. H. 66
Fletcher, Joyce 72
Freakonomics 302
Freud, Sigmund 74
Friedrich, Bernadette 12, 139–140, 149, 171, 179–180, 324–325

G

Gardner, John 390
Generation X 107, 120, 121, 128, 131, 134–136, 373
Georgia Institute of Technology 14, 180, 311, 385
Glick, Len 37
goals for educators 9–10
Godin, Seth 191
Guelph, University of 271

H

Hammer, Michael 389
Harvard University 5, 389
Hersey-Blanchard situational leadership theory 294
Herzberg, Frederick 176
Herzberg's theory of motivation 176
Holland, John 73
Howe, Neil 121

I

integration 70, 78–80, 89, 94, 295, 370
international students 9, 20, 158, 165–168, 183–184, 186
interviewing
    common problems and how to solve them 240
    conducting and critiquing practice interviews 235–244
    teaching in groups 198–201
Introduction to Professional Practice: Centennial Edition 189, 401

J

Jarvis, Peter 66
JobMine 42
Johnston, Nancy 9, 36, 59–60, 66, 69, 70, 71, 77, 78, 80, 85, 91, 112–113, 126, 181–182, 263, 284, 290, 297, 299, 305–306, 307, 326–327, 329, 393, 394
Journal of Cooperative Education 72, 90, 402
Journal of Vocational Behavior 72
Joyce, James 95
Jung, Carl 74

K

Kane, Mary 92, 116, 132, 188, 208–209, 284, 300
knowledge transfer 394–399
Kolb, David 66, 69

L

Labovitz, George 18
LaGuardia Community College 183, 205, 296, 302, 386
Lane Community College 13, 62, 181, 184, 249, 276, 311, 315, 365
Lave, Jean 66, 67, 72
learning
    facilitating 65–80
    less obvious forms of 271–273
    losing sight of 97–99
    maximizing on the job 270–275
    roadblocks 392–394
learning theory 66–72, 77, 79, 94, 126
LeMaster, Brenda 61, 90–91, 92, 328
Levitt, Steven D. 302
Lichtenberg, Georg Christoph 35
Likert scale survey 195
Linn, Patricia L. 72
Littlefield, Homer ("Doc") 10
Locke, John 66
Lotus Notes 45

M

Machiavelli, Niccolo 333
Mahoney, Kerry 145, 159, 178, 205, 207, 210–211, 223, 319

Mamook 42
McLaughlin, Kate 12–13, 91, 116–117, 173, 179, 296, 297–298, 316–317, 322–323, 325
Mezirow, Jack 70
Michigan State University 12, 139, 179, 324
Middendorf, Renee v
Millan, Cesar 146
Millennial Generation 22, 42, 107, 119–134, 138, 144, 193, 258, 302, 373, 376
    characteristics of
        high expectations 125
        highly attached to parents 130
        highly technological 128
        preference for structure 127
        team-oriented 131
Mini-Millennials 133
mistakes 95–118
moments-of-truth scenarios
    A Second Chance? 322–326
    A Transsexual Student's Resume 319–321
    Is This Sexual Harassment? 315–319
    Playing God 326–330
    Quitting Time? 310–315
multiple resumes 164, 221
Munze, Bill 195
Munze exercise 195
Myers, Isabel Briggs 74
Myers-Briggs 20, 21, 34, 74–75, 85, 103, 132, 158, 171, 211

N

National Society for Experiential Education 40

O

online calendars 45
Outlook 11, 45, 125

P

paperless class 206, 207, 213
Patterson, Kirk 31, 34, 81, 245–246, 250, 322, 339, 344, 348, 353, 353–354, 356–357, 364, 366, 367, 384–385
Peck, M. Scott 309
PeopleSoft 42

Pinkas, Tamara 13–14, 62, 157, 175, 181, 184–185, 218, 223, 249–250, 275, 276–277, 311–312, 315–316, 365
PlacePro 42
playing God 104, 326
Pollio, Marcus Vitruvius 66
Porter, Ronnie 10–12, 16, 81, 88–89, 139, 169, 182, 290, 296, 301, 327–328, 336, 354
practice interviews 235
preparation course 52, 53, 78, 108, 123, 126, 178, 187, 210, 292, 294, 297
professional behavior
    phases of development (orientation, navigation, mastery, excellence, closure) 257–262
    preventative measures 255–256
    teaching in groups 202–205

Q

Q & A 199
questioning everything in your program 36–39
quid pro quo 269

R

reflection
    causes of dissatisfaction 283–285
    formal classroom integration 294–295
    journals and papers 295–296
    one-on-one meetings 290–294
    online assessments, portfolios, and seminars 296–297
    small-group seminars 285–289
resume writing
    critiquing one-on-one 216–234
    resume as movie trailer 247–248
    teaching in groups 196–198
RoboTechnologies 42
Rocky Mountain College 122

S

Sacino, Marie 183–184, 205, 211–212, 285, 296, 299, 302, 386–387
Saltmarsh, John 72
Schneider, Herman 66
Schön, Donald 69, 305

Schopenhauer, Arthur 283
self-concept theory 76
sexual harassment 268–270
Simms, Mel 6, 9
Simon Fraser University 9, 36, 59, 66, 91, 112, 126, 181, 263, 305, 326, 402
Simplicity CRM 42, 59
situated learning theory 67–69, 69, 72
Sloane, Bill 2, 6, 227
Sophocles 253
St. Thomas, University of 109
Strauss, William 121
Strong-Campbell Interest Inventory 73, 171
students
    as "pre-colleagues" 29–30
    as job developers 366
    as works-in-progress 391–392
    choices and consequences 160–163
    in assessing program 8–9
    international 165–168, 183–184
    most common job complaints 266–270
    relationships with 22–24, 81–82, 101–107, 151–156
    with disabilities 157, 169–170, 182–183
student whisperer 145
Super, Donald 76
Swift, Jonathan 17
SWOT analysis 18

T

teaching courses
    philosophy of 192–194
    setting the tone 195–196
technology 41–52
    in teaching classes 205–208
Tillman, Bob 6, 29–30, 34, 36, 43, 53, 60–61, 72, 100, 113–114, 193, 196, 203, 209, 284, 298, 303–304, 307
time management 52–59, 80–81
Todd, Anita 24, 30, 89, 138, 221, 247–248, 251, 320–321
Total Quality Management 18–19, 96–97
TQM. *See* Total Quality Management
transitioning from student to employee 203
transparency 27, 30, 34, 156–158, 321, 363

V

Van Gyn, Geraldine 72
Victoria, University of 42, 72
vision, fundamentals of for educators 22–29

W

WACE. *See* World Association of Cooperative
  Education
Waterloo, University of 31, 40, 42, 72, 80, 145,
  178, 205, 210, 245, 248, 250, 253, 278, 319,
  322, 339, 353, 356, 360, 366, 384
Wenger, Etienne vi, 66, 67, 72, 288
Wiles, Isabelle 200
Williams, Steve 19
Wilson, Woodrow 143
Wooster School 392
work/life balance 28–29, 58–59
workload viii, 21, 26, 102, 107, 143, 187, 192,
  215, 253, 318, 333, 372, 392, 393
World Association of Cooperative Education
  40

Y

Yalom, Irvin 148

Z

Zold, Ellen 168

ABOUT THE AUTHOR

Scott Weighart is a Senior Coordinator of Cooperative Education on the faculty at Northeastern University. He has been working with co-op students and employers since 1995. Author of *Find Your First Professional Job: A Guide For Co-ops, Interns, And Full-Time Job Seekers* and *Exceeding Expectations: Mastering the Seven Keys to Professional Success*, Weighart has appeared on network television as an interviewing expert and delivered workshops on co-op topics such as the Millennial Generation and teaching co-op preparation courses at local and national conferences. He lives in Brookline, Massachusetts.